The New NORMAL

D0075232

The New NORMAL

Finding a Balance between Individual Rights and the Common Good

Amitai Etzioni

Transaction Publishers

New Brunswick (U.S.A.) and London (U.K.)

Copyright © 2015 by Transaction Publishers, New Brunswick, New Jersey.

All rights reserved under International and Pan-American Copyright Conventions. No part of this book may be reproduced or transmitted in any form or by any means, electronic or mechanical, including photocopy, recording, or any information storage and retrieval system, without prior permission in writing from the publisher. All inquiries should be addressed to Transaction Publishers, 10 Corporate Place South, Piscataway, New Jersey 08854. www.transactionpub.com

This book is printed on acid-free paper that meets the American National Standard for Permanence of Paper for Printed Library Materials.

Library of Congress Catalog Number: 2014009845
ISBN: 978-1-4128-5477-1
Printed in the United States of America

Library of Congress Cataloging-in-Publication Data

Etzioni, Amitai.
    The new normal : finding a balance between individual rights and the common good / by Amitai Etzioni.
        pages cm.
    Includes bibliographical references and index.
    ISBN 978-1-4128-5477-1
    1. Privacy, Right of--United States. 2. Civil rights--United States. 3. Public interest--United States. 4. Common good. 5. Terrorism--United States.
6. Terrorism--Prevention--Government policy--United States. 7. National security--Law and legislation--United States. I. Title.
    JC596.2.U5E795 2015
    320.97309'051--dc23
                                                                        2014009845

For Patricia,
Michael, Ethan, Oren, David, Benjamin
Lainie, Hedva, Ivone, Shiri, Ruth
Danielle, Shira, Eli, Noah, Noa, Jonathan, Max, Zacharia,
Maya, Marena, Michael-Lo.

My pride and joy—the Etzionis.

Contents

Preface

When I asked the audience at a TED conference if they needed an inflatable Santa Claus on their rooftop, they chuckled. And when I wondered if they could do without a plastic pink flamingo on their front lawn, they laughed dismissively. However, when I next asked if they *needed* a 5s smartphone—the response was a cold silence (http://www.youtube.com/watch?v=FN3z8gtDUFE). The old economic system worked by conditioning us to feel that we "needed" things that, a few years before, simply did not exist. However, these additional items did not make us more content than did our previous acquisitions. True, for those on the lower rungs of the income ladder, basic necessities are missing, and obtaining them enhances the poor's well-being. However, the higher the income, the less one benefits from overextended materialism.

The recent nearly global economic crisis provides an opportunity to ask, can we and should we return to the old system or fashion a "new normal" where those whose basic needs are well sated focus on other sources of contentment? (See chapter 1.)

Societies must work out a balance between individual rights (such as privacy, freedom to assemble, and travel) and the common good (e.g., security, protection of the environment, and public health). The point of balance changes as new technologies develop, as the natural and international environment changes, and as new social forces arise. After 9/11 the United States moved sharply to shore up national security. Some now hold that, in the process, the United States unduly shortchanged individual rights, and these now need to be better protected. Specifically, we ask, should the press be granted more protection, or should its ability to publish state secrets be limited? Should surveillance of Americans and others be curtailed? Should American terrorists be treated differently from others? Addressing these particular questions allows one to potentially answer the more general questions: where is the new proper point of balance between rights and security? Is the current balance in need of adjustment? In what direction and how much? (See chapters 2–4.)

The right to privacy is particularly besieged, not just because of new security-driven interventions but also because of major technological developments. There seems to be a need for a rather different conception of privacy in the cyber age, a new privacy normal that is different in kind, rather than a mere adaptation of the old conception (see chapter 5). Such a theory of privacy must apply not merely to protecting privacy from the intrusion of the government, as assumed by earlier theories of privacy, but also from the intrusion of private agents. This is the case not merely because those who make the marketing of private information their main business are quite intrusive but also because they often work, in effect, for the government (see chapter 6).

The new normal politics are said to be characterized by intensifying partisan conflict and gridlock. Data presented in chapter 7 show that this understanding is erroneous and that what we observe is, in fact, a strong conservative-libertarian political force confronting a weak liberal one. Above all, evidence reveals that a new high level of legalized corruption is the new normal (see chapter 8), and that narrowly-based special interest groups have captured much of public treasures (see chapter 9). Further study shows that relying on enhanced transparency to clean up public life and restore a reasonable level of accountability is a fool's errand (see chapter 10). A study of the debate over whether or not Medicare and Social Security, the proverbial social safety networks, need to be curtailed, provides an additional opportunity to study the way in which politics are practiced in the new age (see chapter 11).

In a previous book of mine (*Hot Spots: American Foreign Policy in a Post-Human-Rights World*), I argued that shifting the focus of American foreign policy from the Middle East to the Far East was premature. This analysis is here extended by addressing the domestic forces in the United States that push for preparations for a war with China and do so without proper review by the highest civilian authorities (see chapter 12).

The major principle that organized the "old world order" was the respect for sovereignty, that is, that no nation is entitled to use force to interfere in the internal affairs of other nations. Whether this principle can be upheld when terrorists treat borders (e.g., between Pakistan and Afghanistan) as a minor inconvenience, is a key issue, particularly when it comes to domestic deliberations over whether the use of drones and other forms of extrajudicial killing are justified (see chapters 13–14). A much less aggressive foreign policy approach toward the Far East is outlined in chapter 15.

Communitarianism calls attention to the essential observation that social life is not limited to two realms, namely the state and the market, but, rather, that there is an important third sector: that of the community. This sphere includes families, voluntary associations, places of worship, not-for-profits, and much more. Moreover, the new normal involves a growing fusion between the private and the public sector, both driven in part by the third one, a development that has numerous important implications for public philosophy, ideology, and politics (see chapter 16).

The New Normal: Making a Silk Purse out of a Sow's Ear

Large segments of the world experienced a major financial shakeup in 2008, followed by a major economic downturn in the United States and Europe, especially southern Europe and Ireland. Unemployment has remained high, especially among the young, and many millions of people lost not merely their jobs but also their homes, their investments, and their pension funds. Many more have had to settle for low-paying jobs that provide little to no benefits. While emerging economies initially held up much better, they too experienced a significant slowdown in their economic growth rates. This economic downturn (and rising inequality) has contributed to the rise of political alienation; the rise in a variety of right-wing expressions, including xenophobia, racism, and anti-Semitism; and support for radical right-wing parties and politicians. What do these developments portend?

One possibility is that economic development will return to a high-growth pathway. As a result, what might be called the "legitimacy of affluence" will be restored. The overwhelming majority of people will again be content with their condition, their society, and their polity. However, a considerable number of scholars hold that due to increased automation and a greater extraction of labor from fewer workers, it may prove impossible to return to a high-growth economy that can provide sufficient employment opportunities. Others cite sustainability issues, believing that we face a world in which high growth rates (and hence, affluence) cannot serve as the source of human contentment, due to environmental conditions, as well as social tensions resulting from growing inequality and rising demands. From the perspective of the affluent society, if the future unfolds in one of these less favorable ways, one must wonder if we shall bear witness to the continued rise in prominence of right-wing fringe groups (e.g., The Golden Dawn, English Defense League, Geert Wilders's Freedom Party , the Jobbik party, and an increasingly radical Tea Party in the United States). Or can one identify other sources of contentment for those who, while having achieved an income level that enables them to meet their "basic" needs, will still live in a more austere, less growth-centered environment? What other sources

[handwritten marginalia: Says you? Looks more like the media crying wolf]

of legitimacy can be developed that are not based on a continually rising standard of living?

In exploring these matters, this chapter draws primarily on data from the United States. However, we shall see that the problems it raises—as well as their possible treatments—are universal. Part I shows that since the onset of the Great Recession, many millions of Americans have experienced a taste of a less affluent, more austere life. Given their reactions, there is empirical support for the concern that austerity can lead to high levels of alienation. Part II asks whether continued affluence, even if it can be achieved, will provide a return to contentment. Part III points to the forces that help explain why higher income is not the engine of satisfaction its champions assume it is. Part IV finds that in many historical periods, high levels of contentment were not associated with high consumption, thus further supporting the thesis that these two factors are not necessarily correlated and that in the future one might well be able to find a less consumeristic culture that still engenders high levels of happiness. Part V provides a Maslovian escape from the trap set by expectations of affluence in an age of slower growth, high unemployment/underemployment, and declining marginal utility of income. Part VI introduces a culture that allows people to flourish, even in an age of austerity. Finally, Part VII points to the environmental and social justice implications of this "capped" culture.

I. Reactions to the Great Recession

The Great Recession forced the majority of Americans to consume less, and many responded by adapting in ways that entailed a less consumeristic life, rather than one of deprivation. In 2010 over seven in ten Americans reported to have bought less-expensive brands,[1] three in ten cut back on alcohol or cigarettes, 57 percent either cut back or canceled vacation plans, and others opted to go to the hairdresser less often (38 percent) or cut down on dry cleaning (24 percent). One in five Americans cancelled or cut back cable television service, and one in five stopped purchasing their morning coffee.[2] An August, 2010, survey found that 44 percent of adults were going out to eat less often than they did six months previously, while only 8 percent were eating out more often.[3] Many young people stayed longer in their parents' home than in previous periods, and there was an increase in the sharing of residential space.

These changes in consumption patterns were accompanied by gains in environmental sustainability. In her book *Plenitude: The New Economics of True Wealth*, economist Juliet Schor argued that many Americans found ways to reduce both consumption and environmental impact at the same time.[4] A June, 2010, poll found that more Americans were brown-bagging lunch instead of purchasing it (48 percent); using refillable water bottles rather than purchasing bottles of water (39 percent);[5] and 12 percent of Americans who previously drove to work began carpooling or using mass transit.[6]

In short, many Americans responded to slower growth by reducing needless consumption without suffering major deprivation. In contrast, many others—such as those who lost their homes or could not find employment—suffered far more serious setbacks.

Hence, there are some signs that the Great Recession has led people to reexamine the belief that contentment can be found in an ever-rising standard of living and whether there is merit in pursuing other sources of happiness. A 2009 survey found that 79 percent of Americans worried that society had become too shallow,[7] and 60 percent were afraid that people had become disconnected from the natural world.[8] It showed that 57 percent desired to be part of a truly important cause,[9] that 67 percent of Americans felt the recession had served to remind people of what's really important in life,[10] and that 48 percent were actively trying to figure out what made them happy.[11]

Seventy-nine percent of Americans respected or admired people who live simply (with minimal purchases, no debt, etc.), while only 15 percent felt the same way about people with high-luxury lifestyles.[12] Seventy-eight percent said that most of us would be better off if we lived more simply,[13] and 66 percent stated that they no longer desired a lot of "bells and whistles" on the products they purchase; they would rather just have them serve the functions they really need.[14]

Polls, however, have revealed that only a minority of the American population aspires to turn their recession-era behavior into the new normal. An April, 2009, poll found that only a third of Americans (32 percent) that had spent less in recent months intended to solidify this behavior as their new normal pattern in the years ahead.[15] In addition, when asked by a May, 2010, Pew study to predict their financial behaviors once the economy recovers, only 31 percent planned to spend less, and only 30 percent planned to borrow less.[16]

In short, only a minority of Americans seem to view the austere life as an opportunity to redefine what constitutes a good life. At the same time, over two-thirds of Americans hold that the nation is on a wrong course.[17] Many feel alienated from major institutions, with only 9 percent approving of Congress (a record low),[18] and only 36 percent expressing confidence in the presidency, 34 percent expressing confidence in the Supreme Court, 32 percent in the public schools, 28 percent in the criminal justice system, 26 percent in the banks, and 23 percent in television news and newspapers.[19] There has also been an increase in populism on both the right (the Tea Party) and the left (Occupy Wall Street), though these developments have also been driven by other, noneconomic factors. In other nations with higher levels of unemployment and deeper, more prolonged recessions, the rise of right-wing and antisocial behavior has been significantly more common and radicalized than in the United States.

As Benjamin Friedman notes, growth correlates strongly with greater tolerance toward both immigrants and people of different ethnicities and *i would hate to point fingers here but... Progressives have been in charge of culture for awhile now and were still sucking humor is crippled, they've also had a Prez for the last 8 years so...*

religions, greater levels of charitable giving to help the disadvantaged, and the fostering of democratic values and institutions.[20] He concludes that it is the shared sense of growing prosperity fostered by growth, and hence affluence, that makes such democratic attitudes possible, noting that historical periods of economic stagnation and retreat can undermine such attitudes and values, often "with disastrous consequences both to a country's own population and to many others besides."[21]

One would therefore predict that either the nations of the world will find a way back to a high-growth pathway, leading to ever higher and more widely distributed levels of affluence—or they will face an undemocratic future, with the majority of the people exhibiting intolerant attitudes and behavior on both the social and political level. However, one must note that the data exhibit diminishing marginal returns with respect to income and happiness—that even if one can ensure the attainment of ever higher levels of income, it will purchase ever less contentment (see next section). Even if all the nations of the world can resume course on the high-growth path, it may not suffice to ensure social peace and, above all, human flourishing. Hence, one turns to ask what other sources of contentment—ones unrelated to high and growing affluence—may provide new forms of happiness and legitimacy. *← why do you care about what others do? R you going to make them?*

II. Income and Happiness

Data suggest that once a certain threshold of income is reached, additional accumulation of income creates little additional contentment. On the whole, social science findings, which have well-known limitations and do not all run in the same direction, seem to support this notion of diminishing returns of happiness relative to income growth (with the important exception of the poor). Findings by Frank M. Andrews and Stephen B. Withey support the notion that one's socioeconomic status has a meager effect on one's sense of well-being and no significant effect on one's life satisfaction.[22] A survey of over 1,000 participants who rated their sense of satisfaction and happiness on both a seven-point scale and a three-point scale concluded that there was no correlation between socioeconomic status and happiness. In fact, the second-highest socioeconomic group was consistently among the least happy of all seven brackets measured. In addition, Jonathan Freedman discovered that levels of reported happiness do not vary greatly among the members of different economic classes, with the exception of the very poor, who tend to be less happy than others.[23]

Additional evidence suggests that economic growth does not significantly affect happiness (though at any given time the people of poor countries are generally less happy than those of wealthy ones). David G. Myers and Ed Diener reported that while per-capita disposable (after-tax) income in inflation-adjusted dollars almost exactly doubled between 1960 and 1990, almost the same proportion of Americans reported that they were "very happy" in 1993

Yes, yes money isn't everything... but it is something...↓

So many problems I'm bored already whats the solution... the reason for writing

Please tell me how your solution would've stoped Stephen from killing himself, would it have stoppe Josh?!

(32 percent) as did in 1957 (35 percent).[24] Although economic growth has slowed since the mid-1970s, Americans reported happiness has been remarkably stable (nearly always between 30 and 35 percent) across both high-growth and low-growth periods.[25] Moreover, in the same period (1960–1990), rates of depression, violent crime, divorce, and teen suicide all rose dramatically.[26]

In a 1973 study,[27] Richard Easterlin reported on a phenomenon that has since been labeled the "Easterlin paradox." At any given time, higher income generates more happiness, though over the longer run (10 years or more), happiness fails to increase alongside national income. In other words, long-term economic growth does not improve the overall happiness of citizens. Japan is an often-cited example of the Easterlin paradox. Between 1962 and 1987, the Japanese economy grew at a rapid rate, more than tripling its GNP per capita, yet Japan's overall happiness remained constant over that period.[28] Similarly, in 1970, the average American income could buy over 60 percent more than it could in the 1940s, yet average happiness did not increase.[29] A survey of those whose income had increased over a ten-year period revealed that these individuals were no happier than those whose incomes had stagnated.[30]

Interest in the Easterlin paradox was revived in the late 1990s and early 2000s as the publication of a number of scholarly articles called into question Easterlin's findings. A 2006 paper by Ruut Veenhoven and Michael Hagerty explained some of the reasons for the discrepancy among happiness researchers.[31] First, changes in happiness tend to be small and must be aggregated over long periods of time. As very little data span more than a few decades, its significance is open to interpretation. Also, average happiness tends to fluctuate, making it difficult to separate the overall trends from the statistical noise. Furthermore, there is a lack of uniformity among happiness surveys; methodologies and questions have changed over time, possibly skewing results. Hence, social scientists may choose to limit their data to only identical surveys (as Easterlin did) or take into account additional data from a variety of other surveys that may cause results to be skewed in one direction or another (as Veenhoven and Hagerty did).

While such issues can be raised about most social science studies of this kind (especially longitudinal studies), a more serious challenge is Veenhoven and Hagerty's finding that both happiness and income increased in the second half of the twentieth century, indicating a correlation between the two.[32] A 2008 paper by Betsey Stevenson and Justin Wolfers found a similar correlation between income growth and happiness.[33]

In December 2010, Easterlin and his associates published a direct response to the challenge raised by Stevenson and Wolfers.[34] The reply showed that much of the data from Stevenson and Wolfers's paper focused on a short period (six years instead of ten) and argued that the trends from the longer-term data were attributable to factors other than economic growth. They also added data from a number of non-Western, developing countries and found renewed support for the Easterlin paradox. They cited the examples of China, South Korea, and Chile to contradict claims of a positive correlation between long-term GDP growth and happiness, as all three countries have very high growth rates. China's growth rate led to a doubling of per capita income in less than ten years; South Korea's in thirteen; and Chile's in eighteen years. However, none of these countries showed a statistically significant increase in happiness. The authors wrote:

> With incomes rising so rapidly in these three different countries, it seems extraordinary that there are no surveys that register the marked improvement in subjective well-being that mainstream economists and policy makers worldwide would expect to find.[35]

There is one important exception to these findings—when incomes of the poor are increased, happiness is significantly enhanced. This is important because otherwise the data cited could be used to argue that seeking to improve the lot of the poor is pointless, as it would not contribute to happiness. Thus, as Richard Layard's 2005 book *Happiness: Lessons from a New Science* shows, when a country's average income exceeds $20,000 a year per person, it does add significantly to contentment.[36] Layard used happiness data from three major long-term public opinion surveys[37] to calculate an average happiness measure for each country, which was compared to average income per capita. (Critics of these data argue that it used absolute rather than proportional measurements.)[38]

A later study came up with a cutoff point for the correlations between individual income and happiness. A 2010 study identified $75,000 as the threshold after which additional income produces little additional happiness.[39] The study found that while having a high income improved individuals' life evaluation (their thoughts about their life), it did not improve emotional well-being, defined as "the frequency and intensity of experiences of joy, stress, sadness, anger, and affection that make one's life pleasant or unpleasant."[40] Hence, whereas life evaluation rises steadily with increases in income, emotional well-being does not progress once an annual income of $75,000 is reached.[41]

In short, although the data do not all point in one direction, the preponderance of the evidence suggests that, at the very least, high levels of income do not buy much happiness. Thus, the legitimacy bestowed by affluence is questionable, regardless of whether or not a high-growth pathway is achievable and sustainable.

III. The Sisyphean Nature of Affluence

One reason high-wage earners derive less happiness from additional income is that the goods that high incomes allow one to buy reportedly do not have *absolute* value in terms of the happiness they provide. Rather, they are judged *relative* to other goods available. Indeed, this is the explanation Easterlin himself offers, namely, that individual happiness seems to be determined by one's income relative to others rather than the absolute level of earning.

One interpretation of this claim is the familiar concept of "keeping up with the Joneses," an expression that captures the use of goods in a status competition among members of the community. Goods are used as visible markers of one's standing in this never-ending race.

The claim also explains why an increase in a nation's collective wealth often fails to increase reported happiness. If what makes people happy is having *more* wealth relative to others, then it follows that happiness is more dependent on whom one compares himself to rather than his absolute income—and one can typically find someone who earns more than he does.

Other social scientists have posited that it is not explicit social competition that is the problem. Rather, people judge the value of a given consumer good based upon a contextual assessment that factors in the goods possessed by their neighbors.[42] In thinking about the competitive consumption that characterizes "keeping up with the Joneses," one notes that the motives underlying the behavior make explicit reference to one's peers. One doesn't just want a "big" house, but rather one that is "bigger than that of the Joneses." By contrast, the contextual valuation of goods prevents collective improvements in wealth from generating collective improvements in happiness even absent any feelings of jealousy, envy, or any explicit reference being made to the conditions of others. Instead, the suggestion is that the value one derives from a given consumer good—that is, the extent to which one considers it to be of good or high quality—depends upon the goods possessed by one's peers. Thus, one does not need to want a "better" house than one's neighbors to be affected; rather, one might just want a "good" house, but such a judgment is inevitably influenced by similar goods possessed by one's neighbors. To illustrate this point, Robert Frank uses the example of how one would feel about owning a 1979 Chevrolet Nova.[43] The answer to this question, he argues, depends upon *context*: to those living in Cuba, such a car would seem a luxury while those living in the California would likely find such a car embarrassing or unwieldy.[44] Similarly, regarding whether one judges a living space to be "large enough," one's teeth to be in good shape from an orthodontic standpoint, or one's clothes to be "nice," Frank argues that the determination is made by comparing what one has with similar goods possessed by one's peers.[45]

Studies have shown how contextual judgments affect reported subjective well-being: people taking happiness surveys in the presence of someone in a wheelchair rate themselves as 20 percent happier on average than those in a control group.[46] Given this evidence, increasing the total wealth of a given society would not necessarily increase the happiness of its members since more or "better" consumer goods would merely raise the bar for what people judged to be "good"—a rising standard that would leave people perpetually dissatisfied with their material objects, even as the quality and quantity of those goods increased. At the same time, it would also explain why providing money to the poor *would* have a positive effect upon their reported well-being as such a transfer would improve their material well-being *relative* to the societal standard.

The same factor seems to help explain why people in small towns are happier than those in big cities.[47] Daniel Gilbert thus notes:

> Now, if you live in Hallelujah, Arkansas, the odds are good that most of the people you know do something like you do and earn something like you earn and live in houses something like yours. New York, on the other hand, is the most varied, most heterogeneous place on earth. No matter how hard you try, you really can't avoid walking by restaurants where people drop your monthly rent on a bottle of wine and store windows where shoes sit like museum pieces on gold pedestals. You can't help but feel trumped.[48]

Another explanation for why increased income often does not improve happiness is that human beings as consumers are doomed to run on a "hedonic treadmill."[49] There are a number of different accounts regarding what constitutes the hedonic treadmill.[50] One account suggests that people psychologically acclimatize to changes in well-being, gravitating to a set level of happiness regardless of external stimulus. It is this usage that characterizes the results of the study that led to the coining of the term. Conducted by Philip Brickman, Dan Coates, and Ronnie Janoff-Bulman, this study found that people who had won the lottery were no happier than a control group of nonwinners.[51] Similarly, a survey found that those on the *Forbes* list of the 100 wealthiest Americans were only "modestly" happier than a control group selected randomly from the same geographic areas.[52]

Alternatively, the "hedonic treadmill" is understood as a rise in aspirations that accompanies improvements in material well-being that offsets any accompanying hedonic gains. Thus, a study of rural Chinese people found that while a rising income improved subjective well-being, it also raised income aspirations, which lowered well-being.[53] The authors propose that this "partial hedonic treadmill" explains why China's rapid economic growth has not translated into gains in subjective well-being.[54] It would also explain Amartya Sen's findings that subjective well-being in poor countries often surpasses what is found in rich countries as those living in poor nations will have often adjusted their expectations to match their circumstances while the citizens of wealthy nations continue to aim for a higher quality of life than they can realistically attain.[55]

Either way, there is no way to find contentment in the high-growth, high-consumption, high-affluence way of life if one's well-being is determined not by the satisfaction of one's needs but by what others have gained—or if the more one buys, the more one feels the need to buy.

IV. Historical Precedents for Nonaffluence-Based Contentment

In seeking alternatives to growth-driven happiness (or lack thereof), one can turn to historical movements and previous cultures and modes of legitimacy that eschewed consumerism and viewed the good life as based on other core values. As Jeffrey Sachs notes, "the essence of traditional virtue ethics—whether in Buddhism, Aristotelianism, or Roman Catholicism—is that happiness is achieved by harnessing the will and the passions to live the right kind of life. Individuals become virtuous through rational thought, instruction, mind training, and habits of virtuous behavior."[56] Thus, consider the way happiness is understood within the Buddhist tradition. According to this view, happiness is not a phenomenological state, but rather "a way of interpreting the world," and thus is more akin to a skill or ability than a sensation.[57]

For centuries the literati of imperial China came to prominence not through acquisition of wealth but through pursuit of knowledge and cultivation of the arts. This group of scholar-bureaucrats dedicated their early lives to rigorous study in preparation for the exams required for government service. They spent years memorizing the Confucian classics. Having passed the imperial exams, the literati were qualified for government service but elected instead to dedicate their lives to the arts or retired early to follow artistic pursuits. They played music and composed poetry, learned calligraphy, and gathered with like-minded friends to share ideas and discuss great works of the past.

Reinhard Bendix writes that in keeping with Confucian teachings,

> the educated man must stay away from the pursuit of wealth . . . because acquisitiveness is a source of social and personal unrest. To be sure, this would not be the case if the success of economic pursuits was guaranteed, but in the absence of such a guarantee the poise and harmony of the soul are jeopardized by the risks involved. . . . The cultured man strives for the perfection of the self, whereas all occupations that involve the pursuit of riches require a one-sided specialization that acts against the universality of the gentleman.[58]

The Ancient Greeks—aside from the Epicureans[59]—generally took "happiness" to be not just a feeling but a way of living.[60] For example, in Aristotle's philosophy the sort of "happiness" discussed is not hedonistic but rather can also be translated as "flourishing" and is based in the manifestation of various virtues. It is a way of being that can be cultivated, and it involves finding a balance between "excess and deficiency" as well as experiencing "emotions at the right times and on the right occasions and towards the right persons and for the right causes and in the right manner."[61] Indeed, Aristotle believed that happiness is comprised of acting in accordance with excellence, in particular the greatest and richest variety of excellence available.[62] In addition to viewing happiness as including the "activity of soul in accordance with virtue," Aristotle's conception of happiness is much broader than that of many contemporary thinkers, amounting to "flourishing human living, a kind of living that is active, inclusive of all that has intrinsic value, and complete, meaning lacking in nothing that would make it richer or better."[63] It thus stands in contrast to the sort of well-being used by most contemporary economists, whose conception of happiness lines up much more with Bentham's hedonistic account of happiness.[64]

Saint Thomas Aquinas presents a conception of happiness grounded in Christian tradition and questions of teleology. For Aquinas, happiness is not a pleasurable psychological state but rather the attainment of one's final good (as opposed to instrumental goods that may help one attain this final good).[65] For Aquinas this final good "consists in the vision of God," meaning that true happiness cannot be attained on Earth but can be only approximated.[66] Though people may get moments of temporary satisfaction after achieving short-term goals, true happiness comes only with the attainment of union with God.[67]

During the Middle Ages, knights were expected to adhere to an exacting code of chivalry. The tenets they were expected to live by are well-captured in *The Song of Roland*, an eleventh-century poem. Throughout the poem the worthy knight is shown to gladly and faithfully serve his liege lord, to protect the weak and the defenseless, to show proper reverence for God, to respect and honor women, to be truthful and steadfast, and to view financial reward with revulsion and disdain. (In traditional Jewish communities, studying the Torah was considered the preferred way of life.)

In recent ages, numerous social movements and communities have pursued other forms of the good life within capitalist societies. The Shakers, who left Manchester, England, for America in the 1770s, founded religious communities characterized by a simple ascetic lifestyle.[68] Other such communities (some secular, some religious) include the Brook Farm Institute, the Harmony Society, the Amana Colonies, and the Amish. In Britain, John Ruskin founded the Guild of Saint George in the 1870s, which he intended to guide the formation of agrarian communities that would lead a simple and modest life. Jewish refugees who emigrated to Palestine starting early in the twentieth century established kibbutzim, in which the austere life was considered virtuous, consumption was held down, communal life promoted, and advancing a socialist and Zionist agenda was a primary goal of life. Numerous religious orders also started with an ascetic life.

In the 1960s, a counterculture "hippie" movement rose on both sides of the Atlantic. Its core values were anticonsumerism, communal living, equality, environmentalism, free love, and pacifism. Timothy Leary encapsulated the hippie ethos when he advised a crowd to "turn on, tune in, and drop out."[69] The British iteration of the hippie movement manifested itself in London's underground culture, a "community of like-minded anti-establishment, anti-war, pro-rock'n'roll individuals, most of whom had a common interest in recreational drugs," and many who opted out of mainstream consumerist culture.[70]

Many of these movements and communities sought to buy out of both the consumption and work system of capitalism and to form an alternative universe committed to an ascetic lifestyle, while dedicating themselves to transcendental activities including spiritual, religious, political, or social elements. They sought to replace capitalism rather than to cap it and graft it on a different society.

Most important, these various movements and communities failed to lay a foundation for a new contemporary society—let alone civilization—and practically all of them either disintegrated, shriveled, or lost their main alternative features. It seems that most people cannot abide an ascetic, severe, and austere life in the longer run. Hence, it seems that if the current environment calls for a new attempt to form a society less centered around consumption, the endeavor will have to graft the new conception of a good life onto the old one. It should seek not to replace consumption but to cap and channel some of its resources and energies and apply them to other pursuits. When one knows that income can be capped without frustrating basic human needs is a question Maslow helps in addressing.

V. The Maslovian Exit

Though published in 1943, Abraham Maslow's "A Theory of Human Motivation" nevertheless speaks directly to our current predicament. Maslow argued that humans have a hierarchy of needs. At the bottom are basic human necessities. Once these are sated, affection and self-esteem are next in line, and finally we can reach the pinnacle of human satisfaction by attending to what he calls "self-actualization." It follows that so long as the acquisition and consumption of goods satisfies basic creature comforts such as safety, shelter, food, clothing, health care, and education, then rising wealth is contributing to genuine human contentment. However, once consumption is used to satisfy the higher needs, it turns into consumerism, which then becomes a social disease.

In historical terms, the turning point for Americans with incomes well above the poverty line came in the decades following WWII. Around the time of WWII, economists held that individuals have fixed needs. Once satisfied, people would allocate additional income toward savings rather than consumption. During the war, however, economists noted that the American productive capacity had greatly expanded. They feared that with the end of the war, the idling of the assembly lines that produced thousands of tanks, planes, and many other war-related materials would lead to massive unemployment—a return to the kind of depression the US had faced prior to WWII—because there was nothing that the assembly lines could produce that people needed, given that fixed, peacetime needs were sated.

In this context, David Riesman published a widely-discussed essay called "Abundance For What?"[71] He suggested that the "surplus" be used for projects such as paying the people of New Orleans to continue to maintain their 1955 lifestyle, so future generations of children could come and visit this sociological Disneyland to see what life was like in earlier ages, much as we do today in colonial Williamsburg.[72] Social scientists thus held that they had to go to creative extremes to protect society from its "excess" capacity. However, this conventional wisdom was soon to change when Vance Packard's *The Status Seekers* called attention to the purveyors of large scale advertising, the producers of artificial, unbounded wants.[73]

In the decades that followed WWII, industrial corporations discovered that they could "manufacture" artificial needs for whatever products they were marketing. For instance, first women and then men were taught that they smelled bad and needed to purchase deodorants. Men, who used to wear white shirts and grey flannel suits, learned that they "had to" purchase a variety of shirts and suits, and that last year's wear was not proper in the year that followed. Soon it was not just suits but also cars, ties, handbags, sunglasses, watches, and numerous other products that had to be constantly replaced to keep up with the latest trends. More recently, people have been convinced that they have various illnesses (such as restless leg syndrome) that require the purchase of medications.

One cannot stress enough that the quest for a new characterization of the good life is a project for those whose creature comforts have been well and securely sated. Urging such a project on individuals, classes, or societies that have not reached that stage of development is to promote what sociologists call "status acceptance," to urge the have-nots to love their misery. It provides a rationale to those who have all they need and more, and who deny such basics to others. Such a position hardly comports with any definition of a good life.

To reiterate, consumption *per se* is not the issue. Maslow does not suggest an austere life of sacks and ashes, nor does he promote making virtue out of poverty. Rather, his theory holds that gaining the material resources needed to provide for basic creature comforts is fully legitimate. However, consumption turns into an obsession when—after necessities are provided—people use the means suitable for attending to creature comforts to try to buy affection, esteem, and even self-actualization. The point is the subject of a considerable number of plays and novels, most dramatically *Death of a Salesman*. In the play, the husband (the context is of earlier generations, in which the breadwinner typically was the man of the house) neglects his spouse, children, and community by investing his time and energy in "bringing home the bacon." In the process, he and his family are shortchanged.

Maslow's conception of the good life falls short, however, in its characterization of self-actualization as the highest good. It is far from clear what he means by this concept, although leading with the "self" serves as a warning signal. Maslow does not find that self-actualization is best achieved by finding meaning in or serving anything greater than self. Any and all forms of self-expression seem equally valued.

More recently, Robert and Edward Skidelsky, in their book *How Much Is Enough?: Money and the Good Life*, written after the onset of the Great Recession, lay out a specific re-characterization of what counts as a good life in the new normal age. They argue that we should leave the rat race by working fewer hours, consuming fewer material goods, and finding contentment from other sources. They list seven goods that are neither labor nor capital-intensive, yet are intrinsically satisfying rather than driven by the consumerist quest to live up to the Joneses and the advertisers demands.

Richard Posner has criticized this approach, arguing that Americans require "expensive leisure" such as "foreign travel, movies and television, casinos, restaurants, . . . having cosmetic surgery, and improving health and longevity."[74] However, one can actually enjoy chess played with plastic pieces about as much as playing with mahogany-carved ones; Shakespeare, the Bible, and Stephen King read about as well in a paperback (or e-reader) edition as in a leather-bound one; and playing dominoes or bocce ball is just as pleasurable as golf. (When an article on this subject was published in Polish, Andrzej Lubowski added, "You do not need a BMW to drive to a picnic.") One can travel by bike and couch surf. Meditation and praying cost even less. In effect, millions of Americans who retire before they must are choosing to work less and thus reduce their lifelong earnings, settling for more leisure time and a less costly lifestyle. And contra Posner, millions of parents of young children choose to curtail their gainful employment and enjoy more time with their kids, showing that such a life is not just possible but also satisfying. So far, so good.

Skidelsky and Skidelsky's seven elements of a good life are decoupled from consumerism but not necessarily from self-centeredness. Two goods are dedicated to creature comforts, namely *security* and good *health*. In their rendering, security is of the person, not the nation; health is that of the individual, with little attention to public health. The inclusion of *respect* and *friendship* (akin to Maslow's self-esteem and affection) in the list of goods is a major step forward, as gaining these goods is disassociated from buying things to enhance one's status or to express friendship.

Skidelsky and Skidelsky enrich Maslow by adding three goods. First is *harmony with nature*, which for them is not an expression of concern for the environment, but rather a quest fort inner tranquility of the individual.[75] Next on the list is *personality*, which is "the ability to frame and execute a plan of life reflective of one's tastes, temperament and conception of the good . . . as well [as] an element of spontaneity, individuality and spirit."[76] Both are self-centered. Finally, while Maslow put self-actualization at the pinnacle, Skidelsky and Skidelsky crown *leisure* at the top of the list of the goods. Leisure is defined as "self-directed activity" and "purposiveness without purpose."[77] It is an intrinsic good wherein people can and should flourish by doing well in whatever they choose to undertake: "The sculptor engrossed in cutting marble, the teacher intent on imparting a difficult idea, the musician struggling with a score . . . such people have no other aim than to do what they are doing well."[78]

This idea has very long roots, going all the way back to Aristotle, who is said to have argued that:

> every substance not only possess a form; one could say it is also possessed by a form, for it naturally strives to realise its inherent form. It strives to become a perfect specimen of its kind. Every substance seeks to actualize what it is potentially.[79]

On first reading, there is something quite appealing about this idea. There is something endearing, maybe even ennobling, in a sculptor struggling with a block of marble, etching out the form that is, thus far, only in his mind, and one which the marble is "resisting," or in a musician working hard to marshal his cello so it will play the music in the way the musician feels it ought to sound. A life so lived is indeed better lived than one centered around shopping for the latest iPhone, Martha Stewart towel, or this year's ties mandated via advertising, so as to keep up with the Joneses. However, what is missing is crucial: attention to others and the common good. For Skidelsky and Skidelsky, it seems that so long as the activity involves a true effort and pleases the individual, it qualifies as good.

Aristotle greatly enriched this teleological way of thinking by adding the assumption that people are social animals by nature. Hence, for them to fully develop and flourish, they must seek to participate in public life. In contrast, Skidelsky and Skidelsky write, "the first goal of the individual is to realize the good life for himself."[80] They never get around to discussing the higher goals because to them "enjoyment"—albeit a sophisticated joy—is the good life. What they extol is ultimately a nonmaterialistic form of consumerism.

VI. True Flourishing—A Communitarian, Postmodern Culture.

Cultures that highly value the following activities and purposes are referred to here as "communitarian," as each activity involves forming and nurturing bonds of affinity to others, and service to the common good.[81] The term postmodern is used because reference is made not to earlier communities that often were overwhelming and oppressive (what Erving Goffman called total institutions[82]), but to new, more liberal ones.

There are three major sources of nonmaterialistic contentment that also provide for a life that reaches beyond the self. They are all compatible with the Maslovian hierarchy of human needs; however, they also add a dimension— a requirement to the particular way these needs are to be stated. These sources of contentment are briefly summarized as follows.

1. The Contentment of Mutuality

Spending time with those with whom one shares bonds of affinity—children, spouses, friends, or members of one's community—has often been shown to make people happier.[83] Indeed, approval from those with whom a person is bonded is a main source of affection and esteem, and is Maslow's second layer of human needs. However, more is involved in engaging in social relations than simply making the ego happy. These relationships are based on mutuality in which two people "give" and "receive" in one and the same act. Those who engage in lasting, meaningful, and effective relationships find them to be a major source of mutual enrichment, which can be achieved with very little expenditure or material costs. (Note that much of the literature contrasts ego-centered activities with altruistic ones.[84] Much more attention should be paid to mutuality, because it is much more common and stable than altruism.)

Both introverts and extroverts report feeling happier when they are with other people.[85] Derek Bok writes that "several researchers have concluded that human relationships and connections of all kinds contribute more to happiness than anything else."[86] Conversely, people who are socially isolated are less happy than those who have strong social relationships. As one study put it, "Adults who feel socially isolated are also characterized by higher levels of anxiety, negative mood, dejection, hostility, fear of negative evaluation, and perceived stress, and by lower levels of optimism, happiness, and life satisfaction."[87] Research shows that married people are happier than those who are single, divorced, widowed, separated, or cohabiting.[88] In addition, the presence of close friendships can have nearly as strong an impact on happiness as a successful marriage.[89]

2. Happiness from Community Involvement

Researchers who examined the effect of community involvement (as opposed to merely socializing with friends or family) also found a strong correlation with happiness. One study, which evaluated survey data from 49 countries, found that membership in (nonchurch) organizations has a significant positive correlation with happiness.[90] Bok notes, "Some researchers have found that merely attending monthly club meetings or volunteering once a month is associated with a change in well-being equivalent to a doubling of income."[91] Other studies have found that individuals who devote substantial amounts of time to volunteer work have greater life satisfaction.[92]

Political participation too yields the fruits of bonding and meaningful activities. As one scholar notes, using the terms of an economist, "Citizens do not only gain utility from the outcome of the political process and its material consequences but also from the democratic process itself."[93] This is particularly true when the political climate is perceived as fair, and thus even those whose preferred candidates are defeated feel as though they had an opportunity to have their political preferences considered.[94] Also, research has found that adolescents who have a greater commitment to contributing to society or pursuing some meaningful end have positive experiences of greater depth and intensity than their less politically-engaged peers.[95]

3. Transcendental Pursuits (Religious, Spiritual, and Intellectual)

Extensive evidence indicates that people who consider themselves religious, express a belief in God, or regularly attend religious services are more content than those who do not. According to one study, agreement with the statement "God is important in my life," was associated with a gain of 3.5 points on a 100-point scale of happiness.[96] (For comparison, unemployment is associated with a 6-point drop on the same scale.) Other studies show that Americans with a deep religious faith are healthier, live longer, and have lower rates of divorce, crime, and suicide.[97] In their 2010 book *American Grace*, Robert Putnam and David Campbell reported that "a common finding [of happiness researchers] is that religiosity is among the closest correlates of life satisfaction, at least as strong as income."[98] They found that the difference in happiness between a person who goes to church once a week and someone who does not attend church was "slightly larger than the difference between someone who earns $10,000 a year and his demographic twin who earns $100,000 a year."[99]

There is some debate as to whether the effect of religiosity on happiness is attributable to participation in religious activities (attending church services, involvement with a religious community) or religious belief. Layard character-izes the correlation between belief in God and life satisfaction as "one of the most robust findings of happiness research,"[100] whereas Putnam and Campbell argue, "The religious edge in life satisfaction has less to do with faith itself than with communities of faith."[101] Whichever is correct, one still learns that religious life is positively correlated with happiness.

There is little research on transcendental activities other than religious pur-suits. However, the evidence that exists indicates that participation in activities that have profound meaning to the individual is associated with happiness. For example, "two studies that examined groups that chose to change their lifestyle to achieve personal values such as 'environmental friendliness' and 'voluntary simplicity' found that both experienced higher levels of well-being."[102] A study used survey data from over 500 subscribers of a back-to-the-land magazine to measure participants' sense of well-being and determine whether they lived up to their sustainability values. The researchers found that those who were able to put their values into practice (live in a sustainable, ecologically friendly manner) were more satisfied with their lives than those who did not.[103]

Much like social activities, volunteering, and political action—which are inherently communitarian—transcendental activities also provide noncon-sumerist sources of contentment. Although some can be isolating and self-centered, many do uphold the values of communitarianism.

VII. Contributions to Sustainability and Social Justice

If postmodern societies could develop a culture of capping that expects every-one to be able to attain sufficient income to provide for a secure flow of the goods needed to attend to their basic creature needs, but otherwise center life around nonmaterialistic, social, and transcendental goods, that culture would provide one obvious major contribution to higher levels of contentment (and hence less alienation and anti-social behavior), as well as one that is far from obvious.

Obviously, a good life that combines caps on consumption and work with a dedication to transcendental pursuits is much less taxing on the environment than consumerism and the level of work needed to pay for it. This is the case because transcendental activities require relatively few scarce resources, fossil fuels, or other sources of physical energy. Social activities (such as spending more time with one's children) require time and personal energy but not large material or financial outlays. (Often those who spend large amounts of money on their kids' toys or entertainment bond less with them than those whose relations are less mediated by objects.) The same holds for cultural and spiritual activities such as prayer, meditation, enjoying and making music, art, sports, and adult education. True, consumerism has turned many of these pursuits into expensive endeavors. However, one can break out of this mentality and find that it is possible to engage in most transcendental activities quite profoundly using a moderate amount of goods and services. One does not need designer clothes to enjoy the sunset or shoes with fancy labels to benefit from a hike. The Lord does not listen better to prayers read from a leather-bound Bible than to those read from a plain one printed on recycled paper. In short, the transcendental society is much more sustainable than consumer capitalism.

Much less obvious are the ways the capped culture serves social justice. Social justice entails transferring wealth from those disproportionally endowed to those who are underprivileged. A major reason such reallocation of wealth has been surprisingly limited in free societies is that those who command the "extra" assets tend also to be those who are politically powerful. Promoting social justice by organizing those with less and forcing those in power to yield has had limited success in democratic countries and led to massive bloodshed in others. However, one must expect that if those in power were willing to embrace the capped culture, they would be much more ready to share than otherwise. This thesis is supported by the behavior of middle class people who are committed to the values of giving and attending to the least among us—values prescribed by many religions and by left-wing liberalism. This important thesis requires a whole distinct study and is included here merely to mention a major side benefit of the new culture rather than document it.

In Conclusion

The Great Recession is one major reason for the rise of alienation and radical political forces in many nations. It is not clear that we can return to a high-growth, job-rich pathway. Even if we could, increasing the income of those whose basic needs have already been sated would buy ever-less contentment. Hence, a question arises as to which other sources of contentment can be found. History has shown that people can find a meaningful and rich life without consumerism, referencing not a life of poverty, but one that caps consumption, allowing the surplus resources to shift to other pursuits, in particular to communitarian pursuits that are neither labor nor capital intensive. That is, that are environmentally friendly, sustainable, and supportive of social justice.

Notes

1. "Coming to an Office Near You," *The Economist* (January 18, 2014), http://www.economist.com/news/leaders/21594298-effect-todays-technology-tomorrows-jobs-will-be-immenseand-no-country-ready, 7.
2. Ibid.
3. Julie Jargon, "Wealthy Take Bigger Helping of Fast Food," *Wall Street Journal* (September 30, 2010), http://online.wsj.com/article/SB1000142405274870 343160457552208069507478.html.
4. Juliet Schor, *Plenitude: The New Economics of True Wealth* (New York: Penguin Press, 2010).
5. "Americans Still Cutting Back on the Little Things to Save Money," Harris Interactive, poll no. 91 (July 21, 2010), http://www.harrisinteractive.com/Default.aspx?tabid=447&ctl=ReadCustom%20Default&mid=1508&Articl eId=442.
6. Ibid.
7. "Prosumer Report: The Emergence of the New Consumer," Euro RSCG Worldwide, (2010), http://www.thenewconsumer.com/wp-content/uploads/2010/11/Prosumer_Report_New_Consumer_Presentation.pdf: 20.
8. Ibid., 24.
9. Ibid., 31.
10. Ibid., 30
11. Ibid., 17.
12. Ibid., 50.
13. Ibid., 47.
14. Ibid.
15. Frank Newport, "In U.S., 32% Say Spending Less Is Their 'New Normal," Gallup (April 27, 2009), http://www.gallup.com/poll/118003/say-spending-less-new-normal.aspx.
16. "How the Great Recession Has Changed Life in America," Pew Social & Demographic Trends (June 30, 2010), http://www.pewsocialtrends.org/2010/06/30/how-the-great-recession-has-changed-life-in-america/.
17. Mike Dorning, "Americans Turn on Washington, 68% Say Wrong Track in Poll," *Bloomberg* (September 25, 2013), http://www.bloomberg.com/news/2013-09-25/americans-turn-on-washington-68-say-wrong-track-in-poll.html.
18. Katy Steinmetz, "The 9%: Congress's Approval Rating Hits the Single Digits," *Time*, (November 12, 2013), http://swampland.time.com/2013/11/12/the-9-congress-approval-rating-hits-the-single-digits/.
19. "Confidence in Institutions," Gallup (June 1–4, 2013), http://www.gallup.com/poll/1597/confidence-institutions.aspx#1.
20. Benjamin Friedman, "The Moral Consequences of Economic Growth," *Society* 43 (January/February 2006): 5–8, 6–7.

21. Ibid., 7.
22. Frank M. Andrews and Stephen B. Withey, *Social Indicators of Well-Being: Americans' Perceptions of Life Quality* (New York: Plenum Press, 1976).
23. Jonathan L. Freedman, *Happy People: What Happiness Is, Who Has It, and Why* (New York: Harcourt Brace Jovanovich, 1978).
24. David G. Myers and Ed Diener, "Who Is Happy," *Psychological Science*, 6, no.1 (January 1995): 12–13.
25. Ibid.
26. Ibid.
27. Richard Easterlin, "Does Money Buy Happiness," *The Public Interest*, 30 (Winter 1973).
    Also: Richard Easterlin, "Does Economic Growth Improve the Human Lot? Some Empirical Evidence," in *Nations and Households in Economic Growth: Essays in Honor of Moses Abramovitz* eds. Paul A. David and Melvin W. Reder (New York: Academic Press, Inc., 1974).
28. Richard Easterlin, "Diminishing Marginal Utility of Income? Caveat Emptor," *Social Indicators Research* 70, (2005): 243–55.
29. Richard Easterlin, "Does Money Buy Happiness," *The Public Interest*, 30 (Winter 1973).
30. David G. Myers and Ed Diener, "The Pursuit of Happiness," *Scientific American*, 274, no. 5 (1996): 70–72.
31. Ruut Veenhoven and Michael Hagerty, "Rising Happiness in Nations 1946–2004," *Social Indicators Research* 79, no 3 (2006): 421–36.
32. Ibid.
33. Betsey Stevenson and Justin Wolfers, "Economic Growth and Subjective Well-Being: Reassessing the Easterlin Paradox," *Brookings Papers on Economic Activity*, 39 (Spring 2008): 69.
34. Easterlin, et al., "The Happiness-Income Paradox Revisited," *PNAS* 107, no. 52 (December 2010): 22463–68.
35. Ibid., 22467.
36. Richard Layard, *Happiness: Lessons from a New Science* (New York: Penguin, 2005), 32–35.
37. The Eurobarometer for Western Europe, the General Social Survey for the United States, and the World Values Survey for Eastern Europe and developing nations.
38. "Economic Focus: The Joyless or the Jobless," *The Economist* (November 27, 2010): 84.
39. Daniel Kahneman and Angus Deaton, "High income improves evaluation of life but not emotional well-being," *Proceedings of the National Academy of Sciences of the United States of America* 107, no. 38 (September 21, 2010): 16489–93.
40. Ibid., 16489.
41. The two figures ($20,000 per year and $75,000 per year) are not directly comparable. The first measures a nation's average income; the second comments on individual income.
42. See, for example: Robert H. Frank, *Falling Behind: How Rising Inequality Harms the Middle Class* (Berkeley: University of California Press, 2007), 29–42.
43. Ibid., 32.

44. Ibid., 32–33.

45. Ibid., 29–42.

46. Fritz Strack, et al. "Salience of Comparison Standards and the Activation of Social Norms: Consequences for Judgements of Happiness and their Communication," *British Journal of Social Psychology* 29, no. 4 (1990): 303–314.

    Further evidence supporting that such judgments are contextual can be found in: Norbert Schwarz and Fritz Strack, "Reports of Subjective Well-Being: Judgmental Processes and Their Methodological Implications," *Well-being: The Foundations of Hedonic Psychology*, eds. D. Kahneman, E. Diener, N. Schwarz (New York: Russell Sage Foundation, 1999): 61–84.

47. Jennifer Senior, "Some Dark Thoughts on Happiness," *New York Magazine* (July 17, 2006), http://nymag.com/news/features/17573/.

48. Ibid.

49. See note 33 at 69.

50. Daniel Kahneman, "Objective Happiness," in *Well-Being: The Foundations of Hedonic Psychology*, eds. D. Kahneman, E. Diener, N. Schwarz (New York: Russell Sage Foundation, 1999), 3–25.

51. Philip Brickman, Dan Coates, and Ronnie Janoff-Bulman, "Lottery Winners and Accident Victims: Is Happiness Relative?" *Journal of Personality and Social Psychology* 36, no. 8 (1978): 917–27.

    Also: Jennifer Senior, "Some Dark Thoughts on Happiness," *New York Magazine* (July 17, 2006), http://nymag.com/news/features/17573/.

52. Ed Diener, Jeff Horwitz, and Robert A. Emmons, "Happiness of the Very Wealthy," *Social Indicators Research* 16, no. 3 (April 1985): 263–74.

53. John Knight, and Ramani Gunatilaka, "Income, Aspirations and the Hedonic Treadmill in a Poor Society," *Journal of Economic Behavior & Organization* 82, no. 1 (2012): 67–81.

54. Ibid.

55. Amartya Sen, *Development as Freedom* (New York: Knopf, 1999).

56. Jeffrey D. Sachs, "Restoring Virtue Ethics in the Quest for Happiness," in *World Happiness Report 2013*, eds. John Helliwell, Richard Layard, and Jeffrey Sachs (New York: UN Sustainable Development Solutions Network, 2013), 85.

57. Matthie Ricard, Happiness: *A Guide to Developing Life's Most Important Skill* (New York: Little Brown and Company, 2000), 19.

58. Reinhard Bendix, *Max Weber: An Intellectual Portrait* (Berkeley: University of California Press, 1977), 124.

59. Martha Nussbaum, "Mill Between Aristotle and Bentham," *Economics and Happiness: Framing and Analysis*, eds. Luigino Bruni and Pier Luigi Porta, (New York: Oxford University Press, 2005), 173.

    Nussbaum notes that throughout almost the entire canon of Western philosophy, almost all schools of thought refuse to identify "happiness" with psychological "pleasure,"

60. Martin Seligman, cited in Jennifer Senior "All Joy and No Fun," *New York Magazine* (July 4, 2010), http://nymag.com/news/features/67024/index5.html#print.

61. Jeffrey D. Sachs, "Restoring Virtue Ethics in the Quest for Happiness," *World Happiness Report 2013*, John Helliwell, Richard Layard, and Jeffrey Sachs, (New

York: UN Sustainable Development Solutions Network, 2013): 84. He quotes Aristotle, *The Niocomachean Ethics* (Amherst: Prometheus Books, 1987), 54.

62. Martha Nussbaum, "Mill Between Aristotle and Bentham," *Economics and Happiness: Framing and Analysis*, eds. Luigino Bruni and Pier Luigi Porta, (New York: Oxford University Press, 2005): 175.

63. Ibid., 171.

64. Luigino Bruni and Pier Luigi Porta, "Introduction," *Economics and Happiness: Framing the Analysis*, eds. Luigino Bruni and Pier Luigi Porta, (New York: Oxford University Press, 2005): 20.

65. Stephen Wang, "Aquinas on Human Happiness and the Natural Desire for God," *New Blackfriars* 88, no. 1015, (May 2007): 322–334, 322.

66. Ibid., 323.

67. Ibid., 326.

68. "The Shakers," *National Park Service*, http://www.nps.gov/nr/travel/shaker/shakers.htm.

69. *American Experience* episode "Summer of Love" film transcript, accessed May 29, 2014, http://www.pbs.org/wgbh/amex/love/filmmore/pt.html.

70. Barry Miles, "Spirit of the Underground: The 60s Rebel," *The Guardian*, January 30, 2011, http://www.guardian.co.uk/culture/2011/jan/30/underground-arts-60s-rebel-counterculture.

71. David Riesman, "Abundance for What?" *Abundance for What?* (New Brunswick, New Jersey: Transaction, 1993).

72. Ibid., 305.

73. Vance Packard and Brian Abbott, *The Status Seekers: An Exploration of Class Behaviour in America* (Harmondsworth: Penguin, 1963).

74. Richard A. Posner, "Working 9 to 12," *The New York Times* (August 17, 2012), http://www.nytimes.com/2012/08/19/books/review/how-much-is-enough-by-robert-skidelsky-and-edward-skidelsky.html.

75. Robert Skidelsky and Edward Skidelsy, *How Much is Enough? Money and the Good Life* (New York: Other Press, 2012), 162–63.

76. Ibid., 160.

77. Ibid., 9.

78. Ibid.

79. Richard Tarnas, *The Passion of the Western Mind: Understanding the Ideas That Have Shaped Our World View* (Ballantine Books, 1991), 58.

80. See note 75 at 169.

81. Amitai Etzioni, *The New Golden Rule: Community and Morality in a Democratic Society* (New York: Basic Books, 1996).

82. Goffman, Erving, and William B. Helmreich, *Asylums: Essays on the Social Situation of Mental Patients and Other Inmates*, vol. 277 (New York: Anchor Books, 1961).

83. Robert Sugden, "Correspondence of Sentiments: An Explanation of the Pleasure of Social Interaction," *Economics and Happiness: Framing the Analysis*, ed. Luigino Bruni and Pier Luigi Porta, (New York: Oxford University Press, 2005): 97–98.

Also: Robert E. Lane, "Does Money Buy Happiness?" *Public Interest* (Fall 1993): 58.

Also: Robert D. Putnam, "Bowling Alone: America's Declining Social Capital," *Journal of Democracy* 6, no. 1 (1995): 65–78.

84.   See, for example: Gary S. Becker, "Altruism, Egoism, and Genetic Fitness:
       Economics and Sociobiology," *Journal of Economic Literature* 14, no. 3 (1976):
       817–26.
          Also: Jeffrey Harrison, "Egoism, Altruism, and Market Illusions: The
       Limits of Law and Economics," *UCLA Law Review* 33 (1986).
          Also: Daniel C. Batson and Adam A. Powell, "Altruism and Prosocial
       Behavior," *Handbook of Psychology* (2003).
          Also: Amitai Etzioni, *The Moral Dimension: Toward a New Economics*
       (New York: The Free Press, 1988).
85.   Derek Bok, *The Politics of Happiness: What Government Can Learn from
       the New Research on Well Being* (Princeton, NJ: Princeton University Press,
       2010), 19.
86.   Ibid.
87.   Cacioppo and Hawkley, "Social Isolation and Health, with an Emphasis on
       Underlying Mechanisms," *Perspectives in Biology and Medicine*, 46.3 (2003):
       S39–S52
88.   Ibid., 17.
89.   Ibid., 19.
90.   John F. Helliwell, "Well-Being, Social Capital and Public Policy: What's
       New?" *Economic Modelling*, 20:2 (March 2003): 331–360.
91.   Ibid., 20.
92.   Ibid., 22.
93.   Bruno S. Frey and Alois Stutzer, "Happiness Prospers in Democracy," *Journal
       of Happiness Studies* 1 (2000): 79–102, 82.
94.   Ibid.
95.   Zipora Magen, "Commitment Beyond the Self and Adolescence: The Issue
       of Happiness," *Social Indicators Research* 37, no. 3 (March 1996): 235–67.
96.   See note 59 at 64.
97.   Derek Bok, The Politics of Happiness: What Government Can Learn from
       the New Research on Well Being (Princeton, NJ: Princeton University Press,
       2010): 21–22.
98.   Robert D. Putnam and David E. Campbell, *American Grace: How Religion
       Divides and Unites Us* (New York: Simon and Schuster, 2010), 490.
99.   Ibid., 491.
100.   See note 60 at 72.
101.   Putnam and Campbell, 491–92.
102.   See note 97 at 22.
          See also: Kirk Warren Brown and Tim Kasser, "Are Psychological and
       Ecological Well-Being Compatible? The Role of Values, Mindfulness, and
       Lifestyle," *Social Indicators Research*, 74 (2005): 349–68.
103.   Jeffrey C. Jacob and Merlin B. Brinkerhoff, "Values, Performance and
       Subjective Well-Being in the Sustainability Movement: An Elaboration of
       Multiple Discrepancy Theory," *Social Indicators Research*, 42, no. 2 (October
       1997): 171–204.

I

Individual Rights versus the Common Good

1

Limit Freedom of the Press?

Introduction

In 2013, following the publication of classified information gleaned from top secret documents leaked to the press, the US government conducted several investigations into these unauthorized disclosures.[1] The government eventually extended these investigations to the press, collecting phone records and subpoenaing reporters, not to prosecute the reporters, but to identify the leakers.[2] These actions were widely criticized by the media, civil libertarians, liberals, and others who decried the government as constraining freedom of the press.[3] At the same time, government officials and their defenders argued that clamping down on leaks was necessary in order to preserve ongoing national security efforts.[4] This chapter asks the following questions about this topic: What normative framework should one apply in finding the proper balance between the freedom of the press and national security? What effect, if any, should the change in historical conditions have on this balance?[5] When highly sensitive national security information is leaked to the press, who has the authority to render the weighty decisions about whether to publish such information?[6] To what extent has the publication of classified information damaged national security?[7] To what extent have the subsequent leak investigations undermined freedom of the press?[8] What mechanisms are available if the balance between liberty and security needs to be recalibrated?[9] What steps can be taken to narrow the conflict between freedom of the press and national security?[10] What role must moral dialogues play before major legal and institutional changes can be introduced?[11]

This chapter argues that (a) the harm to national security caused by published leaks seems greater than most of the media is willing to acknowledge, and (b) that there are better ways to protect the public's right to know and the press's right to publish than those that are currently in place.

I. Advocacy versus the Communitarian Approach

1. The Advocacy Model

Deliberations about public policy often follow the advocacy model characteristic of the American courts. In this model there are only two sides, and each side presents its interpretation of the facts in the way that most strongly supports its position.[12] The case of Bradley Manning, who was charged with leaking hundreds of thousands of secret military documents to WikiLeaks in 2010, illustrates this mode of deliberation.[13] The defense presented the young soldier as "naïve but good-intentioned."[14] To his champions in the media and on the left, Manning is a heroic whistleblower and a victim of government overreach.[15] By contrast, the government contended that Manning is a traitor, guilty of aiding the enemies of the United States.[16] The prosecutor asserted that Manning "used his military training to gain the notoriety he craved."[17]

These positions reflect the state of the debate over government secrecy more broadly. Law Professor David E. Pozen notes that,

> for every governmental assertion of leaks "that have collectively cost the American people hundreds of millions of dollars, and . . . done grave harm to national security," one finds the rebuttal that "there has not been a single instance in the history of the United States in which the press's publication of a 'legitimate but newsworthy' government secret has gravely harmed the national interest"—indeed, that there have been few destructive leaks anywhere in the world.[18]

Many public policy deliberations follow the same pattern of strong, often extreme, one-sided advocacy between two conflicting positions. Key examples include the debates between pro-life and pro-choice advocates,[19] those who favor gun control and those who defend an individualized right to own guns,[20] and free market champions and those who favor strong regulations[21]. Data show that American media and politics have become more polarized in recent years. That is, they are drawing more on the advocacy model and focusing less on finding common ground, forging compromises, and devising "third way" solutions.[22]

In public discourse, the give-and-take about freedom of the press and the way publishers ought to handle leaks has taken a particular turn. In the media, which usually seeks[23] to keep news reporting separate from editorializing, coverage of the recent leak investigations has been loaded with emotive terms criticizing the way these investigations have been conducted. News reports concerning the Department of Justice's investigations into James Rosen and its seizure of *Associated Press* phone records include such editorializing terms as "unprecedented,"[24] "sweeping,"[25] and "aggressive."[26] Further, the editorial pages of many newspapers and magazines have been particularly partisan in their rhetoric. They refer to a "war" on free speech,[27] contend that the Rosen investigation is "as flagrant an assault on civil liberties as anything done by George W. Bush's administration,"[28] and declare that the Obama administration "uses technology to silence critics in a way Richard Nixon could only have dreamed of."[29] The editors of the *New York Times* assert that "the Obama administration has moved beyond protecting government secrets to threatening fundamental freedoms of the press to gather news."[30] Nick Gillespie of *The Daily Beast* writes that the Obama administration's crusade "declares 'war on journalism' by essentially criminalizing the very act of investigative reporting."[31] At the *San Francisco Chronicle*, the editors write, "The feds seemed to have conflated journalism with espionage."[32] Ron Fournier claims in the *National Journal* that "the leak inquiry threatens national security."[33]

The media has given little room, even on the op-ed pages presumably set aside for views opposed to those of a newspaper's own editorials, for articles that explain, let alone seek to justify, the government's viewpoint. One of the media's own, former *NBC* anchorman Tom Brokaw, noted that "many of the same reporters who are tough on the gun lobby when it comes to second amendment rights, run behind the shield of the first amendment, without doing it in a way that is qualitatively analytical, and not just a knee-jerk reaction."[34] Similarly, *Washington Post* reporter Walter Pincus lamented the "circling of the media wagons."[35] In response to the White House Correspondents' Association's statement that "our country was founded on the principle of freedom of the press and nothing is more sacred to our profession,"[36] Pincus wrote, "I worry that many other journalists think that last phrase should be 'nothing is more sacred *than* our profession.'"[37]

In contrast, the government has been unusually ambivalent in defending its position. At first Attorney General Eric Holder stated that the leak to the AP "put the American people at risk," and that trying to determine who was responsible "required very aggressive action."[38] However, soon thereafter he struck a conciliatory tone, saying in an interview with the *Daily Beast* that "while both of these cases were handled within the law and according to Justice Department guidelines, they are reminders of the unique role the news media plays in our democratic system, and signal that both our laws and guidelines need to be updated."[39] President Obama recently stated that "we must keep information secret that protects our operations and our people in the field."[40] But in the same speech, he also said that he was "troubled by the possibility that leak investigations may chill the investigative journalism that holds government accountable"[41] and that "journalists should not be at legal risk for doing their jobs."[42]

The government's hesitant defense of its actions seems to reflect several factors: The administration is highly vulnerable to criticism from the press;[43] it faces pushback from both sides of the political and ideological spectrum;[44] there exists a high level of distrust in the government;[45] and Americans have long been suspicious of the federal government's accumulation of power at the expense of individual rights.[46] As a result, the government seems wary of picking a fight with those "who buy ink by the barrel."[47] All said and done, in this case public discourse is hampered not merely by the advocacy approach but also by the fact that the voice of one of the two sides, that of government speaking for national security, is muted.

5

2. A Liberal Communitarian Approach

The liberal communitarian philosophy holds that the advocacy model is flawed in that it assumes that the clash of two strong one-sided views will lead to a just conclusion, reasonable judgments and sound public policies.[48] The liberal communitarian approach favors the model exemplified by the *agora* in ancient Greece,[49] the *jirgas* of Afghanistan,[50] and the US Senate in earlier decades.[51] This model is one of dialogue, in which opposing sides engage in a civil give-and-take and commit to finding a course acceptable to all concerned.[52]

In contrast to the advocacy model, this chapter draws on a liberal communitarian philosophy, which assumes that as a nation we face two fully legitimate normative and legal claims: protecting national security and the freedom of the press. Neither can be maximized nor fully reconciled, as there is an inevitable tension between these two claims. It thus follows that some balance must be worked out between the conflicting claims. That is, the liberal communitarian model assumes from the outset that the nation is committed to both individual rights and the advancement of the common good, and that neither should be assumed *a priori* to trump the other.[53] The liberal communitarian philosophy is dedicated to achieving a balance between individual rights and social responsibilities, which emanates from the need to serve the common good.[54]

The Fourth Amendment provides an important text for the liberal communitarian philosophy when it states that "[t]he right of the people to be secure in their persons, houses, papers, and effects, against unreasonable searches and seizures, shall not be violated."[55] By banning only *unreasonable* searches and seizures, it recognizes that there are *reasonable* ones—those that serve the common good (or, to use a term more familiar to the legal community, the public interest).

Liberal communitarians thus take it for granted that deliberations about legitimate public policy ought to start with the assumption that the public's "right to know" and the freedom of the press must be balanced with concern for national security, rather than from the position that limitations on the press are *ipso facto* a violation of a basic right or freedom.

3. Within History

Achieving a communitarian balance, however, does not mean invariably opting for the *same* golden middle ground between rights and responsibilities, or freedom and security. Rather, it requires consideration of how changes in historical conditions might shift the equilibrium point. The September 11, 2001, attacks against the United States heightened the country's need to attend to homeland security. One can argue over the severity of the threat that terrorism now poses and how far the government should reach while seeking to protect the United States from future attacks. However, one cannot deny that the combination of less-than-fully-secured nuclear arms in Pakistan and Russia and the existence of many thousands of people around the world who seek to harm the United States continues to pose a security risk.[56]

A second set of factors that affects the historically appropriate balance between national security and freedom of the press is the technological developments that have taken place since the advent of the "cyber age" around 1990.[57] This revolution in computing technologies has made classified information more broadly accessible, retrievable from remote locations, and easily transferrable.[58] Bradley Manning, a young soldier stationed in the middle of the desert in Iraq, was able to download and share many thousands of top secret documents, undetected by his superiors.[59] In the age of ink and paper, such a feat would have been physically impossible. Moreover, the Internet and the twenty-four-hour news cycle put pressure on reporters to publish as soon as they receive a story. In times past, a newspaper that received classified information had time, at least until printing the next edition, to weigh whether or not to publish and to consult with the authorities. Today the same newspaper, fearing being "scooped" by the competition, often posts the story online, where it becomes instantly available not only to a domestic audience but also to declared enemies of the United States.

These developments seem to justify *some* rebalancing. A liberal communitarian holds that deliberations should focus both on the extent of this recalibration and on ensuring that corrective measures are neither excessive nor irreversible as historical and technological conditions change again.[60] However, to simply ignore these new historical developments seems unreasonable. We have not reached the point where we can declare, with regard to the campaign against terrorism and the need to protect the United States from future attacks, "mission accomplished".

II. Who Decides?

Who decides whether the information contained in a particular classified document—or a collection of many thousands of such documents—ought to be published? Currently this decision ultimately rests with the editors of the press.[61] If the government happens to find out that such information is about to be published, or the reporters choose to consult with the government before the presses roll, officials may present their case to the editors and request that they not proceed.[62] The editors then consider whether to grant the government's request.[63] The final judgment is theirs though.

There is a very strong presumption in the American legal tradition, as well as a normative consensus, against punishing editors or publications that air classified or even top-secret information and against the application of prior restraint (preventing publication by court order).[64] As a result, editors—not Congress or the courts, and certainly not the White House—currently have the ultimate authority in the matter.[65]

7

Jack Goldsmith summarizes:

> The way the system works, for better or worse, is that the government makes the case to the media about the national security harms of publication, and the media assesses the government's arguments, weighs the perceived national security harm against the perceived benefits of publication, and decides whether and how to publish.[66]

Bill Keller, former executive editor of the *New York Times*, and Dean Baquet, former managing editor at the *Los Angeles Times*, described this decision-making process as follows: "We weigh the merits of publishing against the risks of publishing. There is no magic formula, no neat metric for either the public's interest or the dangers of publishing sensitive information. We make our best judgment."[67]

Former *Washington Post* Executive Editor Leonard Downie, Jr. stated, "Very, very seldom do we decide not to publish a story at all. But quite often we will leave out specific details, technical details, location details that would put lives or programs in jeopardy unnecessarily."[68] Part of the editor's job, he says, is "weighing how to publish significant stories about national security without causing unnecessary harm."[69]

David Ignatius of the *Washington Post* raises a valuable point when he writes, "We journalists usually try to argue that we have carefully weighed the pros and cons and believe that the public benefit of disclosure outweighs any potential harm. The problem is that we aren't fully qualified to make those judgments."[70] Editors are typically trained in the humanities (often English literature) or journalism rather than in security studies or international relations.[71] Most of the leading editors, those who render pivotal decisions on the matter at hand, gained the bulk of their experience in the world of media rather than in military service or through a stint in the intelligence or diplomatic communities.[72] Their motivation, and that of the profit-making corporations that own most of the media, is not limited to serving the public's right to know.[73]

After the *New York Times* exposed the George W. Bush administration's secret monitoring of suspected terrorist financial transactions,[74] then-Secretary of the Treasury John Snow wrote to Keller:

> The fact that your editors believe themselves to be qualified to assess how terrorists are moving money betrays a breathtaking arrogance and a deep misunderstanding of this program and how it works . . . the paper has given itself free license to expose any covert activity that it happens to learn of—even those that are legally grounded, responsibly administered, independently overseen, and highly effective.[75]

Further, the editors only have access to the leaked information on the particular secret at hand, forcing them to render their decisions mainly on the basis of whatever the leaker chose to reveal. As Steven Coll, a former managing editor at the *Washington Post*, puts it, "You're in the fog all the time, always groping . . . you're always concerned that you're missing something."[76] Such awareness of their own limitations, though, often does not suffice to stop editors from ignoring the government's pleas. Editors state that they ultimately must rely on "their gut" and "instinct."[77] Moreover, when pleading with them not to publish, the government often cannot divulge more information, lest additional state secrets be published.

Sometimes editors suggest that they have acted responsibly, indeed magnanimously, by granting the government a short reprieve and delaying the publication of a national security leak. For example, the *Associated Press* withheld a story about an operation to foil a bomb plot until the operation was complete.[78] Nevertheless, it later revealed that the successful operation had relied on a mole that had infiltrated al Qaeda and was passing vital intelligence on to the United States.[79] This report compromised his identity and denied the US any further life-saving information he could have gained while undercover.[80]

Furthermore, even when the media outlets that consider themselves responsible, such as the *New York Times*, the *Washington Post*, and *National Public Radio*, refrain from publishing a particular piece of classified information, other news outlets, which in the cyber age include Internet publications and amateur bloggers, are less careful. Initially, upon receiving leaked military and diplomatic documents, WikiLeaks worked with the *Guardian*, the *New York Times, Der Spiegel, Le Monde* and *El Pais*, all of which published redacted versions to protect the identities of sources, human rights workers and informants.[81] However, in 2011 around one hundred thousand secret cables were "either released by WikiLeaks by accident, or 'recklessly' published by the *Guardian*," prompting WikiLeaks to post its full archives online.[82] Papers that had worked with the organization issued a joint statement, saying, "We deplore the decision of WikiLeaks to publish the unredacted state department cables, which may put sources at risk. . . . We cannot defend the needless publication of the complete data—indeed, we are united in condemning it."[83] As another example, in the mid-1980s when reporters at the *Washington Post* uncovered a US operation to intercept Soviet cable communications, called "Ivy Bells,"[84] the *Washington Post* delayed publication of the story in response to government requests—but NBC still carried the story.[85] News organizations that have published leaked National Security Agency documents have inadvertently disclosed the names of at least six intelligence workers and other government secrets they never intended to give away.[86]

Unlike doctors or lawyers, journalists need no license to practice; anyone, including bloggers and even foreign spies, can claim that they are journalists, solicit classified information, and publish it. The *New York Times* labeled two teenagers who wrote an article for their high school newspaper about school security "student journalists."[87] It seems to follow that those considered neither informed enough to vote nor responsible enough to drive or have a drink could decide on their own whether to publish top secret information if someone leaked it to them. Should all these persons and outlets be free to proceed unchecked and be shielded from the consequences of their actions? Or is the responsible media willing to make a list of legitimate editors and outlets that can assume the mantle of making these fateful decisions? Will "the" press then hold that the government should enjoin or punish the "irresponsible" publishers? Robert D. Epstein writes that not only journalists but also "lobbyists, academics, think-tank experts, and others, particularly in Washington," make their stock in trade of "often secret or classified" information.[88] Would they all be entitled to the same special status as the "responsible" press?

The term used most often to describe the role of the government in dealing with the media on these matters is particularly telling. President Bush and his aides are reported to have "plead[ed]" with the *New York Times* "for more than a year" not to publish the article about the NSA's highly classified wiretapping program.[89] The term "pleaded" is very appropriate because currently editors have the final authority when it comes to publishing information.[90] There is no place the government can appeal if editors reject the government's petitions.[91] Editors have, as a matter of practice, absolute authority over what they publish and are rarely punished even if it becomes clear after the fact that the harm they caused by doing so is substantial.[92]

Thomas Powers argues that "you could ransack the literature and not come up with three examples" of leaks that harmed national security.[93] David Wise, an author and former White House correspondent who has written extensively on the intelligence community, claims that "[i]t's a phony business, the whole secrecy racket. It's a racket designed to allow political leaders to maintain information control."[94] How valid are these claims?

In line with the liberal communitarian quest for balance, the chapter turns next to asking whether publications of classified information significantly damaged national security, and whether the government's countermeasures unduly curbed the freedom of the press?

III. Harm to National Security?

In order to assess the security implications of media reporting on classified information, consider the following notable leaks:

- In 1942 the *Chicago Tribune* reported that the "Navy had Word of Jap Plan to Strike At Sea," revealing to the Japanese that the United States had broken their naval code.[95]
- In 1943 the press reported that Japanese depth charge attacks were ineffective because they were set to explode at too shallow a depth. This allowed the Japanese military to adjust the depth of their attacks, which cost the US Navy at least ten submarines.[96]

- In 1974, after leaving the CIA, Victor Marchetti co-authored with John D. Marks, a former State Department officer, *The CIA and the Cult of Intelligence*,[97] a book highly critical of the organization, which also included sensitive information about intelligence collection methods and sources.[98]

- In 1975 former CIA agent Philip Agee published *Inside the Company: CIA Diary*,[99] in which he included in the book the names and positions of about two hundred and fifty CIA officers and foreign agents.[100] He later uncovered approximately one thousand agents all over the world and inspired followers.[101] On November 17, 1975, Richard Welch was assassinated by a terrorist organization while working in Greece after the American magazine *CounterSpy* exposed his identity as a CIA agent.[102] An official at the American Embassy in Jamaica fell victim to an armed assault after being identified by *Covert Action Information*, another publication dedicated to such outings.[103]

- In 1979, the *Progressive* published a detailed technical account[104] of how to build a nuclear bomb by piecing together mostly public information. By compiling the disparate pieces of information, the publication made it significantly easier for those seeking to build a bomb to proceed.[105]

- In 1984, Samuel Morison provided *Jane's Defence Weekly*, a British magazine at which he sought employment, with top secret pictures of Soviet military sites obtained through US reconnaissance.[106]

- In 1998 a leak published in the *Washington Times*[107] is reported to have alerted Osama bin Laden to the fact the United States was using his satellite phone to monitor him, leading him to stop using the phone and all other such devices.[108]

- In 2005 the *New York Times* reported on an NSA program of warrantless domestic spying on Americans.[109] Democratic and Republican lawmakers alike condemned the *Times* for "damag[ing] critical intelligence capabilities."[110]

- In 2005 Dana Priest of the *Washington Post* chronicled the George W. Bush administration's use of secret prisons in Eastern Europe, though she heeded the government's request not to publish the names of the countries involved.[111]

- In 2006 the *New York Times* exposed details of a secret Treasury Department program (SWIFT) for monitoring terrorist financial transactions.[112]

- In his 2009 report that the North Koreans were about to launch another nuclear test, *FOX News* reporter James Rosen "alerted the North Koreans that the United States had penetrated their leadership circle,"[113] thus compromising a highly placed source of intelligence.

- In 2010 Bob Woodward exposed numerous highly classified details about the Obama administration's activities in his book, *Obama's Wars*.[114] Among the disclosed details were the existence of a secret CIA paramilitary group, the code names of NSA programs, and a "retribution plan" in case of a Pakistani terrorist attack on the United States.[115]

- In 2010 Private Bradley Manning is reported to have given WikiLeaks classified video footage of a US airstrike that resulted in civilian deaths, Afghanistan and Iraq war logs, files from Guantanamo Bay, and hundreds of thousands of diplomatic cables.[116]
- In 2011 Shakil Afridi, a Pakistani doctor who helped the CIA find Osama bin Laden, was caught by the Pakistani intelligence agency and sentenced to thirty-three years in prison.[117] Some charge that he was identified as a result of a leak that came directly from the White House.[118]
- In his 2012 book *Confront and Conceal*,[119] excerpts of which were published in the *New York Times*, David E. Sanger revealed that "President Obama secretly ordered increasingly sophisticated attacks on the computer systems that run Iran's main nuclear enrichment facilities," intensifying the "Olympic Games" program started under the previous administration.[120] This was the first time the United States was identified as a nation using cyber weapons for a major kinetic attack.[121]
- An AP story in 2012 about a foiled terrorist plot originating in Yemen[122] alerted al Qaeda that the United States had succeeded in infiltrating its ranks.[123]
- In the summer of 2013, former National Security Agency contractor Edward Snowden leaked an estimated 1.7 million documents from official databases to the media. The leaks led to stories about previously secret operations of the NSA, including its phone metadata collection and PRISM programs. According to John Sawers, the head of the British intelligence agency MI6, the Snowden leaks "have put our operations at risk."[124] A senior US intelligence official reports that several terrorist groups changed their communication behaviors as a result[125]. Until the Snowden leaks, it was widely assumed that computers not connected to the Internet were safe from surveillance. Snowden leaked the information that the NSA has developed means to access computers not even connected to the Internet.[126]

Snowden provided specific details of US-based cyber-attacks launched against Hong Kong targets, including the Chinese University of Hong Kong, students, and public officials.[127] He also revealed that the NSA was hacking "major Chinese telecommunications companies, a Beijing university and the corporate owner of the region's most extensive fiber-optic submarine cable network."[128]

A preliminary overview of these leaks seems to suggest that many of them did considerable harm to national security. In some cases, Americans who volunteered to risk their lives in service of their country were killed (e.g., CIA agents and those operating the ten submarines sunk by the Japanese [129]). In other cases, the United States and its allies were left more vulnerable to terrorist attacks (e.g., when the mole in Yemen was exposed[130])—and, arguably, even to nuclear attacks (e.g., when the existence of a mole inside North Korea was exposed[131]).

This does not account for the less tangible effects: allies may think twice about assisting the United States in the campaign against terrorism, and foreign diplomats may no longer speak candidly for fear of reading their revelations in the *New York Times*.[132] Moreover, "leaks about our methods tip our hand to our adversaries and give them the opportunity to adapt their defenses against those methods."[133] Edward Snowden reportedly told China exactly which of its computers the NSA had accessed.[134]

David Ignatius points out the "the CIA claimed at the time that it had suffered great damage from [Philip] Agee's revelations, but it's still very much in business."[135] This is clever rhetoric. Although the CIA never claimed that the death of one of its agents and the identification of about one thousand others put it out of business, it nevertheless seems reasonable to conclude that significant harm was done to its work—and most assuredly to the assassinated agent and his family.[136]

On the same first reading, it also seems that only a small minority of leaks shed light on instances of government abuse or illegal activities. In fact, in many cases, such as Ivy Bells,[137] planting moles in North Korea,[138] and al Qaeda,[139] the revelations painted the government in a positive light, whereas in others the public seemed to gain very little insight at a great expense to national security. For instance, the public gained very little by reading a technical article on assembling nuclear bombs[140] while nations bent on making bombs gained a great deal.

On closer examination all of these cases turn out to be much more complicated and are open to different interpretations and assessments, especially given that the public does not know all the details. To the extent that details are known, it is often difficult to reach a simple summary judgment. Thus although the report that US submarines greatly benefitted from Japan's miscalculation of the range of its depth charges[141] would seem to be a straightforward instance of the press causing significant harm to national security, a media advocate can point out that the information was released by a careless member of Congress, not a journalist.[142] An advocate of more stringent prosecution of leaks may then respond that the Japanese were extremely unlikely to attend the meeting in which the Congressman revealed this information, and hence they would not have known about it without the help of the press. A free press advocate may respond that there is no hard evidence that the Japanese learned about the press story and that, regardless, it is not the job of the press to protect the nation from members of Congress or anyone else that speaks out of turn.

Likewise, press advocates may point out that the 1979 *Progressive* article[143] providing information on how to build a bomb merely pieced together previously published articles and therefore revealed no new information. Security advocates may well respond that by compiling information and creating a comprehensive publication, the *Progressive* made assembling a hydrogen bomb much easier.

Press advocates say that information about US surveillance of Internet traffic overseas was well known and hence writing about it was harmless; critics are likely to point out that terrorists tend to become careless and eventually use the Internet to communicate, and the publication of leaks reminds them to be more cautious.

The AP points to the fact that it withheld a story for a week at the government's request, but moved forward with publication against the wishes of the White House after the operation was complete and those involved were out of harm's way.[144] However, "we shouldn't pretend that this leak of an unbelievably sensitive, dangerous piece of information is okay because nobody died," former White House national security spokesman Tommy Vietor warns.[145] Officials say that the CIA was unable to keep the same double agent in al Qaeda's Yemeni branch after his cover was blown by the AP's story.[146] Even if the United States can find another agent willing to risk his life as a mole, al Qaeda has undoubtedly learned from the incident and will be harder to infiltrate.

In short, although there seems to be considerable evidence of harm, it is very difficult for a nonspecialized observer without access to classified information that has not been leaked to render a definitive judgment on the extent of the harm in many of the cases.

Finally, on further deliberation, one realizes that an important part of the judgment about the various leaks—and hence about in which direction the balance between security and freedom of the press ought to be recalibrated—is the basic normative assumptions that underlie our laws and public policies.[147] One cannot separate consideration of the facts from consideration of their meaning in terms of the values we hold dear. At the foundation of the American constitutional democracy is the principle that the government needs to be checked and held accountable to the people in the particular sense that it should not be trusted but rather supervised.[148] However, how far this distrust is permitted to extend must still be resolved. If one assumes that all government statements are misleading, including those by inspectors general, congressional oversight committees, and investigations by independently appointed prosecutors, there remain very few ways besides the press by which one can discern the actual situation. The system of checks and balances is composed of the three branches of government. If one cannot trust any one of them—or all of them in combination—one faces a much greater challenge than protecting the freedom of the press.

Similarly, when leaks reveal that the government engaged in spying, initiated cyber attacks, formed secret prisons, and perpetrated targeted killing and torture, they raise issues that are not merely factual. Their evaluation depends on the values we hold, according to which some of these acts may be deemed quite tolerable (and best kept in the shadows) and others completely reprehensible (and best aired and stopped).

My response to these fundamental questions follows in three major steps. I ask: (1) What effect have the investigations into news outlets and reporters to find and deter leakers had on the freedom of the press? To what extent did they, as the media repeatedly claims, "chill" the press's sources in the government?; (2) What changes in policy and institutions can reduce the tension between security and press freedom?; and (3) Is there a way to come to a new shared understanding as to which principles should guide the recalibration of whatever imbalance exists?

IV. Limiting of the Press?

When the Justice Department's decision to subpoena James Rosen and investigate the *Associated Press* surfaced in 2013,[149] the media held that "there's no question that this has a chilling effect. People who have talked in the past are less willing to talk now. Everyone is worried about communication and how to communicate, and [asking if there] is there any method of communication that is not being monitored."[150] Gary Pruitt, president of the AP, stated that the government's message to officials is "that if you talk to the press, we're going to go after you" and that "people we would talk to in the normal course of news gathering, are already saying to us that they're a little reluctant to talk to us; they fear that they will be monitored by the government."[151] The *New York Times'* Margaret Sullivan wrote,

> The ability of the press to report freely on its government is a cornerstone of American democracy. That ability is, by any reasonable assessment, under siege. Reporters get their information from sources. They need to be able to protect those sources and sometimes offer them confidentiality. If they can't be sure about that—and it looks increasingly like they can't—the sources will dry up. And so will the information.[152]

Jill Abramson, an editor at the *Times*, told Bob Schieffer on CBS's *Face the Nation* that "the reporters who work for the Times in Washington have told me many of their sources are petrified even to return calls."[153] *The Washington Post's* Leonard Downie, Jr. warns that "the Obama administration's steadily escalating war on leaks, the most militant I have seen since the Nixon administration, has disregarded the First Amendment and intimidated a growing number of government sources of information—most of which would not be classified—that is vital for journalists to hold leaders accountable."[154]

Actually, there is strong evidence that the American press continues to be freer than that of most, if not all, other countries in the world.[155] Even amid Obama's "war on leaks,"[156] the press has regularly carried reports based on insider and classified information, including top secret documents, and there is very little indication that their government sources have been scared into silence.[157] Forty-two percent of government officials that responded to a survey conducted by scholars at Harvard stated that they "fe[lt] it appropriate to leak information to the press" at least once,[158] leading the architects of the survey to conclude that leaks "are a routine and generally accepted part of the policymaking process."[159] The Senate Intelligence Committee analyzed eight prominent newspapers and found evidence of 147 unauthorized disclosures of classified information over a six month period.[160] Although these studies are dated, over the past decades the prevalence of leaks seems to be on the rise. The media correctly reports that the Obama administration has conducted more leak investigations than all previous administrations combined. However, the number of these investigations is six, which amount to a tiny fraction of all the illegal leaks.[161]

Moreover, very few leakers have been punished, and no editor or media outlet has been penalized.[162] Pozen reports that "the thousands upon thousands of" leaks over the decades "have yielded a total of roughly a dozen criminal prosecutions," a "degree of 'underenforcement' [that] is stunning," given that every president since at least Truman has considered leaks "a major threat to national security and good government."[163] A generous estimate of the prosecution rate of leak-law violators is 0.3 percent, though, "the actual rate is probably far closer to zero."[164] Also, note that indictments and prosecutions do not necessarily result in convictions.[165]

Hence it is not surprising that Washington continues to leak like a sieve. In the same month in which newspapers carried a considerable number of editorials and op-eds chastising the Obama administration for the chilling effects of its "war on leaks," two major national security programs were exposed in the media. On June 5, 2013, the *Guardian* published a top-secret Foreign Intelligence Surveillance Court order authorizing the NSA to collect the phone records of millions of Americans.[166] The document contained detailed information about the program.[167] The next day, the *Washington Post* and the *Guardian* revealed that the NSA and FBI, under a top secret program code-named PRISM, had partnered with nine of the biggest Internet companies to monitor foreign communications traffic.[168] Then on June 20, the *Guardian* published two top secret documents that detailed NSA surveillance and data minimization procedures.[169] More leaks followed in rapid succession.[170]

In short, it is hardly the case that the government is plugging the leaks and the press is left out dry. One may argue that this is the way the balance should be tilted, but one cannot deny the direction in which it is leaning. Even if one reaches the conclusion that the leaks so far have caused little harm to national security and that investigations greatly undermine the ability of the press to do its job, all that follows still holds.

V. "There Ought to Be a Law"

What is the current state of the law? Are there too many or too few legal measures to decrease harmful leaks and deter the irresponsible press from publishing them? In responding to these questions, three channels for enhancing government secrecy emerge: going after the leakers directly, investigating the press in order to find and punish the leakers, and stopping the press directly or deterring them from running by punishing those who publish classified information.

1. Investigating and Punishing the Leakers

Extensive administrative rules against leaking classified information are already on the books in most government agencies. Executive orders *require* "sanctions for every knowing, willful, or negligent disclosure of properly classified information to unauthorized persons,"[171] and federal agencies have the authority "to conduct their own investigations into suspected leaks and to impose a wide range of sanctions, including removal, suspension without pay, and denial of access to classified information."[172] Government officials who leak "national defense" information to the press break the law and the terms of their employment,[173] and in the words of former national security policy adviser Daniel J. Gallington, "the government clearly has the right—and even the obligation—to investigate."[174] However, "numerous agencies that work on national security and foreign policy-related issues hardly ever impose such punishments."[175]

Contract law also provides an avenue for stemming the flow of leaks. Intelligence and national security officials sign secrecy agreements as a condition of employment and access to sensitive information—a limitation on free speech repeatedly affirmed by the courts.[176] If an agency is alerted to a potential leak, it can go to court to have the contractual obligations enforced.[177] The CIA did exactly this when, in 1973, former employee Victor Marchetti sought to publish a book critical of the Agency.[178] Before the book was published the government obtained a court order temporarily enjoining publication, and Marchetti was forced to submit the manuscript to the CIA for redaction.[179] Of the 166 passages that the CIA sought to suppress, the US Court of Appeals for the Fourth Circuit compelled Marchetti to remove 26.[180] And in 1977, Frank Snepp, a former CIA analyst, published an account of the agency's involvement in Vietnam without submitting the manuscript for the contractually required review and approval.[181] His case reached the Supreme Court, which sided with the government, ordering that the CIA receive all royalties from the book that profited at the agency's expense.[182] But the book and the secrets had been published.[183]

Moreover, though labeling leakers as spies has been criticized, the courts have affirmed the constitutionality of prosecuting government officials that disclose "national defense" information to the press under the Espionage Act of 1917.[184] Section 793 "prohibits the gathering, transmitting, or receipt of defense information with the intent or reason to believe the information will be used against the United States or to the benefit of a foreign nation."[185] Other portions of the law criminalize specific types of disclosures. Sections

795 and 797, for example, prohibit "unauthorized creation, publication, sale or transfer of photographs or sketches of vital defense installations or equipment as designated by the President."[186]

In the foundational case *United States v. Morison*,[187] the Fourth Circuit rejected Samuel Morison's argument that the prohibitions of the Espionage Act "are to be narrowly and strictly confined to conduct represented 'in classic spying and espionage activity' by persons who . . . transmitted 'national security secrets to agents of foreign governments with intent to injure the United States.'"[188] Rather, the "statutes plainly apply to 'whoever' having access to national defense information . . . 'willfully communicate[d], deliver[ed] or transmit[ted] . . . to a person not entitled to receive it.'"[189] The court added that to invoke the freedom of speech to justify leaking classified information "would be to prostitute the salutary purposes of the First Amendment."[190]

Some legal scholars argue that the 1917 law is "notoriously vague."[191] According to Benjamin Wittes, "it contains no limiting principle in its apparent criminalization of secondary transmissions of proscribed material,"[192] thereby suggesting that anyone who talks, tweets, or blogs about illegally disclosed information could be prosecuted under its provisions.[193] One remedy would be to more precisely define the ambiguous terms of the statute, including what falls under "information relating to the national defense"; who is considered a "person not entitled to receive"; and how to demonstrate that one had "reason to believe [that such information] could be used to the injury of the United States or to the advantage of any foreign nation."[194] This vagueness, however, does not make it more difficult to charge leakers; on the contrary, it could make it too easy—if the law were actually applied that is.

Later amendments to the Espionage Act and other related statutes can and have been used to prosecute leakers of specific categories of sensitive information. The Comint Act (Section 798 of the Espionage Act),[195] passed in 1950 in response to the wartime leak of US code breaking, applies to unauthorized disclosures of cryptographic systems or communications intelligence that are "in any manner prejudicial to the safety or interest of the United States or for the benefit of any foreign government to the detriment of the United States."[196] Following the fatal Agee episode,[197] Congress passed the Intelligence Identities Protection Act of 1982,[198] which made disclosing "any information identifying" covert agents "to any individual not authorized to receive classified information" punishable with up to fifteen years in prison.[199] Under 18 U.S.C. § 1924, any government employee that knowingly removes classified documents or materials "without authority and with the intent to retain such documents or materials at an unauthorized location" is subject to a fine and up to a year in prison.[200] In addition, 18 U.S.C. § 1030 prohibits disclosing information obtained by knowingly accessing a "computer without authorization or exceeding authorized access . . . with reason to believe that such information so obtained could be used to the injury of the United States."[201]

In addition to the Espionage Act, Morison was convicted under 18 U.S.C. § 641, which prohibits the unauthorized theft or conversion of government property.[202]

Though not exhaustive, this sampling of relevant laws demonstrates that "there is ample statutory authority for prosecuting individuals who elicit or disseminate many of the documents at issue, as long as the intent element can be satisfied and potential damage to national security can be demonstrated."[203] Still, over the years lawmakers have introduced additional laws that specifically target the unauthorized disclosure of classified information that does not fit within the definition of traditional espionage.[204] Thus, in 2001, Congress passed the Classified Information Protection Act,[205] a provision of the Intelligence Authorization Act, which penalized the unauthorized disclosure of any classified national security information "regardless of whether the violator intended that the information be delivered to and used by foreign agents."[206] Instead of requiring the government "to prove that damage to the national security has or will result from the unauthorized disclosure,"[207] the bill aimed "to ease the government's burden" in going after leaks by simply requiring the government to demonstrate that the information "is or has been properly classified."[208] Despite easily passing in the House (with over four hundred votes) and Senate (with a voice vote) after an "extremely well-timed media lobbying blitz,"[209] the bill was vetoed by President Clinton, who worried that the provision might "create an undue chilling effect."[210]

Nevertheless, a 2002 review by the Attorney General of existing anti-leak legislation concluded:

> Current statutes provide a legal basis to prosecute those who engage in unauthorized disclosures, if they can be identified. It may be that carefully drafted legislation specifically tailored to unauthorized disclosures of classified information generally, rather than to espionage, could enhance our investigative efforts. The extent to which such a provision would yield any practical additional benefits to the government in terms of improving our ability to identify those who engage in unauthorized disclosures of classified information or deterring such activity is unclear, however.[211]

In short, the main issue is not the absence of legal tools to curb the leaks, but rather their employment. One may argue whether leaks are harmful or vital, but it is clear that there are legal means to curb them, if this is what is called for and if there was the political will to proceed.

2. Investigating the Press to Find the Leakers

Much attention was paid by the media to the Department of Justice's labeling of *Fox News* reporter James Rosen as "an aider, abettor and/or co-conspirator" for his role in the leak of classified information concerning North Korea by Stephen Jin-Woo Kim.[212] *Fox News* issued a statement in his defense stating that it was "outraged to learn today that James Rosen was named a criminal co-conspirator for simply doing his job as a reporter," and pledging to "unequivocally defend his right to operate as a member of what up until now has always been a free press."[213] However, claims that the administration is "criminalizing journalism"[214] rest on a misunderstanding of the law. Calling Rosen a "co-conspirator provides a probable cause for the judge to grant the warrant"[215] for the government to collect his phone records—but does not make him the object of prosecution.

Many in the press have called on Congress to pass a media shield law that would greatly limit the investigation of reporters by requiring prosecutors to convince a judge "that they had no other way to find the leak, that they would not cast their net so widely as to intrude on other reporting operations, and that identifying the leak was more important than the public value of the story" before compelling journalists to identify their sources.[216]

No such law has been enacted. However, the Justice Department's internal guidelines grant journalists special standing and extra protections, and as a result, members of the press are *very rarely* subject to leak investigations.[217] Before subpoenaing evidence from the press, the Justice Department must (a) "take all reasonable steps to attempt to obtain the information through alternative sources or means"[218] and, in most cases, (b) alert the news organization of the subpoena so it may appeal the decision in court.[219] Additionally, the subpoena must be (c) "fashioned as narrowly as possible to obtain the necessary information in a manner as minimally intrusive and burdensome as possible,"[220] and (d) authorized by the Attorney General.[221] According to former federal prosecutor Peter Zeidenberg, the process is so onerous that the government rarely tries to subpoena reporters' records: "It takes an extremely long time, and there's a lot of pushback. So to think that this is a rubber stamp, it couldn't be further from the truth."[222]

The Supreme Court held in *Branzburg v. Hayes*[223] that "the [First] Amendment does not reach so far as to override the interest of the public in ensuring that neither reporter nor source is invading the rights of other citizens."[224] Thus, like any other citizen or third-party provider, "when crimes are being investigated, and journalists possess information about the crime, they are in many (but not all) circumstances obliged to obey subpoenas."[225]

Some in the media point out that the Justice Department's own guidelines have not been observed in even a single case. For instance, Steve Coll writes in the *New Yorker* that "Justice offered the AP no chance to appeal the action, and only by authoritarian twists of logic could a secret subpoena seeking such diverse records be construed as the narrowest course possible."[226] One can look beyond such rhetorical flourishes to recognize that, indeed, the internal guidelines may not have been heeded—but this is almost inevitable given how tightly they have been formulated. Furthermore, it goes without saying that the Justice Department should abide by its own guidelines and that it misleads the press by implying that the internal rules put journalists' sources off-limits.

These guidelines, however, do not have the standing of a constitutional right or even a law enacted by Congress. What the Department has given, the Department can take away—if there is a stronger will to curb leaks.

3. Prior Restraint and State Secrets

So far we have seen that the government has ample legal foundations for deterring leakers, and for investigating the press in its pursuit of leakers. However, if officials are alerted about an impending publication of national security secrets, under what circumstances, if any, can the government compel the press to not to publish a leaked information? That is, what is the current status of the prior restraint doctrine? The American legal tradition draws on English common law in its strong presumption against prior restraint:

> The liberty of the press is indeed essential to the nature of a free state: but this consists in laying no *previous* restraints upon publications, and not in freedom from censure for criminal matter when published. Every freeman has an undoubted right to lay what sentiments he pleases before the public: to forbid this, is to destroy the freedom of the press.[227]

The Supreme Court took up this issue in the 1931 case *Near v. Minnesota*.[228] At issue was a gag law that allowed state officials to prevent the publication of "malicious, scandalous and defamatory" content by newspapers, magazines and periodicals deemed to have created a "public nuisance."[229] The Court ruled in favor of Near, who wrote scandalous pieces about government officials (not issues of national security) but noted that "the protection even as to previous restraint is not absolutely unlimited," though "the limitation has been recognized only in exceptional cases."[230] Thus, while the Court affirmed "the immunity of the press from previous restraint in dealing with official misconduct,"[231] it also maintained that the "government could enjoin speech or press" in extreme cases involving "obscenity, incitement to violence, and opposition to the conduct of war."[232]

In the case of Victor Marchetti,[233] the former CIA agent who sought to expose the agency's secret inner workings, the Fourth Circuit upheld the government's contractual secrecy agreements as one permissible ground for the application of prior restraint.[234] However, the government has been unsuccessful at making the case for injunctions aimed directly at the press or private citizens. For instance, when the Nixon administration sought to enjoin the publication of the Pentagon Papers in the *New York Times* and *Washington Post*, the Supreme Court ruled that "[t]he First Amendment tolerates absolutely no prior judicial restraints of the press predicated upon surmise or conjecture that untoward consequences may result."[235] Though the government failed to meet the "heavy burden of showing justification for the imposition of such a restraint," the Court did not rule out the possibility of allowing prior restraint if a publication would "surely result in direct, immediate, and irreparable damage to our Nation or its people."[236]

This extremely high standard for allowing prior restraint sets the United States apart from most democracies in the world. The United Kingdom, Canada, Israel, and most European countries have some version of an "official secrets act," which makes it a crime to publish classified information.[237] Though the United States never adopted a state secrets law, some argue that certain interpretations of the Espionage Act come close.[238] While the Court rejected the government's attempt to prevent the publication of the Pentagon Papers, Justice White, upon reviewing the legislative history of the Espionage Act, wrote that newspapers should be "on full notice" that the Court "would have no difficulty in sustaining convictions under these sections [of the Espionage Act] on facts that would not justify . . . the imposition of a prior restraint."[239] That is, while the court did not enjoin the publication of the classified papers, "the editors of the newspaper had already opened themselves up to criminal prosecution."[240] In the wake of the *New York Times*' 2005 exposé[241] on the Bush administration's warrantless eavesdropping program, former Attorney General Alberto Gonzales stated that "there are some statutes on the book which, if you read the language carefully, would seem to indicate that" prosecuting journalists who publish classified national security information "is a possibility."[242] Doing so would have "the effect of a de facto American Official Secrets Act on the press."[243]

4. In Conclusion

We have seen that (a) although each case is subject to different interpretations and assessments, the level of harm that leaks cause seems considerable; (b) leaks are very common and there is very little evidence to support claims that leaks have been "chilled" or that as a result of the leak investigations the press is unable to do its job; and (c) there are ample laws to provide for the prosecution of leakers, the investigation of reporters, and even for the imposition of prior restraint. These laws, however, are so rarely applied that leaking remains routine and the press solicits classified information with impunity.

Moreover, there is a strong normative consensus in the media, supported by leading public intellectuals and elected officials across much of the ideological spectrum, against applying these laws. (Polls show that the public at large is much more supportive of such an application.)[244] In other words, if the present circumstances call for greater secrecy in matters of national security, such rebalancing between the national security and the right of the public to know is not hindered by law but by the opposition of the media, supported by select public mavens, and lack of political will on the part of many key elected officials. In short, the press has never been stopped by the government even though the law allows for such action. Norms and politics are the media's strongest shield as it wields its sword.

VI. Narrowing the Gap

There are several important reforms that can be introduced to significantly narrow the distance between those who hold that security is seriously harmed by unauthorized disclosures and those who believe that the freedom of the press is under attack. In other words, there are ways to alleviate—though not fully abate—the conflict between the two core elements of the liberal communitarian equation, national security and freedom of the press.

1. Declassification

Major voices in the media hold that one reason its representatives are soliciting leaks is that the excessive classification of information prevents the media from doing its job of keeping the public informed—an essential function in a democratic polity.[245] Stephen Vladeck, of the American University Washington College of Law, goes so far as to maintain that over-classification, not leaks, is the crux of the problem.[246] The "elephant in the room" is that the federal government—in order to advance a certain policy agenda or cover up misconduct, or because of bureaucratic inertia—regularly labels information as top secret "that should never have been classified in the first place."[247] One need not put the case that strongly to agree that the press cannot do its job of holding government officials accountable if much of the information that the public needs or has a right to know is classified. Furthermore, one can find many examples of information that was classified without clear security reasons.[248] However, the solution is not to tacitly condone illegal activity by treating national security leaks as a necessary part of the trade.[249] Rather, Congress should reform the classification system and provide the additional funds needed for an accelerated review of classified files.[250] Classifiers should be required to "detail their reasons for classification, have those decisions audited, and face sanctions for severe or recurring overclassification."[251] In addition, senior-level managers should be held accountable for excessive classification, in particular when it is used for political benefit rather than protecting security.[252] Incentives could be offered to those who successfully challenge the improper or erroneous classification of information.[253] Such measures alone would not prevent national security leaks, but they would enable the press to report on many more subjects without seeking leaks and may help to convince members of the media as well as elected officials that "goad[ing]" government officials to hand over classified documents is neither in the public interest nor a sacred right of the press.[254]

2. Revised AUMF

We have seen that the search for the proper liberal communitarian balance between security and the freedom of the press must be undertaken "within history," and that the September 11, 2001 attacks against the United States called attention to the need to strengthen the former. While there have been no major terrorist attacks against the United States since 2001, grave challenges remain. Al Qaeda has regrouped and established new affiliates in Africa, the Arabian Peninsula, and in other parts of the world.[255] Many thousands of people across the globe harbor strong anti-American sentiments and consider using violence against the United States an act of martyrdom.[256] Pakistan is unable or unwilling to combat terrorists within its borders and has experienced at least six serious terrorist attempts to penetrate its nuclear facilities.[257] All this suggests that the time has not yet come for the United States to declare mission accomplished or terminate its transnational counterterrorism campaign.[258] During a *defined* period of heightened vigilance, greater energy and more resources should be dedicated to protecting sensitive national security information.

Defining this period may be accomplished through reissuing and revising the Authorized Used of Military Force (AUMF),[259] a joint resolution passed by Congress on September 14, 2001 that granted the president the power "to use all necessary and appropriate force against those nations, organizations, or persons he determines planned, authorized, committed, or aided the terrorist attacks that occurred on September 11, 2001."[260] There are a variety of reasons, which need not be discussed here, that an updated authorization is called for. In the process of reauthorization, Congress should hold hearings to consider more vigorously protecting national security secrets for the duration of the sanctioned counterterrorism campaign.[261] During such a campaign, as in wartime or a state of emergency, society may tolerate some limitations that it may not abide in more peaceful times. This does not require enacting more laws, which we have seen are quite strong (indeed, too strong, according to some), but rather enhancing the level of enforcement and assigning higher priority to identifying and penalizing leakers. The revised AUMF would include a "sunset" clause so that, *if not renewed*, the enhanced enforcement policy would expire in, say, five years.[262]

3. Classification Appeals Court (CAC)

The press often argues that it is asked to hold back a story not because the leaked information would "really endanger lives," but "for reasons of policy, partisanship or embarrassment."[263] It further holds that the government's attempts to track down leakers by investigating the press are unwarranted, and, thus, seeks to protect reporters and records from such incursions.[264] Rather than taking it upon themselves to decide whether or not a given governmental claim for secrecy is legitimate, editors should have an opportunity to appeal to a court, modeled after the Foreign Intelligence Surveillance Administration (FISA) court, composed of people with high-level security clearance, to sort out the matter.[265] Like FISA, such a panel would need to be always "on call" because of time pressures. If this court rules against a news source, but the source proceeds to publish the story anyway, it may face informal censure (e.g., loss of readership), sanctions (e.g., denial of access to White House briefings), or more serious consequences, the nature of which cannot be spelled out until a new shared moral understanding is reached about such leaks.[266] If the court rules against the government, the press would be free to proceed with publication and would not be required to reveal its sources.

There are some who hold that the FISA court acts as a rubber stamp for the government, and similar criticisms would likely be raised against a classification appeals court.[267] According to one study, of the 8,591 applications submitted to FISA between 2008 and 2012, only two were rejected.[268] However, defenders of FISA point out that the court is actually very demanding, and that the low rejection rate is attributable to the extensive give-and-take between the judges and applicants before a request is submitted for final approval.[269] Before an application reaches the court it is "signed by a high-ranking official in the executive branch, such as the director of the FBI, the secretary of defense, and then it's signed by the attorney general."[270] Then, the judge may raise questions and concerns, allowing the executive authority to fine-tune the request for approval.[271] In short, the FISA approval rate reflects a strong selection bias. Nevertheless, both FISA and a CAC would benefit from another layer of accountability, discussed next, to ensure that judges do not simply acquiesce to all government demands in the name of national security.

At a minimum, one should expect that the professional association of editors will form a panel to formulate what they consider the proper normative (not legal) guidelines to follow. One obvious guideline is to avoid endangering the lives of our agents overseas or their local collaborators. Another is to avoid divulging ongoing operations. In addition, editors struggling with the question of whether or not to publish a given state secret may wish to consult with this panel which should be composed of retired editors, select respected public intellectuals, and maybe a few former security officials. If the panel concurs with their preferences, editors could then draw on the panel's conclusions to help legitimate their decision when they face critics from the public or within their publication or profession. If the panel urges that publication should be avoided, then the editors would need to carefully reexamine their preferences.

Above all, the society of editors should determine who may legitimately claim to be the editor of a bona fide publication. Otherwise anybody with a

Twitter account or a blog—including foreign agents—could claim they can publish state secrets with impunity.

Finally, one may wonder if editors who proceed to publish secrets and directly cause harm should be subject to post hoc (as distinct from prior restraint) accounting. For instance if the family of a CIA agent was shot after his name was revealed by a press, should he not have the right to sue for damages in a civil court?

4. Accountability versus Transparency

In the wake of major leaks about the government collection of phone records of American citizens and surveillance of foreign Internet traffic, officials provided various justifications for these programs, including the claim that they comport with laws enacted by Congress, are supervised by congressional committees that are regularly briefed about the programs, and above all, that they have been instrumental in foiling more than fifty potential terrorist events in the United States and over twenty other countries since 9/11.[272] Some strong critics have argued that these programs are unconstitutional on their face because, among other reasons, they entail warrantless searches.[273] One federal judge and a civic review board found that the NSA programs are in violation of the constitution. More moderate critics and the media have asked for more details about the terrorist attacks that officials claim these programs have prevented.[274]

Something often called for in this context is "scrutiny."[275] This can be achieved in two major ways: by more transparency or by more accountability (and, of course, by various combinations of the two). Transparency entails releasing more information to the press and, thus, the public. Accountability entails more oversight by elected representatives and trusted public figures. The first, in effect, assumes a direct democracy model: the public will know, judge, and either approve or reject the secret programs. The second assumes representative democracy in which the public will trust select members of Congress or other public authorities to review the programs and vote them up or down. The press naturally favors transparency over accountability because it sees its job as informing the public and not leaving the assessments at issue in the hands of closed bodies of representatives.

A high level of transparency has two serious problems. The first problem reflects the well-known difficulties associated with direct democracy. There are sharp limits to the capacity of the public, busy making a living and leading a social life, to learn the details of any government program and evaluate it—especially given that, in the end, they cannot vote for any particular program, but have only one "holistic" vote for their representative, based on all that he or she favors and opposes. Second, high transparency is, on its face, incompatible with keeping secrets that must be kept secrets.

Moreover, when the government responds to calls for more scrutiny with the release of more information—so as to demonstrate that the secret acts did, in fact, improve security—this release encounters several difficulties. First, each piece of information released potentially helps the adversaries.[276] This is, in effect, the way intelligence work is often done: by piecing together details released by various sources.[277] Thus, the publication of information about which past operations of terrorists the government aborted could allow those groups to find out which of their plots failed because of US government interventions as opposed to those that failed because of technical flaws, the weakness of their chosen agents, or some other reason. Second, it is nearly impossible to spell out how these cases unfolded without giving away details about our sources and methods.[278] Finally, however much information about specific cases the government releases, skeptics are sure to find details that need further clarification and documentation. (This is the reason public relations experts urge those whose misdeeds are under public scrutiny to "tell all" right from the start, a strategy that may serve well politicians who cheat on their spouses, but not those who deal with combating terrorism.)

Thus, following the uproar over the revelations that technology companies were handing over customer information to the government as part of a secret national security program, the companies sought to reassure users by releasing reports on the frequency of government data requests.[279] The result, the *New York Times* reported, was that "rather than provide clarity, some of the disclosures have left many questions unanswered."[280] When General Keith Alexander, Director of the NSA, released details about how the Agency's surveillance programs had thwarted terrorist plots, the media immediately asked for more detailed information.[281] Also, there is no way for the media to determine whether the released cases are typical or were chosen because they reflect well on the government.

Instead, increased accountability should serve to reassure the public that leaks to the press are being curbed for valid reasons. Briefing many more members of Congress may not be the best way to proceed, as most members of Congress do not have the security clearance that members and key staffers of the Congressional intelligence committees have, and many are known to be notorious leakers themselves.[282] Rather, the public and the press would benefit from a regular review to be conducted by a new civilian review board. Such a review board would be composed of the kind of people who served on the 9/11 Commission: bipartisan, highly respected by the public, able to work together, not running for office, and with security clearance.[283] Although not everyone agreed with that Commission's conclusions, they were well-respected and largely trusted.[284]

The new board would issue reports, possibly annually, that would state whether the government unduly withheld information, improperly investigated leaks, and pressured the press not to publish stories for political and not security reasons. They would also report if leaks in fact caused considerable harm to national security and the press therefore acted irresponsibly by publishing classified information. However, instead of revealing detailed case studies, the civilian review board would provide statistics. For example, if it reported that there were a large number of cases in which serious threats were averted, such as the planned attack on New York City's subway,[285] the public would learn that the threats to national security warrant increased efforts to enforce anti-leak legislation. If, on the other hand, the board reported that many cases involve fairly minor threats, this would tilt the consensus the other way.[286] If the current Civil Liberties and Privacy Protection board would be properly staffed, funded, and its powers increased, it might serve in such a function.[287]

Those who trust neither the government nor independent commissions should fight for institutional changes until they gain a system they *can* trust. However, demanding that the government, which they do not trust, release more information just so whatever information it does release can then be questioned makes sense only if one denies that security requires keeping some information from the public at large.

5. *Protect True Whistleblowers*

The media claims that the investigations of leaks and the "sweeping nature" of laws against leaking silence whistleblowers who seek to reveal government abuse or illegal activities.[288] Whistleblower protections were first introduced in the Civil Service Reform Act (CSRA) of 1978,[289] which established the Merit Systems Protection Board on the principle that federal employees "should be protected against reprisal for the lawful disclosure" of government misconduct.[290] The Whistleblower Protection Act of 1989 closed loopholes contained in the CSRA, for example, "changing protection of 'a' disclosure to 'any' disclosure" that the "applicant reasonably believes is credible evidence of waste, fraud, abuse, or gross mismanagement."[291] In 2012, President Obama signed into law the Whistleblower Protection Enhancement Act,[292] which protects federal workers from retaliation when they report government corruption or wrongdoing. While this bill does not cover national security officials, Obama later signed a Presidential Policy Directive that "prohibits retaliation against employees [in the Intelligence Community] for reporting waste, fraud, and abuse."[293] This directive does not, however, protect those who leak legitimate national security secrets.[294] The directive itself may need to be expanded, and it should be made into law by the Congress, because until then, as Tom Devine of the Government Accountability Project warns, "no one whose new rights are violated will have any due process to enforce them."[295]

The whistleblower defense should be taken into account by judges or juries only if the leaker exhausted other reasonable means to address his or her concerns without revealing classified information. These may include appealing to superiors, the Inspector General, members of Congress with proper security clearance, or the FBI. For example, Daniel Ellsberg approached three senators with his concerns about the information contained in the Pentagon Papers, including George McGovern, who was sympathetic but demurred because of his presidential aspirations.[296] Only "after months of frustration" working within official channels did Ellsberg leak the documents to the press.[297] In contrast, both Manning and Snowden seem to have retrospectively invoked the whistleblower defense without showing that they did first try to correct the system according to established procedures.[298]

VII. Needed: A Moral Dialogue

All the above measures combined will not obviate the need for a moral dialogue about the principles the nation should embrace and the extent to which terrorism still constitutes a threat, although they may well facilitate the dialogue's progress. For such a discussion to take place, both sides must stop engaging in one-sided advocacy, by which one side claims that the press is committing treason and the other that the government has killed the First Amendment. The dialogue would benefit from building on the liberal communitarian assumption that we face two legitimate claims, and seek a new balance, one that will take into account changes in technology and international security conditions.

Unlike the "cool," reasoned deliberations that democratic theory envisions, moral dialogues have space for substantive convictions and foundational values, and tend to be passionate, emotionally engaging, and disorderly. These dialogues are often without a clear beginning or end and can occur within small communities and nations as well as transnationally. Prevailing values are examined and challenged, for instance, by arguments that they are inconsistent with other values the party holds or that they lead to normative conclusions the party could not possibly seek. When moral dialogues are successfully advanced, members of communities arrive at new shared normative understandings.[299]

Currently, the moral dialogue is hindered by an unusual condition. Typically the press reflects (and feeds) the full array of different public views (albeit not necessarily with equal voice[300]). However, when it comes to covering the press and its rights and privileges, the press serves as both plaintiff and jury, while giving little voice to the defense.[301] The voices which hold that leaks ought to be curbed are largely holding back because the government finds it politically unwise and even futile to argue with the media about the media.[302] Under these circumstances, the effort to gain a revised consensus is left to those not politically engaged—legal scholars, public intellectuals, and leaders willing to risk the wrath of the media—to call it the way they see it and to thus balance the moral dialogue.

The revised moral dialogue has to cover the following questions: First, does the nation—and the media—basically agree in principle to the liberal communitarian position that the public's right to know and the media's right to publish must be balanced with legitimate national security needs? That is, do we agree that there is no absolute right to publish anything and everything? If the response to this question is in the affirmative, the next step is to ask whether the current threat level from terrorists justifies some extra protections for the secrecy of anti-terrorism programs for as long as Congress regularly reaffirms that the said higher threat level is still in place.

Next, do we agree that, currently, leaks are rampant, and that many cause harm to security, while the ample regulations and laws to better protect state secrets are very rarely enforced? If so, do we agree that either the press has to restrain itself more, or that the enforcement of the laws that punish leakers and investigations of the press to find the leakers must be enhanced rather than curtailed? Are there any conditions in which prior restraint and deterring the press from irresponsibly disclosing classified information are justified? Should the United States follow other democracies and enact a state secrets act? And last but not least, are true whistleblowers, who reveal government illegality or abuse, sufficiently protected?

Notes

1. Sharon LaFraniere, "Math Behind Leak Crackdown: 153 Cases, 4 Years, 0 Indictments," *The New York Times* (July 21, 2013), A1.
2. See, e.g., Charlie Savage & Scott Shane, "Justice Dept. Defends Seizure of Phone Records," *The New York Times* (May 15, 2013), A15.
3. See, e.g., "NAA President and CEO Caroline H Little Comments on the Justice Department's Seizure of Associated Press Confidential Telephone Records," *Newspaper Association of America* (May 13, 2013), http://www.naa.org/News-and-Media/Press-Center/Archives/2013/Caroline-Little-Comments-on-Justice-Department-Seizure-of-AP-Phone-Records.aspx ("These actions shock the American conscience and violate the critical freedom of the press protected by the US Constitution and the Bill of Rights,").
4. See note 2.
5. See Part I.
6. See Part II.
7. See Part III.
8. See Part IV.
9. See Part V.A-C.
10. See Part VI.
11. See Part VII.
12. See, e.g., David A. Garvin & Michael A. Roberto, "What You Don't Know About Making Decisions," *Harvard Business Review* 79, no. 8 (2001): 108, 110 (likening the advocacy model to a contest).
13. See, e.g., Ashley Fantz & Paul Courson, "Prosecutors: Bradley Manning 'Craved' Notoriety," *CNN* (June 3, 2013), http://www.cnn.com/2013/06/03/US/manning-court-martial.
14. Ibid.
15. Ibid.

16. Ibid.

17. Ibid.

18. David E. Pozen, "The Leaky Leviathan: Why the Government Condemns and Condones Unlawful Disclosures of Information," *Harvard Law Review* 127 (2013): 512, 542–43 (citations omitted).

19. See Lydia Saad, "'Pro-Choice' Americans at Record-Low 41%," Gallup (May 23, 2012), http://www.gallup.com/poll/154838/pro-choice-americans-record-low.aspx (highlighting the close divide between pro-choice and pro-life Americans).

20. See "Gun Control: Key Data Points," Pew Research Center (July 27, 2013), http://www.pewresearch.org/key-data-points/gun-control-key-data-points-from-pew-research (reporting that the division among Americans on the gun rights debate is virtually even).

21. See "Market Troubles," *The Economist* (April 6, 2011), http://www.economist.com/blogs/dailychart/2011/04/public_opinion_capitalism (noting a split in Americans' opinion of the free market).

22. For more discussion on the fragmentations of the media, see Rebecca Chalif, "Political Media Fragmentation: Echo Chambers in Cable News," *Electronic Media & Policy* 1 (July 2011): 46, available at http://www.emandp.com/site_content_uploads/main_content/Political Media Fragmentation - Echo Chambers in Cable News (1).pdf.

    For more evidence of political polarization, see David R. Jones, "Party Polarization and Legislative Gridlock," *Political Research Quarterly* 54 (2001): 125.

    Also: Amitai Etzioni, "Gridlock?" *The Forum* 10, no. 3 (2012), available at http://icps.gwu.edu/files/2013/01/Gridlock.pdf.

23. I choose the word "seeks" deliberately because the media endeavors, but does not necessarily achieve, this goal.

24. Ann E. Marimow, "A Rare Peek into a Justice Department Leak Probe," *The Washington Post* (May 19, 2013), http://www.washingtonpost.com/local/a-rare-peek-into-a-justice-department-leak-probe/2013/05/19/0bc473de-be5e-11e2-97d4-a479289a31f9_story.html.

25. Mark Hosenball & Tabassum Zakaria, "AP Records Seizure Just Latest Step in Sweeping U.S. Leak Probe," *Reuters* (May 15, 2013), http://www.reuters.com/article/2013/05/16/us-usa-justice-ap-investigation-idUSBRE94F01F20130516.

26. Charlie Savage & Leslie Kaufman, "Phone Records of Journalists Seized by U.S.," *The New York Times* (May 14, 2013), A1.

27. See, e.g., Nick Gillespie, "Obama's War on Journalism: 'An Unconstitutional Act'," *The Daily Beast* (May 22, 2013), http://www.thedailybeast.com/articles/2013/05/22/obama-s-war-on-journalism-an-unconstitutional-act.html.

28. Dana Milbank, "In AP, Rosen Investigations, Government Makes Criminals of Reporters," *The Washington Post* (May 21, 2013), http://articles.washingtonpost.com/2013-05-21/opinions/39419370_1_obama-administration-watergate-benghazi.

29. Ibid.

30. "Another Chilling Leak Investigation," *The New York Times* (May 21, 2013), A26.

31. See note 27.
32. "Justice Department Run Amok on Journalists' Sources," *The San Francisco Chronicle* (May 22, 2013), http://www.sfchronicle.com/opinion/editorials/article/Justice-Department-run-amok-on-journalists-4540632.php.
33. Ron Fournier, "You Know What Really Risks National Security? Leak Investigations," *National Journal* (May 30, 2013), http://www.national-journal.com/politics/you-know-what-really-risks-national-security-leak-investigations-20130517.
34. Alex Weprin, "Tom Brokaw: 'The Press Always Has to Be Careful About Having a Glass Jaw,'" *TVNewser* (May 29, 2013), http://www.mediabistro.com/tvnewser/tom-brokaw-on-the-brokaw-files-the-state-of-media-and-the-presidents-press-policy_b181138.
35. Walter Pincus, "A Knee-Jerk Circling of the Media Wagons," *The Washington Post* (May 28, 2013), A9.
36. "Correspondents' Association Statement on Monitoring of Journalists," *Fox News* (May 21, 2013), http://www.foxnews.com/politics/2013/05/21/correspondents-association-statement-on-monitoring-journalists/.
37. See note 35.
38. Tom Curry, "Holder Addresses AP Leaks Investigation, Announces IRS Probe," *NBC News* (May 14, 2013), http://nbcpolitics.nbcnews.com/_news/2013/05/14/18253923-holder-addresses-ap-leaks-investigation-announces-irs-probe?lite.
39. Daniel Klaidman, "Holder's Regrets and Repairs," *The Daily Beast* (May 28, 2013), http://www.thedailybeast.com/articles/2013/05/28/holder-s-regrets-and-repairs.html.
40. Barack Obama, "Remarks at the National Defense University," (May 23, 2013) (transcript available at http://www.whitehouse.gov/the-press-office/2013/05/23/remarks-president-national-defense-university).
41. Ibid.
42. Ibid.
43. See note 18 at 577.
44. Ibid., 514.
45. See Jeffrey M. Jones, "Americans' Trust in Government Generally Down this Year," Gallup (September 26, 2013), http://www.gallup.com/poll/164663/americans-trust-government-generally-down-year.aspx (reporting that trust in the executive branch fell to fifty-one percent in 2013).
46. See note 18 at 573.
47. Matthew Cooper, "Why a Media Shield Law Isn't Enough to Save Journalists," *National Journal*, May 29, 2013, http://www.nationaljournal.com/politics/why-a-media-shield-law-isn-t-enough-to-save-journalists_20130529.
48. See Amitai Etzioni, *The Common Good* (Cambridge: Polity Press, 2004), 3–4.
49. See, e.g., Kostas Vlassopoulos, "Free Spaces: Identity, Experience and Democracy in Classical Athens," *Classical Quarterly* 57 (2007): 33, 39–47.
50. See "Q&A: What is a Loya Jirga?" *BBC News* (July 1, 2002), http://news.bbc.co.UK/2/hi/south_asia/1782079.stm.
51. See Dylan Matthews, "It's Official: The 112th Congress was the Most Polarized Ever," *The Washington Post* (January 17, 2013),

http://www.washingtonpost.com/blogs/wonkblog/wp/2013/01/17/its-official-the-112th-congress-was-the-most-polarized-ever/.

52. See generally Amitai Etzioni, "Communitarianism," *Encyclopedia Britannica Online*, http://www.britannica.com/EBchecked/topic/1366457/communitarianism (accessed January 13, 2014).

53. Amitai Etzioni, *The Common Good* (Cambridge: Polity Press, 2004).

    In contrast, authoritarian and East Asian communitarians tend be concerned with the common good and pay heed to rights mainly insofar as they serve the rulers' aims. *See* ibid and note 151. At the opposite end of the spectrum, contemporary liberals emphasize individual rights and autonomy over societal formulations of the common good. Ibid.

54. Ibid.

55. US Const. amend. IV.

56. See generally "National Terrorism Advisory System," Department of Homeland Security, http://www.dhs.gov/national-terrorism-advisory-system (accessed January 15, 2014) (stating that "Americans . . . should always be aware of the heightened risk of terrorist attack in the United States").

57. See "The Comprehensive National Cybersecurity Initiative," The White House, http://www.whitehouse.gov/issues/foreignpolicy/cybersecurity/nationa-initiative (accessed January 14, 2014) (identifying "cybersecurity as one of the most serious economic and national security challenges we face as a nation, but one that we as a government or as a country are not adequately prepared to counter").

58. Ibid.

59. See, e.g., Marc Ambinder, "WikiLeaks: One Analyst, So Many Documents," *National Journal* (November 29, 2010), http://www.nationaljournal.com/whitehouse/wikileaks-one-analyst-so-many-documents-20101129.

    Mark Feldstein writes that Wikileaks' "instantaneous global reach poses a challenge not only to state secrets everywhere, but even perhaps to the very idea of government itself," Mark Feldstein, "The Implications of Wikileaks," *American Journalism Review* (December 14, 2010), http://www.ajrarchive.org/Article.asp?id=4999.

60. See note 53.

61. To save ink I use the term editors to include publishers and owners.

62. Rachel Smolkin, "Judgment Calls," *American Journalism Review* 28 (October/November 2006): 22, 23, 25–26.

63. Ibid., 26.

64. See generally Douglas E. Lee, "Prior Restraint," First Amendment Center (September 13, 2002), http://www.firstamendmentcenter.org/prior-restraint.

65. Ibid.

66. Jack Goldsmith, "The Patriotism of the American Media," *Lawfare* (February 28, 2011), http://www.lawfareblog.com/2011/02/the-patriotism-of-the-american-media/#.Ut6MICg8ly4.

67. Dean Baquet & Bill Keller, "When Do We Publish a Secret?" *The New York Times* (July 1, 2006), A15.

68. See note 62 at 26.

69. Leonard Downie, Jr., "Leonard Downie: Obama's War on Leaks Undermines Investigative Journalism," *The Washington Post* (May 23, 2013), http://www.washingtonpost.com/opinions/leonard-downie-obamas-war-on-

leaks-undermines-investigative-journalism/2013/05/23/4fe4ac2e-c19b-11e2-bfdb-3886a561c1ff_story.html.

70. David Ignatius, "Beyond 'Trust Us," *The Washington Post* (July 5, 2006), A13.

71. Jean Folkerts, John Maxwell Hamilton & Nicholas Lemann, "Educating Journalists: A New Plea for the University Tradition," Columbia Journalism *School* (October 2013), 1, 12.

72. See Killian Young & Matthew Kovac, "Journalists and Military History: A Caution," *Medill National Security Zone*, (March 4, 2013), http://nationalsecurityzone.org/site/journalists-and-military-history-a-caution/.

73. See, e.g., Victor Pickard, "Take the Profit Motive out of News," *The Guardian*, (July 23, 2009), http://www.theguardian.com/commentisfree/cifamerica/2009/jul/23/newspapers-internet-advertising.

74. Eric Lichtblau & James Risen, "Bank Data Sifted in Secret by US to Block Terror," *The New York Times*, (June 23, 2006), A1.

75. "Letter from John W. Snow, Secretary, US Department of the Treasury, to Bill Keller, Managing Editor, New York Times" (June 26, 2009), http://www.treasury.gov/press-center/press-releases/Pages/4339.aspx.

76. See note 62 at 25. (quoting Coll).

77. Ibid., 30.

78. "A Look at Public Statements about AP Story about Foiled Terror Plot," *Fox News*, (May 14, 2013), http://www.foxnews.com/us/2013/05/14/look-at-public-statements-about-ap-story-about-foiled-terror-plot/.

79. Scott Neuman, "Leaks, Bombs and Double Agents: More on That AP Story," *NPR* (May 15, 2013), http://www.npr.org/blogs/thetwo-way/2013/05/15/184274166/leaks-bombs-and-double-agents-more-on-that-ap-story.

80. Matt Smith, "Bomb Plot Story at Heart of Probe, AP Says," *CNN* (May 14, 2013), http://www.cnn.com/2013/05/14/us/justice-ap-plot/.

81. Dylan Byers, "'New York Times,' 'Guardian' Condemn WikiLeaks: Former partners say leak endangers sources," *AdWeek* (Sept. 2, 2011), http://www.adweek.com/news/press/new-york-times-guardian-condemn-wikileaks-134586.

82. Elizabeth Flock, "WikiLeaks Posts All Cables Unredacted," *The Washington Post* (September 2, 2011), http://www.washingtonpost.com/blogs/blogpost/post/wikileaks-publishes-full-cache-of-unredacted-cables-online/2011/09/02/gIQAHAhWwJ_blog.html.

83. James Ball, "WikiLeaks Publishes Full Cache of Unredacted Cables," *The Guardian*, (September 2, 2011), http://www.guardian.com/media/2011/sep/02/wikileaks-publishes-cache-unredacted-cables.

84. See note 62 at 29.

85. Ibid.

86. "Media Sometimes Try, Fail to Keep NSA's Secrets," *The New York Times* (February 8, 2014), http://www.nytimes.com/aponline/2014/02/08/world/europe/ap-us-nsa-surveillance.html?partner=rss&emc=rss&_r=0.

87. Al Baker, "Seeking Exposé, Students End Up in Handcuffs," *The New York Times* (June 15, 2013), A1.

88. Robert D. Epstein, "Balancing National Security and Free-Speech Rights: Why Congress Should Revise the Espionage Act," *CommLaw Conspectus* 15 (2007): 483, 505 (citation omitted).

89. Gabriel Schoenfeld, *Necessary Secrets: National Security, the Media, and the Rule of Law* (New York: W.W. Norton, 2010), 17.

90. See generally Robert A. Sedler, "The Media and National Security," *Wayne Law Review* 53 (2007): 1025, 1026-27 (stating that the First Amendment presents a formidable obstacle to government efforts to regulate media expression).

91. Ibid., 1027–29.

92. See Geoffrey R. Stone, "Government Secrecy vs. Freedom of the Press," *Harvard Law & Policy Review* 1 (2007): 185, 185–86.

93. See note 62 at 28.

94. Ibid.

95. See Dina Goren, "Communication Intelligence and the Freedom of the Press. The Chicago Tribune's Battle of Midway Dispatch and the Breaking of the Japanese Naval Code," *Journal of Contemporary History* 16 (1981): 663, 663–64.

96. See note 89 at 124.

97. Victor Marchetti, John D. Marks, and Melvin L. Wulf, *The CIA and the Cult of Intelligence* (New York: Knopf, 1974).

98. See note 89 at 196.

99. Philip Agee, *Inside the Company: CIA Diary* (Penguin Books, 1975).

100. Scott Shane, "Philip Agee, 72, Dies; Exposed other C.I.A. Officers," *The New York Times* (January 10, 2008), A28.

101. Vanessa Bauza, "CIA Leak Comes Full Circle," *Sun Sentinel* (August 21, 2005), http://articles.sun-sentinel.com/2005-08-21/news/0508200650_1_cia-diary-philip-agee-white-house.

102. Richard Immerman et al., "Biographies of Important CIA Administrators: Philip Agee," in *The Central Intelligence Agency: Security Under Scrutiny*, ed. Athan Theoharis et al. (Westport, CT: Greenwood, 2006), 235.

103. See note 89 at 205.

104. Howard Morland, "The H-bomb Secret," *The Progressive* (November 1979), 3.

105. Ibid.

106. See *Morison v. United States*, 486 US 1306 (1988)
     Also: Stephen Engelberg, "Spy Photos' Sale Leads to Arrest," *The New York Times* (October 3, 1984), A8.

107. Martin Sieff, "Terrorist is Driven by Hatred for U.S., Israel," *The Washington Times* (August 21, 1998), A1.

108. This claim is controversial; some disagree that it was a press leak that led bin Laden to abandon his phone. See Glenn Kessler, "File the Bin Laden Phone Leak Under 'Urban Myths'," *The Washington Post* (December 22, 2005), A2.

109. See James Risen & Eric Lichtblau, "Bush Lets U.S. Spy on Callers Without Courts," *The New York Times* (December 16, 2005), A1.

110. See note 89 at 31.

111. Dana Priest, "CIA Holds Terror Suspects in Secret Prisons," *The Washington Post* (November 2, 2005), A1.

112. See note 74.

113. See note 35.

114. Bob Woodward, *Obama's Wars* (New York: Simon and Schuster, 2010).

115. Ibid., 8, 10, 46.

116. See "What Did WikiLeaks Reveal?" Private Manning Support Network (August 16, 2011), http://www.privatemanning.org/news/what-did-wikileaks-reveal.

117. Habibullah Khan & Muhammad Lila, "Pakistani Doctor Who Aided Bin Laden Hunt Gets 33 Years," *ABC News* (May 23, 2012), http://abcnews.go.com/Blotter/shakil-afridi-pakistani-doctor-aided-bin-laden-hunt/story?id=16412064.

118. See, e.g., Donna Cassata, "McCain Says Classified Leaks Done to Boost Obama," *Associated Press* (June 5, 2012), http://bigstory.ap.org/article/mccain-says-classified-leaks-done-boost-obama.

    Also: Felicia Sonmez, "Paul Ryan Suggests White House Leaked Identity of Pakistani Doctor," *The Washington Post* (September 12, 2012), htrp://www.washingtonpost.com/blogs/post-politics/wp/2012/09/12/paul-ryan-suggests-white-house-leaked-identity-of-pakistani-doctor.

119. David E. Sanger, *Confront and Conceal: Obama's Secret Wars and Surprising Use of American Power* (New York: Random House, 2012).

120. David E. Sanger, "Obama Order Sped Up Wave of Cyberattacks Against Iran," *The New York Times* (June 1, 2012), A1.

121. Ibid.

122. See note 78.

123. See note 78.

124. Lee Ferran and Marcus Wilford, "Al Qaeda 'Gleeful' Over Snowden Leaks, MI6 Head Says," *ABC News* (Novermber 7, 2013), http://abcnews.go.com/Blotter/al-qaeda-gleeful-snowden-leaks-mi6-head/story?id=20816271.

125. Pierre Thomas et al., "Officials: How Edward Snowden Could Hurt the U.S.," *ABC News* (June 24, 2013), http://abcnews.go.com/blogs/headlines/2013/06/officials-how-edward-snowden-could-hurt-the-u-s/.

126. David E. Sanger and Thom Shanker, "N.S.A. Devises Radio Pathway Into Computers," *The New York Times* (January 14, 2014), http://www.nytimes.com/2014/01/15/us/nsa-effort-pries-open-computers-not-connected-to-internet.html.

127. Ibid.

128. Kurt Eichenwald, "How Edward Snowden Escalated Cyber War With China," *Newsweek* (November 1, 2013), http://www.newsweek.com/how-edward-snowden-escalated-cyber-war-1461.

129. See note 89 at 124-5.

    Also: see note 102 at 235.

130. See note 80 (quoting United States Attorney General Eric Holder as saying that the leak "put the American people at risk").

131. See note 35 (arguing that the person who leaked information disclosing that the United States had a mole in North Korea "harmed national security").

132. See, e.g., David Batty, "Afghan's Finance Minister Warns Leaked Cables Will Damage Relations with US," *The Guardian* (December 4, 2010), http://www.theguardian.com/world/2010/dec/04/afghan-finance-minister-leaked-cables-damage.

    Also: "Saudi Prince Turki bin Faisal on Wikileaks: 'People Will No Longer Speak to American Diplomats Frankly," *Spiegel Online* (December 5, 2010), http://www.spiegel.de/international/world/saudi-prince-turki-bin-faisal-on-wikileaks-people-will-no-longer-speak-to-american-diplomats-frankly-a-732950.html.

    Also: Mary Beth Sheridan, "Calderon Cites 'Serious Damage' to U.S. Ties," *The Washington Post* (March 4, 2011), A9.

133. "National Security Leaks and the Law: Hearing Before the Subcommittee on Crime, Terrorism, & Homeland Security of the H. Comm." On the Judiciary, 112th Congress 13 (2012) (statement of Kenneth L. Wainstein, Cadwalader, Wickersham & Taft LLP).

134. David Firestone, "Snowden's Questionable New Turn," *The New York Times* (June 17, 2013), http://takingnote.blogs.nytimes.com/2013/06/17/snowdens-questionable-new-turn/.

135. David Ignatius, "Snowden Knows Best?" *The Washington Post* (June 13, 2013), A21.

136. See note 102 at 235.

137. See notes 84–86 and accompanying text.

138. See note 35 and text accompanying note 131.

139. See notes 114–5, 122–3 and accompanying text.

140. See note 104–05 and accompanying text.

141. See note 89 at 124–125.

142. See, e.g., ibid., 125 ("If appalling stupidity like [Kentucky Congressman Andrew Jackson] May's was one facet of the security problem, its even more significant side came as a nasty brew of one part recklessness and nine parts politics,").

143. See note 104.

144. Carol D. Leonnig & Julie Tate, "Some Question Whether Leak to AP Put Nation 'At Risk," *The Washington Post* (May 16, 2013), A8.

145. Ibid.

146. See Ted Barrett & Kate Bolduan, "Leaks in Foiled Plot Compromised Mole, Alerted al Qaeda, Lieberman Says," *CNN*, (May 10, 2012), http://www.cnn.com/2012/05/10/us/lieberman-terror-leak/.

147. See generally Martin Linsky, *Impact: How the Press Affects Federal Policymaking* (W.W. Norton, 1986), 181–222 (discussing the impact of leaks, why some people choose to leak confidential information, various politicians' and journalists' views on the value of leaking, and how it all informs policymaking).

148. See generally Cecelia M. Kenyon, "Men of Little Faith: The Anti-Federalists on the Nature of Representative Government," *William & Mary Quarterly* 12 (1955): 3, 37–38 (noting that both Federalists and Anti-Federalists alike displayed a "profound distrust of man's capacity to use power wisely and well," and believed a "political machinery" was necessary to supervise government).

149. See notes 212–215 and accompanying text.

150. Greg Mitchell, "Obama's War on Leaks: Already Having 'Chilling Effect' on the Media?" *The Nation* (May 22, 2013), http://www.thenation.com/blog/174477/obamas-war-leaks-already-having-chilling-effect-media (quoting Mark Mazzetti, a *New York Times* reporter, as interviewed by the *Washington Post*).

151. Ravi Somaiya, "Head of The A.P. Criticizes Seizure of Phone Records," *The New York Times* (May 20, 2013), B8 (quoting Pruitt).

152. Margaret Sullivan, "Leak Investigations Are an Assault on the Press, and on Democracy, Too," *The New York Times* (May 14, 2013, 5:40 PM), http://publiceditor.blogs.nytimes.com/2013/05/14/leak-investigations-are-an-assault-on-the-press-and-on-democracy-too/.

153. See "Jill Abramson on DOJ Investigations: 'News Gathering Is Being Criminalized,'" *The Huffington Post* (June 2, 2013), http://www.huffington-post.com/2013/06/02/jill-abramson-doj-eric-holder-meeting_n_3375035.html.
154. See note 69.
155. Robert Epstein points to the United States' poor ranking on the Worldwide Press Freedom Index (57th out of 168 countries in 2006) as evidence that "freedom of the press in this country has drastically eroded in recent years," See note xx, xx. This conclusion ignores the fact that many of the "freer" countries, such as those in Northern Europe, do not face the same threat from terrorists as the United States, nor shoulder the responsibility for going after global terrorist networks. *Ibid.*
156. See note 69.
157. See notes 95–128 and accompanying text.
158. See note 147 at 238.
159. Ibid.,197.
160. See Mark Lawrence, "Executive Branch Leads the Leakers," *The Washington Post* (July 28, 1987), A13.
161. See note 69.
162. See Leonard Downie, Jr. & Sara Rafsky, "The Obama Administration and the Press: Leak investigations and Surveillance in post-9/11 America" Committee To Protect Journalists (October 10, 2013), http://cpj.org/reports/2013/10/obama-and-the-press-us-leaks-surveillance-post-911.php.
163. See note 18 at 534–36.
164. Ibid., 536.
165. See Jim Young, "State Dept. Contractor to go to Jail Under Espionage Act for Tipping Off Journalist," *Reuters* (February 7, 2013), http://rt.com/usa/stephen-kim-espionage-plea-104/.
166. See Jonathan Turley, "Obama's Verizon Surveillance Reveals Massive Erosion of US Civil Liberties," *The Guardian* (June 6, 2013), http://www.theguardian.com/commentisfree/2013/jun/06/obama-verizon-surveillance-erosion-liberties (summarizing and interpreting the Verizon record seizure and identifying Judge Roger Vinson as having signed the order).
167. "Verizon Forced to Hand over Telephone Data—Full Court Ruling," *The Guardian* (June 5, 2013), http://www.theguardian.com/world/interactive/2013/jun/06/verizon-telephone-data-court-order.
   Also: see note 270.
168. See Barton Gellman & Laura Poitras, "U.S. Mines Internet Firms' Data, Documents Show," *The Washington Post* (June 7, 2013), A1.
   Also: Glenn Greenwald & Ewen MacAskill, "NSA Prism Program Taps in to User Data of Apple, Google and Others," *The Guardian* (June 6, 2013), http://www.theguardian.com/world/2013/jun/06/us-tech-giants-nsa-data.
169. Glenn Greenwald & James Ball, "The Top Secret Rules that Allow NSA to Use US Data Without a Warrant," *The Guardian*, (June 20, 2013), http://www.guardian.co.uk/world/2013/jun/06/nsa-phone-records-verizon-court-order.
170. See "Timeline: Guardian Announces Leak of Classified NSA Documents," *Aljazeera America*, (June 5, 2013), http://america.aljazeera.com/topics/topic/organization/nsa.html (click and drag the timeline feature to view a visual chronology of the news stories detailing the Snowden leaks).

171. See note 18 at 540.
172. Ibid.
173. See notes 176–83 and accompanying text.
174. Daniel J. Gallington, "There Is No Scandal in Tracking Down Leaks," *U.S. News & World Report*, (May 20, 2013), http://www.usnews.com/opinion/blogs/world-report/2013/05/20/obama-is-right-to-target-ap-national-security-leaks.
175. See note 18 at 542 (noting that administrative punishments for leakers are rare).
176. See Genelle Belmas & Wayne Overbeck, *Major Principles of Media Law* (Boston: Cengage Learning, 2013), 65–67 (discussing CIA employment contracts that require employees to seek prior approval before publishing anything about their employment).
177. Ibid., 66.
178. See *United States v. Marchetti*, 466 F.2d 1309 (4th Cir. 1972), cert. denied, 409 U.S. 1063 (1972).
    Also: see note 176 at 66.
179. See note 76, Ch. 13 n. 110.
    Also: see note 174, preface n. 65.
180. See note 176 at 66.
181. See *Snepp v. United States*, 444 U.S. 507 (1980).
    Also: see note 176 at 66.
182. Ibid., 516
    Also: see note 176 at 66.
183. See note 176 at 66.
184. See note 18 at 534–35 & n.115 (citing *United States v. Rosen*, 445 F. Supp. 2d 602 (E.D. Va. 2006), *aff'd*, 557 F.3d 192 (4th Cir. 2009)).
185. 18 U.S.C. § 793 (2006).
    See also: Jennifer K. Elsea, "Criminal Prohibitions on the Publication of Classified Defense Information" Congressional Research Service, R41404 (2013), 8.
186. 1 8 U.S.C. §§ 795, 797 (2006).
    See also: Jennifer K. Elsea, "Criminal Prohibitions on the Publication of Classified Defense Information" Congressional Research Service, R41404 (2013), 11.
187. 844 F.2d 1057 (4th Cir. 1988).
188. Ibid., 1063 (footnote omitted) (quoting Appellant's brief).
189. Ibid., (alterations in original) (quoting 18 U.S.C. § 793).
190. Ibid., 1070.
191. E.g., see note xx, xx (testimony of Nathan A. Sales, Assistant Professor of Law, George Mason University).
192. Benjamin Wittes, "Problems with the Espionage Act," *Lawfare* (December 2, 2010), http://www.lawfareblog.com/2010/12/problems-with-the-espionage-act/.
193. Ibid.
194. 18 U.S.C. § 793(d)-(e) (2006).
195. 18 U.S.C. § 798 (2006).
196. Section 798(a).
197. See notes 99–103 and accompanying text.

198. Intelligence Identities Protection Act of 1982, 50 U.S.C. § 3121 (formerly cited as 50 U.S.C. § 421).
199. Section 3121(a) (formerly cited as 50 U.S.C. § 421(a)).
200. 18 U.S.C. § 1924(a) (2006).
201. Section 1030(a)(1).
202. Section 641.
203. Jennifer K. Elsea, "Criminal Prohibitions on the Publication of Classified Defense Information" Congressional Research Service, R41404 (2013), 6.
204. See notes to follow.
205. H.R. 2943, 107th Cong. (1st Sess. 2001), available at https://www.fas.org/sgp/congress/2001/hr2943.html.
206. Jennifer K. Elsea, "Protection of National Security Information" Congressional Research Service, RL33502 (2006), 14, available at http://www.au.af.mil/au/awc/awcgate/crs/rl33502.pdf.
207. Ibid., 15 (quoting H.R. Rep. No. 106-969, at 44 (2000)).
208. Jennifer Elsea, "Protection of National Security Information: The Classified Information Protection Act of 2001," Congressional Research Service, RL31245 (2002), 2 available at http://stuff.mit.edu/afs/sipb/contrib/wikile-aks-crs-wikileaks-crs-reports/RL31245.pdf.
209. "Intelligence Authorization Act for Fiscal Year 2001," National Archives (December 6, 2000), http://www.archives.gov/iwg/about/intelligence-authorization-act-2001.html.
210. "Statement by the President," White House Office of the Press Secretary (November 4, 2000), available at http://www.fas.org/sgp/news/2000/11/wh110400.html.
211. "Letter from John Ashcroft, U.S. Attorney Gen., to the Honorable J. Dennis Hastert, Speaker of the House, U.S. House of Representatives" (October 15, 2002), available at http://www.fas.org/sgp/othergov/dojleaks.html.
212. See, e.g., "DOJ Targets Fox News, Accuses Reporter of a Crime . . . and We Stand By James Rosen's Right as a Member of the Free Press," *Fox News* (May 20, 2013), motion.foxnews.com/james-rosen/2013/05/20/report-doj-investigated-fox-news-reporter-2009-leak-probe.
213. Ibid., (quoting Michael Clemente, Fox News' executive vice president of news).
214. See, e.g., Michael Calderone & Ryan J. Reilly, "DOJ Targeting of Fox News Reporter James Rosen Risks Criminalizing Journalism," *The Huffington Post* (May 20, 2013), http://www.huffingtonpost.com/2013/05/20/doj-fox-news-james-rosen_n_3307422.html.
215. See note 35.
216. Bill Keller, "Op-Ed, Secrets and Leaks," *The New York Times*, (June 3, 2013), A21.
217. See, e.g., RonNell Andersen Jones, "Avalanche or Undue Alarm? An Empirical Study of Subpoenas Received by the News Media," *Minnesota Law Review* 93 (2008): 585, 596–602 (discussing the infrequency of investigative subpoenas issued by the Justice Department under the guidelines).

See also note 121, 534 ("All those thousands upon thousands of national security-related leaks to the media have yielded a total of roughly a dozen criminal prosecutions in U.S. history,").

218. U.S. Dep't of Justice, Criminal Resource Manual 9-13, 400, available at http://www.justice.gov/usao/eousa/foia_reading_room/usam/title9/13mcrm.htm#9-13.400.
219. Ibid.
220. Ibid.
221. Ibid. (however, prior authorization to interrogate or arrest a member of the news media is not necessary "in cases involving exigent circumstances").
222. Carrie Johnson, "Why Shield Laws Don't Always Help Media's Position," *NPR* (May 30, 2013), http://www.npr.org/2013/05/30/187227982/why-shield-laws-don't-always-medias-position (transcript of NPR Morning Edition interview between Carrie Johnson and Peter Zeidenberg).
223. 408 U.S. 665 (1972).
224. Ibid., 691–92.
225. See note 89 at 235.
226. Steve Coll, "The President and the Press," *The New Yorker* (June 10, 2013), http://www.newyorker.com/talk/comment/2013/06/10/130610taco_talk_coll.
227. William Blackstone, *Commentaries on the Laws of England* (Oxford: Clarendon Press, 1765–1769): 151 3;52
228. 283 U.S. 697 (1931).
229. Ibid., 701–02 (quoting § 1 of the state statute).
230. Ibid., 716.
231. Ibid., 720.
232. James L. Oakes, "The Doctrine of Prior Restraint Since the Pentagon Papers," *University of Michigan Journal of Law Reform* 15 (1982): 497, 499.
233. *United States v. Marchetti*, 466 F.2d (4th Cir.), *cert. denied*, 409 U.S. 1063 (1972).
234. Ibid., 1316–17.
235. *N.Y. Times Co. v. United States*, 403 U.S. 713, 725–26 (1971) (Brennan, J., dissenting).
236. Ibid., 730 (White, J., concurring).
237. See generally "Constitutional Provisions, Laws and Regulations," Right2Info.org, http://www.right2info.org/laws/#canada (last updated Oct. 24, 2011, 4:30 PM) (click particular country of inquiry on digital map for breakdown of pertinent official secrecy laws).
238. See, e.g., note 192, 508 (discussing the opinion of "some outspoken critics" on the use of the Espionage Act in the prosecution of Steven Rosen).
239. *N.Y. Times Co.*, 403 U.S. at 737–38.
240. See note 89 at 181.
241. See note 109.
242. Adam Liptak, "Gonzales Says Prosecutions Of Journalists Are Possible," *The New York Times* (May 22, 2006), A14.
243. See note 88 at 509.
244. According to a USA TODAY/Pew Research Center Poll conducted in June 2013, fifty-four percent of American believe NSA leaker Edward Snowden should be criminally prosecuted for sharing classified documents with the press. Susan Page, "Poll: Snowden Should be Prosecuted for NSA Leaks," *USA Today* (June 18, 2013), http://www.usatoday.com/story/news/politics/2013/06/17/americans-say-snowden-should-be-prosecuted-for-nsa-leaks-in-usa-today-poll/2430583/.

245. E.g., see note Stephen Vladeck. "National Security Leaks and the Law: Hearing Before the House Committee on the Judiciary Subcommittee on Crime, Terrorism, and Homeland Security" (July 11, 2012), 32–34 (testimony of Stephen I. Vladeck, Professor of Law and Associate Dean for Scholarship, American University Washington College of Law).

246. Ibid.

247. Ibid., 34.

248. E.g., Elizabeth Goitein & David M. Shapiro, "Reducing Overclassification Through Accountability" Brennan Center for Justice (2011), 1–2, available at http://www.brennancenter.org/sites/default/files/legacy/Justice/LNS/Brennan-Overclassification_Final.pdf (listing three "notable examples").

249. See note 18 (examining, *inter alia*, the federal government's vast tolerance of illegal national security leaks).

250. See note 248 at 43.

251. Ibid., 33.

252. Ibid.

253. Ibid.

254. Sarah Chayes, "When Journalists Seek Secrets, Do They Grasp the Risks?: *The Washington Post* (June 2, 2013), B3.

255. Ashley Fantz, "Still Out There and Growing–al Qaeda on the Rebound, Experts Say," *CNN* (December 28, 2013), http://www.cnn.com/2013/12/28/world/meast/al-qaeda-growing/.

256. Ibid.

257. See: Shaun Gregory, "The Terrorist Threat to Pakistan's Nuclear Weapons," *CTC Sentinel* (U.S. Military Acad., West Point), (July 2009), 3.

258. In May 2013, President Obama stated that "our systematic effort to dismantle terrorist organizations must continue. But this war, like all wars, must end. That's what history advises. It's what our democracy demands," Peter Baker, "A Pivot from War," *The New York Times*, (May 24, 2013), A1 (quoting President Obama).

259. Authorization for Use of Military Force, Pub. L. No. 107–40, § 2(a), 115 Stat. 224, 224 (2001).

260. Ibid.

261. Charles E. Berger, "AUMF: Rewrite and Renew," *The National Interest* (December 13, 2013), http://nationalinterest.org/commentary/aumf-rewrite-renew-9552.

262. The NSA surveillance program is already limited by such a defined period. *See* Scott Shane & Jonathan Weisman, "Debate on Secret Data Looks Unlikely, Partly Due to Secrecy," *The New York Times* (June 11, 2013), A1.

263. See note 62 at 26.

264. Ibid., 25.

265. "Foreign Intelligence Surveillance Court," Federal Judiciary Center, http://www.fjc.gov/history/home.nsf/page/courts_special_fisc.html (accessed February 2, 2014).

266. See Part I.

267. See, e.g., Claire Cain Miller, "Secret Ruling Put Tech Firms In Data Bind," *The New York Times* (June 14, 2013), A1.

268. Ibid.

269. See "Interviews-James Baker: Spying on the Home Front," *PBS Frontline* (May 15, 2007), http://www.pbs.org/wgbh/pages/frontline/homefront/interviews/baker.html (edited transcript of an interview conducted March 2, 2007).

270. Ibid.

271. Ibid.

272. See Spencer Ackerman, "NSA Chief Claims 'Focused' Surveillance Disrupted More than 50 Terror Plots," *The Guardian* (June 19, 2013), http://www.guardian.com/world/2013/jun/18/nsa-surveillance-limited-focused-hearing.

273. Laura K. Donohue, "NSA Snooping is Legal. It Isn't Constitutional," *The Washington Post* (June 23, 2013), B1.

274. Spencer Ackerman, "Senators Press NSA Director for Answers on Secret Surveillance Program," *The Guardian* (June 12, 2013), http://www.theguardian.com/world/2013/jun/12/senate-nsa-director-keith-alexander.

275. See, e.g., "Obama Vows More Transparency in Response to Scrutiny Over Surveillance Programs," *PBS Newshour* (August 9, 2013), http://www.pbs.org/newshour/bb/white_house/july-dec13/obama_08-09.html.

276. See note 274.

277. Ibid.

278. Ibid. That is, unless the government releases misleading details. But, sooner or later, some whistleblower would likely expose the ploy, undermining the whole enterprise, which is meant to build trust in government.

279. Vindu Goel & Claire Cain Miller, "More Data on Privacy, But Picture Is No Clearer," *The New York Times* (June 18, 2013), B1.

280. Ibid.

281. See note 274.

282. See Emma Roller, "Do Tell!" *Slate* (June 14, 2013), http://www.slate.com/articles/news_and_politics/explainer/2013/06/senate_intelligence_hints_at_prism_can_members_of_congress_be_tried_for.html.

283. See "Investigating Sept. 11," *PBS Newshour* (November 27, 2002), http://www.pbs.org/newshour/bb/terrorism/july-dec02/investigation_11-27.html.

284. Ibid.

285. See note 274.

286. In 2001, six men from Buffalo, NY, took a trip to Pakistan for a spiritual retreat sponsored by Tablighi Jamaat—a group that, while associated with radicalism, was not designated as a terrorist organization. While there, however, the six men were accused of attending a terrorist training camp called Al Farooq and supposedly listened to a speech delivered by Osama bin Laden. No evidence was presented of a forthcoming plot on their part. There were no weapons found, no history of violence uncovered, nor was there any "clear and convincing evidence" that the six men were planning any sort of terrorist act. Yet they were still charged under the Antiterrorism and Effective Death Penalty act with a possible fifteen years in prison and $250,000 fine for their activities. See JoAnn Wypijewski, "Living in an Age of Fire," *Mother Jones* (March/April 2003), 66, 69.

287. See Larry Greenemeier, "Obama to Speak on NSA Surveillance Controversy," *Scientific American* (January 16, 2014), http://www.scientificamerican.com/article.cfm?id=obama-to-speak-out-on-nsa-surveillance-controversy.

288. Michael Calderone & Matt Sledge, "Obama Whistleblower Prosecutions Lead to Chilling Effect on Press," *The Huffington Post* (April 16, 2013), http://www.huffingtonpost.com/2013/04/16/obama-whistleblower-prosecutions-press_n_3091137.html.

289. Civil Service Reform Act of 1978, Pub. L. No. 95–454, 92 Stat. 1111.

290. Ibid.

291. 147 Cong. Rec. 10,207 (2001).

292. Whistleblower Protection Enforcement Act of 2012, Pub. L. No. 112–199, 126 Stat. 1465.

293. "Presidential Policy Directive on Protecting Whistleblowers with Access to Classified Information" (October 10, 2012), available at http://www.whitehouse.gov/sites/default/files/image/ppd-19.pdf.

294. Ibid.

295. Joe Davidson, "Security Intelligence Workers Get Whistleblower Protection," *The Washington Post* (October 12, 2012), B4.

296. See note 89 at 174.

297. Ibid.

298. "Snowden could claim whistle-blower protection only if he took his concerns to the NSA's inspector general or to a member of one of the congressional intelligence committees with the proper security clearances"—which he did not. Pete Williams, "Analysis: Why Edward Snowden Isn't a Whistle-Blower, Legally Speaking," *NBC News* (June 18, 2013), http://usnews.nbcnews.com/_news/2013/06/18/19024443-analysis-why-edward-snowden-isnt-a-whistle-blower-legally-speaking?lite.

    See also: Jeffrey Toobin, "Edward Snowden Is No Hero," *The New Yorker*, (June 10, 2013), http://www.newyorker.com/online/blogs/comment/2013/06/edward-snowden-nsa-leaker-is-no-hero.html.

299. Amitai Etzioni, *From Empire to Community: A New Approach to International Relations* (Palgrave Macmillan, 2004), 67–68.

300. Conservative Fox News' primetime audience in 2011 was more than twice the size of liberal MSNBC—a median viewership of 1.9 million. *See* Jesse Holcomb, Amy Mitchell & Tom Rosenstiel, "State of the News Media 2012: Cable: By the Numbers," Pew Research Center for Excellence in Journalism (2012), available at http://stateofthemedia.org/2012/cable-cnn-ends-its-ratings-slide-fox-falls-again/cable-by-the-numbers/.

301. See notes 19–37 and accompanying text.

302. See notes 43–47 and accompanying text.

2

How Much Surveillance
Is Legitimate?

This chapter deals with the issues following the disclosures in 2013 about two surveillance programs the NSA is conducting. One is known as "Bulk Collection of Telephone Metadata," which collects, stores, and analyzes the records of a significant portion of the phone calls made and received in the United States (from here on "phone surveillance"). The other, known as PRISM, collects private electronic communications from a number of major online providers such as Google and Facebook and is focused on non-Americans.[1] This chapter focuses on the specific issues raised by these two programs, although they have attributes and raise issues that are also relevant to other national security programs. The chapter draws on a liberal communitarian approach in assessing the issues at hand. This approach will be discussed in part I of this chapter. Part II responds to critics of the programs who hold that such surveillance is neither needed nor effective. Part III examines major specific grounds on which phone surveillance has been criticized and justified. Part IV lays out similar analysis regarding the PRISM program. Part V examines the alternative ways both surveillance programs may be better controlled, on the grounds that *the more the government surveils, the more it needs to be surveiled.* Part VI closes the chapter with a discussion about the potential danger these program pose if the US government is overtaken by a McCarthy-like figure or even a tyrant.

I. A Liberal Communitarian Approach

The liberal communitarian philosophy (as developed by the author[2]) assumes that nations face several fully legitimate normative and legal claims. Attention to none of these claims can be maximized nor can these claims be fully reconciled, as there is an inevitable tension among them. It follows that some balance must be worked out among the conflicting claims rather than assuming that one will always trump the others. This chapter applies this approach to the balance between national security and individual rights, in particular the right to privacy in the context of the revelations regarding the United States' phone surveillance and its PRISM programs.[3]

In contrast to this balancing approach, libertarians, civil libertarians, and a fair number of contemporary liberals tend to emphasize individual rights and autonomy over considerations of the common good.[4] And at the opposite end of the spectrum are authoritarian communitarians (mainly in East Asia)[5], who privilege the common good a priori and pay mind to rights mainly to the extent that they serve the rulers' aims.[6] In that sense liberal communitarianism occupies the middle of the spectrum between libertarianism and authoritarianism, especially of the kind of communitarianism that draws mainly on social pressures rather than state coercion.

The Fourth Amendment text provides a strong expression of the liberal communitarian philosophy. It states, 'the right of the people to be secure in their persons, houses, papers, and effects, against unreasonable searches and seizures, shall not be violated.' By banning only *unreasonable* searches and seizures, it recognizes, by extension, that there are reasonable ones, namely those that serve the common good.

Public intellectuals, elected officials, and segments of the media tend to adopt a one-sided advocacy position whereby they champion one of the two core values of society, arguing that some individual right, such as privacy or freedom of speech, is being violated, and the laws or actions responsible should be halted. They often argue that "it is against the law, hence it is wrong," or that the court ruling or law on which a particular surveillance program is based violates a core value such as our right to privacy and hence should be rejected. They do not ask whether the service to that other core value, national security, might justify some scaling back of these rights, which have often been recalibrated over the decades. Keep in mind that there was no federal right to privacy until the mid-1960s,[7] and the Supreme Court failed to endorse a single legal claim that the government had violated the (now semi sacred) free speech guaranteed by the First Amendment until 1919—and even then it endorsed such protection only in a dissenting opinion.[8]

In contrast to the one-sidedness of advocates, the courts (often using the term "public interest"[9] rather than the common good") regularly weigh both core values.[10] In several cases, they concluded that the level of threat to the public interest justified some redefinition or even curbing of rights, while, in others, they found that the threat level did not justify such infringement.

For example, in *New York Times Co. v. United States* the court ruled that, in attempting to suppress the Pentagon Papers, the government failed to meet the "heavy burden of showing justification for the imposition of [prior judicial] restraint," though such restraint might be justified if the court believed that the release of the information would "surely result in direct, immediate, and irreparable damage to our Nation or its people."[11] In contrast, a court held in *United States v. Hartwell* that, although TSA screenings violated privacy, they were nonetheless permissible, as "preventing terrorist attacks on airplanes is of paramount importance" and, thus, such screenings "advance the public interest" to the point where some violation of privacy is justified.[12] This chapter follows the balanced approach taken by the courts rather than the one-sided advocacy of libertarians and authoritarians.

II. Basic Challenges and Responses

Critics of the phone surveillance and PRISM programs argue that terrorism has subsided and hence these programs were not needed.[13] For instance, many statements about the NSA surveillance programs start with arguing that these programs infringe on this or that right, and hence are unconstitutional and should be canceled.[14] In effect, the House of Representatives, even after extensive pleading by the president, the Republican Speaker of the House, and senior members of those congressional committees familiar with the programs and who have proper security clearance, came within 12 votes (205–217) of completely defunding the phone records collection program.[15] Others stated that, in establishing many of the antiterrorist measures enacted since September 11, including the NSA programs in question, Congress was "reckless," as the powers granted have proven "unnecessary and overbroad."[16] Others argue that terrorists can be handled by existing law authorities and procedures like other criminals. This is a position taken by the director of the Center on National Security, Karen J. Greenberg,[17] and the ACLU's Anthony D. Romero,[18] as well as Attorney General Eric Holder.[19] This view is also widely held in Europe.[20] Still others argue that these surveillance programs are ineffectual, and that the phone surveillance program in particular has no proven benefits.

1. Threat Assessments

Those who hold that terrorism has much subsided can draw on President Obama's statements. The President announced in May of 2013 that "the core of al Qaeda in Afghanistan and Pakistan is on the path to defeat. Their remaining operatives spend more time thinking about their own safety than plotting against us,"[21] and he echoed this sentiment in August when he stated that "core al Qaeda is on its heels, has been decimated."[22] Administration officials have been similarly optimistic regarding the diminished terror threat.[23] The president has since "pivoted" US foreign policy away from a focus on the Middle East in favor of a focus on East Asia.[24] However, since then there has been a steady stream of reports suggesting that much remains to be done in facing terrorism, and indeed that al Qaeda is rebuilding its strength and that the pivot to the Far East may well have been premature.

Core al Qaeda is regrouping under the banner of "al Qaeda in the Arabian Peninsula" (AQAP). Ayman al-Zawahiri has taken over Osama bin Laden's vacated position. It has expanded from between two hundred and three hundred members in 2009 to over one thousand today.[25] This group was behind the "most specific and credible threat" since the attacks on 9/11, which led to the closure of dozens of American embassies across the Middle East,[26] and it managed to capture and control significant territory in Yemen.[27]

Al Qaeda increasingly is relying on a decentralized network of collaborating terrorist affiliates,[28] and these affiliates are growing in strength and spreading into additional nations.[29] They include groups in Africa (a network that spans Algeria, Mali, Niger, Mauritania, and Libya),[30] the Caucasus, Syria, and Somalia.[31] Taken together, "al-Qaeda franchises and fellow travelers now control more territory and can call on more fighters, than at any time since Osama bin Laden created the organization 25 years ago."[32] Al Qaeda in Iraq has recently started a bombing campaign that killed over 300 people in 3 months.[33] The campaign has escalated, with the most recent monthly death toll (July 2013) estimated at 700 people killed by the group.[34] In addition the group has transformed Iraq into a staging point for incursions into the Syrian civil war.[35]

At the same time, Syria is turning into a haven and breeding ground for terrorists. Experts report that Syria has become a center for terrorists in the form of "an even more powerful variant of what Afghanistan was more than thirty years ago,"[36] with non-al Qaeda imitator groups emerging in the country. The radical Islamist Nusra Front has over three hundred fighters and has claimed responsibility for a number of bombings, kidnappings, and suicide bombings across the country.[37] It is estimated that there are as many as seventeen thousand foreign fighters in the country, most from Saudi Arabia and Tunisia.[38] Western intelligence officials are therefore worried that Syria is becoming a terrorist haven and might be "developing into one of the biggest terrorist threats in the world today."[39]

Al Qaeda has also staged a series of major prison breaks. In Iraq, militants used a combination of aggressive mortar fire, suicide bombers, and an assault force to free hundreds of prisoners from two separate prisons.[40] Over one thousand prisoners, including some terrorist suspects, escaped from a Libyan prison,[41] and in Pakistan, over 250 inmates were freed by some 150 militants.[42] In total, over two thousand prisoners, many of whom were al Qaeda-trained militants, were freed in the raids.[43]

In September 2013 al Shabaab, an al Qaeda linked terrorist organization based in Somalia, carried out a massive, well-planned and sophisticated attack in Nairobi, Kenya. In a three-day standoff in a shopping mall, the group killed over 65 people and left almost two hundred others injured.[44] Al Qaeda and its subsidiaries showed their agility and ability to adapt when they used of ink cartridges as a bomb and "implanted" explosives undetectable by airport scanners.

Finally, terrorists have been trying to get their hands on nuclear weapons. Both Russia and Pakistan have less-than-fully-secured nuclear arms within their borders,[45] and Pakistan has experienced at least six serious terrorist attempts to penetrate its nuclear facilities.[46]

A rule that applies here is that if the disutility of a particular event is very high, some carefully-designed security measures are justified even if the probability is very low. This point requires some elaboration. There is a tendency to assume that if it is very unlikely that one will face a given risk, then it is rational to ignore it. It makes little sense to carry an umbrella if the likelihood that it will rain is one in a thousand, let alone one in ten thousand. One reason (other than the charge of racial profiling) why the New York court ruled that the police procedure of stop-and-frisk should not be allowed was that it resulted in the apprehension of few wrongdoers.[47] Indeed, the main justification for stop-and-frisk is that it gets guns off the street, yet illegal guns were seized in only 0.15 percent of all stop-and-frisk searches.[48] However, this rule of thumb ignores the magnitude of the risk. The larger the risk—even if the probability remains unchanged and very low—the more security measures it justifies.

In short, the level of risk posed by terrorists, particularly if they acquire WMDs, provides justification for some enhancements of security measures, a core element of the liberal communitarian balance. This is especially true, as we shall see, if the measures are minimally intrusive or not intrusive at all. That is, they do not diminish the other core element—individual rights.

2. Terrorists Cannot Be Handled Like Criminals

Critics argue that terrorists could be handled like other criminals and hence no special counterterrorism programs are needed.[49] There are, however, strong counterarguments that suggest that terrorists should be treated as a distinct category. First and foremost, dealing with terrorists requires a focus on *preventing* attacks before they occur. This point is particularly evident in light of the concern that terrorists may acquire WMDs. Whatever deterrent benefit might be gained[50] by bringing terrorists to trial after they turn part of a major city into a radioactive desert is vastly outweighed by the magnitude of the harm already done.[51] In any case, there is little reason to think that those willing to commit suicide during their attack can be deterred at all; such people have little to lose. None of the nineteen people who attacked the US homeland in 2001, terrorized a nation, and left a deep mark on the American psyche can be brought to trial. Even terrorists not bent on committing suicide attacks are often "true believers" who are willing to proceed despite whatever punishments the legal system may throw at them.[52] Law enforcement assumes that punishment after the fact serves to deter future crimes (the intent is not to eliminate them but to keep them at a socially acceptable level).[53] This premise does not hold when it comes to acts of terror because the first priority of counterterrorism is to thwart terrorist designs beforehand, rather than to try in vain to capture and prosecute terrorists in the aftermath of an attack that is often much more damaging than most criminal acts.

Affording terror suspects the right to legal counsel prior to undergoing interrogation imposes a severe cost: information that can no longer be acquired through questioning. One may suggest that a terrorist could refuse to talk, even if not granted this privilege. However, adhering to the regular law enforcement procedures would require that, if a terrorist asks for a legal counsel, the authorities no longer talk to him, offer deals, or give incentives, let alone apply pressure. Given that terrorists often act in groups and pose more harm than most criminals, the notion of legally binding investigators such that they cannot adequately question a terrorist who has been caught—at least, until an attorney is found—tilts too far from protecting the common good.[54] One may say there is already a "public safety" exception that applies to emergency situations. When dealing with transnational terrorists, this should be the rule, not the exception.[55]

In addition, the criminal procedures of open arrest records, charging suspects within 48 hours under most circumstances, and the guarantee of a speedy trial all undermine the fight against terrorism. Counterterrorism requires time to capture other members of the cell before they realize that one of their members has been apprehended, to decipher their records, and to prevent other attacks that might be underway. Also security demands that authorities do not reveal their means and methods, hence it is often the case that one cannot allow terrorists to face their accusers. Just imagine having to bring in a CIA agent or Muslim collaborator—who the United States has successfully placed high in the Al Qaeda command—in order to have that operative testify in open court in the United States.

Next, the nature of the evidence likely to be presented in a terrorist trial is problematic. Much of it is classified and highly sensitive, which puts the government in the position of having to choose between jeopardizing national security in order to gain a conviction, or letting terrorists off easy, if not completely, lest they give away vital sources and methods. For example, Mounir el-Motassadeq, a member of the Hamburg cell which included four 9/11 hijackers, was brought to trial in Germany for abetting mass murder. His conviction was successfully appealed and a judge ordered his immediate release because without being able to verify the statements made by the prisoners there was not "sufficient proof in either direction."[56]

To avoid all these traps, the government, when forced to deal with civilian courts, often turns to plea bargaining. It is estimated that over 80 percent of the guilty terrorist convictions achieved in civilian courts since 2001 have been the result of plea bargains.[57] Although guaranteeing a guilty verdict, plea deals result in light sentences[58]

In short, there seem to be strong arguments as to why curbing terrorism justifies additional and, above all, different security measures than those employed in going after criminals. These arguments do not justify any particular security measure or surveillance program, but rather support the category of extraordinary public safety measures to which they belong. An examination of the two specific programs under consideration, the phone surveillance program and PRISM, follows.

3. Not Effective

A common claim against the NSA programs under discussion and other national security programs is that they are not effective.[59] This is a particularly potent argument for those opposed to these measures because if the programs are ineffectual, presumably nobody will seek to support them no matter how little they infringe upon rights. If, by contrast, the programs are proven to be effective, then at least some may begin to wonder if the associated gain in security does not justify some recalibration of rights.

The government argues that PRISM and the collection of phone company metadata disrupted fifty-four terrorist plots, one fifth of which were to be carried out within the borders of the United States.[60] However, critics have questioned these statistics, expressing skepticism regarding the reliability of government officials' testimony[61] and the adequacy of the thwarted plots as a metric of efficacy.[62] The question of how to ensure the validity of these and other government claims is addressed below in part IV.

Critics especially wonder about phone surveillance.[63] Some point out that the program was not the "primary" tool in averting any terrorist attack.[64] However, this criticism can be leveled against any program or instrument used by law enforcement authorities or national security agencies. Surely police cruisers or FBI files or even the whole Air Force are often but separate instruments that, in conjunction with others, bring about the required outcomes.

There are obviously scores of situations in which phone records would be of much help, even if they alone were not sufficient in preventing an attack or in finding those who committed acts of terror. To illustrate: when the authorities caught one of the two Tsarnaev brothers (the pair responsible for the Boston Marathon bombing), there was reason to suspect that they were cooperating with others, and surely that they planned more attacks, specifically in New York City. It does not take a PhD in counterterrorism to realize that under those circumstances it was very useful to know who they were previously in contact with over the phone. The same holds for the efforts to find out if they acted on their own or were supplied, guided, or financed from overseas, and if so by whom.

One telling piece of evidence regarding the effectiveness of the electronic surveillance programs is the way they hobbled bin Laden. When he found out that he was unable to use any modern communication device to run his terror organizations that had branches in three continents,[65] he was reduced to using the same means of communication used 5,000 years ago—a messenger. This was a very slow, low volume, cumbersome, and unreliable method of communication and command, which in effect prevented bin Laden from serving as an effective commander in chief of al Qaeda. Moreover, once the CIA deduced that using a messenger was the only way left for him to communicate, tracking the messenger led to bin Laden's downfall.[66]

Additional, publically-available evidence that the NSA programs forced terrorists to limit their communications is gleaned from reports that following the revelation that the United States had intercepted the communications of Ayman al-Zawahri, there was a sharp decline in al Qaeda's electronic communications.[67]

In short, we have seen that terrorism continues to pose a serious threat to national security; that terrorists cannot be handled like other criminals, and the use of distinct, special measures is the best way to counter them; and that surveillance programs like PRISM and the phone surveillance programs make a significant contribution to curbing terrorism. Therefore, these programs do enhance one core element of the liberal communitarian balance. The next question the chapter addresses is the extent they undermine the other core element.

III. Phone Surveillance of Americans

The NSA's phone surveillance program is a program involving the bulk collection of metadata from major telephone providers. These records, collected from at least three major phone companies,[68] include the numbers dialed by Americans and the duration of each call, but not the content of the calls.[69] The phone surveillance program has been deemed as violating individual rights on several different grounds, which are next reviewed.

1. Third-Party Doctrine

The collection of phone records has been justified on the basis of the third-party doctrine. It holds that once a person voluntarily discloses a fact to another party, he or she forfeits all Fourth Amendment protection when it comes to the disclosed information, as he or she no longer has a reasonable expectation of privacy once that information has been disclosed.[70] Relevant cases include *United States v. Miller* (1976) wherein the Supreme Court ruled that bank depositors forfeit their reasonable expectation of privacy when they hand over personal information to a bank. Moreover, sharing such information to a third party necessarily entails the risk that the third party might voluntarily turn over the information to the government.[71] Another example is *Smith v. Maryland* (1979), in which the Court held that the voluntary disclosure of information to telephone companies entailed the forfeiture of a reasonable expectation of privacy when it came to telephone records.[72] According to the Office of the Director of National Intelligence General Counsel Robert Litt "as a result, the government can get this information without a warrant, consistent with the Fourth Amendment."[73]

Though the third-party doctrine is the accepted law of the land, it is controversial,[74] and thus will not serve as the basis for the following defense of government surveillance. My main reason for moving away from the third-party doctrine is that in the cyber age much of our private lives are lived in a cyber world of cloud computing operated by third parties like Google and Facebook. As a result, a massive amount of information that once resided in the private sphere is now in the hands of third parties. If one accepts the third-party doctrine as the basis for a defense of government surveillance, one leaves very little in terms of what is considered reasonably private information protected from search.[75]

In short, we had best determine whether phone surveillance can be justified on grounds other than the third-party doctrine, because if the doctrine must be employed, one may well conclude that the privacy sacrifices the doctrine legitimates are too high a price to pay for whatever security gains these programs offers. (This may not be the case if one considers what might be called a partial third-party doctrine that excludes sensitive information, as is already the case for medical and financial information and some other such information).

2. 'Traffic' versus Content Analysis

Many critics of the phone records collection program refer to it explicitly or implicitly as if the government was listening to American phone calls and hence violating the privacy of millions of people. For example, Glenn Greenwald claims that 'the NSA frequently eavesdrops on Americans' calls and reads their e-mails without any individualized warrants—exactly that which NSA defenders, including Obama, are trying to make Americans believe does not take place.'[76] Similarly, Conor Friedersdorf suggests that to believe the NSA *isn't* listening to our calls requires 'trusting that the NSA is telling us the truth. But they've lied to us repeatedly.'[77] Among the public, a nearly two-to-one majority (63 percent) of Americans believe that the government was collecting the content of Americans' phone calls and e-mails—with 27 percent stating that they believed the government was listening to their phone calls or reading their e-mails.[78]

However, given the massive amount of communications content that is generated every day, it would be impossible for the NSA to examine even a small portion of that content unless its employees numbered in the millions. According to one source, "It would take 400 million people to listen and read" through all of the global communications traffic.[79] As NSA Director Keith Alexander put it, "If you think that we would listen to everybody's telephone calls and read everybody's e-mails to connect the dots, how do you do that? And the answer is, that's not logical."[80]

Actually, the program collects phone *records* that show who called what other number, the times the calls were placed, and their duration, but nothing more. (Note that even the various leakers did not claim that the content of the messages, the voice transmissions, were collected). This is akin to collecting the information from envelopes that Americans mail to each other—as opposed actually reading their mail—a practice that is, in fact, regularly carried out in bulk by the United States Postal Service. Indeed, the Postal Service "photographs the exterior of every piece of paper mail that is processed in the United States," and saves the recorded data for an unknown amount of time.[81]

The government reports that it collects and stores these records in order to have rapid access when needed and to stitch together various data. The phone companies also keep the records, but only for only short periods of time,[82] while security concerns require longer storage,[83] a rather weighty consideration.

In short, given the security that comes with gains engendered by ready access to this information—and the fact that storing this information intrusiveness is low—phone surveillance, like mail surveillance, passes this part of the liberal communitarian test. It is justified on both prudential (pragmatic, technical) grounds and on legal ones.

3. General Search and Individualized Suspicion

Privacy advocates often argue that before the government searches anyone, it should be required—indeed is required, according to the Constitution—to present evidence to a court of law demonstrating that there exists strong reason (enough to convince a judge) for believing that the particular person is likely to be a criminal or a terrorist. Only then, according to these advocates, can said person can be subjected to surveillance.[84] The phone surveillance program violates this rule on the face of it, because it collects records of millions for whom no particularized suspicion has been articulated, nor has a search been approved by a court. Thus, the ACLU filed a lawsuit seeking to halt the program on the grounds that the surveillance carried out is "warrantless and unreasonable."[85]

However, the courts have long established (employing, in effect, a rather similar line of analysis to the liberal communitarian one outlined above) that when there is both a clear public interest and the privacy intrusion is small, "administrative searches"—that is, searches that are executed without either a warrant or probable cause—are legal and are needed.[86]

One important subset of administrative search is the "dragnet" search where some agent of the government "searches or seizes every person, place, or thing in a specific location or involved in a specific activity based only on a showing of a generalized government interest."[87] Dragnet searches include checkpoints where drivers are stopped to check for the purposes of investigating a crime,[88] sobriety checkpoints,[89] and airport screening.[90]

In *Camara v. Municipal Court* the court held that routine government inspections of homes to ensure they were in compliance with housing code was permissible—this despite the fact that such searches covered every house in a particular area without any sort of particularized suspicion.[91]

In *Michigan Department of State Police v. Sitz*, the court approved of a sobriety checkpoint where every vehicle was stopped (at which point drivers demonstrating visible signs of impairment were pulled aside for further screening) on the grounds that the state has a strong interest in curbing drunk driving while the degree of intrusion involved in a brief traffic stop is minor.[92] The court held that, given the short duration of the stop and the minimal intensity of the search, the fact that the stops furthered the stated interests of the state rendered the searches reasonable under the Fourth Amendment.[93]

In *Illinois v. Lidster*, the court held that a traffic stop for the purposes of investigating a recent hit-and-run accident was permissible, given that "the gravity of the public concerns served by the seizure" and "the degree to which the seizure advances the public interest" outweighed "the severity of the interference with individual liberty" in that context.[94] And in *United States v. Hartwell*, the Third Circuit Court of Appeals held that TSA screenings, despite lacking individualized suspicion and being conducted without a warrant, are permissible as they further a key state interest while also being minimally invasive. According to the court, "preventing terrorist attacks on airplanes is of paramount importance," and thus, given the empirical evidence, screening checkpoints "advance the public interest" in a way that no measure relying upon individualized suspicion could.[95] At the same time, the court held that, in addition to protecting the public, the searches were "minimally intrusive" as the procedures used "were well-tailored to protect personal privacy, escalating in invasiveness only after a lower level of screening disclosed a reason to conduct a more probing search. The search began when Hartwell simply passed through a magnetometer and had his bag x-rayed, two screenings that involved no physical touching."[96] (TSA screening was also upheld on similar grounds in previous rulings, most notably *United States v. Davis*[97] and *United States v. Pulido-Baquerizo*[98]).

General search was further legitimized by section 215 of the Patriot Act and the National Security letters that it authorizes. This legislation allows the government to conduct surveillance without first identifying some individual as a suspected terrorist while also granting it the authority to search through third-party databases without notifying suspects—as long as the 'information is relevant to a terrorism investigation.'[99]

Specifically, Section 215 of the Patriot Act stripped FISA's business records provision of the requirement that requests for such records involve "specific and articulable facts" if these records pertain to "a foreign power or an agent of a foreign power."[100] However, it provides communications providers with an option for judicial review whereby they might contest the legality of a records request as well as any associated nondisclosure orders.[101] Section 215 has been cited in a ruling by a FISC court upholding the legality of the NSA's phone records collection program.[102] Section 215 also prohibits the collection of records for an investigation based solely on the basis of a protected First Amendment activity. A US citizen cannot be the subject of NSA surveillance simply because of what that person says or believes.[103] No evidence has been presented, even following all the leaks, that this section has been violated by NSA, in contrast to reports that the IRS has targeted Tea Party groups. Indeed, in late December of 2013, US District Judge William Pauley ruled that the NSA phone records collection program did not violate the Fourth Amendment, noting in particular that there was no evidence that the program had been used for any purpose aside from disrupting terrorist attacks.[104]

Most important, and often ignored by critics, the phone surveillance program does follow the Fourth Amendment rule of particularized search. Although the government collects and stores phone records, the calls of no person can be legally scrutinized until it has been established that there are "facts giving rise to a reasonable articulable suspicion" that the number to be searched is associated with a foreign terrorist organization.[105] The basis for that suspicion has to be documented in writing and approved by one of twenty-two highly-vetted NSA officers.[106] Far from granting many such searches, in 2012, fewer than three hundred proposed searches met the "reasonable, articulable suspicion" standard.[107]

In short, given that phone surveillance does not violate the constitution or the law, and since its intrusiveness is low, it should be tolerated. (The term "tolerated" is used to remind that one need not be enamored with such programs to consider them necessary and legitimate).

Given this cardinal observation, the question comes down to whether collecting and storing records in computers amounts to a search, general or otherwise. This point is discussed next.

D. Computers Don't Search. A major, indeed critical, feature of the phone surveillance program, ignored by many critics, is that it merely stores the records and that in order to access them and examine the records of any individuals (and those they called), particularized suspicion and a court order is required. It is hence important to note that computers *per se* do not violate privacy, although they vastly increase the risk that it might be violated. (How to best address and mitigate that risk is discussed below in part V.)

Computers do not gossip. They see no evil, hear no evil, and speak no evil. They do not engage in pillow talk, leak information to the press, or sell information to the Cubans, Chinese, or anyone else.

Hence, those who are concerned with finding a reasonable balance between security and privacy should focus on the interface between computers and human agents. That is, they ought to seek to ensure that once the computers flag particular individuals, this information is revealed only to law enforcement authorities and used by them in legal and accountable ways. (More about this below).

In short, privacy advocates would have good reason for concern if the massive collection of records (a) included content of the calls, and (b) if the records of who called whom would be available to all comers or even to various law enforcement agencies or regularly scrutinized by counterterrorism agents. However, if these records are merely collected and stored so that they will be readily available once a court order is granted for an individualized search, then most of the issue is moot beyond the question of how to ensure that access to the computers themselves is under tight surveillance.

E. Keep in Private Hands?. Critics argue that rather than collect and store phone records in bulk, the government should wait until it has a particularized suspicion and a court order and *then* collect the relevant records of that person from the phone companies.[108] However, both prudential and principled reasons favor the government position on this point.

Most important, currently phone companies are not required to keep these records and they keep them for only a short period of time.[109] That is, if the government will not store these records, they very often will not be available. This alone justifies the collection program.

One may argue that we could have our privacy cake and gain all the security we need if instead of collecting the records, the phone companies would be required to keep them say for seven years. But this idea raises three problems.

First of all, Terrorists, and more generally criminals, use a large variety of phones, including landlines and cell phones, managed by different phone companies. Indeed, some carry pocketfuls of cell phones so as to rapidly switch between them. If the government needs to rapidly trace the calls of a terrorist who has been apprehended in order to find their partners, it would have to approach different companies, put together different databases, and input them into its computers—all in short order. Anybody who has combined large databases from several different sources can attest to the fact that such combinations are time-consuming and challenging. There are strong reasons to have these combinations take place before searches actually need to be carried out. In addition, these large bases are needed for attempts to find patterns.

Second, if the phone companies were to keep the records for as long as the government might need them and to make them available whenever the government comes calling, the difference between such an arrangement and the status quo would be largely cosmetic. Indeed, I have shown elsewhere that, while privacy advocates strongly oppose (for good reason) the possibility of the government maintaining dossiers with detailed and private information about most Americans—including those not charged with anything—these advocates seem much less agitated when such databases are kept by private companies. Too often these advocates ignore that these private databases are merely a click (and a check) away from government agencies (including the Department of Justice, the IRS, and the INS), which have scores of contracts to this effect.[110]

This is far from a hypothetical idea. Currently, major private corporations keep very detailed dossiers on most Americans, hundreds of millions of dossiers. These include information on "income, net worth, real property holdings, social security number [sic], current and previous addresses, phone numbers and fax numbers, names of neighbors, driver records, license plate and VIN numbers, bankruptcy and debtor filings, employment, business and criminal records, bank account balances and activity, stock purchases, and credit card activity."[111] What is more, they make them available to the government for a fee, without any court order or review.[112] We are conditioned to hold that the private sector and privacy go hand in hand while the public sphere is closely associated with the violation of privacy, but actually, in the cyber age, these boundaries have been blurred. If the government has ready access to private data banks, they do not, by definition, provide extra privacy protection—and if they are not readily accessible, they hinder counterterrorism drives.

Third, one may say that the phone companies could review the government requests and thus serve as a sort or privacy-protecting screen. However, on what basis could a phone company lawyer deny government access in the face of government claims that protecting national security requires such access? Should the government reveal to company lawyers—who would lack security clearance and the relevant experience and training when it comes to such matters—why it is interested in particular set of records? Should the phone companies set up their own FISA-like courts to second-guess the government? The answer seems clear: the companies are not in a position to second-guess the government.

In short, not only is assured access to the records, sometimes on short order, a necessity, and not only are there technical reasons for allowing the government to keep them, but one should also recognize that keeping these records in private hands adds little to privacy protection.

Taking into account all of these considerations, it seems that the phone surveillance program's "correction" to the liberal communitarian balance between individual rights—especially privacy—and national security is (a) limited and not excessively intrusive, (b) abides by the constitution and prevailing law, (c) is structured in a reasonable manner (compared to the alternative of leaving the records only in private hands) and (d) contributes to the protection of national security. Whether it is subject to the level of oversight and accountability necessary for ensuring that it is not abused as a way to spy on people because of their political views, to wantonly ensnaring innocent people, or for any other variety of misuse is less clear. This question deserves separate treatment, which is provided in the following section where it can be applied to the PRISM program as well.

IV. PRISM

The PRISM program acquires electronic communications (including, e-mails, chat logs, videos, VoIP, file transfers, social networking details) from American-based Internet Service Providers (ISPs), including Microsoft, Apple, Google, Yahoo, and Facebook.[113] The program targets non-US persons outside the United States. PRISM can be used for various national intelligence purposes, such as keeping under surveillance the communications of militaries of nations' hostile to the United States. Here, only its use as a counterterrorism measure is under review.

The program is authorized by Section 702 of the FISA Amendments Act (FAA) of 2008.[114] Under Section 702, the United States Government does not unilaterally obtain information on foreign targets from the servers of US ISPs. All information is collected is for counterterrorism purposes and is gathered with the knowledge of the ISP. These actions are authorized by written directives from the US Attorney General and the Director of National Intelligence, which are approved by FISC for a period of one year, and can subsequently be renewed. The NSA, thus, does not need an individualized court order to gather intelligence on a suspected overseas intelligence targets.[115]

In addition to facilitating the Government's surveillance of the live communications and stored data of foreign targets operating outside the United States, PRISM also collects the electronic data of select Americans who communicate with foreign targets.[116]

1. The Legal Basis for PRISM's Surveillance of Foreign Nationals Abroad

Collecting the phone records of Americans concerned many American critics; the collection of information about foreigners received much less attention. The question though stands: what are the rights of non-Americans under Constitutional, domestic, and international law?

a. Under the US Constitution. As with the phone records collection program, critics have charged the government with a violation of Fourth Amendment rights. NSA officials have asserted that non-US persons do not enjoy Fourth Amendment protections.[117] This reasoning is backed by the courts: in *United States v. Verdugo-Urquidez*, the court held that the "Fourth Amendment does not apply to the search and seizure by United States agents of property owned by a nonresident alien and located in a foreign country," on the grounds that "the people" protected by The Constitution's Fourth Amendment "refers to a class of persons who are part of a national community or who have otherwise developed sufficient connection with this country to be considered part of that community."[118] The majority did not offer a clear definition of "sufficient connection" but maintained that the Fourth Amendment did not apply to property located abroad and belonging to a foreign national with no residential connection to the United States.[119]

As former Attorney General William Barr put it "our conventional criminal justice system is designed to apply to people within our political community, but it doesn't make sense to extend those rights to foreign enemies who are trying to slaughter us. These people are just like the Nazi saboteurs."[120] On what ground can terrorists, who are willing to kill and die to undermine the values that undergird the American system of justice, claim to enjoy the very rights and privileges they seek to destroy?[121]

In contrast, the dissenting Justices, Brennan and Marshall, challenged the majority's interpretation and contended that the respondent, Verdugo-Urquidez, had developed a sufficient connection with this country because "our Government, by investigating him and attempting to hold him accountable under United States criminal laws, has treated him as a member of our community for purposes of enforcing our laws. He has become, quite literally, one of the governed."[122]

In short, Brennan and Marshall argued that the government's authority to criminalize, investigate, and prosecute both domestic and foreign conduct originates in the Constitution. As such, the actions the government takes in enforcing that authority is similarly subject to constitutional constraints. The two justices further affirmed that in light of the increasingly globalized reach of American law enforcement and the government's efforts to "hold foreign nationals criminally liable under federal laws for conduct committed entirely beyond the territorial limits of the United States that nevertheless has effects in this country," the extension of constitutional protections to foreign nationals was particularly critical.[123]

The majority, however, maintained that such an interpretation would have a detrimental impact on not just law enforcement's but also the military's activities abroad, as non-Americans with no substantive links to the United States would flood American courts with lawsuits for damages related to Fourth Amendment violations in foreign countries. Furthermore, they argued, the executive and legislative branches would be "plunged into a sea of uncertainty as to what might be reasonable in the way of searches and seizures conducted abroad."[124]

These divergent views on the extraterritorial application of the Constitution can be traced to the distinct theories invoked in defense of these clashing interpretations of the Fourth Amendment. Social contract theory, on one hand, contends that "the people" in the Constitution refers to a voluntary party to the social contract (i.e., citizens or "a class of persons who are part of a national community or who have otherwise developed sufficient connection with this country to be considered part of that community").[125] In contrast, the natural rights theory views the Constitution as a constraint on the American government's activities everywhere—limits on the actor rather than rights given to a specific kind of victim.[126] At present, the prevailing legal consensus supports the former theory and foreign nationals abroad are consequently excluded from the protection of the Constitution's Fourth Amendment.

b. Domestic Law. Section 702 of the Foreign Intelligence Surveillance Act, enacted in 2008, authorizes the PRISM program to collect, without a warrant, the electronic communications of foreign targets reasonably believed to be both non-US citizens and outside the United States.[127] Furthermore, according to the FISA Amendments Act, any foreign national outside the United States can be targeted for surveillance as long as the government's objective is to collect foreign intelligence.[128] FISA broadly defines "foreign intelligence collection" as "information with respect to a foreign power or foreign territory that relates to *the conduct of the foreign affairs of the United States.*"[129]

In accordance with FISA, the attorney general and director of national intelligence can issue one-year blanket authorizations for the surveillance of noncitizens who are reasonably believed to be outside the United States.[130] Along with this authorization, the attorney general also provides the Foreign Intelligence Surveillance Court with a "written certification containing certain statutorily required elements."[131] The court reviews the certification as well as the targeting and minimization procedures mandated by FISA regulations.[132] If the judge determines that the targeting and minimization procedures adequately restrict the acquisition, retention, and dissemination of private information related to US persons and are consistent with the requirements of the FISA subsections and the Fourth Amendment, the judge enters an order approving the certification.[133] If, on the other hand, the court decides that the Section 702 application does not meet the aforementioned requirements, the judge will "issue an order directing the government to, at the government's election and to the extent required by the court's order, either correct any deficiency identified by the Court's order not later than 30 days after the date on which the Court issues the order, or cease, or not begin, the implementation of the authorization for which the certification was submitted."[134]

Ergo, PRISM meets not only the Constitutional requirements as they are widely understood, but is also in accordance with the relevant laws concerning FISA and related matters.

c. International Law. Article 12 of the Universal Declaration of Human Rights, of which the United States is a signatory, affirms that "no one shall be subjected to arbitrary interference with his privacy, family, home or correspondence, nor to attacks upon his honor and reputation. Everyone has the right to the protection of the law against such interference or attacks."[135] And the Universal Declaration of Human Rights, described by Professor Richard Lillich as the 'Magna Carta of contemporary international human rights law,'[136] is widely accepted as customary international law. The International Covenant on Civil and Political Rights (ICCPR), ratified by the

United States in March 1976, reaffirms this principle in nearly identical terms. International law has recognized the right to privacy as a fundamental human rightOne must nevertheless take into account that the Universal Declaration of Human Rights is not legally binding and signatories are consequently not legally responsible for violations of the Declaration's provisions. Furthermore, although the United States Congress ratified the ICCPR, they did so with an "unprecedented number of reservations, understandings, and declarations," effectively "rendering the treaty powerless under domestic law."[137]

Most important, because spying has been practiced since the beginning of history, and is very frequently and regularly practiced by one nation against others, disregarding the privacy rights of foreign nationals is widely and tacitly accepted as part of "normal," albeit not normative, international life.[138] It is considered uncouth to submit friendly nations to surveillance, but it is not considered a serious violation of the prevailing standards of international relations. PRISM fits into a world that is rife with many more serious violations of the UDHR.

2. Americans Abroad

FISA bans monitoring the Internet activity of American citizens abroad by mandating that activities authorized under Section 702 "not intentionally target a United States person reasonably believed to be located outside the United States."[139] James Clapper, the director of national intelligence, has noted that the NSA's surveillance activities are subject to oversight by the Foreign Intelligence Surveillance Court, the executive branch, and Congress, and he has stated that the program is not be used to "intentionally target any US citizen, any other US person, or anyone located within the United States."[140]

These statements sound much more absolute than they should sound. People are hardly required to show their passports when they "travel" in cyberspace, and it is therefore far from obvious when the NSA is surveiling people overseas, what their nationality is. The NSA follows a special procedure to deal with this attribution problem. The process of acquiring data on a foreign target begins when an NSA analyst 'tasks' the PRISM system for information about a new surveillance target.[141] The request to add a new target is subsequently reviewed by a supervisor who must endorse the analyst's "reasonable belief," defined as 51 percent confidence, that the specified target is a foreign national who is overseas at the time of collection.[142]

NSA analysts examine the following three categories of information to make the above determination:

(1) They examine the lead information they have received regarding the potential target or the facility that has generated interest in

conducting surveillance to determine what the lead information discloses about the person's location. For example, has the target stated that he is located outside the United States? With whom has the target had direct contact, and what do we know about the location of such persons?

(2) They conduct research in NSA databases, available reports, and collateral information to determine whether the NSA knows the location of the person, or knows information that would provide evidence concerning that location. For example, the NSA will review their own databases as well as databases of other intelligence and law enforcement agencies to determine if the person's location is already known.

(3) They conduct technical analyses of the facility or facilities to determine or verify information about the person's location. For example, the NSA may examine Internet content repositories for records of previous Internet activity that may indicate the location of the target.[143]

In addition, the NSA maintains records of telephone numbers and electronic accounts, addresses, and identifiers that they have reason to believe are being used by US persons. Before targeting an individual for surveillance, a telephone number or electronic communications account is checked against these records in order to ascertain whether the NSA has reason to believe the target is a US person.[144] However, "in the absence of specific information regarding whether a target is a US person, a person reasonably believed to be located outside the US or whose location is not known will be presumed to be a non-US person unless such person can be positively identified as a United States person, or the nature or circumstances of the person's communications give rise to a reasonable belief that such person is a US person."[145]

Critics contend that these standards and procedures are far from rigorous and do not satisfactorily ensure that targeted persons are not American citizens or residents.[146] Numbers are difficult to come by, as the intelligence community maintains that it is "not reasonably possible to identify the number of people located in the United States whose communications may have been reviewed under the authority" of the FISA Amendments Act that authorizes PRISM.[147] John D. Bates, the chief judge of the Foreign Intelligence Surveillance Court has noted that, given the scale of the NSA's data collection, "the court cannot know for certain the exact number" of wholly domestic communications collected under the act.[148]

Critics cite an NSA internal audit dated May 2012, which found 2,776 incidents in the preceding twelve months of unauthorized collection, storage, access to or distribution of protected communications. Most of these incidents were unintended, with many involving failures of due diligence or violations of operating procedures. However, "the most serious incidents included a violation of a court order and unauthorized use of data about more than 3,000 Americans and green-card holders."[149]

Other reports show that (a) these violations make up just a tiny fraction of 250 million communications that are collected by the NSA each year[150]; (b) practically all were inadvertent, mostly technical mistakes such as syntax errors when making database queries[151] or the programming error that interchanged the Washington D.C. area code 202 with the international dialing code for Egypt which is 20;[152] (c) measures were taken to reduce error rate;[153] (d) willful violations of privacy led to termination of the offending employees,[154] and (d) the NSA was responsive to internal audits and deferred to court guidance, which shows that oversight works.[155]

Moreover, if an NSA analyst incidentally obtains information that involves a US person he or she has to follow 'minimization' protocols. If the communication has no foreign intelligence value he or she cannot share or disseminate it unless it is evidence of a crime. Even if a conversation has foreign intelligence value, that information can only be disseminated to someone with an appropriate need to know the information pursuant to his or her mission.[156]

The NSA put it as follows: "We're a human-run agency operating in a complex environment with a number of different regulatory regimes, so at times we find ourselves on the wrong side of the line . . . [If you] look at [the] number [of violations] in absolute terms that looks big, and when you look at it in relative terms, it looks a little different."[157]

The Supreme Court has not ruled on the applicability of the Fourth Amendment to US citizens abroad but, in April of 2000, a federal district judge decided in *United States v. Bin Laden* that an exception to the warrant requirement for Americans abroad existed for foreign intelligence searches.[158] Citing 'the president's constitutional power over foreign affairs, the policy costs of imposing a warrant requirement, and the absence of a warrant procedure'—as well as the fact that FISA explicitly specifies that it limits the president's authority to collect foreign intelligence only within the borders of the United States—the judge held that the warrantless phone surveillance and search of the home of an American citizen living in Kenya (who was in communication with al Qaeda) was permissible.[159] The judge, however, additionally required that there be probable cause to suspect that the defendant was an agent of a foreign power and that the searches or seizures were first authorized by the president or attorney general for the foreign intelligence exception to be applicable.

3. Cross-border Communications

The government's initial position has been that PRISM is not targeting Americans or those known to reside within the borders of the United States.[160] In addition, the NSA cannot target a foreign communication with the intention of tracing it back to a person in the U.S.[161]

However, critics of the PRISM program, such as Senator Ron Wyden (D-OR), have argued that a loophole in Section 702 allows the government to conduct 'backdoor' or warrantless searches of Americans' communications.[162] Specifically, critics argue that the incidental collection of data belonging to Americans who communicate with foreign nationals abroad further increases the potential pool of Americans being electronically monitored by the government. When the NSA collects information on a foreign target, it "means, at minimum, that everyone in the suspect's inbox or outbox is swept in." Furthermore, "intelligence analysts are typically taught to chain through contacts two "hops" out from their target, which increases 'incidental collection' exponentially."[163] Additionally, the 2008 amendment to FISA removed the warrant requirement for any communication involving a foreign target—even if the communication involved an American sender or recipient.[164]

Much of the legal reasoning that justifies the collection of phone records (e.g., the general acceptance of "checkpoint searches" as being in accordance with the Fourth Amendment), can also be used to justify PRISM's incidental collection of communications between Americans and those across the border. In addition, the fact that these communications occur at the cyberequivalent of a border also could be used to justify this kind of search. The Supreme Court has held that "searches made at the border, pursuant to the longstanding right of the sovereign to protect itself by stopping and examining persons and property crossing into this country, are reasonable simply by virtue of the fact that they occur at the border."[165] The court has similarly maintained that such searches without probable cause are reasonable not just at the physical borders, but at the "functional equivalents" of the border as well.[166] These searches are all justified by the fact that the United States has an "overriding interest, and authority, to protect its 'territorial integrity' as well as preserve national security."[167] More broadly, the exception is based on the Government's "sovereign right to protect itself from terrorist activities, unlawful migration, and contraband."[168] Whether PRISM should be applied to deal with acts other than terrorism is a very weighty normative and legal issue that calls for a separate treatment not provided in this book.

The review so far suggests that PRISM is a lawful program and a reasonable one. This assumes that it is employed as depicted by the government. How to ensure that this is the case, and that the program will be properly contained and held accountable in the future, is explored next.

V. Accountability vs. Transparency

1. Serious Charges

So far, the article has assumed that the main features of the two surveillance programs are those that have been reported. One can have some confidence in the information because it largely emanates not from the government, but from leakers who have proven themselves to be quite willing to reveal the governments flaws and misdeeds. The evidence so far suggests that the government basically follows the procedures indicated, and moreover, even liberal critics had to admit that there are no specific cases in which an innocent person was actually harmed by these programs. As the *New Yorker*'s Hendrik Hertzberg has observed, "In the roughly seven years the programs have been in place in roughly their present form, no citizen's freedom of speech, expression, or association has been abridged by them in any identifiable way. No political critic of the Administration has been harassed or blackmailed as a consequence of them. They have not put the lives of tens of millions of Americans under 'surveillance' as that word is commonly understood."[169]

Two very serious specific charges have been leveled against the NSA. One concerns the report that the NSA often failed to comply with the laws that are supposed to govern its operations.[170] "For several years, the National Security Agency unlawfully gathered tens of thousands of e-mails and other electronic communications between Americans," via the "upstream" collections—a program authorized by Section 702 of FISA. This program is distinct from both PRISM and the phone surveillance program.[171] However, such violations raise questions about the extent to which the NSA can be trusted to heed the law.

The second serious charge is that the NSA has misled the public and watchdogs regarding the extent and nature of its program. A FISC judge charged the government with providing misleading statements, noting that "the government has now advised the court that the volume and nature of the information it has been collecting is fundamentally different from what the court had been led to believe."[172] In a particularly sharply-worded footnote, the judge, John Bates, stated that "the court is troubled that the government's revelations regarding NSA's acquisition of Internet transactions mark the third instance in less than three years in which the government has disclosed a substantial misrepresentation regarding the scope of a major collection program."[173]

Similarly, Judge Reggie B. Walton accused the NSA of having repeatedly provided the Foreign Intelligence Surveillance Court with misinformation with respect to how the telephone metadata was being used.[174] Walton wrote that the "government has compounded its noncompliance with the court's orders by repeatedly submitting inaccurate descriptions of the alert list process," and that "it has finally come to light that the FISC's authorizations of this vast collection program have been premised on a flawed depiction of how the NSA uses the phone call data."[175]

Given these findings one can either hold that these programs ought to be canceled (a position taken by a considerable number of members of Congress on both the right and the left[176]), or that NSA needs to be more closely monitored. The preceding discussion suggests that given that threat level and the need for enhanced security measures, one should at least closely test the thesis that a better monitored NSA could be made to fully function within the law before one considers canceling either the phone surveillance or PRISM programs. One can accord the government more license to surveil the population commensurate with the degree to which its surveillance programs are *themselves* subject to surveillance. This approach is explored next.

There are two major ways to implement such guarding of the guardians: increasing transparency and increasing accountability. While I cannot stress enough that both have a contribution to make, I shall attempt to show that enhanced accountability ought to be relied upon much more than enhanced transparency. I will also suggest a particular means for strengthening accountability.

2. The Limits of Enhancing Transparency

Enhanced transparency entails releasing more information about the details of the surveillance programs to the media and, hence, to the public, as well as to members of Congress in general, rather than only to a select few with security clearance who serve on specialized committees. Following the revelations of the NSA programs in 2013 there was a very considerable demand for such disclosures and increased transparency. Over a quarter of the Senate signed a letter urging the White House to be more transparent about its surveillance practices.[177] The president's aides stated that they were going to try to be even more transparent,[178] and additional information was released by the government,[179] on top of the continued stream of leaks.

There are some potential ways that transparency could be enhanced. For example, the government might release summaries of the FISA rulings that justifies its programs without going into the details of the facts about specific suspects on which these cases are based. Since the revelations in 2013, the government has begun to make moves toward such transparency. For example, judge on the nation's intelligence court directed the government to review the possibility of publicly releasing some of the court's presently-classified opinions regarding the NSA's phone records collection program.[180] In addition, the Office of the Director of National Intelligence has developed a webpage where it makes public formerly-classified material that helps to explain the functioning of the programs in question.[181] James Clapper, the director of national intelligence also stated that his office would release additional information regarding the number of secret court orders and national security letters sent out each year in the process of collecting data, as well as the number of people affected by such searches.[182]

However, high transparency is, on the face of it, incompatible with keeping secret that which must be kept secret. Moreover, when the government responds to calls for more scrutiny with the release of more information, so as to demonstrate that the secret acts did, in fact, improve security and did not unduly violate privacy, these releases encounter several difficulties. First, each piece of information released potentially helps the adversaries. This is, in effect, the way intelligence work is often done: by piecing together details released by various sources. Thus, the publication of information about which past terrorist operations were aborted by the government could allow those terrorist groups to find out which of their plots failed because of US government interventions versus those that failed because of technical flaws, the weakness of their chosen agents, or some other reason.[183] Second, it is next to impossible to spell out how these cases unfolded without giving away details about sources and methods which could aid the enemy. One intelligence official reports that the leaks regarding the NSA snooping programs have already led to terrorist groups "changing their communications behavior based on these disclosures," meaning that we might "miss tidbits that could be useful in stopping the next plot."[184]

Moreover, however much information about specific cases the government releases, skeptics are sure to find details that need further clarification and documentation. Thus, following the uproar over PRISM, technology companies sought to "reassure users" by releasing reports on the frequency of government data requests. The result, the *New York Times* reports, was that "rather than provide clarity, the companies' disclosures have left many questions unanswered."[185] As another example, when NSA Director General Keith Alexander released details about how the agency's surveillance programs had thwarted terrorist plots, the media immediately asked for more.[186] Moreover, there is no way for the media to determine whether the released cases are typical or were chosen because they reflect well on the government.

3. Increasing Accountability

A considerable number of suggestions have been made regarding how greater oversight could be implemented to hold the government to account. These include:

- A panel of high-level, independent experts who would review the technologies being used by the NSA and who could provide recommendations regarding how to balance privacy and security.[187]
- FISA to include a "privacy advocate" who would add an adversarial element to requests made to the courts.[188] Legislation to this effect has been introduced by two members of the House who propose creating an 'Office of the Constitutional Advocate' to be lead by an advocate appointed by the judicial branch.[189]
- Annual reports by inspectors general regarding the activities of the NSA.[190]
- Stronger laws protecting whistleblowers—a category that should be limited to those who go through established channels rather than leak information to the public and the press.[191]
- Subjecting the NSA to closer oversight by various congressional committees.[192] One should note though the danger of over correcting the current problems. Famously the Department of Homeland Security is

subject to so many committees that is senior staff is spending a very large proportion of their time testifying before Congress and preparing for such appearances.

- Reforming how the FISA court judges are selected to ensure greater independence from government and creating multiple judge panels that might allow for dissents.[193]
- Senator Dianne Feinstein has suggested that the government keep records for only two or three years rather than the present five-year retention period.[194] However, there is no apparent evidence for thinking that such a short period is sufficient. Sleeper cells often stay inactive for ten years or longer. A case in point is the Russian spy ring that was broken up in 2010.[195]
- The implementation of audit trails to ensure that only the proper authorities have access to any given piece of information.[196]

A powerful example is provided by a report on the operation of the Terrorist Finance Tracking Program (TFTP). A project developed by the United States Treasury, TFTP collects large amounts of data from a financial messaging system called SWIFT that records data on financial transfers. TFTP has used this information to uncover terrorist networks and to prevent multiple attacks.[197] Crucially, TFTP was subjected to significant oversight, with only narrowly-focused searches and analysis of the data being permitted and with two different groups of independent auditors ensuring that those restrictions were being strictly adhered to.[198] Moreover, any time a government analyst wanted to query the system, they would have to submit a reason for their query which could then be approved or denied by a SWIFT representative.[199] (It is not obvious that this arrangement is scalable to the NSA level. Queries by analysts are already reviewed by managers at NSA. Select queries are subject to a "two person" rule.)

Other suggestions involve Congress, such as increasing the number of members of Congress who are being briefed and changing the committees charged with oversight of NSA.

Each and all of these measures deserve close study. Some such moves are clearly necessary to further ensure that the NSA abides by all the laws and regulations, and to assure the public that it does so. Given the current level of distrust of the government in general, one must wonder if all these measures taken together will suffice, or if some extraordinary steps need to be taken.

4. Civic Oversight

Consideration should be given to introducing a greater role for nongovernmental civic bodies that help with oversight, such as a regular review conducted by an independent civilian review board. (Critics of this proposal may suggest that these missions are already coerced by the Civil Liberties Board and the President's Intelligence Advisory Board).

However, these bodies have not been sufficiently composed and given enough power for important segments of the public (those segments that have legitimate concerns as opposed to those who automatically distrust everything the government does and says) to feel confident that the level of accountability is adequate.

The new board would issue reports, say annually, that would state whether or not the government collected information for legitimate and legal goals or for political reasons or in the pursuit of minor crimes rather than terrorists. However, instead of revealing detailed case studies, the civilian review board would provide statistics. For example, if it reported that there were a large number of cases in which serious threats were averted, such as the planned attack on New York City's subway, the public would learn that the threats to national security warranted increased efforts to enforce anti-leak legislation. If, on the other hand, the board reported that many cases involve fairly minor threats, this would tilt the consensus the other way.[200] If the current Civil Liberties and Privacy Protection board would be properly staffed, funded, and its powers increased, it might serve in such a function.

The board should ensure that the government is adequately kept in check while also ensuring that the system of accountability does not tilt too far in the opposite direction by placing too many restraints on the NSA. One does not, for example, want to impose procedures like those that prevented the FBI from setting up a sting operation to capture Tamerlan Tsarnaev, one of the Boston bombers. According to US officials, a sting operation can only be undertaken if there is "evidence that someone is already contemplating violence"—an evidentiary threshold that Tsarnaev's activities did not pass before the bombing of the Boston Marathon. This restriction that prevented the FBI from sharing relevant information about the terrorist brothers with the Boston police department.[201] The liberal communitarian balance can be lost in either direction—too much security or too many limitations on security. Indeed, oversteering in one direction often leads to overcorrections in the opposite direction.

VI. The Coming Tyrant?

A common claim among civil libertarians is that even if little harm is presently being inflicted by government surveillance programs, the infrastructure is in place for a less-benevolent leader to violate the people's rights and set us on the path to tyranny. For example, it has been argued that PRISM "will amount to a 'turnkey' system that, in the wrong hands, could transform the country into a totalitarian state virtually overnight. Every person who values personal freedom, human rights and the rule of law must recoil against such a possibility, regardless of their political preference."[202] Similarly, *The Atlantic's* Conor Friedersdorf argued that, thanks to PRISM and the collecting of phone records, "the people in charge will possess the capacity to be tyrants—to use power oppressively and unjustly—to a degree that Americans in 1960, 1970, 1980, 1990, or 2000 could've scarcely imagined," and emphasized that "it could happen here, with enough historical amnesia, carelessness, and bad luck."[203] In addition, Senator Rand Paul (R-KY) has been "careful to point out that he is concerned about the possible abuses of some future, Hitler-like president."[204]

A few things might be said in response to these concerns. First, all of the data that the government is collecting is already being archived (at least for short periods—as discussed above) by private corporations and other entities. It is not the case that PRISM or other such programs entail the collection of new data that was not previously available. Second, if one is truly concerned that a tyrant might take over the United States, one obviously faces a much greater and all-encompassing threat than a diminution of privacy. Likewise, the response must be similarly expansive. One can join civic bodies that seek to shore up democracies or work with various reform movements and public education drives. Or one can join groups that prepare to retreat to the mountains, store ammunition and essential foods, and plan to fight the tyrannical forces. But it makes no sense to oppose limited measures to enhance security on the grounds of potential tyranny.

Conclusion

Revelations about two surveillance programs—collecting phone records of Americans, and digital communications by foreigners overseas—should be assessed by drawing on a liberal communitarian paradigm that seeks a balance between security and privacy (and other individual rights). Such an evaluation shows that (a) we do face a significant terrorist threat, hence the continued need for enhanced security; (b) that this threat cannot be mitigated by dealing with terrorists as criminals; and (c) that the government reports that the said programs are effective.

At the same time the means used to surveil Americans are either not intrusive or only lowly intrusive. Records need be collected because otherwise they are not maintained or readily accessible. Computers that store these records do not *per se* violate privacy. Before any individual records can be searched, probable cause must be established. In short, the program seems to qualify on both constitutional and legal grounds. Furthermore, the program that surveils foreigners overseas does not violate American laws, to the extent that it does not ensnare Americans.

Finally the extent to which the government can be accorded more surveillance powers should be combined with great surveillance of its surveillance programs. Several suggestions are made to increase the accountability of NSA, above all by drawing on a civilian security review board that is independent of the government. Thus two balances must be maintained: that between rights and the common good, and that between the need to act and the need to ensure that action is in accordance with our liberal communitarian values.

71

Notes

1. To qualify as legal, the program is required to not target Americans. Thus, PRISM searches are carried out only when there is at least 51 percent confidence in a target's 'foreignness.'

   Timothy B. Lee, "How Congress unknowingly legalized PRISM in 2007," *The Washington Post* (June 6, 2013), http://www.washingtonpost.com/blogs/wonkblog/wp/2013/06/06/how-congress-unknowingly-legalized-prism-in-2007/.

2. Amitai Etzioni, *The New Golden Rule: Community and Morality in a Democratic Society* (New York: Basic Books, 1996).

3. I have previously discussed this balance in the context of privacy and public health, public safety, sex offenders, and freedom of the press, among other rights. See: Amitai Etzioni, *The Limits of Privacy* (New York: Basic Books, 1999); "The Privacy Merchants: What Is To Be Done?" *Journal of Constitutional Law* 14/4 (2012), 929–951; and *How Patriotic is the Patriot Act?: Freedom Versus Security in the Age of Terrorism* (New York: Routledge: 2004).

4. Gerald Gaus and Shane D. Courtland, "Liberalism," The Stanford Encyclopedia of Philosophy ed. Edward N. Zalta (Spring 2011), http://plato.stanford.edu/entries/liberalism/. Also: John Rawls, A Theory of Justice (Cambridge: Belknap Press, 1999).

5. For example: Lee Kuan Yew, "Jinken gaiko wa machigatteiru [Human Rights Diplomacy Is Wrong]," *Shokun* (September 1993), 140–149.

   Also: Bilahari Kausikan, "Asian versus 'Universal' Human Rights," *The Responsive Community* 7, no. 3 (Summer 1997).

6. For a broader discussion of this strand of communitarianism, see: Russell A. Fox, "Confucian and Communitarian Responses to Liberal Democracy," *The Review of Politics* 59, no. 3 (1997): 561–592.

   Also: Daniel Bell, "Daniel Bell on Confucianism & free speech," audio interview with Free Speech Debate (February 16, 2012), http://freespeech-debate.com/en/media/daniel-bell-on-confucianism-free-speech/.

   Also: Francis Fukuyama, "Confucianism and Democracy," *Journal of Democracy* 6, no. 2 (1995): 20–33.

7. Jed Rubenfeld, "The Right of Privacy," *Harvard Law Review* 102, no. 4 (1989): 740.

   The development of a right to privacy with respect to torts dates back a bit further to 1890 with the publication of Warren and Brandeis' "The Right to Privacy." See: Richard A. Posner, "The Right of Privacy," *Georgia Law Review* 12, no. 3 (1978): 409.

   Also: Samuel D. Warren and Louis D. Brandeis, "The Right to Privacy," *Harvard Law Review* 4, no. 5 (1890): 193–220.

   The exact emergence of the notion of a *Constitutional* right to privacy is a bit more difficult to exactly pinpoint. For a more genealogy of constitutional right, see: William M. Beaney, "The Constitutional Right to Privacy in the Supreme Court," *The Supreme Court Review* (1962): 212–251.

8. Anthony Lewis, *Freedom for the Thought We Hate: A Biography of the First Amendment* (New York: Basic Books, 2007): 23.

9. Black's Law Dictionary, "What is the Public Interest?" *Black's Free Online Legal Dictionary*, no. 2, http://thelawdictionary.org/public-interest/.

10. See, for example: *United States v. Hartwell*, 436 F.3d 174, 180 (3d Cir. Pa. 2006).
    Also: *Skinner v. Railway Labor Executives' Association*, 489 US 602 (1989).
    Also: *National Treasury Employees Union v. Von Raab*, 489 US 656 (1989).

11. *New York Times Co. v. United States*, 403 U. S. 713 (1971).

12. *United States v. Hartwell*, 436 F.3d 174, 180 (3d Cir. Pa. 2006).

13. See, for example: Bruce Schneier, "It's Smart Politics to Exaggerate Terrorist Threats," *CNN* (May 20, 2013), http://www.cnn.com/2013/05/20/opinion/schneier-security-politics/index.html.

14. See, for example: Randy E. Barnett, "The NSA's Surveillance is Unconstitutional," *The Wall Street Journal* (July 11, 2013), http://online.wsj.com/article/SB10001424127887323823004578593591276402574.html.
    Also: Conor Friedersdorf, "Lawbreaking at the NSA: Bring on a New Church Committee," *The Atlantic* (August 16, 2013), http://www.theatlantic.com/politics/archive/2013/08/lawbreaking-at-the-nsa-bring-on-a-new-church-committee/278750/.

15. Frank Thorp and Carrie Dann, "House Narrowly Votes Down Move to Gut NSA Data-Collection Program," *NBC News* (July 24, 2013), http://nbcpolitics.nbcnews.com/_news/2013/07/24/19658896-house-narrowly-votes-down-move-to-gut-nsa-data-collection-program?lite.

16. For example: "President Obama's Dragnet," *The New York Times* (June 6, 2013), http://www.nytimes.com/2013/06/07/opinion/president-obamas-dragnet.html?pagewanted=all.

17. Karen J. Greenberg, Susan Quatrone, et al., "Terrorist Trial Report Card: September 11, 2001 - September 11, 2011," Center on Law and Security, NYU School of Law (2011), http://www.lawandsecurity.org/Portals/0/Documents/TTRC%20Ten%20Year%20Issue.pdf.

18. Anthony D. Romero, "Terrorists are Criminals and Should be Tried in Civilian Court," *U.S. News & World Report* (February 16, 2010), http://www.usnews.com/opinion/articles/2010/02/16/terrorists-are-criminals-and-should-be-tried-in-civilian-court.

19. Paige Lavender, "Eric Holder Defends Civilian Trials for Terrorists," *The Huffington Post* (June 16, 2011), http://www.huffingtonpost.com/2011/06/16/eric-holder-civilian-trials-terrorism_n_878750.html.

20. Melanie Getreuer, "Why Civilian Courts are Best for Terror Trials, Especially Boston Bombing Suspect," *The Christian Science Monitor* (April 30, 2013), http://www.csmonitor.com/Commentary/Opinion/2013/0430/Why-civilian-courts-are-best-for-terror-trials-especially-Boston-bombing-suspect.

21. Barack Obama, "Remarks by the President at the National Defense University," *The White House Office of the Press Secretary* (May 23, 2013), http://www.whitehouse.gov/the-press-office/2013/05/23/remarks-president-national-defense-university.

22. Barack Obama, as quoted in "Obama's Remarks at a News Conference," *The New York Times* (August 9, 2013), http://www.nytimes.com/2013/08/10/us/politics/obamas-remarks-at-a-news-conference.html?pagewanted=all&_r=0.

23. Mark Mazzetti, "Interpol Asks Nations to Help Track Terror Suspects Freed in Prison Breaks," *The New York Times* (August 3, 2013),

http://www.nytimes.com/2013/08/04/world/interpol-issues-alert-on-prison-breaks-in-9-nations.html?_r=0.

24.   Hillary Clinton, "America's Pacific Century," *Foreign Policy* (2011), http://www.foreignpolicy.com/articles/2011/10/11/americas_pacific_century?print=yes&hidecomments=yes&page=full.

25.   Douglas A. Pryer, "The Rise of the Machines," *Military Review* (2013): 17, http://usacac.army.mil/CAC2/MilitaryReview/Archives/English/MilitaryReview_20130430_art005.pdf.

26.   Lindsey Boerma, "Al Qaeda Embassy Plot Among 'Most Specific and Credible Threats' Since 9/11, McCaul says," *CBS News* (August 4, 2013), http://www.cbsnews.com/8301-3460_162-57596909/al-qaeda-embassy-plot-among-most-specific-and-credible-threats-since-9-11-mccaul-says/.

27.   Katherine Zimmerman, "Al Qaeda and its Affiliates in 2013," *American Enterprise Institute* (2013): 2, http://www.criticalthreats.org/al-qaeda/al-qaeda-affiliates.

28.   Oren Dorell, "Al-Qaeda on the run? No Way, Say Experts," *USA Today*, (August 6, 2013), http://www.usatoday.com/story/news/world/2013/08/06/al-qaeda-middle-east/2623475/.

29.   There is a debate regarding the nature of the relationship between al Qaeda and what are often designated its subsidiaries. For more on this point, see: Leah Farrall, "Forward focus: Assessing Al-Qaeda's in-theater capabilities," *IHS Defense, Security and Risk Consulting* (2012): 14–19, http://allthingsct.files.wordpress.com/2012/03/janes-article-2012.pdf.

30.   Sara Carter, "Al Qaeda Gaining Strength in Mali, North Africa," *The Washington Times* (March 26, 2013), http://www.washingtontimes.com/news/2013/mar/26/key-mali-lawmaker-challenges-obama-on-al-qaida-thr/?page=all.

    See also: Sudarsan Raghavan, "Nigerian Islamist Militants Return From Mali with Weapons, Skills," *The Washington Post* (May 31, 2013), http://articles.washingtonpost.com/2013-05-31/world/39642133_1_northern-mali-boko-haram-nigerian-islamist.

    See also: Adam Entous, Drew Hinshaw, and David Gauthier-Villars, "Militants, Chased from Mali, Pose New Threats," *The Wall Street Journal* (May 24, 2013), http://online.wsj.com/article/SB10001424127887323336104578503464066163002.html.

31.   See note 27, 3.

32.   "The Unquenchable Fire," *The Economist*, (September 28, 2013), 21–23.

33.   See note 27, 3.

34.   "Al Qaeda in Iraq Scores Big," *The New York Times* (July 29, 2013), http://www.nytimes.com/2013/07/30/opinion/al-qaeda-in-iraq-scores-big.html?_r=0.

35.   See note 27, 3.

36.   Ibid.

37.   Justin Vela and Liz Sly, "In Syria, Group Suspected of Al-Qaeda Links Gaining Prominence in War to Topple Assad," *The Washington Post* (August 19, 2012), http://www.washingtonpost.com/world/middle_east/in-syria-group-suspected-of-al-qaeda-links-gaining-prominence-in-war-to-topple-assad/2012/08/19/c7cffd66-ea22-11e1-9ddc-340d5efb1e9c_story.html.

38. Liz Sly, "Al-Qaeda expands in Syria via Islamic State," *The Washington Post* (August 12, 2013), available at http://www.washingtonpost.com/world/al-qaeda-expands-in-syria-via-islamic-state/2013/08/12/3ef71a26-036a-11e3-9259-e2aafe5a5f84_story.html.
39. Ibid.
40. Mark Mazzetti, "Interpol Asks Nations to Help Track Terror Suspects Freed in Prison Breaks," *The New York Times* (August 3, 2013), http://www.nytimes.com/2013/08/04/world/interpol-issues-alert-on-prison-breaks-in-9-nations.html?_r=0.
41. Ibid.
42. Ibid.
43. Carol J. Williams, "Spree of Jailbreaks Stirs Fear of New Al Qaeda Threat," *The Los Angeles Times* (July 31, 2013), http://www.latimes.com/news/world/worldnow/la-fg-wn-prison-breakouts-al-qaeda-20130730,0,3702148.story.

    See also: Kareem Raheem and Ziad al-Sinjary, "Al Qaeda prison break: Hundreds of Militants Flee Iraq's Notorious Abu Ghraib Jail," *NBC News* (July 22, 2013), http://worldnews.nbcnews.com/_news/2013/07/22/19615653-al-qaeda-prison-break-hundreds-of-militants-flee-iraqs-notorious-abu-ghraib-jail?lite.
44. See note 30.
45. For a detailed discussion of this point, see: Paul K. Kerr and Mary Beth Nikitin, "Pakistan's Nuclear Weapons: Proliferation and Security Issues," *Congressional Research Service* RL34248 (March 19, 2013), http://www.fas.org/sgp/crs/nuke/RL34248.pdf.

    And: Amy F. Woolf, "Nonstrategic Nuclear Weapons," Congressional Research Service RL32572 (2012), http://www.fas.org/sgp/crs/nuke/RL32572.pdf.
46. Shaun Gregory, "The Terrorist Threat to Pakistan's Nuclear Weapons," *CTC Sentinel* 2, no.7, (2009).

    See also: Dean Nelson and Tom Hussain, "Militants Attack Pakistan Nuclear Air Base," *The Telegraph* (August 16, 2012), http://www.telegraph.co.uk/news/worldnews/asia/pakistan/9479041/Militants-attack-Pakistan-nuclear-air-base.html.

    Also: Kapil Komireddi, "Take Pakistan's Nukes, Please," *Foreign Policy* (May 24, 2011), http://www.foreignpolicy.com/articles/2011/05/24/take_pakistans_nukes_please.
47. Joseph Goldstein, "Judge Rejects New York's Stop-and-Frisk Policy," *The New York Times* (August 12, 2013), http://www.nytimes.com/2013/08/13/nyregion/stop-and-frisk-practice-violated-rights-judge-rules.html?pagewanted=all&_r=0.
48. "Stop-and-Frisk on Trial," *The New York Times* (May 21, 2013), http://www.nytimes.com/2013/05/22/opinion/stop-and-frisk-on-trial.html?ref=stopandfrisk.
49. Adam Serwer, "Holder Defends Civilian Courts," *The American Prospect* (March 16, 2010).

    Also: Lavender, "Eric Holder Defends Civilian Trials for Terrorists."

    Also: The Associated Press, "Eric Holder: Critics of Civilian Courts Handling Terrorism Cases 'Are Simply Wrong,'" *The Huffington Post*

(May 11, 2013), http://www.huffingtonpost.com/2013/05/11/eric-holder-terrorism-cases_n_3260432.html.

50. See Matthew Kroenig and Barry Pavel, "How to Deter Terrorism," *The Washington Quarterly* 35/2 (2012): 21–36, http://dx.doi.org/10.1080/01636 60X.2012.665339. (In contrast [to the Cold War], deterrence against terrorism can only be partial at best. The United States cannot deter all terrorist activity, but as long as Washington can deter certain types of terrorists from engaging in certain types of terrorist activity, deterrence can contribute to national security goals.")

51. Robert Pape, *Dying to Win: The Strategic Logic of Suicide Terrorism* (New York, NY: Random House, 2006), 2, 5.

52. Clearly jihadists do not have a monopoly on this type of fanaticism, and the American criminal court system handles domestic terrorists, like Wade Michael Page who killed six worshippers in a Sikh temple in 2012. But zealots such as these are also best dealt with in a preventative measure, and while they make up a tiny percentage of American criminals, they are a large part of the terrorist population, large enough to justify a different level of legal protection.

53. Matthew Waxman writes, "Criminal justice also has a preventive component . . . criminal law is generally retrospective in focus, in that it addresses past acts" in "Administrative Detention of Terrorists: Why Detain, and Detain Whom?" *Journal of National Security Law and Policy* 3 (2009): 12–13.

54. Coleen Rowley, "Memo to FBI Director Robert Mueller," (May 21, 2002), http://globalresearch.ca/articles/ROW205A.html.

55. The FBI "provides guidance for law enforcement officers confronted with an emergency that may require interrogating a suspect held in custody about an imminent threat to public safety without providing Miranda warnings." Carl A. Benoit, "The 'Public Safety' Exception to Miranda," *FBI Law Enforcement Bulletin* (2011), http://www.fbi.gov/stats-services/publications/law-enforcement-bulletin/february2011/legal_digest.

56. El-Motassadeq was later re-tried and convicted but the case demonstrates that "even in the most obvious and dramatic instances of terrorist involvement, substantial conviction cannot always be achieved."
Brian Whitaker, "Member of 9/11 Terror Cell Jailed," *Guardian* (August 19, 2005), http://www.guardian.co.uk/world/2005/aug/20/september11.usa.

57. Lucian E. Dervan, "The Surprising Lessons from Plea Bargaining in the Shadow of Terror," *Georgia State University Law Review* 27, no.2 (2011): 239–298.

58. "Ali Saleh Kahlah al-Marri," *The New York Times* (May 1, 2009), http://topics.nytimes.com/top/reference/timestopics/people/m/ali_saleh_kahlah_al_marri/index.html.

59. See, for example: Jameel Jaffer, "Needles are Harder to Find in Bigger Haystacks," *The New York Times* (June 10, 2013), http://www.nytimes.com/roomfordebate/2013/06/09/is-the-nsa-surveillance-threat-real-or-imagined.
Also: Ron Wyden and Mark Udall, "Wyden, Udall Issue Statement on Effectiveness of Declassified NSA Programs," (June 19, 2013), http://www.wyden.senate.gov/news/press-releases/wyden-udall-issue-statement-on-effectiveness-of-declassified-nsa-programs.

Also: Kevin Drum, "The NSA's Massive Call Record Surveillance Program Barely Accomplishes Anything," *Mother Jones* (July 31, 2013), http://www.motherjones.com/kevin-drum/2013/07/nsa-surveillance-call-record-program.

Also: Robert Zubrin, "PRISM Costs Lives," *National Review Online* (June 21, 2013), http://www.nationalreview.com/article/351622/prism-costs-lives-robert-zubrin.

60. Keith Alexander, as quoted in "House Select Intelligence Committee Holds Hearing on Disclosure of National Security Agency Surveillance Programs," *Federation of American Scientists* (June 18, 2013): 5, 11–13, https://www.fas.org/irp/congress/2013_hr/disclosure.pdf.

61. See note 59.

62. Matthew Waxman, "How to Measure the Value of NSA Programs?" *Lawfare*, (August 12, 2013), http://www.lawfareblog.com/2013/08/how-to-measure-the-value-of-nsa-programs/.

63. Wyden and Udall, "Wyden, Udall Issue Statement on Effectiveness of Declassified NSA Programs"

Also: Drum, "The NSA's Massive Call Record Surveillance Program Barely Accomplishes Anything."

Also: Josh Gerstein, "The Metadata Muddle: How effective is call-tracking?" *Politico* (June 19, 2013), http://www.politico.com/story/2013/06/nsa-surveillance-93075.html.

64. Ibid.

Also: see note 60.

65. Peter L. Bergen, *The Osama bin Laden I Know* (New York: Free Press, 2006), 397.

Also: Jason Burke and Ian Black, "Al-Qaida: Tales from Bin Laden's Volunteers," *The Guardian* (September 10, 2009), http://www.theguardian.com/world/2009/sep/10/al-qaida-terrorism-bin-laden.

Also: Matthew Schofield, "Osama Bin Laden was Angry, Increasingly Irrelevant in Final Years, Letters Show," *McClatchy* (May 3, 2012), http://www.mcclatchydc.com/2012/05/03/v-print/147573/letters-show-bin-laden-was-angry.html.

66. Peter Finn and Anne E. Kornblut, "Al-Qaeda Couriers Provided Trail that Led to bin Laden," *The Washington Post* (May 2, 2011), http://articles.washingtonpost.com/2011-05-02/national/35264458_1_al-qaeda-couriers-osama-bin-laden-abu-faraj.

67. Eric Schmitt and Michael S. Schmidt, "Qaeda Plot Leak has Undermined U.S. Intelligence," *The New York Times* (September 30, 2013): A1.

68. Sibohan Gorman, Evan Perez, and Janet Hook,"U.S. Collects Vast Data Trove," *The Wall Street Journal* (June 7, 2013) http://online.wsj.com/article/SB10001424127887324299104578529112289298922.html.

69. Dianne Feinstein, "Make NSA Programs More Transparent," *The Washington Post* (July 30, 2013), http://articles.washingtonpost.com/2013-07-30/opinions/40893423_1_nsa-analyst-national-security-agency-fisa-court.

Also: Bob Cesca, "CNET Reporter Posts Wildly Inaccurate Yet Totally Viral 'Bombshell' About NSA Eavesdropping," *The Daily Banter* (June 16, 2013), http://thedailybanter.com/2013/06/cnet-reporter-posts-wildly-inaccurate-yet-totally-viral-bombshell-about-nsa-eavesdropping/.

Examples of critics include: Glenn Greenwald, "Fisa Court Oversight: a Look Inside a Secret and Empty Process," *The Guardian* (June 18, 2013), http://www.theguardian.com/commentisfree/2013/jun/19/fisa-court-oversight-process-secrecy.

Also: Conor Friedersdorf, "The NSA Scandal Is *All That*: A Polite Rebuttal to Marc Ambinder," *The Atlantic* (August 22, 2013), http://www.theatlantic.com/politics/archive/2013/08/the-nsa-scandal-is-em-all-that-em-a-polite-rebuttal-to-marc-ambinder/278886/.

70. Information voluntarily handed over to another party does not receive Fourth Amendment protection "even if the information is revealed on the assumption that it will be used only for a limited purpose and the confidence placed in the third party will not be betrayed." *United States v. Miller*, 425 U.S. 435, 443 (1976).

See also: Orin Kerr, 'The Case for the Third Party Doctrine', *Michigan Law Review* 107 (2009): 561, 569–70. Earlier cases that built up this doctrine include *Lee v. United States* 343 U.S. 747 (1952) and *Couch v. United States* 409 U.S. 322 (1973).

71. *United States v. Miller*, 425 U.S. 435 (1976).

72. *Smith v. Maryland*, 442 U. S. 735 (1979).

73. Robert Litt, "General Counsel Litt's Remarks on Intelligence Collection," *Council on Foreign Relations* (July 18, 2013), http://www.cfr.org/intelligence/general-counsel-litts-remarks-intelligence-collection/p31130?cid=rss-primarysources-general_counsel_litt_s_remarks-071813.

74. As Orin Kerr notes, "The third-party doctrine is the Fourth Amendment rule scholars love to hate. It is the *Lochner* of search and seizure law, widely criticized as profoundly misguided . . . The verdict among commentators is has been frequent and apparently unanimous: The third-party doctrine is not only wrong, but horribly wrong. Even many state court judges have agreed. Over a dozen state Supreme Courts have rejected the doctrine under parallel provisions of their state constitutions. . . . Remarkably, even the U.S. Supreme Court has never offered a clear argument in its favor. Many Supreme Court opinions have applied the doctrine; few have defended it." Kerr, "The Case for the Third-Party Doctrine," 563–564.

Though Kerr highlights the many criticisms of the doctrine, the cited paper attempts to defend the doctrine by defusing prominent criticism and presenting positive reasons for accepting the doctrine, e.g., it preserves the Fourth Amendment's technological neutrality and ensures its ex ante clarity.

75. Matthew Tokson, "Automation and the Fourth Amendment," *Iowa Law Review* 96 (2011): 581, 586.

76. See note 67.

77. Conor Friedersdorf, "The NSA Scandal Is *All That*: A Polite Rebuttal to Marc Ambinder," *The Atlantic* (August 22, 2013), http://www.theatlantic.com/politics/archive/2013/08/the-nsa-scandal-is-em-all-that-em-a-polite-rebuttal-to-marc-ambinder/278886/.

78. Pew Research, "Few See Adequate Limits on NSA Surveillance Programs," (July 26, 2013), http://www.people-press.org/2013/07/26/few-see-adequate-limits-on-nsa-surveillance-program/.

79. David Ignatius, "NSA Weighs its Options," *The Washington Post* (July 26 2013), http://articles.washingtonpost.com/2013-07-26/

opinions/40859128_1_national-security-agency-surveillance-programs-calling-records.

80.	Keith Alexander, as quoted in "Clear and Present Danger: Cyber-Crime; Cyber-Espionage; Cyber-Terror; and Cyber-War," *Aspen Security Forum* (July 18, 2013), http://www.nsa.gov/public_info/_files/speeches_testimonies/ GEN_A_Aspen_Security_Forum_Transcript_18_Jul_2013.pdf.

81.	Ron Nixon, "U.S. Postal Service Logging All Mail for Law Enforcement," *The New York Times* (July 3, 2013), http://www.nytimes.com/2013/07/04/ us/monitoring-of-snail-mail.html?pagewanted=all.

82.	The data retention policies of the U.S. telecommunication giants vary from company to company and depending on the type of information. In 2011, the ACLU of North Carolina obtained through a FOIA request a chart created by the Department of Justice that details how long six major cellular service providers kept their data. Cell tower information was kept on a rolling one-year basis by Verizon; for 18–24 months by Sprint; and indefinitely since 2008 by AT&T. In contrast, the content of text messages was not retained at all by four of the companies, and kept for 3–5 days by Verizon and 90 days by Virgin Mobile (but only accessible to law enforcement with a warrant). See: Allie Bohm, "How Long Is Your Cell Phone Company Hanging On To Your Data?" *American Civil Liberties Union* (September 28, 2011), http:// www.aclu.org/blog/technology-and-liberty/how-long-your-cell-phone-company-hanging-your-data.

    Similarly, on *Washington Week* with Gwen Ifill, Pete Williams said that, "the phone companies only keep this data for 30 to 90 days. They don't have any reason. There's no business reason for the phone company to keep six-month old phone records. So they throw it away. Unless the government gets it, it's not going to keep it." See: Pete Williams as quoted in "Transcript, Washington Week with Gwen Ifill," (June 7, 2013), http://www.pbs.org/weta/ washingtonweek/watch/transcript/39902.

83.	Mike Rogers, "'This Week' Transcript: Sen. Dianne Feinstein and Rep. Mike Rogers," *ABC This Week* (June 9, 2013), http://abcnews. go.com/Politics/week-transcript-sen-dianne-feinstein-rep-mike-rogers/ story?id=19343314&page=4#.Udsm2jtilJl.

84.	Legal Information Institute, "Fourth Amendment," *Cornell University Law School* (accessed July 12, 2013) http://www.law.cornell.edu/wex/fourth_ amendment.

85.	American Civil Liberties Union "ACLU Motion for Preliminary Injunction in ACLU v. Clapper," (2013): 4, https://www.aclu.org/national-security/ aclu-v-clapper-legal-documents.

86.	Eve Brensike Primus, "Disentangling Administrative Searches," *Columbia Law Review* 111 (2011): 256, http://www.columbialawreview.org/wp-content/uploads/2011/03/111-2_Primus.pdf.

87.	Ibid., 263.

88.	*Illinois v. Lidster*, 540 U.S. 419, 427 (2004).

89.	See Michigan Department of State Police v. Sitz, 110 S. Ct. 2481 (1990).

90.	See: United States v. Hartwell, 436 F.3d 174, 180 (3d Cir. Pa. 2006). Also: *Electronic Privacy Information Center v. United States Department of Homeland Security*, 653 F.3d 1, 10–11 (D.C. Cir. 2011).

91.	See note 86 at 263–4.

92. *Michigan Department of State Police v. Sitz*, 496 U.S., 455.
93. Ibid., 451.
94. See, for example: Illinois v. Lidster, 540 U.S. 419, 427 (2004) (quoting Brown v. Texas, 443 U.S. 47, 51 (1979).
95. *United States v. Hartwell*, 436 F.3d 174, 180 (3d Cir. Pa. 2006).
96. Ibid.
97. *United States v. Davis*, 482 F.2d 893, 908.
98. *United States v. Pulido-Baquerizo* 800 F.2d 899, 901.
99. Jeffrey Rosen, "The Naked Crowd: Balancing Privacy and Security in an Age of Terror," *Arizona Law Review* 46 (2004): 613.
100. United States Foreign Intelligence Surveillance Court, "In Re Application of the Federal Bureau of Investigation for an Order Requiring the Production of Tangible Things From [Redacted]," *American Civil Liberties Union* (2013): 13–14, https://www.aclu.org/files/assets/br13-09-primary-order.pdf.
101. Ibid., 15.
102. Ibid.
103. Robert Litt, "Privacy, Technology, & National Security: An Overview of Intelligence Collection," *Brookings Institution* (July 19, 2013), http://www.dni.gov/index.php/newsroom/speeches-and-interviews/195-speeches-interviews-2013/896-privacy,-technology-and-national-security-an-overview-of-intelligence-collection.
104. Jonathan Stempel, "U.S. Judge Says NSA Phone Surveillance is Lawful," *Reuters* (December 27, 2013), http://www.reuters.com/article/2013/12/27/us-usa-security-aclu-idUSBRE9BQ0DA20131227.
105. Charlie Savage, "Senate Panel Presses N.S.A on Phone Logs," *The New York Times* (July 31, 2013), http://www.nytimes.com/2013/08/01/us/nsa-surveillance.html?pagewanted=all.
     Also: Section 215 White Paper, U.S. Department of Justice: 3, http://www.nytimes.com/interactive/2013/08/10/us/politics/10obama-surveillance-documents.html?_r=0.
106. United States Foreign Intelligence Surveillance Court, "In Re Application of the Federal Bureau of Investigation for an Order Requiring the Production of Tangible Things From [Redacted]," *American Civil Liberties Union* (2013): 7, https://www.aclu.org/files/assets/br13-09-primary-order.pdf.
107. Section 215 White Paper, U.S. Department of Justice, http://www.nytimes.com/interactive/2013/08/10/us/politics/10obama-surveillance-documents.html?_r=0.4, 4.
108. See, for example: Mark Udall and Ron Wyden, "The White House Should End the Bulk Collection of Americans' Phone Records," *The Washington Post* (July 26, 2013), http://articles.washingtonpost.com/2013-07-26/opinions/40864658_1_phone-records-collection-program-americans.
109. See note 106.
110. Marc Rotenberg and Chris Jay Hoofnagle, open letter to Reps. Adam Putnam and William Clay, Electronic Privacy Information Center (2003), http://epic.org/privacy/profiling/datamining3.25.03.html.
     Also: Arshad Mohammed and Sara Kehaulani Goo, "Government Increasingly Turning to Data Mining," *The Washington Post* (June 15, 2006), http://www.washingtonpost.com/wp-dyn/content/article/2006/06/14/AR2006061402063.html.

And: Heidi Boghosian, "The Business of Surveillance," *Human Rights Magazine* 39 (2013), http://www.americanbar.org/publications/human_rights_magazine_home/2013_vol_39/may_2013_n2_privacy/the_business_of_surveillance.html.

111. Christopher Slobogin, "Government Data Mining and the Fourth Amendment", *The University of Chicago Law Review* 75 (2008): 317, 320.

112. Ibid.

113. Glenn Greenwald and Ewen MacAskill, "NSA Prism Program Taps in to User Data of Apple, Google and Others," *The Guardian* (June 6, 2013), http://www.theguardian.com/world/2013/jun/06/us-tech-giants-nsa-data.

114. Cover Letter and 2009 Report on the National Security Agency's Bulk Collection Program for USA Patriot Act Reauthorization, Office of the Director of National Intelligence, Washington, DC (2013), http://www.dni.gov/files/documents/2009_CoverLetter_Report_Collection.pdf.

115. Letters to the House Permanent Select Committee on Intelligence and the Senate Select Committee on Intelligence Leadership regarding Section 702 Congressional White Paper "The Intelligence Community's Collection Programs Under Title VII of the Foreign Intelligence Surveillance Act," Office of the Director of National Intelligence, Washington, DC, (2013,): 6, http://www.dni.gov/files/documents/Ltr%20to%20HPSCI%20Chairman%20Rogers%20and%20Ranking%20Member%20Ruppersberger_Scan.pdf.

116. Glenn Greenwald and Ewen MacAskill, "NSA Prism Program Taps in to User Data of Apple, Google and Others," *The Guardian*, (June 6, 2013), http://www.theguardian.com/world/2013/jun/06/us-tech-giants-nsa-data.

    With respect to the Americans whose data is collected, the *Washington Post* reports that "The surveillance may not 'intentionally target' an American, but the NSA can obtain the private communications of Americans as part of a request that officially 'targets' a foreigner."

    Timothy B. Lee, "'Here's everything we know about PRISM to date.'" The Washington Post, (June 12, 20130, http://www.washingtonpost.com/blogs/wonkblog/wp/2013/06/12/heres-everything-we-know-about-prism-to-date/

117. See note 100.

118. *United States v. Verdugo-Urquidez*, 856 F.2d 1214, 1218 (9th Cir. 1988).

119. It was initially unclear whether *Verdugo* would evolve into a general rule or a fact-specific finding, so I think a clarifying point is in order. In order to draw the conclusion that the finding does in fact limit Fourth Amendment rights this broadly, it would be necessary to also provide evidence that the finding has since been interpreted as a general rule rather than a fact-specific finding. A wide range of dissenting and concurring opinions written by the various justices has apparently "muddied the water" and led *Verdugo* to be understood to apply in a "diverse array" of situations.

120. This is a reference to the eight Nazis who came entered the United States via submarine with explosives and instructions to destroy vital war-time infrastructure. President Roosevelt set up a military commission for their prosecution. Stuart Taylor Jr., "The Bill To Combat Terrorism Doesn't Go Far Enough," *National Journal*, (October 29, 2001), http://www3.nationaljournal.com/members/buzz/2001/openingargument/102901.htm.

121. Anderson makes a similar point. The constitutional rights and criminal protections granted to American citizens "have developed *within* a particular political community, and fundamentally reflect decisions about rights within a fundamentally domestic, democratic setting in which all of us have a stake in both side of the equation . . . because we are part of the political community which must consider both individual rights and collective security . . . Terrorist who come from outside this society . . . cannot be assimilated into the structure of the ordinary criminal trial."

     Kenneth Anderson, "What to do with Bin Laden and Al Qaeda Terrorists?: A Qualified Defense of Military Commissions and United States Policy on Detainees at Guantanamo Bay Naval Base," *Harvard Journal of Law and Public Policy* (2001–2002): 610.

122. *United States v. Verdugo-Urquidez*, 856 F.2d 1214, 1218 (9th Cir. 1988).

123. Ibid.

124. Ibid.

125. Mary Lynn Nicholas, "United States v. Verdugo-Urquidez: Restricting the Borders of the Fourth Amendment," *Fordham International Law Journal* 14, no.1 (1990): 270.

126. Ibid.

127. H.R. 6304 (110th): FISA Amendments Act of 2008, http://www.govtrack.us/congress/bills/110/hr6304/text (accessed September 17, 2013).

128. Ibid.

129. 50 USC § 1801 – Definitions, Legal Information Institute, http://www.law.cornell.edu/uscode/text/50/1801 (accessed September 17, 2013).

130. Barton Gellman and Laura Poitras, "U.S., British Intelligence Mining Data from Nine U.S. Internet Companies in Broad Secret Program," *The Washington Post* (June 6, 2013), http://www.washingtonpost.com/investigations/us-intelligence-mining-data-from-nine-us-internet-companies-in-broad-secret-program/2013/06/06/3a0c0da8-cebf-11e2-8845-d970ccb04497_story_1.html.

131. "Letter from the Honorable Reggie B. Walton to Senator Patrick Leahy," (2013), https://www.fas.org/irp/news/2013/07/fisc-leahy.pdf.

132. Ibid.

133. Ibid.

134. Ibid.

135. The Universal Declaration of Human Rights, The United Nations, http://www.un.org/en/documents/udhr/.

136. Richard B. Lillich as quoted in David Cole, "Are Foreign Nationals Entitled to the Same Constitutional Rights as Citizens?" *Georgetown Law Faculty Publications and Other Works* 297 (2003): 372, http://scholarship.law.georgetown.edu/facpub/297.

137. William A. Schabas, "Invalid Reservations to the International Covenant on Civil and Political Rights: Is the United States Still a Party?" *Brooklyn Journal of International Law* 21 (1995): 277, 280. as quoted in Kristina Ash, "U.S. Reservations to the International Covenant on Civil and Political Rights: Credibility Maximization and Global Influence," *Northwestern Journal of International Human Rights* (2005), http://scholarlycommons.law.northwestern.edu/cgi/viewcontent.cgi?article=1018&context=njihr.

138. For more on this *tu quoque* argument, see: Jack Goldsmith, "Spying on Allies," *Lawfare*, (July 1, 2013), http://www.lawfareblog.com/2013/07/spying-on-allies/.

Goldsmith notes that there is even some reason for thinking that widespread spying provides a normative and legal defense of privacy violations, quoting a 1999 Department of Defense Report wherein it was contended that "The lack of strong international legal sanctions for peacetime espionage may also constitute an implicit application of the international law doctrine called 'tu quoque' (roughly, a nation has no standing to complain about a practice in which it itself engages)."

This claim would also defuse more specific criticisms that PRISM is spying even on our allies. See, for example: Steven Erlanger, "Outrage in Europe Grows Over Spying Disclosures," *The New York Times*, (July 1, 2013), http://www.nytimes.com/2013/07/02/world/europe/france-and-germany-piqued-over-spying-scandal.html?pagewanted=all.

139. H.R. 6304 (110th): FISA Amendments Act of 2008, http://www.govtrack.us/congress/bills/110/hr6304/text (accessed September 17, 2013).

140. "DNI Statement on Activities Authorized Under Section 702 of FISA," Office of the Director of National Intelligence, http:/www.dni.gov/index.php/newsroom/press-releases/191-press-releases-2013/869-dni-statement-on-activities-authorized-under-section-702-of-fisa (accessed September 15, 2013).

141. "NSA Slides Explain the PRISM Data-Collection Program," *The Washington Post* (June 6, 2013), http://www.washingtonpost.com/wp-srv/special/politics/prism-collection-documents/.

142. Ibid.

143. "Procedures Used by NSA to Target Non-US Persons: Exhibit A — Full Document," *The Guardian* (June 20, 2013), http://www.theguardian.com/world/interactive/2013/jun/20/exhibit-a-procedures-nsa-document.

144. Ibid.

145. Ibid.

146. Spencer Ackerman and James Ball, "NSA Loophole Allows Warrantless Search for U.S. Citizens' Emails and Phone Calls," *The Guardian* (August 9, 2013), http://www.theguardian.com/world/2013/aug/09/nsa-loophole-warrantless-searches-email-calls#.

147. Ron Wyden and Mark Udall, "Open letter to Keith Alexander," (June 24, 2013), http://www.fas.org/irp/congress/2013_cr/wyden-nsa.pdf.

148. Ellen Nakashima, "NSA Gathered Thousands of Americans E-mails Before Court Ordered it to Revise its Tactics," *The Washington Post* (August 21, 2013), http://articles.washingtonpost.com/2013-08-21/world/41431823_1_court-opinion-chief-judge-government-surveillance.

149. Barton Gellman, "NSA Broke Privacy Rules Thousands of Times Per Year, Audit Finds," *The Washington Post* (August 15, 2013), http://www.washingtonpost.com/world/national-security/nsa-broke-privacy-rules-thousands-of-times-per-year-audit-finds/2013/08/15/3310e554-05ca-11e3-a07f-49ddc7417125_story.html.

150. Benjamin Wittes, "The NSA, the Washington Post, and the Administration," *Lawfare* (August 18, 2013), http://www.lawfareblog.com/2013/08/the-nsa-the-washington-post-and-the-administration/.

This point also made by Jennifer Rubin who argues, "If there are 20 million inquiries each month over a year span that works out to 240,000,000. That equates to an error rate of .00001156666. If the NSA figures are accurate this is the most airtight surveillance program in history "NSA scandal or near-perfection?" *The Washington Post* (August 18 2013), http://www.washingtonpost.com/blogs/right-turn/wp/2013/08/18/nsa-scandal-or-near-perfection/.

151. Ibid.
152. Benjamin Wittes, "The NSA, the Washington Post, and the Administration," *Lawfare* (August 18, 2013), http://www.lawfareblog.com/2013/08/the-nsa-the-washington-post-and-the-administration/.
153. Ibid., 146.
154. Andrea Peterson, "LOVEINT: When NSA officers use their spying power on love interests," *The Washington Post*, August 24, 2013, http://www.washingtonpost.com/blogs/the-switch/wp/2013/08/24/loveint-when-nsa-officers-use-their-spying-power-on-love-interests/.
155. See note 152.
156. See note 103.
    Also: Sean Mirski and Benjamin Wittes, "The NSA Documents Part VI: The 2011 Minimization Procedures," *Lawfare*, August 23, 2013, http://www.lawfareblog.com/2013/08/the-nsa-documents-part-vi-the-2011-minimization-procedures/.
157. See note 149.
158. Corey M. Then, "Searches and Seizures of Americans Abroad: Re-examining the Fourth Warrant Clause and the Foreign Intelligence Exception Five Years After United States V. Bin Laden," *Duke Law Journal* 55 (2005): 1064.
159. Ibid, 1065–1068.
160. Zeke J. Miller, "Obama Administration Declassifies Details On 'PRISM,' Blasts 'Reckless' Media and Leakers," *TIME* (June 8, 2013), http://swampland.time.com/2013/06/08/obama-administration-declassifies-details-on-prism-blasts-reckless-media-and-leakers/.
161. Edward Liu, "Reauthorization of the FISA Amendments Act," Congressional Research Service, Washington, DC (April 2013): 5, http://www.cfr.org/intelligence/crs-reauthorization-fisa-amendments-act/p30877.
162. See note 146.
163. See note 130.
164. H.R. 6304 (110th): FISA Amendments Act of 2008, http://www.govtrack.us/congress/bills/110/hr6304/text (accessed September 17, 2013).
165. *United States v. Ramsey*, 431 U.S. 606, 616 (1977).
166. *Almeida-Sanchez v. United States*, 413 U.S. 266, 272, (1973).
167. "Will the Fourth Amendment Protect Your Laptop at the Border?" *American Bar Association* (September 17, 2013), http://www.americanbar.org/publications/gp_solo/2012/november_december2012privacyandconfidentiality/will_fourth_amendment_protect_your_laptop_border.html.
168. Yule Kim, "Protecting the US Perimeter: Border Searches Under the Fourth Amendment," Congressional Research Service (2009), http://www.fas.org/sgp/crs/homesec/RL31826.pdf.
169. Hendrik Hertzberg, "Snoop Scoops," *The New Yorker* (June 24, 2013), http://www.newyorker.com/talk/comment/2013/06/24/130624taco_talk_hertzberg.

170. Luke Johnson, "Obama Defends NSA Programs, Says Congress Knew About Surveillance," *The Huffington Post* (June 7, 2013), http://www.huffingtonpost.com/2013/06/07/obama-nsa_n_3403389.html.
171. See note 148.
172. Ibid.
173. John D. Bates, "April 2011 Submissions," *The Washington Post* 16, Footnote 14, http://apps.washingtonpost.com/g/page/national/fisa-court-documents-on-illegal-nsa-e-mail-collection-program/409/.
174. Scott Shane, "Court Upbraided N.S.A. on Its Use of Call-Log Data," *New York Times* (September 10, 2013), http://www.nytimes.com/2013/09/11/us/court-upbraided-nsa-on-its-use-of-call-log-data.html?pagewanted=all.
175. Ibid.
176. Eyder Peralta, "Senators Announce Bill That Ends NSA Phone Records Collection," *NPR* (September 25, 2013), http://www.npr.org/blogs/thetwo-way/2013/09/25/226263270/senators-announce-bill-that-ends-nsa-phone-records-collection.
177. Ellen Nakashima, "Bipartisan group of senators urges transparency on phone record surveillance," *The Washington Post* (June 28, 2013), http://articles.washingtonpost.com/2013-06-28/world/40251889_1_phone-records-bulk-collection-senators.
178. Peter Baker, "After Leaks, Obama Leads Damage Control Effort," *The New York Times* (June 28, 2013) http://www.nytimes.com/2013/06/29/us/politics/after-leaks-obama-leads-damage-control-effort.html?pagewanted=all.
179. Trevor Timm, "The NSA Leaks Are Forcing More Transparency on Both Companies and the Government," Freedom of the Press Foundation (June 15, 2013), https://pressfreedomfoundation.org/blog/2013/06/nsa-leaks-are-forcing-more-transparency-both-companies-and-government.
180. Scott Shane, "U.S. Is Urged To Consider Releasing Data on Calls," *The New York Times* (September 14, 2013): A10.
181. Ibid.
182. Scott Shane, "New Leaked Document Outlines U.S. Spending on Intelligence Agencies," *The New York Times* (August 29, 2013), http://www.nytimes.com/2013/08/30/us/politics/leaked-document-outlines-us-spending-on-intelligence.html?pagewanted=all.
183. Intelligence official report that a leak to the press regarding the government's capability to intercept al Qaeda's electronic communications prompted the group to immediately and dramatically change the way in which they communicated and the sorts of information that passed through electronic channels to avoid U.S. surveillance. See: Eric Schmitt and Michael S. Schmidt, "Qaeda Plot Leak has Undermined U.S. Intelligence." The New York Times (September 29, 2013) http://www.nytimes.com/2013/09/30/us/qaeda-plot-leak-has-undermined-us-intelligence.html?pagewanted=all&_r=0.
184. Scott Shane and David E. Sanger, "Job Title Key to Inner Access Held by Snowden," *The New York Times* (June 30, 2013), http://www.nytimes.com/2013/07/01/us/job-title-key-to-inner-access-held-by-snowden.html?pagewanted=all.
185. Vindu Goel & Claire Cain Miller, "More Data on Privacy, but Picture Is No Clearer," *The New York Times* (June 17, 2013), http://www.nytimes.com/2013/06/18/technology/more-data-on-privacy-but-picture-is-no-clearer.html.

186. Spencer Ackerman, "Senators Press NSA Director For Answers on Secret Surveillance Program," *The Guardian* (June 12, 2013), http://www.guardian.co.uk/world/2013/jun/12/senate-nsa-director-keith-alexander.

187. Andrea Peterson and Scott Wilson, "Former U.S. Officials to Assess Surveillance Policy," *The Washington Post* (August, 23 2013): A2.

    Such a board might also take the form of something along the lines of the Privacy and Civil Liberties Oversight Board. See: Garrett Hatch, "Privacy and Civil Liberties Oversight Board: New Independent Agency Status," Congressional Research Service RL34385 7-5700 (2012), http://www.fas.org/sgp/crs/misc/RL34385.pdf.

188. Janet Hook and Carol E. Lee, "Obama Plan to Revamp NSA Faces Obstacles," *The Wall Street Journal* (August 12, 2013): A4.

    See also: Dan Roberts, "US must Fix Secret FISA Courts, Says Top Judge Who Granted Surveillance Orders," *The Guardian* (July 9, 2013), http://www.theguardian.com/law/2013/jul/09/fisa-courts-judge-nsa-surveillance.

    President Obama, himself, proposed such a measure. See: "President Obama Weighs in on Information-Gathering," *The Washington Post* (August 9, 2013), http://articles.washingtonpost.com/2013-08-09/opinions/41237761_1_president-obama-government-surveillance-technologies.

189. Andrea Peterson, "The House is Divided Over Almost Everything. But FISA Court Reform Might be Able to Unite it," *The Washington Post* (October 1, 2013), http://www.washingtonpost.com/blogs/the-switch/wp/2013/10/01/the-house-is-divided-over-almost-everything-but-fisa-court-reform-might-be-able-to-unite-it/.

    This proposal would have the advocate assist communications companies and analyze all requests sent before the FISA court—though judges could exclude the advocate from certain cases. The advocate would have the option to appeal cases to the FISA Court of Review.

190. See, for example: Matthew C. Waxman, in an interview with Jonathan Masters, "Has the FISA Court Gone Too Far?" Council on Foreign Relations (July 1, 2013), http://www.cfr.org/intelligence/has-fisa-court-gone-too-far/p31095.

191. Such a measure might resemble the Whistleblower Protection Enhancement Act. See: Government Accountability Project, "Whistleblower Protection Enhancement Act (WPEA)," available at http://www.whistleblower.org/program-areas/legislation/wpea.

192. See: 50 U.S.C.S. §§ 413, 413a, 413b(c), (e). (2007).

193. Bruce Ackerman, "Surveillance and the FISA Court," *Los Angeles Times*, (September 24, 2013), http://www.latimes.com/opinion/commentary/la-oe-ackerman-fisa-reform-20130924,0,5246449.story.

194. Dianne Feinstein, "Make NSA Programs More Transparent," *The Washington Post*, (July 30, 2013), http://articles.washingtonpost.com/2013-07-30/opinions/40893423_1_nsa-analyst-national-security-agency-fisa-court.

195. Ken Dilanian, "Russian Spies Were Succeeding, FBI Official Says", *Los Angeles Times*, (October 31, 2011), http://articles.latimes.com/2011/oct/31/nation/la-na-russian-spies-20111101.

196. Such a measure is proposed in: Kenneth L. Wainstein, "Memorandum for the Attorney General," (November 20, 2007), http://www.emptywheel.net/wp-content/uploads/2013/06/111120-Wainstein-memo.pdf (accessed August 27, 2013): 9.

However, it has been noted that the efficacy of audit trails can be compromised through the introduction of loopholes. For more on this point, see: Patrick C. Toomey, "Raiding the 'Corporate Store': The NSA's Unfettered Access to a Vast Pool of Americans' Phone Data," American Civil Liberties Union, 2, August 2013, available at https://www.aclu.org/blog/national-security/raiding-corporate-store-nsas-unfettered-access-vast-pool-americans-phone-data.

197. Leonard H. Schrank and Juan C. Zarate, "Data Mining, Without Big Brother," *The New York Times*, 2 (July 2013), http://www.nytimes.com/2013/07/03/opinion/data-mining-without-big-brother.html?_r=0.
198. Ibid.
199. Ibid.
200. In 2001, six men from Buffalo, NY took a trip to Pakistan for a spiritual retreat sponsored by Tablighi Jamaat—a group that, while associated with radicalism, was not designated as a terrorist organization. While there, however, the six men were accused of attending a terrorist training camp called Al Farooq and supposedly listened to a speech delivered by Osama bin Laden. No evidence was presented of a forthcoming plot on their part. There were no weapons found, no history of violence uncovered, nor was there any "clear and convincing evidence" that the six men were planning any sort of terrorist act. Yet they were still charged under the Antiterrorism and Effective Death Penalty act with a possible fifteen years in prison and $250,000 fine for their activities. JoAnn Wypijewski, "Living in an Age of Fire," *Mother Jones* (March/April 2003), http://www.motherjones.com/politics/2003/03/living-age-fire.
201. Greg Miller and Sari Horwitz, "Boston Case Highlights Limitations of U.S. Counterterror Network," *The Washington Post* (May 4, 2013), http://articles.washingtonpost.com/2013-05-04/world/39025322_1_boston-marathon-national-counterterrorism-center-terrorist-bomb-plot/2.
202. Kim Dotcom, "Prism: Concerns Over Government Tyranny are Legitimate," *The Guardian* (June 13, 2013), http://www.guardian.co.uk/commentisfree/2013/jun/13/prism-utah-data-center-surveillance.
203. Conor Friedersdorf, "All the Infrastructure a Tyrant Would Need, Courtesy of Bush and Obama," *The Atlantic* (June 7, 2013), http://www.theatlantic.com/politics/archive/2013/06/all-the-infrastructure-a-tyrant-would-need-courtesy-of-bush-and-obama/276635/.
204. Micahel Gerson, "Rand Paul Masks His True Worldview," *The Washington Post* (March 12, 2013), http://articles.washingtonpost.com/2013-03-11/opinions/37621773_1_rand-paul-drone-policy-drone-program.

3

Should American Terrorists Be Tried Differently from Others?

This chapter argues that there are strong normative reasons to treat American terrorists—abroad and within the United States—as individuals who have committed treason. American terrorists are widely held as commanding rights above and beyond those to which other terrorists are entitled. However, American terrorists also commit a serious offense when they raise their arms against their nation, a crime that other terrorists are incapable of committing. To put it differently, when Americans attack the U.S., they commit two offenses: the act of terror (as defined in Title 18, Section 2331 of the US Code[1]), and the undermining of the trust Americans invest in each other—trust which serves as a basis for a robust civil society. Whether or not a particular suspect actually committed treason should be determined through the distinct set of processes that the Constitution explicitly lays out (the only crime treated so thoroughly in the main body of text): "on the Testimony of two Witnesses to the same overt Act, or on Confession in open Court."[2] The forum in which these witnesses are to present their evidence depends on whether or not these terrorists can be captured and brought before a tribunal without subjecting our troops to undue risk.

I should note from the onset that the terms treason and traitor tend to raise the hackles of reasonable people because they remind one of accusations all too quickly hurled by demagogues. Especially progressive people are likely to associate these terms with right-wing political rabble rousing. At the same time, one cannot ignore that members of a community can and do betray the trust their fellow members put in them. It might help if readers would think about the acts of treason considered in the following lines as referencing assaults on the community and actual terrorists attacks—rather than trumped-up charges of disloyalty. Unfortunately, the word treason itself cannot be avoided in what follows, as it is the term that the Constitution employs.

I. Focus on Americans

To proceed, it is important to note that often when the issue of American terrorists is debated, the objections raised concern the targeted killing of anyone, not just US citizens. These objections include questions about the legitimacy of killing terrorists either outside of a declared zone of war, without a declaration of war, or without a trial in a civil court.[3] However, the question about American citizens arises only if one agrees that such killings are legal in general, when the targeted individual is not a US citizen. If no terrorist may be killed in such a way, then logically the same would hold true for Americans. It is an elementary syllogism: if all A's (American terrorists) are B's (terrorists), and no B (terrorist) is a C (a legitimate target for assassination), then no A (American terrorist) is a C (legitimate target). This chapter takes for granted that killing terrorists, if they cannot be captured without undue risk to our troops, is legal and legitimate, on the grounds of self-defense;[4] that membership in a declared terrorist organization suffices to qualify an individual as a terrorist; and that Congress' Authorization for Use of Military Force (AUMF) authorized the use of lethal force by the president and those he commands.[5] One may disagree about any or all of these points. However, they are not relevant to the question whether of American terrorists should be treated differently from others.

If one accepts, even merely for sake of argument, the preceding points, one should then note that the 2012 Justice Department white paper, which purports to explain when the government can "use lethal force in a foreign country outside the area of active hostile activities against a US citizen," fails to deliver that which it set out to accomplish.[6] The three conditions listed—that the person be a senior operational leader of al Qaeda or an associated force, that his capture be deemed infeasible, and that the US follow the applicable law of war principles—apply to all terrorists and hence do not explain why one should set aside the special standing Americans command, the "extra" protections granted to them as citizens, above and beyond those of all persons.[7]

There is disagreement about whether Americans overseas possess *all* constitutional rights, but not whether they have at least some protections not granted to foreign nationals. In the 1957 ruling for *Reid v. Covert,* a plurality (as opposed to an authoritative majority) of Supreme Court justices wrote that "When the Government reaches out to punish a citizen who is abroad, the shield which the Bill of Rights and other parts of the Constitution provide to protect his life and liberty should not be stripped away just because he happens to be in another land."[8] Two other justices concurred that the Fifth and Sixth Amendments protect American's outside the U.S., but did not go so far as to affirm that the same was true of all rights enumerated in the Constitution. In 2007, a US Court of Appeals held that only part of the Fourth Amendment applied to citizens overseas.[9] In contrast, the Supreme Court held in *United States v. Verdugo-Urquidez* that "The Fourth Amendment does not apply to the search and seizure by United States agents of property owned by a non-resident alien and located in a foreign country."[10] In 2003 the Supreme Court ruled that alien residents convicted of "aggravated felonies" can face mandatory detention—a double standard justified by the fact that "Congress regularly makes rules that would be unacceptable if applied to citizens."[11]

Hence the normative and legal question stands: Should American terrorists be treated differently from others? What distinct procedures are to be employed in determining their treatment and in what legal forum should they be tried?

II. The Normative Grounds

Libertarianism and some forms of liberalism are normative systems that are centered on individuals and their rights. Communitarianism is a normative system centered on the common good and the responsibilities that emanate from this shared understanding that the members of the community are expected to uphold. Liberal (or responsive) communitarianism seeks to balance these two sets of normative concerns, and determine when individual rights or social responsibilities should take precedence when the two cannot be reconciled.[12] This chapter describes, from a liberal communitarian perspective, the circumstances under which American terrorists can be legally subjected to targeted killings while outside the United States and the proper procedures for dealing with those who can be captured.

Liberal communitarianism grants that Americans have "extra" rights but stresses that they also have responsibilities to the national community that foreigners do not have. Note that reference is not merely to the civic obligations due to the state, e.g., observing the laws, paying taxes, serving in a jury, and serving in the armed forces if there is a draft. Communitarians view nations as communities invested in states, of which people are not merely citizens by also members. Economists may see here a matter of implicit contract and incentives. Thus, neighbors will watch over the property of those who live next door when they are away on travel, merely on the implicit assumption that the favor will be returned. This holds for scores of other matters, from watching out for children, to maintaining the front lawns in order to ensure each other's property values, to making donations to keep the community center open. Sociologists, by contrast, will suggest that these communal obligations rest not so much on economic calculations of costs and benefits, but on a sense of internalized responsibility. In effect both considerations interact. One may start with a sense of obligation but if not reciprocated, it will diminish, though a perfect symmetry or "a clearing of the books" is not expected.[13] Most revealing, community members, including those of imagined communities (e.g., "the nation"), have a sense of commitment to one another based on the sense that they have a shared identity, history, future and fate. True, some people have such a sense toward communities more expansive than the nation, and some to much smaller ones, such as their ethnic or confessional group. However, in modern nations this sense of respect for the community and its welfare is particularly strong at the national level, as revealed by the fact that many citizens are willing to die for the preservation of their country, in particular when defending it against attacks by outsiders.

From this communitarian viewpoint, when an American terrorist attacks the United States (or threatens to attack it, or joins a group whose goal is to terrorize the United States) that person commits an additional normative violation above and beyond that committed by other terrorists. He raises arms against his own kind, he betrays the community which he is committed to uphold, he fails to live up to responsibilities he has assumed, and he undermines the community of which he is a member—a community which has protected and nurtured him and his loved ones. This is on the face of it a serious normative violation, and, to reiterate, one that only Americans can commit against their own nation.

Moreover, such assaults sow distrust. If the members of a community find that they cannot trust their own kind, they are particularly likely to feel terrorized and be suspicious of one and all. It is enough to recall the poisonous social climate at the height of the McCarthy era, when people felt that there was "a communist under every bed," even though there were only a very tiny number of Americans who actually betrayed their country, to sense the kind of social malaise that would arise if a large number of Americans did indeed aid and abet the enemy. Also American terrorists are more likely than others to successfully carry out an attack, given that they command American passports, and are familiar with American ways, culture, and modes of communication. Thus, deterring them is of special value to US security.

III. A Legal Expression

Which legal expression is most suitable to the communitarian normative precept just presented? This chapter first discusses the legal category and then the attending procedures and forums for prosecution.

1. The Legal Foundation

If one relies simply on the actual text of the Constitution, one will note that it clearly and quite explicitly treats treason as an offense different from all others. Article III, Section 2 of the Constitution speaks of "all crimes," while the whole of Section 3 is set aside to deal with treason. It states, "Treason against the United States, shall consist only in levying War against them, or in adhering to their Enemies, giving them Aid and Comfort."[14] Federal law runs along the same lines: "Whoever, owing allegiance to the United States, levies war against them or adheres to their enemies, giving them aid and comfort within the United States or elsewhere, is guilty of treason."[15] The fact that the text considers two types of betrayal—war or merely adhering to enemies—speaks directly to those who claim that the US can use its military only against nations and not against nonstate actors. These include for instance Wayne McCormack who argues that "Until the international community defines terrorist crimes as being violations of the law of war, the US system should commit that these persons be tried in civilian courts rather than by military commissions . . . because there is no coherent distinction between the alleged terrorist and the ordinary street criminal"—American or otherwise.[16] One can dismiss such concerns as a rather bad case of legalism, given that a group of terrorists armed with WMD poses a much greater threat to the US than do quite a few nations. In effect, it is a long time since any nation reaped as much destruction and terror on the US as nineteen attackers did on 9/11. One can suggest that those who hold this view of the law are aware of these basic facts but are concerned that the president will use military force without the authorization of Congress, which only wars with nations are said to require. However, this door can be closed by assuming that employing lethal force against nonstate actors also requires a declaration by Congress, as indeed happened three days after 9/11 with passage of the AUMF. One should note that those who hold the AUMF to be too vague or otherwise in need of revision are, in effect, arguing for a new AUMF, and not against the legitimacy of engaging in armed conflict with nonstate actors. One cannot hold, though, that such a declaration must be limited to particular theaters of war, as several scholars do.[17] This an obsolete concept in a world in which terrorists consider borders to be only a minor inconvenience, and cyber space is rapidly emerging as a vulnerable, transnational, borderless arena.

It is true that throughout American history, very few individuals have been charged with treason, and of those, most were eventually acquitted (and several others pardoned). However, treating American terrorists as individuals guilty of treason is far from unprecedented. Herbert Hans Haupt, a naturalized citizen of German descent, was convicted of treason by a military tribunal and executed for his participation in a failed Nazi-backed sabotage plot.[18] Tomoya Kawakita, a dual US-Japanese citizen was convicted of treason for torturing American prisoners of war during World War II.[19] More recently, in 2006, Adam Gadahn became the first American indicted for treason since WWII. Gadahn, who was raised in California, converted to Islam and moved to Pakistan where he "chose to join our enemy and to provide it with aid and comfort by acting as a propagandist for al-Qaeda."[20]

In considering the suggestion that the United States could charge American terrorists with treason by drawing upon the highly relevant and exceptionally clear lines of the Constitution regarding this subject, one best recall that each generation finds texts within the Constitution that speak to its unique challenges and needs—to its own communitarian balance. In the 1920s, the ACLU championed and succeeded in applying the text of the First Amendment to define free speech as we now understand it. In the 1960s, the Supreme Court fashioned a federal right to privacy.[21] And in 2008, the Roberts Court broke from 200 years of precedent by interpreting the Second Amendment as an individualized right to own guns, as opposed to a right limited only to well-regulated militias.[22]

2. Procedure and Forum

What procedures should be followed and in what forum should American terrorists be tried if they are charged with treason? Many civil libertarians strongly hold that all terrorists should be treated like other criminals—tried in civilian courts and granted all the procedural protections afforded to other criminals. These libertarians seem not to be mindful of the fact that, in order for terrorists to be tried in this way, they must first be captured and hauled into court. They are, after all, most unlikely to respond to an invitation to the present themselves, and the American legal tradition prohibits trying a person *in absentia* who was not at least present at the beginning of the trial.[23] However, many terrorists, say those in North Waziristan, northern Yemen, and considerable parts of Africa, cannot be captured without undue risk to our troops. Hence, a requirement to capture them is in effect a suggestion—however unwitting—to grant immunity to most if not all of them. Thus, one needs to consider separately two categories of American terrorists: those that cannot be captured and those who have been successfully detained.

3. For those not captured

For those who cannot be captured, the procedures outlined in the Constitution apply. It states that "No Person shall be convicted of Treason unless on the Testimony of two Witnesses to the same overt Act, or on Confession in open Court." (Title 18, Section 2381 of the US Code uses identical wording). Witness "ordinarily means one who gives evidence under oath or affirmation, in person or by affidavit or deposition, in any proceeding in any court of justice, or before any officer thereof, or before any tribunal or officer created by law, or in any proceeding in regard to any matter or thing in or respecting which an oath or affirmation is or may be required or authorized by law."[24] That is, witness testimony need not take place in civilian court.

The Justice Department white paper that lays out when the government can supposedly legally "use lethal force in a foreign country outside the area of active hostile activities against a US citizen," oddly does not mention that the United States is already approximating the Constitution's process in dealing with those terrorists whose capture is in effect infeasible. For an individual to be added to the "kill list," there must be two independent sources of intelligence that confirm that he is a terrorist.[25] This condition seems to satisfy the requirement that there be two witnesses. The question remains whether they testify to "the same overt act." If one source of intelligence establishes that a particular person was preparing bombs on Monday, and a second source finds the same person placing the explosives beside a road on Tuesday, is this the same act? Presuming the response is in the affirmative, one might argue that the basic evidentiary conditions for establishing treason laid out by the Constitution are being met for all terrorists, Americans included.

In effect, the procedures currently followed by the US do better by terrorists that cannot be captured than those accused of treason, by conducting a semi-trial. Before a person is put on the kill list, administration lawyers review the evidence against him to determine whether the target is legally appropriate based upon whether he constitutes a significant threat.[26] President Obama is reported to personally review the cases, a review not granted to Americans otherwise subjected to the death penalty.[27] As I see it, one could further strengthen this procedure by appointing one of the lawyers (with proper security clearance) to act as if he represents the prospective target, like a guardian, without further requiring all the procedural steps of a normal trial—which the Constitution does not call for in judging those suspected of treason as it does for other crimes. The main purpose of providing such a "guardian" is to ensure the validity of the two (or more) witnesses and the reliability of the evidence they provide.

Kristen Eichensehr argues that slipping away from the protections of criminal process "is nearly impossible in the treason context" because the Constitution "provides specific procedural and evidentiary requirements for treason that establish a nonderogable floor of protections."[28] Indeed, when the government overreached, the Supreme Court has overturned treason convictions that did not follow precise definition and procedures laid out in the Constitution.[29] In *Cramer v. United States*, the Supreme Court overturned the government's conviction of Anthony Cramer, who was charged with supporting Nazi saboteurs, writing that the requirement that "Every act, movement, deed, and word of the defendant charged to constitute treason must be supported by the testimony of two witnesses" had not been met, thereby setting a "high bar for what constitutes an overt act of aid and comfort." This case shows that, far from being automatic or incontestable, treason hearings can be thorough and reliable.

Civil libertarians charge that the government's targeted killing program allows the executive to act as the accuser, judge, and executioner, and thus argue that a judicial authority should be involved. A *New York Times* editorial in 2010 called for setting up a FISA-like court, made up of judges appointed by Congress, to review additions to the terrorist kill list.[30] In 2013, several senators raised this possibility and the administration responded that this might be "worthy of discussion."[31] (One notes in passing that civil libertarians often criticize FISA for approving practically all of the many thousands of surveillance requests brought before it and for not being sufficiently transparent.) In any case, such a court might be established, although this is not what the Constitution requires. Moreover, retired federal judge James Robertson has objected to involving the judiciary in the preapproval of targeted killings, writing that such a case "is necessarily considered in absentia and in secret. An American judge cannot do American justice in such a case. If he did, his independence would be severely compromised."[32] As it is a matter of policy, as opposed to a truly "justiciable" case, Robertson argues that deciding who constitutes a legitimate target for a drone strike is the job of Congress and the executive.

Congress, one must assume, will of course continue to oversee all such actions by the administration.[33] Congress would do best not to second-guess individual cases, but to review the procedures and criteria used to ensure that the witnesses are reliable and that examination of the evidence by whoever makes the kill ruling is judicious.

As I see it, it is particularly troubling is when the United States defines speech as treason. During World War II, in both the United States and Great Britain, propagandists for Germany and Japan, including radio personalities, were charged with treason and had their convictions affirmed in court. Mildred Gillars was convicted of treason for recording a radio drama which was "broadcast by the German Radio Broadcasting Company to the United States and to its citizens and soldiers at home and abroad as an element of German propaganda and an instrument of psychological warfare."[34] Herbert John Burgman was also charged with treason for his radio broadcasts addressed to the US armed forces which allegedly sought "to impair the morale of those forces and to dissuade them from support of this country."[35] These precedents "facilitated" al Qaeda propagandist Gadhan's indictment half a century later.[36] However, one wonders whether these acts truly assaulted the community. Did they lead to the kind of mutual distrust and corrosion of the social fabric that violent acts by Americans against American would engender? I tend to join those who hold that sticks and stones will break our bones but words we should be able to handle.

Eichensehr warns that "without a clear definition of 'aid and comfort' that encompasses those who work for an enemy to produce propaganda but excludes those who engage in political dissent by independently agreeing with, but not working with, the enemy, treason may be expanded without limit."[37] She argues that the government can avoid this slippery slope by instead charging propagandists under the "levying war" prong of the Treason Clause as this would "limit treason more clearly to those cases in which the defendant has acted in concert with the enemy in a program of warfare, and prevent the government from raising treason prosecutions against individuals who make independent statements in support of ideas endorsed by the enemy."[38]

One way or another, we should let Americans speak unless there is hard and specific evidence that their words effectively incite terror. Otherwise, American terrorists that cannot be captured should be subject to a review of the kind that is already being carried out.

4. If Captured

There are many reasons that those American terrorists that are captured should not be brought to trial before civilian courts in the US and that their cases be disposed in another forum—call it a security review board.[39] The reasons have been previously spelled out by Benjamin Wittes, Mark Gitenstein, Jack L. Goldsmith, Neal Katyal, Philip Bobbits, and me.[40] Hence they are here only quickly reviewed. From the onset it should be noted that the United States (and other free societies) already have several distinct judicial authorities to deal with different kinds of people. The implication of the civilian libertarian position that all people ought to be judged in the same way does not take into account the fact that the US has drug courts, immigration courts, family courts, debtor courts, juvenile courts, Social Security Administrative courts, and military commissions among others. Each of these adheres to different procedures and standards of evidence (e.g., some require proof beyond a reasonable doubt, some only a preponderance of evidence). There seems to be strong reasons to add a separate forum for dealing with those who commit treason.

Many of the reasons why Americans indicted for treason should not stand trial in civilian court also apply to foreign terrorists. Both classes are often captured in combat zones or ungoverned regions where it is difficult to collect evidence that would meet the standards of the ordinary criminal justice system. The nature of available evidence is likely to be classified and highly sensitive, or obtained in a way whose legality is not fully consolidated and liable to be thrown out by a civilian judge. For example, a federal appeals court threw out Salim Hamdan's conviction for providing material support for terrorism, not because he was innocent, but because he committed his crime before the Military Commissions Act of 2006 was enacted.[41] Reading terror suspects their Miranda rights and allowing them to "lawyer up" may forestall the collection of intelligence needed to prevent a future attack. Allowing terrorists to face their accusers would expose the means and methods of counterterrorism authorities and jeopardize their safety and efforts.[42]

In order to reduce the possibility of a failed conviction—which would put the government in the difficult position of having to either set free someone strongly suspected harming or intending to harm the U.S., or undermine the legitimacy of the American legal system by detaining the suspect despite their acquittal—prosecutors often rely on plea bargains, which guarantee the conviction but generally result in lighter sentences.[43] This is regrettable even when dealing with ordinary criminals but difficult to accept when one deals with terrorists, especially those who, in addition to their terrorist act, have committed treason.

Like all human beings, American terrorists convicted of treason are entitled to some basic rights. They should not be killed if they can be captured without undue risks to innocent lives, nor should they be tortured. Instead of suspending *habeas corpus*, they should be subject to a defined period of administrative detention,[44] which could be extended if necessary upon proper review. In Great Britain, for example, the 2006 Terrorism Act permitted a 28 day period (shortened to 14 days in 2010) of pre-charge detention for those reasonably suspected of being terrorists.[45] The specific numbers are not so important, as long as there is an initial period characterized by less judicial scrutiny, which allows for the disruption of possible additional attacks, debriefing of the terrorist, and deciphering of encrypted documents.

A security review board would be made up of federal judges with life tenure and "expertise in applying rules that protect classified information and national security concerns."[46] Suspects would retain the right to fair counsel and to appeal decisions to a second set of select federal judges. However, detainees would not be afforded all the protections to which ordinary criminals are entitled, such as facing their accusers, if those protections would compromise counterterrorism efforts. Next, the standards for admissible evidence would be lower than those of criminal cases. While evidence obtained through torture would be inadmissible, "probative material—even hearsay or physical evidence whose chain of custody or handling would not be adequate in a criminal trial—ought to be fair game."[47]

An American found to have committed an act of terrorism should not be privileged compared to other terrorists, but on the contrary subjected to harsher punishment, as he committed an additional crime. The US Code clearly indicates that treason should be strongly punished: those convicted of treason "shall suffer death, or shall be imprisoned not less than five years and fined under this title but not less than $10,000; and shall be incapable of holding any office under the United States." In addition, the Federal Sentencing Guidelines "assign treason the highest possible base offense level," which "requires life imprisonment, regardless of the offender's criminal history; a death-qualified jury would, of course, be necessary to impose the death penalty."[48] Clear enough.

5. Stripping citizenship?

Several legal scholars and voices in the media who seem to share my concern that Americans suspected of having committed treason will be provided with undue legal protection suggest that such Americans should be stripped of their citizenship. For instance, David French argues that the current law, under which Americans "in the armed forces of a foreign state engaged in hostilities against the U.S." forfeit their citizenship, should be expanded to include those who join "any armed force (state or nonstate) engaged in armed conflict (as designated by Act of Congress) against our nation."[49] Charles Krauthammer agrees that "Once you take up arms against the United States, you become an enemy combatant, thereby forfeiting the privileges of citizenship and the protections of the Constitution, including due process."[50] In 2010, Senator Joe Lieberman proposed legislation that would revoke the citizenship of Americans who purposely provide material support to foreign terrorist organizations or engage in hostilities against the U.S.[51] Obviously if such Americans were to lose their citizenship they would be subject to the same treatment as foreign terrorists.

At first blush, this approach seems promising. Treason is one of the seven actions included in the Immigration and Nationality Act for which "a person who is a national of the United States whether by birth or naturalization, shall lose his nationality." However, the act must be done voluntarily "with the intention of relinquishing United States nationality." Furthermore, in *Vance v. Terrazas* the Supreme Court ruled that the actions themselves to did not establish intent; a "preponderance of evidence" is required to establish that the action was done with the intention of giving up citizenship.[52] Finally, the loss of nationality will occur only "if and when the national thereafter takes up a residence outside the United States and its outlying possessions."[53] Terrorists are most unlikely to accommodate the prosecution by showing such intent. Hence, either Congress will have to change the act and eliminate this provision—and have the Supreme Court rule that such a move is constitutional—or one ought to instead avoid this highly-controversial course.[54] Instead, assign American terrorists to be judged by a security review board, following the procedures clearly laid out by the Constitution.

Notes

1.   Terrorism is defined as activities that "a) involve violent acts or acts dangerous to human life that are a violation of criminal laws . . . b) appear to be intended—(i) to intimidate or coerce a civilian population; (ii) to influence the policy of a government by intimidation or coercion; or (iii) to affect the conduct of a government by mass destruction, assassination, or kidnapping; and c) occur primarily outside the territorial jurisdiction of the United States," 18 U.S.C. § 2331(1) (2012), http://www.law.cornell.edu/uscode/text/18/2331.
2.   US Const. art. III, § 3.
3.   Kenneth Anderson, "Targeted Killing and Drone Warfare: How We Came to Debate Whether There is a 'Legal Geography of War,'" *Future Challenge in National Security and Law,* ed. Peter Berkowitz (April 26, 2011).
     Also: Afsheen John Radsan and Richard W. Murphy, "Due Process and Targeted Killing of Terrorists," *Cardozo Law Review* 31 (2009): 405.
     Also: Beau Barnes, " Reauthorizing the 'War on Terror': The Legal and Policy Implications of the AUMF's Coming Obsolescence," *Military Law Review* 211 (2012): 57.
4.   Jordan J. Paust, "Self-Defense Targetings of Non-State Actors and Permissibility of U.S. Use of Drones in Pakistan," *Journal Transnational Law & Policy* 19 (2010): 237.
5.   David Glazier, "Playing by the Rules: Combating Al Qaeda within the Law of War," *William & Mary Law Review* 51 (2010): 957.
6.   Lawfulness of a Lethal Operation Direction Against a U.S. Citizen Who is a Senior Operational Leader of Al-Qa'ida of An Associated Force, Department

of Justice White Paper, accessed at http://msnbcmedia.msn.com/i/msnbc/sections/news/020413_DOJ_White_Paper.pdf.

7. David Cole, "Are Foreign Nationals Entitled to the Same Constitutional Rights As Citizens?" Thomas Jefferson Law Review 25 (2003): 367, 382.
      Also: Gerald L. Neuman, "The Extraterritorial Constitution after Boumediene v. Bush," Harvard Public Law Working Paper no. 08–39 (September 14, 2008).

8. *Reid v. Covert*, 354 U.S. 1 (1957).

9. In re Terrorist Bombings of U.S. Embassies in E. Africa, 552 F.3d 157, 167 (2d Cir. 2008).

10. *United States v. Verdugo-Urquidez*, 494 U.S. 259 (1990).

11. *Demore v. Kim*, 538 U.S. 510 (2003).

12. Amitai Etzioni, *The New Golden Rule: Community And Morality In A Democratic Society* (1998). See also, "The Responsive Communitarian Platform," available at http://communitariannetwork.org/about-communitarianism/responsive-communitarian-platform/.

13. H. Lorne Carmichael and W. Bentley MacLeod, "Gift Giving and the Evolution of Cooperation," *International Economic Review* 38 (1997): 3, 485.

14. US Constitution article III, § 3.

15. 18 U.S.C. § 2381.

16. Wayne McCormack, "Military Detention and the Judiciary: Al Qaeda, the KKK, and Supra-State Law," *San Diego International Law Journal* 5 (2004): 7, 71, cited in Carlton F.W. Larson, "The Forgotten Constitutional Law of Treason and the Enemy Combatant Problem," *University of Pennsylvania Law Review* 154, note 1 (2006) 863, 864.

17. Vincent-Joël Proulx, "If the Hat Fits, Wear It, If the Turban Fits, Run for Your Life: Reflections on the Indefinite Detention and Targeted Killing of Suspected Terrorists," *Hastings Law Journal* (2005): 56801, 804; Mary Ellen O'Connell, "When is a War not a War? The Myth of the Global War on Terror," *ILSA Journal of International & Comparative Law* 12 (2005): 2; Paul R. Pillar, "The Limitless Global War," *National Interest*, (June 19, 2012), http://nationalinterest.org/blog/paul-pillar/the-limitless-global-war-7094.

18. "German Espionage and Sabotage Against the U. S. in World War II: George John Dasch and the Nazi Saboteurs" (FBI Handout), Naval Historical Center, (March 1984), http://www.history.navy.mil/faqs/faq114-2.htm (accessed March 18, 2013).

19. *Kawakita v. United States*, 343 US 717 (1952).

20. Dan Eggen and Karen DeYoung, "U.S. Supporter of Al-Qaeda Is Indicted on Treason Charge," *The Washington Post*, (October 12, 2006), http://www.washingtonpost.com/wp-dyn/content/article/2006/10/11/AR2006101101121.html.

21. *Griswold v. Connecticut*, 381 US 479 (1965).

22. *District of Columbia v. Heller*, 554 US 570 (2008). Robert Barnes, "Justices Reject D.C. Ban on Handgun Ownership—5-4 Ruling Finds 1976 Law Incompatible With Second Amendment," *The Washington Post*, June 27, 2008 A1 ("The court's landmark 5 to 4 decision split along ideological grounds and wiped away years of lower court decisions that had held that the intent of the amendment, ratified more than 200 years ago, was to tie the right of gun possession to militia service,").

23. Federal Rules of Criminal Procedure: Rule 43. Defendant's Presence, available at http://www.law.cornell.edu/rules/frcrmp/rule_43.
24. Definition provided by Justice Rawlings of the Supreme Court of Iowa in his opinion for *State v. Gilroy*. *State v. Gilroy*, 199 N.W.2d 63 (Iowa 1972).
25. Jane Mayer, "The Predator War: What are the Risks of the C.I.A.'s Covert Drone Program?" *The New Yorker*, October 26, 2009, http://www.newyorker.com/reporting/2009/10/26/091026fa_fact_mayer#ixzz2MCx8Wqsc ("According to the recent Senate Foreign Relations Committee report, the U.S. military places no name on its targeting list until there are "two verifiable human sources" and "substantial additional evidence" that the person is an enemy,").
26. Benjamin McKelvey, "Due Process Rights and the Targeted Killing of Suspected Terrorists: The Unconstitutional Scope of Executive Killing Power," *Vanderbilt Journal of Transnational Law* 44 (2011): 1353, 1358.
27. Doyle McManus, "Who Reviews the U.S. 'Kill List'?" *Los Angeles Times* (February 5, 2012), http://articles.latimes.com/2012/feb/05/opinion/la-oe-mcmanus-column-drones-and-the-law-20120205.
28. Kristen E. Eichensehr, "Treason in the Age of Terrorism: An Explanation and Evaluation of Treason's Return in Democratic States," *Vanderbilt Journal of Transnational Law* 42 (2009): 1443, 1495.
29. Ibid, 1454.
30. "Lethal Force Under Law," *The New York Times* (October 9, 2010), http://www.nytimes.com/2010/10/10/opinion/10sun1.html.
31. Open Hearing on the Nomination of John O. Brennan to be Director of the Central Intelligence Agency, US Senate Select Committee on Intelligence (Washington DC: February 7, 2013), transcript available at http://intelligence.senate.gov/130207/transcript.pdf.
32. James Robertson, "Judges Shouldn't Decide About Drone Strikes, *The Washington Post*, (February 15, 2013), http://www.washingtonpost.com/opinions/judges-shouldnt-decide-about-drone-strikes/2013/02/15/8dcd1c46-778c-11e2-aa12-e6cf1d31106b_story.html.
33. Ken Dilanian, "Congress Keeps Closer Watch on CIA Drone Strikes," *Los Angeles Times* (June 25, 2012), http://www.latimes.com/news/nationworld/world/middleeast/la-na-drone-oversight-20120625,0,7967691,full.story.
34. *Gillars v. United States.*, 182 F.2d 962 (D.C. Cir. 1950).
35. *United States v. Burgman*, 87 F. Supp. 568, 569–70 (D.D.C. 1949).
36. See note 28 at 1455.
37. Kristen Eichensehr, "Treason's Return," *Yale Law Journal Pocket Part* 116 (2007): 229, 231–232, http://thepocketpart.org/2007/01/16/eichensehr.html.
38. Ibid., 232.
39. The term "board" may be preferred to "court" as it signals a break from the civilian justice system. However, the name matters little as long as it is a distinct authority with its own rules and procedures.
40. Jack L. Goldsmith and Neal Katyal, "The Terrorists' Court," *The New York Times* (July 11, 2007), http://www.nytimes.com/2007/07/11/opinion/11katyal.html?_r=0; Benjamin Wittes and Mark Gitenstein, *A Legal Framework for Detaining Terrorists: Enact a Law to End the Clash Over Rights, Opportunity 08: Independent Ideas for Our Next President* (2008); Philip Bobbitt, *Terror and Consent: The Wars for the Twenty-First Century* (2008), 125.

41. Charlie Savage, "In Setback for Military Tribunals, Bin Laden Driver's Conviction is Reversed," *The New York Times* (October 16, 2012), http://www.nytimes.com/2012/10/17/us/politics/dispute-over-clothing-dominates-guantanamo-hearing.html?_r=0.

42. Philip Bobbitt write that because the prosecution of terrorists is "unlikely to succeed with the current rules of trial practice and evidence, the U.S. administration has taken the position that they can simply be held indefinitely, much like other prisoners of war who await the end of the conflict in which they participated. Yet terrorists can also be interrogated like a spy or partisan or tried like a criminal before a military tribunal (which of course no ordinary criminal could be). This simply amounts to a refusal to follow existing law or create new law that is more responsive to our new situation," Philip Bobbitt, *Terror and Consent: The Wars for the Twenty-First Century* 266 (2008).

43. Lucian E. Dervan, "The Surprising Lessons from Plea Bargaining in the Shadow of Terror," *Georgia State University Law Review* 27 (2011): 239.

44. "Treaties have long recognized that a state may detain without trial not only opposing armed forces, but also civilian and others who pose threats to its security . . . these rules [governing detention] impose a high standard for a state to initially detain a person, require the state immediately review that detention, permit the detainees, to appeal the detention decision, requires the state to review the detention periodically, and obligate the state to release the detainee when the reasons for his detention have ceased," Ashley S. Deeks, "Administrative Detention in Armed Conflict," *Case Western Reserve Journal of International Law* 40 (2009): 403.

45. Gavin Berman and Alexander Horne, Pre-Charge Detention in Terrorism Cases, Commons Library Standard Note (March 16, 2012), http://www.parliament.uk/briefing-papers/SN05634.

46. Wittes and Gitenstein, *A Legal Framework for Detaining Terrorists*, 4.

47. Benjamin Wittes, *Law and the Long War: The Future of Justice in the Age of Terror* 19 (2008).

48. Eichensehr, *Treason in the Age of Terrorism*, 1502.

49. David French, "Yes, the Military Can and Should Target American Members of Al-Qaeda," *National Review Online* (February 6, 2013), http://www.nationalreview.com/corner/340008/yes-military-can-and-should-target-american-members-al-qaeda-david-french.

50. Charles Krauthammer, "In Defense of Obama's Drone War, *The Washington Post* (February 4, 2013), http://www.washingtonpost.com/opinions/charles-krauthammer-in-defense-of-obamas-drone-war/2013/02/14/3a69d76c-76e5-11e2-aa12-e6cf1d31106b_story.html.

51. Terrorist Expatriation Act, S. 3327 (111th), available at http://www.govtrack.us/congress/bills/111/s3327/text.

52. *Vance v. Terrazas*, 444 US 252 (1980).

53. Restrictions on loss of nationality , 8 USC § 1483.

54. Members of Congress Propose Bill To Strip Citizenship From American Terrorism Suspects, ACLU, (May 6, 2010), http://www.acluct.org/downloads/ACLUReactionLieberman.pdf; Statement Opposing the Terrorist Expatriation Act, The Constitution Project, (May 20, 2010), http://www.constitutionproject.org/manage/file/402.pdf.

II

Privacy

4

A Cyber Age Privacy Doctrine

A privacy doctrine built for the cyber age must address a radical change in the type and scale of violations that the nation—and the world—face, namely that the greatest current threats to privacy come not at the point that personal information is collected, but rather from the secondary uses of such information. Often cited court cases, such as *Katz, Berger, Smith, Karo, Knotts, Kyllo,* and most recently *Jones,* concern whether or not the initial collection of information was in compliance with the constitution. They do not address the fact that personal information that was legally obtained may nevertheless be used later to violate privacy—that the ways such information is stored, collated with other pieces of information, analyzed, and distributed or accessed often entails very significant violations of privacy.[1] Moreover, although a considerable number of laws and court cases cover these secondary usages of information, they do not come together to make a coherent doctrine of privacy, and most assuredly not one that addresses the unique challenges of the cyber age.[2]

True, collected personal information was subject to secondary abuses even when it was largely paperbound (e.g., in police blotters or FBI files). Indeed, when Warren and Brandeis published their groundbreaking 1890 article in the *Harvard Law Review,* considered the "genesis of the right of privacy," they were not concerned about gossip *per se* (a first order privacy violation) but about the wider distribution of intimate details through the media (a secondary violation).[3] However, the digitization of information, the widespread use of the Internet and computers, and the introduction of artificial intelligence systems to analyze vast amounts of data have increased the extent, volume, scope, and kinds of secondary usages by so many orders of magnitude that it is difficult to find a proper expression to capture the import of this transformation.[4] The main point is not that information can now be processed at a tiny fraction of the cost and with incomparably faster speeds than when it was paper bound, which is certainly the case, but that modes of analysis that are common today —which divine new personal information out of personal data previously collected—were simply inconceivable when most personal information was paper bound.[5] Because these observations are critical to all that follows, and because the term "secondary usages" (which implies usages less important than the first or primary ones) is a rather weak one, I employ from here on the term *cybernation* to refer to information that is digitized, stored, processed, and formatted for mass distribution. Cybernated data can be employed in two distinct ways, and both represent a serious and growing threat to privacy. A discrete piece of personal information, collected at one point in time, called "spot information," may be used for some purpose other than that for which it was originally deemed constitutional, or it may be pieced together with other data to generate new information about the person's most inner and intimate life.

The cyber age privacy doctrine must lay down the foundations on which Congress can develop laws and the courts can accumulate cases that will determine not merely what information the government may legally collect, but also what it might do with that data. According to some legal scholars, the D.C. Circuit's decision in *Maynard* and the concurring opinion by the Supreme Court's justices in *Jones* provide the building blocks for this new edifice, sometimes referred to as a mosaic theory of the Fourth Amendment, under which "individual actions of law enforcement that are not searches for Fourth Amendment purposes may become searches when taken together en masse."[6] This observation is based on Justice Alito's argument that the GPS tracking of a vehicle on a public highway constituted a search because of the length of time over which the monitoring took place (28 days). This opens the door to taking into account the volume of information collected, and presumes that, while limited amounts of collection may be permissible, large amounts could constitute a violation of privacy. *Jones*, however, still only deals with collection. Hence, most of the work of laying down the foundations for the protection of privacy from cybernation remains to be carried out.

This chapter first suggests that we cannot rely on the privacy expectations of individuals or society—principles introduced in *Katz*—in developing a new privacy doctrine for the cyber age (Part I, A). The chapter then briefly indicates that a return to the home as the major focus of privacy will not serve either, and that we are to consider privacy as a protective sphere that follows the individual regardless of place (Part I, B). This is followed by an introduction to a "social policy model" of the Fourth Amendment to move us forward.[7] Within this model, we shall see that defining what is minimally intrusive becomes a key issue. Instead of treating intrusiveness as a discrete variable, we find it must be treated as a continuous one. That is, the intrusiveness of an act may be considered higher or lower rather than either minimal or not (Part I, C).

Having cleared the way through these deliberations, this chapter outlines the three dimensions of a cyber age privacy cube: volume, sensitivity, and cybernation (Part II). The last section of this chapter deals with the issue of defining when the collection and cybernation of information along these dimensions violates privacy (Part III).

I. Assumptions

1. Moving Beyond Katz

Since 1967, the US legal system has drawn on the twin concepts of personal and societal expectations of privacy to determine whether a Fourth Amendment "search" has taken place. This chapter assumes that relying on both or either expectations of privacy, as articulated by Justin Harlan in his concurring opinion in *Katz*, is indefensible and that it should be allowed to fade from legal practice. Indeed, Justice Harlan himself adopted rather quickly a critical view of his two-pronged test. Four years after *Katz*, in his dissent for US *v. White*, Harlan wrote, "While these formulations represent an advance over the unsophisticated trespass analysis of the common law, they too have their limitations and can, ultimately, lead to the substitution of words for analysis. The analysis must, in my view, transcend the search for subjective expectations."[8]

The reasonable expectation of privacy standard has since faced a range of strong criticisms.[9] In his widely cited article on the Fourth Amendment, Anthony G. Amsterdam writes,

> An actual, subjective expectation of privacy obviously has no place in a statement of what Katz held or in a theory of what the fourth amendment protects. It can neither add to, nor can its absence detract from, an individual's claim to fourth amendment protection. If it could, the government could diminish each person's subjective expectations of privacy merely by announcing half-hourly on television that 1984 was being advanced by a decade and that we were all forthwith being placed under comprehensive electronic surveillance . . . Fortunately, neither Katz nor the fourth amendment asks what we expect of government. They tell us what we should demand of government.[10]

A leading scholar of the Fourth Amendment and privacy, Orin Kerr concedes, "What counts as a 'reasonable expectation of privacy' is very much up for grabs,"[11] and hightly respected students of privacy Charles Whitebread and Christopher Slobogin charge that the Supreme Court has sent "mixed signals" on how to apply this standard.[12]

The absurdity of *Katz* is revealed by contemplating the following example: Assume a municipal government announces that, for public health reasons, anyone who relieves themselves in a public pool would be charged with a misdemeanor. This government would then insert a dye (which unfortunately only exists in Hollywood's fertile imagination) that would form a dark blue cloud around anyone who violates the ordinance, but would not announce the introduction of this dye. By *Katz*, surely a person could argue that their expectation of privacy has been grossly violated, as they did not expect to be detected when peeing in the pool. Would it be therefore reasonable to rule this ordinance unconstitutional and to dismiss the charges against them?

107

And once the introduction of the dye is made public, how many people would have to know about it before it is no longer reasonable to expect privacy in the matter? Who determines what is a reasonable expectation, and how? Would one announcement about the new dye suffice, or must it be regularly advertised?

Or, take those who speak in a sizeable political meeting. They may well have no expectation of privacy. However, surely they should be protected from government surveillance in such a setting under most circumstances, to protect their privacy (among other reasons).[13] And do new technologies change what is expected, with, say, Facebook lowering the standards of privacy because so many people post so much private information? The Electronic Communications Privacy Act (ECPA) only protects e-mails for 90 days, during which time a warrant is needed for the government to read them. After that, a subpoena from any prosecutor will do, without judicial oversight, because in 1986 the thought of keeping e-mails around that long was ridiculous because the cost of storing them was so high. Does anyone expect that their e-mails are private (to the extent that they are) for 90 days but not for more?

As to the societal expectation of privacy, a sociologist is keen to know which, if any, communities will be polled to establish what this expectation is.[14] Is it the privacy expected by the community of which the defendant is a member—say Spanish Harlem? Or is it the city of New York, or the United States, or the judge's country club? The fact that judges are free to assume they can rely on their sociological instincts as to what the community expects seems a strange foundation to rely on to determine when a search violates the Constitution.[15]

Finally, the whole notion is circular. Mr. Katz and all others either have or do not have an expectation of privacy *depending on what the Supreme Court rules.* Jim Harper put it well when he wrote: "Societal expectations are guided by judicial rulings, which are supposedly guided by societal expectations, which in turn are guided by judicial rulings, and so on."[16]

Four years after the Supreme Court ruled that the police had violated Katz's Fourth Amendment rights by bugging a public pay phone without a warrant, the Court held in *United States v. White* that no warrant was needed to record a conversation in a private home![17] Any reasonable person would expect that Mr. White has a higher expectation of privacy in his home than Mr. Katz has in a public phone booth, and there no reason to believe that "society" found the government's surveillance to be more reasonable in White's home than in the public booth.

Particularly relevant to what follows is that various court cases that draw on *Katz* seem not to recognize what might be called a "split condition"—that is, situations in which the government collects information in a way that would be considered constitutional because it was "expected," but then uses and distributes it in "unexpected" ways, which would, thus, be in violation of the constitution. There are, of course, many such split situations, and these situations should be covered by any comprehensive theory of privacy.

In short, it is difficult for a reasonable person to make sense out of *Katz*. Court rulings on whether a collection of personal information is a "search" by Justice Harlan's formula seem to be highly dependent on what judges divine a person or "society" would expect without determining in any half-objective way what these expectations actually are. At the same time, such standards ignore that rulings on privacy recast these expectations. It may take a long time before *Katz* is repealed. Meanwhile more reasonable criteria for privacy need to be developed and used to replace *Katz*.

2. But Not Back to "The Castle"

To suggest that the time has come to leave behind the reasonable expectation of privacy standard is not to say that the courts should revert to pre-*Katz* Fourth Amendment analysis, which gave considerable weight to the home as the locus of privacy. In *Katz* the majority ruled that "the Fourth Amendment protects people, not places," rejecting the "trespass" doctrine enunciated in *Olmstead*. However, even after this, the home remained largely inviolable in the eyes of the courts. It seems *Katz* did not detach Fourth Amendment safeguards from the home but rather extended the sphere of privacy beyond it to other protected spaces. Information collected about events in one's home is still often considered *a priori* a violation of privacy, while much more license is granted to the state in collecting information about conduct in public and commercial spaces. As Justice Scalia put it, "'At the very core' of the Fourth Amendment 'stands the right of a man to retreat into his own home and there be free from unreasonable governmental intrusion.' With few exceptions, the question whether a warrantless search of a home is reasonable and hence constitutional must be answered no."[18] This is an idea that has deep roots in American and English common law: "Zealous and frequent repetition of the adage that "a man's house is his castle," made it abundantly clear that both in England and the colonies, "the freedom of one's house" was one of the most vital elements of English liberty."[19] In *Dow Chemical Company v. United States,* the Court established that the expectation of privacy was lower in an industrial plant than a home because the latter "is fundamentally a sanctuary, where personal concepts of self and family are forged, where relationships are nurtured and where people normally feel free to express themselves in intimate ways."[20]

Feminist scholars correctly and roundly criticized the inviolability of the home and the private/public distinction in privacy law. Catharine MacKinnon writes the problem with granting the home extra protection is that "while the private has been a refuge for some, it has been a hellhole for others, often at the same time."[21] Linda McClain points out that freedom from state interference in the home "renders men unaccountable for what is done in private-rape, battery, and other exploitation."[22]

Moreover over, this chapter draws on the findings that the private/public distinction is rapidly declining in importance in general[23] and with regard to privacy in particular.[24] Marc Jonathon Blitz made the case compelling with regard to the cyber age and hence is quoted here at some length:

> The 1969 case Stanley v. Georgia forbade the government from restricting the books that an individual may read or the films he may watch "in the privacy of his own home." Since that time, the Supreme Court has repeatedly emphasized that Stanley's protection applies solely within the physical boundaries of the home: While obscene books or films are protected inside of the home, they are not protected en route to it—whether in a package sent by mail, in a suitcase one is carrying to one's house, or in a stream of data obtained through the Internet.
>
> However adequate this narrow reading of Stanley may have been in the four decades since the case was decided, it is ill-suited to the twenty-first century, where the in-home cultural life protected by the Court in Stanley inevitably spills over into, or connects with, electronic realms beyond it. Individuals increasingly watch films not, as the defendant in Stanley did, by bringing an eight millimeter film or other physical copy of the film into their house, but by streaming it through the Internet. Especially as eReaders, such as the Kindle, and tablets, such as the iPad, proliferate, individuals read books by downloading digital copies of them. They store their own artistic and written work not in a desk drawer or in a safe, but in the "cloud" of data storage offered to them on far-away servers.[25]

Privacy, it follows, is hence best viewed as a personal sphere that follows an individual irrespective of location. This is a version of what Christopher Slobogin refers to as the protection-of-personhood theory of privacy, which "views the right to privacy as a means of ensuring individuals are free to define themselves."[26] Privacy plays the same role whether one is in the home or out in public: "Because a substantial part of our personality is developed in public venues, through rituals of our daily lives that occur outside the home and outside the family, cameras that stultify public conduct can stifle personality development."[27] If the government uses a long distance "shotgun mic" to eavesdrop on the conversations of two persons walking in a public park, such a search is clearly more intrusive than if the government measured the heat setting in their kitchen. This is the case because conversations are much more revealing about the person, including their medical condition, political views, and so on, than is their preferred heat setting.[28] In short, privacy is best not home bound but person centered.

3. A "Social Policy" Model of the Fourth Amendment

The cyber age privacy doctrine concerns the normative principles that underlie both the evolving interpretations of the Constitution and the laws enacted by Congress, reflecting changes in the moral culture of the society. It hence deals both with the Fourth Amendment and public policy. Such comprehensive normative changes have occurred in other areas. For instance, the civil rights movement has led to changes in the position of the Supreme Court (e.g., from *Plessy v. Ferguson* to *Brown v. Board of Education*) and–to acts of Congress (e.g., the Voting Rights Act of 1965). More recently, changes were introduced both by the courts and by various legislatures reflecting changes in the characterization of same-sex marriage in the moral culture. Now such a change is called for with regard to the concept of privacy. This chapter next discusses the normative principles of such a reconstituted concept.

(i) In seeking to base a privacy doctrine neither on expectations of privacy nor on location, this chapter draws on a liberal communitarian philosophy that assumes that individual rights, such as the right to privacy, must be balanced with concerns for the common good, such as those about public health and national security.[29] (By contrast, authoritarian and East Asian communitarians tend to be exclusively concerned with the common good or to pay mind to individual rights only to the extent that they serve the rulers' aims.[30] At the opposite end of the spectrum, libertarians and many contemporary liberals privilege individual rights and autonomy over societal formulations of the common good.) Although the term "common good" is not one often found in legal literature, its referent is rather close to what is meant by "public interest," which courts frequently recognize, and a similar concept is found in the US Constitution's reference to the quest for a "more perfect union."

The Fourth Amendment reads: "The right of the people to be secure in their persons, houses, papers, and effects, against *unreasonable* searches and seizures, shall not be violated."[31] This is a prime example of a liberal communitarian text because it does not employ the absolute, rights-focused language of many other amendments (e.g., "Congress shall make *no* law"), but recognizes on the face of it that there are reasonable searches, understood as those in which a compelling public interest takes precedence over personal privacy.

(ii) This chapter assumes that the communitarian balance is meta-stable. That is, for societies to maintain a sound communitarian regime with a careful balance between individual rights and the common good, societies must constantly adjust their public policies and laws in response to changing external circumstances (e.g., 9/11) and internal developments (e.g., FBI overreach). Moreover, given that societal steering mechanisms are rather loose, societies tend to over-steer and must correct their corrections with still further adjustments. For example, in the mid-1970s, the Church and Pike Committees investigated abuses by the CIA, FBI and NSA, uncovering "domestic spying on Americans, harassment and disruption of targeted individuals and groups, assassination plots targeting foreign leaders, infiltration and manipulation of media and business."[32] As a result, Congress passed the Foreign Intelligence Surveillance Act of 1978 (FISA) and created the Foreign Intelligence Surveillance Court to limit the surveillance of American citizens by the US government.[33] After 9/11, several reports concluded that the reforms had gone too far by blocking the type of interagency intelligence sharing that could have forestalled the terrorist attacks.[34] As a result, the Patriot Act was enacted in a great rush and, according to its critics, sacrificed privacy excessively in order to enhance security and "correct" what are considered the excesses of the reforms the Church and Pike committees set into motion. Since then, the Patriot Act itself has been recalibrated.[35]

At each point in time, one must hence ask whether society is tilting too far in one direction or the other. Civil libertarians tend to hold that rights in general and privacy in particular are not adequately protected. The government tends to hold that national security and public safety require additional limitations on privacy. It is the mission of legal scholars, public intellectuals, and concerned citizens to nurture dialogues that help sort out in which direction corrections must next be made.[36] Note that often some tightening in one area ought to be combined with some easing in others. For instance, currently a case can be made that TSA screening regulations are too tight, while the monitoring of whether visitors and temporary residents committed to leaving the US actually do so is too loose.

Orin Kerr and Peter Swire engage in an important dialogue on whether the issues presented above are best suited for treatment by the courts or by Congress, and whether they are largely viewed through the prism of the Fourth Amendment or Congressional acts. The following discussion treats both as if they were an amalgam.

(iii) Four criteria help specify the liberal communitarian approach to privacy.[37] First, a liberal democratic government will limit privacy only if it faces a well-documented and large scale threat to the common good (such as to public safety or public health), not merely a hypothetical threat or one limited to few individuals or localities. (I avoid the term "clear and present danger," despite the similarity in meaning, because it has a specific legal reference not here intended.) The main reason this threshold must be cleared is because modifying legal precepts—and with them the ethical, social, public philosophies that underlie them—endangers their legitimacy. Changes, therefore, should not be undertaken unless there is strong evidence that either the common good or privacy has been significantly undermined.

Second, if the finding is that the common good needs shoring up, one had best seek to establish whether this goal can be achieved without introducing new limits on privacy. For instance, this is achieved by removing personally identifying information such as names, addresses, and social security numbers when medical records are needed by researchers, thus allowing access to data previously not accessible. True, various technical difficulties arise in securing the anonymity of the data. Several ingenious suggestions have been made to cope with this challenge.[38] Conversely, if privacy needs shoring up, one should look for ways to proceed that impose no "losses" to the common good, such as introducing audit trails.

Third, to the extent that privacy-curbing measures must be introduced, they should be as unintrusive as possible.[39] For example, many agree that drug tests should be conducted on those directly responsible for the lives of others, such as school bus drivers. Some employers, however, resort to highly intrusive visual surveillance to ensure that the sample is taken from the person who delivers it. Instead, one can rely on the much less intrusive procedure of measuring the temperature of the sample immediately following delivery.

Fourth, measures that ameliorate the undesirable side effects of necessary privacy-diminishing measures are to be preferred over those that ignore these effects. Thus, if contact tracing is deemed necessary to curb the spread of infectious diseases to protect public health, efforts must be made to protect the anonymity of those involved. A third party may inform those who were in contact with an affected individual about such exposure and the therapeutic and protective measures they ought to next undertake, without disclosing the identity of the diagnosed person.

The combined application of these four balancing criteria helps to determine which correctives to a society's course are both needed and not excessive. This chapter focuses on the third criteria and seeks to address the question: What is least intrusive?

II. Privacy as a Three Dimensional Cube

In this section I attempt to show that to maintain privacy in the cyber age, boundaries on information that may be used by the government should be considered along three major dimensions: The level of sensitivity of the information, the volume of information collected, and the extent of cybernation. These considerations guide one to find the lowest level of intrusiveness holding constant the level of common good. A society ought to tolerate more intrusiveness if there are valid reasons to hold that the threat to the public has significantly increased (e.g., there is an outbreak of a pandemic), and reassert a lower level of intrusiveness when such a threat has subsided.

1. Sensitivity

One dimension is the level of sensitivity of the information.[40] For instance, data about a person's medical condition is considered highly sensitive, as is information about one's political beliefs and conduct (e.g., voting) and personal thoughts. Financial information is ranked as less sensitive than medical information, and publically presented information (e.g., license plates) and routine consumer choices are ranked even less so.

These rankings are not based on "expectations of privacy" or on what this or that judge divines as societal expectations.[41] Rather, they reflect shared social values and are the product of politics in the good sense of the term, of liberal democratic processes, and of moral dialogues.[42] Different nations may rank differently what they consider sensitive. For example, France strongly restricts the collection of information by the government about race, ethnicity, and religion (although its rationale is not the protection of privacy but rather a strong assimilationist policy and separation of church and state). For those who analyze the law in terms of the law and economics paradigm, disclosure of sensitive data causes more harm to the person by objective standards than does the disclosure of data that is not sensitive. Thus, disclosure of one's medical condition may lead one to lose one's job or not be hired, to be unable obtain a loan, or to incur higher insurance costs, among other harms. By contrast, disclosure of the kinds of bread, cheese, or sheets one buys may affect mainly the kind and amount of spam one receives.

A re-examination of *Kyllo* helps highlight this principle. If one goes by *Katz*, the legality of a thermal imaging search from outside the home depends on what one presumes personal and societal expectations to be. At least in middle class American suburbs, people may consider such a heat reading a violation of their expectations. If one clings to the idea that "my home is my castle," measuring the heat inside the home is indeed a major violation of privacy. However, if one goes by the cyber age privacy doctrine outlined here, such readings rank very low on the sensitivity scale because they reveal very little or nothing about the resident's medical, financial, or political preferences, let alone their thoughts. Furthermore, they detect an extremely low bandwidth of information. The information revealed is less consequential than what kind of cereal or which brand of coffee the person purchased. In contrast, taping a person's phone calls is much more revealing. Hence both *Kyllo* and *White* deserve to be reversed.

One may argue that information about the heat inside a home is actually particularly sensitive because it reveals that a crime is being committed. Preventing crime is obviously a contribution to the common good. Given that in 2011 fewer than half of violent crimes and 20 percent of property crimes in the US were resolved, some may well hold that public authorities are not excessively indulged when dealing with crime.[43] As to the rights of the individuals involved, they would be harmed only if they had a right to commit a crime. As to the presumption of innocence, there is the public safety exception. The arguments against the notion that crime committed in a home (e.g., spousal abuse) deserves more protection than one committed in public were already presented above. What is new here is that historically, when the Constitution was written, searching a home required a person to enter or peep, which would entail a high level of intrusiveness because the intruder could not but note other potentially sensitive information besides whether or not a crime was being committed. However, technologies that have a very narrow and crime-specific bandwidth (e.g., dogs that sniff for bombs or sensors that measure abnormal levels of heat) and are, hence, very lowly-intrusive should be allowed. One may disagree with this line of analysis but still accept the basic point that the less-intrusive collection of less-sensitive information should be tolerated, while the collection of highly-sensitive information should be banned under most circumstances.

Many court cases treat the voluntary release of information to others (and by them to still others, discussed below under the third party doctrine) as if the information disclosed—including phone numbers dialed,[44] copies of written checks,[45] documents given to an accountant,[46] newspaper records,[47] and even papers held by a defendant's attorney[48]—all had the same level of sensitivity.[49] A privacy doctrine that follows the principles here outlined would grant persons more say about the cybernization of sensitive information, while recognizing that the less sensitive information may be used and passed on without the individual's explicit consent.

Over the years, Congress has pieced together privacy law by addressing the protection of one kind of sensitive information at a time, rather than treating all kinds in a comprehensive fashion. Thus, in 1973 the Department of Health, Education and Welfare developed the Code of Fair Information Practices to govern the collection and use of information by the federal government. The principles of the code were incorporated in the Privacy Act of 1974, which "prohibits unauthorized disclosures of the records [the federal government] protects. It also gives individuals the right to review records about themselves, to find out if these records have been disclosed, and to request corrections or amendments of these records, unless the records are legally exempt."[50] The Privacy Act applies only to the federal government and has not been expanded to include records kept by the private sector. In 1986, the Electronic Communications Privacy Act restricted wiretapping, regulated government access to electronic communication stored by third parties, and prohibited the collection of communications content (i.e., what was said, but not who was called) by pen registers. After the Supreme Court ruled in the 1976 case *United States v. Miller* that there was no reasonable expectation of privacy for records at financial institutions, Congress passed the Right to Financial Privacy Act,[51] which extended Fourth Amendment protections to these records. As required by the 1996 Health Insurance Portability and Accountability Act (HIPAA), in 2002 the Department of Health and Human Services published the final form of "the Privacy Rule," which set the "standards for the electronic exchange, privacy and security of health information."[52] This accumulation of privacy protections includes laws covering specific sectors—or responding to specific events—but did not provide an overarching design. A well-known case in point is Congress' enactment of the Video Privacy Protection Act after the video rental records of Supreme Court nominee Judge Robert Bork were obtained by a Washington, D.C., newspaper.[53]

Congress could help to establish a privacy doctrine for the cyber age by reviewing what by now has been fairly called an incomplete "patchwork of federal laws and regulations" and providing a comprehensive overall ranking of protections based on the sensitivity of the data.[54] However, many of the building blocks needed for such an edifice are already in place. To develop sensitivity as a criterion for a privacy doctrine, does not require a major leap.

2. Volume

The second dimension on which a cyber age privacy doctrine should draw is the volume of information collected. Volume refers to the total amount of information collected about the same person holding constant the level of sensitivity. Volume reflects the extent of time surveillance is applied (the issue raised in *Jones*), the amount of information collected at each point in time (e.g., only e-mails sent to a specific person or all e-mails stored on a hard drive), and the bandwidth of information collected at any one point in time (e.g., only the addresses of e-mail sent or also their content). A single piece of low-sensitivity data deserves the least protection, and a high volume of sensitive information should receive the most protection.

Under such a cyber age privacy doctrine, different surveillance and search technologies differ in their intrusiveness. Least intrusive are those that collect only discrete pieces of information of the least sensitive kind. These include speed detection cameras, tollbooths, and screening gates, because they all reveal, basically, one piece of information of relatively low sensitivity. Radiation detectors, heat reading devices, and bomb and drug-sniffing dogs belong in this category, not only because of the kind of information they collect (low or not sensitive), but also because the bandwidth of the information they collect is very low (just one facet, indeed a very narrow one, and for a short duration).

Typical closed-circuit televisions (CCTVs)—privately owned, mounted on one's business, parking lot, or residential lobby—belong in the middle range because they pick up several facets (e.g., location, physical appearance, who one associates with), but do so for only a brief period of time and in one locality. The opposite holds for Microsoft's Domain Awareness System, first tested in New York City in 2012. The program collates thousands of piece of information about the same person from public sources—such as that from the city's numerous CCTV cameras, arrest records, 911 calls, license plate readers, and radiation detectors—and makes them easily and instantly accessible to the police. While the system does not yet utilize facial recognition, it could be readily expanded to include such technology.

Phone tapping—especially if not minimized and continued for extended period of time—and computer searches collect considerable volume. (This should not be conflated with considerations that come under the third dimension: Whether these facts are stored, collated, analyzed and distributed—the elements of cybernation). Drones are particularly intrusive because they involve much greater bandwidth and have the potential to engage in very prolonged surveillance at relatively low costs compared to, say, a stake out. These volume rankings must be adapted as technologies change. The extent to which combining technologies is intrusive depends on the volume (duration and bandwidth, holding sensitivity constant) of information collected. High volume searches should be much more circumscribed than low volume ones.

When the issue of extending privacy protection beyond spot collection arose in *Jones*, several legal scholars, in particular Orin Kerr, pointed to the difficulties of determining when the volume of collection was reasonable and when it became excessively intrusive. Kerr writes:

> In *Jones*, the GPS device was installed for 28 days. Justice Alito stated that this was 'surely' long enough to create a mosaic. But he provided no reason why, and he recognized that 'other cases may present more difficult questions.' They may indeed. If 28 days is too far, how about 21 days,or 14 days,or 3.6 days? Where is the line?[55]

In response, one notes that there are many such cut off points in law, such as the number of days suspects may be detained before they must be charged or released, the voting and driving ages, the number of jurors necessary for due process, and so on. One may say that they reflect what a "reasonable" person would rule. Actually, they reflect what judges consider a compromise between a restriction that is clearly excessive and one that's clearly inadequate—a line that has been adjusted often. There is no reason the volume of collection should not be similarly governed.

3. Cybernation: Storing, Analysis, and Access

The third dimension is the one that is increasing in importance and regarding which law and legal theory have the most catching up to do. To return to the opening deliberations of this article, historically, much attention was paid to the question of whether the government can legally collect certain kinds of information under specific conditions. This was reasonable because most violations of privacy occurred through search and surveillance that implicated this first-level collection, that of spot information. True, some significant violations also occurred in the paper age as a result of collating information, storing it, analyzing it, and distributing it. However, to reiterate, as long as records were paper bound, which practically all were, these secondary violations of privacy were inherently limited when compared to those enabled by the digitization of data and the use of computers.

To illustrate the scope and effects of cybernation a comparison follows: In one state, a car passes through a tollbooth, a picture of its license plate (but not the driver or others on the front seat) is taken. This information is

117

immediately deleted from the computer if the proper payment has been made. In another state, the same information, augmented with a photo of the passengers, is automatically transmitted to a central data bank. There, it is combined with many thousands of other pieces of information about the same person, from locations they have visited (e.g., based on cell tower triangulation) to their magazine subscriptions, recent purchases, and so on. The information is regularly analyzed by artificial intelligence systems to determine if people are engaged in any unusual behavior, what places of worship they frequent (e.g., flagging Mosques), which political events they attend (e.g., flagging those who have participated in protests), if they stop at gun shows, and so on. The findings are widely distributed to local police and the intelligence community and can be gained by the press and divorce lawyers.

Both systems are based on the same spot information—that is, pieces of information pertaining to a very limited, specific event or point in time. However, if such information is combined with other information, analyzed, and distributed, as depicted in the second scenario, it provides a very comprehensive and revealing profile of one's personal life. In short, the most serious violations of privacy are often perpetuated not by surveillance or information collection *per se*, but by combination, manipulation, and data sharing—by cybernation. The more that information is cybernated, the more intrusive it becomes.

III. Limiting Intrusion by Cybernation

There two major systematic approaches in place for dealing with privacy violations that result from secondary uses: The third party doctrine and the EU Data Protection Directive (DPD). The third party doctrine holds that once a person voluntarily discloses a fact to another party, that party is free to pass on (or sell) this information to third parties, and those various third parties are free to further process this information, collate it with other data, draw inferences, and so on—in short, to cybernate it.[56]

This approach is challenged by critics who note that in the cyber age much of our private lives are lived in a cyber world operated by third parties like Google and Facebook. Thus, Matthew Lawless writes:

> The third party doctrine gives effect to the criticism often aimed at the "reasonable expectation of privacy" principle, by holding that individuals can only reasonably expect privacy where the Court gives them that privacy. Because the third party doctrine fails to address true societal expectations of privacy (as evident by its failure to protect any information entered into a search engine), it reinforces the privacy norms of a politically and temporally insulated judiciary: [O]nce people know their searches are exposed, then—by the time these cases are contested—there will, in truth, be no expectation of privacy.[57]

However, even without drawing on whatever the societal expectation of privacy is, one notes that considerable harm will come to people and that core societal values will be violated if the third party doctrine is given free rein. This observation is strengthened by the fact that various exceptions to the third party doctrine are already in place, such as special rules for medical and financial information. However, according to Greg Nojeim, these rules do not provide the same level of protection granted by the Fourth Amendment. He notes that "privacy statutes that protect some categories of sensitive personal information generally do not require warrants for law enforcement access."[58] Furthermore, Matthew Tokson argues that "the conflation of disclosure to automated Internet systems with disclosure to human beings" has led the court to exclude from Fourth Amendment protection a great deal of personal information, including "Internet protocol ('IP') addresses, e-mail to/from information, information about the volume of data transmitted to a user, name, address, and credit card information, and even the contents of a user's e-mails."[59] In short, the third party doctrine provides very little privacy protection and the less so the more cybernation is developed and extended.

The European Union's DPD in effect takes the opposite view, namely, that any secondary use of personal information released by a person or collected about him requires the explicit *a priori* approval of the original individual "owner" of the information, and that this consent cannot be delegated to an agent or machine.[60] The details of DPD are complex and changing.[61] For instance, it made exceptions from this rule for many areas, such as when the data is needed for the purposes of research, public health, or law enforcement, among others. In January 2012, the European Commission passed draft legislation that would update the existing data protection law. This legislation includes an "opt in" provision: "As a general rule, any processing of personal data will require providing clear and simple information to concerned individuals as well as obtaining specific and explicit consent by such individuals for the processing of their data." Data show that information about a person is used many times each day by a large variety of users. Hence, if such a policy were systematically enforced, each Internet user would have to respond to scores if not hundreds of requests per day even for uses of nonsensitive information. It seems that in this area, as in many others, the way DPD rules survive is by very often not enforcing them. Whenever I meet Europeans, and following public lectures in the EU, I ask if anyone has been ever asked to consent to the use of personal information that they had previously released. I have found only one person so far. He said that he got one such request—from Amazon. Other sources indicate that compliance is at best "erratic."[62] The penalties for violating the DPD seem to be miniscule and rarely collected. No wonder a large majority of the EU public—70 percent—fear that their personal data may be misused.[63] In short, neither of these approaches is satisfactory.

In addition, there are in place a large number of laws, regulations, and guidelines that deal with limited particular usages of personal information beyond the collection point. However, a very large number of them deal with only one dimension of the cube and often with only one element of cybernation, limiting either storage, or analysis, or distribution. The laws reflect the helter-skelter way they were introduced and do not provide a systematic doctrine of cyber privacy. They are best viewed as building blocks that, if subjected to considerable legal scholarship and legislation, could provide the needed doctrine. They are like a cast of characters in search of an author.

One of the key principles for such a doctrine is that the legal system can be more tolerant of the primary spot collection of personal information (a) the more limited the volume (duration and bandwidth) of the collection[64] and (b) the more limited and regulated cybernation is—holding constant the level of sensitivity of the information. That is, much more latitude can be granted to the collection and cybernation of nonsensitive information, stricter limitations can be placed on highly sensitive information, and a middle level of protection can be established in between.

In other words, a cyber age privacy doctrine can be much more tolerant of primary collection conducted within a system of laws and regulations that are effectively enforced to ensure that cybernation is limited, properly supervised, and employed for legitimate purposes—and much less so if the opposite holds. One may refer to this rule as the positive correlation between the level of permissiveness in primary collection and the strictness of controls on secondary usage of personal information.

Another key principle is a ban on using nonsensitive information to divine the sensitive (e.g., using information about routine consumer purchases to divine one's medical condition) because it is just as intrusive as collecting and employing sensitive information.[65] This is essential because currently such behavior is rather common.[66] Thus, under the suggested law, Target would be prevented from sending coupons for baby items to a teenage girl after the chain store's analysis of her recent purchases suggested she might be pregnant.[67] To further advance the cyber age privacy doctrine, much more attention needs to be paid to private actors. Privacy rights, like others, are basically held against the government, to protect people from undue intrusion by public authorities. However, cybernation is increasingly carried out by the private sector. There are corporations that make shadowing Internet users—and keeping very detailed dossiers on them—their main line of business. According to Slobogin,

> Companies like Acxiom, Docussearch, ChoicePoint, and Oracle can provide the inquirer with a wide array of data about any of us, including: Basic demographic information, income, net worth, real property holdings, social security number, current and previous addresses, phone numbers and fax numbers, names of neighbors,

driver records, license plate and VIN numbers, bankruptcy and debtor filings, employment, business and criminal records, bank account balances and activity, stock purchases, and credit card activity.[68]

These data are routinely made available to government agencies, including the FBI. Unless this private cybernation is covered, the cyber age privacy doctrine will be woefully incomplete.[69]

Given that private actors are very actively engaged in cybernation and often tailor their work so that it might be used by the government (even if no contract is in place and they are, hence, not subject to the limits imposed on the government), extending the privacy doctrine beyond the public/private divide is of pivotal importance for the future of privacy in the cyber age. Admittedly, applying to the private sector restrictions and regulations similar to those that control the government may well be politically unfeasible in the current environment. However, as one who analyzes the conditions of society from a normative viewpoint, I am duty-bound to point out that it makes ever less sense to maintain this distinction.[70] Privacy will be increasingly lost in the cyber age, with little or no gain to the common good, unless private actors—and not just the government—are more reined in. To what extent this may be achieved by self-regulation, changes in norms, increased transparency, or government regulation is a question not addressed here.

For this doctrine to be further developed, laws and court rulings ought to be three dimensional.[71] These laws and court cases had best specify not only whether a particular collection of personal information is a "search," but also what level of sensitivity can be tolerated and to what extent the information may be stored, analyzed, and distributed. This is a tall, if not impossible, order. However, as is next illustrated, a considerable number of measures are already in place that are, in effect, at least two-dimensional. These, though, suffer from the fact that they have been introduced each on their own and do not reflect an overarching doctrine of privacy; hence, they reveal great inconsistencies that need to be remedied. I cannot stress enough that the following are but selective examples of such measures.

One should note that a very early attempt to deal with the issue by banning a form of cybernation utterly failed. In 2003, Congress shut down the Pentagon's Total Information Awareness (TIA) program, which was created to detect potential terrorists by using data mining technologies to analyze unprecedented amounts of personal transaction data. However, a report by the *Wall Street Journal* in 2008 revealed that the most important components of TIA were simply "shifted to the NSA" and "put in the so-called black budget, where it would receive less scrutiny and bolster other data-sifting efforts."[72]

Minimization is one way of addressing the volume issue, as Swire pointed out in his groundbreaking article on *Jones* and mosaic theory.[73] Accordingly, when the FBI taps a phone, even for an extended period of time, the intrusion can be reduced significantly if the FBI either stops listening when it hears that the conversation is not relevant to the investigation (e.g., a child is calling the suspect under surveillance) or locks away those segments of the taped correspondence that turn out to be irrelevant.[74] For this rule to be integrated into the doctrine, it may be waived for nonsensitive information. That is, there would be no need to minimize if the child asked, say, to watch TV, but activated if she asked, say, about medical news concerning a family member.

Another example of a safeguard against excessive privacy intrusions is the requirement that certain content be deleted after a specific time period. Most private companies that utilize CCTV erase video footage after a set number of days, such as after a week. Admittedly, their reasons for doing so may be simply economic; however, the effect is still to limit the volume of collection and potential for subsequent abuse. Note that that there are no legal requirements to erase these tapes. However, such laws ought to be considered (Europeans are increasingly recognizing a "right to be forgotten"). It would be in the public interest to require that footage be kept for a fixed period of time (as it has proven useful in fighting crime and terrorism), but also ban under most circumstances the integration of the video feed into encompassing and cybernated systems of the kind Microsoft has developed.

The treatment of private local CCTVs should be examined in the context of the ways other such spot collection information is treated. Because the bandwidth of information collected by tool booths, speed cameras, and radiation detectors is very narrow, one might be permitted to store it longer and feed it into cybernated systems. By contrast, cell phone tracking can be utilized to collect a great volume and bandwidth of information about a person's location and activities. People carry their phones to many places they cannot take their cars, where no video cameras or radiation detectors will be found, including sensitive places such as political meetings, houses of worship, and residences. These rules must be constantly updated as what various technologies can observe and retain constantly changes.

Regulations to keep information paper bound have been introduced for reasons other than protecting privacy, but these requirements still have the effect of limiting intrusiveness. For example, Congress prevents the Bureau of Alcohol, Tobacco, Firearms and Explosives (ATF) from computerizing gun records when such information is collected during background checks.[75] In 2013, an amendment to the anti-insider trading STOCK Act exempted 28,000 executive branch staff from having to post their financial disclosure forms "online in a searchable, sortable and downloadable format."[76] These bans serve as reminders that not all the privacy measures that are in place are legitimate and that some are best scaled back rather than enhanced.[77]

A related issue is raised by the cybernation of arrest records. Arrest records should be but are not considered highly-sensitive information. When these records, especially those concerning people who were subsequently released without any charges, were paper bound, the damage they inflicted on most people's reputations was limited. However, as a result of cybernation, they have become much more problematic. Under the suggested doctrine, arrest records of people not charged after a given period of time would be available only to law enforcement officers. The opposite might be said about data banks that alert the public to physicians that have been denied privileges for cause, a very high threshold that indicates serious ethical shortcomings.

Many computer systems ("clouds" included) encrypt their data and a few have introduced audit trails. The cyber age privacy doctrine might require that all data banks that contain sensitive information be encrypted and include at least some rudimentary form of an audit trail.

Technologies can be recalibrated to collect the "need to know" information while shielding extraneous but highly sensitive information from observation. For example, when law enforcement collects DNA samples from convicted criminals or arrested individuals, FBI analysts create DNA profiles using so-called "junk DNA" "because it is not 'associated with any known physical or medical characteristics,' and thus theoretically poses only a minimal invasion of privacy."[78] Storing these "genetic fingerprints" in national databases is much less intrusive than retaining data produced by blood samples, which "reveal sensitive medical or biological information."[79] In 2013, the TSA stopped its use of body scanners that revealed almost-nude images, using instead scanners that produce "cartoon-like" images on which the scanners mark places hidden objects are found.[80] This did not affect the volume of collection, but lessened the sensitivity of the content.

Other measures must address the fact that often data can be "re-identified" or "de-anonymized." For example, in 2006, AOL released the search records—stripped of "personal identifiers"—of over six hundred thousand people. An investigation by the *New York Times*, however, demonstrated that intimate information—including names and faces—can be gleaned from such purportedly anonymous data. This risk is mitigated by the development of statistical methods that prevent such undertakings, such as "differential privacy," which allows curators of large databases to release the results of socially beneficial data analysis without compromising the privacy of the respondents who make up the sample.[81]

Many more examples could be provided. However, the above list may suffice to show that while there are numerous measures in place that deal with various elements of the privacy cube, these have not been introduced with systematic attention to the guiding principles needed for the cyber age.

Notes

1.   Amitai Etzioni, "The Privacy Merchants: "What Is To Be Done?" *University of Pennsylvania Journal of Constitutional Law* 14 (March 2012): 929.

2.   Peter P. Swire, "Katz is Dead. Long Live Katz," *Michigan Law Review* 102 (2002): 904, 912. ("The increasing storage of telephone calls is part of the much broader expansion since 1967 of stored records in the hands of third parties. Although there are no Supreme Court cases on most of these categories of stored records, the Miller and Smith line of cases make it quite possible that the government can take all of these records without navigating Fourth Amendment protections").

        Some scholars have suggested that Fourth Amendment restrictions should apply to subsequent use, although the analysis is not sufficiently developed in the courts to constitute a meaningful privacy doctrine. Harold J. Krent, "Of Diaries and Data Banks: Use Restrictions Under the Fourth Amendment," *Texas Law Review* 74 (1995–1996): 49. ("If the state can obtain the information only through means constituting a search or seizure, then use restrictions should apply, confining the governmental authorities to uses consistent with the [Fourth] Amendment's reasonableness requirement").

3.   Samuel D. Warren and Louis D. Brandeis, "The Right of Privacy," *Harvard Law Review* 4 (1890): 193.

4.   For an excellent overview of how advances in information and communication technologies have rendered obsolete the privacy laws (and the doctrines on which these laws are based) of the 1980s and 1990s, see Omer Tene, "Privacy: The New Generations," *International Data Privacy Law* 1 (2011): 15. For a discussion of how these changes have particularly affected the privacy expectations of the 'Facebook generation,' see Mary Graw Leary, "Reasonable Expectations of Privacy for Youth in a Digital Age," *Mississippi Law Journal* 80 (2011): 1033.

5.   This is of course not a terribly new position—legal scholars have been discussing the implications for privacy and the Fourth Amendment of the Internet since its introduction as publically available technology. See Lawrence Lessig, *Code and Other Laws of Cyberspace* (1999), 222–23 and Laurence H. Tribe, The Constitution in Cyberspace, Keynote Address at the First Conference on Computers, Freedom, & Privacy (March 26, 1991) (transcript available at www.sjgames.com/SS/tribe.html).

6.   Erin Smith Dennis, "A Mosaic Shield: Maynard, the Fourth Amendment, and Privacy Rights in the Digital Age," *Cardozo Law Review* 33 (2012): 737. *See also* Orin Kerr, "The Mosaic Theory of the Fourth Amendment," *Michigan Law Review* 111 (2012): 311, 320 ("Under mosaic theory, searches can be defined collectively as a sequence of discrete steps rather than as individualized steps. Identifying Fourth Amendment search requires analyzing police actions over time as a collective 'mosaic' of surveillance"); Madelaine Virginia Ford, "Mosaic Theory and the Fourth Amendment: How Jones Can Save Privacy in the Face of Evolving Technology," *American University Journal Gender, Social Policy, and Law* 19 (2011): 1351; Bethany L. Dickman, "Untying Knots: The Application of Mosaic Theory to GPS Surveillance in United States v. Maryland," *American University Law Review* 60 (2011): 731.

7. Orin S. Kerr, "Four Models of Fourth Amendment Protection," *Stanford Law Review* 60 (2007): 503, 519.

8. *United States v. White*, 401 U.S. 745, 786 (1971).

9. Shaun B. Spencer, "Reasonable Expectations and the Erosion of Privacy," *San Diego Law Review* 39 (2002): 843; Jim Harper, "Reforming the Fourth Amendment Privacy Doctrine," *American University Law Review* 57 (2008): 5; Haley Plourde-Cole, "Back to Katz: Reasonable Expectation of Privacy in the Facebook Age," *Fordham Urban Law Journal* 38 (2010): 571; Christopher Slobogin & Joseph E. Schumacher, "Reasonable Expectations of Privacy and Autonomy in Fourth Amendment Cases: An Empirical Look at Understandings Recognized and Permitted by Society," *Duke Law Journal* 42 (1993): 727; Richard G. Wilkins, "Defining The 'Reasonable Expectation Of Privacy': An Emerging Tripartite Analysis," *Vanderbilt Law Review* 40 (1987): 1077, 1108; Sherry F. Colb, "What Is A Search? Two Conceptual Flaws in Fourth Amendment Doctrine And Some Hints Of A Remedy," *Stanford Law Review* 55 (2002): 119, 122; Silas Wasserstom & Louis Michael Seidman, "The Fourth Amendment as Constitutional Theory," *Georgetown Law Journal* 77 (1988): 19.

10. Anthony G. Amsterdam, "Perspectives on the Fourth Amendment," *Minnesota Law Review* 58 (1974): 349, 383.

11. Orin S. Kerr, "The Fourth Amendment and New Technologies: Constitutional Myths and the Case for Caution," *Michigan Law Review* 102 (2004): 801, 808.

12. Charles H. Whitebread & Christopher Slobogin, *Criminal Procedure: An Analysis of Cases and Concepts* 3 (1993), 116.

13. Further, what is considered a reasonable expectation is in constant flux due to technological changes. Thus, as the use of the Internet for personal communications grew, the Electronic Communications Privacy Act of 1986 failed protect stored private e-mails because it was passed in a time when most e-mails were related to business records, which are expected to be afforded a lesser degree of privacy. See Deirdre L. Mulligan, "Reasonable Expectations in Electronic Communications: A Critical Perspective on the Electronic Communications Privacy Act," *George Washington Law Review* 72 (2004) 1557.

14. Christopher Slobogin & Joseph E. Schumacher, "Reasonable Expectations of Privacy and Autonomy in Fourth Amendment Cases: An Empirical Look at Understandings Recognized and Permitted by Society," *Duke Law Journal* 42 (1993): 727, 732 ("A sense of how (innocent) US citizens gauge the impact of police investigative techniques on their privacy and autonomy is highly relevant to current Fourth Amendment jurisprudence. This Article describes an effort to obtain some preliminary data in this regard").

15. Robert M. Bloom, *Searches, Seizures, and Warrants* 46 (2003) ("Because there is no straightforward answer to this question, 'reasonable' has largely come to mean what a majority of the Supreme Court Justices say is reasonable").

16. Jim Harper, Reforming Fourth Amendment Privacy Doctrines, *American University Law Review* 57 (2008): 1381, 1382. See also Jeffrey Rosen, *The Unwanted Gaze: The Destructive Privacy in America* 60 (2001) (" Harlan's test was applauded as a victory for privacy, but it soon became clear that it was

entirely circular,"); Michael Abramowics, "Constitutional Cicularity," *UCLA Law Review* 49: 1, 60–61 (" Fourth Amendment doctrine, moreover, is circular, for someone can have a reasonable expectation of privacy in an area if and only if the Court has held that a search in that area would be unreasonable").

17. Cloud, *Symposium: Rube Goldberg Meets the Constitution: The Supreme Court, Technology and the Fourth Amendment*.

18. *Kyllo v. United States*, 533 U.S. 27, 31 (2001) (quoting Silverman v. United States, 365 U.S.) 505, 511 (1961).

19. *Payton v. New York*, 445 U.S. 573, 591–98 (1980).

20. *Dow. Chem. Co. v. United States*, 749 F.2d 307, 314 (6th Cir. 1984), *aff'd*, 476 U.S. 227 (1986).

21. Catharine A. MacKinnon, "Reflections on Sex Equality Under Law," *Yale Law Journal* 100 (1991): 1281–1311.

22. Linda C. McClain, Inviolability and Privacy: The Castle, the Sanctuary, and the Body," *Yale Law Journal & Human* 7 (1995): 195–209.

23. Amitai Etzioni, "The Bankruptcy of Liberalism and Conservatism," *Political Science Quarterly* 128 (2013): 39.

24. Christopher Slobogin, "Public Privacy: Camera Surveillance of Public Places and The Right to Anonymity," *Mississippi Law Journal* 72 (2002), 213.

    Also: Scott E. Sundby, "Everyman's Fourth Amendment: Privacy or Mutual Trust between Government and Citizen?" *Columbia Law Review* 94 (October, 1994):1751, 1758–9, Bethany L. Dickman, Untying Knotts: "The Application of Mosaic Theory to GPS Surveillance in United States v. Maryland," American University Law Review 60 (2011): 731.

25. Marc Jonathan Blitz, "Stanley in Cyberspace: Why the Privacy Protection of the First Amendment Should Be More Like That of the Fourth," *Hastings Law Journal* 62 (2010): 357.

26. Christopher Slobogin, "Public Privacy: Camera Surveillance of Public Places and The Right to Anonymity," *Mississippi Law Journal* 72 (2002), 256.

27. Ibid., 257.

28. I discuss below the question of whether information that reveals that one is committing a crime deserves extra protection. See infra, Part II.A.

29. Amitai Etzioni, "Community," *Encyclopedia of Political Thought, First Edition* eds. Michael Gibbons, (John Wiley & Sons, Ltd., 2015).

30. Ibid.

31. US Constitution, Amendment XIV.

32. Mary Ferrell Foundation, *Post-Watergate Intelligence Investigations*, http://www.maryferrell.org/wiki/index.php/Post-Watergate_Intelligence_ Investigations.

33. Mary Ferrell Foundation, *Post-Watergate Intelligence Investigations*, http://www.maryferrell.org/wiki/index.php/Post-Watergate_Intelligence_ Investigations.

34. Thomas B. Hunter, "The Challenges of Intelligence Sharing," *Operational Studies* (December 2004): 3.

35. For a critical analysis of the "Information Sharing Paradigm" that has arisen in law enforcement and intelligence community since 9/11, see Peter P. Swire, "Privacy and Information Sharing in the War on Terrorism," *Villanova Law Review* 51 (2006): 260.

36. Alexander Aleinikoff, writing in 1987, argued that the courts had entered the "age of balancing," "Balancing has been a vehicle primarily for weakening earlier categorical doctrines restricting governmental power to search and seize," T. Alexander Aleinikoff, "Constitutional Law in the Age of Balancing," *Yale Law Journal* 96 (1987): 943, 965. Many civil libertarians have argued that post-9/11, Fourth Amendment rights are being systematically eroded in the name of national security. See Jay Stanley, "Reviving the Fourth Amendment and American Privacy," ACLU (May 28, 2010), http://www.aclu.org/blog/national-security-technology-and-liberty/reviving-fourth-amendment-and-american-privacy. *See also* Orin S. Kerr, "An Equilibrium-Adjustment Theory of the Fourth Amendment," *Harvard Law Review* 125 (2011): 476, 478 ("[t]he theory of equilibrium-adjustment posits that the Supreme Court adjusts the scope of Fourth Amendment protection in response to new facts in order to restore the status quo level of protection. When changing technology or social practice expands government power, the Supreme Court tightens Fourth Amendment protection; when it threatens government power, the Supreme Court loosens constitutional protection).
37. Amitai Etzioni, *The Limits of Privacy* (New York: Basic Books, 1999), 5.
38. Jack Nicas, "TSA to Halt Revealing Body Scans at Airports," *Wall Street Journal* (January 18, 2013).
39. "This point is virtually identical to the demand that courts make of government legislation when they are applying heightened scrutiny—that is, strict or intermediate scrutiny—in First Amendment or Equal Protection Clause cases. The court has also hinted at such a proportionality of means requirement, albeit much less clearly, in its Fourth Amendment 'special needs' cases," Marc Blitz, Professor of Law, Oklahoma City University School of Law, (January 17, 2014).
40. "ABA Standards for Criminal Justice, 3rd Edition: Law Enforcement Access to Third Party Records Standards" *American Bar Association* (2013), http://www.americanbar.org/content/dam/aba/publications/criminal_justice_standards/third_party_access.authcheckdam.pdf.
41. Shaun Spencer raises concerns around legislating privacy protections. See note 9 ("Given the powerful influence of various lobbies opposed to strong privacy protection, that role may best be described as a sine qua non. That is, unless the public has a strong desire for privacy in a particular area, attempts to pass legislation establishing that area as a private sphere are doomed to fail . . . To the extent that legislatures base privacy legislation on social values and norms, they necessarily rely on the same changing expectations as the judicial conception of privacy").
42. Amitai Etzioni, *From Empire to Community: A New Approach to International Relations* (2004), 67–71.
43. "Offenses Cleared," *Uniform Crime Report: Crime in the United States 2011*, Federal Bureau of Investigation (October 2012).
44. *Smith v. Maryland*, 442 US 735, 745 (1979).
45. *United States v. Miller*, 425 US 435 (1976).
46. *Couch v. United States*, 409 US 322 (1973).
47. *Zurcher v. Stanford Daily*, 436 US 547 (1978).
48. *Fisher v. United States*, 425 US 391 (1976).

49. The preceding examples are laid out in Swire. See note 2 at 908–09.
50. Privacy Act of 1974, *as amended*, Federal Trade Commission, http://www. ftc.gov/foia/privacy_act.shtm (accessed April 7, 2013).
51. The Right to Financial Privacy Act of 1978, 12 U.S.C. §§ 3401–3402 (West 2011).
52. Summary of the HIPAA Privacy Rule, Department of Health and Human Services, http://www.hhs.gov/ocr/privacy/hipaa/understanding/summary (last visited March 4, 2014).
53. The Video Privacy Protection Act of 1988, 18 U.S.C. § 2710 (West 2013).
54. Gina Stevens, Congressional Research Services, R41756, Privacy Protections for Personal Information Online (2011).
55. Ibid., 24.
56. Information voluntarily handed over to another party does not receive Fourth Amendment protection "even if the information is revealed on the assumption that it will be used only for a limited purpose and the confidence placed in the third party will not be betrayed," *United States v. Miller*, 425 US 435, 443 (1976); *see also* Orin Kerr, "The Case for the Third Party Doctrine," *Michigan Law Review* 107 (2009): 561, 569–70. Earlier cases that built up this doctrine include *Couch v. United States* 409 US 322 (1973); *Lee v. United States* 343 US 747 (1952).
57. Matthew D. Lawless, "The Third Party Doctrine Redux: Internet Search Records and the Case for a "Crazy Quilt" of Fourth Amendment Protection," *UCLA Journal Law & Technology* 2 (2007): 1.
58. Orin Kerr and Greg Nojeim, "The Data Question: Should the Third-Party Records Doctrine Be Revisited?" *ABA Journal* (August 1, 2012), http://www. abajournal.com/magazine/article/the_data_question_should_the_third-party_records_doctrine_be_revisited.
59. Matthew Tokson, "Automation and the Fourth Amendment," *Iowa Law Review* 96 (2011) 581, 586.
60. Daniel Cooper, "Consent in EU Data Protection Law," *European Privacy Association* http://www.europeanprivacyassociation.eu/public/download/ EPA%20Editorial_%20Consent%20in%20EU%20Data%20Protection%20 Law.pdf (accessed April 7, 2013).
61. "Why do we need an EU data protection reform?" *European Commission* http://ec.europa.eu/justice/data-protection/document/review2012/fact-sheets/1_en.pdf (accessed April 7, 2013).
62. Erica Newland, "CDT Comments on EU Data Protection Directive," *Center for Democracy and Technology*, (January 20, 2011), https://www.cdt.org/ blogs/erica-newland/cdt-comments-eu-data-protection-directive.
63. "Data protection reform: Frequently asked questions," *Europa* (January 25, 2012), http://europa.eu/rapid/press-release_MEMO-12-41_en.htm?locale=fr.
64. In the wake of *Jones*, Professor Susan Freiwald identified four factors that the courts use to extend Fourth Amendment protection to new surveillance technologies that "make sense," These include whether the target is unaware of the surveillance; it covers items that the people consider private; it is continuous; and it is indiscriminate (covers more information than is necessary for establishing guilt). Susan Freiwald, "The Four Factor Test," *The Selected Works of Susan Freiwald*, http://works.bepress.com/ susan_freiwald/11.

65. People often trust assurances that their sensitive information (names and social security number) can be deleted when their data is collected in large databases. In fact, scientists have shown that individuals can be easily "deanonymized." Paul Ohm writes that this misunderstanding has given the public a false sense of security and has led to inadequate privacy protections, laws and regulations. See Paul Ohm, "Broken Promises of Privacy: Responding to the Surprising Failure of Anonymization," *UCLA Law Review* 57 (2010): 1701. See also Marcia Stepanek, "Weblining," *Business Week* (April 3, 2000), http://www.businessweek.com/2000/00_14/b3675027.htm; Jennifer Golbeck, Christina Robles & Karen Turner, "Predicting Personality with Social Media," *CHI Extended Abstracts* (2011): 253–262.

66. Marcy Peek, "Passing Beyond Identity on the Internet: Espionage and Counterespionage in the Internet Age," *Vermont Law Review* 28 (2003): 91, 94 (evaluating ways to resist discriminatory marketing in cyberspace); Marcia Stepanek, "Weblining," *Business Week*, (April 3, 2000), http://www.businessweek.com/2000/00_14/b3675027.htm ([a] data broker company Acxiom matches names against housing, education, and incomes in order to identify the unpublicized ethnicity of an individual or group.); Nicholas Carr, "Tracking Is an Assault on Liberty, With Real Dangers," *Wall Street Journal* (August 7–8, 2010): W1 ("[i]t used to be . . . you had to get a warrant to monitor a person or a group of people. Today, it is increasingly easy to monitor ideas,"); Etzioni. See note 1 at 929, 948–50.

67. "How Target Figured Out A Teen Girl Was Pregnant Before Her Father Did," *Forbes* (February 16, 2012), http://www.forbes.com/sites/kashmirhill/2012/02/16/how-target-figured-out-a-teen-girl-was-pregnant-before-her-father-did.

68. Christopher Slobogin, "Government Data Mining and the Fourth Amendment," *University of Chicago Law Review* 75 (2008): 317, 320.

69. For further discussion on these matters, see Amitai Etzioni, *The Privacy Merchants: What Is To Be Done?*, 14 Penn. J. Const. L. 929 (March 2012); Amitai Etzioni, *The Bankruptcy of Liberalism and Conservatism*, 128 PSQ 39 (2013) (discussing the collapse of the public-private divide).

70. Ibid.

71. Kerr sees a greater role here for Congress, while Swire for the courts. See note 2 at 904, 912 and note 11. This chapter is unable to add to these deliberations other than to recognize that both are needed and neither seems able to keep up with changing technologies.

72. Siobhan Gorman, "NSA's Domestic Spying Grows as Agency Sweeps up Data," *The Wall Street Journal* (March 10, 2008).

73. Peter P. Swire, "A Reasonableness Approach to Searches After the Jones GPS Tracking Case," *Stanford Law Review Online* 64 (2012): 57.

74. Gary T. Marx, "Ethics for the New Surveillance", *The Information Society: An International Journal* 14 (1998): 171, 178.

75. Erica Goode and Sheryl Gay Stolberg, "Legal Curbs Said to Hamper A.T.F. in Gun Inquiries," *The New York Times* (December 25, 2012).

76. Tamara Keith, "How Congress Quietly Overhauled Its Insider-Trading Law," *NPR* (April 16, 2013), http://m.npr.org/news/Politics/177496734.

77. See note 37.

78. Anna C. Henning, Congressional Research Service, R40077, Compulsory DNA Collection: A Fourth Amendment Analysis 2 (2010) (quoting *United States v. Kincade*, 379 F.3d 813, 818 (9th Cir. 2004) (en banc).
79. Ibid., 13.
80. See note 38.
81. Cynthia Dwork, *Differential Privacy: A Survey of Results*, in M. Agrawal et al., eds. TAMC, LNCS 4978, (2008): 1–19 ([r]oughly speaking, differential privacy ensures that the removal or addition of a single database item does not (substantially) affect the outcome of any analysis. It follows that no risk is incurred by joining the database, providing a mathematically rigorous means of coping with the fact that distributional information may be disclosive").

5

The Privacy Merchants

Rights have been long understood, first and foremost, as protection of the private from the public, the individual from the state. True, we also recognize positive rights (such as socioeconomic rights) and the government's duty to protect citizens from violations of rights by other actors besides the state. However, when violations of privacy are discussed, the first violator that typically comes to mind is "Big Brother"—that is, the state.[1]

This chapter focuses on the growing threat to privacy from private actors, specifically profit-making corporations. It briefly outlines a range of options aimed at protecting individual privacy against encroachment by private actors—and evaluates them within the prevailing normative, legal, and political context in the United States.

I. Corporate Surveillance, Tracking, Data Mining, and Profiling

Most informed citizens probably know by now that corporations collect information about them, but they may well be unaware of the extent and scope of the invasions of privacy that are now widespread. Many may be aware of tracking tools referred to as "cookies," which are installed on one's computer by visited websites. Cookies are used to identify the person and to remember his or her preferences. Some people learned to protect themselves from such tracking by employing software that allows one to clear cookies from one's computer. However, corporations have recently begun to install "supercookies" that are very difficult to detect, and if removed, secretly reinstall themselves.[2] As one report concluded: "This means that privacy-sensitive consumers who 'toss' their HTTP cookies to prevent tracking or remain anonymous are still being uniquely identified online by advertising companies."[3]

Major cell phone and mobile technology companies offer services that allow lovers, ex-spouses, lawyers, or anyone else to find out where a person is—and track their movements—by using the GPS capabilities of their cell phone.[4] A German politician who inquired about location storage information discovered that over a six-month period, his longitude and latitude had been recorded over 35,000 times.[5]

There are two kinds of corporations that keep track of what Internet users buy, read, visit, drink, and who they call, email, date, and much else. Some merely track users' activity on their site as part of their regular business; recording purchases and viewed products helps them increase sales. This is true for nearly every major online retailer. Other corporations make shadowing Internet users—and keeping very detailed dossiers on them—their main line of business. One can call these the "privacy merchants." They sell information to whoever pays the required price. In 2005, one such company—Choicepoint—had records on over 220 million people.[6] Professor Christopher Slobogin notes that the amount of information culled by corporate data miners

> can provide the inquirer with a wide array of data about any of us, including basic demographic information, income, net worth, real [sic] property holdings, social security number, current and previous addresses, phone numbers and fax numbers, names of neighbors, driver records, license plate and VIN numbers, bankruptcy and debtor filings, employment, business and criminal records, bank account balances and activity, stock purchases, and credit card activity.[7]

In 2009, a law professor at Fordham University gained minor notoriety when he gave his class an assignment to create a dossier on Justice Antonin Scalia using only the information they could find online—resulting in a 15-page file "that included the justice's home address and home phone number, his wife's personal e-mail address and the TV shows and food he prefers."[8] Some privacy merchants even keep dossiers on a person's marital status, political leanings, as well as interests in topics including religion, the Bible, gambling, and adult entertainment.[9]

Although several data mining companies allow individuals to opt out of their databases, each separate company must be contacted individually, and even then information may still linger in some search results or web sites: Google, for example, generally does not remove search results if the information contained is truthful and not illegal.[10]

Privacy merchants are limited by laws Congress (and states) have enacted that carve out subsets of data that they cannot freely trade in, especially medical and financial records. So far though, very little attention has been paid to the fact that information is fungible. Through a process that might be called "privacy violating triangulation" (PVT), one can readily derive much about a person's medical, financial, or other protected private information by using "innocent facts" not privileged by law. A piece of seemingly benign information—for instance, the number of days a person failed to show up for work, or if the person made special purchases, such as a wig—suggests volumes about one's medical condition. By building a portfolio of many such apparently innocuous facts, one could infer a great deal, effectively violating the realm of privacy surrounding individuals' most sensitive information. Thus, a study of Facebook shows "how the on-line social network data could be used to predict some individual private trait that a user is not willing to disclose (e.g. political or religious affiliation)."[11] This will be discussed in further detail below.

Some individuals may think that they can protect themselves from tracking and dossiers by using pseudonyms and multiple "mailboxes." However, some companies have developed software to match pseudonyms used on message boards and blogs with real names and personal email addresses.[12] The subjects of this tracking, who are unaware that their anonymity has been stripped, include people who use online pseudonyms to discuss sensitive topics like mental illness.[13] As Eli Pariser reports, "Search for a word like 'depression' on Dictionary.com, and the site installs up to 223 tracking cookies and beacons on your computer so that other websites can target you with antidepressants."[14] It should be noted that the privacy of medical records is protected by law, but not "visits" to medical web sites or chat groups.

Many companies claim that they do not collect names or that they disassociate names from dossiers. However, some companies keep a database of names on file. One such company, RapLeaf, states that it does not share its subjects' names with advertisers; but an investigation found that it does link those names to "extraordinarily intimate databases . . . by tapping voter-registration files, shopping histories, social-networking activities and real estate records."[15] And although the company indeed refrains from specifically sharing *names* with its clients, it did share personally identifiable information with them, such as unique Facebook account numbers that can be traced back to the account holder's name.[16]

Privacy advocates have sharply objected to the government's use of deep packet inspection (DPI)—a powerful tool used to analyze the contents of communications transmitted over the Internet—in large part because it is much more intrusive than merely tracking who is communicating with whom. (The difference is akin to reading letters versus examining the outside of an envelope to see who sent the letter and to whom it is addressed.) Now private companies are offering to perform DPI for Internet service providers to facilitate targeted advertising.[17]

In 2010, Facebook became the most visited website in the United States,[18] nearing 700 million users in June 2011.[19] Facebook users put great amounts of personal information on their individual profiles, including their religious and political views, educational and professional background, interests, as well as photos and videos of themselves. Most important, unlike most other websites where individuals employ usernames or pseudonyms, Facebook is designed for people to use their real names. This makes it vastly more valuable to data miners who seek to gather personally identifiable information in order to assemble dossiers on the individuals. Furthermore, each individual's profile is linked to the profiles of their "friends," who may have different privacy settings allowing for broader access to shared data, such as photographs or group membership, than the individual chooses to exhibit on his or her own profile.

Facebook provides customizable privacy tools and some privacy protection, but it has faced consistent criticism that those protections are difficult to manipulate.[20] As Facebook has introduced third-party applications such as games to its site, it has faced mounting difficulties in keeping its end of the bargain.

In a July 2010 letter to Representative John Conyers of the US House Judiciary Committee, a Facebook official stated, "The question posed in your letter asks whether Facebook shares users' personal information with third parties without the knowledge of users... The answer is simple and straight-forward: we do not. We have designed our system and policies so that user information is never shared without our users' knowledge."[21] It was a few months later, in October 2010, that the *Wall Street Journal* broke the story of extensive user privacy breaches by Facebook.[22] It discovered that popular Facebook applications were "providing access to people's names and, in some cases, their friends' names" to Internet tracking companies.[23] According to the *Journal*, the breach affected "tens of millions" of users, including those who were vigilant in setting their privacy protections, and was in violation of Facebook's stated policies.[24] In the same month, the *New York Times* reported on two studies that found that "in certain circumstances, advertisers—or snoops posing as advertisers [on Facebook]—may be able to learn sensitive profile information, like a person's sexual orientation or religion, even if the person is sharing that information only with a small circle of friends."[25]

In addition, the nearly ubiquitous Facebook "Like" and Twitter "Tweet" buttons on websites "notify Facebook and Twitter that a person visited those sites even when users don't click on the buttons."[26] These widgets have been added to millions of web pages and they appear on more than one-third of the world's top one thousand websites, allowing sites with those widgets to track specific Facebook users.[27] The tracking, which is used for targeted advertising, continues until the user specifically logs out of their account, even if the user turns off their computer.[28]

One may argue that the private sector merely uses this information for commercial purposes, while the government may use it to jail people, suppress free speech, and otherwise violate their rights. However, one must note that the violation of privacy by private agents has some similar effects to violations committed by government agents, effects that lead to discrimination and "chilling" of expression and dissent. Thus, when gay people who seek to keep their sexual orientation private are "outed" by the media, or banks call in loans of those they find out have cancer, or employers refuse to hire people because they learn about their political or religious views, privacy is violated in a manner about as consequential as if the same violations had been carried out by a government agency.

II. Privacy Merchants in the Service of Big Brother

Even if one disregards the facts already cited, showing that corporate violations of privacy are far-reaching and chilling, one must note that the information corporations amass is available to the government. Laws prevent the government from ordering a private company to conduct surveillance on innocent citizens not suspected of anything, or from generating dossiers that the government itself is banned from generating. In other words, when corporations act as government agents, they may be subject to the same or similar limitations the government must abide by. However, the government can and does use data already amassed by privacy merchants for their own sake. Nor do prevailing laws prevent private corporations from analyzing online activity with an eye towards the government's needs and shaping their privacy-violating data in ways to make them more attractive to government purchasers of their services. Indeed, because the government is such a large and reliable client, corporate data banks have a strong financial interest in anticipating its needs. The thesis that what is private does not stay private is far from hypothetical. As Professor Chris Hoofnagle notes, even though Congress limited the executive branch's amassing of personal information in the 1974 Privacy Act, "those protections have failed to meet Congress' intent because the private sector has done what the government has been prohibited from doing."[29]

According to Professor Daniel Solove, "for quite some time, the government has been increasingly contracting with businesses to acquire databases of personal information. Database firms are willing to supply the information and the government is willing to pay for it."[30] Solove points out that the government can "find out details about people's race, income, opinions, political beliefs, health, lifestyle, and purchasing habits from the database companies that keep extensive personal information on millions of Americans."[31]

Hoofnagle similarly warns that "private sector commercial data brokers have built massive data centers with personal information custom-tailored to law enforcement agents."[32] ChoicePoint, a major privacy merchant, has at least thirty-five contracts with government agencies, including the Department of Justice (through which it provides its databases to the FBI), as well as the DEA, the IRS, and the Bureau of Citizenship and Immigration Services.[33]

Another corporate data miner, Florida-based SeisInt, ran a massive database called MATRIX (Multi-State Anti-Terrorism Information Exchange), in a joint effort among several US states to coordinate counterterrorism efforts.[34] The federal government paid $12 million to support the program, which SeisInt developed with extensive amounts of data, including individuals' "criminal histories, photographs, property ownership, SSNs, addresses, bankruptcies, family members, and credit information."[35] Even before the 9/11 attacks, the US Marshals Service alone performed up to forty thousand searches every month using private data banks.[36] The exact number of contracts the government has made with corporate data miners is unknown, because many of the contracts are classified.[37] However, one 2006 government study found that at least fifty-two federal agencies had launched—or were planning to launch at the time of the study—at least 199 data-mining projects that rely on the services and technology of commercial data banks.[38]

Other government tracking and surveillance efforts have relied on private corporations. In 2006, it was disclosed that three major telecommunications providers, AT&T, Verizon, and BellSouth, had cooperated with the NSA to provide it with the phone call records of "tens of millions of Americans"—a program which, according to one source, was "the largest database ever assembled in the world."[39] The companies which agreed to work with the NSA provide phone service to over two hundred million Americans, leading the program significantly closer to its ultimate goal: creating a database of every phone call made within the United States.[40] Other government projects relying on private sources include efforts by Homeland Security to secure air travel and the nation's borders and a Pentagon program which collects data on teenagers to better target military recruitment efforts.[41]

Moreover, the trend is to extend this use, as evidenced by a 2011 FBI manual that enables agents to search for private citizens in commercial databases without prior authorization or even notification.[42] In 2011, Google revealed that the US government made the most requests for Internet users' private data in 2010, with Google complying with 94 percent of these orders.[43]

One may well hold that some of the usages of private data banks by the government serve legitimate purposes, even if they are loaded with extensive dossiers on most adult Americans, rather than just those for whom there is some evidence or reason to suspect that they are violating the law. However, one must still note that from here on, whether such data banks are in the FBI headquarters or in some corporate office matters little. At most, they are just a click—and a payment—away.

The next segment of this article outlines differing approaches to the protection of privacy in the new world in which the traditional distinction between public and private realms, on which many normative and legal conceptions build, in particular those that concern privacy, are much less important and are becoming still less significant. The new amalgamated social world calls for cross-realm or holistic modes of deliberations and policymaking.

III. The Main Alternatives

The following deliberations draw on my sociological training and normative considerations and not on any legal preparation. I merely chart the "big picture" because, as will become clear shortly, most if not all the alternatives are facing major hurdles. It therefore seems premature to spell out any of the alternative approaches before strategies and political forces are developed that will make it possible to overcome these hurdles. The alternatives are evaluated not on the basis of what would best protect privacy from privacy merchants, but which measures might be taken in the prevailing context in the United States.

1. Change the Norm: A World without Privacy?

One major response to privacy merchants' expanding reach has been well encapsulated by the CEO of Sun Microsystems, Scott McNealy, who stated, "You have zero privacy . . . Get over it."[44] Facebook's founder, Mark Zuckerberg, argues that social norms undergirding privacy law are obsolete.[45] That is, instead of finding new ways to protect individuals from corporations, individuals should learn to accept changed—in effect, much lower—levels of privacy. He elaborated, "People have really gotten comfortable not only sharing more information and different kinds, but more openly and with more people . . . That social norm is just something that has evolved over time."[46] Zuckerberg continued: "We view it as our role in the system to constantly be innovating and be updating what our system is to reflect what the current social norms are."[47] He thus implies that the privacy erchants are not undermining the norm, but merely accommodating their wares to already in-place changes in norms.

As I see it, it is true that the privacy norms are eroding due to other factors than the corporate drive to use private information for profit making, as one sees with people going on talk shows to reveal much about themselves, a form of exhibitionism. However, there can be little doubt that corporations, especially the new social media, led by Facebook, are aiding, abetting, and seeking to legitimate the erosion of privacy.

The *Wall Street Journal* editorial page, which reflects that publication's philosophy, argues that the change in norms indicates that the introduction of new laws or regulations to better protect privacy is not called for.[48] L. Gordon Crovitz pointed out that, as of March 2011, more than half of Americans over age twelve have Facebook accounts.[49] He proceeded to ask: "If most Americans are happy to have Facebook accounts, knowingly trading personal information for other benefits, why is Washington so focused on new privacy laws? There is little evidence that people want new rules."[50]

Furthermore, Crovitz argues, consumers value the benefits of information gathering, including better-targeted ads, specific recommendations for customers, and huge troves of data for research, such as in Google Flu Trends, which tracks search terms about illnesses to assist epidemiologists. "People are increasingly at ease with sharing personal data in exchange for other benefits," he argues.[51]

However, some public opinion polls, including recent ones, show that the American people care a great deal about their privacy. Others show that various segments of the public vary in the way they feel about this right. For example, according to a 2009 survey, 73 to 86 percent of Americans object to the tracking methods used to personalize their advertisements.[52] Furthermore, the study found that 82 percent of young people—who are generally believed to be apathetic about privacy—had at some point refused to provide information to a company because it was too personal.[53] Eighty-six percent of Americans—84 percent among respondents aged eighteen to twenty-four—felt that their permission should be sought before pictures of them were posted online.[54]

Other data reveal a more varied picture. In a 1995 survey, Alan Westin divided the public into three "camps" with regard to privacy concerns.[55] About 25 percent of respondents were "Privacy Fundamentalists," who value privacy especially highly; 55 percent were "Privacy Pragmatists," who adjust their expectations based on the relative value of information types and trust in specific companies; and 20 percent were "Privacy Unconcerned," who have no problem with giving out personal information.[56]

A 2002 study found that while 70 percent of consumers were concerned about their privacy, 82 percent were willing to give out personal information in exchange for the chance to win a hundred dollars in a sweepstakes.[57] The rise in popularity of location-tracking social networking sites such as Foursquare, Facebook Places, and Gowalla, which offer discounts to users who log visits to various businesses and restaurants, suggests that people are indeed willing to trade information once considered private (their locations and consumption habits) for certain benefits. According to one survey, the coupon reward systems on these sites were the main incentive for users to join.[58]

One must take into account though that it is very likely that those who have relatively little concern about privacy are unaware that their less sensitive information can be used for PVT. Furthermore, privacy is a right, not subject to majority rule. Even if only a minority cherishes it, it is still a birthright of all Americans.

2. The Self-Regulation Option

The prevailing system in the United States—and the *de facto* prevailing system in the EU—relies to a significant extent on self-regulation and individual choice. That is, the assumption is that consumers will choose the services and products of those corporations that protect privacy at the level the consumers seek, that users can set their privacy controls to the level they prefer, and that, as a result, corporations that provide less privacy protection than the public seeks will lose business and be incentivized to enhance their privacy protection. Additionally, some scholars have argued that marketing in this vein is protected as free speech under the First Amendment, an argument not addressed in this paper.[59] These ideas are founded on the standard libertarian argument, as noted by Susanna Kim Ripken: "Respect for individual autonomy, responsibility, and decision-making is deeply entrenched in our culture and law. We believe that people can order their own economic affairs and, given sufficient information, can make their own personal assessments of the risks and benefits of transactions."[60]

None of these assumptions withstand sociological scrutiny. The thesis that consumers are rational actors who make decisions in their best interests, in line with their personal preferences and available information, has been disproven beyond reasonable doubt by the studies of behavioral economists.[61] For this very reason, transparency does not work. That is, the suggestion that if corporations simply declare what their privacy standards are, consumers could choose those that suit them, is erroneous if not misleading. The statements are written in legalese, in terms few can penetrate, and the privacy settings provided are complex, cumbersome, and frequently revised after the users have posted information on the site, which they cannot erase.

Furthermore, without regulation, there is no assurance that corporations will adhere to their privacy declarations, at least to their implied promise.[62] This does not refer necessarily to outright false statements, but to carefully crafted yet misleading commitments to privacy that end up entrapping the consumer. For instance, after public outcry over the iPhone's hidden location tracking, Apple released a statement denying that they tracked users' locations, claiming that they instead maintained "a database of WiFi hot spots and cell phone towers around your current location."[63] As Mark Rotenberg of the Electronic Privacy Information Center (EPIC) pointed out, this database is precisely how the company tracks locations, even if it is not tracking the device itself.[64] A study by DoubleVerify surveyed five billion advertisements and found that an icon explaining the privacy policy was clicked on only 0.002 percent of the time. Even then, after users reviewed the advertisers' information practices, only 1 percent opted out of the targeted advertising.[65] "That's an opt-out rate of just 0.00002 percent," Crovitz notes,[66] concluding that "people seem to have adjusted to this new technology faster than regulators are willing to admit."[67] Crovitz argues that the fact that few consumers read these statements shows they do not care; in actuality, data already cited strongly suggests that they do not use them because they find them impenetrable.[68] Another national survey found that 57 percent of adult Americans were under the false impression that if a website merely had a privacy policy, then it would not share their information with other companies.[69] Moreover, individuals cannot protect themselves from corporations that employ covert tools such as Flash cookies, supercookies, and widgets.

Large corporations, which do business in all fifty states as well as overseas, find it in their interest to promote regulation that would provide some modicum of privacy. This is the case because such corporations incur considerable costs when they have to adjust their way of doing business to different state laws, and deal differently in various segments of the market, some of which are more regulated than others under the current patchwork of privacy laws.

Hence some large corporations once opposed to legislation now favor a federal omnibus privacy law that would simplify the patchwork of federal sector-specific laws and preempt state specific statutes. A Microsoft white paper from 2005 advised, "Federal privacy legislation should pre-empt state laws that impose requirements for the collection, use, disclosure, and storage of personal information."[70] Such a law would likely set standards and ceilings (for instance, caps on damages for privacy violations), which states could not exceed. State laws demanding higher privacy standards than a federally mandated norm would be invalidated, or at least weakened significantly. Indeed, it seems they would accept only legislation that included preemption. Former CEO of eBay Meg Whitman explicitly testified before Congress, "Legislation without preemption would make the current situation possibly worse, not better, by creating additional uncertainty and compliance burdens."[71]

The ideal legislation, for Microsoft and similar entities, would provide "baseline privacy protection" over which companies would be encouraged to "compete on the basis of more robust privacy practices"[72] to essentially regulate themselves. According to Microsoft Deputy General Counsel Erich Anderson's testimony before Congress, a federal law should be crafted only as "an effective complement to" self-regulation.[73]

State and sectoral laws have already addressed a number of privacy issues (e.g. setting limits on tracking consumers for targeted advertising[74]) while Congress has been largely inactive in this area.[75] Hence, following a course of self-regulation would in effect reduce privacy standards in those states that lifted them and may prevent them from adding protections in the future.[76] Moreover, the corporate proposal does involve some federal legislation rather than merely relying on self-regulation. Indeed, it seems impossible to restrain the privacy merchants without calling in Big Brother.

3. Consent for Secondary Use: Opt in Rather than Out?

A rather different approach holds that individuals who release information about themselves for a specific purpose or transaction, for example to purchase a book from Amazon, would be understood to still "own" this information, and that Amazon could use it for other purposes or sell that information to other parties only with the explicit consent of the consumer, rather than on the basis of a privacy statement on its web pages or presumed consent. The same idea is referred to in other words, namely that consumers would have to opt in to grant secondary and additional use of private information rather than opt out.[77] In American discourse, the term "owned" is used because information is treated as property and private information as private property. In Europe the same idea is embraced, but privacy is treated more as an individual right—as part of one's personhood—which is violated when one's private sphere is violated.

In 1995, in an effort to establish minimum protections for Internet user privacy and establish a baseline consistency among the data protection laws of EU member states, the European Council issued what is commonly called the "Data Protection Directive." The directive, which scholars have called "aggressive"[78] and "extraordinarily comprehensive,"[79] took effect in October 1998. Based on a legal tradition that "expressly recognizes the fundamental right to the protection of personal data,"[80] the directive is credited with having established the most influential and prominent data protections in the world to date.[81] However, it has proven difficult to ensure compliance in those countries governed by the directive. Although the law set out ambitious goals for the standardization of privacy protection in Europe, it has been hampered from the start by significant gaps in member states' compliance and enforcement. According to one observer, "Although the EU Data Privacy Directive has been approved by the EU itself, it is not self-implementing. Before taking effect in individual nations, each of the fifteen EU member countries must pass its own implementing legislation. As of the effective date, only five had done so."[82]

The directive requires that personal data be processed "only with the consent of the data subject,"[83] with limited exceptions carved out for national security, law enforcement, and some basic state functions such as taxation.[84] The intentionally broad language of the directive includes—but is not limited to—such actions as collecting, storing, recording, adapting, retrieving, and erasing data,[85] and "data" itself is defined broadly enough to include not just text, but also photographs, video, and sound.[86] Its restrictions recognize that certain kinds of data are particularly sensitive and vulnerable to abuse. Thus, it contains heightened restrictions on the processing of data which would reveal the subject's personal traits, such as race, ethnicity, religious beliefs, or health background. In most cases, collecting and passing on these kinds of information require the subject's written consent, or they cannot be processed.[87]

The law also requires a degree of transparency: data processors must disclose to subjects of processing the ways in which they intend to use the data.[88] Finally, in one of the directive's most restrictive and controversial portions, the drafters attempted to address the "borderless" nature of the Internet and the likelihood that user data could be processed in or transmitted to countries not subject to the law's protections. To protect against this vulnerability, the directive contains a provision requiring member states to prohibit the transfer of data to other countries that have not adopted an "adequate level of protection" for personal data.[89] However, as we have seen, implementing these protections has proven difficult, and enforcement across Europe has proven inconsistent at best.

According to a 2011 report from the Center for Democracy and Technology, "although it is comprehensive in many ways, the [European] Data Protection Directive has significant weaknesses. Erratic enforcement and uneven implementation have left consumers and industry confused as to how the Directive's principles apply to emerging practices."[90] In 2011, various EU authorities called for new, stronger privacy protection measures, especially in response to Facebook; however, so far those have not been translated into new laws or regulations, not to mention enforcement.

Limiting the involuntary secondary use of private information is much more popular in Europe than in the United States, as evidenced by the directives enacted relatively early in the Internet's lifespan, while a comprehensive American approach has yet to be articulated. However, the differences between the American and European approaches are much less pronounced than they may first seem. This is the case because (a) Europeans do allow involuntary secondary use for a variety of purposes, including national security, prevention of criminal activity, journalistic freedom of speech, and personal use (for instance, an address book);[91] (b) the United States has set limits on a variety of secondary use of what might be called "sensitive information;" and (c) there exists what is called a "compliance gap"—a gap between what is mandated by European laws and the extent to which the various governments enforce these laws.[92] The EU's privacy protections suffer from this gap.

The ban on involuntary secondary use burdens the consumers, who have limited capacity to evaluate various privacy statements and assurances that these are indeed heeded. They are unaware of the risks of PVT. Furthermore, business lobbies tend to strenuously oppose this approach, which makes it very unlikely to be enacted in the United States or heeded in Europe. In addition, differences in laws and enforcement levels among countries across whose borders the same information readily flows greatly limit the value of this way of better protecting privacy from private invasions.

4. Ban Public Use of Private Information?

Those who adhere to the traditional distinction between the public and private realm, and the precept that the main danger to privacy comes from Big Brother, may suggest that the way to proceed is to ban the government from using private data banks. The 1974 Privacy Act already states that the government may not *maintain* records of certain types of personal data for citizens who are not the subjects of investigations;[93] it would be relatively simple to add that they also may not *use* existing records in the private sphere. Still, this would not be necessary if privacy merchants were limited to trading only in less sensitive information, and of little use if this were not the case. In the latter case, such a law would in effect assume that it is acceptable for data banks to be used for profit-making—but not for enhancing the common good, such as public health and security. (Security these days often brings to mind measures taken to prevent terrorist attacks. A considerable number of civil liberty advocates hold that these dangers have been exaggerated and hence rights are unduly curtailed. However, one should note that security also encompasses criminal justice systems, which have utilized data banks to curb criminals.[94])

5. Increased Public Regulation of Sensitive Information?

A limited approach to curbing privacy merchants entails expanding the American patchwork of sectoral laws that limit the violation of privacy in one specific area or another. As Gina Stevens catalogues, "Federal laws and regulations extend protection to consumer credit reports, electronic communications, federal agency records, education records, bank records, cable subscriber information, video rental records, motor vehicle records, health information, telecommunications subscriber information, children's online information, and customer financial information."[95] One could add some more areas to this long but seemingly arbitrary list.

The patchwork of laws can be viewed as based on a rationale that treats differently three main areas: private information gleaned from public records (e.g. house ownership), relatively sensitive information (especially medical and financial), and information that is in effect deemed less sensitive (most consumer choices). The patchwork can be seen as largely based on the level of sensitivity of the information. Public records, therefore, are open for dissemination online because this information was not private in the first place; less sensitive information is considered in need of little protection because no or little harm is inflicted when it is used by third parties; and sensitive information is protected. And to the extent that one finds that some area is not well protected, the argument runs that one can add another "patch" of legislation to cover this area.

The patchwork approach has two serious defects, one often cited and one less often noted. It is widely recognized that the patchwork lags woefully behind technological developments in the private sector. Thus, legislation attempting to cover uncovered areas is "proposed" and "drafted" but not enacted. Thus, as of mid-2011, one suggested bill calls for a federal requirement of a "Do Not Track" option for online advertising.[96] Another suggested bill would deal with the relatively new technology of geolocation and mobile privacy.[97] The Federal Trade Commission is reportedly working on a regulatory framework governing social networking sites in the wake of high-profile FTC complaints against Google Buzz and Twitter.[98] The FTC also plans to target smart phones, a market virtually untouched by regulation thus far.[99] However, these laws lag considerably behind the new technological developments employed by privacy merchants, and given the current anti-regulatory climate, are unlikely to be enacted.

Less often noted is the problem that the distinction between "sensitive" and "less sensitive" information is much less tight than it seems, and it is likely to further weaken in the near future. Even if sensitive information such as medical or financial records is better protected online, less sensitive—and therefore, less protected—information can reveal volumes of sensitive information through PVT. As Marcy Peek points out, "The Internet has allowed commercial decision-makers to manipulate technology in such a way as to identify persons according to a multitude of variables and categories."[100] Unique IP addresses are tracked by each page people visit and ad they click on to create a detailed portrait of the offline persona. Peek explains, "Through various means such as 'cookies,' Web bugs, and personal data input such as zip codes, corporate marketers can obtain a person's demographic and other information and 'tag' an individual on the basis of such information."[101] The individual is then categorized and ranked against other users. The result is "Weblining," an online version of the offline discriminatory practice of "redlining" individuals by denying or increasing the cost of services based on their demographic.[102] After the Fair Housing Act of 1968 prohibited redlining, which used a mortgage applicant's neighborhood to discriminate along racial lines, banks used instead other markers of race, such as which social club people joined or church they attended, as a basis for racial discriminations.[103] That is, an item of information that is not sensitive was used to divine another item meant to be private. The easy access to this type of nonsensitive information online streamlines this practice.

As early as 2000, *Business Week* highlighted a PVT service offered by data broker company Acxiom called "InfoBase Ethnicity System," which matched names against housing, education, and incomes in order to identify the unpublicized ethnicity of an individual or group.[104] More recently, a computer consultant named Tom Owad wrote a simple piece of software allowing him to download public wish lists that Amazon.com customers post to catalog products they plan to buy.[105] He downloaded over 250,000 wish lists in one day, used Yahoo People Search to identify addresses and phone numbers, and published a detailed map showing the locations of people interested in certain books or themes. Owad explained, "It used to be... you had to get a warrant to monitor a person or a group of people. Today, it is increasingly easy to monitor ideas. And then track them back to people."[106] And most people who put simple items of information about their preferences on their Facebook profiles are unlikely to know that it can be used to divine their personality traits with 90 percent accuracy, as if they had taken personality tests.[107]

All this suggests that laws that ban the use of sensitive information (without requiring any action by the millions of affected citizens), the way medical, financial, and select other records are now protected, could be reinforced by banning PVT of protected areas. That is, the wall that separates more sensitive and less sensitive information could be shored up. (Granted, the debate about what is sensitive and what is not would continue.) That is, the law would ban privacy merchants from using "less" sensitive information, such as what one purchases, to divine "more" sensitive information, such as one's medical condition.

Given the current pro-business and anti-regulatory climate in Congress, the Supreme Court, and, it seems, among the voters, enactment of such laws in the United States (and their enforcement in Europe, if enacted) may seem very unlikely. The prospect of such legislation improves if one notes that they would mainly curb those few corporations that make selling private information their main lines of business. Other corporations that merely keep profiles of their own customers' consumeristic preferences would not be affected, although their ability to sell this information to other parties might be limited (to reduce the risk of PVT), and their advertising would be set back because corporations could not use sensitive information in their targeting. Nevertheless, if such laws against the use of PVT to divine sensitive information could be enacted, they would serve as part of system that would shore up privacy to reasonable levels in the future. If they are not enacted, however, I expect PVT to be greatly extended. It is better to ban this approach before it catches on widely than try to eradicate it once it is widespread.

Conclusion

Corporations, especially those that make trading in private information their main line of business—the privacy merchants—are major violators of privacy, and their reach is rapidly expanding. Given that the information these corporations amass and process is also available to the government, it is no longer possible to protect privacy by only curbing the state. Suggesting that norms have changed and that people are now more willing to give up their privacy may be true, but only up to a point. The extent to which private aspects of one's medical and even financial conditions are revealed is unlikely to be widely accepted as a social good. Furthermore, violation of the privacy of dissenters and, more generally, of anyone's political and social views (e.g., by tracking what people read) has chilling effects, whether or not the majority of the public understands the looming implications of unbounded profiling of most Americans. Self-regulation cannot come to the rescue because it assumes that individuals can sort out what corporations are doing behind the veil of their privacy statements, an unrealistic assumption. Banning the use of less sensitive information (in particular about purchases) for divining more sensitive information (e.g., medical)—that is, outlawing Privacy Violating Triangulation—may serve, if combined with laws that add "patches" to the current patchwork of legislation, to cover new technological developments (e.g., social media). If such twin progress is possible, there will be much less reason to prevent the government from drawing on the databanks maintained by privacy merchants, because they would be limited to less sensitive information, and PVT of innocent Americans would be banned. Without such progress, one must assume that what is private is also public in two senses of these words: that one's privacy (including sensitive matters) is rapidly corroded by the private sector, and that whatever it learns is also available to the government.

Notes

1. See, e.g., Shane Harris, *The Watchers: The Rise of America's Surveillance State* (Penguin, 2010), 2 (identifying the "little-known and little-understood band of mavericks who've spent most of their careers working in the intelligence and national security agencies of the government,").

2. See Julia Angwin, "Latest in Web Tracking: Stealthy Supercookies," *The Wall Street Journal* (August 18, 2011), http://online.wsj.com/article/SB10001424 053111903480904576508382675931492.html (citing cookies used through Flash software as an example of this practice).

3. Ashkan Soltani et al., *Flash Cookies and Privacy* 2 (Summer Undergraduate Program in Engineering Research at Berkeley, Working Paper, 2009), http:// papers.ssrn.com/sol3/papers.cfm?abstract_id=1446862 (describing how Flash cookies operate).

4. See Justin Scheck, "Stalkers Exploit Cell Phone GPS," *The Wall Street Journal* (August 3, 2010), http://online.wsj.com/article/SB100014240527487034673 04575383522318244234.html (reporting how GPS systems "have unexpectedly made it easier for abusers to track their victims").

5. Noam Cohen, It's Tracking Your Every Move, And You May Not Even Know, *The New York Times* (March 26, 2011), A1 (noting that Deutsche Telekom "traced him from a train on the way to Erlangen at the start through to that last night, when he was home in Berlin,").

6. "They're Watching You," *Business Week* (January 24, 2005), http://www. businessweek.com/magazine/content/05_04/b3917056_mz005.htm (book review).

7. Christopher Slobogin, "Government Data Mining and the Fourth Amendment," *University of Chicago Law Review* 75 (2008): 317, 320 (describing how the government "routinely makes use" of these "commercial data brokers").

8. Noam Cohen, "Law Students Teach Scalia About Privacy and the Web," *The New York Times* (May 18, 2009), B3.

9. See Emily Steel, "A Web Pioneer Profiles Users by Name," *The Wall Street Journal* (October 25, 2010), http://online.wsj.com/article/SB1000142405 2702304410504575560243259416072.html (profiling the online tracking company RapLeaf Inc.).

10. See Riva Richmond, "How to Fix (Or Kill) Web Data About You," *The New York Times* (April 14, 2011), B6 (explaining Google's policy for removing information from it search engines).

11. Jack Lindamood et al., "Inferring Private Information Using Social Network Data," (Paper presented at the 18th International World Wide Web Conference, Madrid, April 20–24 2009), http://www.utdallas.edu/~muratk/ publications/www09pp242-lindamood.pdf.

12. Julia Angwin and Steve Stecklow, "'Scrapers' Dig Deep for Data on Web," *The Wall Street Journal* (October 12, 2010), A18 (describing software that "matches people's real names to the pseudonyms they use on blogs, Twitter, and other social networks").

13. Ibid., A1 (describing a forum in which "people exchange highly personal stories about their emotional disorders, ranging from bipolar disease to a desire to cut themselves").

14. Eli Pariser, "What the Internet Knows About You," *CNN* (May 22, 2011), http://articles.cnn.com/2011-05-22/opinion/pariser.filter.bubble.

15. Emily Steel, "A Web Pioneer Profiles Users by Name," Wall Street Journal, Oct. 25, 2010.

16. Ibid., A16.

17. Steve Stecklow and Paul Sonn, "Shunned Profiling Technology on the Verge of Comeback," *The Wall Street Journal* (November 24, 2010), A1.

18. Jessica Guynn, "T. Rowe Price invests in Facebook," *The Los Angeles Times* (April 15, 2011), http://latimesblogs.latimes.com/technology/2011/04/t-rowe-price-invests-in-facebook.html.

19. Pascal Emmanuel Gobry, "Facebook: Now 700 Million Strong?" *Business Insider* (May 31, 2011), http://www.businessinsider.com/facebook-700-million-2011-5.

20. "Facebook Faces Criticism Over Privacy Change," *BBC News* (December 10, 2009), http://news.bbc.co.uk/go/pr/fr/-/2/hi/technology/8405334.stm.

21. Juliana Gruenwald, "Facebook Defends Privacy Policies," *National Journal Subscriber* (July 27, 2010), http://techdailydose.nationaljournal.com/2010/07/facebook-defends-privacy-polic.php (internal quotation marks omitted).

22. See Emily Steel and Geoffrey A. Fowler, "Facebook in Privacy Breach," *The Wall Street Journal*, (October 18, 2010), A2 (investigating Facebook apps and their unauthorized transfer of private user data).

23. Ibid.

24. Ibid ("Facebook prohibits app makers from transferring data about users to outside advertising and data companies, even if a user agrees").

25. Miguel Helft, "Marketers Can Glean Private Data On Facebook," *The New York Times* (October 23, 2010), B1.

26. Amir Efrati, "'Like' Button Follows Web Users," *The Wall Street Journal* (May 19, 2011), B1.

27. See Ibid. (evaluating a study by former Google engineer, Brian Kennish of the 1,000 most popular websites).

28. See Ibid. (concluding that widgets are a powerful way to track Internet users).

29. Chris Hoofnagle, "Big Brother's Little Helpers: How ChoicePoint and Other Commercial Data Brokers Collect, Process, and Package Your Data for Law Enforcement," *North Carolina International Law and Commercial Regulation* 29 (2004): 595, 636.

30. Daniel Solove, *The Digital Person: Technology and Privacy in the Information Age* (2004), 169.

31. Ibid., 167.

32. Chris Hoofnagle, "Big Brother's Little Helpers: How ChoicePoint and Other Commercial Data Brokers Collect, Process, and Package Your Data for Law Enforcement," North Carolina International Law and Commercial Regulation 29 (2004): 637.

33. Jay Stanley, "The Surveillance-Industrial Complex: How the American Government Is Conscripting Businesses and Individuals in the Construction of a Surveillance Society," *American Civil Liberties Union* (August 2004): 26, http://www.aclu.org/FilesPDFs/surveillance_report.pdf (discussing government customers' large contracts with data companies).

34. "Report to the Public Concerning the Multistate Anti-Terrorism Information Exchange (MATRIX) Pilot Project," Department of Homeland Security, December 2006, Accessed at http://www.dhs.gov/xlibrary/assets/privacy/privacy-matrix-122006.pdf
35. Ibid.
36. Slobogin, Christopher, "Government Data Mining and the Fourth Amendment," University of Chicago Law Review, Forthcoming: 320; Available at SSRN: http://ssrn.com/abstract=1001972 (highlighting the variety of data available in these banks including demographic information, net worth, employment and criminal records and credit card activity).
37. Arshad Mohammed & Sara Kehaulani Goo, "Government Increasingly Turning to Data Mining," *The Washington Post* (June 15, 2006), D03, available at http://www.washingtonpost.com/wp-dyn/content/article/2006/06/14/AR2006061402063.html ("It is difficult to pinpoint the number of such contracts because many of them are classified . . . ,").
38. Ibid.
39. Leslie Cauley, "NSA Has Massive Database of Americans' Phone Calls," *USA Today* (May 11, 2006), 1A http://www.usatoday.com/news/washington/2006-05-10-nsa_x.htm (internal quotation marks omitted).
40. Ibid.
41. See Shad Mohammed & Sara Kehaulani Goo, "Government Increasingly Turning to Data Mining," Washington Post, June 15, 2006, available at http://www.washingtonpost.com/wp-dyn/content/article/2006/06/14/AR2006061402063.html (discussing the increase in federal government spending for personal data within the private sector).
42. Charlie Savage, "FBI Agents Get Leeway to Push Privacy Bounds," *The New York Times* (June 13, 2011), A1, http://www.nytimes.com/2011/06/13/us/13fbi.html ("The new rules add to several measures taken over the past decade to give agents more latitude . . . ,").
43. "Google Transparency Report, July to December 2010," (June 2011) http://www.google.com/transparencyreport/governmentrequests/userdata/?p=2010-12.
44. Polly Sprenger, "Sun On Privacy: 'Get Over It,'" *Wired* (Jan. 26, 1999), http://www.wired.com/politics/law/news/1999/01/17538.
45. See Bobbie Johnson, "Privacy No Longer a Social Norm, Says Facebook Founder," *The Guardian* (January 10, 2010), http://www.guardian.co.uk/technology/2010/jan/11/facebook-privacy ("The rise of social networking online means that people no longer have an expectation of privacy, according to Facebook founder, Mark Zuckerberg,").
46. Bobbie Johnson, "Privacy No Longer a Social Norm, Says Facebook Founder," *The Guardian* (January 11, 2010), http://www.guardian.co.uk/technology/2010/jan/11/facebook-privacy (internal quotation marks omitted).
47. Ian Paul, "Facebook CEO Challenges the Social Norm of Privacy," *PC World*, (January 11, 2010), http://www.pcworld.com/article/186584/facebook_ceo_challenges_the_social_norm_of_privacy.html (internal quotation marks omitted).
48. L. Gordon Crovitz, "The 0.00002% Privacy Solution," Wall Street Journal (March 28, 2011): A15.
49. Ibid.

50. Ibid.

51. Ibid.

52. Joseph Turow et al., "Americans Reject Tailored Advertising and Three Activities that Enable It," *University of Pennsylvania Scholarly Commons* (September 1, 2009): 15, http://repository.upenn.edu/asc_papers/137.

53. Chris Jay Hoofnagle et al., "How Different are Young Adults from Older Adults When it Comes to Information Privacy Attitudes and Policies?" (April 14, 2010): 10, http://ssrn.com/abstract=1589864.

54. Ibid.

55. Alan Westin, "'Whatever Works': The American Public's Attitudes Toward Regulation and Self-Regulation on Consumer Privacy Issues," *Privacy and Self-Regulation in the Information Age* 1 (Nat'l Telecomm. & Info. Admin., 1997): 52–53, http://www.ntia.doc.gov/reports/privacy/selfreg1.htm#1F.

56. Ibid.

57. Bob Tedeschi, "E-Commerce Report: Everybody Talks About Online Privacy, But Few Do Anything About It," *New York Times* (June 3, 2003), C6.

58. Matt Carmichael, "What Consumers Want From Brands Online," *Advertising Age* (February 27, 2011): 20, http://adage.com/article/digital/consumers-seek-brand-discounts-facebook-preferred-platform/149095 (discussing coupons as the "main driver listed for users of location-based check-in services").

59. For further discussion, see A. Michael Froomkin, "The Death of Privacy?" *Stanford Law Review* 52 (2000): 1461; and Eugene Volokh, "Freedom of Speech and Information Privacy: The Troubling Implications of a Right to Stop People from Speaking About You," *Stanford Law Review* 52 (2000): 1049.

60. Susanna Kim Ripken, "The dangers and drawbacks of the disclosure antidote: toward a more substantive approach to securities regulation," *Baylor Law Review* 139 (2006): 195–96.

61. For further discussion on this subject, see Dan Ariely, *Predictably Irrational: The Hidden Forces That Shape Our Decisions* (2008), 243.

62. Chris Hoofnagle, "Can Privacy Self-Regulation Work for Consumers?" *TAP* (January 26, 2011), http://www.techpolicy.com/CanPrivacySelf-RegulationWork-Hoofnagle.aspx (providing examples of organizations that failed to abide by their own privacy policies).

63. Apple Q&A on Location Data, Apple Press Info, (April 27, 2011), http://www.apple.com/pr/library/2011/04/27Apple-Q-A-on-Location-Data.html.

64. Adam Satariano and Katie Hoffmann, "Apple Denies Tracking IPhone Locations, Will Update Software," *Bloomberg* (April 27, 2011), http://www.bloomberg.com/news/2011-04-27/apple-denies-tracking-iphone-locations-will-reduce-data-storage-capacity.html.

65. L. Gordon Crovitz, "The 0.00002% Privacy Solution," Wall Street Journal, March 28, 2011, accessed at http://online.wsj.com/news/articles/SB10001424052748704474804576222732361366712

66. Ibid.

67. Ibid.

68. Federal Trade Commission, FTC Staff Issues Privacy Report, Offers Framework for Consumers, Businesses, and Policymakers (December 1, 2010), http://www.ftc.gov/opa/2010/12/privacyreport.shtm. ("Although many companies use privacy policies to explain their information practices, the policies have become long, legalistic disclosures that consumers usually don't read and don't understand if they do,").

69. Joseph Turow, "Americans and Online Privacy: The System is Broken," *Annenberg Public Policy Center Report* (June 2003), http://www.asc.upenn. edu/usr/jturow/internet-privacy-report/36-page-turow-version-9.pdf.

70. Paul M. Schwartz, "Preemption and Privacy," *Yale Law Journal* 118 (2009): 902, 921 (internal quotation marks omitted).

71. Ibid., 929 (internal quotation marks omitted).

72. The Need for a Comprehensive Approach to Protecting Consumer Privacy: Hearing on the State of Online Consumer Privacy Before the Senate Comm. on Commerce, Science & Transp., 112th Congress 6 (2011) (statement of Erich Anderson, Deputy General Counsel, Microsoft Corporation).

73. Ibid., 5 (emphasis in original).

74. Raised B. 5765, Gen. Assemb., Feb. Sess. (Conn. 2008).

75. See Schwartz, supra note 64 at 946.

76. Hoofnagle, supra note 58.

77. See Julie E. Cohen, "Information Rights and Intellectual Freedom," *Ethics and the Internet* (Anton Vedder, ed., 2001), 11–32 (discussing consent-based approaches to privacy and information "ownership").

78. Julia M. Fromholz, "The European Union Data Privacy Directive," *Berkeley Technology Law Journal* 15 (2000): 461, 462.

79. Fred H. Cate, *Privacy in the Information Age* (Washington, DC: Brookings Institution Press 1997), 36.

80. Background: EU Data Protection Directive, Electronic Privacy Information Center, http://epic.org/privacy/intl/eu_data_protection_directive.html.

81. Erica Newland, "CDT Comments on EU Data Protection Directive," Center for Democracy & Technology, (January 20, 2011), http://www.cdt. org/blogs/erica-newland/cdt-comments-eu-data-protection-directive; see also Comments of the Center For Democracy & Technology to the European Commission in the Matter of "Consultation on the Commission's Comprehensive Approach on Personal Data Protection in the European Union, *Center for Democracy & Technology*," 7 (January 15, 2011), http://cdt. org/files/pdfs/CDT_DPD_Comments.pdf (noting the "very strong top-level principles embodied in the Directive").

82. Julia M. Fromholz, The European Union Data Privacy Directive, 15 BERKELEY TECH. L.J. 467-8 (2000). 467–8.

83. Fred H. Cate, Privacy in the Information Age 37 (1997).

84. Ibid., (noting that other exemptions allowing for the processing of personal data include monetary and budgetary considerations for a Member State of the European Union or the EU itself).

85. Ibid., 36.

86. Ibid.

87. Ibid., 37 ("Personal data may be used only for the legitimate purpose for which they were collected.... The processing of data... is severely restricted and in most cases forbidden without the written permission of the data subject,").

88. Ibid., (discussing the requirements of processing personal data in compliance with national laws).

89. Fred H. Cate, "The EU Data Protection Directive, Information Privacy, and the Public Interest," *Iowa Law Review* 80 (1995): 431, 437 (internal quotation marks omitted).

90. Erica Newland, "CDT Comments on EU Data Protection Directive," Center for Democracy & Technology, (January 20, 2011), http://www.cdt.org/blogs/ erica-newland/cdt-comments-eu-data-protection-directive

91. Directive 95/46/EC of the European Parliament and of the Council of October 24,1995 on the Protection of Individuals with regard to the Processing of Personal Data and on the Free Movement of Such Data, 1995 O.J. (L 281), 31, 42.

92. For a discussion of this topic, see Ellen Mastenbroek, "EU Compliance: Still A 'Black Hole?'" *Journal of European Public Policy* 1103–1120; see also Maria Mendrinou, "Non-compliance and the European Commission's Role in Integration," *Journal of European Public Policy* (1996): 1–22.

93. 5 U.S.C. § 552a(e)(7) (2006) ("Each agency that maintains a system of records shall . . . maintain no record describing how any individual exercises rights guaranteed by the First Amendment unless expressly authorized by statute or by the individual about whom the record is maintained or unless pertinent to and within the scope of an authorized law enforcement activity,").

94. See Amitai Etzioni, "DNA Tests and Databases in Criminal Justice: Individual Rights and the Common Good," *DNA and the Criminal Justice System* (David Lazer ed., 2004): 197 (discussing "several issues raised by the extensive use of DNA tests and databases in advancing public safety").

95. Gina Stevens, Congressional Research Service, R41756, Privacy Protections for Personal Information Online 7 (2011) (footnotes omitted).

96. See Katie Kindelan, "John McCain and John Kerry Propose 'Online Privacy Bill of Rights,'" *Social Times* (March 10, 2011), http://socialtimes.com/ john-mccain-and-john-kerry-propose-online-privacy-bill-of-rights_b41604 (discussing proposed legislation that would govern online privacy).

97. Ibid.

98. Tony Romm, "Will FTC Get the Funds It Needs to Police Internet?" *Politico* (June 3, 2011), http://www.politico.com/news/stories/0611/56134.html (discussing the implications of Congressional allotment of funds to the FTC on the FTC's potential to expand its regulatory powers).

99. Ibid.

100. Marcy Peek, "Passing Beyond Identity on the Internet: Espionage & Counterespionage in the Internet Age," *Vermont Law Review* (2003): 91, 98 (evaluating ways to resist discriminatory marketing in cyberspace).

101. Ibid., 95.

102. Ibid., 91–92.

103. Ibid., 91 (explaining the practice and history of redlining).

104. Marcia Stepanek, "Weblining," *Business Weekly* (April 3, 2000), http://www. businessweek.com/2000/00_14/b3675027.htm (assessing companies' practices of using personal data to take advantage of customers online).

105. Nicholas Carr, "Tracking is an Assault on Liberty, With Real Dangers," *The Wall Street Journal* (August 7–8, 2010): W1 (arguing for the need for greater privacy protection online).

106. Ibid.

107. Jennifer Golbeck, Cristina Robles & Karen Turner, "Predicting Personality with Social Media," *CHI* (2011): 253, 254 (discussing a study conducted to determine to what extent information on an individual's Facebook page can accurately reflect the individual's personality).

III

The New Politics

6

Is There a Gridlock?

One common way to analyze the current condition of the American polity concludes that the system is "gridlocked"[1] and "dysfunctional."[2] Various reasons are provided to explain the current condition, which is viewed as a perversion of the system of checks and balances.[3] These include gerrymandering,[4] polarization,[5] the influence of interest groups,[6] media fragmentation,[7] and structural hurdles presented by the bicameral system.[8] Others argue that the polity is experiencing a "stalemate" between "two visions of where the country needs to go": a conservative one championed by the GOP and a liberal/progressive vision championed by the Democrats.[9]

Election results are seen as indicating that the two camps represent more or less equal numbers, especially when one considers independent voters who can be swayed in either direction. Thus according to the *New York Times* "we live in a highly polarized, evenly divided nation."[10] In some elections one side gains more, in some the other side. But, so the argument holds, none has enough power to direct the polity its way. While a measure of gridlock has long been observed,[11] it is widely held to have been particularly severe and damaging during the 111th and 112th Congresses, between 2008 and 2012.

In contrast, this article argues that the American polity is functioning properly, in the specific sense that it serves the expressed conservative preferences of the popular majority. Gridlock exists when party A wants to move east and party B seeks to move west, and thus nothing budges. However, when party A wants to move east and party B wants to stay put, and nothing moves, what seems like a gridlock is in effect a victory for party B. In this sense, the fact that the 112th Congress enacted only half as many laws as other Congresses on average[12] is not an indication of gridlock, but instead one measure of conservative success. The discussion below provides evidence that between 2008 and 2012, conservatives not only blocked, weakened, and eliminated government actions and programs, but also that they enacted laws that favored their constituencies and ideology.

The thesis of this article is not that there was no gridlock or that the conservative majority won all the confrontations. I merely contend that much was achieved from a conservative viewpoint and little from a liberal one over this period. That is, as we shall next see, the elected officials and more generally the political system were responsive to the expressed conservative preferences of the majority of American voters, thereby meeting a fundamental criterion of democracy.

This observation does not answer the remaining questions as to whether the polity was dysfunctional despite being responsive; that is, whether it attended to specific national needs such as gaining a higher level of economic growth, a lower level of unemployment, and lower deficits that many independent experts hold are essential for its well-being. Furthermore, we shall see that the majority of the voters have been deeply dissatisfied with the polity during this period, which seems on its face to be incompatible with the suggestion that the polity responded to their preferences. This thesis, we shall see, holds for economic and foreign policy, homeland security, and public safety, but not for cultural issues, which are not further discussed here.

These observations do raise fundamental questions about democratic theory. Did the voters make rational choices? Did they gain what they voted for? Were they uninformed or misinformed? Manipulated by demagogues? Or was the government captured by special interests? How is one to explain the fact that the government is responsive to the majority's expressed preferences, but the country is nevertheless headed in the wrong direction, even according to the majority of voters? Can a government be responsive, democratic, and yet dysfunctional? If so, what does this conclusion entail for our understanding of democratic theory? Part I of the article seeks to demonstrate that the American polity is responsive to the majority's expressed preferences. Part II explores the implication of these findings for democratic theory.

I. The Conservative "Party," Popular Majority, and Political Responsiveness

The often used categories of Democrat and Republican are misleading for the purposes of this analysis. The main reason for this claim is that elected officials in the United States, unlike those in many other democracies, are not required to follow their party line when they vote for particular bills. Hence, the fact that a given party has a majority in a given house does not mean that its positions will prevail. Most relevant, in the period under study, many Democratic members of Congress voted with Republicans in support of conservative bills—and very few Republicans voted with Democrats for liberal bills.

Democrats often refrained from even raising liberal positions (such as on gun control or a single-payer healthcare plan), and vastly diluted others in order for them even to be considered. The few relatively liberal acts that were passed were later watered down or not enforced, and liberals allowed procedural changes that made current and future conservative moves more likely to succeed. Hence, it often makes more sense to think about divisions between a majority conservative "party" and a minority liberal "party". Readers who agree that there was no overarching gridlock between 2008 and 2012 and that conservatives often prevailed may wish to skip to Part II. Those who question these conclusions may wish to review the evidence that follows.

The terms liberal and conservative are used in this article as they are used in contemporary public discourse and not as they are used in political theory. They are also used as they are in the United States as distinct from the ways these terms are used in Europe. One may argue that one must take into account that the meanings of these terms have changed in public American discourse, that the whole political spectrum has moved to the right,[13] and hence one cannot use these terms as fixed reference points. However, for the period under study—four years—and even for much of the flashback period since WWII, the terms continue to retain several key meanings.

Conservatism (that is economic or laissez-faire conservatism; this article does not deal with social conservatism) holds that the government that governs least, governs best. Liberals, on the other hand, see a major positive role for the state. Several observers hold that during the period under study, conservatives have become more radical under the influence of the Tea Party and other developments, and moved from being "compassionate conservatives" (such as George W. Bush) to "severe conservatives" (Mitt Romney). However, these are differences in conservative leanings and not in the liberal/conservative ideological spectrum.

1. The Public and the Voters

In the 2008 Presidential election, the Democratic candidate, Barack Obama, received 53 percent of the popular vote compared to 45.7 percent for his Republican rival. US presidential elections of the past 20 years have witnessed the Democratic candidate command the majority of the popular vote, by margins ranging between 0.5 percent and 8.5 percent, excepting the 2004 election, when the Republican candidate received 2.4 percent more of the popular vote than his Democratic challenger. Furthermore, studies show consistently that more Americans identify themselves as Democrats than as Republicans. Over the past 20 years, Democratic affiliation has accounted for

U.S. Political Ideology -- 1992-2011 Annual Averages

How would you describe your political views -- very conservative, conservative, moderate, liberal, or very liberal?

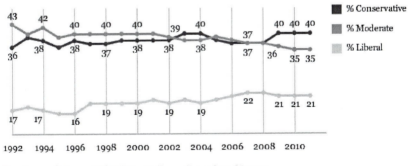

Based on 20 Gallup and USA Today/Gallup polls conducted in 2011

Ideological Self-Identification of American Public

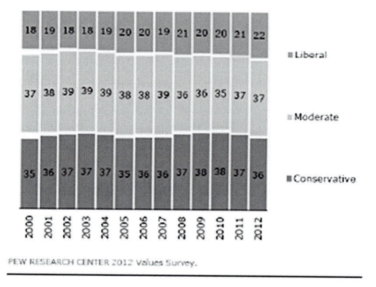

PEW RESEARCH CENTER 2012 Values Survey.

31–33 percent of the electorate (32 percent in 2012), while the Republican party has declined from about 30 percent to 24 percent in 2012.[14] One could hence expect the Democrats to prevail often in making public policy, especially when they held the White House and controlled both houses of Congress, at times even with a filibuster-proof majority in the Senate. And given that the Democrats are more liberal than the Republicans, one would thus expect liberal policies to prevail.

However, for the issues at hand, party affiliation is often not the crucial issue. Much more important was that for every one voter who identified as liberal, there were nearly two who identified as conservative. This conservative majority is not just a recent phenomenon. This finding is true not only for the period under study, but also holds with only moments of minor exception as far back as 1984,[15] with a less marked conservative plurality stretching back further.[16] Between 1992 and 2011 the percentage of Americans who identified as conservative ranged from 35 percent to 40 percent, while those identifying as liberal was below 22 percent.[17]

The data regarding how big the conservative plurality is, and whether it consists of a majority, vary from study to study but at a minimum, there is a consensus that conservatives outnumber liberals by wide margins. Specifically, between 2008 and 2012, the proportion of the voting-age public self-identifying as liberal hovered around a mere 20 percent of the electorate, while those who identified as conservative accounted for between 35 percent and 40 percent,[18]

Ideological Self-Identification by Political Party

Profile of Republicans - % Who Self-Identify as...				
	2000	2004	2008	2012
% of electorate	28%	30%	25%	24%
Conservative	60	63	68	68
Moderate	29	29	26	26
Liberal	7	5	5	5

Profile of Democrats - % Who Self-Identify as...				
	2000	2004	2008	2012
% of electorate	33%	33%	36%	32%
Conservative	24	24	25	20
Moderate	41	42	37	38
Liberal	28	29	34	38

Profile of Independents - % Who Self-Identify as...				
	2000	2004	2008	2012
% of electorate	30%	30%	32%	38%
Conservative	28	27	30	30
Moderate	45	46	45	43
Liberal	20	22	20	22

depending on the study. Moreover, conservatives are strongly represented in both major parties, as well as among independents. Only 5 percent of Republican voters identify as liberals, whereas six times more—30 percent—of independents and four to five times more Democratic voters consider themselves conservatives. Indeed, between 2008 and 2012, the proportion of Democrats who considered themselves ideologically conservative was roughly equal to, and at times higher than, the percentage of the overall American population which identified as liberal.[19]

Also worth noting is that more Americans consider themselves conservative on economic issues relative to social issues. Poll data from 2012 demonstrate that when asked about economic and social issues independently, 46 percent of Americans responded that they were economically conservative (with 20 percent choosing liberal), against 38 percent of those who said that they were socially conservative. A poll of likely voters, which does not offer respondents the option to identify as "moderate," repeatedly finds that a majority of Americans identify as somewhat or very conservative. For instance, in spring of 2012, 58 percent describe themselves as conservative, compared to 37 percent as liberal.[20]

In short, the data show that American voters are significantly more conservative than liberal, a fact which is by and large obscured by the rough equivalence in electoral successes between the two parties, by the larger Democratic following, and by the notion that Democrats are liberals. Hence for many purposes, one had best consider the American electorate as containing a majority conservative party, consisting of practically all Republicans, at least half of the independents, and significant segments of the Democrats versus a minority liberal party, consisting of parts of the Democratic Party and some independents.

2. The Executive Branch

Flashback: Arthur Schlesinger, Jr., famously held that American politics go through liberal and conservative phases.[21] Other notable scholars have adopted a similar cyclical approach to American politics, discussing presidential power,[22] the influence of private interest groups,[23] and congressional voting patterns[24] as the product of oscillations between liberal and conservative temperaments. Related to this view is the thesis that American public philosophy from the outset reflected a tension between a Hamiltonian communitarian perspective and a Jeffersonian individualist one.[25] The public opinion data explored above could thus be read to indicate that we are now merely in a Jeffersonian phase, soon to give way to a Hamiltonian phase. However, many observers point out that Americans are much more Jeffersonian than Europeans, not to mention the citizens of most other societies.[26] Moreover, those who espouse conservative positions do better for rather extended periods than those who express liberal ones.

One may argue that this "cycle" thesis is supported by the fact that since World War II, the White House was held for thirty-six years by Republicans and thirty-two years by Democrats as of the end of Obama's first term. However, these numbers underestimate the conservative control of the White House, because when Democrats were elected as presidents, they often advanced few major liberal policies and tended to support relatively conservative ones. Eric Alterman and Kevin Mattson, researchers for the Center for American Progress, point out that each of the most recent Democratic presidents, Carter, Clinton, and Obama, "found it necessary to become a far more conservative president, both in foreign and domestic policy, than the candidate who actually won the race."[27]

President Carter put a very high premium on balancing the budget and curbing inflation, but did little to advance liberal causes. Douglas Brinkley, in his biography of Carter, concludes that he left the White House "as perhaps the most conservative Democratic commander in chief since Grover Cleveland."[28] Carter himself wrote in his diary that "In many cases I feel more at home with the conservative Democratic and Republican members of Congress."[29] President Clinton capped social programs for five years in order to balance the budget and ended "welfare as we know it," while his healthcare initiative failed.[30] The record of the Obama Administration reflects the fact that liberals are a minority and conservatives dominate. Key details follow.

Economic policy: Reviving the economy was a major concern when President Obama took office. The preferred liberal treatment was a large stimulus. Christina Romer, Chairman of the Council of Economic Advisors, advocated a stimulus of $1.2 trillion, mostly in the form of government spending.[31] Other liberals held that even a larger stimulus was needed. Lawrence Summers, Director of the National Economic Council, presented the president with four stimulus plans of varying size: $550 billion, $665 billion, $810 billion, and $890 billion, but did not include Romer's liberal option. This was because he believed that this option could not pass Congress.[32] The final stimulus package approved was $787 billion, which, by the standards of Keynesian economics to which most liberals ascribe, was too small and explains the economy's continued slow growth and thus its political consequences.[33] Moreover, to pass even this stimulus, about a third of the package—$286.9 billion[34]—had to be diverted to conservative preferences, namely tax cuts, which, according to Keynesian economics, are much less simulative than government spending.

The Affordable Care Act (ACA) is considered by some a liberal victory. Yet it was proposed without even granting a hearing to the preferred liberal option of a single-payer system. Even more moderate liberal proposals for a public option, where citizens could potentially 'buy into Medicare,' were quickly jettisoned as the Obama Administration sought to secure the support of powerful interest groups. One of the first steps the administration undertook was to promise the hospital and health insurance industries that a public option would not be advanced.[35] To bolster support for the ACA, the Obama Administration made major concessions to lobbyists from the Pharmaceutical Research and Manufacturers of America, guaranteeing them that the ACA would not allow Medicare to import prescription drugs at lower prices from foreign suppliers.[36] The individual mandate that requires all citizens to have health insurance, a key element of the ACA, was originally proposed by the conservative Heritage Foundation in the 1990s as an antidote and alternative to a single-payer system.[37] It was later implemented in Massachusetts by Mitt Romney.[38] True, the ACA promises to provide health insurance to some 30 million citizens over the otherwise expected total by 2020, a significant liberal gain. Yet it would still leave approximately 30 million others without coverage

Public safety: The liberal Brady Campaign to Prevent Gun Violence gave President Obama an "F" rating on issues related to background checks, closing the gun show loophole, gun trafficking, guns in public, and the federal assault weapons ban, calling his record on gun control "an abject failure."[39] Moreover, President Obama signed more repeals of federal gun laws than President George W. Bush did during his two terms.[40] Even in the wake of two shootings in mid-2012, the Obama Administration did not propose any new legislation related to gun control or even wish to reopen the debate.[41]

Regarding immigration, the Obama administration deported in less than four years nearly as many undocumented immigrants as in the eight-year Bush administration.[42] Obama expanded a program to check the immigration status of people booked into jails, continued to build the "virtual fence" along the US border, and increased the ranks of border patrol agents, all policies favored by conservatives. In 2012, President Obama did make a liberal move when he allowed children of immigrants who came to the US under age sixteen, stayed five years, graduated from high school, and had a clean record, to apply for a two-year waver on deportation.

The American justice system relies heavily on incarceration to maintain public order, keeping 2.2 million Americans locked up, more than are jailed in China.[43] The Obama Administration has continued this policy, through a steady expansion of the budget for federal prisons, bringing the total to $6.9 billion in his 2013 budget proposal.[44] At the same time, President Obama's Justice Department has failed to prosecute any of the executives responsible for the financial crisis,[45] even when they presided over massive and systematic fraud. In August of 2012, Goldman Sachs became the latest company to be let off the hook, despite its major role in causing the meltdown.[46]

On matters relating to national security and terrorism, President Obama followed or extended the conservative policies of the George W. Bush Administration. He signed an extension of the Patriot Act in 2011,[47] and he continued and expanded Bush-era policies of domestic surveillance.[48] Obama was unable to close the detention facilities at the Guantanamo Bay Naval Base, or try terrorists in civil courts, as preferred by liberals. After initially suspending trials by military commissions for terror suspects, Obama resumed them in 2009.[49]

Defense: President Obama withdrew the US forces from Iraq but authorized a surge in Afghanistan, moving to reduce troops in that nation toward the end of his term. This was certainly a liberal victory, yet it was made politically possible by the fact that by this time, a strict majority of Americans, including many conservatives, favored ending these wars.[50] Despite initially setting limited goals for that war (eradicating Al-Qaeda), his administration spent $385 billion on nation-building efforts favored by neo-conservatives in a failed attempt to turn Afghanistan into a stable state and a viable democracy.[51] In May of 2012, a coalition of 222 House Republicans and 77 Democrats passed the National Defense Authorization Act, which provides the Defense Department with $642 billion—$8 billion over the limits mandated by the 2011 budget deal[52] and $4 billion more than President Obama requested.[53]

The Bush administration interpreted the 2001 AUMF (Authorization for the Use of Military Force) broadly, to mean that the United States could ". . . act as though it were in an armed conflict in every part of the globe wherever a terrorist might be found."[54] The Obama administration has continued to operate using this definition,[55] opposed by liberals who hold that such acts must be limited to declared theaters of war.[56] The Obama administration carried out five times more drone strikes than the Bush administration (250 compared to 44), and it has utilized them in areas not declared as theaters of war, such as Yemen and Somalia.[57] Obama authorized and defended the targeted killing of US citizens abroad, never authorized by Bush.[58]

Foreign policy: Initially, Obama pursued a policy of multilateralism and engagement regarding North Korea and Iran, approaches favored by liberals. When these nations rebuffed his overtures, the Obama administration moved to isolate one and impose sanctions on the other, similar to actions taken by the Bush Administration, albeit with more European cooperation and fewer threats to employ the military option. Obama's China policy is also similar to that of Bush. The American "pivot" toward Asia has entailed a more aggressive posture toward China and sown distrust between the two powers.[59]

Russia appears to be an exception, as the administration was able to reach a new treaty that entails a significant reduction in strategic weapons, the New START, a rare liberal win. Otherwise, though, President Obama pledged in the first year of his presidency to prioritize nuclear nonproliferation, including "immediately and aggressively" pushing for ratification of the Comprehensive Nuclear Test-Ban Treaty. Given the conservative opposition, this treaty was not presented to the Senate for consideration. In addition, foreign aid, a favored liberal tool of foreign policy which president Obama promised during his election campaign to double to about $50 billion, was somewhat increased, as it was under George W. Bush.

James Mann concluded that Obama's foreign policy is "strikingly" similar to that of George W. Bush, although in some areas it was more "hawkish" and in some more multilateral.[60] Some argue that Obama is a pragmatist and does not follow any particular ideology. However, if one means by pragmatism adapting to domestic politics and not merely to the reality of international relations, and one does not try to convince the public of a new foreign policy course (as Roosevelt did at the eve of WWII and Truman did regarding containment), this means that in the American context between 2008 and 2012 that a fairly conservative foreign policy was pursued.

Appointments: The justices President Obama appointed to the Supreme Court, Sonia Sotomayor and Elena Kagan, were both moderate liberals compared to candidates the liberals favored, such as federal appeals court judge Diane P. Wood.[61] Similarly, Obama passed over Elizabeth Warren, a prominent liberal, in favor of Richard Cordray for the position of head of the Consumer Financial Protection Bureau.[62] All these and other such moderate appointments were largely forced on the White House by the "conservative party" in Congress, though the president never put up a strong fight to appoint strong liberals.

With regards to lower-court nominations, the Obama Administration appointed about 40 fewer justices than previous administrations (over an equal time span), leaving posts open to be filled by another administration. Moreover, his appointments included fewer liberals and more moderates than those before, such that Obama will leave "less of a lasting ideological imprint on the judiciary than many liberals had hoped for and many conservatives had feared."[63]

On many of these issues, one may suggest that President Obama had no choice but to follow the course he did, given the conservative tilt of the country, of Congress, and of the interest groups. Others may argue that he could have gained more liberal results if he had fought harder. Here, however, the point is that whatever the cause and the processes, the results were often relatively conservative.

3. The Legislative Branch

From the viewpoint of the issues at hand, there was a difference between the 111th and 112th Congresses, though it is much less important than may at first seem. In the 111th, Democrats held the majority but in several important matters conservative Democrats voted with the GOP to ensure conservative victories. Indeed, in the 111th Congress, approximately 25 percent of those Congressional votes where Republicans prevailed were made possible by conservative Democratic votes.[64] In the 112th Congress, Republicans held the majority in the House, as many of the conservative Democrats were defeated. Because practically all members of the GOP vote conservative, the "conservative party" continued to prevail. Moreover, conservative Democrats helped the GOP carry the day in 10 percent of the votes, including the Senate's extension of the Patriot Act for another four years and their passage of free trade agreements with Columbia, Panama, and South Korea.[65] Very few liberal victories were made possible by votes from the GOP, in either house of Congress, and those that were relied overwhelmingly on the same two or three legislators.

A methodological digression is needed here. The terms liberal and conservative are here used as these terms are used in contemporary social and political public philosophy in the United States. Hence, when the article states that a given member of Congress voted as a liberal or conservative, votes are assessed against a *fixed* ideological spectrum. This contrasts with those who use a relative standards, which maps politicians along a spectrum of theoretical policy space, assessing their ideology based upon their proximity to like legislators or party averages, rather than upon specified criteria as to what constitutes a liberal or conservative. Many often-used measures of politicians' leanings, such as the NOMINATE scores, are relative measures in this way. As such, they are not well suited for comparing the level of following either liberals or conservatives have over time.

Despite having a clear majority in both the House and the Senate during the 111th Congress, along with a Democrat as the President, even during the two brief periods during which the Democratic majority was filibuster-proof,[66] these Democrats passed little liberal legislation. This is largely because of the conservative Democrats. For example, a 2009 vote in the Senate over an amendment to the 2010 budget, expanding the amount of wealth exempt from the estate tax to over $5 million and capping that tax at 35 percent for the remainder of the deceased's wealth constituted a boon to the rich, and anathema to liberals. This amendment received support from all 41 Republicans, as well as the support of 10 Democrats, giving it the slightest of majorities needed to pass. Not only did the Democratic votes line up to pass this conservative amendment, but no attempt was made by the liberals to filibuster the bill, a tactic they faced all too often and that blocked many of their bills, to the point that it made little sense even to bring them up.

Another key example occurred during the Dodd-Frank debates, when twenty-two Democrats in the Senate voted to help pass a Republican-sponsored bill exempting automotive dealers from regulation by the Consumer Financial Protection Agency. Moreover, in 2009, twenty-four Democratic Senators voted for a Republican proposal to establish a sixty-vote threshold for the imposition of any new energy taxes during the budget deliberations for the following year. And a Republican proposal to ban the use of federal funds by the EPA in enforcing lead paint regulations against specific contractors was passed with the help of nineteen Democrats. Moreover, it took Democrats to carry a vote denying federal funding for Amtrak unless it allowed guns to be brought on trains.

Procedural Challenges: Between 2008 and 2012, the conservative "party" introduced several procedural changes over the objections of the liberal minority, changes that further enhanced the conservatives' power. In these years, the Senate greatly extended threats of the filibuster which fundamentally altered the voting dynamics in the Senate, making a sixty-vote majority a near necessity for passing nontrivial legislation. Up to 2008, the filibuster was a rarely used tool for demonstrating a particularly strong opposition to a measure, such as when Southern Democrats filibustered to protest civil rights legislation in the 1960s. In 2009 alone, however, there were twice as many filibusters (67) as in the twenty-year period between 1950 and 1969.[67] In addition, the number of cloture motions doubled between 2008 and 2012, as compared to the average number during the Bush Administration.[68]

This aggressive use of the filibuster meant that oftentimes bills enacted were modified to suit conservative preferences, even when the Democrats held clear majorities. To illustrate: we already saw that the ACA was not the healthcare policy liberals favored. In addition to concessions made to the relevant industries by the White House, conservative Democrats in Congress gained several concessions. Pro-life Democrats granted their "yes" votes in return for gaining an executive order that strictly prohibited federal funds from being used to cover abortions.[69] To secure Sen. Joe Lieberman's vote, a provision that would have allowed those aged fifty-five to sixty-four to buy into Medicare was removed from the Act.[70] The bill did require insurance companies to cover people who had preexisting conditions and to include people younger than twenty-six in their parents' insurance, but it set only minor limits on what the insurance companies could charge and will provide only a moderate degree of cost control.[71]

In terms of the sheer number of laws passed, Congress was less active in the period under study—an outcome favored by the conservatives. In 2011, Congress passed only ninety bills, an unprecedentedly low number, and this behavior has persisted into 2012, with Congress being on track toward another record low. Furthermore, several of the bills passed could not be considered major legislation—more than 20 percent of these bills renamed federal buildings and offices.[72] 2011 was found to be the least active year in Congressional history.[73]

Another procedural change that favored conservative positions involved raising the debt ceiling, which used to be a routine and nonpartisan move. Since 1962, it has been done seventy-four times, under both Democratic and Republican administrations and legislatures.[74] However, during the 111th Congress, conservatives refused to raise the debt ceiling until they were granted major concessions, mainly in the form of cutting funding for programs favored by liberals. Thus, in the 2011 deal, in exchange for a $2.1 trillion increase over the next six months in potential borrowing, the Obama Administration agreed to cut $55 billion per year from nondefense programs between 2013 and 2021.[75] A disproportionate amount of these cuts will come from programs favored by liberals; $38.6 billion per year, over a third of the total cuts agreed to, will be taken from the nondefense discretionary budget, which comprises only 15 percent of the Federal budget. Programs and organizations such as the EPA, low-income housing assistance, child care supports, and re-employment training will all face deeper cuts proportionally than any other program.[76]

Economic policies: We already saw that at least by some liberal standards, the stimulus Congress agreed to enact was too small, which had major consequences for all that followed in terms of domestic economic recovery, the global position of the US, and the 2010 and 2012 elections. Second to the stimulus in importance was the question of whether or not the Bush tax cuts would be renewed, and if so, if they were to apply to all Americans or just those making under $250,000 (or $1 million) as the liberals preferred. In 2010, Obama worked closely with Republican legislators to renew the Bush tax cuts for all income levels. The cost of these tax cuts in loss of revenue came to $858 billion.[77] The continuation of the Bush tax cuts for the duration of the Obama years represents a major and ongoing conservative victory.

When in July of 2012 President Obama called for extending the Bush tax cuts for everyone who earns $250,000 or less—98 percent of the public—the opposition included, not only Republicans but also 19 Democrats in the House, while 3 Democratic senators indicated support for the Republican/conservative plan for an extension of tax cuts to all levels of income.[78] Some wanted to exclude from the tax hike those earning $1 million or less, and some simply joined the conservative Republican position that nobody should be required to pay more taxes.

Another indication of the direction the polity is tilting is in the change of the position of the president and the Democrats on entitlements. Defense of these programs, especially Social Security and Medicare, used to be the strongest source of support for the "liberal party". However, during 2008–12, the White House and the Democrats increasingly indicated their willingness to cut entitlements.

Liberals hold that a major factor in causing the Great Recession was deregulation, plus the repeal of the Glass-Steagall Act that limited commercial banks from acting as "investment" banks or as securities dealers. Thus the repeal allowed banks to engage in what has been called a great financial casino, playing the markets on Wall Street rather than truly investing. Liberals also hold that banks were too big, and hence those which had to be bailed out by taxpayers would have to be cut back. However, in the face of conservative opposition, restoring the Glass-Steagall Act was not ever seriously considered, banks were allowed to become even bigger,[79] and the regulation that was enacted—a liberal victory—was weakened while still being formed by Congress and designed in such a way as to be further weakened as it was implemented.

The Dodd-Frank Act, passed in 2010, introduced new rules to regulate the complicated financial products traded on Wall Street and created the Consumer Financial Protection Bureau. Yet the original text of Dodd-Frank was weakened considerably over the course of its time on the congressional floor.[80] Exemptions were made for many banks with less than $10 billion in deposits, and an amendment that sought to break up banks risking over 2 percent of US GDP, intended to prevent another "too big to fail" scenario, was defeated on the floor, with twenty-seven Democratic "nays."[81] Within the prodigious text of the bill, there were inserted a number of clauses and exceptions to major regulations on derivative trading which, according to a former Consumer Financial Protection Bureau official, make it such that "violating them is risk-free." Additionally, the bill left most of the details to be decided by the regulatory agencies.

As of May of 2012, nine bills were pending in Congress that would weaken its regulation of derivatives, none of which would make regulation stronger;[82] as of June 1, 2012, only 110 of Dodd-Frank's 348 rulemaking requirements were finalized.[83] In June of 2012, the House Appropriations committee moved to reduce the administration's requested funding for the Commodity Futures Trading Commission by 41 percent.[84] The committee approved an increase of only $50 million of a requested $245 million for the Securities and Exchange

Commission's budget—and stipulated that the additional funds were not to be used for Dodd-Frank implementation.[85]

Attempts to pass the environmental cap-and-trade legislation during this period were defeated. When voting on a needed procedural move to push cap-and-trade forward, all forty-one Republicans were joined by twenty-six Democrats opposing that legislation's advance. Various liberal legislators have proposed raising the minimum wage to between $9.50 and $10 an hour, yet no raise was enacted in the period under study. The Disclose Act, which would have increased the transparency of campaign donations and limited the donation abilities of foreign-owned corporations, did not pass the Senate. Other liberal reforms, like an attempt to stop granting tax exemptions to oil companies with annual revenues in excess of $1 billion, were similarly stalled.

The conservative "party" did not gain all it sought, especially what its radical wing favored. This includes failing to adopt the Paul Ryan budget, which passed in the House but was defeated in the Senate; failing to adopt privatization of Medicare and Social Security; and failing to repeal the ACA. Some analysts argue that both the Democrats and the GOP are internally divided and held back by their radical wings, and that the right-center and the left-center could coalesce.[86] Yet one should note that the division within the GOP is between radical and moderate conservatives, while that within the Democratic Party is between conservatives and liberals. This is ultimately the reason centralist coalitions seem unlikely, while conservative Democrats are likely to continue to vote with the almost completely conservative GOP.

4. The Judicial Branch

Supreme Court: Some see the Supreme Court as consisting of four conservatives, four liberals, and a swing vote, first Sandra Day O'Connor, then Anthony Kennedy. Others see it as five conservatives and four weak liberals, one of whom is an occasional swing vote. An analysis of the court's major rulings in the period under study suggests that the second interpretation is closer to the facts, showing that this branch of government, like the two others, is in line with the voters' majority.[87] The Supreme Court is traditionally more independent from voters than both the White House and Congress, but it usually also seeks to be not too far removed from the positions of the majority of the public.

Nor did the Court gridlock other branches during the period under study. Instead, it has been clearing the way for one issue after the other. Its rulings on campaign finance, gun control, and other issues have widely affected public laws, rulings which far exceed the scope of the cases at hand. A 2010 analysis of the Roberts court described it as the "most conservative in decades," noting that four of the current justices are among the top six most conservative justices since 1937 and that Justice Kennedy is in the top 10.[88] Justice Kennedy, who regularly acts as the court's swing vote, sides with the conservatives about two-thirds of the time.[89]

From the viewpoint of the issue at hand, the 2010 Supreme Court ruling in *Citizens United v. Federal Election Commission* is particularly consequential. A 5-4 ruling overturned McCain-Feingold and most of modern campaign finance law.[90] The ruling allows corporation, labor unions, and rich individuals in effect to inject unlimited amounts of money into the election of public officials, and enables them to do so secretly. Moreover, in June of 2012, the Supreme Court's conservative majority ruled to restrict the fundraising capabilities of labor unions.[91]

The Court deviated from all precedent throughout its own history when it for the first time interpreted the 2nd Amendment, in the 2008 ruling *District of Columbia v. Heller*, as an individualized right to bear arms rather than that of a "well regulated militia." This ruling was expanded to include all fifty States in the 2010 ruling of *McDonald v. Chicago*. This is the position favored by conservatives and the NRA. Though Chief Justice Roberts unexpectedly sided with the liberals on the court to uphold the Affordable Care Act, his ruling that the law's mandate was not valid under the commerce clause, on which he was joined by the four dissenting judges, has been interpreted as a conservative move to limit Congress's authority to regulate domestic affairs.[92]

The import of the conservative leaning of the court ranges beyond the specific cases. If the polity would have merely responded to the conservative majority of the electorate, we would have a flawed form of democracy, one that is subject to a tyranny of the majority. However, given that the court mostly supported and in effect amplified and extended the conservative tilt of the polity, one cannot deny that this constitutional democracy produced a conservative wave. If one speculates what the nation's direction would have been in all the matters at hand if the election results would have been the same and Congress has acted in the same way, but the court would have had a strong liberal majority, one sees the importance of the conservative court. It greatly extended and legitimated the conservative direction of the polity. And it was rather active—a far cry from a gridlock.

5. Regulatory Agencies

Flashback: Liberals tend to view the enactment of most regulations, especially with regard to Wall Street, as a victory. One should note, though, that regulations that are enacted are often later significantly weakened. For example, Congress passed the Sarbanes–Oxley Act of 2002, establishing a new, firmer accounting regime for corporations. One part of the Act required companies regularly to audit their own internal anti-fraud and bookkeeping safeguards, and set up the Public Company Accounting Oversight Board to audit these auditors. Businesses lobbied this rule, and in 2006, after the Enron-inspired public outcry had subsided, the SEC greatly curtailed the regulations involved.

Instead of requiring auditors to investigate any accounting issues that had a "more than remote" chance of turning out to be an error or fraud, the new rule requires auditors to investigate only issues that had a "reasonable possibility" of fraud.[93] Many other details were eliminated as reflected in the fact that the regulations now run to only 65 pages rather than the original 180.

We have already seen how the financial regulations created by the Dodd-Frank Act were significantly weakened while that law was enacted. Like many other laws, it was further weakened while it was implemented. Thus, in 2011, the Commodity Futures Trading Commission, responding to pressure from the financial industry and conservative lawmakers, weakened a provision intended to limit commodity speculation by large organizations.[94] A key component of Dodd-Frank, the Volker Rule, was intended to stop banks from engaging in proprietary trading, which was considered one of the main causes of the 2008 crisis. Lobbying by the financial industry filled the regulations with exemptions and complications that left it "as good as dead."[95]

Dodd-Frank did accord a liberal win in the formation of the Consumer Financial Protection Bureau, which moved to require greater transparency from credit card companies and which monitors their behavior in response to customer complaints to ensure that they do not levy excessive or inaccurate charges. An investigation conducted by the *New York Times* found fifty-one cases between 1996 and 2011 in which nineteen Wall Street firms broke anti-fraud laws they had promised not to break. These firms include Goldman Sachs, Morgan Stanley, JPMorgan Chase, and Bank of America. When faced with these multiple violations, the SEC simply reached another settlement and extracted another promise, rather than bringing a contempt charge in court.[96]

6. The States

There are of course significant differences in the ways the fifty state assemblies and governors conduct their business. However, here too a conservative tilt is visible on at least two major fronts. The power of labor unions, historically a key part of the liberal base, has been systematically curtailed before and during the period under study.[97] Governor Scott Walker survived a recall election in Wisconsin that was launched by the unions when he greatly curtailed the collective bargaining rights of state workers.[98] His success served as a signal to other governors, leading them to enact similar measures in their own states. These governors included Democratic governors such as Andrew Cuomo (NY), who is working to reduce the benefits of unionized public sector workers, and Jerry Brown (CA), who is working to cut public sector pensions.[99]

In 2012, there were twenty-nine Republican state governors and twenty Democratic state governors, but these numbers conceal the fact that a majority of state governments have embraced conservative economic principles. Since 2008, thirty-five states have worked to reduce pension benefits for public-sector workers, and eighteen have curtailed or cut completely cost-of-living adjustments to public salaries.[100]

New immigration laws by Alabama, Georgia, and Arizona over this period have pushed immigration policy in a more conservative direction, as well as challenging the federal government's authority over immigration policy. Although most of the provisions of these laws have been struck down in the courts, some were let stand, such as a stipulation in Alabama which prevents illegal immigrants from engaging in a "business transaction" with a state or municipal agency. These moves have not only pushed immigration law in a more conservative direction than the federal government preferred, but they have also pushed the Obama Administration to demonstrate its strong commitment to enforcing immigration law, with some of the consequences being the high rates of deportation noted above.[101]

Public Sector Labor Force: Conservatives gained reductions in the governmental labor force, freezes on salaries, and reductions in benefits as part of their quest for a smaller government—according to some because these workers tend to vote Democratic and liberal. Between December of 2008 and August of 2012, the total number of government employees has declined by 655,000.[102] The National League of Cities found in 2010 that more than half of US cities had, since the start of this period, either frozen or cut pay for city employees.[103]

In sum, we have seen so far that in the overwhelming majority of public policy issues, including foreign policy, defense, homeland security, and economic policies the polity is not gridlocked, but instead often produces the policies and institutional changes sought by the conservative majority of the voters. This finding holds for all three branches of federal government, the regulatory agencies, and for a majority of state governments. There are liberal "moments" and policy outcomes, but they are much fewer and last for shorter periods.

II. Implications for Democratic Theory

If one is ready to assume for argument's sake that the American political system is basically responsive to the expressed preferences of the majority of the electorate rather than gridlocked, then what are the implications of these observations for democratic theory? One may suggest that the answer is all too evident: the voters spoke; the government followed; and democracy worked, at least in the period under study (2008–2012).

However, a considerable amount of data show that an overwhelming majority of the people are deeply troubled not just by the direction of the country but also by the actions of the government. Public opinion polls show that:

(a)   The proportion of respondents who thought the country was headed in the "wrong direction" grew steadily from 2008 until a peak in October of 2011, with 75 percent saying the country was moving in the

wrong direction, and after that steadied around 60 percent.[104] (There
was a brief intermission during what might be called an 'Obama high',
in the first months of his administration, when about 45 percent said
"wrong direction" and 45 percent said "right direction").

(b) The public is extremely critical of political institutions. Congressional
approval ratings have been below 30 percent throughout the 2008-
2012 period (excluding that brief moment of higher approval just
after Obama's inauguration)[105], reaching a low point of 11 percent
approval in December of 2011.[106] Public opinion of the Supreme
Court has also been declining and reached a twenty-five-year low in
April of 2012, with about half (52 percent) of respondents approving.[107] When asked their overall opinion of the federal government,
the proportion of Americans responding with an "unfavorable"
appraisal grew from 46 percent in 2007 to 50 percent in 2009 and
2010 to 62 percent in 2012. By the end of the period in question, the
percentage responding with a 'favorable' rating was at a fifteen-year
low and those with a 'very unfavorable' response at a fifteen-year
high (representing 25 percent of those surveyed). There has been
a similar, if slightly more muted, decline in the favorability of state
governments over this period.[108]

(c) The rise of protest movements, especially the Tea Party, but also
Occupy Wall Street, whose populist critical messages found broad
support among the general populace, is another indication of
widespread disaffection.[109] In October of 2011, when both movements were fresh on the political scene, 32 percent of Americans
supported the Tea Party and 39 percent supported the Occupy
movement, with 10 percent supporting both, and only 14 percent
opposing both.[110]

(d) By the observation of a considerable number of independent observers, including academics in other nations, the US government has not
functioned well in the period under study, as measured by such key
indicators as the low level of economic growth, high unemployment,
and ballooning deficits.[111] Moreover, the majority of the public lost
significant parts of its wealth during this period, with the median net
worth of American families declining by 39 percent between 2007
and 2010.[112] Over the period in question, an additional ten million
Americans have fallen to, or below, the poverty line, with over twenty
million in 2012 being in "deep poverty" with an income less than half
of the poverty line.[113] Millions lost their homes, their life-long savings,
and their jobs, or are close to someone who did.

These considerations bring us to a query. The majority of Americans are
deeply dissatisfied with the general course of the nation, as well as with its
political institutions. At the same time, they continue to vote for a conservative
course (and the polity is basically delivering what their expressed preferences
indicate), rather than vote for changes that would bring the polity to a pathway the majority of the voters appear to find more satisfying. These changes

could be for a more conservative policy, for a liberal alternative, or for a still different course, but one cannot but wonder why the majority voted to stay the course? As we saw, the change in Congress following the 2010 elections, which led to the replacement of conservative Democrats with Republicans, made little difference in the often conservative course of foreign, defense, homeland security, and economic policies. I refer to this combination as the big disconnect.

True, people may be distressed if they find that their country is on a wrong course because it has been pushed there by strong external forces, despite the best efforts of the political system. However, under these conditions, one would expect them to rally behind the government rather than be deeply critical of it. We see this, for instance, when a nation is attacked. In the period under study, the public has shown some understanding that economic difficulties were due in part to developments in Europe and elsewhere. For instance, when asked about who was most at fault for rising gas prices, people responded with 38 percent pointing at oil/energy companies, 28 percent blaming instability in the Middle East, and only 14 percent blaming the president[114]. However, in the period under study, the voters clearly also held that the government was acting wrongly or ineffectually, even as it was responding to their expressed preferences.

Did the majority hold that the government was not conservative enough? Did they not have time to digest the information? Did they draw the wrong conclusions? Or how else is one to reconcile (in terms of democratic theory) a responsive government that functions poorly both from the viewpoint of the majority and of independent observers? I provide next a set of possible explanations for this big disconnect. All of them leave questions to be answered. The same holds if one looks for the answer in the combination of several factors. The reasons no review of literature follows for each of these hypotheses are as follows: Firstly, the literature is enormous, and it would require volumes and years to review it. Second, the hypotheses are familiar. However, this may not be the case for the questions the period under study raised about these hypotheses by the period under study. These questions will be the only focus of the following discussion.

1. Rational Actors?

In democratic theory, it is a common assumption that the people are sovereign, and hence can direct the state in any way they prefer (or even misdirect it). However, it is also often assumed at least implicitly that the people are reasonable, that they will learn from their mistakes, and that they will not support policies that undermine their values and interests, again at least in the longer run. Hence also the expectation that good citizens will not merely vote but also inform themselves and engage in public affairs on the basis of what they learned.

The "public choice" school in effect took this idea a step further and assumed that people are rational actors, who know their self interests and vote accordingly.[115] The school drew on the assumptions of neoclassical economics that take it for granted that consumers and investors are rational and assumed likewise for voters.[116] When public choice scholars sought to collect evidence in support of this assumption, they run into considerable difficulties.[117] As two scholars critical of the approach put it, "a large proportion of the theoretical conjectures of rational choice theorists have not been tested empirically. Those tests that have been undertaken have either failed on their own terms or garnered theoretical support for propositions that, on reflection, can only be characterized as banal."[118] However, there are still scholars who hold that people vote "correctly," that is for representatives and policies that serve their values and self interests.

One of the few recent studies that examined how many people in a given election voted "correctly,"[119] claims that 75 percent of voters in the elections between 1972 and 2004 voted in accordance with their values and self-interests.[120] However, it is important to note that this study used a model of correct voting which was described by the authors as "naïve" in the sense that they measured votes against the expressed political preferences of the voters. This confronts the issue of incomplete information, but wholly ignores the more fundamental issue of whether voter preferences themselves accord with their actual interests. I return to this below in the discussion of the split self.

If one seeks to understand the period under study in these terms, one would conclude that voter disaffection is due to the fact that the government was not conservative enough (e.g., it did not cut the deficit and entitlements and did not reduce taxes and regulations sufficiently). These interpretations would be supported if (a) in the future, more voters come to favor more radically conservative candidates and policies and will favor, and (b) if this would lead to improved conditions of the nation and a reduction in disaffection. This hypothesis may seem as self-evident to a Tea Party conservative as it will seem absurd to a liberal. Empirically, it remains to be seen whether a further shift to the right would resolve the big disconnect.

2. Rational but Misinformed?

Neoclassical economics used to assume that people absorb information instantaneously and without efforts or costs, which is needed if they are to act rationally. However, economists have relaxed this assumption. They now tend to assume that if people stopped collecting and processing more information, it is because they reached a point at which the costs of gaining more knowledge are higher than the benefits that might be obtained in this way (though it is not quite clear how economic actors know that they have reached this point). Some economists have further relaxed this assumption and hold that people act rationally as long as they use the information available to them but do not necessarily possess all of the revelant information. This is known as "bounded rationality"[121]. This interpretation is supported by the findings that most people are unaware of many basic relevant facts, such as the name of their representatives and what they voted for.[122]

In line with this hypothesis, the big disconnect is explained by the fact that people do not understand the way the economy works and how it is best managed, especially given the high level of complexity involved in these issues. Otherwise they would have supported policies that would have put the nation on a different course, say, a bigger stimulus in the short run and a commitment to reduce the deficit once the economy grew again more vigorously.

To validate this hypothesis, one would have to determine whether people who are more informed vote differently than those less informed. It has often been suggested that educated people are more likely to hold liberal political beliefs,[123] and this finding is supported by some data. However, the link between liberal attitudes and education is tenuous. Although educated people are more likely to vote in a liberal manner, those who vote liberal in America are not likely to be highly educated. That is to say, although a majority of those with college and post-secondary degrees have a liberal outlook, among the liberal coalition as a whole, the majority of voters are poorly educated.[124] Also, the fact that followers of the Tea Party, far from being the redneck hicks their critics make them out to be, are more educated than average,[125] raises doubts about this hypothesis. Thus, the data on this question is inconclusive.

The findings of behavioral economics cast additional doubts on this line of reasoning, because very robust findings show that people are unable to process information rationally and are hard wired to make systematic cognitive errors.[126] So far behavioral economics has not spelled out the implications of these findings for democratic theory. However, this suggests that voters are not rational actors and that their misconceptions may have caused the great disconnect. Basic cognitive limitations could lead voters to support policies that damage their interests and values—and not notice it when the results hit them. However, to reiterate, there seems to be no definitive study that shows a correlations between levels of political ignorance and voting preference from one policy direction or another. For example, the Obama high was not based on an improvement in conditions—the economy actually got worse over this time—but the high was instead based upon hope and anticipation.

A form of voting that might be called holistic relies on a much lower level of knowledge than does economics or public choice theory, along with less knowledge than that assumed by democratic theory as it is typically understood. The holistic voting approach focuses on the observation that people have only one vote. Hence, however much they learn about the various policies and the various positions of different candidates for office, the voters cannot employ this knowledge.[127] They instead look at the two or three policies most important to them and determine whether they trust a specific candidate to make the kind of choices they favor, and then vote accordingly. This version of the hypothesis that knowledge matters (and that its absence causes the big disconnect, as it leads people to vote for policies and candidates they would reject if they knew more at least about the issues most important to them) faces the same test and questions as the previous ones. Do voters who are better informed, at least about the policies they most care about, vote systematically for policies that narrow the great disconnect? And if not, what are the implications for democratic theory?

3. The Split-Self Hypothesis

A rather different approach suggests that the great disconnect reflects the fact that the voters have a "split self". The idea is that the American polity is responsive to the preferences of the majority, which are *philosophically conservative*, but it is not responsive to their *operational preferences*, which are liberal. Hence the discontent. An early study by Lloyd Free and Hadley Cantril in the 1960s showed that while about 50 percent of Americans are philosophically conservative and only 16 percent philosophically liberal (according to their responses to generalized value questions), 65 percent of Americans are "operational liberals," based on their responses to questions about specific government actions and policies, while only 14 percent of Americans were operationally conservative.[128]

More recent data came to similar conclusions. James A. Stimson finds that "When Americans are asked if they want government to do more and spend more—and implicitly tax more—they generally say "yes" a lot more often than "no." That conclusion springs from the hundreds of different sorts of survey questions that we have. The pattern is not universal. Most Americans do not want government to spend more on "welfare," for example. But over all issues and controversies "more" dominates "less." Americans are operationally liberal: given a choice of more government or less, they generally choose more."[129]

Using poll results on a series of specific policy platforms taken from the American National Election Study, Stimson finds that voters who self-identify as conservatives are still highly likely to support a variety of government programs when asked about them individually. Poll data from 2011 show that among Republicans who make less than $75,000 a year, (i.e., the bottom 70 percent of US earners[130]) a majority prefer government benefits over deficit reduction, do not think that Medicare recipients should take on a greater responsibility for their own healthcare, and oppose reduced funding for roads and education.[131] This split political self was famously captured by a man at a town hall meeting in South Carolina who demanded that his representative "keep your government hands off my Medicare."[132] This would explain why the majority of the voters would be dissatisfied with whatever course the government followed, because it would either violate their philosophical or their operational preferences.

However, this hypothesis does not square with the fact that the people were much less discontented, despite their ostensible split political personalities, in earlier periods. For example, comparing public opinion from early 1997 (during the middle of the Clinton presidency) to 2010, there were an equal proportion of Americans who were "frustrated" with the national government in both years (56 percent). Moreover, the proportion Americans who were "angry" with the government was 10 percentage points higher in 1997 than in 2010, yet the proportion of Americans who considered government's effect on their daily life to be positive was 12 percentage points higher in 1997 than in 2011.

All this seems to suggest that other factors are at work, even though the fact that people are of two minds may make it rather difficult to satisfy many of them. Bigger government will antagonize their ideational self, while smaller government will antagonize their operational self. Their elected officials seem all too aware of this split and hence are often on both sides of the issue, talking budget cuts while increasing the deficit, for example. This in turn may have alienated both sides of the same voters, especially if they are unaware of their split selves.

4. The Voters are Not the Public

Another hypothesis is that the big disconnect reflects the difference between the voters and the public. Only 62 percent of eligible voters cast a ballot in the 2008 Presidential election,[133] and this number dropped off to 41 percent during the 2010 congressional election.[134] Because the government presumably responds to those who do vote, while public opinion polls that measure the disconnect include nonvoters—this could account for the difference. If most of these nonvoters were more liberal than those who voted, this might explain why voters support policies that displease large segments of the general public.

A poll taken in 2010 finds that 26 percent of those unlikely to vote identify as liberal, as opposed to 21 percent of the voting public. The proportion of conservatives among nonvoters was found to be 31 percent, which was 15 points lower than conservatives among polled voters. Comparing these groups further, we find that 52 percent of nonvoters support programs for increased governmental services, compared to 32 percent of voters, while 57 percent of nonvoters desire greater levels of gun control, against 42 percent among voters.[135] Of the estimated 90 million unlikely voters, polls show that 43 percent of them prefer Obama to either Romney (who has the support of 18 percent) or a third-party candidate.[136]

On the other hand, we see that although the nonvoting pubic is more liberal than the voting one, the difference is too small to explain the big disconnect. In addition, one needs to know the proportion of nonvoters who choose relatively freely not to vote, (whose preferences, according to Lipset and others, should be ignored[137]) versus those who are hindered through voter suppression efforts and various socioeconomic factors. The more there are of the second kind, the more weight must be given to this factor as explaining why the public would not be content with what the voters chose, although for the reasons indicated, this factor could at most account for a segment of the big discontent.

5. Weak Liberal Message

Others hold that major differences in the conservative and liberal messages are a key factor. They find that the liberal message is weaker than the conservative one by several indicators. William Forbath finds that "conservatives dominate the debate not because they have a killer theory (they do not), but chiefly because they have a bold, clear account of past constitutional commitments, adding up to a vision the Constitution promises to promote and redeem individualism, small government, godliness, and private property. Liberals have too often been complacent and purely defensive."[138] Michael Kazin contends that in this day and age, liberals have become a "defensive breed," who "now dedicate themselves to defending the reforms enacted from FDR to LBJ's administration and rebutting free-market fantasies, rather than proposing fresh models or theories."[139]

George Packer writes: "liberals are no less cynical, short sighted, and parochial than anybody else, and they understand their fellow Americans just as badly as they themselves are understood."[140] Michael Walzer observes that "the Democrats are weak-minded these days. No band of intellectuals is directing their thinking or writing their platform. They are almost as much in thrall to corporate wealth as the Republicans are – but without an ideological commitment to their thralldom."[141]

There is some evidence that the conservative message is easier to communicate to masses of people than the liberal one. CNN's Gloria Borger reported that when she asked Democratic voters what the Republican message was, they regurgitated it easily and correctly. When Borger asked them what the Democratic message was, the voters had greater difficulty in responding. The essence of the conservative message is for less government and more private sector freedom. The liberals do not counter with an opposing simple message, for more government and less freedom, but instead with a more nuanced and complex position.[142] For instance, President Clinton stated that the "age of big government is over", and President Obama has stated that "the question we ask today is not whether our government is too big or too small, but whether it works."[143] President Obama told that Democratic national convention in 2012 that the "We don't think the government can solve all our problems. But we don't think that the government is the source of all our problems"—hardly the sort of catchy rhetoric capable of replacing that of Reagan.

Conservatives have won the think-tank competition since the 1980s. Institutions such as the Cato Institute, the American Enterprise Institute, and the Heritage Foundation helped develop the conservative message, while liberal think tanks, such as the Center for American Progress and the Center on Budget and Policy Priorities, were much less effective.[144] Among the top ten think tanks in the United States in 2011, three were overtly conservative or libertarian and none explicitly liberal or progressive.[145] Of the fifteen largest think tanks, three are conservative but none is liberal.[146] Three of the top five most influential think tanks were conservative. Out of twenty-seven think tanks ranked by 125 congressional staffers and journalists as the most influential with regard to policymaking in Washington, only one was liberal.[147] Seventy-seven percent of op-eds were written by scholars at conservative think tanks, 18 percent from centrist ones, and only 5 percent by authors from left-leaning think tanks.[148]

The conservative messages, at least in the period under study, seem to have been stronger and more influential than the liberal ones. However it is far from clear whether this is due to the fact that the majority was more open to conservative messages because of its values and interests, or that they have been swayed by the messages. Most likely there were both conservative predispositions and message enforcement, but it matters a great deal which was more consequential. There seems to be next to no evidence to answer that question.

6. Misled by Media and Demagogues

According to this hypothesis, the great disconnect is due to the fact that voters are misled through persuasion by media and by demagogues who foster a false consciousness. Thomas E. Mann and Norman Ornstein argue that the media has become much more ideological and less responsible, news items are less informative, and the media has become fragmented, which enables people to choose their sources for information and thus never listen to the other side. Above all, media has become sensationalistic and inflammatory. All this causes Mann and Orenstein to suggest that "These phenomena help the conservative message, as those media forms most liable to sensationalism and a self-serving distortion of the facts, namely radio programs and e-mail chains, are dominated by conservative messages.[149]

Conservative Fox News's primetime audience in 2011 was more than twice the size of liberal MSNBC—a median viewership of 1.9 million compared to 773,000—and its daytime audience was nearly three times as large (1.1 million vs. 358,500).[150] All of the top-ten talk-radio hosts in 2011 were conservative or libertarian,[151] while Al Gore's attempt at a progressive talk-radio counterpoint, Air America, collapsed.[152] The left-leaning Pacifica Radio Network consists of only five radio stations with an extremely small audience.[153] There are no liberal programs comparable to those of Rush Limbaugh, Sean Hannity, and Bill O'Reilly in terms of audience size or impact.

The conservative advantage is even attributed to differences in inventing code words and images. Renaming the estate tax a "death tax" is credited with helping conservatives cut the estate tax. Liberals have been trying to match these efforts by calling federal expenditures "investments" and tax increases 'revenue raises.'[154]

Conservatives are also said to be more willing than liberals to engage in negative attacks. Although there are large amounts of negative ads from both sides, those run by "independent" super PACs are specifically notable in this regard. "Swift boating" in the 2004 presidential race is given as a key example, as are ads about Willie Horton in 1988. In the 2012 election campaign, several major liberal donors, such as George Soros, have been reluctant to donate to candidate-oriented super PACs that mushroomed after the *Citizens United* ruling, as these organizations are reported to specialize in negative ads. These donors focused instead on grassroots efforts, voter registration and turnout, and research.[155] However, negative attacks can be more effective than their promotional counterparts,[156] especially when they are put forth by "independent" PACs which do not provoke as much backlash as do attack ads released by candidates themselves.[157]

It is impossible to review here the very considerable literature on the effects of the media on politics, a literature which studies the extent to which the media "dumbs down" the public and biases it. One can note though that the public attitudes regarding their conservative versus liberal preferences have changed little since the advent of the new media, including CNN and especially Fox. For instance the proportion of Americans who self-identified as conservatives was 35 percent in 2000 and 36 percent in 2012.[158] In addition, the public is much more educated and informed than it was in earlier generations, with over 30 percent of American adults having a college degree.[159] Furthermore, people's preferences are affected by numerous factors, including their economic and social conditions and the general social fabric—not just the media.[160] Lastly, a good part of what is considered the media effect actually reflects self-selection. That is, the fact that more people watch Fox than MSNBC reflects not only the persuasive power of Fox but also that there are more conservatives to begin with, and they flock to Fox. The media thus seems more to reinforce than to convert.

Moreover, people have a choice to follow either liberal, conservative, or "neutral" media, such NPR, public television, and the *New York Times* and *Washington Post,* with their longer and more nuanced news stories. Nobody is forcing people to watch dumbed-down media.

7. Interest Groups

Another alternative hypothesis is that the polity is mainly responsive to *special interests*, a position associated with Mancur Olson[161] and Robert Tollison,[162] and more recently laid out by Kay Lehman Schlozman.[163] During the mid-20th century, several theorists held that on the whole, because all special interests are free to organize themselves politically and because interest groups are only powerful when citizens participate or donate to their cause, their involvement in politics expressed the popular will and made for sound policy.[164] What has been referred to as "interest group pluralism" suggested that the needs and preferences of various segments of the public do find expression in one interest group or another, and hence all are represented such that no one group can lord over the others or ignore their concerns.[165]

Since then, this view has given way to a new consensus, which maintains that some interest groups are systematically better situated to influence the polity than others. Following the classic account of Schattschneider, who argued that "the flaw in the pluralist heaven is that the heavenly chorus sings with a strong upper-class accent," contemporary political scientists have paid much more attention to the differing levels of power held by distinct interest groups.[166] Specifically, those interests that favor conservative policies (e.g., large corporations, banks, real estate, farmers, the NRA) are significantly stronger than those that favor liberal policies (e.g., labor unions, social workers, nursing associations and students).[167] Other scholars have noted how certain issues which are of low salience for the majority of voters but high salience for a select few (such as the estate tax or gun control) feature wealthy or well-connected interest groups exerting powerful influences on public policy against the majority of public opinion.[168] In this view, the difference in leverage that the various interests gain can be measured by the amount of donations they make to PACs and super PACs.

Political scientists differ in the extent to which they hold that monies affect the outcome of elections.[169] However, note that many of these analyses compare the donations that are made to Republicans to those made to Democrats, and they find that one party gains more during one election and the other more in the other, and that one party gained more from the rank and file and PACs and the other more from affluent individuals and via Super PACs. However, for the current analysis, one needs to compare the funds that flow to *liberal* versus *conservative* representatives whatever actual party they belong to. There seems to be no systematic study of this difference, but just a few anecdotes.

The answer to the question of whether the polity is responsive to conservative voters or conservative special interests is obvious: It seems responsive to both. However, when one considers those situations in which the demands of these two groups diverge, one finds that conservative interest groups are granted their preferred legislation more often than are conservative voters. Thus, conservative interest groups continue to gain large federal outlays and tax exemptions for their constituencies while demanding a reduction in deficits.

For example, in 1996, Congress passed legislation that stipulated that only when oil prices were low should the US government offer oil companies drilling rights to prime locations without collecting royalties. Enforcement of this legislation was assigned to the Minerals Management Service, which is reported to be under the lobbying influence of the oil industry. As a result, between 1996 and 2012, 24 companies were granted royalty free leases that violated the conditions set out by Congress. The loss in revenues is estimated to exceed $50 billion by 2035.[170] Large subsidies to farmers, who tend to vote conservative and strongly oppose big government and corporate welfare, is another key case in point. Far from serving to keep the small farmer alive, an American ideal, the overwhelming bulk of subsidies is channeled to large agri-businesses, to the tune of about $30 billion a year. There are numerous other examples behind most tax exemptions in the 1200-page-long IRS code, plus thousands of earmarks, subsidies, and other forms of interest group privilege.

The result, one may hypothesize, is that the polity is following policies that alienate the majority. Clearly, interest groups swell the deficit, which particularly troubles conservative voters. They also make voters feels as if they are pulling levers that are disconnected. Thus the majority may favor certain forms of gun control, such as a ban on high-capacity magazines and semi-automatic weapons,[171] but the NRA prevents the polity from responding. The majority believes that wealth in America should be more evenly distributed,[172] and that wealthier Americans should pay more into Social Security.[173] Twice as many Americans believe increasing taxes for those making $250,000 a year or more would help the economy as think it would hurt the economy.[174] Over two-thirds of voters agree that the influence of Super-PACs is corrupting our national government.[175]

One can readily expect that the workings of these interests groups, occurring so often behind the scenes, is the cause of a significant part of the big disconnect. However, what is puzzling is that the majority does not view them as the main culprit, a role reserved for the government (though interest groups remain on many people's list of issues they find troubling).[176] Additionally, there seem to be little if any data to suggest that the majority understands that not all interest groups have the same leverage, and which ones have more.

In Conclusion

So far, this article has dealt with various possible explanations for the big disconnect by examining one approach at a time. Obviously, more than one factor is likely to be at work—possibly several or even all of them. Thus lack of information, media biases, interest group power, and the voters' "split selves" may each account for some of the disconnect. However, unless one can attribute some weights to each of the various factors, establishing which are most significant as well as how they interact, we do not have much of an explanation. As far as I can tell, no such scale exists, and the challenge posed to democratic theory by the facts before us stands.

All these hypotheses, whether examined one at a time or in some combination, do have one common element. They implicitly compare the way the American polity functions to some ideal state, in which voters know their preferences, they command the relevant information, their preferences are not conflicted, and they are not swayed by the media or by demagogues. That is, the comparison is drawn between a democratic system that functions in a complex sociological reality and some abstract ideal. The results are so unfavorable that they have led some people seriously to suggest a shift from a democratic polity to a technocracy or even to the Chinese regime. Thus, Peter Orszag argues that "to solve the serious problems facing our country, we need to minimize the harm from legislative inertia by relying more on automatic policies and depoliticized commissions for certain policy decisions. In other words, radical as it sounds, we need to counter the gridlock of our political institutions by making them a bit less democratic,"[177] such that "the best we can do to avoid gridlock may be to expand the degree of 'automaticity' in the legislative process."[178] More radically, Thomas Friedman argues that "There is only one thing worse than one-party autocracy, and that is one-party democracy, which is what we have in America today. One-party autocracy certainly has its drawbacks. But when it is led by a reasonably enlightened group of people, as China is today, it can also have great advantages."[179]

I guess the best one can do for now is to fall back on Churchill, who famously pointed out that, compared to all other systems which function in the real world, democracy works the least poorly. Importantly, other systems are much more prone to resort to violence when people are disaffected. In contrast, during the period under study, the strong protest of the Tea Party was absorbed by the political system, leading it to lobby, raise funds, run candidates, and caucus, all peaceful and legitimate democratic expressions. Other polities may function well as long as the autocrat is benign, as the Prime Minister of Singapore arguably was for his people, yet there is no institutionalized way to restrain them or to replace them when they turn out to be a Hitler or Stalin. And corruption, while far from unknown in democracies, is even more debilitating in other regimes.

The challenge the United States faces is hence, on the face of it, not to find another regime but how to make democracy work better, a challenge that is likely to benefit us all if we better understand why the voters—whose expressed preferences are heeded—are so deeply disaffected.

Notes

1. See Thomas E. Mann and Norman J. Ornstein, *It's Even Worse Than It Looks* (New York: Basic Books, 2012).
   Also: Francis Fukuyama, "Oh for a Democratic Dictatorship and Not a Vetocracy," *Financial Times* (November 22, 2011), http://www.ft.com/intl/cms/s/0/d82776c6-14fd-11e1-a2a6-00144feabdc0.html#axzz1vtTUgOBV.
   Also: Peter Orszag, "The Looming Showdown," *Democracy* 25 (Summer 2012), http://www.democracyjournal.org/25/the-looming-showdown.php?wpisrc=nl_wonk.
2. For example: William Galston, "Political Dysfunction and Economic Decline," Brookings Institution (January 13, 2012), http://www.brookings.edu/research/papers/2012/01/13-economy-galston.

Also: Francis Fukuyama, "American Political Dysfunction," *The American Interest* (November/December 2011).

3. Sarah A. Binder, *Stalemate: Causes and consequences of Legislative Gridlock* (Washington DC: Brookings Institution Press, 2003). Binder argues that the current state of gridlock is only partly derived from the constitutional system of checks and balances. Changes in the political system since these checks and balances were created, particularly the rise of senatorial power and the establishment of interbranch political parties.

4. "How to Rig an Election," *The Economist* (April 25, 2002), http://www. economist.com/node/1099030?story_id=E1_TDJJDPD.
   Also: Brookings Institution, http://www.brookings.edu/blogs/up-front/posts/2010/06/15-gerrymandering-frankel.

5. David R. Jones, "Party Polarization and Legislative Gridlock," *Political Research Quarterly* 54, no. 1 (March 2001): 125–141.

6. Thomas T. Holyoke, "Interest Group Competition and Legislative Gridlock," Paper prepared for Annual Meeting of the Western Political Science Association (April 2010), http://papers.ssrn.com/sol3/papers.cfm?abstract_id=1580602.

7. Rebecca Chalif, "Political Media Fragmentation: Echo Chambers in Cable News," *Electronic Media and Politics* 1, no. 3 (July 2011): 46–65.

8. Sarah A. Binder, "The Dynamics of Legislative Gridlock, 1947–96," *The American Political Science Review* 93, no. 3 (September 1999): 519–533.

9. Barack Obama, "Remarks by the President at a Campaign Event," The White House (July 5, 2012), http://www.whitehouse.gov/the-press-office/2012/07/05/remarks-president-campaign-event.

10. David Brooks, "Ryan's Biggest Mistake," *The New York Times* (August 24, 2012), A21.

11. Sarah A. Binder, *Stalemate: Causes and consequences of Legislative Gridlock* (Washington DC: Brookings Institution Press, 2003). In particular, see Chapter 3.

12. Susan Davis, "This Congress could be Least Productive Since 1947," *USAToday* (August 15, 2012), http://www.usatoday.com/news/washington/story/2012-08-14/unproductive-congress-not-passing-bills/57060096/1.

13. Marc Fisher, "Over the Past Half-Century, a Strong Shift to the Right," *The Washington Post* (August 29, 2012), A1, A8.
    Also: "Political Scientist: Republicans Most Conservative they've been in 100 Years," *NPR* (April 13, 2012), http://www.npr.org/blogs/itsallpolitics/2012/04/10/150349438/gops-rightward-shift-higher-polarization-fills-political-scientist-with-dread.

14. Pew Research Center, "Partisan Polarization Surges in Bush, Obama Years: Trends in American Values, 1987–2012." Pew Research Center for the People and the Press (June 4, 2012), http://www.people-press.org/files/legacy-pdf/06-04-12%20Values%20Release.pdf, 13.

15. Donald R. Kinder and Nathan P. Kalmoe, "The Nature of Ideological Identification in Mass Publics Part II: Formation and Consolidation," American Political Science Association 2009, Toronto Meeting Paper. Available at SSRN: http://ssrn.com/abstract=1464961.
    Also: Christopher Ellis and James A. Stimson, *Ideology in America* (New York, New York: Cambridge University Press, 2012), Chapters 1 and 4.

16. Lydia Saad, "Conservatives Remain the Largest Ideological Group in U.S.," Gallup (January 12, 2012), http://www.gallup.com/poll/152021/conservatives-remain-largest-ideological-group.aspx.

17. Ibid.

18. Data for the two graphic shown above from Pew Research Center, "Partisan Polarization Surges in Bush, Obama Years: Trends in American Values, 1987–2012."

19. Pew Research Center, "Partisan Polarization Surges in Bush, Obama Years: Trends in American Values, 1987–2012." Pew Research Center for the People and the Press, (June 4, 2012,: http://www.people-press.org/files/legacy-pdf/06-04-12%20Values%20Release.pdf, 13–15.

20. "Battleground 2012 (XLVII)," *Politico*, George Washington University (May 2012), http://images.politico.com/global/2012/05/bg_47_questionnaire.html, 13.

21. Arthur J. Schlesinger Jr., "The Cycles of American Politics," in *The Cycles of American History* (New York: First Mariner Books, 1999): 23–48.

22. Stephen Skowronek, "Presidential Leadership in Political Time," in *The Presidency and the Political System*, 2nd edition, ed. Michael Nelson, Washington, DC: Congressional Quarterly Press, 1988), 115–119.

23. Andrew S. McFarland, "Interest Groups and Political Time: Cycles in America," *British Journal of Political Science* 21 (1991): 257–284.

24. Samuel Merrill, III, Bernard Grofman, and Thomas L. Brunell, "Cycles in American National Electoral Politics, 1854–2006: Statistical Evidence and an Explanatory Model," *American Political Science Review* 102, no. 1 (February 2008): 1–17.

25. See E.J. Dionne, *Our Divided Political Heart* (New York: Bloomsbury, 2012).

26. Pew Research Center, "The American-Western European Values Gap," Pew Global Attitudes Project (February 29, 2012), http://www.pewglobal.org/2011/11/17/the-american-western-european-values-gap/.
    Also see Geert Hofstede on National Culture, his research shows the United States to have the highest ratio on the measure of individualism versus collectivism.

27. Eric Alterman and Kevin Mattson, *The Cause: The Fight for American Liberalism from Franklin Roosevelt to Barack Obama* (New York: Viking, 2012), 460.

28. Douglas Brinkley, *The Unfinished Presidency: Jimmy Carter's Journey Beyond the White House* (New York: Penguin Books, 1998). For this assessment of Cater as a conservative Democrat, at odds with his more liberal colleagues, see chapter 1, available at http://www.nytimes.com/books/first/b/brinkley-unfinished.html.

29. Ibid.

30. See Eric Alterman and Kevin Mattson, *The Cause: The Fight for American Liberalism from Franklin Roosevelt to Barack Obama* (New York: Viking, 2012).

31. Ryan Lizza, "The Obama Memos," *The New Yorker* (January 30, 2012), http://www.newyorker.com/reporting/2012/01/30/120130fa_fact_lizza?currentPage=all.

32. Andrew Goldman, "Larry Summers: Un-King of Kumbaya," *The New York Times* (May 12, 2011), http://www.nytimes.com/2011/05/15/magazine/larry-summers-un-king-of-kumbaya.html.

33. Ryan Lizza, "The Obama Memos," *The New Yorker* (January 30, 2012), http://www.newyorker.com/reporting/2012/01/30/120130fa_fact_lizza?currentPage=all.

34. "Tax Stimulus Report Card: Conference Bill," Urban-Brookings Tax Policy Center (February 13, 2009).

35. David Kirkpatrick, "Obama Is Taking an Active Role in Talks on Health Care Plan," *The New York Times* (August 12, 2009), http://www.nytimes.com/2009/08/13/health/policy/13health.html?pagewanted=all.

36. Peter Baker, "Obama was Pushed by Drug Industry, E-mails Suggest," *The New York Times* (June 8, 2012), http://www.nytimes.com/2012/06/09/us/politics/e-mails-reveal-extent-of-obamas-deal-with-industry-on-health-care.html?pagewanted=all.

37. Michael Cooper, "Conservatives Sowed Idea of Health Care Mandate, Only to Spurn it Later," *The New York Times* (February 14, 2012), http://www.nytimes.com/2012/02/15/health/policy/health-care-mandate-was-first-backed-by-conservatives.html.

38. Nicholas Wapshott, "Secret Emails Show Romney's Approval of Health Mandate," *Reuters* (June 8, 2012), http://blogs.reuters.com/great-debate/2012/06/08/secret-emails-show-romneys-approval-of-health-mandate/.

39. "President Obama's First Year: Failed Leadership, Lost Lives," Brady Center to Prevent Gun *Violence* (January 2010), http://www.bradycampaign.org/xshare/reports/fedleg/obama-1styear-report.pdf, 1.

40. Ibid.

41. Kate Andersen Brower and Roger Runningen, "Obama Resists Gun Control Advocates' Call for Legislation," *Bloomberg News*,(August 6, 2012), http://www.businessweek.com/news/2012-08-06/obama-resists-gun-control-advocates-call-for-stemming-violence#p1..

42. Molly O'Toole, "Analysis: Obama deportations raise immigration policy questions," *Reuters* (September 20, 2011), http://www.reuters.com/article/2011/09/20/us-obama-immigration-idUSTRE78J05720110920.

43. Adam Liptak, "Inmate Count in US Dwarfs Other Nations," *The New York Times* (April 23, 2008), http://www.nytimes.com/2008/04/23/us/23prison.html?pagewanted=all.

44. Kevin Johnson, "2011 Budget Gives Federal Prisons $528," *USAToday* (February 4, 2010), http://www.usatoday.com/news/washington/2010-02-03-prison-budget_N.htm.
    Also: James Ridgeway and Jean Casella, "Obama Budget: Grow Prisons and keep Gitmo," *Mother Jones* (February 22, 2012), http://www.motherjones.com/politics/2012/02/obama-federal-prison-budget.

45. William J. Quirk, "Too Big to Fail and Too Risky to Exist," *The American Scholar* (Autumn 2012): 31–43.

46. David Ingram and Aruna Viswanatha, "Justice Department Drops Goldman Financial Crisis Probe," *Reuters* (August 9, 2012), http://www.reuters.com/article/2012/08/10/us-usa-goldman-no-charges-idUS-BRE8781LA20120810.

47. Charlie Savage, "Senators Say Patriot Act Is Being Misinterpreted," *The New York Times* (May 26, 2011), http://www.nytimes.com/2011/05/27/us/27patriot.html.

48. Andy Pasztor and John Emshwiller, "Drone Use Takes Off on the Home Front," *The Wall Street Journal* (April 21, 2011), http://online.wsj.com/article/SB10001424052702304331204577354331959335276.html.

49. Peter Finn, "Obama Set to Revive Military Commissions," *The Washington Post* (May 9, 2009), http://www.washingtonpost.com/wp-dyn/content/article/2009/05/08/AR2009050804228.html.

50. On Iraq, see: Jeffrey M. Jones, "Three in Four Americans Back Obama on Iraq Withdrawal," Gallup (November 2, 2011), http://www.gallup.com/poll/150497/Three-Four-Americans-Back-Obama-Iraq-Withdrawal.aspx.
On Afghanistan, see: Lydia Saad, "Americans Broadly Favor Obama's Afghanistan Pullout Plan," Gallup (June 29, 2011), http://www.gallup.com/poll/148313/Americans-Broadly-Favor-Obama-Afghanistan-Pullout-Plan.aspx.

51. Helene Cooper, "Cost of Wars a Rising Issue as Obama Weighs Troop Levels," *The New York Times* (June 21, 2011), http://www.nytimes.com/2011/06/22/us/politics/22costs.html?pagewanted=all.
Also: Anthony H. Cordesman, "The US Cost of the Afghan War: FY2002-FY2013," Center for Strategic and International Studies (May 14, 2012), http://csis.org/files/publication/120515_US_Spending_Afghan_War_SIGAR.pdf.

52. Jonathan Weisman, "House Vote Upholds Indefinite Detention of Terror Suspects," *The New York Times* (May 18, 2012), http://www.nytimes.com/2012/05/19/us/politics/house-votes-to-preserve-a-power-of-indefinite-detention.html.

53. David Alexander, "House-Backed Defense Budget Sets up Clash with Obama," *Reuters* (May 18, 2012), http://www.reuters.com/article/2012/05/18/us-usa-defense-budget-idUSBRE84G1IM20120518.

54. Mary Ellen O'Connell, "When is a War not a War? The Myth of the Global War on Terror," *ILSA Journal of International & Comparative Law* 12, no. 2 (2005), http://www.pegc.us/archive/Articles/O%27Connell_22_ILSA_J_Intl_Comp_L_2005.pdf.

55. John O. Brennan, "The Ethics and Efficacy of the President's Counterterrorism Strategy," Remarks at the Woodrow Wilson International Center for Scholars, Washington, DC (April 30, 2012), http://www.wilsoncenter.org/event/the-efficacy-and-ethics-us-counterterrorism-strategy.

56. Daniel Klaidman, *Kill or Capture: the War on Terror and the Soul of the Obama Presidency*, (New York, New York: Harcourt, 2012).

57. Paul Harris, "Drone Wars and State Secrecy—How Barack Obama Became a Hardliner," *The Guardian* (June 2, 2012), http://www.guardian.co.uk/world/2012/jun/02/drone-wars-secrecy-barack-obama.

58. Eric Holder, "Attorney General Eric Holder Speaks at Northwestern University School of Law," (May 5, 2012), http://www.justice.gov/iso/opa/ag/speeches/2012/ag-speech-1203051.html.

59. Martin S. Indyk, Kenneth G. Lieberthal, and Michael O'Hanlon, *Bending History: Barack Obama's Foreign Policy* (Washington D.C.: Brookings Institution Press, 2012).

60. James Mann, *The Obamians: The Struggle Inside the White House to Redefine American Power* (New York, New York: Penguin Books, 2012).

61. Charlie Savage, "Obama Weighs Supreme Court Nominees, and Each Potential Battle," *The New York Times* (April 16, 2010), http://www.nytimes.com/2010/04/17/us/politics/17court.html?pagewanted=all.

62. Binyamin Appelbaum, "Former Ohio Attorney General to Head New Consumer Agency," *The New York Times* (July 17, 2011), http://www.nytimes.com/2011/07/18/business/former-ohio-attorney-general-picked-to-lead-consumer-agency.html?pagewanted=all.

63. Charlie Savage, "Obama Lagging on Filling Seats in the Judiciary," *The New York Times* (August 18, 2012), A1.

64. For these figures, only votes where Republicans won despite Democratic opposition were counted. Non-partisan votes were not counted. This statistic provided by Ryan Kelly, from the Congressional Quarterly.

65. Binyamin Appelbaum and Jennifer Steinhauer, "Congress Ends 5-Year Standoff on Trade Deals in Rare Accord," *The New York Times* (October 12, 2011), http://www.nytimes.com/2011/10/13/business/trade-bills-near-final-chapter.html?pagewanted=all.

66. This includes the cooperation of the 2 Independent Senators in the 60 vote total. The first of these 'moments' was in July 2009, lasting for over a month, the second in September 2009, lasting until early February 2010.

67. Emmet J. Bondurant, "The Senate Filibuster: Politics of Obstruction," *Harvard Journal on Legislation* 48, no. 2 (2011), 478.

68. United States Senate, "Senate Actions on Cloture Motions," http://www.senate.gov/pagelayout/reference/cloture_motions/clotureCounts.htm.

69. Andrea Seabrook, "Health Care Passage Hinged on Abortion Language," *NPR* (March 22, 2012), http://www.npr.org/templates/story/story.php?storyId=125004701.

70. Adam Nagourney, "Leiberman Disputes Reid's Account of Health Bill Wrangling," *The New York Times* (January 13, 2010), http://thecaucus.blogs.nytimes.com/2010/01/13/lieberman-disputes-reids-account-of-health-bill-wrangling/.

71. "Fact Checking Health Insurance Premiums," *FactCheck.org* (October 24, 2011), http://www.factcheck.org/2011/10/factchecking-health-insurance-premiums/.

72. Josh Boak, "Do Nothing Congress Did Something: Named Buildings," *The Fiscal Times* (August 15, 2012), http://www.thefiscaltimes.com/Articles/2012/08/15/Do-Nothing-Congress-Did-Something-Named-Buildings.aspx#page1.

73. Stephan Dinan, "Congress Logs Most Futile Legislative Year on Record," *The Washington Times* (January 15, 2012), http://www.washingtontimes.com/news/2012/jan/15/congress-logs-most-futile-legislative-year-on-reco/.

74. Alan Silverleib, "Debt Ceiling Votes: From Routine to Radioactive," *CNN* (July 7, 2011), http://articles.cnn.com/2011-07-06/politics/debt.ceiling.fight_1_debt-ceiling-federal-debt-limit-crs?_s=PM:POLITICS.

75. United States Government Accountability Office, "Debt Limit: Analysis of the 2011-2012 Actions Taken and Effect of Delayed Increase on Borrowing Costs," Government Accountability Office (July 2012), http://www.gao.gov/assets/600/592832.pdf.

76. Richard Kogan, "How the Potential Across-the-Board Cuts in the Debt-Limit Deal Would Occur," Center on Budget and Policy Priorities (November 22, 2011), http://www.cbpp.org/files/8-4-11bud.pdf.

77. Ryan J. Donmoyer and Peter Cohn, "Congress Passes $858 Billion Tax-Cut Extension, Sends to Obama for Signing," *Bloomberg* (December 17, 2010),

http://www.bloomberg.com/news/2010-12-17/house-votes-to-debate-obama-s-858-billion-tax-cut-deal-with-republicans.html.

78. Jonathan Weisman, "House Approves One-Year Extension of the Bush-era Tax Cuts," *The New York Times* (August 1 2012), http://www.nytimes.com/2012/08/02/us/politics/house-votes-to-extend-bush-era-tax-cuts.html. Also: Brian Beutler, "Senate Dems Jam House Republicans, Pass Bush Tax-Cut Extension for Middle Class," *TalkingPointsMemo* (July 25, 2012), http://tpmdc.talkingpointsmemo.com/2012/07/senate-dems-jam-house-republicans-pass-bush-tax-cut-extension-for-middle-class.php.

79. William J. Quirk, "Too Big to Fail and Too Risky to Exist," *The American Scholar* (Autumn 2012): 31–43.

80. Marian Wang, "Regulators Weaken Dodd-Frank Draft Regs, Allow More Risk," *ProPublica.org* (September 22, 2011), http://www.propublica.org/blog/item/regulators-loosen-limits-on-risk-in-latest-drafts-of-dodd-frank-rules.

81. Matt Taibbi, "Wall Street's War," *Rolling Stone* (May 26, 2010), http://www.rollingstone.com/politics/news/wall-streets-war-20100526.

82. Taylor Lincoln, "Forgotten Lessons of Deregulation: Rolling Back Dodd-Frank's Derivative Rules Would Repeat a Mistake that Led to the Financial Crisis," Public Citizen (May 2012), http://www.citizen.org/documents/forgotten-lessons-of-deregulation-derivatives-report.pdf, 3.

83. "Dodd-Frank Progress Report," (June 2012), DavisPolk Regulatory Tracker, http://www.davispolk.com/files/Publication/867cc356-a624-49e9-b1fc-529db6946e6e/Presentation/PublicationAttachment/97a3eb90-7d31-41fe-a2a7-815c28e874f5/Jun2012_Dodd.Frank.Progress.Report.pdf, 2.

84. Jonathan Weisman, "House Bill Takes Scythe to Spending," *The New York Times* (June 5, 2012), http://www.nytimes.com/2012/06/06/us/house-bill-takes-a-scythe-to-spending.html.

85. Ibid.

86. David Brooks, "Ryan's Biggest Mistake," *The New York Times* (August 24, 2012), A21.

87. Robert Barnes, "After Supreme Court Term, Line between 'Liberal' and 'Conservative' is Blurrier," *The Washington Post* (June 30, 2012), http://www.washingtonpost.com/politics/after-supreme-court-term-line-between-liberal-and-conservative-is-blurrier/2012/06/30/gJQAbumcEW_story.html.

88. Adam Liptak, "Court Under Roberts Is Most Conservative in Decades," *The New York Times* (July 24, 2010), http://www.nytimes.com/2010/07/25/us/25roberts.html?pagewanted=all.

89. "Conservative majority emerges on court," The Washington Times, July 1, 2007, accessed at http://www.washingtontimes.com/news/2007/jul/1/conservative-majority-emerges-on-court/#ixzz39jzMZxgJ

90. Jeffrey Toobin, "Money Unlimited," *The New Yorker* (May 21, 2012), http://www.newyorker.com/reporting/2012/05/21/120521fa_fact_toobin?currentPage=all.

91. Alana Samuels, "Supreme Court Clamping Down on Unions' Political Fundraising," *Los Angeles Times* (June 21, 2012), http://www.latimes.com/news/politics/la-pn-supreme-court-clamping-down-on-unions-political-fundraising-20120621,0,6066157.story.

92. Brad Plummer, "Supreme Court Puts New Limits on Commerce Clause. But Will It Matter?" *The Washington Post* (June 28, 2012), http://www.washingtonpost.com/blogs/ezra-klein/wp/2012/06/28/the-supreme-court-put-limits-on-commerce-clause-but-does-it-matter/.

Also: Tom Scocca, "Obama Wins the Battle, Roberts Wins the War," *Slate* (June 28, 2012), http://www.slate.com/articles/news_and_politics/scocca/2012/06/roberts_health_care_opinion_commerce_clause_the_real_reason_the_chief_justice_upheld_obamacare_.html.

93. Carrie Johnson, "Plan Unveiled to Scrap a Sarbanes-Oxley Rule," *The Washington Post* (December 20, 2006), http://www.washingtonpost.com/wp-dyn/content/article/2006/12/19/AR2006121901433.html.

94. Sarah N. Lynch, "Watchdog Backs Down on Commodities Rules," *Reuters* (September 22, 2011), http://www.reuters.com/article/2011/09/22/us-financial-regulation-limits-idUSTRE78L11P20110922.

95. Jesse Eisinger, "The Volker Rule, Made Bloated and Weak," *The New York Times* (February 22, 2012), http://dealbook.nytimes.com/2012/02/22/the-volcker-rule-made-bloated-and-weak/.

96. Edward Wyatt, "Promises Made, and Remade, by Firms in SEC Fraud Cases," *The New York Times* (November 7, 2011), http://www.nytimes.com/2011/11/08/business/in-sec-fraud-cases-banks-make-and-break-promises.html?pagewanted=all.

97. Steven Greenhouse, "Strained States Turning to Laws to Curb Labor Unions," *The New York Times* (January 3, 2011), http://www.nytimes.com/2011/01/04/business/04labor.html?pagewanted=all.

98. Peter Whoriskey and Dan Balz, "Wisconsin Gov. Scott Walker's Victory Deals Blow to Unions," *Washington Post* (June 6, 2012), http://www.washingtonpost.com/business/economy/wisconsin-gov-scott-walkers-victory-deals-blow-to-unions/2012/06/06/gJQAAIWVJV_story.html.

99. David Gergen and Michael Zuckerman, "A Victory for Curbs on Public Worker Unions," *CNN.com* (June 6, 2012), http://www.cnn.com/2012/06/04/opinion/gergen-zuckerman-walker/index.html.

100. Mark Miller, "Five things to Consider Before Cutting Pension Benefits," *Reuters.com* (June 20, 2012), http://www.reuters.com/article/2012/06/20/us-column-miller-idUSBRE85J0N120120620.

101. "Court Blocks Provisions in Immigration Laws, Lets some Controversial Ones Stand," *CNN.com* (August 20, 2012), http://articles.cnn.com/2012-08-20/justice/justice_state-immigration-laws_1_attorney-general-sam-olens-immigration-laws-national-immigration-law-center.
Also: Robert Barnes, "Supreme Court to Hear Challenge to Arizona's Immigration Law," *The Washington Post* (December 12, 2011), http://www.washingtonpost.com/politics/supreme-court-to-hear-challenge-of-arizonas-restrictive-immigration-law/2011/12/12/gIQA4UYepO_story.html.

102. Bureau of Labour Statistics, "All Employees, Government," US Department of Labour (September 7, 2012), http://research.stlouisfed.org/fred2/data/USGOVT.txt.

103. Steven Greenhouse, "More Workers Face Paycuts, Not Furloughs," *The New York Times* (August 3, 2010), http://www.nytimes.com/2010/08/04/business/economy/04paycuts.html?_r=1&pagewanted=all.

104. "Direction of Country," *Real Clear Politics*, http://www.realclearpolitics.com/epolls/other/direction_of_country-902.html.

105. Frank Newport, "Congress Approval Ties All-Time Low at 10%," Gallup (August 14, 2012), http://www.gallup.com/poll/156662/Congress-Approval-Ties-Time-Low.aspx.

106. Frank Newport, "Congress Ends 2011 with Record-Low 11% Approval," Gallup (December 19, 2011), http://www.gallup.com/poll/151628/congress-ends-2011-record-low-approval.aspx.

107. "Supreme Court Favorability Reaches New Low," The Pew Research Center for People and the Press (May 1, 2012), http://www.people-press.org/files/legacy-pdf/5-1-12%20Supreme%20Court%20Release.pdf.

108. Pew Research Center, "Partisan Polarization Surges in Bush, Obama Years: Trends in American Values, 1987–2012," Pew Research Center for the People and the Press (June 4, 2012), http://www.people-press.org/files/legacy-pdf/06-04-12%20Values%20Release.pdf, 117–118.

109. Gerald F. Seib, "Populist Movements Rooted in Same Soil," *The Wall Street Journal* (November 15, 2011), http://online.wsj.com/article/SB100014240 52970203503204577037980400569026.html.

110. Pew Research Center, "Public Divided Over Occupy Wall Street Movement," Pew Research Center for the People and the Press (October 24, 2011), http://www.people-press.org/2011/10/24/public-divided-over-occupy-wall-street-movement/.

111. David Wessel, *Red-Ink: Inside the High-Stakes Politics of the Federal Budget* (New York: Random House, 2012).

112. Ylan Q. Mui, "Americans Saw Wealth Plummet 40 Percent from 2007 to 2010, Federal Reserve Says," *The Washington Post* (June 11, 2012), http://www. washingtonpost.com/business/economy/fed-americans-wealth-dropped-40-%0b%0bpercent/2012/06/11/gJQAllsCVV_story.html.

113. Sasha Abramsky, "The Other America, 2012: Confronting the Poverty Epidemic," *The Nation* (April 25, 2012), http://www.thenation.com/article/167564/other-america-2012-confronting-poverty-epidemic.

114. Matthew Cooper, "Poll Shows Public Supports Obama on Gas Prices" *National Journal* (March 12, 2012). http://www.nationaljournal.com/daily/poll-shows-public-supports-obama-on-gas-prices-20120312

115. I disregard that at least two leading members of this school wondered why people vote at all, because the cost of voting—such as standing in line and missing work or leisure time—was a tangible cost while they cannot reasonably expect that they will see a benefit to voting, namely, that their vote will make a difference. They expect that people would get a free ride on the outcomes of the votes of others in all but very close elections. See Anthony Downs, *An Economic Theory of Democracy* (Harper and Row: New York, 1957).

116. Jane S. Shaw, "Public Choice Theory," *The Concise Encyclopedia of Economics*, 1st Ed., (1993).

117. Geoffrey Brennan and Alan Hamlin, "Revisionist Public Choice Theory," *New Political Economy* 13, no. 1 (March, 2008): 77–88.

118. Donald Green and Ian Shapiro, *Pathologies of Rational Choice Theory: A Critique of Applications in Political Science* (New Haven, CT: Yale University Press, 1994), 6.

119. They determined a vote to be "correct" if the voter cast a ballot for the same candidate they would have endorsed had they had complete information. Voters' political preferences were determined by answers and priority rankings they gave on a policy and political values survey, and the positions of the candidates were determined by independent political experts.

120. Richard R. Lau, David J. Andersen, and David P. Redlawsk, "An Exploration of Correct Voting in Recent US Presidential Elections," *American Journal of Political Science* 52, no. 2 (April 2008): 395–411.
121. Herbert Simon, *Models of Bounded Rationality, Vol. 1* (Cambridge, MA: MIT Press, 1984).
122. For example: Only 40% of voters can name all three branches of the federal government; 60% do not realize that federal judicial appointments rely on approval by the Senate; 65% do not know that Congress holds the power to declare war. See Rick Shenkman, *Just How Stupid are we? Facing the Truth About the American Voter* (New York, NY: Basic Books, 2008).
123. Seymour Martin Lipset, *Political Man: The Social Bases of Politics* (New York, NY: Doubleday and Co., 1960), 109–115.
    Also: Herbert H. Hyman and Charles Wright, *Education's Lasting Influence on Values* (Chicago, IL: University of Chicago Press, 1979), 60–62.
    Also: Eamonn Callan, *Creating Citizens: Political Education and Liberal Democracy* (New York, NY: Oxford University Press, 2004), Chapter 1.
124. In a 2011 study by Pew, which divided the American electorate into eight groups, the two most well-educated groups were the two most liberal, however the third most well-educated were "staunch conservatives," so any correlation here is not indicative of much. Moreover, the group of more moderate democrats, who hold predominately but not exclusively liberal views, was the least well educated of those groups who are likely to vote. See Pew Research Center, "Beyond Red vs. Blue: Political Typology," Pew Research Center for the People and the Press (May 4, 2011), http://www.people-press.org/files/legacy-pdf/Beyond-Red-vs-Blue-The-Political-Typology.pdf.
125. Brian Montopoli, "Tea Party Supporters: Who they are and What they Believe," *CBSnews.com* (April 14, 2010), http://www.cbsnews.com/8301-503544_162-20002529-503544.html.
    Also: Kate Zernike, *Boiling Mad: Inside Tea Party America* (New York: Times Books, 2010).
    Also: Jill Lepore, *The Whites of Their Eyes: The Tea Party's Revolution and the Battle Over American History* (Princeton: Princeton University Press, 2010), 14.
126. Daniel Kahneman, *Thinking, Fast and Slow* (New York, NY: Farrar, Straus, and Giroux, 2011).
127. This point stands out if one contrasts the current situation with a hypothetical scenario where people could vote for or against a given line of policy, say one vote for economic policy, one for foreign policy and so on, or even elect directly the heads of each government agency including that of the Federal Reserve system.
128. Scott Keeter, "Review: Albert H. Cantril and Susan Davis Cantril. *Reading Mixed Signals: Ambivalence in American Public Opinion about Government*," *Public Opinion Quarterly* 64, no. 4 (Winter 2000): 543–546.
129. James A. Stimson, *Tides of Consent: How Public Opinion Shapes American Politics* (New York, NY: Cambridge University Press, 2004), 84.
130. "Income Breaks, 2011," TaxPolicyCenter.org (May 12, 2011), http://taxpolicycenter.org/numbers/displayatab.cfm?DocID=2970.
131. Pew Research Center, "Public Wants Changes in Entitlements, Not Changes in Benefits," Pew Research Center for the People and the Press, (July 7, 2011).

Also: Pew Research Center, "More Blame Wars than Domestic Spending or Tax Cuts for Nation's Debt," Pew Research Center for the People and the Press (June 7, 2012).

132. Philip Rucker, "Sen. DeMint in S.C. Is Voice of Opposition to Health-Care Reform," *Washington Post* (July 28, 2009), http://www.washingtonpost.com/wp-dyn/content/article/2009/07/27/AR2009072703066.html?hpid=topnews&sid=ST2009072703107.

133. "2008 General Election Turnout Rates," United States Elections Project (March 31, 2012), http://elections.gmu.edu/Turnout_2008G.html.

134. "2010 General Election Turnout Rates," United States Elections Project (December 28, 2011), http://elections.gmu.edu/Turnout_2010G.html.

135. Pew Research Center, "The Party of Nonvoters," Pew Research Center for the People and the Press (October 29, 2010), http://pewresearch.org/pubs/1786/who-are-nonvoters-less-republican-educated-younger.

136. Susan Page, "Why 90 Million Americans Won't Vote in November," *USAToday.com* (August 15, 2012), http://www.usatoday.com/news/politics/story/2012-08-15/non-voters-obama-romney/57055184/1.

137. Seymour Martin Lipset, *Political Man: The Social Bases of Politics* (New York, NY: Doubleday and Co., 1960), Chapter 6.
Also: Richard R. Lau, David J. Andersen, and David P. Redlawsk, "An Exploration of Correct Voting in Recent US Presidential Elections," *American Journal of Political Science* 52, no. 2 (April 2008): 395–411.

138. William E. Forbath, "Workingman's Constitution," *The New York Times* (July 6, 2012), http://query.nytimes.com/gst/fullpage.html?res=9F04EFD81E3DF935A35754C0A9649D8B63&pagewanted=all.

139. Michael Kazin, "Why Don't Liberals Write Big Books Anymore?" *The New Republic* (February 28, 2012), http://www.tnr.com/article/books-and-arts/101171/liberal-books-thinkers-friedan-hitchens-krugman-critics.

140. George Packer, "The New Liberalism," *The New Yorker* (November 17, 2008), http://www.newyorker.com/reporting/2008/11/17/081117fa_fact_packer.

141. Michael Walzer, "Social Movements and Election Campaigns," *Dissent* (Summer 2012): 25–28.

142. Beverly Gage, "Why is there no Liberal Ayn Rand?" *Slate* (August 13, 2012), http://www.slate.com/articles/news_and_politics/history/2012/08/paul_ryan_and_ayn_rand_why_don_t_america_liberals_have_their_own_canon_of_writers_and_thinkers_.html.

143. "Barack Obama's Economic Record," *The Economist* (September 1, 2012), 26.

144. Andrew Rich, "War of Ideas: Why Mainstream and Liberal Foundations and the Think Tanks They Support Are Losing in the War of Ideas in American Politics," *Stanford Social Innovation Review* (Spring 2005): 18–25.

145. James G. McGann, "The Global Go-To Think Tanks Report 2011," Think Tanks and Civil Society Program, International Relations Program, University of Pennsylvania (January 20, 2012): 37–38.

146. Andrew Rich, *Think Tanks, Public Policy, and the Politics of Expertise* (Cambridge, U.K.: Cambridge, University Press, 2004): 224.

147. As Rich discusses, the selection of list of think tanks was not randomized and cannot be considered to be an objecting ranking of the influence of the think tanks listed. However, the results still provide a useful depiction of the relative standing of many well-known think tanks. Ibid., 230.

148. Samuel P. Jacobs, "The Right-Wing Op-Ed Insurgency," *The Daily Beast* (August 1, 2009), http://www.thedailybeast.com/articles/2009/08/01/the-right-wing-op-ed-insurgency.html.
    A 2008 survey of references to think tank produced studies in news stories published in major media outlets revealed a similar disparity between conservative and liberal think thinks. See Michael Dolny, "The Incredible Shrinking Think Tank," *Extra!* (March/April 2008), http://www.fair.org/index.php?page=3322.
    Also: John Michlethwait and Adrian Wooldridge, *The Right Nation: Conservative Power in America* (New York: Penguin Books, 2004): 166–167.
149. Thomas E. Mann and Norman J. Orenstein, *It's Even Worse than It Looks* (New York: Basic Books, 2012), 67.
150. Jesse Holcomb, Amy Mitchell, Tom Rosentiel, "Cable: By the Numbers," *The State of the News Media 2012*, Pew Research Center's Project for Excellence in Journalism (2012), http://stateofthemedia.org/2012/cable-cnn-ends-its-ratings-slide-fox-falls-again/cable-by-the-numbers/.
151. Laura Houston Santhanam, Amy Mithcell, and Tom Rosentiel, "Audio: How Far Will Digital Go?" *The State of the News Media 2012*, Pew Research Center's Project for Excellence in Journalism (2012), http://stateofthemedia.org/2012/audio-how-far-will-digital-go/.
152. Brian Stelter, "Liberal Radio, Even Without Air America," *The New York Times* (January 24, 2010), http://www.nytimes.com/2010/01/25/arts/25radio.html?_r=1.
153. "About the Pacifica Network," *Pacifica Affiliates Network* (2012), http://www.pacificanetwork.org/radio/content/section/4/81/.
154. George Lakoff, *Moral Politics: How Liberals and Conservatives Think* (Chicago: University of Chicago Press, 1996).
155. Nicholas Confessore, "Liberals Steer Outside Money to Grass-Roots Organizing," *The New York Times* (May 7, 2012), http://www.nytimes.com/2012/05/08/us/politics/liberals-putting-super-pac-money-into-grass-roots.html.
156. For a summary overview of the literature on negative advertisements, and the complexities with assessing their efficacy, see: Richard R. Lau, Lee Sigelman, and Ivy Brown Rovner, "The Effects of Negative Political Campaigns: A Meta-Analytic Reassessment," *Journal of Politics* 69, no. 4 (November 2007): 1176–1209.
157. Deborah Jordan Brooks and Michael Murov, "Assessing Accountability in a Post-Citizens United Era: The Effects of Attack Ad Sponsorship by Unknown Independent Groups," *American Politics Research* 40, no. 3 (May 2012): 383–418.
158. Pew Research Center, "Partisan Polarization Surges in Bush, Obama Years: Trends in American Values, 1987–2012." *Pew Research Center for the People and the Press* (June 4, 2012), http://www.people-press.org/files/legacy-pdf/06-04-12%20Values%20Release.pdf.
159. "Bachelor's Degree Attainment Tops 30 Percent for the First Time," US *Census Bureau* (February 23, 2012), http://www.census.gov/newsroom/releases/archives/education/cb12-33.html.
160. For an overview of this literature, see Michael MacKuen and Courtney Brown, "Political Context and Attitude Change," *American Political Science Review* 81, no. 2 (June 1987): 471–490.

Also: Jeffrey Lyons, "Where You Live and Who You Know," *American Politics Research* 39, no. 6 (November 2011): 963–992.
Also: Scott D. McClurg, "Social Networks and Political Participation," *Political Research Quarterly* 56, no. 4 (December 2003): 449–464.

161. Mancur Olson, *The Logic of Collective Action* (Cambridge, MA: Harvard University Press, 1971), and *The Rise and Decline of Nations* (New Haven, CT: Yale University Press, 1982).

162. Robert D. Tollison, W. Mark Crain, and Thomas H. Deaton, "The Price of Influence in an Interest-Group Economy," *Rationality and* Society 3, no. 4 (October 1991): 437–449.
Also: Robert D. Tollison, "The Interest Group Theory of Government: Problems and Prospects," *Kyklos* 54, no. 2 (May 2001): 465–472.

163. Kay Lehman Schlozman and John T. Tierney, *Organized Interests and American Democracy* (New York, NY: Harper and Row, 1986).
Also: Kay Lehman Schlozman, Sidney Verba, and Henry E. Brady, *The Unheavenly Chorus* (Princeton, NJ: Princeton University Press, 2012).

164. Frank R. Baumgartner and Beth L. Leech, *Basic Interests: The Importance of Groups in Politics and in Political Science* (Princeton, NJ: Princeton University Press, 1998).
Also: Jeffrey M. Berry and Clyde Wilcox, *The Interest Group Society*, 5th *ed.* (New York, NY: Pearson-Longman, 2009). Classically: Mancur Olson, *The Logic of Collective Action*.

165. Robert A. Dahl, *Who Governs?* (New Haven, CT: Yale University Press, 1961). David B. Truman, *The Governmental Process: Political Interests and Public Opinion* (New York, NY: Knopf, 1951).
Also: Andrew S. MacFarland, "Interest Groups and Theories of Power in America," *British Journal of Political Science* 17, no. 2 (April 1987): 129–147.

166. Elmer Schattschneider, *The Semi-Sovereign People: A Realist's View of Democracy in America* (New York: Holt, Rinehart and Winston, 1960).

167. Kay Lehman Schlozman, "What Accent the Heavenly Chorus? Political Equality and the American Pressure System," *Journal of Politics* 46, no. 4 (November 1984): 1006–1032. Kay Lehman Schlozman and John T. Tierney, *Organized Interests and American Democracy* (New York, NY: Harper and Row, 1986).

168. Ian Shapiro, *The Real World of Democratic Theory* (Princeton, NJ: Princeton University Press, 2011) Chapter 6.
Also: Christopher Witko, "PACs, Issue Context, and Congressional Decisionmaking," *Political Research Quarterly* 59, no. 2 (June 2006): 283–295.

169. Influence is noted in Doug Roscoe and Shannon Jenkins, "A Meta-Analysis of Campaign Contributions' Impact on Roll Call Voting," *Social Science Quarterly* 86 no. 1 (March 2005): 52–68. However, some find the evidence to be inconclusive, such as Richard A. Smith, "Interest Group Influence in the US Congress," *Legislative Studies Quarterly* 20, no. 1 (February 1995): 89–139.

170. "Oil Royalties: Giving Away Government Money Accidentally On Purpose," *The Economist* (February 22, 2011). http://www.economist.com/blogs/democracyinamerica/2011/02/oil_royalties/.

171. Polling Report, "Guns," *PollingReport.com* (August 8, 2012), http://www.pollingreport.com/guns.htm.

172. Frank Newport, "Democrats, Republicans, Differ Widely on Taxing the Rich," *Gallup.com* (April 14, 2011), http://www.gallup.com/poll/147104/Democrats-Republicans-Differ-Widely-Taxing-Rich.aspx.

173. Jeffrey M. Jones, "Americans Look to Wealthy to Help Save Social Security," *Gallup.com* (July 29, 2010), http://www.gallup.com/poll/141611/Americans-Look-Wealthy-Help-Save-Social-Security.aspx.

174. Pew Research Center, "Raising Taxes on Rich Seen as Good for Economy, Fairness," *Pew Research Center for the People and the Press* (July 16, 2012), http://www.people-press.org/2012/07/16/raising-taxes-on-rich-seen-as-good-for-economy-fairness/.

175. "National Survey: Super PACs, Corruption, and Democracy," *Brennan Center for Justice* (April 24, 2012), http://brennan.3cdn.net/5d2ff3bdfc12b2eb27_pym6b9cdv.pdf.

176. Brian Montopoli, "Alienated Nation: Americans Complain of Government Disconnect," *CBSNews.com* (June 28, 2011), http://www.cbsnews.com/8301-503544_162-20074813-503544.html.

177. Peter Orszag, "Too Much of a Good Thing," *The New Republic* (September 14, 2011), http://www.tnr.com/article/politics/magazine/94940/peter-orszag-democracy.

178. Peter Orszag, "The Looming Showdown," Democracy 25 (Summer 2012): 34.

179. Thomas L. Friedman, "Our One-Party Democracy," *The New York Times* (September 8, 2009), http://www.nytimes.com/2009/09/09/opinion/09friedman.html.

7

The Scope of Corruption

This chapter seeks to provide a preliminary design, to set the agenda for a major collaborative political science project to study the level and scope of political corruption in the United States. Reference is not to a formal collaboration, but to one in which different colleagues independently contribute both to the project's overarching design and the building blocks that the design calls for. This involves suggesting revisions and additions to the design, carrying out some of the research it calls for, and sharing one's findings with both political scientists and the public. Such collaboration is needed due to the magnitude of the subject, the limited (albeit growing) amount of available research on the subject, and the inherent difficulties in studying behavior that is concealed by those who engage in it. The social significance of the subject is self-evident, especially if one holds, as I do, that political corruption in the United States is much more prevalent, consequential, and resistant to correction than is often assumed.

Competing Definitions

Political scientists have devoted considerable attention to the ways political corruption is defined.[1] In 1978, two political scientists wrote that "the systematic study of corruption is hampered by the lack of an adequate definition. What may be 'corrupt' to one citizen, scholar, or public official is 'just politics' to another, or 'indiscretion' to a third" (Peters and Welch 1978, 974). Since then, much deliberation has gone into how to best resolve this difficulty. Mark Philip's (1997) "Defining Political Corruption" is an excellent starting point for a discussion of the numerous issues raised by definition. Benson, Maaranen, Heslop (1978); Heidenheimer, Johnston, and LeVine (2001); and Svensson (2005) have also made important contributions to the subject.

A focus on first pinning down the concept at issue is well justified because, as is the case with much research, measurements of the observed phenomenon will depend upon how the measured variable is defined. Thus, if one defines being 'in poverty' as all those whose annual income is below $15,000, one will find far fewer people living in poverty than if the threshold is set at $30,000. This issue is particularly challenging in the study of political corruption because the subject is defined in rather discrete ways, and each definition reflects—as we shall see—distinct political theories. A definition can make corruption seem less widespread than it is, for instance, if it excludes practices that some consider legalized bribery. Theoretically at least, the opposite could also happen (see Olken and Pande (2011, 13)).

Although there is no practical way for the discipline to formulate and agree on a single definition of political corruption, this need not impede the proposed endeavor. One turns to the second-best option: editors of political science publications should urge authors to clearly state which definition they are employing, and those who review these contributions should help to foster such a norm. In the following discussion, three proposed definitions—along with their theoretical underpinnings—are employed to provide a first approximation of a research design. The concept will be delineated according to whether political corruption is viewed as personal (e.g. accepting bribes and stealing public assets, known as graft) (discussed in Part I), the illegal deflection of public goods into coffers of private special interest groups (Part II), or not merely illegal but also illicit or unethical conduct (Part III). This is by no means an exhaustive list of definitions. However, it suffices to demonstrate the need to indicate up front which definition-cum-theory is employed, and what this implies for subsequent evaluations of the level of political corruption.

Several scholars have voiced the concern that political scientists have neglected the study of political corruption in the United States by any definition (DeLeon 1993; Johnston 2006; Meier and Holbrook 1992; Tevfik, Price and Weber 1986).[2] Interest in the subject tends to spike after a particularly egregious scandal such as Watergate or the prosecution of notorious lobbyist Jack Abramoff. In recent years, a great deal of academic research on corruption has focused on the so-called "developing world" and cross-national comparisons, especially as they relate to economic growth (Olken and Pande, 2011). However, as we shall see shortly, the analytical apparatus used in these studies cannot be automatically applied to the United States because of features that are unique to the American political system, especially those included in the US Constitution.

For outlining the agenda for a collaborative study of American corruption, it seems necessary to draw not only on empirical research but also on highly informal sources, including reports by investigative journalists (e.g., those published by the *New York Times* and *Washington Post*) and even the mass media (e.g., *60 Minutes*). Such anecdotal evidence serves to identify factors that may warrant further exploration and can be used to build hypotheses, though it may not establish the validity of those hypotheses.

I. Less Corrupt Politicians, More Corrupt Politics?

According to one relatively narrow definition, political corruption entails the illegal use of *public* power and resources for *personal* gain. The obvious examples would be elected representatives or civil servants ("public officials" from here on) accepting bribes and handing out favors in return. Those who have studied political corruption using this definition include Nye (1967), Meier and Holbrook (1992), Van Klaveren (1989), Sheifer and Vishny (1993), Fackler and Lin (1995), and Banerjee et al. (2012).[3] For a review of several empirical economic analyses of personal corruption and the factors that can incentivize or combat it, see studies by Sheifer and Vishny (1993), Besley and McLaren (1993), and Ades and Di Tella (1997). In effect, their analyses treat corruption as either bribes or theft of government funds, but do not focus on the deflection of resources to interest groups.[4]

There seems to be no systematic study by political scientists of the changes in congressional rules that seek to reign in the personal corruption of public officials.[5] Over the years, Congress has introduced a number of regulations that limit the gifts members can legally accept. For instance, after the 2006 scandal surrounding lobbyist Jack Abramoff—which ended the careers to two congressmen and led to criminal charges against several other public officials—Congress passed the Honest Leadership and Open Government Act of 2007, which bans essentially all gift-giving from registered lobbyists (previously Congress members and staff could accept gifts valued less than $50) and prohibits members of Congress and staffers from accepting private travel from lobbyists (though exceptions may be approved by the House Committee on Ethics). However, there is a need to study the extent to which these rules are followed and enforced—as well as the loopholes that are hidden within them. For instance, media reports point to an exemption in the 2007 bill for "foreign-financed cultural-exchange trips," whereby despite the fact that "registered foreign lobbyists can't buy a $2 cup of coffee for a congressional staffer in Washington, they are allowed to invite, plan and accompany a staffer on a trip costing $10,000 or more" (Farnam 2013). Similarly, when one classifies lobbying activities as "campaign events," they are not subject to the same strict guidelines. In addition, hiring or directing business to spouses is still quite common (Kindy, Fallis, and Higman 2012). Congress is also reported to exempt its members from rules applying to others, such as bans on insider trading. An investigation by *The Washington Post* revealed that members of Congress regularly benefit from stock trades and business deals based on nonpublic information, a practice that Peter Schweizer of the Hoover Institution calls "honest graft" (*60 Minutes* 2011). In response to the criticism generated by this and similar reports, Congress passed the Stop Trading On Congressional Knowledge Act of 2012, which bans insider trading by members of Congress. However, such regulation still leaves open other avenues for Congressmen to profit from their position, e.g., investing in the very industries that they regulate. The *Washington Post* reported in June 2012 that "one-hundred-thirty members of Congress or their families have traded stocks collectively worth hundreds of millions of dollars in companies lobbying on bills that came before their committees, a practice that is permitted under current ethics rules" (Keating et al. 2012). All things considered, if one draws on media reports, it seems that Congress has tightened the rules regulating personal conduct over the last decades, but opportunities for personal corruption remain or have emerged in new forms. Neither the current scope nor the net effect of this kind of corruption in the national legislature has been established by political science research.

The executive branch has had its share of corruption-related scandals (Genovese 2010). In 2009, Darleen Druyun, civilian chief of Air Force acquisition, was sentenced to nine months in prison for favoring Boeing while negotiating future employment with the company (Cahlink 2004). Bush Administration officials in the Department of the Interior, Labor and Justice pleaded guilty to accepting bribes from Jack Abramoff. It might therefore seem that corruption in the executive branch is similar in scope to the level in Congress.

However, one must take into account that while there are only 535 members of Congress and some thirty thousand legislative employees, the executive branch employs nearly 2.8 million people (Copeland 2011). Even if a similar number of incidents of personal corruption were found in both branches, the prevalence of corruption in the executive branch would be much less. Importantly, the two possess different incentive structures. Members of Congress are under a great deal of pressure to raise large amounts of money in order to avert or survive primary elections and to triumph in the general election. It is much easier to achieve this end by appealing to a few large donors. Thus, members of Congress have a much greater incentive to grant favors to generous contributors than civil servants who need not fundraise to hold onto their jobs.

To add a note based on experience, thirty-five years of personal observation in Washington DC, including one year in the White House, have convinced me that the executive branch of the government is much less corrupt than the legislative branch. Moreover, most parts of it, with notable exceptions, are corruption-free to a point that if the other branches of government were as "clean," corruption would cease to be a systematic, institutionalized issue. Furthermore, I suggest, that the executive branch should serve as a demonstration to skeptics that a clean government is possible. In my experience, when I had lunch with civil servants, they insisted on paying for their own meals. When I sent a book to a high-ranking official of the FBI (after we served together on a commission and became quite friendly), she returned it on the grounds that she could not accept gifts. I had numerous similar experiences. In contrast, I was asked to give talks at top-of-the-line resorts where members of Congress, their families, and staffers were wined and dined and had their golf, tennis, and room and board paid for. Keys to rental cars and monogrammed pieces of luggage were handed out by various industrial groups, including those who promote the consumption of cotton, cigarettes, and alcohol. True, in recent years this kind of spending has been reigned in, however at the same time some new ways of rewarding members of Congress have been found. I am not suggesting that there are no corrupt members of the executive branch, but do raise the hypothesis that they are the outliers, as opposed to Congress where such personal corruption remains significantly more widespread. The data on this point, however, are scant. The federal judiciary seems also much "cleaner" than Congress. These are, however, merely hypotheses.

Even if research reveals that there has been some decline in *personal* corruption in the federal legislative branch over the last forty years (much ethics reform came to pass in the mid and late 1970s) and that there is considerable integrity in the executive and judiciary on the federal level, it does not follow that the American political system has grown less corrupt in recent decades— at least not if one draws on a more encompassing definition of corruption.

II. Captured?

A broader definition of corruption views it as an illegal use of public power and resources for private gain, which includes not only or even primarily personal gain, but the deflection of public resources and employment of public power to advance the causes of one or more private special interest groups (Berg, Hahn, and Schmidhauser 1976, 98; Fackler, Tim, and Lin 1995). It should be noted that this definition of corruption reflects a particular theoretical position that not all political scientists, let alone all other social scientists, share. It assumes public officials should be concerned with the common good or the public interest. For instance, Carl Friedrich (1966, 74) writes that corruption exists when a "power-holder" "is by monetary or other rewards not legally provided for, induced to take actions which favour whoever provides the rewards *and thereby does damage to the public and its interests.*" At the opposite side of the spectrum is the position that the very concept of the common good or public interest is illusory, that politics is by nature a vying of various private interests over resources distributed by the political system and that the legislature acts as clearing house in which parties work out these allocations (Bentley 1908; Golembiewski 1960; Posner 1974; Stigler 1971, 11; Tollison 1991). In such a system, assertions that some acts serve the common good are viewed as veiled attempts by private parties to legitimate their claims. Lobbying that involves campaign contributions, in contrast, is considered a legitimate activity used by private actors to further their interests (Fatka and Levien 1998, 586). Many acts that are considered corrupt under the assumption that the government does and should promote the common good are seen as acceptable under the interest group theory of governance.

Many theoretical positions concerning the ways in which the polity functions—and ought to function—fall somewhere between these two extremes. For instance, some hold that that politics serves to reconcile various private interests with the common good by satisfying the private ends in ways that advance the shared interest (Ackerman 1991, 273). Failing that, good polities attempt to at least balance the public interest with private ones. The following discussion assumes that a functional polity must operate under some basic shared understanding about the common good (Etzioni 2004).

According to standard liberal democratic theory, laws and the regulations that specify and implement them are a major way that the common good (or public interest) is advanced. However, according to a counter-theory advanced by many economists, laws and above all the regulators who implement them are typically "captured" by the very same interest groups that are meant to be reined in—and are thereby prevented from serving the intended public end. In his frequently cited article "The Economic Theory of Regulation," George Stigler (1971) writes that, "as a rule, regulation is acquired by the industry and is designed and operated primarily for its benefit."[6] (This work builds upon Stigler's previous essay with Claire Friedland (1962), "What can Regulators Regulate? The Case of Electricity," which finds that setting prices for electricity by public authorities to prevent it from rising detrimentally affected consumers.) A considerable number of subsequent studies reached similar conclusions (Becker 1976; Peltzman 1976; Posner 1974).

Many of these studies are limited to capture of the regulation or law itself, that is, the way it was initially formulated (Dal Bo 2006). For instance, lobbyists representing the pharmaceutical industry literally composed parts of the 2003 bill that governs drug benefits for Medicare recipients. This benefit was initially estimated to cost $400 billion over ten years. More recent estimates range as high as $1.2 trillion, in part because the law prohibits the government from negotiating with pharmaceutical companies over the price of drugs (Hall and Van Houweling 2006).[7] However, capture takes many other forms. In the following lines, I list some of its most prominent variants and provide brief illustrative examples. As far as I can establish, there are no studies examining how widespread such capture actually is, whether it is increasing or on the decline, or its societal consequences.

1. Diluting Regulation

In the wake of the 2001 Enron scandal, Congress passed the 2002 Sarbanes-Oxley Act. Hailed by *The Economist* (2003) as, "the most sweeping reform of corporate governance in America since the Great Depression," the law left it to the Securities and Exchange Commission (SEC) to work out the details of its new regulations. Following intense lobbying by the accounting industry, the SEC employed a definition of auditing that created a loophole such that accountants can continue practices initially targeted for prohibition.

Sarbanes-Oxley was further weakened in 2006. Whereas it initially required auditors to investigate any accounting issues that had a "more than remote" chance of damaging a company's finances, the rules were revised to only require auditors to investigate issues that have a "reasonable possibility" of doing so.

Moreover, in 2009, small businesses were permanently exempted from two of the act's key provisions—the first requiring executives to confirm the integrity of their firms' internal accounting procedures, and the second requiring an outside audit of these procedures. This gradual dilution of regulations is reflected in the size of the regulatory text of the law, which was reduced from 180 pages to a mere 65 (Winkler 2009).

2. Debilitating Restrictions

Under the influence of the National Rifle Association (NRA), Congress has repeatedly limited the ability of the Bureau of Alcohol, Tobacco, Firearms and Explosives (ATF) to enforce gun laws. The Firearms Owners' Protection Act of 1986 bans the ATF from inspecting gun dealers more than once in any twelve month period, even if violations are uncovered, and reduces record-keeping violations from a felony to a misdemeanor offense. As a result, gun dealers are very rarely prosecuted. The 2003 and 2004 "Tiahrt amendments" require that records from the background checks of gun buyers be destroyed within 24 hours, bar the ATF from requiring gun dealers to conduct inventory checks to monitor gun thefts, and prevent crime gun trace data from being used in court even when a dealer has broken the law. In addition, Congress prohibited the creation a computerized database by the ATF, which means that when a gun is recovered at a crime scene, agents must manually search through boxes of paper records to trace the firearm to its dealer or purchaser. Finally, Congress has left the ATF without a permanent director for six years. (See Langbein and Lotwis (1990) and Kahane (1999) for empirical studies of regulation capture by the gun lobby.)

3. Weakened Enforcement

The ability of the Federal Election Comission (FEC) to enforce campaign finance laws has eroded in recent years in large part because the three Republicans on the commission "take a hands-off attitude on campaign finance law" (Knot 2011). From 2006 to 2010 the average fine levied by the FEC fell from $180,000 to $42,000, and the number of conciliation agreements resulting in penalties for violators dropped from ninety-one in 2007 to only twenty-nine in 2010. Critics of the "toothless" commission contend that it is "exactly the weak and ineffective agency that members of Congress, whose campaign finance activities it oversees, intended it to be" (Wertheimer and Simon, 2013).[8]

4. Weakened Penalties

The low penalties often imposed by regulatory agencies are not accidental but are reflective of what might be called "second order corruption," which takes place when those charged with fighting corruption are themselves co-opted by other interests. To clarify the concept, consider the following illustrative example. In 1989, the US Sentencing Commission drafted new guidelines for the punishment of corporate crime. The guidelines introduced a huge fine, up to $364 million, for crimes that had previously resulted in fines of tens of thousands of dollars. The commission's recommendations came under severe criticism from major corporations and trade associations. The commission withdrew its initial recommendations and in March 1990 released revised guidelines that drastically scaled back most of the penalties—in some cases by as much as 97 percent. For example, the maximum proposed penalty dropped from $364 million to $12.6 million. Under pressure from liberal groups, certain penalties were increased in the final report, but the guidelines also included a list of extenuating circumstances that provided offending corporations with the means to substantially reduce, if not completely avoid, the remaining penalties (Etzioni 1993). One empirical study of this sort of second order corruption found that "fraudulent firms involved in lobbying are 38 percent less likely to be detected by regulators than those not involved in lobbying" (Yu and Yu 2011, 2).

In short, there is some reason to hypothesize that corruption by capture is rather common in the contemporary United States,if one takes into account the various forms it takes, above and beyond the manipulation of the processes by which laws and regulations are initially laid out. It remains to be determined whether these assessments are correct and whether such capture is accelerating or decelerating. Moreover, one sees that even if there is little personal corruption there can be a rather high level of systematic corruption, whereby legislators do not enrich themselves but rather some private interests, which often are not those of their constituents.

III. Illegal *and* Illicit

According to a third definition, political corruption encompasses the use of public power and resources for illegal and illicit or unethical purposes (Rogow and Lasswell 1963; Rundquist and Hansen 1976; Warren 2006).[9] One need not agree with John Gardiner who went so far as to contend that, "if an act is harmful to the public interest, it is corrupt even if it is legal; if it is beneficial to the public, it is not corrupt even if it violates the law."[10] In other words, some forms of corruption may be legalized but still be illicit. If studies of corruption follow this definition, rather than one of the narrower definitions introduced above, one would expect rather different findings. Many practices that were once illegal and considered corrupt have been legalized and/or normalized since the 1970s, but still involve what some consider the unethical use of public power and assets (Thurber 2010; Wilson 2010).[11] Reference is specifically to the 1976 case *Buckley v. Valeo*, in which the Court struck down several parts of the Federal Election Campaign Act of 1971, ruling that restrictions on independent and candidate expenditures amounted to "direct and substantial restraints on the quantity of political speech." The decision provided legal grounds to the popularly expressed view that "money is speech" (Blasi 1994; Smith 2010).[12] In the 2008 case of *Citizens United v. Federal Election Commission*, the Supreme Court went a major step further, ruling that corporations and labor unions can make unlimited contributions to political campaigns. As a result, there are few limits left on the amount of money that corporations and labor unions can donate to election campaigns.[13]

This is an area of possible political corruption to which political science has paid considerable attention, but the findings of the discipline have varied considerably. On the one hand, there are those who find that private donations to campaigns buy very little in the way of private favors and do not lead elected officials to deviate from their public duties (Smith 2000). A meta-analysis of forty studies by Snyder et al. (2002) concluded that there is little correlation between campaign contributions and legislator voting patterns; that people make donations not as an investment (or payments) for outcomes, but as a mode of political participation or consumption, akin to giving to a favorite charity. The fact that there is a huge discrepancy between the amounts given (often in tens of thousands of dollars) and the legislative "payoffs" (often worth billions) suggests to these researchers that people are not motivated by making an economic return. In a competitive marketplace, a "rational" corporation would continue to expend resources, for example, to secure a government contract, until they "break even"—but firms rarely do so. (See more about such "rent" see section IV below). In 2012, a record amount of independent money, largely from super PACs, was poured into the presidential and congressional campaigns. However, according to at least one analyst, it "had no discernible effect on the outcome of most races," and, in fact, two-thirds of the funds spent by outside groups backed losing candidates (Eggen and Farnam 2012). Amy McKay (2012, 1) tested the effect of lobbyists' resources on policy outcomes and found "surprisingly little relationship between organizations' financial resources and their policy success."

In contrast, other political scientists have reached the conclusion that contributions from PACs can influence voting behavior among members of congress (Baumgartner et al. 2009; Drope and Hansen 2004; Magee 2002; McGarity and Wagner 2008). Richard Fleisher (1993, 402) found that PAC contributions from defense contractors had a statistically significant impact on defense voting, and that while the effect was marginal, "even at the margins, PAC contributions from defense contractors can influence the outcome of legislative deliberations." Another study found that contributions from labor PACs to lawmakers did translate into support for labor issues among recipients (Wilhite and Theilmann 1987). More funds are donated to party leaders and members of Congress who chair or serve in powerful committees than to less-influential legislators, suggesting that donors seek to maximize the return on their investment by contributing to those who "control the purse strings" (Grier and Munger 1986; Romer and Snyder 1994; Ansolabehere and Snyder

1999). One study of voting behavior within the Ways and Means Committee found that the "total number of lobbying contacts representatives received"— not campaign contributions—best explained voting decisions (Wright 1990, 417). Other studies have looked at whether contributions, rather than directly swaying votes, instead "buy" access and lawmakers' time and energy (Austen-Smith 1996; Chin, Bond, and Geva 2000; Hall and Wayman 1990; Langbein 1986; Kau and Rubin 1982). Other research has revealed that, while firms do lobby financial regulatory agencies (such as the SEC, GAO, and IRS) directly, they spend much more on the campaigns of members of Congress who control the regulators (Yu and Yu 2011).

One can readily see that it is not possible to reach a consensus about the scope of corruption in the United States unless one can reconcile these rather conflicted findings. Indeed, if one proceeds with the kind of collaborative project here envisioned, it may well start with assembling those interested in PACs and trying to work out a research design that will move us closer to agreement on this issue.

Measurement issues also need to be resolved. For instance, if one takes into account only those funds donated before a particular vote was cast, and not those given after the favorable act, one will potentially reach different conclusions than if both are taken into account. Also, one must take into consideration funds that flow from special interests to law firms or lobbyists, which then make contributions to members of Congress on behalf of their clients.

Finally, some argue that correlations between donations and legislative outcomes are of little importance because, regardless of contributions, lawmakers vote in line with their political dispositions (i.e., a conservative Senator may have received money from the NRA, but would have voted against gun control regardless). However, an empirical study on the effect of the NRA's lobbying activities leading up to the passage of the Firearm Owners Protection Act suggests that "campaign contributions affected member's subsequent votes, even when other variables, including ideology, member's prior position, and constituency characteristics, are held constant" (Langbein and Lotwis 1990, 413). This finding is supported by at least one other study (not conducted by a professional social scientist), which shows that donations can lead Congress members to vote against to their declared beliefs (Etzioni 1984).[14]

Given that there are more studies in this area than most others, the possibility for secondary analysis and additional meta-reviews could bring the discipline closer to a consensus on whether aspects of campaign finance constitute illicit corruption even though they are legal.

IV. High "Rents" and Predicting the Future

A rather different approach to the study of corruption draws on the concept of rent seeking, or "the process of expending resources in an attempt to influence public policy outcomes" (Mbaku 1998, 195; see also Tullock 1967). (While bribery is an obvious example of such behavior, not all rent seeking, such as lobbying, is necessarily corrupt, nor is all corruption a form of rent seeking.) According to the original economic theory on the subject, firms will "invest in political activity so long as the expected benefits exceed the expected costs" (Pasour 1987, 129). That is, competitive rent seeking for public goods will leave private actors in "zero-profit" equilibrium.

However, empirical studies suggest that firms that expend resources to influence public policy do not just "break even." A tax provision in the American Jobs Creation Act of 2004 provided researchers with a unique opportunity to measure the 'rate of return' earned by money spent on lobbying. They found that "for every dollar spent on lobbying, there was a tax savings from the firm equal to about $220. In percentage terms, this is a 22,000 percent return" (Alexander, Mazza, and Scholz 2009, 30). Another study found that "taking into account the initially [sic] lobbying investment, for each additional $1 spent on lobbying the mean firm receives somewhere in the range of $6 to $20 of tax benefits" (Richter, Samphantharak, and Timmons 2009, 907). Given that firms stand to profit a great deal from lobbying, various scholars are surprised by the relatively low level of rent-seeking behavior (Ansolabehere, de Figueiredo, Snyder 2002).

Various explanations have been given for the lower than expected rent in the United States. A study of the kind here suggested should actively explore and attempt to synthesize those explanations. I add the hypothesis that there is a cultural lag. That is, once activities that were formerly considered corrupt are legalized, segments of the public still consider them off-limits, and hence many potential rent-seekers are *initially* reluctant to proceed. However, as the newly-legalized behavior becomes more common, more join in. This is what happened with PACs, which were fully legalized in 1974. The number of PACs has grown from just 608 in 1974 to 4,234 in 2008 (U.S. Federal Election Commission 2008).

Second, many corporations have customers of various political persuasions and fear being perceived as having aligned themselves with one political camp. However, once these corporations take full advantage of the fact that they can now make such contributions in secret (via super PACs), and come to believe that such secrecy is assured, they are likely to increase their contributions. If these hypotheses are correct, one can expect more private money flowing into public hands in the future.

V. Other Subject Areas

A full study of the subject at hand had best include a number of additional areas only briefly listed here.

1. Regulatory Agencies: Watch Dogs or Lap Dogs?

One of the key roles of regulatory commissions is to enforce rules that help curb corruption. To the extent that they are captured—some critics in the media refer to these bodies as "lap dogs"—they become an extension of what I have called second order corruption. This charge is often levied against the FEC and the SEC. A typical media item follows. In fifty-one cases over the past fifteen years, nineteen Wall Street firms broke anti-fraud laws that they had promised not to break. These firms included Goldman Sachs, Morgan Stanley, JPMorgan Chase, and Bank of America. When first faced with such violations, the SEC settled the cases after the corporations promised not to break the law again. When faced with repeat violations, the SEC simply opted for another settlement coupled with another promise, rather than pursue contempt or fraud charges in court. As the report notes, to outsiders this all appears odd given that the firms are "merely promising not to do something that the law already forbids" (Wyatt 2011).

Andrew Baker (2010, 663) argues "that a form of multilevel regulatory capture was both a principal political cause of the financial crisis of 2007–2009 and one of the central political issues and challenges raised by the financial crash. However, it has not been confronted directly or explicitly in current reform efforts, and has been touched upon in only a somewhat piecemeal, incidental and indirect fashion in the changes emerging in the field of global financial governance."

One common explanation for the weakness of regulatory agencies is the 'revolving door' phenomenon (Gormley 1979; Makkai, Toni, and Braithwaite 1992). Frédéric Boehm (2007) provides a useful overview of the various explanations that economists give for corruption-via-regulatory capture and its implications.

2. States and Cities

Some view states and cities as social laboratories in which political innovation takes place and where new designs can be tested before they are adopted at the national level—designs that may include ways to curb corruption. Because there are fifty states and numerous cities, comparative studies can be carried out more readily than when one deals with national polities.[15]

At first blush, one notes many reasons one would expect state and city governments to be more corrupt than the executive, judiciary, or legislative branches at the federal level. In an influential article, James Q. Wilson (1960) argues that, because people are generally less-informed about state governance, and local officials face less voter and media scrutiny, local corruption is far worse than federal corruption. He also suggests that state officials have fewer inhibitions when it comes to misusing federal transfer payments because the money comes from outsiders—not their constituents.[16] Further, many members of state and city legislative bodies only serve part-time and thus are allowed by law to gain outside income, including from the industries they legislate and regulate.

208

Some research in this area has been undertaken. For instance, in 2011, a consortium of nonpartisan groups began the "State Integrity Investigation" (2013), a data-driven analysis of governance at the state level. States were given grades in categories such as lobbying disclosure, campaign finance laws, and ethics enforcement. No state gained an "A" and only five earned "B's." (The Justice Department's Public Integrity Section also keeps track of public corruption convictions which the publication *Governing* compiled by state from 2001–2010.)

Goel and Nelson (1998, 117) found a "positive relationship between corruption and the size of state-local governments and a negative relationship between government salaries and corruption," suggesting "that policy makers looking to reduce corruption by cutting government spending should be reducing expenditures other than those on employee salaries." Meier and Holbrook (1992, 4) "detect higher [corruption] conviction rates in more urban states with less educated citizenries, larger fractions of citizens with Irish or Italian ancestries, lower voter turnout, and higher total government employment." One study found a "link between isolated capitals and corruption," noting that such cities tend to have lower levels of public and media accountability, greater expenditures on state-level campaigns, and lower levels of spending on public goods (Campante and Do 2012, 28). In addition there are several solid cross-state studies (Adsera, Boix, and Payne 2003; Alt and Lassen 2010; Glaeser and Saks 2004; Hill 2003; Johnston 1983; Maxwell and Winters 2005; Schlesinger and Meier 2000) whose findings need not to be here reviewed.[17]

As far as I can establish, these various findings have not been compiled to provide overarching conclusions regarding whether corruption (in accordance with the various definitions) is (a) higher at the state and local level than it is at the national level (which one would expect on the basis of structural and incentive considerations); (b) rising or falling; (c) much lower in some states and local institutions than it is in others; and, above all, (d) what accounts for these differences.

3. State Judiciaries

Most judges used to be appointed. However, over the past decades, more judgeships have become subject to competitive elections, thereby increasing the need to raise funds from private hands. From 2000–09, state supreme court candidates raised $206.4 million nationally, more than double the $83.3 million spent in 1990–99 (Puiszis 2011, 12). There is some reason to hold that, as a result, judges have become increasingly indebted to those who make large donations, leading the former to favor the latter in their rulings.[18] Retired Supreme Court Justice Sandra Day O'Connor stated that "in too many states, judicial elections are becoming political prizefights where partisans and special interests seek to install judges who will answer to them instead of the law and the Constitution" (Justice at Stake 2007). In contrast, one study found that "having elected, rather than appointed, state supreme court judges is also associated with lower corruption," affirming the authors' hypothesis that "because corruption comes at the expense of (almost) all voters . . . a judiciary accountable to voters should be more concerned about curbing corruption" (Alt and Lassen 2005, 38, 56). It follows, then, that one must raise similar questions about campaign contributions to judges as those presented above regarding how donations influence Congress, so as to fully assess the scope and changing extent of political corruption in America.

4. The Private Sector

At first blush, one may wonder if there is any reason to study corruption in the private sector given that the subject at hand is political corruption, which is, by definition, limited to the abuse of public power. For instance, private schools that claim to base admission merely on merit but actually admit children whose families made major donations to the school would obviously fall outside of this study's scope. However, because there is such a high level of interpenetration between the public and the private sector, it seems that major parts of the private sector would have to be studied. For instance, inappropriate billing by Medicare providers as well as defense and other contractors, corrupt behavior that leads to pension and corporate failures that the government has to bail out, fraudulent medical practices that lead to treating more illness at the public's expense, and numerous other such examples need to be studied because their prevalence is, in part, a reflection of the fact that they are tolerated by the public sector. This tolerance can be explained by ideological considerations, technological limitations and other factors, but political corruption also seems a plausible explanation. Hence, these private acts are to be included in a comprehensive study of political corruption in the American system.

An illustrative example follows. Health Management Associates, the fourth-largest for-profit hospital chain in the United States, was found to set hospital admission benchmarks (20 percent of all patients, and 50 percent of those over sixty-five years of age) in order to increase revenue. Before a patient is even seen by a doctor, the company's software may order unnecessary tests and suggest that he or she be admitted. Doctors are evaluated on the basis of how many patients they admit and how many procedures they order. The result is not merely bilking billions from Medicare, but exposing people who do not need hospitalization to both infection via the pathogens common in hospitals, as well as to what one doctor termed "medical misadventures"—errors and mistakes made by hospital staff that often result in severe consequences for those affected. *60 Minutes* (2012), which reported all this in an episode that aired on December 2, 2012, noted that the Department of Justice is investigating the matter, but so far no HMA executive has been charged with any wrongdoing, nor has the corporation been fined or required to return the funds fraudulently extracted from Medicare and Medicaid.

In short, given the high level of interpenetration of the private and the public realm, it might not be possible to gain an accurate account of the level of political corruption without studying not merely the illicit inroads the private sector may make in the public realm but also the level of corruption in the private sector—a tall order.

5. Culture

Corruption in general, and that of public institutions in particular, is not merely affected by the level of punishment meted out to those caught acting illegally (and the probability that these punishments will be actually enforced) but also by the moral culture. The latter can treat corruption as a great evil, tolerate but deplore it, view low levels of it as functional, or accept it as common and expected. This point is illustrated by an account of the conduct of Wall Street corporations in the years leading up to the savings and loan crisis of the late 1980s and early 1990s—which cost taxpayers approximately $124 billion—wherein the corporations were found to have had little difficulty circumventing federal laws, regulations and oversight, easily evading regulations set up by their own industry. However, one major Wall Street firm refused to participate in the racket. When offered the chance to sell junk bonds, its partners responded with a "we do not do this kind of thing here" attitude (Stewart 1992). That is, their internal culture and shared values served as a major anti-corruption bulwark.

I observed for more than a year a medical partnership whose members decided to practice medicine "the old fashioned way." Most times they do not rush patients and do not order procedures primarily to supplement their income or to protect themselves from possible lawsuits. New physicians who seek to join the practice are warned that "here you are not going to make it rich" and if they do not abide by the norms, they are not made partners and are soon eased out. It is not sheer altruism. The practice's members gain considerable psychic income from their way of conducting themselves and their reputation. Nevertheless, they illustrate the role of culture in undergirding integrity.

Granted these two illustrative examples seem like outliers. However, few would question that, in all social settings, people's values and the moral culture of the community or communities of which they are members affect the level of corruption.[19]

One reason culture (and the informal social controls that undergird it) seems significant is that many billions of transactions occur in society each year, including economic, political, and social ones. There is no practical way to ensure that all the relevant laws (not to mention informal ethical standards) are enforced by accountants, inspectors, custom agents, police, and other such agents. Not only is the volume too high and the cost prohibitive, but the famous question arises: Who would guard the guardians? Thus, even if one could get, say, all of the Canadians to work as anti-corruption enforcers for the United States, who would monitor the Canadians? In short, culture must play a key role in fostering voluntary compliance and, thus, limiting corruption.

One can gain some sense of the power of culture by noting that law enforcement in Japan relies much more on the moral culture and informal social pressures than do other societies and it "incarcerates its citizens at a far lower rate than most developed countries: 55 per 100,000 people compared with 149 in Britain and 716 in America" (*Economist* 2013). (It goes without saying that other variables are also at play, such as the ways nonviolent offenders— including drug abusers and white collar criminals—are treated.)

An early review of the literature on this subject by Alan Lewis (1982) is still valuable. He shows that, as long as people hold that tax revenues are spent legitimately and that the burdens are fairly distributed, most individuals pay taxes voluntary. Another study found that in the "more civic regions" of Italy, citizen-government interactions tended to concern public issues, while in "less civic regions" citizens' contact with public officials "overwhelmingly involve requests for jobs and patronage" (Putnam 1993, 101). Edward Banfield's account of one Italian town demonstrated that a lack of public-spiritedness "resulted in an indifferent and corrupt government . . . Voter choices were not based on class, ideology, or the public interest, but simply rewarded the party providing jobs or other particularistic favors" (Knack 2002, 774).

In short, the content of the moral culture—and not just incentive structures— must be taken into account. However, there seems to be little systematic data on what the American culture tell us about corruption. It ought to be included in the design of a master study of corruption in contemporary America.

VI. Is Some Corruption Functional?

In the 1960s, some political scientists suggested corruption (at least at a low level) is "functional" because bribery can not only increase efficiency by reducing red tape and 'greasing' the bureaucratic wheels, but also may integrate otherwise-excluded constituencies into the political system (Anechiarico and Jacobs 1996; Huntington 1968; Leff 1964; Meón and Weill 2010; Nye 1967).[20] Olken and Pande (2011, 3–4) note that "just knowing the magnitude of corruption does not tell us how serious the problem is. Others argue that corruption represents a transfer from one party (say, the government) to another party (say, bureaucrats), with little efficiency cost. In fact, if bureaucrats' official salaries were less than their market wage in expectation of the corrupt rents they would obtain—and there is evidence that this is indeed exactly what happens—there could be no net costs of corruption at all." Curbing it, it seems to follow, might harm rather than benefit the polity.

This position is held by some economists who view corruption as efficient or neutral. For example, a study of public sector salaries in Ukraine found that while government employees made less than their private sector equivalents, bribes to civil servants exactly offset this wage differential. Whether or not this is an "efficient" outcome depends—some economists hold—on whether the bribes create more or less "deadweight loss" than the tax increase that would be necessary to pay the higher salary (Gorodnichenko and Peter 2007). Others point out that some highly-corrupt nations (as indicated by Transparency International's perceived corruption index) have very high rates of economic growth.

One notes that it remains to be established whether a "healthy" level of corruption can be contained or tends to increase, an issue similar to the question of whether or not a low level of inflation can be good for the economy (Elster 1989). Moreover, the studies do not examine the effects of corruption on variables other than economic growth, including extra-institutional expressions of alienation, cultural corrosion, and the trust that people put into their government.

Hence a side project of a comprehensive study of political corruption in the United States might be to further test the proposition that corruption can be functional.

VII. Reforms

It would take a whole separate design or agenda-setting endeavor to outline what would be required to lower the level of corruption in the United States if it was found to be unduly high. There are a fair number of studies of such drives in other countries, including India, Haiti, Uganda, and Indonesia (Jenkins Goetz 1999; Klitgaard 2010; Olken 2007; Reinikka and Svensson 2004). Most of those efforts are based in countries that have rather different polities, economies, and cultures than those of the United States. Furthermore, practically all of these drives failed. (Among the few exceptions are Botswana (Theobald and Williams 2006) and Hong Kong (Lo 1999).) In some cases, those driving the anticorruption efforts were found to be corrupt themselves or to be using the drive for political purposes, such as to defeat a particular opponent rather than reform the polity.

Political scientists may be more interested in earlier American reform drives, especially the Progressive moment (Glaeser and Goldin 2004). However, even here one must wonder if what worked more than one hundred years ago could work again today. Here I must leave this as a very preliminary effort, leaving the design question completely open-ended.

213

Notes

1. John Peters and Susan Welch identify three categories of political corruption: "definitions based on legality, definitions based on the public interest, and definitions based on public opinion," Michael Genovese draws a distinction between "personal corruption" (i.e., a "bad apple" selling his vote) and "systemic corruption" (i.e., illicit campaign financing that "is embedded in day-to-day operations of the system").

2. Johnston (2006) offers several explanations for the dearth of studies on corruption by American political scientists, which he considers an unfortunate "blind spot," Meier and Holbrook (1992, 135) assert there has not been extensive "systematic empirical research on political corruption," and DeLeon (1993, 14) writes that "political science [seems] unwilling to address frontally the questions posed by political corruption, and more critically, what can be done to reduce it and its effects,"

3. Nye (1967) defines corruption as "behavior which deviates from the formal duties of a public role (elective or appointive) because of private-regarding (personal, close family, private clique) wealth or status gains: or violates rules against the exercise of certain types of private-regarding influence," Van Klaveren (1989, 25–26) states, "corruption means that a civil servant abuses his authority in order to obtain an extra income from the public,"). Shleifer and Vishny (1993, 599) "define government corruption as the sale by government officials of government property for personal gain,"

4. McCann and Redlawsk (2006, 797) suggest that the "small-d democratic conception of corruption is much broader; it goes beyond mere violations of established rules. Political scientists, however, have tended to focus on corruption as illegal activity on the part of public officials,"

5. Thurber (2010, 26) raises numerous pressing questions that need to be resolved in this regard, and his preliminary analysis suggests that "major lobbying and ethics reforms in 2007 (HLOGA) and President Obama's new regulations over lobbyists do not seem to have reduced public and media suspicion of lobbyists and campaign consultants or unethical behavior,"

6. For a review of some major works on regulatory capture, see Nixon, David C., Robert M. Howard, and Jeff R. DeWitt. 2002. "With Friends Like These: Rulemaking Comment Submissions to the Securities and Exchange Commission," *Journal of Public Administration Research and Theory* 12 (January): 59–76.

7. Hall and Van Houweling (2006, 4) develop a model to test the effect of hard and soft money on the legislators who crafted and passed the 2003 MMA and conclude that in "one of the most important public health reforms of our lifetime . . . private money enjoyed robust representation,"

8. Correia (2012, 3) finds that firms that contribute to congressman connected to the SEC and that spend money directly lobbying the SEC "are less likely to be involved in an SEC enforcement action and face lower penalties on average,"

9. Warren (2006, 804) characterizes such behavior as duplicitous exclusion: "political corruption attacks democracy by *excluding* people from decisions that affect them" and is duplicitous because the corrupt violate the very norms and standards they profess to uphold. Rogow and Lasswell (1963, 132–133) argue that "[a] corrupt act violates responsibility toward at least one system of public or civic order and is in fact incompatible

with (destructive of) any such system," Rundquist and Hansen (1976, 2–3) write, "[p]olitical corruption [is] behavior by an individual or group (party, administration) which violates citizens' conceptions of acceptable official behavior within their political community,"

10. John A. Gardiner, "Defining Corruption," *Corruption and Reform*, vol. 7, no. 2 (1993): 111–124.

11. Wilson (2010, 740–741) writes, "The Court's emphasis on quid pro quo corruption fails to account for the potential for other corruptive influences stemming from unlimited campaign spending. Specifically, the relationship between money and potentially manipulative communication strategies arguably supports a more expansive definition of "corruption," See also, Thurber (2010).

12. Smith (2010, 76) writes that "the century-old effort to constrict the ways our elections are funded has, from the outset, put itself at odds with our constitutional tradition. It seeks to undermine not only the protections of political expression in the First Amendment, but also the limits on government in the Constitution itself — as well as the understanding of human nature, factions and interests, and political liberty that moved the document's framers," See also, Blasi (1994).

13. According to Farrar-Myers and Skinner (2012) the case "scaled back on the definition of corruption or the appearance of corruption to focus on a more traditional sense of quid pro quo corruption . . . [and] broaden[ed] what constituted a permissible independent expenditure that could be made free of governmental restriction or regulation," See also, Issacharoff (2010) argue that "the threat [of *Citizens United*] to democratic governance may come from the emergence of a 'clientelist' relation between elected officials and those who seek to profit by relations to the state,"

14. This study by Ralph Nader—done many years ago and by an advocate—has little academic merit. But it addresses a question that ought to be revisited.

15. Several cross-national analyses have addressed the relationship between corruption and democratization: De Leon (1993); Kunicova and Susan Rose-Ackerman (2005); Goldsmith (1999); Montinola and Jackman (2002); Treisman (2000).

16. Fisman and Gatti (2002, 33) corroborate Wilson's argument, finding "that the rate of prosecutions for abuse of public office is greater in states with higher rates of federal transfers,"

17. Adsera, Boix, and Payne (2003, 445) find that "the presence of a well-informed electorate in a democratic setting explains between one-half and two-thirds of the variance in the levels of government performance and corruption,"

18. This is manifest in what Shortell (2010) calls 'acute' or 'systemic' judicial corruption. The former involves judges taking bribes or granting favors to friends, while in the latter the judiciary is coopted by a particular political regime—a far more corrosive situation.

19. Girling (2002, 123) writes that, "the gentlemanly ideal of political and social leadership contributed as much as any other factor to prevent British material success from 'corrupting' the approved standards of public behavior,"

20. For example, Meón and Weill (2010, 3) suggest corruption "may be positively associated with efficiency in countries where institutions are ineffective,"

For those interested in further pursuing the subjects discussed in this chapter, what follows is a list of the complete citations of all the works mentioned in the preceding text. They are listed in alphabetical order by last name.

Ackerman, Bruce. 1991. *We The People: Foundations.* Cambridge: The Belknap Press.

Ades, Alberto, and Rafael Di Tella. 1997. "The New Economics of Corruption: a Survey and some New Results." *Political Studies* 45: 496–515

Adsera, Alicia, Carles Boix, and Mark Payne. 2003. "Are You Being Served? Political Accountability and Quality of Government." *Journal of Law, Economics and Organization* 19 (October): 445–490.

Alexander, Raquel M., Stephen W. Mazza, and Susan Scholz. 2009. "Measuring Rates of Return on Lobbying Expenditures: An Empirical Case Study of Tax Breaks for Multinational Corporations." *Journal of Law and Policy* 25 (April): 401–458.

Alex Knott, "FEC Falls Short on Enforcement, Commissioner Says," *Roll Call,* 27 May, 2011, http://www.rollcall.com/news/FEC_falls_short_enforcement_commissioner_Weintraub-206027-1.html.

Alt, James E., and David E. Lassen. 2007. "Political and Judicial Checks on Corruption: Evidence from American State Governments." *Economics and Politics* 20 (September): 33–61.

Alt, James E., and David D. Lassen. 2010. "Enforcement and Public Corruption: Evidence from US States." Harvard University and University of Copenhagen. Typescript.

Anechiarico, Frank, and James B. Jacobs. 1996. *The Pursuit of Absolute Integrity: How Corruption Control Makes Government Ineffective.* Chicago: University of Chicago Press.

Ansolabehere, Stephen and James M. Snyder, Jr. 1999. "Money and Institutional Power." *Texas Law Review* 77 (June): 1673–1704.

Ansolabehere, Stephen, John M. de Figueiredo, and James M. Snyder, Jr. 2002. "Why is there so Little Money in U.S. Politics?" *NBER Working Paper* No. 9409 (December).

Austen-Smith, David. 1996. "Campaign Contributions and Access." *American Political Science Review* 89 (September): 566–81.

Baker, Andrew. 2010. "Restraining regulatory capture? Anglo-America, crisis politics and trajectories of change in global financial governance." *International Affairs* 83 (May): 647–663, 663.

Banerjee, Abhijit, Sendhil Mullainathan, and Rema Hanna. 2012. "Corruption." *NBER Working Paper* No. 17968 (April).

Baumgartner, Frank R., Jeffrey M. Berry, Marie Hojnacki, David C. Kimball, and Beth L. Leech. 2009. *Lobbying and Policy Change: Who Wins, Who Loses, and Why.* Chicago: University of Chicago Press.

Becker, Gary, and George Stigler. 1974. "Law Enforcement, Malfeasance and the Compensation of Enforcers." *Journal of Legal Studies* 3(January): 1–19.

Becker, Gary. 1976. "Toward a More General Theory of Regulation." *Journal of Law and Economics* 19 (April): 245–248.

Benson, George C. S., Steven A. Maaranen, and Alan Heslop. 1978. *Political Corruption in America*, Lexington: Lexington Books.

Bentley, Arthur. 1908. *The Process of Government*. Chicago: Chicago University Press.

Berg, Larry, Harlan Hahn, John R. Schmidhauser. 1976. *Corruption in the American Political System*. Morristown: General Learning Press.

Besley, Timothy, and John McLaren. 1993. "Taxes and Bribery: The Role of Wage Incentives." *Economic Journal* 103 (January): 119–141.

Blasi, Vincent. 1994. "Free Speech and the Widening Gyre of Fund-Raising: Why Campaign Spending Limits May Not Violate the First Amendment after All." *Columbia Law Review* 94 (May): 1281–1325.

Boehm, Frédéric. 2007. "Regulatory Capture Revisited – Lessons from Economics of Corruption." Internet Centre for Corruption Research. Working paper.

Campante, Felipe R., and Quoc-Anh Do. 2012. "Isolated Capital Cities, Accountability and Corruption: Evidence from US States." Research Collection School of Economics Paper No. 1387 (May).

Chin, Michelle, Jon R. Bond, and Nehemia Geva. 2000. "A Foot in the Door: An Experimental Study of PAC and Constituency Effects on Access." *Journal of Politics* 62 (May): 534–49.

Copeland, Curtis W. 2011. "The Federal Workforce: Characteristics and Trends," *Congressional Research Service* (April).

Correia, Maria M. 2012. "Political Connections, SEC Enforcement and Accounting Quality." *Rock Center for Corporate Governance at Stanford University Working Paper* No. 61 (August).

Crimes and Criminal Procedures: Licensing, 18 U.S.C. § 923.

Dal Bo, Ernesto. 2006. "Regulatory Capture: A Review." *Oxford Review of Economic Policy* 22 (Summer): 203–225.

Dan Keating, David S. Fallis, Kimberly Kindy and Scott Higham, "Members of Congress Trade in Companies While Making Laws That Affect Those Same Firms," *Washington Post*, 23 June, 2012, http://articles.washingtonpost.com/2012-06-23/politics/35460140_1_stock-act-trades-lawmakers.

David Eggen and T.W. Farnam, "Spending by independent groups had little election impact, analysis finds," *Washington Post*, 7 November, 2012, http://articles.washingtonpost.com/2012-11-07/politics/35505345_1_presidential-race-attack-ads-wealthy-political-groups.

De Leon, Peter. 1993. *Thinking about Political Corruption*. Armonk, NY: Sharpe.

Drope, Jeffrey M., and Wendy L. Hansen. 2004. "Purchasing Protection? The Effect of Political Spending on US Trade Policy." *Political Research Quarterly* 57 (March): 27–37.

"Eastern porridge," *Economist*, February 23, 2013, http://www.economist.com/news/asia/21572257-even-japanese-criminals-are-orderly-and-well-behaved-eastern-porridge.

Elster, Jon. 1989. *The Cement of Society: A Survey of Social Order*, Cambridge: Cambridge University Press.

Etzioni, Amitai. 1984. *Capital Corruption: The New Attack on American Democracy*. New Brunswick: Transaction Publications, citing "Nader Study Links Oil Contributions to Pro-Oil House Vote." 1979. Washington D.C.: Public Citizen's Congress Watch.

Etzioni, Amitai. 1993. "U.S. Sentencing Commission on Corporate Crime: A Critique," *Annals of the American Academy of Political and Social Science* 525 (January): 147–156.

Etzioni, Amitai. 2004. *The Common Good.* Cambridge: Polity Press.

Etzioni, Amitai. 2009. "The Capture Theory of Regulations—Revisited." *Society* 46 (July-August): 319–323.

Fackler, Tim, and Tse-mon Lin. 1995. "Political Corruption and Presidential Elections, 1929–1992." *Journal of Politics* (November): 971–993.

Farrar-Myers, Victoria A., and Richard Skinner. 2012. "Super PACs and the 2012 Elections." (August). Available at SSRN: http://ssrn.com/abstract=2131279 or http://dx.doi.org/10.2139/ssrn.2131279.

Fatka, Stacie L., and Jason Miles Levien. 1998. "Protecting the Right to Petition: Why a Lobbying Contingency Fee Prohibition Violates the Constitution." *Harvard Journal on Legislation* 35 (Summer): 559–587.

Firearms Owners' Protection Act, 18 U.S.C. § 921.

Fisman, Raymond, and Roberta Gatti. 2002. "Decentralization and Corruption: Evidence from U.S. Federal Transfer Programs." *Public Choice* 113 (October): 25–35.

Fleisher, Richard. 1993. "PAC Contributions and Congressional Voting on National Defense." *Legislative Studies Quarterly* 18 (August): 391–409.

Friedrich, Carl J. (1966) "Political Pathology." *Political Quarterly* 37 (January): 70–85. Cited in, *Political Corruption: A Handbook,* eds. Arnold Heidenheimer, Michael Johnston, Victor T. LeVine. New Brunswick: Transaction Publishers (1989) at 10.

Gardiner, John. 1989. "Defining Corruption." In P*olitical Corruption: A Handbook,* eds. Arnold Heidenheimer, Michael Johnston, and Victor T. LeVine. New Brunswick: Transaction Publishers: 25–8.

Genovese, Michael A., and Victoria Farrar-Myers, eds. 2010. *Corruption and American Politics.* Amherst, NY: Cambria Press.

Genovese, Michael A. 2010. "Presidential Corruption: A Longitudinal Analysis." In *Corruption and American Politics,* eds. Michael A. Genovese and Victoria Farrar-Myers. New York: Cambria Press.

George Cahlink, "Ex-Pentagon procurement executive gets jail time," *Government Executive,* 1 October, 2004, http://www.govexec.com/defense/2004/10/ex-pentagon-procurement-executive-gets-jail-time/17737/.

Girling, John. 2002. *Corruption, Capitalism, and Democracy.* New York: Routledge.

Glaeser, Edward L., and Claudia Goldin. 2004. "Corruption and Reform: An Introduction." In *Corruption and Reform: Lessons from America's Economic History.* Chicago: University of Chicago Press.

Glaeser, Edward L., and Raven Saks. 2004. "Corruption in America." Harvard Institute of Economic Research Discussion Paper No. 2043.

Goel, Rajeev K., and Michael A. Nelson, 1998. "Corruption and Government Size: A Disaggregated Analysis." *Public Choice* 97 (October):107–120.

Goldsmith, Author A. 1999. "Slapping the Grasping Hand: Correlates of Political Corruption in Emerging Markets." *American Journal of Economics and Sociology* 58 (October): 865–883.

Golembiewski, Robert J. 1960. "The Group Basis of Politics: Notes of Analysis and Development." *American Political Science Review* 54 (December): 962–971.

Gormley, William T. Jr. 1979. "A Test of the Revolving Door Hypothesis at the FCC." *American Journal of Political Science* 23 (November): 665–683.

Gorodnichenko, Yuriy, and Klara Sabirianova Peter. 2007. "Public Sector Pay and Corruption: Measuring Bribery from Micro Data." *Journal of Public Economics* 91 (June): 963–991.

Grier, Kevin, and Michael Munger. 1986. "The Impact of Legislator Attributes on Interest-Group Campaign Contributions." *Journal of Labor Research* 7 (Winter): 349–361.

Hall, Richard L., and Frank W. Wayman. 1990. "Buying Time: Moneyed Interests and the Mobilization of Bias in Congressional Committees." *American Political Science Review* 84 (March): 797–82.

Hall, Richard L. and Robert P. Van Houweling. 2006. "Campaign Contributions and Lobbying on the Medicare Modernization Act of 2003." Presented at the Annual Meeting of the American Political Science Association, Philadelphia.

Hill, Kim Quaile. 2003. "Democratization and Corruption: Systematic Evidence from the American States." *American Politics Research* 31 (November): 613–663.

Huntington, Samuel P. 1968. "Modernization and corruption." In *Political Order in Changing Societies*, ed. Samuel P. Huntington. New Haven: Yale University Press, 59–71.

Issacharoff, Samuel. 2010. "On Political Corruption." *Harvard Law Review* 124 (August): 118–144.

Jenkins, Rob, and Anne-Marie Goetz. 1999. "Constraints on Civil Society's Capacity to Curb Corruption," *IDS Bulletin* 30 (October): 39–49.

Johnston, Michael. 1983. "Corruption and political culture in America: An empirical perspective." *Publius* 13 (Winter): 19–39.

Johnston, Michael. 2002. "Party Systems, Competition, and Political Checks Against Corruption." In *Political corruption: Concepts and Contexts*, eds. Arnold J. Heidenheimer and Michael Johnston. New Brunswick: Transaction Publishers.

Johnston, Michael. 2006. "From Thucydides to Mayor Daley: Bad Politics, and a Culture of Corruption?." *PS: Political Science & Politics* 39 (October): 809–819.

Justice at Stake. "Money and Elections." http://www.justiceatstake.org/issues/state_court_issues/money-and-elections/ (accessed April 3, 2013).

Kahane, Leo H. 1999. "Gun Lobbies and Gun Control: Senate Voting Patterns on the Brady Bill and the Assault Weapons Ban." *Atlantic Economic Journal* 27 (December): 384–393.

Kau, James B., and Paul H. Rubin. 1982. *Congressmen, Constituents, and Contributors: Determinants of Roll Call Voting in the House of Representatives.* Boston: M. Nijhoff.

Kindy, Kimberly, David S. Fallis and Scott Higham, "Congress members back legislation that could benefit themselves, relatives," *Washington Post*, 7 October, 2012.

Klitgaard, Robert. 2010. "Addressing Corruption in Haiti." *AEI Working Paper Series on Development Policy* No. 2 (April).

Knack, Stephen. 2002. "Social Capital and the Quality of Government: Evidence from the States." *American Journal of Political Science* 46 (October):772–785, citing Banfield, Edward C. 1958. *The Moral Basis of a Backward Society.* Chicago: The Free Press.

Krueger, Anne O. 1974. "The Political Economy of Rent Seeking Society." *American Economic Review* 64 (June): 291–303.

Kunicova, Jana, and Susan Rose-Ackerman. 2005. "Electoral Rules and Constitutional Structures as Constraints on Corruption." *British Journal of Political Science* 35 (October): 575–606.

Langbein, Laura I. 1986. "Money and Access: Some Empirical Evidence." *Journal of Politics* 48 (November): 1052–1062.

Langbein, Laura I., and Mark A. Lotwis. 1990. "The Political Efficacy Of Lobbying and Money: Gun Control in the US House, 1986." *Legislative Studies Quarterly* 15 (August): 413–440.

Leff, Nathaniel H. 1964. "Economic Development through Bureaucratic Corruption." *American Behavioral Scientist* 8 (November): 8–14.

Lewis, Alan. 1982. *The Psychology of Taxation.* London: Palgrave MacMillan.

Lo, T. Wing. 1999. "The Political-Criminal Nexus: The Hong Kong Experience." *Trends in Organized Crime* 5 (Spring): 60–80.

Magee, Christopher. 2002. "Do Political Action Committees Give Money to Candidates for Electoral or Influence Motives?" *Public Choice* 112 (September): 373–99.

Maxwell, Amanda E., and Richard F. Winters. 2005. "Political Corruption in America." Presented at the American Politics Seminar, Hanover, NH.

Mbaku, John M. (1998). "Corruption and rent-seeking." In *The Political Dimension of Economic Growth,* eds. S. Borner and M. Paldam. London and New York: Macmillan Press and St. Martins Press, 193–211.

Makkai, Toni, and John Braithwaite. 1992. "In and out of the revolving door: making sense of regulatory capture." *Journal of Public Policy* 12 (January): 61–78.

McCann, James A., and David P. Redlawsk. 2006. "As Voters Head to the Polls, Will They Perceive a 'Culture of Corruption?'" *PS: Political Science and Politics* 37 (October): 797–802.

McGarity, Thomas O., and Wendy E. Wagner. 2008. *Bending Science: How Special Interests Corrupt Public Health Research.* Cambridge: Harvard University Press.

McKay, Amy. 2012. "Buying Policy? The Effects of Lobbyists' Resources on Their Policy Success." *Political Research Quarterly* 65 (December): 908–923.

Meier, Kenneth J., and Thomas M. Holbrook. 1992. "I Seen My Opportunities and I Took 'Em: Political Corruption in the American States." *The Journal of Politics* 54 (February): 135–155.

Meón, Pierra-Guillaume, and Laurent Weill. 2010. "Is Corruption an Efficient Grease?" *World Development* 38 (December): 244–259.

Montinola, Gabriella, and Robert Jackman. 2002. "Sources of Corruption: A Cross-Country Study." *British Journal of Political Science* 32 (January): 147–170.

Nice, David C. (1983). "Political Corruption in the American States." *American Politics Quarterly* 11(October): 507–517.

Nixon, David C., Robert M. Howard, and Jeff R. DeWitt. 2002. "With Friends Like These: Rulemaking Comment Submissions to the Securities and Exchange Commission." *Journal of Public Administration Research and Theory* 12 (January): 59–76.

Nye, Joseph S. 1967. "Corruption and political development." *American Political Science Review* 61 (June): 417–427.

Olken, Benjamin A. 2007. "Monitoring Corruption: Evidence from a Field Experiment in Indonesia," *Journal of Political Economy* 115 (April): 200–248.

Olken, Benjamin A., and Rohini Pande. 2011. "Corruption in Developing Countries." *NBER Working Paper* No. 17398 (September).

Pasour, Ernest C. 1987. "Rent Seeking: Some Conceptual Problems and Implications." *Review of Austrian Economics* 1 (March): 123–145.

Peltzman, Sam. 1976. Toward a more general theory of regulation. *Journal of Law and Economics*, 19 (April): 211–240.

Peters, John G., Susan Welch. 1978. "Political Corruption in America: A Search for Definitions and a Theory, or If Political Corruption Is in the Mainstream of American Politics Why Is It Not in the Mainstream of American Politics Research?" *The American Political Science Review* 72 (September): 974–984."

Philip, Mark. 1997. "Defining Political Corruption." *Political Studies* 45: 436–462.

Posner, Richard A. 1974. "Theories of Economic Regulation." *Bell Journal of Economics and Management Science* 5 (Autumn): 355–358.

"Public Corruption Convictions: State Totals, 2001-2010." *Governing: The States and Localities,* http://www.governing.com/gov-data/politics/public-corruption-case-convictions-state-data.html (accessed March 13, 2013).

Puiszis, Steven M. 2011. "Developments in Judicial Selection Methods and Campaign Financing." In *Without Fear or Favor in 2011: A New Decade of Challenges to Judicial Independence and Accountability.* Chicago: DRI.

Putnam, Robert, Robert Leonardi and Raffaella Y. Nanetti. 1993. *Making Democracy Work: Civic Traditions in Modern Italy.* Princeton: Princeton University Press.

Reinikka, Ritva, and Jakob Svensson. 2004. "Local Capture: Evidence from a Central Government Transfer Program in Uganda." *The Quarterly Journal of Economics* (May): 679–705.

Richter, Brian K., Krislert Samphantharak, and Jeffrey F. Timmons. 2009. "Lobbying and Taxes." *American Journal of Political Science* 53 (October): 893–909.

Rogow, Arnold A., and Harold Lasswell. 1963. *Power, Corruption and Rectitude.* Englewood Cliffs: Prentice-Hall.

Rolfe Winkler, "The race to the regulatory bottom continues," *Reuters,* Option ARMageddon Blog, 4 November, 2009, http://blogs.reuters.com/rolfewinkler/2009/11/04/the-race-to-the-regulatory-bottomcontinues/ (Accessed March 28, 2013).

Romer, Thomas, and James M. Snyder, Jr. 1994. "An Empirical Investigation of the Dynamics of PAC Contributions." *American Journal of Political Science* 38 (August): 745–769.

Rundquist, Barry S., and Susan Hansen. 1976. "On Controlling Official Corruption: Elections vs. Laws." Unpublished manuscript.

Schlesinger, Thomas, and Kenneth J. Meier. 2000. "Variations in Corruption Among the American States." University of Wisconsin-Milwaukee and Texas A&M University. Typescript.

"Setting the rules." *Economist,* 24 January, 2003.

Shleifer, Andrei, and Robert W. Vishny.1993. "Corruption." *The Quarterly Journal of Economics* 108 (August): 599–617.

Shortell, Christopher. 2010. "When Justice is Not Blind: Corruption in the Courts." *Corruption and American Politics,* Michael A. Genovese and Victoria Farrar-Myers Amherst. New York: Cambria Press, 209–242.

Smith, Bradley A. 2010. "The Myth of Campaign Finance Reform." *National Affairs* (Winter): 75–91.

Smith, Mark A. 2000. *American Business and Political Power: Public Opinion, Elections, and Democracy*. Chicago: University of Chicago Press.

State Integrity Investigation, http://www.stateintegrity.org/ (accessed March 13, 2013).

Steve Kroft, "Congress: Trading stock on inside information?" *60 Minutes*, CBS News, aired November 13, 2011, transcript available at http://www.cbsnews.com/8301-18560_162-57323527/congress-exempt-from-insider-trading-laws/.

Stigler, George J., and Claire Friedland. 1962. "What can Regulators Regulate? The Case of Electricity." *Journal of Law and Economics* 5 (October): 1–16.

Stigler, George. 1971. "The Theory of Economic Regulation." *Bell Journal of Economic and Management Science* 2 (Spring): 3–21.

Stewart, James B. 1992. *Den of Thieves*. New York: Touchstone.

Tevfik, Nas, Albert C. Price, and Charles T. Weber. 1986. "A Policy-Oriented Theory of Corruption." *American Political Science Association* 80 (March): 107–119.

Theobald, Robin, and Robert Williams. 2006. "Combating Corruption in Botswana: Regional Role Model or Deviant Case?" *Commonwealth & Comparative Politics* 44 (March): 117–134.

Thurber, James A. 2010a. "Changing the Way Washington Works? President Obama's Battle with Lobbyists." Presented at the Conference on The Early Obama Presidency, London.

Thurber, James A. 2010b. "Corruption and Scandal in Washington: Have Lobbying and Ethics Reform Made a Difference? Exploring the Relationship Among Candidates, Campaign Consultants, Lobbyists, and Elected and Appointed Public Officials." In *Corruption and American Politics*, eds. Michael A. Genovese and Victoria Farrar-Myers. Amherst, NY: Cambria Press, 177–208.

Treisman, Daniel. 2000. "The Causes of Corruption: A Cross-national Study." *Journal of Public Economics* 76 (June): 399–457.

Tollison, Robert D. 1991. "Regulation and Interest Groups." In *Regulation*, ed. Jack High. Ann Arbor: University of Michigan Press, 59–76.

Tullock, Gordon. 1967. "The Welfare Costs of Tariffs, Monopolies and Theft." *Western Economics Journal* (June): 224-232.

T.W. Farnam, "Congressional Staffers Often Travel on Tabs of Foreign Governments," *Washington Post*, 17 February, 2013.

U.S. Federal Election Commission. 2008. *PAC Count: 1974 to Present*. Washington, D.C.: Federal Election Commission, http://www.fec.gov/press/press2008/20080117paccount.shtml (accessed March 26, 2013).

Van Klaveren, Jacob. 1989. "The Concept of Corruption." In *Political Corruption: A Handbook*, eds. Arnold Heidenheimer, Michael Johnston, and Victor T. LeVine. New Brunswick: Transaction Publishers: 25–28.

Warren, Mark E. 2006. "Political Corruption as Duplicitous Exclusion." *PS: Political Science and Politics* 37 (October): 803–807.

Wertheimer, Fred, and Don Simon. 2013. "The FEC: The Failure to Enforce Commission." *American Constitution Society Issue Brief* (January): 1–22.

Wilhite, Allen, and John Theilmann. 1987. "Labor PAC contributions and labor legislation: A simultaneous logit approach." *Public Choice* 53 (June): 267–276.

Wilson, James Q. 1966. "Corruption: The Shame of the States." *Public Interest* 2 (Winter): 28–38.

Wilson, Molly J. Walker. 2010. "Behavioral Decision Theory and Implications for the Supreme Court's Campaign Finance Jurisprudence." *Cardozo Law Review* 31:649–747, 740–741.

Wright, John R. 1990. "Contributions, Lobbying, and Committee Voting in the U.S. House of Representatives." *American Political Science Review* 84 (June): 417–38.

Wyatt, Edward, "Promises Made, and Remade, by Firms in S.E.C. Fraud Cases," *New York Times*, November 7, 2011.

Yalof, David Alistair. 2012. *Prosecution Among Friends: Presidents, Attorneys General, and Executive Branch Wrongdoing.* College Station, TX: Texas A&M University Press.

Yu, Frank, and Xiaoyun Yu. 2011. "Corporate Lobbying and Fraud Detection." *Journal of Finance and Quantitative Analysis* 46 (December): 1865–1891.

8

Regulatory Capture

I. The Problem

Liberals tend to favor regulations as expressions of the public will and the common good, and as a way to protect children, patients, mortgage holders, airline passengers, and many other consumers from abuse by unscrupulous actors in the private sector. Laissez-faire conservatives and libertarians tend to oppose regulations because they view them as an abusive use of the government's power and as harmful to the economic well-being of the nation.

I write "tend" because liberals recognize that some regulations are poorly crafted or not needed, and some conservatives and libertarians admit that some regulations are beneficial. However, each side demands that the other demonstrate why a deviation from their preferred default position is merited— and they set a fairly high bar that the introduction of regulations (or their removal) must first clear.

In addition, this is a case of pluralistic ignorance, in which various observers note incidents that deviate from their core assumptions, but neither generalize nor draw overarching conclusions from these incidents. Thus, liberals are quite aware of regulations that end up serving private interests rather than the public, but they still strongly favor regulations. For instance, they considered the enactment of the Dodd-Frank financial reform bill in 2010 to be one of the major achievements of the Obama administration, despite the fact that the bill had already been greatly diluted by lobbyists working for the industries it is supposed to regulate, and despite the fact that the law, as enacted by Congress, is particularly open-ended, leaving it to various agencies to shape the needed specifications, under conditions particularly favorable to lobbyists. Conservatives too may note incidents in which regulations serve those usually allied with them in the private sector, but nevertheless continue to be strongly opposed to regulation in general.

Both sides share one key assumption: they view regulations as acts of the government, largely aimed at the private sector, although they recognize that regulations do not always work in this way. In fact, the ways regulations are formulated and enforced are often deeply affected by the private sector. Economists and political scientists refer to this phenomenon as "regulatory capture."

They show that regulations are often captured by those they are supposed to regulate, making the regulators and the regulated march more or less in tandem. Thierer and other scholars have found that regulatory capture has occurred "in various arenas: transportation and telecommunications; energy and environmental policy; farming and financial services; and many others."

Nobel Laureate economist George Stigler, who is credited with having made major contributions to the study of capture, concludes that "as a rule, regulation is acquired by the industry and is designed and operated primarily for its benefit." I refer from here on to those who capture regulations as "special interests" in order to denote that these are often not groups which represent major segments of the electorate.

II. The Research Evidence

Some of those who have written about capture imply that it governs most, if not all, regulations and that capture is complete. Some have concluded from this observation that regulation is generally ineffective. In fact, however, there are considerable differences among different regulatory areas in the extent to which capture occurs. And although the level of capture is often significant, it is still far from complete. There follows here a brief illustration: a case study of a substantial—but not complete—capture of important regulations.

In 2001, Enron Corporation and its accounting firm Arthur Andersen were found to have used irregular accounting practices to conceal a significant amount of Enron's debts and losses. As these practices came to light, Enron's stock plummeted from over $90.00 to less than $.50 per share, forcing the company to declare bankruptcy, causing substantial losses to many thousands of investors, and leaving thousands of Enron employees without their retirement savings accounts and other benefits. Enron was not alone; similar scandals involved major other American corporations such as Tyco and WorldCom.

In response to these abuses, Congress passed the Sarbanes-Oxley Act in 2002. At the time, the law was considered by *The Economist* magazine to be "the most sweeping reform of corporate governance in America since the Great Depression in the 1930s." The law left working out the details of the new regulations to the Securities and Exchange Commission (SEC), which was subjected to extensive lobbying by the accounting industry, which was able to weaken its regulatory impacts. The bill initially banned auditors from providing their clients with advice on tax shelters (a particularly lucrative practice) because of fears that auditors would be inclined to soften their reviews in order not to lose the tax businesses, as well as concerns noted by *The Economist* that "if auditors were allowed to design tax shelters, they would end up auditing their own work, a conflict of interest." However, lobbyists convinced the SEC to allow auditors to provide tax services (though they must now obtain permission from the audit committee of the company's board of directors). The accounting industry's lobbyists won another victory when they used the

SEC rule-writing process to weaken an older compromise they had made in 2000. That compromise required auditors to categorize their work as either auditing or nonauditing, and disclose to regulators the specific amounts they were paid for each. During the rule-writing process for Sarbanes-Oxley, the accountants modified this compromise to expand the definition of "auditing" work to include some tasks as "audit-related" and hence minimize the amount of "nonauditing" work they appeared to be doing.

Sarbanes-Oxley was further weakened in 2006. Instead of requiring auditors to investigate any accounting issues that have a "more than remote" chance of damaging a company's finances, the rules were revised to only require auditors to investigate issues that have a "reasonable possibility" of doing so. (The various thinning out of regulations are reflected in the size of the regulatory text of the law—it was reduced from 180 pages to 65 pages.) In 2009, small businesses were permanently exempted from two of the acts key provisions—one requiring executives to confirm the integrity of their firm's internal accounting procedures, and another requiring an outside audit of these procedures.

Nevertheless, the law has achieved some of its goals. As John C. Coates of Harvard Law School has concluded, Sarbanes-Oxley "created new incentives for firms to spend money on internal controls, above and beyond the increases in audit costs that would have occurred after the corporate scandals of the early 2000s." Furthermore, Coates found, "Sarbanes-Oxley promises a variety of long-term benefits. Investors will face a lower risk of losses from fraud and theft, and benefit from more reliable financial reporting, greater transparency, and accountability," even if the difficulty of calculating the law's costs and benefits means that judgments of it "must be tentative and qualitative." In short, regulatory capture can frequently be substantial, but capture is far from complete or all-encompassing. It is a major way in which the private and the public are intertwined without their separation being obliterated.

Aside from diluting regulations, capture is achieved in several other ways, briefly illustrated here.

a) *Special interests compose the regulations.* Lobbyists representing the pharmaceutical industry literally composed the text of the 2003 bill that governs drug benefits for Medicare recipients. This benefit was initially estimated to cost $400 billion over 10 years; more recent estimates range as high as $1.2 trillion. Also, as composed by the lobbyists, the law prohibits the government from negotiating the prices of these drugs.

b) *Weakening of enforcement.* According to a 2006 report by Schlosser, "cutbacks in staff and budgets reduced the number of food-safety inspections conducted by the FDA to about 3,400 a year from 35,000 in the 1970s," and "the number of inspectors at the Agriculture Department has declined to 7,500 from 9,000."

227

In the late 1980s and early 1990s, the US Sentencing Commission drafted sentencing guidelines that aimed to severely punish corporate crimes. The commission acted after it found that previous penalties for corporations convicted of major crimes were very light. For instance, Eli Lilly & Company, the pharmaceutical manufacturer, was fined a mere $25,000 after pleading guilty to the charge of failing to inform the government of a large number of deaths caused by its arthritis drug Oraflex, as is required by law. In November 1989, the commission published its draft guidelines, introducing large fines up to $364 million for crimes that had previously resulted in fines of just tens of thousands of dollars. The draft led to intense lobbying by major corporations and trade associations. As a result, the commission reduced the suggested penalties by as much as 97 percent. The commission also provided a list of extenuating circumstances that allowed offending corporations to reduce easily the remaining penalties to small amounts, if not to zero.

c) *Gaming the regulators.* Special interests affect the regulatory regime in their favor by switching regulations into a new jurisdiction (e.g., from state to federal) or by pitting the regulators against one another. Thus the *Washington Post* reports that when mortgage lender Countrywide Financial felt "pressured" by the federal agencies charged with overseeing it, executives "simply switched regulators." As a national commercial bank, Countrywide had been under the jurisdiction of the Office of the Comptroller of the Currency. As early as 2005, Countrywide executives engaged in talks with the Office of Thrift Supervision (OTS), known to be a much more "flexible" regulator. Less than two years later, Countrywide redefined itself as a "thrift" instead of a "national commercial bank" and thus became regulated by the OTS. Over the next two years OTS proved to be a very lax regulator of Countrywide's mortgage lending as it also proved to be for IndyMac, Washington Mutual, and other major lenders. They also played a significant role in the financial crisis that followed.

d) *Setting prices and rates.* Regulators are often charged with limiting the profits gained by one industry or another, such as for limiting the rate increases of utilities. However, in several major cases, captured regulations had the opposite effect: they bolstered the profits of a specific industry by setting higher prices and rates than the market would provide. One widely-cited example is the government-created Civil Aeronautics Board, which set airline fares and limited the entry of new airlines into the travel market. After airlines were deregulated in 1978, fares typically fell by 20 percent or more.

e) Close relationships between regulators and industry. After the explosion at Upper Big Branch Mine in West Virginia in 2010 killed twenty-nine people, it was reported that the federal agency responsible for mine oversight, the Mine Safety and Health Administration, was reluctant to close even those mines which repeatedly violated safety rules. Furthermore, the agency rarely imposed large fines and often failed to collect the fines it did impose.

After the explosion at BP's Deepwater Horizon well in 2010, and the resulting oil spill in the Gulf of Mexico, there was widespread consensus that the federal agency responsible for regulating the well, the Minerals Management Service (MMS), had failed in large part because it had been captured. In the Wall Street Journal, Gerald P. O'Driscoll, Jr. wrote, "By all accounts, MMS operated as a rubber stamp for BP. It is a striking example of regulatory capture: Agencies tasked with protecting the public interest come to identify with the regulated industry and protect its interests against that of the public. The result: Government fails to protect the public." The Interior Department's inspector general found that MMS officials responsible for overseeing drilling in the Gulf of Mexico were allowing oil and gas officials to fill out their own inspection forms, and some even considered themselves part of the industry they were tasked to regulate.

All this shows that as far as regulations are concerned, the public and the private realms are often and significantly intertwined, that they change in tandem, and that they are co-determined—although there are no studies that show with any measure of precision the extent to which regulations across the board are captured. It is, however, clear that in those considerable areas in which capture occurs—whether full, substantial, or merely partial—we face the same force from both realms, and that captured regulations neither serve the liberal vision of promoting the common good nor confirm the conservative fear that the government will impose its will on the private sector. Rather, they are instances in which the prevailing powers of the private realm prevail in the public realm as well.

III. Recommendations and Solutions

Regulatory capture cannot be tackled by itself because it is but the tip of the iceberg. Large segments of what Congress does is captured by private interests, including the introduction of hundreds of loopholes into the tax code, earmarks and their functional equivalents, subsidies, and so and on. To overcome this widespread, generic capture would require a major change in the distribution of power within the American political system. Such changes are very difficult to bring about and occur rarely.

In some nations, they have entailed revolutions. In the U. S., they are much more likely to be driven by a major social movement. The progressive movement at the onset of the 20th century, the Civil Rights Movement, and the movement to protect the environment are key examples. Such movements first of all change core values and then mobilize large numbers of citizens to support new norms and policies that reflect these values.

Unfortunately, it seems that it is easier (although still far from easy) to form social movements around substantive issues rather than around procedural ones. Reforming the ways elections are financed—the main way capture takes place—is considered a procedural matter. This seems to be a key reason attempts to mobilize a reform movement around this issue by Common Cause and others have failed. One can argue, though, that Occupy Wall Street movements (and some may argue even the Tea Party) reflect new popular discontent with the political system that may lead to reforms. That is, unless these movements will themselves be captured.

References

Adam Thierer, "Regulatory Capture: What the Experts Have Found," *The Technology Liberation Front* (December 19, 2010), http://techliberation.com/2010/12/19/regulatory-capture-whatthe-experts-have-found/ (Retrieved July 17, 2012).

Applebaum, Binyamin and Ellen Nakashima. 2008. "Banking Regulator Played Advocate Over Enforcer," *Washington Post* (November 23), http://www.washingtonpost.com/wpdyn/content/article/2008/11/22/AR2008112202213.html, (Retrieved July 17, 2012)

Coates, John C., "The Goals and Promise of the Sarbanes-Oxley Act," *Journal of Economic Perspectives* 21, no. 1 (2007): 91–116.

Etzioni, Amitai, *The Moral Dimension: Toward a New Economics* (New York: The Free Press, 1988).

O'Driscoll, Gerald P., Jr. "The Gulf Spill, The Financial Crisis, and Government Failure," *Wall Street Journal* (June 12, 2010), http://online.wsj.com/article/SB10001424052748704575304575296873167457684.html (Retrieved July 17, 2012).

Eric Schlosser, "Has Politics Contaminated the Food Supply?" *New York Times* (December 11, 2006), http://www.nytimes.com/2006/12/11/opinion/11schlosser.html?pagewanted=all (Retrieved July 17, 2012).

George J. Stigler, "The Theory of Economic Regulation," *Bell Journal of Economics and Management Science* 2, no. 1 (1971): 3–21.

The Economist, "Setting the Rules," *The Economist* (January 29, 2003), http://www.economist.com/node/1558898 (Retrieved July 17, 2012).

Rolfe Winkler, "The Race to the Regulatory Bottom Continue," *Reuters, Option ARMageddon Blog* (November 4, 2009) http://blogs.reuters.com/rolfewinkler/2009/11/04/the-race-to-the-regulatory-bottomcontinues/ (Retrieved July 17, 2012).

9

Is Transparency the Best Disinfectant?

Transparency is a highly regarded value, a precept used for ideological purposes, and a subject of academic study. The following critical analysis attempts to show that transparency is overvalued. Moreover, its ideological usages cannot be justified, because a social science analysis shows that transparency *cannot* fulfill the functions its advocates assign to it, although it can play a limited role in their service. We shall see that in assessing transparency, one must take into account a continuum composed of the order of disutility and the level of information costs. The higher the score on both variables, the less useful transparency is. Moreover, these scores need not be particularly high to greatly limit the extent to which the public can rely on transparency for most purposes.

I. Transparency, Weak and Strong, and Other Goods

Transparency is generally defined as the principle of enabling the public to gain information about the operations and structures of a given entity.[1] Transparency is often considered synonymous with openness and disclosure, although one can find some subtle differences among these terms.[2]

In public discourse, transparency is widely considered a "good" on the face of it, similar to privacy and free speech. Transparency is viewed as a self-evident good in Western society to the point that "we might almost say that 'more- transparent-than-thou' has become the secular equivalent of 'holier-than-thou' in modern debates over matters of organization and governance."[3] Transparency International, an organization that promotes transparency in many nations, both developing and industrialized, was founded in 1993 and has won much acclaim.

Several progressive groups in many democratic countries have been promoting the introduction of "sunshine" into legislation.[4] Reports indicate that transparency has been gaining ground "not only in state decision-making bodies but also in states' central banks, the international regimes to which they belong, and even in private companies within their borders."[5] Professor of Government Christopher Hood further documented this trend in a book entitled *Transparency: The Key to Better Governance.*[6] Transparency has gained additional popularity in recent years, since the lack of transparency in financial instruments has been deemed one of the major factors in causing the 2008–2009 near-global economic crisis. Also, President Obama made increasing transparency one of the major themes of his 2008 election campaign. Since his election, there has been a great deal of discussion about the need for more regulation, especially of the financial markets, but so far little new regulation has been enacted, and various draft bills have encountered a great deal of opposition. In contrast, several transparency measures have been introduced. For instance, the website *Data.gov*, which was launched in May 2009, makes statistical information collected by over fifty federal agencies publicly available. In addition, Obama introduced "sunlight before signing," which entails posting new legislation on the web for five days before the president signs the bills into law to allow for public comments.

In addition, transparency has an ideological application. This application makes a much stronger claim than the position that transparency is merely one feature of good government. Ideological advocates of transparency maintain that it can obviate the need for most—if not all—government controls. That is, transparency becomes a tool to fight off the regulations opposed by various business groups[7] and politicians from conservative parties.[8]

The editorial page of the *Wall Street Journal*, which is openly ideological, runs articles with titles such as "Transparency is More Powerful than Regulations"[9] and lines like "transparency is better than draconian regulation."[10] The importance of the latter article is not where it was published, but who wrote it: Professor Cass Sunstein, a highly regarded scholar who has been appointed by President Obama as the head of the White House Office of Information and Regulatory Affairs, which is in charge of regulations, and Richard Thaler, one of the most respected and influential economists in the United States.

Others advance the argument that "better transparency is the surest way to make markets more efficient and less volatile. Market wisdom results when more people access better information."[11] Some argue that disclosure will allow consumers to become "citizen-regulators" and do the job better than the government.[12]

The following analysis deals mainly with this kind of transparency in its strong form rather than with its weak, supplementary form. What is at issue is whether transparency can be the mainstay of delivering the sought-after goods, rather than whether it can make a contribution to their promotion. To put it differently, *the critical question is whether transparency constitutes a reliable mechanism of promoting good governance and sound markets under most circumstances—or whether it is a rather weak means that itself relies on other forms of guidance and can supplement regulation but not serve a main form of guidance.*[13] I find that even the soft version—as just an element of regulation—cannot carry much weight.

I need to make two comments in order to properly focus the following discussion. The transparency I deal with here is public and not social. Communitarianism has long established that informal social controls can be very powerful. People have a profound need for approval from others, especially people to whom they are related by bonds of affection—often members of their family, social group, or community.[14] For such controls to work, these others must know how an ego is behaving. When people conceal their addictions or abuses from others, social control is often held in abeyance, while disclosure activates it. The mechanisms at work in this situation are radically different from the kind of strong transparency studied in this article; social controls are informal and voluntary. The focus here is on transparency mandated by the government, including annual audited statements by corporations and voluntary associations, campaign contribution disclosure, nutrition and ingredient labels for food, warning labels on hazardous materials, disclosure of terms of contracts and privacy policies, and numerous other transparency mechanisms. This kind of transparency is held to provide a substitution for government regulations, not for informal social controls.

Second, even advocates of strong transparency do not claim that it is an absolute value. Clearly there are situations in which transparency must be squared with other values, including security, private property (e.g., trade secrets and copyright protections), and privacy.[15] The best example of the limits of transparency is the rationale for a secret ballot. However, when one is concerned with economic activities, laissez-faire conservatives, libertarians, some kinds of liberals, and many others hold that (a) the market can regulate itself and (b) if it does need regulation, transparency can provide it.

II. The Theory of Transparency

Both popular and academic texts lay out the ways in which transparency is expected to function. Although they are well known, I review these here to lay out the elements and mechanisms on which transparency is believed to rely, and which, we shall see, are in fact absent.

1. In The Economic Realm

According to the popular version of transparency, consumers control the direction of the economy by using their purchasing power to "vote" on which businesses will succeed and which will fail.[16] For this consumer "sovereignty" to work, consumers must be able to know the attributes of the goods they are about to purchase. This explains the introduction of labels that disclose the attributes of various food items, such as their caloric value, types and levels of vitamins, and so on, as well as labels on cigarette boxes and posters in liquor stores. The transparency theory presumes that such disclosure will enable consumers to make informed choices, reward the businesses that provide the preferred products, and discourage or even put out of business those that disregard the informed consumers' preferences.[17]

Furthermore, transparency has a strong normative underpinning. As Chapman University law professor Susanna Kim Ripken notes, "Respect for individual autonomy, responsibility, and decision-making is deeply entrenched in our culture and law. We believe that people can order their own economic affairs and, given sufficient information, can make their own personal assessments of the risks and benefits of transactions."[18] In addition, she says, "Disclosure promotes fairness and empowers the investor with information to make smart investment choices."[19]

2. In The Public Realm

The same basic argument is a very familiar part of the popular theory of democracy. "Greater openness and wider information-sharing enable the public to make informed political decisions," write World Bank economist Tara Vishwanath and the Brookings Institute's Daniel Kaufmann.[20] Specifically, according to political philosopher Onora O'Neill, transparency "is supposed to discipline institutions and their office-holders by making information about their performance more public. Publicity is taken to deter corruption and poor performance, and to secure a basis for ensuring better and more trustworthy performance."[21] In short, "the more strictly we are watched, the better we behave," as Jeremy Bentham put it.[22]

In the 1970s, the US legislature introduced new requirements that mandated the disclosure of campaign contributions. The Federal Election Commission (FEC) was founded in 1975. The FEC requires that campaign contributions over $200 to those running for federal office be reported in a timely manner. The McCain-Feingold Act of 2002 requires public disclosure of large donations to political campaigns and was upheld by the Supreme Court in 2003 on the grounds that disclosure of funding is vital for the American citizen to effectively assert his or her right to choose representatives.[23]

Transparency of medical organizations is critical for improving healthcare, according to Sen. Ron Wyden (D-OR).[24] In 1975, *U.S. World and News Report* began issuing rankings on mortality in various hospitals to allow consumers to select those that perform better and to deny patients to poor performers, assuming that such disclosure would either force them to improve their service or close down.[25] The same argument was made in reference to disclosing data about the relative performance of various public schools.[26]

3. In Academic Discussions

There are a fair number of academic treatments of transparency that parallel, and hence at least indirectly support, the popular theory of transparency. These works are, as a rule, much more qualified and nuanced than the ideological texts, although some works, such as those by Milton Friedman, have a considerable ideological content. For instance, academic works by economists provide a major modification to the theory of transparency with the introduction of transaction costs, including the cost of collecting and processing information. This element allows one to recognize that consumers and voters may not find it efficient to absorb and process all of the disclosed information. That is, sub-optimal processing of revealed information may actually serve to make optimal choices. (This applies to all the cases in which the costs of additional collecting and processing of information—of additional "search"—exceed the expected gains.)

Another major addition to the popular theory of transparency is the thesis that the public can utilize intermediaries, experts, technologies, heuristics, and choice architecture to help process the information.[27] As Jason Zweig points out, a forty-seven-page mortgage can lull people into a false sense of security, as they mistakenly believe that more details means more honesty. However, as he sees it, if the industry were required to offer a standard mortgage with easy-to-understand terms, consumers might receive less direct information but would gain information they would be able to digest and use.[28]

These two brief examples may suffice to illustrate my point that even when some of the academic work on transparency might be said to support the strong transparency thesis, it does so in a much more qualified way than is seen in transparency's ideological usages.[29]

III. Empirical Studies of Transparency

Given the high value put on transparency, its ideological currency, and scholarly interest, it is surprising to find that there are few empirical studies of the effects of transparency, especially of the strong kind under discussion here. Moreover, there seem to be no comparative studies of the use of transparency versus other means of regulation, to determine which is more effective. I am hardly the first or only one who notes this fact. There continues to be a dearth of studies empirically testing the theoretical claims of transparency advocates, even as legislation and institutional support for their case accumulates exponentially.[30]

Some of the handful of available findings deal with communitarian rather than public transparency, namely transparency of the kind used by communities for their members that is voluntary in nature rather than imposed by the government. One case in point is the study of "open book" management. With open book management, financial information is shared with everyone in a company. Moreover, the management also lays out the meaning of the financial information and points to ways the employees can contribute to the company's success. A 2005 survey found that 40 percent of the firms among "the five hundred fastest-growing private companies employed the practice in some fashion—far more than in the business community as a whole."[31] However, this study deals with the internal process of a company, not with the public at large.

The following are typical findings of the few studies that deal with public transparency. A study of nutrition labels[32] examined changes in nutrition labeling in grocery stores in New England from 1986 to 1989. It found that such labels affected consumer purchases. However, the effect was small. For instance, the share of household income devoted to milk labeled "healthy" over unlabeled milk rose slightly in the first year. Moreover, this effect was found only "in those food categories where differences in other quality characteristics (e.g., taste) are relatively small between more and less healthy products."[33] That is, consumers were only likely to switch to healthier food if the healthy and unhealthy products had similar tastes.

Other studies find that the introduction of warning labels enhances awareness of risk, but to a rather limited extent. In the first year after the introduction of alcohol warning labels in 1989, there was a slight increase in the public's perception of the risk associated with consuming alcoholic beverages. About 54 percent of the sample described alcoholic beverages as "very harmful" in 1990, compared to 50 percent a year earlier. The increase was somewhat larger among "heavy" drinkers.[34] Note, however, that this study deals with awareness and not with changes in behavior.

A study of disclosure statements in television ads in 2002 found that such disclaimers provide little clarification for consumers. The study of 258 undergraduate students over a six-week period tested disclaimers in multiple ways. At times the students were explicitly told to pay attention to the disclosure statements, which were then shown multiple times, yet the failure rate for recall remained high.[35] Another scholar concluded with regard to political financial disclosures, "There is no empirical evidence that this has resulted in a more aware electorate."[36]

The quality of 382 commercial HMOs was observed between 1997 and 2000. The study found that the quality significantly improved among those HMOs that publicly disclosed quality information, "suggesting that public release of quality information can serve as a mechanism to improve quality in healthcare."[37] However, there are very few such studies, and there is no evidence that these improvements do not wash out over time.

In short, there are few empirical studies of transparency to begin with, and several of those that are available deal with communitarian rather than government-imposed transparency or with situations in which the information is easy to collect and process and the change in behavior required to benefit is not taxing.

Most important, none of these studies indicate that the effects of transparency are significant enough to obviate the need for regulation, especially in those cases in which the harm done by a given activity or product is considerable (relatively high disutility) and the information is relatively complex (that is, the cost of processing the disclosed information is high for the user). Given the paucity of empirical studies, I move ahead to suggest that strong transparency *cannot* work.

IV. A Critical Examination of Transparency

1. Strong Transparency is a Form of Regulation

The transparency often discussed as an alternative to regulation is, in effect, a form of regulation because it is required by the government. For instance, corporations are required by law to issue annual statements about their financial activities to the Securities and Exchange Commission. Most food manufacturers are required by the Federal Food, Drug, and Cosmetic Act to place nutrition labels on their products, and so on. Politicians who are running for federal offices are required by law to post campaign contributions with the FEC. That is, transparency is *coercive*, a label sometimes affixed by opponents to regulation, but which also applies to transparency.[38]

Additional regulation is required if the information released in order to meet the transparency requirements is to be *understandable* to consumers and voters. Unless the government requires disclosure in forms that the public finds digestible, the information is often released in ways that provide little *de facto* transparency.[39] This is an issue with the small, legalistic, and opaque text on the back of airline tickets and when people take out mortgages, credit cards, and auto loans in the United States.[40]

Still more regulation is required to ensure the *veracity* of the released information. The US Securities and Exchange Commission requires public companies to disclose their financial and operating information as defined by federal statutes, including net sales or operating revenues, income or losses from continuing operations, total assets, long-term obligations and redeemable preferred stock, every six months in the form of a portfolio snapshot at a particular point in time. This snapshot "can easily be manipulated by readjusting the composition just before and after the snapshot is taken—a well-documented practice known as *window dressing*."[41]

Another example of manipulative disclosure concerns hospital mortality rates: "The reduction in standardized mortality ratio . . . observed [after the implementation of disclosure of mortality rates] most likely reflects the changes in palliative care: fewer patients were admitted to die in hospital and more patients were discharged to die elsewhere."[42]

Political Action Committees (PACs), composed by special interest groups, regularly adopt names that very effectively conceal whom they are promoting. For instance, try to guess to which political party the following PACs are linked: "All America," "America's Foundation," "American Dream," "America Works," and "American Leadership Council." (Answers: D, R, R, D, R.) The same holds for lobbies that represent various special interests.

Finally, like other regulations, the requirements to be transparent must be *enforced* by government. Thus, one reason transparency regarding campaign contributions does not disclose much is that when disclosure laws are violated, the matter goes before the deadlocked, minimally staffed, and poorly funded Federal Election Commission. If the commission does manage to find a grossly misleading disclosure, it is often months too late, well after the election is over. Regulators failed to impose penalties on almost five hundred thousand violations by companies that dumped hazardous chemicals in places from which people draw their drinking water, in violation of the Clean Water Act.[43]

In short, transparency is to a significant extent merely a form of regulation by other means. These observations are ignored by those who oppose regulation and argue that transparency obviates the need for regulation.

A less dichotomous proposition is more defensible. Regulations come in different shades and forms. For instance, some regulations are more coercive than others: compare those that impose minor fines (like the $20 fine on text messaging while driving in Virginia) to those that require jailing offenders. Also, some regulations outright ban certain products or activities, while others merely require that safety measures be added to dangerous products but do not ban them outright (e.g., seat belts, motorcycle helmets, and, in some jurisdictions, child locks on guns). In this context, transparency stands out as a relatively light form of regulation, in the sense that meeting its requirements is much less restrictive of producer and consumer choice than other forms of regulations. However, for it to work, consumers and voters must be able to process the released information.

2. The Limits of Knowing

Transparency, unlike other forms of regulation, has a major disadvantage: it assumes that those who receive the information released by manufacturers or public officials can properly process it and that their conclusions will lead them to reasonable action.[44] However, the well-known and often-cited findings of behavioral economics demonstrate that very often the public is unable to properly process even rather simple information because of "wired in," congenital, systematic cognitive biases.[45]

Counterarguments do not seem to hold. The argument that these findings apply only to experimental conditions does not take into account that the same limitations have also been demonstrated in field studies.[46] The suggestion that it is rational for people to stop processing information when the cost of additional processing exceeds the benefit assumes that people can correctly assess the cost of information they have not yet collected, but there is next to no evidence that this is the case.[47]

None of this is to suggest that providing transparency where it is lacking has none of the desired effects, but merely that often it cannot suffice *by itself* to serve the goals set for it, even when consumers and voters must deal with only modestly complex information. And it cannot carry much of the needed public protection under any circumstances. That is, even the merits of the soft position are greatly limited.

In today's "disclosure regime," "disclosure documents . . . are written by corporate lawyers in formalized language to protect the corporation from liability rather than to provide the investor with meaningful information,"[48] notes Susanna Kim Ripken. "The complexity and detail in disclosure documents can make them almost incomprehensible at times . . . Disclosure cannot fulfill its communicative purpose if investors find it impenetrable and therefore ignore it."[49] Aware that "transparency mandates *disclosure* or *dissemination*, but does not require effective communication with any audience,"[50] these advocates state that "to be effective, information should be fair, reliable, timely, complete, consistent, and presented in clear and simple terms."[51] However, such disclosure is rare, and itself requires additional regulation and enforcement. Moreover, if the released information is to serve the goals set for it, there are often limits on the extent to which it can be simplified, as it tends to contain rather complex assumptions, probabilities, and multiple correlations. Hence, we should not be surprised that it is far from demonstrated that information that is reasonably comprehensive can still be digested by most people, even those trained in statistics.[52] Indeed, behavioral economics and other studies consistently show that often people cannot process even relatively simple information.[53]

In response to those who claim that not all investors are "smart," the Efficient Capital Market Hypothesis defends transparency on the grounds that "the biases, errors in judgments, and decision-making shortcomings of uninformed investors are random and will cancel each other out in the market. Even if people are subject to errors and inconsistencies in decision-making, these fallibilities will be exploited and weeded out of the market by the more sophisticated, rational agents."[54] However, this theoretical hypothesis is not supported by evidence. Consumers were not protected by "more sophisticated agents" when they were sold sub-prime mortgages they could not possibly pay for, and millions lost their homes; people who rely on brokers or financial advisers for investment advice are doing worse than those who invest in passive investment instruments such as index funds; consumers are not protected by private intermediaries from those who market foods contaminated with E. coli, melamine, or salmonella. Nor, as the record of the last years reminds us, is the whole economic system protected from major crises by such agents. True, other factors are involved, such as irresponsible acts by consumers who were seeking speculative gains in real estate, individuals who consumed more than they earned by using credit cards, and so on, and theses tendencies are in turn fanned by changes in the culture and by marketing. However, people were not educated about, encouraged to deal with, or protected from these failings by "sophisticated agents."

In short, studies of processing information strongly favor adding stronger forms of regulation than those that merely require transparency, even if requirements to communicate clearly are added.

V. Intermediaries: Evaluation and Trust

1. Reliance on Intermediaries

Advocates of transparency respond to the findings of behavioral economics by suggesting that people need not process the information because they can rely on experts or leaders—the "smart" members of the masses.[55] For instance, people do not need to test appliances; they can rely on reports such as those issued by the Consumer Union or on the Good Housekeeping Seal of Approval. Instead of reading long legalistic statements about a corporation's privacy policy on its website, they can rely on the green TRUSTe icon. However, issues we face in dealing with the absorbability and veracity of what might be called first-order information we also face when dealing with intermediaries or second-order, processed (rather than directly accessed) information.

The public does not have the cognitive capacities to determine which intermediary provides information that is better processed than another. Reference here is not to deliberate manipulation, but to differences in the quality of the information processing due to differences in access to primary information, resources available to the analysts, their skills and training, and the assumptions they make. A case in point is the ranking of colleges provided by various publications such as the *US News and World Report*, *USA Today*, and the *Princeton Review*, whose lists differ from one another and whose rankings have been subject to considerable controversy.[56] There is no evidence that consumers can evaluate the relative reliability of these rankings any better than they can process the raw information on which these ratings draw.

Hospital rankings have been issued by *US News and World Report* and *Healthinsight.org*, among others, based on data compiled by the Centers for Medicare and Medicaid. Drawing on such processed information, users may well wish to avoid hospitals that have high morality rates. But actually, these are likely the best hospitals because they attract patients with severe illnesses. Rankings of high schools issued by *US News and World Report* draw in part on the number of AP classes taken, which in turn correlates with admission to "elite" colleges. However, these data do not inform readers as to whether the schools' success is due to the selection of students (i.e., "successful" schools draw a large number of their students from affluent neighborhoods, which tend to produce more prepared students) or due to the quality of education provided in the school. In short, the users of intermediaries (and the information processed by them) face many of the same problems individuals encounter when they deal directly with raw information.

Second, the old question of who will guard the guardians applies to intermediaries. As long as they are not regulated, the intermediaries can, and in some occasions do, manipulate their rankings. The TRUSTe label is granted practically to all who pay for it.[57] Far from indicating that a corporation that displays such an icon provides strong privacy protection, which is how many interpret it, it merely indicates that the corporation is living up to whatever policy it announces, even when the small print states that it will sell clients' information to third parties. One may say that rankings and labels provided by the federal government can be trusted and save the consumer from having to find out on his or her own what the score is. However, a report on the "USDA Organic" label finds that it often applies to products that do not meet consumer expectations of organic: "foods without pesticides and other chemicals, produced in a way that is gentle to the environment." Instead, many products include ingredients that are neither natural nor environmentally friendly.[58]

In short, consumers and voters cannot evaluate or rely on intermediaries much more than they can rely on the original sources of information—especially if neither is closely regulated.

2. Information versus Choice

Transparency advocates tend to assume that if given information, individuals will use it to make improved decisions. Actually, more than a generation ago, we learned that "a curious feature of the growing demand for more information is the paucity of concrete evidence that past disclosures have made significant differences in consumer or market *behavior*."[59]

Data from psychological studies shows that people "do not make rational choices when it comes to their saving and investing activities . . . information is beneficial only to the extent that it can be understood and utilized by the individual to whom it is directed. . . . Evidence suggests that when people are given too much information in a limited time, the information overload can result in confusion, cognitive strain, and poorer decision-making," concludes Susanna Kim Ripken.[60]

A survey found that only 11 percent of Medicare beneficiaries have sufficient knowledge to make an informed choice between new Medicare+Choice options and the traditional fee-for-service program.[61]

Most importantly, in numerous situations, even a well-informed person may find choice restricted, and must rely on other sources of control for protection. Small investors with pension funds provided by their employers cannot affect the composition of these funds or the selection of funds among which they may choose (if any is provided). In the case of health plans, the selection is likely to be even more limited and changes in the plans even less subject to individual preferences. Theoretically, a person could choose to seek another job with the preferred kind of pension or health plan, but the costs of such a shift are often very high. Hence, a case can be made that beyond being transparent, pension and health plans should be mandated to meet at least minimal standards. Even if one disagrees on this point, there is no denying that transparency has limited consequences when the choice is nil.

VI. The Guidance Continuum

To reiterate, the question is not, as the *Wall Street Journal* put it, whether "transparency is better than regulation" (which should be "better than other forms of regulation"), but how much of the regulatory mission transparency can carry out. The preceding analysis suggests that it is fairly limited. The main factors that determine the extent to which one can rely on transparency without backing it up it with stronger regulatory means (sometimes referred to as substantive regulation[62]) are as follows: the degree of disutility if the information is not heeded, the education level (whether people are likely understand the information released), the culture of compliance (whether people trust and heed the information released), and one's values. Clearly if the harm one seeks to prevent is great, when the education level is low and when there is strong tendency to ignore or mistrust information released by the government or by corporations, transparency can be relied on even less than if all these factors are reversed. Moreover, the preceding data suggest that on the continuum that these variables form (I call it the guidance continuum), the cutoff point—the point at which transparency cannot be relied upon—is fairly close to the low end of the continuum. That is, even if the disutility and distrust are not high, compliance is reasonable, and the level of education is considerable, transparency will often be insufficient for achieving a reasonable level of public protection.

Ultimately though, it is a normative issue. If one values autonomy very highly and considers it morally acceptable for people to suffer various ill effects as long as they were informed about the risks involved (or opportunities they miss), one would lean toward relying more on transparency than if one holds that protecting people who cannot protect themselves from serious disutility is morally justified.

Also, one should note that regulations have an "expressive" function—they express the community's shared values and help to set norms. Relying on transparency indicates that the community considers the matter at hand—public safety, prevention of pandemic, exploitation, manipulation, or fraud—less consequential than if the activities or products at issue are banned or their provision is required.[63]

In Conclusion

Transparency is a very popular concept. It reflects the idea that people are autonomous rational choosers who can govern themselves. Theoretically, transparency could be limited to voluntary disclosures. Thus, it could be promoted by consumers refusing to purchase items from sources that do not disclose their content, and investors refraining from investing in corporations that do not provide financial details. Indeed, some measure of such voluntary, communitarian disclosure is taking place because it generates good will and is considered "good business." However, to ensure the veracity of the information that is released, to promote releases that are comprehensible to the public and comparable to information released by other sources, and to secure that such information will be regularly made available, often requires government regulation.

There are few empirical studies of the effects of transparency, and there seem to be none that compare its effects to other methods of regulation under the same conditions. However, other data, especially evidence assembled by behavioral economists, strongly indicate that people are neither as able to process information nor as likely to act on it as transparency theory presumes. Hence, in situations in which adverse outcomes have a relatively high disutility (e.g., there is a high probability that they will cause death, serious bodily damage, or loss of one's home or life's savings) or the information is complex (e.g., medical information), drawing on other sources of regulation in addition to transparency seems called for. That is, transparency cannot replace other kinds of regulation, and even its "soft" version is overrated; it cannot provide much of the necessary public protection, even when combined with other means of regulation.

Finally, one should note that from a normative viewpoint, the difference between transparency (which is relatively welcomed by laissez-faire conservatives and libertarians and by academics whose assumptions parallel these ways of thinking) and other forms of government regulations (which these same groups consider an anathema) is smaller than it at first seems. Under numerous conditions, transparency has to be mandated or it is not provided, the forms of information disclosed must be prescribed, or else even the more prepared users will be unable to decipher the meaning of the released information, and its veracity must be assured. At the same time, other kinds of regulation are not necessarily highly coercive. Some merely provide incentives for good conduct. Others impose a minor fine and thus leave it to the regulated agent whether or not to comply. And for those regulations that outright ban an activity, enforcement varies a great deal. When all is said and done, there is room for increased, validated, and comprehensive transparency (and vetted intermediaries). However, it is not sufficient protection when the disutility and the information costs are high—and often even when they are not.

Notes

1.   David Heald, "Varieties of Transparency," in *Transparency: The Key to Better Governance?* ed. Christopher Hood and David Heald (Oxford: Oxford University Press, 2006), 26
      Also: Bernard I. Finel and Kristin M. Lord, "The Surprising Logic of Transparency," *International Studies Quarterly* 43 (1999): 315–39, 316.
2.   "Openness might therefore be thought of as a characteristic of the organization, where transparency also requires external receptors capable of processing information made available" David Heald, "Varieties of Transparency," in *Transparency: The Key to Better Governance?* ed. Christopher Hood and David Heald (Oxford: Oxford University Press, 2006), 26.

3. Christopher Hood, "Transparency in Historical Perspective," in *Transparency: The Key to Better Governance?* ed. Christopher Hood and David Heald (Oxford: Oxford University Press, 2006), 9.

4. Transparency International, the National Democratic Institute, and Openthegovernment.org are examples of organizations promoting more transparency in government.

5. Bernard I. Finel and Kristin M. Lord, "The Surprising Logic of Transparency," *International Studies Quarterly* 43 (1999): 315–39, 315.

6. See notes 1–3.

7. Steven Thomma and Kevin G. Hall McClatchy, "President Rolls Out Financial Regulation Proposal," *The Spokesman-Review* (June 18, 2009).

8. Gene Healy, "Obama's Statist Ambitions," *DC Examiner* (June 30, 2009) Also: Mark A. Calabria, "Cato Scholar Comments on the Obama Administration's Financial Regulation Reforms," (June 17, 2009), http://www.cato.org/pressroom.php?display=ncomments&id=242.

9. L. Gordon Crovitz, "Transparency is More Powerful than Regulation," *The Wall Street Journal* (March 30, 2009), http://online.wsj.com/news/articles/SB123837223623167841.

10. Richard H. Thaler and Cass R. Sunstein, "Disclosure is the Best Kind of Credit Regulation," *The Wall Street Journal* (August 13, 2008), http://online.wsj.com/news/articles/SB121858695060335079.

11. L. Gordon Crovitz, "Transparency is more powerful than regulation," *Wall Street Journal*, March 30, 2009.

12. Daniel Roth, "Road Map for Financial Recovery: Radical Transparency Now!" *Wired Magazine* 17 (February 23, 2009), http://www.wired.com/techbiz/it/magazine/17-03/wp_reboot?currentPage=all.

13. I use the term *guidance* rather than *control* because it captures the observation that as a rule regulations merely point to preferred choices and are rarely fully coercive in their adaptation. For more discussion see Amitai Etzioni, *The Active Society* (New York: Free Press, 1968).

14. Dennis Wrong, *The Problem of Order: What Unites and Divides Society* (Cambridge, MA: Harvard University Press, 1995).

15. Patrick Birkinshaw, "Transparency as a Human Right," in *Transparency: The Key to Better Governance?* ed. Christopher Hood and David Heald (Oxford: Oxford University Press, 2006), 50.
Also: Mark Landler, "Experts Say Full Disclosure May Not Always be Best Tactic in Diplomacy," *The New York Times* (June 17, 2009), http://www.nytimes.com/2009/06/07/world/middleeast/07diplo.html?_r=0.
Also: Kristin M. Lord, *The Perils and Promise of Global Transparency* (Albany: State University of New York Press, 2006).
Also: Warren Bennis, "The New Transparency," in *Transparency* (San Francisco: Jossey-Bass, 2008), 11.
For further discussion see also: Albert Breton, Gianluigi Galeotti, Pierre Salmon, and Ronald Wintrobe, *The Economics of Transparency in Politics* (Burlington, VT: Ashgate, 2007), 1.

16. M. Joseph Sirgy and Chenting Su, "The Ethics of Consumer Sovereignty in an Age of High Tech," *Journal of Business Ethics* 28 (2002): 1–14, 2.

17. Ibid., 1.

18. Susanna Kim Ripken, "The Dangers and Drawbacks of the Disclosure Antidote: Toward a More Substantive Approach to Securities Regulation," *Baylor Law Review* 58 (2006): 139–204, 195. See also: Jerry Brito and Jerry Ellig, "An Accountability Agenda," *Regulation* 31 (2008): 4–7, 5.

19. See note 18, 154.

20. Tara Vishwanath and Daniel Kaufmann, "Toward Transparency: New Approaches and their Application to Financial Markets," *The World Bank Research Observer* 16 (2001): 41–57, 41.

21. Onora O'Neill, "Transparency and the Ethics of Communication," in *Transparency: The Key to Better Governance?* ed. Christopher Hood and David Heald (Oxford: Oxford University Press, 2006), 13.

22. Jeremy Bentham, "Farming Defended," *Writings on the Poor Laws*, vol. 1, ed. Michael Quinn (Oxford: Oxford University Press, 2001), 277.

23. *McConnell v. Federal Election Commission* (02-1674), 540 US 93 (2003).

24. Ron Wyden, "Transparency: A Prescription Against Malpractice," *Public Health Reports* 110 (1995), 380–1. Also: Clay Christiensen, "What Obama's Health Care Team can Learn From Massachusetts," *Harvard Business Review* (January 22, 2009), http://blogs. hbr.org/2009/01/what-obamas-health-care-team-c/.

25. Michael B. Rothberg, Elizabeth Morsi, Evan M. Benjamin, Penelope S. Pekow and Peter K. Lindenauer, "Choosing the Best Hospital: The Limitations of Public Quality Reporting," *Health Affairs* 27 (2008), 1680–7.

26. Jay Mathews, "FAQ: Best High Schools," *Newsweek* (May 17, 2008), http:// www.newsweek. com/id/137415/page/1. Also: Andrew J. Rotherman, "In Politics of School Reform, Transparency Doesn't Equal Accountability," US *News and World Report* (May 14, 2009), http://www.usnews.com/ articles/opinion/2009/05/14/in-politics-of-school-reform-transparency-doesnt-equal-accountability.html.

27. Richard H. Thaler and Cass R. Sunstein, *Nudge* (New Haven, CT: Yale University Press, 2008).

28. Jason Zweig, "About Time: Regulation Based on Human Nature," *The Wall Street Journal*, (June 20–21, 2009), http://online.wsj.com/news/articles/ SB124545477468032915.

29. For examples of limited transparency theory, see: "Disclosure as a Legislative Device," *Harvard Law Review* 76, no. 6 (1963): 1273–93, 1277–8. Also: Jon Faust and Lars E. O. Svensson, "Transparency and Credibility: Monetary Policy with Unobservable Goals," *International Economic Review* 42 (2001): 369–97. Also: Andrea Prat, "The Wrong Kind of Transparency," *American Economic Review* 95 (2005): 862–77, 869. Also: Robert Bloomfield and Mareen O'Hara, "Market Transparency: Who Wins and Who Loses?" *Review of Financial Studies* 12 (1999): 5–35.

30. Martin N. Marshall, Paul G. Shekelle, Sheila Leatherman, and Robert H. Brook, "The Public Release of Performance Data," *Journal of the American Medical Association* 283 (2000): 1866–74, 1866.

31. Warren Bennis, "The New Transparency," in *Transparency* (San Francisco: Jossey-Bass, 2008), 108–9.

32. For example: Scott B. Keller, Mike Landry, Jeanne Olson, Anne M. Velliquette, Scot Burton and J. Craig Andrews, "The Effects of Nutrition Package Claims, Nutrition Facts Panels, and Motivation to Process Nutrition Information on Consumer Product Evaluations," *Journal of Public Policy & Marketing* 16 (1997): 256–69.
    Also: Scot Burton, Abhijit Biswas and Richard Netemeyer, "Effects of Alternative Nutrition Label Formats and Nutrition Reference Information on Consumer Perceptions, Comprehension, and Product Evaluations," *Journal of Public Policy & Marketing* 13 (1994): 36–47.
    Also: John C. Kozup, Elizabeth H. Creyer and Scot Burton, "Making Healthful Food Choices: The Influence of Health Claims and Nutrition Information on Consumers' Evaluations of Packaged Food Products and Restaurant Menu Items," *Journal of Marketing* 67 (2003): 19–34.

33. Mario F. Teisl and Alan S. Levy, "Does Nutrition Labeling Lead to Healthier Eating," *Journal of Food Distribution Research* 28 (1997): 19–26.

34. Michael B. Mazis, Louis A. Morris, and John L. Swasy, "Evaluation of the Alcohol Warning Label: Initial Survey Results," *Journal of Public Policy and Marketing* 10 (1991): 229–41, 239–40.

35. Fred W. Morgan and Jeffery J. Stoltman, "Television Advertising Disclosures: An Empirical Assessment," *Journal of Business and Psychology* 16 (2002): 515–35, 535.

36. Jeffrey Kraus, "Campaign Finance reform Reconsidered: New York's Public Finance Program After Fifteen Years," *The Forum* 3 (2006), 20 (article 6).
    See also: Nathaniel Persily and Kelli Lammi, "Perceptions of Corruption and Campaign Finance: When Public Opinion Determines Constitutional Law," *University of Pennsylvania Law Review* 153 (2004): 119–80, 119–20.

37. Kyoungrae Jung, "The Impact of Information Disclosure on Quality of Care in HMO Markets," presented at iHEA 2007 6th World Congress: Explorations in Health Economics, abstract available at http://ssrn.com/abstract=992234.

38. William Walker, "Some Reflections on Transparency in the Contemporary Security Environment," *Disarmament Forum* 2 (2003): 55–9, 56.

39. Communication Research Institute, "Card Statements Blind Consumers to Debt Traps," http://communication.org.au/modules/cri_news/item.php?itemid=16.

40. Sara Hansard, "Insurers, Banks Criticize Obama's Proposed Consumer Watchdog Agency," *Investment News* (June 24, 2009), http://www.investmentnews.com/article/20090624/FREE/906249973.

41. Andrea Prat, "The Wrong Kind of Transparency," *American Economic Review* 95 (2005): 862.
    See also: David Heald, "Transparency as an Instrumental Value," *Transparency: The Key to Better Governance?* ed. Christopher Hood and David Heald (Oxford: Oxford University Press, 2006), 62.
    Also: Kristin M. Lord, *The Perils and Promise of Global Transparency* (Albany: State University of New York Press, 2006), 5.
    Also: see note 26.

42. Kaveh G. Shojania and Alan J. Forster, "Hospital Mortality: When Failure is not a Good Measure," *Canadian Medical Association Journal* 179 (2008):153–7, 155.

43. Charles Duhigg, "Clean Water Laws Neglected, at a Cost," *The New York Times* (September 13, 2009), http://www.nytimes.com/2009/09/13/us/13water.html.
44. Ann Florini, *The Right to Know: Transparency in an Open World* (New York: Columbia University Press, 2007), 4.
45. Daniel Kahneman, J. Knetsch, and Richard Thaler, "Anomalies: The Endowment Effect, Loss Aversion, and Status Quo Bias," *Journal of Economic Perspectives* 5 (1991): 193–206.
    Also: J. Edward Russo and Paul J. H. Shoemaker, *Decision Traps* (New York: Simon and Schuster, 1989).
    Also: Arthur Lefford, "The Influence of Emotional Subject Matter on Logical Reasoning," *Journal of General Psychology* 34 (1946): 127–51.
    Also: Amos Tversky and Daniel Kahneman, "Judgment Under Uncertainty: Heuristics and Biases," *Science* 185 (1974): 1124–31.
    Also: Marco Cipriani and Antonio Guarino, "Herd Behavior and Contagion in Financial Markets," *The B.E. Journal of Theoretical Economics* 8 (2008).
    Also: Robert H. Frank, Thomas Gilovich, and Dennis T. Regan, "Does Studying Economics Inhibit Cooperation?" *Journal of Economic Perspectives* 7 (1993): 159–71.
46. Brigitte Madrian and Dennis Shea, "The Power of Suggestion: Inertia in 401(k) Participation and Savings Behavior," *Quarterly Journal of Economics* 116 (2002): 1149–225.
    Also: Daniel Kahneman, J. Knetsch, and Richard Thaler, "Anomalies: The Endowment Effect, Loss Aversion, and Status Quo Bias," *Journal of Economic Perspectives* 5 (1991): 193–206.
    Also: Uri Gneezy and Also Rustchini, "Incentives, Punishment, and Behavior," *Advances in Behavioral Economics*, ed. C. F. Camerer, G. Lowenstein, and M. Rabin (Princeton, NJ: Princeton University Press, 2004), 573–89.
47. Gordon Malkiel Burton, *A Random Walk Down Wall Street: Including a Life Cycle Guide to Personal Investing*, 7th edn. (New York: Norton, 1999).
48. See note 18, 186.
49. Ibid., 185.
50. Onora O'Neill, "Transparency and the Ethics of Communication," in *Transparency: The Key to Better Governance?*, ed. Christopher Hood and David Heald (Oxford: Oxford University Press, 2006), 81.
51. See note 15, 43.
    Also: Virginia A. Sharpe, "Science, Bioethics, and the Public Interest: On the Need for Transparency," *Hastings Center Report* 32 (2002): 23–6, 24.
52. See note 18, 177–178.
53. See note 39.
54. See note 18, 177–178.
55. Helen Margetts, "Transparency and Digital Government," *Transparency: The Key to Better Governance?* ed. Christopher Hood and David Heald (Oxford: Oxford University Press, 2006), 201.
    Also: Richard H. Thaler, "Mortgages Made Simpler," *The New York Times* (July 5, 2009), http://www.nytimes.com/2009/07/05/business/economy/05view.html.

56. Elizabeth F. Farrell and Martin Van Der Werf, "Playing the Rankings Game," *Chronicle of Higher Education* (May 25, 2007), http://chronicle.com/article/ Playing-the-Rankings-Game/4451.
Also: Glen Kersten, "Grading on the Curve: College Ratings and Rankings," *Points of Reference* (January 2000), http://www.sls.lib.il.us/reference/por/ features/99/collrank.html.
Also: Eric Hoover, "Liberal-Arts College Group Plans to Help Develop Alternative to Commercial Rankings," *Chronicle of Higher Education* (June 20, 2007), https://chronicle.com/article/Liberal-Arts-College- Group/123129/.

57. Wired Blogs, "Report: TrustE Sites Twice as Likely to be Bad Actors," (September 26, 2006), http://www.wired.com/threatlevel/2006/09/report_ truste_s/.

58. Kimberly Kindy and Lyndsey Layton, "Integrity of Federal 'Organic' Label is Questioned," *The Washington Post* (July 3, 2009), http://www.washing- tonpost.com/wp-dyn/content/article/2009/07/02/AR2009070203365.html.
Also: David Heald, "Transparency as an Instrumental Value," *Transparency: The Key to Better Governance?* ed. Christopher Hood and David Heald (Oxford: Oxford University Press, 2006), 70.
See note 18, 159–160.

59. George S. Day, "Assessing the Effects of Information Disclosure Requirements," *Journal of Marketing* 40 (1976): 42–52, 42.

60. See note 19.

61. William M. Sage, "Regulating Through Information," *Columbia Law Review* 99 (1999): 1701–829, 1729.

62. See note 18.

63. Ibid., 149.

10

Cutting "Entitlements"?

Newspapers and magazines do not usually regurgitate ideas that have been bandied about for decades, especially when they are replayed one more time by the same leading author. Hence, it is telling that *The New Republic* republished in mid-2011 the brief by Daniel Callahan (this time co-authored with Sherwin Nuland).[1] The authors call for a ceasefire in America's "war against death," arguing that those who surrender gracefully to death "may die earlier than [is now common], but they will die better deaths." They urge the medical profession—and ultimately, the American people—to undergo a cultural shift that they argue is necessary to prevent the otherwise inevitable financial failure of our health care system. This shift will replace a "medical culture of cure" with a "culture of care." They note that "rationing and limit-setting will be necessary" to bring about this change. Callahan and Nuland point to evidence that little progress has been made in our quest for cures for chronic diseases (like Alzheimer's) or will likely be made in our efforts to significantly extend our life expectancy. Given the marginal benefit and high cost of medical advancements, they argue that we need to invest much more of our limited funds in preventive, affordable care, rather than in strenuous efforts to wring a few more years out of life.

Focusing on care for the elderly, the authors call on us to abandon the "traditional open-ended model" (which assumes medical advances will continue unabated) in favor of more realistic priorities—namely, reducing early death and improving the quality of life for everyone. They further advocate age-based prioritization, giving the highest priority to children and "the lowest to those over 80."

Callahan sometimes comes across as though he advocates providing only palliative care to those who, as summarized by Beth Baker in her 2009 interview with Callahan, "have lived a reasonably full life of, say, 70 to 80 years," offering them "high quality long-term care, home care, rehabilitation and income support, but not extraordinary and expensive medical procedures." That is, we should ration health care for our elders, granting them mainly ameliorative care rather than vainly seeking to cure the unyielding chronic illnesses that plague them. In other texts, his argument is more hedged. However, he tends to hold that quality of life is more important than length of life, especially given that the last years of our lives are miserable, as our minds wander, and we are beleaguered by incurable diseases. Otherwise, our futile battle against death "may doom most of us . . . [to an end] . . . with our declining bodies falling apart as they always have but devilishly—and expensively—stretching out the suffering and decay." They hence determine that the cutoff point, the age at which we should put our elderly on ice, is eighty. As we shall see shortly, whether one reads Callahan's statements as stark or as more nuanced, his argument faces the same basic challenges.

Daniel Callahan is the co-founder of a premier bioethics research institution, the Hastings Center. It has played a major role in the development of bioethics in the United States, and indeed the world. (Callahan's co-author, Sherwin Nuland, was a practicing surgeon for thirty years and has authored several books on life, death, and medicine.) However, this essay (as well as previous writings by Callahan on the same subject) is neither a work of scholarship nor of policy analysis but of political advocacy. It employs emotive terms, rhetorical devices, and vague formulas to advance a cause. Thus, *The New Republic* article recommends that seniors be granted a "primary care" period, which at first blush sounds much less troubling than to argue that elder Americans will be provided only palliative care. However, on second thought, one recalls that primary care is the gate to secondary and tertiary care (such as surgeries, kidney dialysis, hip replacements, and chemotherapy). Hence, if this gate is shut, primary care becomes largely ameliorative care!

As part of their advocacy, the authors frame numbers to alarm us. For instance, they state that the cost of Alzheimer's is expected to reach $189 billion in 2015 and will rise to $1 trillion in 2050. This assumes no improvement in treatments, even of the kind L-Dopa provided for Parkinson's and antiviral medications for HIV (two illnesses that were not cured, but for which the lives of those affected were made much better, longer, and more productive), let alone a partial cure (which have been found for several cancers). It disregards the fact that by 2050 the economy is going to be much larger as well. A nonpropagandist way to deal with such figures is to present them as a percentage of GDP and not as absolute numbers.

In the same vein, the authors keep setting up straw men and then slaying them. Thus, they argue that Americans seek to conquer disease and live forever, citing one source who declares, "We do not appear to be moving to a world where we die without experiencing disease, functioning loss, and disability." No evidence is presented that this is what Americans expect and even if such evidence does exist, such daydreams do not provide a moral foundation for ruling whether we should stop seeking to extend life and curb the ravages of disease.

Callahan and Nuland's exhibit number one is infectious disease. They argue that "forty years ago, it was commonly assumed that infectious disease had all but been conquered . . ." This is false, Callahan and Nuland say, pointing out "the advent . . . of HIV as well as a dangerous increase in antibiotic-resistant microbes." Ergo, we should note that "infectious disease will never be eliminated but only, at best, become less prevalent." "Only less prevalent" is dismissed as if this is an unworthy goal.

The authors obviously deal with the United States because a mountain of good has recently been achieved overseas in exactly this department. In the U.S., the main reason relatively little has been achieved in fighting infectious disease—is because many of them were largely licked in an earlier generation! Spurning efforts to eliminate diseases simply because new ones creep up is like resigning yourself to living in squalor because your home is "only going to get messy again." Oddly, the example the authors cite as a sign that we ought to surrender to the inexorable, the spread of HIV, is a research field in which great achievements were made in the last decade.

Callahan and Nuland express exasperation with "the endless issuing of promissory notes" by medical researchers that have not been paid. With regard to chronic diseases, a major counterexample can be found in the very significant improvements in the treatment of diabetes in recent years.

In short, even if it is true that the pace of progress in medical care is slowing, it is by no means nearly as unproductive as the authors maintain. And the value of the achievable should not be dismissed because it does not meet some elusive dream; it should be appreciated because of the good that it *is* delivering.

I. End of Life—Or Age-Based Rationing?

One of the major findings of the research on health care costs is that Americans use up more medical resources in the last year of their life than in any other previous years. For instance, findings from the 1992–1996 Medicare Beneficiary Survey indicated that "mean annual medical expenditures . . . for persons aged 65 and older were $37,581 during the last year of life versus $7,365 for nonterminal years." These and other such statistics seem at first blush to provide strong support for the Callahan thesis. However, at a second glance, one notes that many of these statistics apply to *all* last years of life—whether that of preemies too small to make it, a young person with advanced cancer or AIDS, or that of select senior citizens. The relevant criteria is not age but rather the likelihood that a person can be cured, or at least restored to a meaningful life, able to love and serve, and whether his or her end is near. To put it differently, Callahan makes it sound as though as soon as the body turns eighty, there is an abrupt change in our medical condition. The opposite is true: our bodies gradually change, both before and after that age, and at a different pace for different people. Much of what Callahan is talking about holds for those in the last months or maybe year of life, not for those who have simply had eighty candles on their birthday cake. And as the average lifespan has been extended by eight to nine years since 1960, many of these years for many of those older than 80 were far from miserable.

251

If ration we must, we should limit care for all those who have a terminal illness and medically determined short time to live—whatever their age. Callahan claims that "Americans" (i.e., all of us) seek immortality, are unwilling to face death, and believe in the ability to extend life forever and a day. Actually, the caring professions have developed and society has embraced a way to proceed, which is not based on age. Namely, once a person is determined, typically by a physician, to have no more than six months to live, they are referred to a hospice (whatever their age), and there they get the Callahan treatment—ameliorative rather than therapeutic care. Moreover, the fact that millions of Americans write living wills, and many ask to sign DNR orders shows that Americans can and do deal with end of life issues.

Closely related is the question of what constitutes a worthy or productive life. Callahan and Nuland draw on a vague concept of being able to "manage society." Once we go down this path, many others will draw, as they already often do, on the stream of earning.

This is a very treacherous basis on which to allocate health care resources. It does not respect assets other than money making, such as the ability to give love (for which grandparents are quite well-suited, I can attest, as someone who has passed eighty and has thirteen grandchildren) or to be creative and serve the community through volunteerism. It suggests that homemakers and those with serious handicaps are less worthy human beings than the money makers. Indeed, if earnings were the basis for rationing health care, the best and most exhaustive care would go to movie stars, heads of hedge funds, those who sell large amounts of fraudulent mortgages, and drug dealers.

We had best continue to respect all life and not allow the government to determine what makes a good life and when it is no longer a worthy one. And we best ensure that enough hospices are available—and of good quality—to those who choose to move there once they find out that their life is nearing a close, whatever their chronological age.

II. Slippery Slopes

Revisiting these ideas now ought to be subject to particularly close scrutiny, because they are republished in the context of alarm about rising deficits and mushrooming health care costs. Hence, this kind of writing is likely to be used as ammunition by those who want to reduce public support for health care in general and for the elderly in particular.

One ought to note that the fact that we are squeezed for funds can be used to justify rationing health care, and to insist that now we simply must limit those above a certain age to receiving mainly or only ameliorative rather than therapeutic care. It logically follows—like a hangover after a night of boozing—that the cutoff age should be lowered if our economic condition further deteriorates. Once we set such a limit and accept the "cultural shift" Callahan and Nuland call for, one that treats age-based rationing as morally justifiable, what is the next step. Sure, one can show that, on average, those who are, say, seventy-seven to eighty, produce less and have greater care costs than those who are younger. But then, we can likewise say that about those who are somewhere between seventy-two and seventy-seven, between sixty-five and seventy-two, and so on. And if other countries are to follow such a model, they will surely have to set a lower age. Say fifty-five for El Salvador? Forty-three for Afghanistan?

The possibility that using age-based rationing will lead to troubling outcomes is far from mere speculation. For example, reports have indicated that in Britain, people older than fifty have been discouraged from seeking kidney dialysis treatment.

Moreover, it is essential to note that the concept of quality of life is a particularly slippery one. Once we cease to respect life *per se* and cherish only life of "good quality," we truly open the door to defining which lives deserve to be saved and which do not, especially in hard economic times. One may say that we are very short of resources, and hence must resort to rationing. However, this should be considered only if there are no other places to reduce health care costs—places where cost-cutting can be much more readily justified. And as I will show shortly, there is a surprisingly long list.

III. No Assured Reallocation

Another major weakness of Callahan's thesis is that it is based either on a complete misunderstanding of the way the American polity works or an unwillingness to face what it would take to introduce a regime of the sort Callahan advocates. Callahan first off treats health care as if it were a hermetically sealed, discrete political and economic system. In this Never Never Land, if fewer funds are allotted to elderly care, *ipso facto*, more will be available for child care and for younger people in general. This assumption ignores that elder care is largely publically financed, while younger care is not. Hence, if tomorrow the government collects, say, $100 billion less in tax revenue from Americans to pay for Medicare, there is no reason to assume that these dollars will be employed for preventive care, youth care, or for any other form of health care. Even if the funds remain within the public sector, it does not follow that reducing the Medicare outlays will not flow to some other expenditure, from ethanol subsidies to paying for the bombing of Libya to food stamps or raises for civil servants or God knows what else.

Some of these are worthy goals, but one best ask not only if they outrank helping the elderly to make even relatively small but high cost health gains, but also what mechanism could be developed to ensure that whatever is cut from senior care will end up where it is supposed to land.

One of Callahan's great merits is that as a fellow communitarian, he recognizes that we have obligations to the common good and not just rights and entitlements. (The issue was raised recently when neither Presidents Bush nor

Obama called on Americans to make any sacrifices in the wake of 9/11 and the wars in which the United States is engaged.) However, before I would call on anyone to give up any beneficial medical interventions they seek, I would ask them—if save we must—to smoke less, drive less, and give up on status goods, among many others. In contrast to those who see our seniors as privileged and our youth as deprived, I see most seniors as having made lifelong contributions to society, while the youths' turn has yet to come. Even if the cuts have to be made within the health care system, there are other ways to proceed.

IV. Other Ways

To argue against age-based rationing and the naïveté of reallocation is not to suggest that the cost of Medicare—or, more precisely, of health care—should not be reduced. However, there are other ways which a normative analysis suggests should be considered long before one turns to reductions in therapeutic care for seniors and, more generally, to cutbacks in medical research and investment in new technologies.

If we must make cuts in Medicare, we ought first to make far more strides in reducing harmful activities. There are an estimated 44,000 to 98,000 preventable deaths due to medical error each year, according to the 1999 US Institute of Medicine report, entitled "To Err is Human." While the report has been highly regarded and frequently cited for the past decade, more recently, 99,000 patients were found to "succumb to hospital-acquired infections" annually, according to a 2009 Centers for Disease Control and Prevention study. Experts hold that nearly all of those deaths are preventable.

Study after study shows that even relatively small changes can reap major benefits. These include measures such as getting health personnel to cut their fingernails shorter, wash their hands even more often, use typed rather than handwritten drug prescriptions, use electrical shavers rather than razors (in preparations for surgery), getting doctors to pay more mind to comments by nurses, and so on. The results are detailed in *Safe Patients, Smart Hospitals*, a book co-authored by Peter Pronovost and Eric Vohr, which advocates integrating strictly followed checklists into health care procedures, as well as abandoning the hierarchical structure of hospitals that often leaves nurses hesitant to challenge doctors when they make mistakes. The book then shows the great reductions in medical errors that follow the introduction of checklists. Atul Gawande, a Harvard Medical School surgical professor, similarly argues for systematic checklists, offering numerous examples of greater success due to checklists, not only in the medical field, but also in fields like aviation, a comparison that John Nance makes extensive use of in his book *Why Hospitals Should Fly*.

Next, we should cut reimbursements for those interventions for which there are no demonstrated benefits. Twenty percent of all medical expenditures were estimated to pay for medical care that is "inappropriate and unnecessary" in a 1990 study by the RAND Corporation. Consistent with these findings, Henry Aaron, a leading expert at Brookings, noted that both 2008 presidential candidates "put forward proposals for curtailing waste in the US health care system . . . based on estimates that various medical procedures are used inappropriately as much as one third of the time in the United States." Among them are testing patients who have advanced, life-threatening illnesses for other diseases for which preventable treatment could not be provided in the time they have left on this earth, and screening for colon cancer, which, according to many experts, is inadvisable for the elderly, as it can result in complications that outweigh the potential benefits. Again, it is unlikely that waste will be completely eradicated, but surely significant strides could be made. And this particular opportunity for cost reduction and improved efficiency has been recognized by Obama's Affordable Care Act, which establishes an advisory board specifically tasked with identifying and recommending policies to eliminate such waste in the Medicare program.

Equally important is to reduce administrative costs. The United States spends at least twice as much on administrative costs for health care as many other countries. For instance, a 2003 comparative study found that US administrative costs amounted to $30 out of every $100 spent on health care, compared to $17 in Canada. There are many reasons we cannot match Canada's ways, but if we cut only part of the difference in administrative overhead, we would save tens of billions each year. One way this may be achieved is by using capitation, rather than reviewing every intervention. Another option is to follow the UK Tory government's example and pursue what is called the Big Society program. It allots a pool of funds to the physicians serving a given area and lets them make the allocation decisions within nationally established guidelines.

Some experts snicker when people argue that one can achieve major savings by reducing fraud and abuse. *60 Minutes*, though, documented that the Medicare fraud industry in South Florida is now larger than the cocaine industry, due to the relative ease of swindling Medicare. There is less risk of exposure and less risk of punishment if caught. Crooks buy patient lists and bill the government for expensive items, ranging from scooters to prostheses, to the tune of some $60 billion a year. Because Medicare is required by law to pay all bills within thirty days and has a small accounting staff, it often cannot vet claims before the checks must be issued. By the time Medicare authorities find out a storefront's bills are phony, the crooks have closed their operation and opened one next door under a different name. It does not seem too difficult to imagine that Medicare could be given more time and more resources to reduce such fraud. In short, one can readily demonstrate that before one denies beneficial health care to people of any age, even if the benefits are limited, there are other major areas to reduce outlays and put our health system on sound economic footing. It is morally repugnant to deny people beneficial health care in order to save money, before one engages in much stronger efforts to reduce harmful and useless interventions and to curb fraud, abuse, and costly paper work. All this can be accomplished without giving up the "war against death"—a war that we know cannot be won, but that nevertheless should be fought, if only to wrestle out of Death's arms as many worthy years for as many people as possible.

Moreover, I have no trouble envisioning an America in which, thanks to improved health care, including changes in lifestyles and in the environment, the average American lives to be one hundred years old and works until he is eighty. The average work week for all Americans would be reduced to, say, 25 hours, so that there would be work for all. Average incomes would be lower, and hence people would buy fewer goods but spend more time in social and transcendental activities that are low in cost, such as hanging out with family, reading, taking walks, meditating, observing sunsets, and praying.

V. The Foundations of Moral Judgments

After I published a brief along the preceding lines about ways to reduce health care costs and thus Medicare outlays, Callahan posted a comment in the Hastings *Bioethics Forum* blog under the title "The Political Use of Moral Language." He raised issues whose importance extends well beyond the future of health care and the ethical ways to reign in its costs, as important as these are in their own right. Callahan wrote:

"Amitai Etzioni, a prominent social scientist and leader of a communitarian movement, published an article in February arguing that it would be 'immoral' to cut Medicare or Social Security benefits unless we first eliminate a range of pathologies in our health care system. 'If we must make cuts,' he wrote, 'we ought first to cut those budget items that in effect pay for harmful activities and then those without discernible social benefits.' He had in mind such long-time villains as excessive administrative overhead, waste and fraud, direct-to-consumer advertising, unnecessary treatments, and medical error.

"He was right to identify those failings, all of which reflect a bad health care system. And as a fellow communitarian, I welcome his support for a solid and equitable social safety net. But are those on the other side of the aisle 'immoral'? At what point does a political issue or position pass from simply being unfair, wrong-headed, or dangerous in some way or other, to being immoral?

"A dictionary definition of immoral is 'not following accepted standards of morality' (Oxford) or 'not conforming to a high moral standard' (Merriam-Webster). The obvious problem in this case is that those most prone to slice away at the social safety net are in a party whose views on what we owe our neighbor represent an enduring part of American history and culture, going back to Thomas Jefferson and noted later by de Tocqueville, that of extreme individualism, market freedom, and hostility to government. I would estimate that at least 50 percent of Americans are in that camp. In the run-up to the passage of the Affordable Care Act, one memorable quote by a constituent of a Republican congressman, was, 'I don't know why I should be expected to pay for someone else's sickness.' I don't know whether Jefferson would have gone as far as that, but I do know that man reflected a deep strain in American life. We would do well to recall that the passage of the Medicare, Medicaid, and Social Security bills were accomplished in the face of the hostility of those in the Jeffersonian tradition, just as the ACA is being challenged by their latter-day loyalists.

"We do not have 'accepted standards of morality' on social safety nets, though even the most conservative Republicans, even if begrudgingly, will accept some – and most are wise enough, save for Paul Ryan, to stay away from schemes that would privatize those programs.

"The trouble with the word immoral is that its connotation is not just that a moral rule has been broken but that it reflects the ideas or actions of a corrupt person, someone of bad character. I thus put the word 'immoral' in the same category as the term 'un-American,' a Tea Party favorite, suggesting a violation of American values and, even worse, someone who does not love our country. And as we well know, Friedrich von Hayek tutored many in their hostility to government to believe that 'socialist' government programs take us straight down the road to serfdom.

"Ad hominem arguments combined with slippery slope predictions have become the accepted rhetorical style of conservative opponents of communitarian, social justice convictions. Nothing is added, and much that is harmful, is introduced into the public debate by the word immoral. My own observation is that neither liberals (aka progressives) nor conservatives have a monopoly on morality. That our communitarian crowd favors a strong social safety net is a tribute to our wise (even if politically controversial) judgment about the common good, not a sign of superior morality."

My response follows:

Daniel Callahan's commentary about my article in *Dissent* shows that even a bioethics giant, and a fellow communitarian, can make a mistake, and not a trivial one. Sadly he is not alone in adopting a culturally relativistic definition of what is moral. (The co-editor of *Dissent*, Michael Walzer, also holds that the community is the ultimate arbiter of that which is right.) And hence, of course, when there is no consensus, there are no moral standards and we are told there is nothing on which to base our moral judgments.

As I see it, there is a limited set of universal moral truths—human rights, for instance. Life and health over death and illness in all but exceptional circumstances, for example. These truths are, as the founding fathers put it so well, self evident. (As a deontologist would put it, these are moral causes that speak to us directly.) In the subject at hand, I need no community to approve a standard that will inform me that if one has a choice between saving money by cutting reimbursement for beneficial procedures, say kidney dialysis, or cutting the funds that pay doctors who run two CTs on the same patient on the same day or blowing money because insurers refuse to use the same claim form—which is the moral direction to go. It may not be politically practical, but there is no question what is right. (And the fact that one may find some very limited conditions under which the suggested statement will not hold just shows that some philosophers are sharp, not that we lack foundations for moral judgments).

Callahan correctly points out that I use normative arguments for a political purpose. All political acts and decisions have a moral dimension and if we do not judge, it will not stop others from laying moral claims, just mute our side. Moreover, is this bad? I am trying to shame and lose votes for those who pass immoral laws that provide obscene profits to health insurers and exorbitant salaries for their executives while cutting funds for health care for poor children and many more such policies. I stand content to be judged accordingly.

Callahan truly crosses a line when he jumps from my position that some people make immoral choices, to argue that they must be bad people (his non sequitur), and therefore accuses me of ad hominem attacks. As I see it there are some bad people, those who have no moral conscience, the psychopaths. Most people struggle between their debased and nobler sides, and I am out to give whatever support I can to their better angels.

Note

1. Daniel Callahan and Sherwin B. Nuland, "The Quagmire:How American medicine is destroying itself." *The New Republic* (May 19, 2011). http://www.newrepublic.com/article/economy/magazine/88631/american-medicine-health-care-costs.

IV

The Politics of Security

11

Who Authorized Preparations for a War with China?

The United States is preparing for a war with China, a momentous decision that so far has failed to receive a thorough review from elected officials, namely the White House and Congress. This important change in the United States' posture toward China has largely been driven by the Pentagon. There have been other occasions in which the Pentagon has framed key strategic decisions so as to elicit the preferred response from the commander in chief and elected representatives. A recent case in point was when the Pentagon led President Obama to order a high level surge in Afghanistan in 2009, against the advice of the Vice President and the US ambassador to Afghanistan. The decision at hand stands out even more prominently because (a) the change in military posture may well lead to an arms race with China, which could culminate in a nuclear war, and (b) the economic condition of the US requires a reduction in military spending, not a new arms race. The start of a new term, and with it the appointment of new secretaries of state and defense, provide an opportunity to review the United States' China strategy and the military's role in it. This review is particularly important before the new preparations for war move from an operational concept to a militarization program that includes ordering high-cost weapon systems and force restructuring. History shows that once these thresholds are crossed, it is exceedingly difficult to change course.

In the following pages I first outline recent developments in the Pentagon's approach to dealing with the rise China. I then focus on the deliberations of the highest civilian authorities. These two sides seemed to operate in parallel universes, at least until November 2011 when the pivot to Asia was announced by the White House—though we shall see their paths hardly converged even after that date. I conclude with an outline of what the much-needed civilian review ought to cover.

I write about the "Pentagon" and the "highest civilian authorities" (or our political representatives) rather than contrast the view of the military and that of the civilian authorities, because the Pentagon includes civilians, who actively participated in developing the plans under discussion. It is of course fully legitimate for the Pentagon to identify and prepare for new threats.

The question that this article raises is whether the next level of government—which reviews such threats while taking into account the input of the intelligence community (which includes nonmilitary agencies such as the CIA and NSA) and other agencies (especially the State Department)—has adequately fulfilled its duties. Have the White House and Congress properly reviewed the Pentagon's approach—and found its threat assessment of China convincing and approved the chosen response? And if not, what are the United States' overarching short and long term political strategies for dealing with an economically and militarily rising China?

I. In the Pentagon

Since the Second World War the United States has maintained a power-projection military, built upon forward deployed forces with uninhibited access to the global commons—air, sea, and space. For over six decades the maritime security of the Western Pacific has been underwritten by the unrivaled naval and air power of the United States. However, starting in the early 1990s, Chinese investments in sophisticated but low-cost weapons—including anti-ship missiles, short and medium range ballistic missile, cruise missiles, stealth submarines, and cyber and space arms—began to challenge the military superiority of the United States, especially in China's littoral waters. These "asymmetric arms" threaten two key elements of the United States' force projection strategy: its fixed bases (such as those in Japan and Guam) and aircraft carriers. Often referred to as anti-access/anti-denial capabilities (A2/AD), these Chinese arms are viewed by some in the Pentagon as raising the human and economic cost of the United States' military role in the region to prohibitive levels. To demonstrate what this new environment means for regional security, military officials point out that in 1996, when China conducted a series of missile tests and military exercises in the Strait of Taiwan, the United States responded by sending two aircraft carriers to the South China Sea, a credible display of force that reminded all parties of its commitment to maintaining the status quo in the region.[1] However, these analysts point out, if in the near future China decided to forcefully integrate Taiwan, the same US aircraft carriers that are said to have once deterred Chinese aggression could be denied access to the sea by PLA anti-ship missiles. Thus, the U.S.'s interests in the region, to the extent that they are undergirded by superior military force, are increasingly vulnerable.

Two influential American military strategists, Andrew Marshall and his protégé Andrew Krepinevich, have been raising the alarm about China's new capabilities and aggressive designs since the early 1990s. Building on hundreds of war games played out over the past two decades, they gained a renewed hearing for their concerns following *Pacific Vision*, a war game conducted by the US Air Force in October 2008. The game was financed in part by Marshall's Office of Net Assessment, a division of the Pentagon focused on identifying emerging security threats to the United States. The *Air Force Magazine* reported at the time that the simulation convinced others in the Pentagon of the need to face up to China, and "when it was over, the PACAF [Pacific Air Force Command] staff set about drawing up its conclusions and fashioning a framework for AirSea Battle"—a plan to develop the new weapons and operation capabilities needed to overcome the challenges posed by A2/AD.[2]

With Marshall's guidance, Secretary of Defense Robert Gates instructed the Chiefs of Staff to begin work on the AirSea Battle (ASB) project and, in September of 2009, Air Force Chief of Staff Gen. Norton Schwartz and Chief of Naval Operations Adm. Gary Roughead signed a classified Memorandum of Agreement endorsing the plan.[3] ASB received Gates's official imprimatur in the 2010 Quadrennial Defense Review which directed the US military to "develop a joint air-sea battle concept . . . [to] address how air and naval forces will integrate capabilities across all operational domains—air, sea, land, space, and cyberspace—to counter growing challenges to US freedom of action."[4] In late 2011 Gates's successor, Secretary of Defense Leon Panetta, also signed off on the ASB and formed the new Multi-Service Office to Advance AirSea Battle. Thus, ASB was conceived, born, and began to grow.

AirSea Battle calls for "interoperable air and naval forces that can execute networked, integrated attacks-in-depth to disrupt, destroy, and defeat enemy anti-access area denial capabilities."[5] The hypothetical battle begins with a campaign to reestablish power projection capabilities by launching a "blinding attack" against Chinese anti-access facilities, including land and sea-based missile launchers, surveillance and communication platforms, satellite and antisatellite weapons, and command and control nodes. US forces could then enter contested zones and conclude the conflict by bringing to bear the full force of their material military advantage. One defense think tank report, "AirSea Battle: A Point-of-Departure Operational Concept," acknowledges that "the scope and intensity of US standoff and penetrating strikes against targets in mainland China clearly has escalation implications," because China is likely to respond to what is effectively a major direct attack on its mainland with all the military means at its disposal—including its stockpile of nuclear arms.[6] The authors make the critical assumption that mutual nuclear deterrence would hold in a war with China. However, after suggesting that the United States might benefit from an early attack on Chinese space systems, they concede in a footnote that "attacks on each side's space early warning systems would have an immediate effect on strategic nuclear and escalation issues . . . However," they continue, "this issue lies beyond the scope of this paper and is therefore not addressed here."[7] Addressing the risk of nuclear war might be beyond the scope of that paper, but not of a proper review of ASB. Although the Chinese nuclear force is much smaller than that of the United States, China nonetheless has the capacity to destroy American cities. According to leading Australian military strategist Hugh White, "we can be sure that China will place a very high priority indeed on maintaining its capacity to strike the United States, and that it will succeed in this."[8] Given this, the United States' development of ASB will likely accelerate China's expansion of both its conventional forces and its nuclear, cyber, and space weapons programs. Joshua Rovner of the US Naval War College notes that deep inland strikes could be mistakenly perceived by the Chinese as preemptive attempts to take out its nuclear weapons, thus cornering them into "a terrible use-it-or-lose-it dilemma." That is, ASB is prone to lead to nuclear war.[9]

As current US technologies and force structures are unable to carry out this hypothetical campaign, its architects urge investments in penetrating, long-endurance ISR (intelligence, surveillance, and reconnaissance) and strike capabilities, aerial tankers, and forward base hardening. Strategists have also encouraged the Navy to "develop and field long-range/endurance UUVs [Unmanned Undersea Vehicles] for multiple missions germane to intelligence preparation of the undersea battle space" and recommended that the Air Force and Navy stockpile precision-guided munitions (PGM) "in sufficient quantities to execute an ASB campaign."[10] ASB also involves a considerable shift of budgetary priorities from the Army and Marines to the Navy and Air Force. A review of the FY 2013 Defense budget finds that "the new budget also shifts the balance of funding among the Services according to the new strategic guidance, which calls for a greater reliance on air and sea power as part of the pivot to the Asia-Pacific region."[11] While all branches face spending cuts, the Army will experience the steepest reduction (8.9 percent); the budgets of the Air Force and Navy/Marines shrink by 5.8 and 4.3 percent respectively. Although this force restructuring initially led to strong protests from the Army, in late 2012 it began carving out its role place in the ASB plan.[12]

AirSea Battle is already beginning to shape acquisition decisions. General Schwartz writes that, "The first steps to implement Air-Sea Battle are already underway here at the Pentagon. In our FY 2012 and FY 2013 budgets we increased investment in the systems and capabilities we need to defeat access threats."[13] Admiral Greenert points to the investments in anti-submarine warfare, electronic warfare, air and missile defense, and information sharing, that were included in the president's 2012 budget as one aspect of ASB's implementation and notes that the 2013 budget "sustains these investments and really provides more resilient C4ISR [Command, Control, Communications, Computers, Intelligence, Surveillance and Reconnaissance] investments."[14] The *New York Times* reported that the new Littoral Combat Ship (LCS), which is able to deftly navigate shallow coastal seas, is "central to President Obama's strategy of projecting American power in the Pacific."[15] So far, two of the planned fifty-five LCSs have been completed, and the first will be deployed in Singapore in 2013. A press report in August 2012 stated that "the Air-Sea Battle concept has prompted Navy officials to make significant shifts in the service's FY2014-FY2018 budget plan, including new investments in ASW, electronic attack and electronic warfare, cyber warfare, the F-35 Joint Strike Fighter (JSF), the P-8A maritime patrol aircraft, and the Broad Area Maritime Surveillance (BAMS) UAV [Unmanned Aerial Vehicle]."[16] Some point out that many of these weapons would have been ordered even if there was no ASB, and that some purchases merely constitute technology updates. However, it also true that a smaller defense budget means making choices about the allocation of resources, and evidence suggests that the Pentagon has made the hardware of ASB a high priority.

In addition, a 2012 report by the Congressional Research Service on the implications of Chinese naval modernization disclosed that there has been a "redeployment of various advanced US nuclear submarines and Aegis SM-3 based missile defense vessels to the Pacific in close cruising distance to China and North Korea. Other vessels in the Pacific were recently moved to Guam and Hawaii to presumably cut transit time to areas of possible conflict. All of this would be helpful if AirSea concepts are employed."[17]

Some argue that ASB is merely a limited "operational concept." However, insofar as it is influencing the Pentagon's "hardware" purchases and is transforming force structure, ASB is moving beyond its conceptual stage. Moreover, even if it is merely a highly influential concept, it still merits high-level review.

One should note that several officials also maintain that ASB is not aimed at China. At a background briefing on ASB one Pentagon official stated, "It is not about a specific actor. It is not about a specific actor or regime."[18] General Norton Schwartz has said that questions about China's place in the concept are "unhelpful."[19] However, the consensus of most observers is that "Air-Sea Battle is billed as the answer to growing anti-access/area-denial capabilities generically, but as everyone knows, specifically China," as former Marine Corps officer J. Noel Williams put it.[20] And according to a senior Navy official overseeing the forces modernization efforts, "Air-Sea Battle is all about convincing the Chinese that we will win this competition."[21]

Indeed, as far as one can determine, the Pentagon decided to embrace the ASB concept over alternative ways for sustaining US military power in the region that are far less likely to lead to escalation. One such is the "war-at-sea" option, a strategy proposed by Jeffrey Kline and Wayne Hughes of the Naval Postgraduate School, which would deny China use of the sea within the first island chain (which stretches from Japan to Taiwan and through the Philippines) by means of a distant blockade, the use of submarine and flotilla attacks at sea, and the positioning of expeditionary forces to hold at-risk islands in the South China Sea. By foregoing a mainland attack, the authors argue that the war-at-sea strategy gives "opportunities for negotiation in which both sides can back away from escalation to a long-lasting, economically-disastrous war involving full mobilization and commitment to some kind of decisive victory."[22] In the same vein, the "Offshore Control Strategy" put forward by

National Defense University's T.X. Hammes, "seeks to use a war of economic attrition to bring about a stalemate and cessation of conflict" by establishing a distant blockade and a maritime exclusion zone within the first island chain, while dominating the surrounding waters "to ensure the continued flow of trade to our allies while tightening the blockade against China."[23] This would not bring a decisive victory, but would allow the US to achieve its objectives of protecting its allies and maintaining free access to sea lanes, while giving China space to back down.

Several defense analysts in the United States and abroad, not least in China, see ASB as being highly provocative. Former Vice Chairman of the Joint Chiefs of Staff General James Cartwright stated in 2012 that, "AirSea Battle is demonizing China. That's not in anybody's interest."[24] An internal assessment of ASB by the Marine Corps commandant cautions that "an Air-Sea Battle-focused Navy and Air Force would be preposterously expensive to build in peace time" and if used in a war against China would cause "incalculable human and economic destruction."[25]

Several critics point out that ASB is inherently escalatory and is likely to accelerate the arms race in the Asia-Pacific. China must be expected to respond to the implementation of ASB by accelerating its own military buildup. Chinese Colonel Gauyue Fan stated that, "If the US military develops AirSea Battle to deal with the [People's Liberation Army], the PLA will be forced to develop anti-AirSea Battle."[26] Moreover, Raoul Heinrichs, from the Australian National University, points out that "by creating the need for a continued visible presence and more intrusive forms of surveillance in the Western Pacific, AirSea Battle will greatly increase the range of circumstances for maritime brinkmanship and dangerous naval incidents."[27]

Other critics argue that ASB operates in a strategic vacuum. Hammes maintains that "ASB is the antithesis of strategy. It focuses on the tactical employment of weapons systems with no theory of victory or concept linking the Air-Sea approach to favorable conflict resolution."[28] Dan Blumenthal of the American Enterprise Institutes agrees that, "ASB is an operational concept detached from a strategy . . . As a result, the US is both making commitments to Asia that it may not be able to afford and articulating a high-risk operational doctrine that does not answer basic strategic questions."[29]

As I see it, the implied strategy is clear: ASB planners aim to make the United States so clearly powerful that not only would China lose if it engaged militarily, but it would not consider engaging because the United States would be sure to win. Krepinevich holds that ASB achieves both deterrence through denial, "designed to convince a would-be aggressor that he cannot achieve his objective, so there is no point in trying," as well as deterrence through punishing, "designed to persuade him that even though he may be able to achieve his objective, he will suffer so much as a result that his anticipated costs will outweigh his gains."[30] The imagined result of ASB is the ability to end a conflict with China in much the same way the United States ended WWII: The US military defeats China and dictates the surrender terms.

This military strategy, which involves threatening to defeat China as a military power, is a far cry from containment or any other strategies that were seriously considered in the context of confronting the USSR after it acquired nuclear arms. The essence of the Cold War was *mutual* deterrence, and the conflict was structured around red lines that not only the Warsaw Pact forces were not to cross (e.g., by moving into the NATO controlled areas) but that the NATO forces were also committed to respect by not crossing into the Soviet realm that included Eastern Europe and East Germany. (This is the reason the United States did not help the freedom fighters who rose against the Communist regimes in Hungary and Czechoslovakia.) First strike (nuclear) strategies were foresworn and steps were taken to avoid a war precipitated by miscommunications, accidents, or miscalculations. In contrast, ASB requires that the US be able to take the war to the mainland with the goal of defeating China, which quite likely would require striking first. Such a strategy is nothing short of a hegemonic intervention.

When Andrew Krepinevich suggested that ASB is simply seeking to maintain stability in the Asia-Pacific, he was asked if this "stability" really meant continued US hegemony in the area. He chuckled and responded, "well, the nations in the area have a choice: either we are number one or China [is]—and they prefer us."[31] Actually, most of the nations in area prefer playing the big powers against each other rather than joining a particular camp. They greatly benefit from trade and investment from China and, at the same time, most are quite keen to receive security backing from the United States. And they realize that in a case of conflict between the United States and China, they stand to lose a great deal. (A common saying in the area: "When the elephant and tiger rumble, the grass gets trampled."). Most important, one must ask if there are other strategies that do not operate on the assumption that our dealings with China represent a zero-sum game. For instance, one should consider if there are strategies in which the superpower pursues its interests by accommodating a rising power—especially when this power is mainly a regional one—by allowing it an increased sphere of influence. This is the way Britain, once a superpower that relied greatly on naval power, accommodated to a rising upstart—the United States.

II. The White House and Congress

To judge by several published reports which will be discussed in greater detail below, including those by government "insiders," there is no indication—not even a passing hint—that the White House has ever considered earnestly preparing the nation for a war with China. Nor is there any evidence that the White House has compared such a strategy to alternatives, and—having concluded that the hegemonic intervention implied by ASB is the course the

United States should follow—then instructed the Pentagon to prepare for such a military showdown. Indeed, as far as one can determine at this stage, the White House and State Department have engaged in largely *ad hoc* debates over particular tactical maneuvers, never giving much attention to the development of a clear underlying China strategy. True, some individuals in the State Department and White House pursued engagement and cooperation, and others advocated "tougher" moves that seem to reflect a vague preference for containment. However, neither approach was embraced as an overarching strategy. The November 2011 presidential announcement that the United States was beginning a "pivot" from the Near to the Far East may at first seem to suggest that a coherent stance on China eventually coalesced within the administration. We will see shortly that this is not the case.

One major source of information regarding the development of China policy in the Obama White House is an insider's report fully dedicated to the subject at hand, *Obama and China's Rise* by Jeffrey A. Bader. Having served as senior director for East Asian affairs on the National Security Council from January 2009 to April 2011, Bader reports in great detail on how the Obama administration approached China policy. When Obama was still a Senator campaigning in the 2008 election—the same time the Pentagon was launching the ASB mission—his philosophy was to engage the nations of the world rather than confront them, to rely on diplomacy rather than on aggressive (let alone coercive) measures, and to draw on multilateralism rather than on unilateral moves. Following his election, the president's key staffers report that, with regard to China, containment was "not an option," nor was the *realpolitik* of power balancing embraced. Instead, the administration pursued a vague three-pronged policy based on: "(1) a welcoming approach to China's emergence, influence, and legitimate expanded role; (2) a resolve that a coherent stance on China eventually coalesced to see that its rise is consistent with international norms and law; and (3) an endeavor to shape the Asia-Pacific environment to ensure that China's rise is stabilizing rather than disruptive."[32]

Once in office, the administration's main China-related policy questions involved economic concerns (especially the trade imbalance, currency manipulation, and the dependence on China for the financing of US debt), North Korea's development of nuclear arms and missiles, sanctions on Iran, Tibet and human rights, and counterterrorism. The fact that China was somewhat modernizing its very backward military is barely mentioned in the book-length report. There is no reference to ASB or to the strategy it implies as being considered, questioned, embraced, or rejected—let alone how it fits into an overarching China strategy, which the Obama administration did not formulate in the first term.

Moreover, Bader's account leaves little doubt that neither the Obama White House nor State Department ever developed a coherent China strategy. In effect, key staff members scoffed at the very idea that such overarching conceptions were of merit or possible (as opposed to reactive responses to ongoing developments). The Obama team, Bader notes, "fine-tun[ed] an approach" that avoided the extremes of, on the one hand, relying "solely on military muscle, economic blandishments, and pressure and sanctions of human rights," and on the other, pursuing "a policy of indulgence and accommodation of assertive Chinese conduct."[33] Not too hot, not too cold makes for good porridge, but is not a clear guideline for foreign policy.

A closer reading of these lines, as well as similar statements issued by the administration that were often fashioned as strategic positions, reveals them to be vague and open to rather different interpretations. They seem more like public rationales than guidelines capable of coordinating policies across the various government agencies, let alone reigning in the Pentagon. The overarching ambiguity is captured by Bader, who first reports that, "for China to directly challenge America's security interest, it would have to acquire ambitions and habits that it does not at present display. The Unites States should not behave in a way that encourages the Chinese to move in that direction." Then, just pages later, he concludes that "the United States needs to maintain its forward deployment, superior military forces and technological edge, its economic strength and engagement with the region, its alliances, and its enhanced relationships with other emerging powers. Chinese analysts are like to consider all these traits to be hostile to China."[34]

Another book describing the same period, *The Obamians: The Struggle Inside the White House to Refine American Power*, by James Mann, reveals that although President Obama sought to engage China, his administration was increasingly "irked" by various Chinese moves, from its assertive declarations about the South China Sea to the cyber-attacks assumed to originate from within its borders. In response, the Obama Administration is reported to have "stiffened" both its rhetoric and diplomatic stance toward China. For example, in response to Beijing's pronouncement that the South China Sea represented one of China's "core interests," Secretary of State Clinton told an audience at the 2010 ASEAN meeting that freedom of navigation in the seas was a "national interest" of the United States. She also delivered a speech criticizing China's abuse of Internet freedom and argued that such nations "should face consequences and international condemnation." It is reported that State Department officials, who generally sought to avoid conflict with China, "absolutely hated" the speech.[35] If such a speech caused tensions to flare up in the department, it is not hard to imagine the outcry that would have followed had the administration approved ASB—that is, if it was considered in the first place. Yet in Mann's account of the period under study there is no reference to either ASB or the strategy it implies—or to what a former Pentagon official called a White House "buy in."[36]

A third book covering the same era, *Bending History: Barack Obama's Foreign Policy*, confirms with much nuance what the other two books report.

It discusses the White House "toughening" its reaction to what were viewed by many as assertive moves by the Chinese, such as its aggressive action in the South China Sea in 2010, and President Hu Jintao's refusal to condemn North Korea's torpedo attack on a South Korean warship.[37] Here again, it is reported that the White House and State Department reacted by changing the tone of the speeches. For instance, in a thinly veiled criticism of China, Obama stated in 2011 that "prosperity without freedom is just another form of poverty."[38] The administration also intensified the United States' participation in ASEAN and the East Asia Summit (EAS) and encouraged—but only indirectly and cautiously—countries in the region to deal with China on a multilateral rather than bilateral basis in resolving territorial disputes. The Obama administration also ramped up US participation in the Trans-Pacific Partnership negotiations, a free trade agreement that at least initially would exclude China, and is thought by many to be a counterbalance to China's extensive bilateral trade relationships in the region. Furthermore, the president paid official visits to both Burma and Cambodia—two nations that have distanced themselves from China in recent years. All these are typical diplomatic moves, some of which have economic implications, but not part of a preparation of the kinds of confrontational relationship ASB presumes.

In his book *Confront and Conceal*, David E. Sanger confirms what these three accounts suggest: the Obama administration never formulated a coherent, consistent, proactive China strategy and its policies were primarily reactive.[39] This highly regarded source also lacks any mention of a review of AirSea Battle and the military strategy it implies.

Congress held a considerable number of hearings about China in 2008 and in the years that followed. However, the main focus of these hearings was on economic issues such as trade, job losses due to companies moving them overseas, the US dependency on China for financing the debt, Chinese currency controls, and Chinese violations of intellectual property and human rights. In his testimony before the Senate Armed Services Committee in February 2012, Admiral Robert F. Willard spoke of the potential challenges posed by China's A2/AD capabilities, but made no mention of ASB. Rep. Randy Forbes (R-VA) founder and co-chair of the Congressional China Caucus, wrote to Secretary of Defense Panetta in November 2011 that "despite reports throughout 2011 AirSea Battle had been completed in an executive summary form, to my knowledge Members of Congress have yet to be briefed on its conclusions or in any way made a part of the process."[40] In the same month, Sen. Lieberman (I-CT) co-sponsored an amendment to the Fiscal 2012 Defense Authorization Bill that required a report on the implementation of and costs associated with the AirSea Battle Concept. It passed unanimously, but as of April 2013, such a report has yet to be released.[41]

In the public sphere there was no ASB debate by either think tanks or public intellectuals like that which is ongoing over whether or not to use the military option against Iran's nuclear program or the debate surrounding the 2009 surge of troops in Afghanistan. ASB did receive a modicum of critical examination from a small number of military analysts. However, most observers who understand the ins-and-outs of using drones or bombing Iran have no position on ASB or its implications for US-China relations and the world order. The reason is they simply do not know about it. A December 11, 2012 search of Google brings up 15,800,000 hits for "U.S. drone strikes"; a search for "AirSea Battle": less than 200,000. In Googlish, this amounts to being unknown, and suggests this significant military shift is simply not on the wider public's radar.

III. The Pivot: An Exception that Proves the Rule

In November 2011, President Obama announced that, with the wars in the Middle East coming to a close, his national security team was to make the US "presence and mission in the Asia-Pacific a top priority."[42] At first blush it might seem that this dramatic change in strategic focus was very much in line with the one the Pentagon has been developing intensely since 2008. In reality, this rebalancing can be interpreted in several ways, none of which support the conclusion that the pivot amounted to an endorsement of ASB.

One possible view of the pivot is that it was very much in line with the President's long-standing view—one he expressed even before he was elected—that Asia, as the heart of the global economy, was of growing importance to the United States. Hence, as he was freeing the United States from its engagement in Iraq and from Afghanistan, the time had come to shift priorities. Moreover, immediately after declaring the Asia-Pacific a top priority, Obama assured that "reductions in US defense spending will not—I repeat, will not—come at the expense of the Asia-Pacific . . . we will allocate the resources necessary to maintain our strong military presence in this region."[43] At the same time, the United States secured an agreement with Australia which provided for the rotation of 2,500 Marines through the northern port city of Darwin and announced that 60 percent of the Navy would be positioned in the Pacific by 2020—up from 50 percent. These moves highlighted that there were indeed a few military accouterments to the pivot.

Critics attacked this take on the pivot from two vantage points. Some saw it as hollow—"all hat and no cattle" as one Texan military officer put it. Sending some 2,500 Marines adds little to overall US forces in the area, which already amount to some 320,000 troops. Some of those Marines are actually being moved away from Okinawa to Australia, some 2,600 miles from China. The reberthing of a few ships does not display a significant power shift. All the rest of the pivot was—to parrot a criticism often raised against Obama—eloquent talk with little follow-through.

Others see the pivot as merely political maneuvering during an intense election campaign, undertaken to fend off the GOP's repeated charge that the Democrats are soft on defense. The Obama administration removed US troops from Iraq, but the unstable Iraqi regime, tilting toward Iran and refusing to allow the United States to keep bases in Iraq, made it difficult to present the withdrawal as a victory. The great difficulties the administration encountered in Afghanistan and Pakistan also did not make for a compelling election picture either. Furthermore, the Arab Awakening was looking more and more like a loss for the US at least in the short run. Nations that used to be reliable allies, in particular Egypt, were (and continue to be) in a state of disarray, and the turmoil in Syria presented the war-weary United States with only poor options. In this context, shifting attention from the Near to the Far East, where the United States could throw its weight around, at least in the short term, was a safe bet, especially as long as no new outlays were involved but merely the repositioning of assets already in hand.

Moreover, in November 2012 during the only presidential election debate dedicated to foreign policy, no reference was made to preparations for a war with China. Governor Romney repeatedly stated that he was going to be tougher on China than President Obama by declaring it a currency manipulator on his first day in office—a hard line stance but one focused exclusively on economic matters. President Obama cited the increased trade sanctions bought against China by his administration and said that his "pivot" policy sent a "very clear signal" to China that the United States is and will remain a Pacific power.[44] But nothing more.

In short, however one interprets the "pivot" to Asia, it clearly does not constitute an endorsement, let alone the implementation of the AirSea Battle concept, and the strategy it implies.

In Conclusion

I am not arguing that the US military is seeking out war or intentionally usurping the role of the highest civilian authorities. Information about the rise of China as an economic and military power is open to a range of interpretations. And the Pentagon is discharging its duties when it identifies new threats and suggests ways to respond to them. Moreover, civilians—including two Secretaries of Defense—have endorsed ASB and arguably the strategy it implies. But while ASB should not be dismissed on the grounds that it is merely an attempt to secure a mission and funds for the military, there is room to question whether the threats have been overstated and to ask if the Pentagon-favored response is the right strategy. The time has come for the White House and Congress to reassess both the threat and the suggested response.

Four areas ought to be considered in such a review process: (1) While the *economy* of China does not by itself determine its military strength, it does constrain its options. One would be wise to take into account that China's per capita GDP is far below that of the United States, and that to maintain support, the Communist Party needs to house, feed, clothe, and otherwise serve four times more people than the United States, on top of dealing with major environmental strains, an aging population, a high level of corruption, and growing social unrest.[45] (2) The *military* modernization of China often provokes concerns that it is "catching up." Although it is true that China has increased military spending, the budget for the PLA started well behind that of the US military and China's defense spending is still dwarfed by that of the United States. (3) Moreover, whatever its capabilities, China's *intentions* are relevant. China shows little interest in managing global affairs or imposing its ideology on other nations. Instead, China has shown a strong interest in securing the flow of raw materials and energy on which is economy depends. However, the US can accommodate this core interest without endangering its security by facilitating China's efforts to secure energy deals in the global marketplace and pathways for the flow of resources (by constructing pipelines, railways, and new ports in places such as Pakistan), rather than seeking to block them. (4) Finally, it is widely agreed that the US can no longer afford to fight two major wars. Hence, one must decide what the most urgent threats to US security are. Certainly almost all of them can be found in the Near and Middle East—not the Far East.[46]

Notes

1. Ronald O'Rourke, "China Naval Modernization: Implications for US Navy Capabilities—Background and Issues for Congress," Congressional Research Service Report for Congress (December 10, 2012), http://www.fas.org/sgp/crs/row/RL33153.pdf, 3.
2. Richard Halloran, "PACAF'S "Vision" Thing," *Air Force Magazine* (January 2009), http://www.airforce-magazine.com/MagazineArchive/Pages/2009/January%202009/0109vision.aspx.
3. Kyle D. Christensen, "Strategic Developments in The Western Pacific: Anti-Access/Area Denial And The Airsea Battle Concept," *Journal of Military and Strategic Studies* 14, no. 3 (2012), 10.
4. US Department of Defense, *Quadrennial Defense Review Report* (Washington DC: Government Printing Office, February 2010), 32.
5. General Norton A. Schwartz, "Air-Sea Battle Doctrine: A Discussion with the Chief of Staff of the Air Force and Chief of Naval Operations," The Brookings Institution (May 16, 2012), http://www.brookings.edu/~/media/events/2012/5/16%20air%20sea%20battle/20120516_air_sea_doctrine_corrected_transcript.pdf.
6. Jan Van Tol et al., *AirSea Battle: A Point-Departure Operational Concept*, (Washington, DC: Center for Strategic and International Studies, 2010), 66.
7. Ibid, 34.
8. Hugh White, *The China Choice: Why America Should Share Power* (Melbourne: Black Inc., 2012), 78.

9. Joshua Rovner, "Three Paths to Nuclear Escalation with China," *The National Interest* (July 19, 2012), http://nationalinterest.org/blog/the-skeptics/three-paths-nuclear-escalation-china-7216?page=1.
10. See note 6, 90–91.
11. Todd Harrison, *Analysis of the FY 2013 Defense Budget and Sequestration* (Washington, DC: Center for Strategic and International Studies, 2012), 4.
12. Kristina Wong, "Foot Soldiers March their Way into New Air Sea Battle Concept" *The Washington Times* (September 30, 2012), http://www.washingtontimes.com/news/2012/sep/30/foot-soldiers-march-their-way-into-new-air-sea-bat/?utm_source=RSS_Feed&utm_medium=RSS.
13. Norton A. Schwartz and Jonathan W. Greenert, "Air-Sea Battle, Promoting Stability in an Era of Uncertainty," *The American Interest* (February 20, 2012), http://www.the-american-interest.com/article.cfm?piece=1212.
14. Admiral Jonathon Greenert, "Air-Sea Battle Doctrine: A Discussion with the Chief of Staff of the Air Force and Chief of Naval Operations," The Brookings Institution (May 16, 2012), http://www.brookings.edu/~/media/events/2012/5/16%20air%20sea%20battle/20120516_air_sea_doctrine_corrected_transcript.pdf.
15. Elizabeth Bumiller, "Smaller Navy Ship Has a Rocky Past and Key Support," *The New York Times* (April 5, 2012), http://www.nytimes.com/2012/04/06/us/politics/a-smaller-navy-ship-with-troubles-but-presidents-backing.html?pagewanted=all&_r=0.
16. See note 1, 92.
17. Harry Kazianis, "AirSea Battle's identity crisis," *The Geopolitical Conflict Report* (September 13, 2011), http://gcreport.com/index.php/analysis/194-airsea-battles-identity-crisis.
18. US Department of Defense, "Background Briefing on Air-Sea Battle by Defense Officials from the Pentagon," (November 9, 2011), http://www.defense.gov/transcripts/transcript.aspx?transcriptid=4923.
19. Philip Ewing, "The Rise and Fall of Air-Sea Battle," *DODBuzz* (May 17, 2012), http://www.dodbuzz.com/2012/05/17/the-rise-and-fall-of-air-sea-battle/.
20. J. Noel Williams, "Air-Sea Battle: An Operational Concept Looking for a Strategy," *Armed Forces Journal* (September 2011), http://www.armedforcesjournal.com/2011/09/7558138/.
21. Greg Jaffe, "U.S. model for a future war fans tensions with China and inside Pentagon," *The Washington Post* (August 1, 2012), http://articles.washingtonpost.com/2012-08-01/world/35492126_1_china-tensions-china-threat-pentagon.
22. Jeffrey Kline and Wayne Hughes, "Between Peace and Air-Sea Battle: A War at Sea Strategy," *Naval War College Review* 65, no. 4 (2012), 36.
23. T.X. Hammes, "Strategy for an Unthinkable Conflict," *The Diplomat* (July 27, 2012), http://thediplomat.com/flashpoints-blog/2012/07/27/military-strategy-for-an-unthinkable-conflict/.
24. Sydney J. Freedberg Jr., "Cartwright Targets F-35, AirSea Battle; Warns of $250B More Cuts," *AOL Defense* (May 15, 2012), http://defense.aol.com/2012/05/15/cartwright-savages-f-35-airsea-battle-warns-of-250-billion-mo/.

25. See note 21 (A reviewer of this chapter from a military think tank commented that "incalculable" was an over statement, that such a war would be only "very destructive," I stand corrected.)

26. "Pentagon to Weigh Sending Extra Subs, Bombers to Asia-Pacific," *Global Security Newswire* (August 2, 2012), http://www.nti.org/gsn/article/pentagon-weighing-sending-extra-subs-bombers-asia-pacific/.

27. Raoul Heinrichs, "America's Dangerous Battle Plan," *The Diplomat* (August 17, 2012), http://thediplomat.com/2011/08/17/america%E2%80%99s-dangerous-battle-plan/.

28. T.X. Hammes, "Offshore Control: A Proposed Strategy for an Unlikely Conflict," *Strategic Forum No. 258* (National Defense University Institute for National and Strategic Studies, 2012), 2.

29. Dan Blumenthal, "The US Response to China's Military Modernization," in *Strategic Asia 2012–13: China's Military Challenge*, ed. Ashley Tellis and Travis Tanner (Washington, DC: The National Bureau of Asian Research, 2013).

30. Andrew F. Krepinevich, "Strategy in a Time of Austerity: Why the Pentagon Should Focus on Assuring Access," Center for Strategic and Budgetary Assessments (November 1, 2012), http://www.csbaonline.org/2012/11/01/strategy-in-a-time-of-austerity-why-the-pentagon-should-focus-on-assuring-access/3/.

31. Andrew F. Krepinevich, interview with author (December 3, 2012).

32. Jeffrey A. Bader, *Obama and China's Rise: An Insider's Account of America's Asia Strategy* (Washington, DC: The Brookings Institution, 2012), 7.

33. Ibid., 3.

34. Ibid., 147–150.

35. James Mann, *The Obamians: The Struggle Inside the White House to Redefine American Power* (New York: Penguin Group, 2012), 245.

36. See note 31.

37. Martin S. Indyk, *Bending History: Barack Obama's Foreign Policy* (Washington, D.C.: The Brookings Institution, 2012), 38–41.

38. "President Obama Speaks at the University of Indonesia," *DipNote: U.S. State Department Official Blog* (November 10, 2010), http://blogs.state.gov/index.php/site/entry/obama_university_of_indonesia.

39. David E. Sanger, *Confront and Conceal: Obama's Secret Wars and Surprising Use of American Power* (New York: Random House, 2012).

40. J. Randy Forbes, "Letter to Secretary of Defense Leon Panetta," (November 7, 2011), http://forbes.house.gov/uploadedfiles/panetta_asb.pdf.

41. None of this prevented the two hawkish senators from championing ASB. See J. Randy Forbes, "AirSea Office Must Battle Through, Or Fail," *AOL Defense* (September 13, 2012), http://defense.aol.com/2012/09/13/airsea-office-must-battle-through-or-fail-rep-j-randy-forbes/.

    Also: Joseph Lieberman, "Peace through Strength American Leadership in Asia Pacific," The Heritage Foundation's Annual B.C. Lee Lecture on US Policy in the Asia-Pacific (November 2, 2012), http://www.realfijinews.com/756328456/peace-through-strength-american-leadership-in-asia-pacific/.

42. "Remarks By President Obama to the Australian Parliament," The White House Office of the Press Secretary, Canberra, Australia (November 17,

2011), http://www.whitehouse.gov/the-press-office/2011/11/17/remarks-president-obama-australian-parliament.

43. Ibid.

44. "Transcript: Presidential Debate on Foreign Policy at Lynn University," *Fox News* (October 22, 2012), http://www.foxnews.com/politics/2012/10/22/transcript-presidential-debate-on-foreign-policy-at-lynn-university/.

45. For more discussion, see Amitai Etzioni, "Accommodating China," *Survival* 55, no. 2 (2013).

46. For more discussion, see Amitai Etzioni, *Hot Spots: American Foreign Policy in a Post-Human Rights World* (New Brunswick, NJ: Transaction Publishers, 2012).

References

Bader, Jeffrey, A. 2012 *Obama and China's Rise: An Insider's Account of America's Asia Strategy*. Washington, DC: The Brookings Institution.

Blumenthal, Dan. 2013. "The US Response to China's Military Modernization." *Strategic Asia 2012-13: China's Military Challenge*.

Etzioni, Amitai. 2012. *Hot Spots: American Foreign Policy in a Post-Human Rights World*. New Brunswick, NJ: Transaction Publishers.

Forbes, Randy, J. 2011. *Randy J. Forbes to Secretary of Defense Leon Panetta, November 7*, Letter. http://forbes.house.gov/uploadedfiles/panetta_asb.pdf.

Greenert, Jonathan. 2012. "Air-Sea Battle Doctrine: A Discussion with the Chief of Staff of the Air Force and Chief of Naval Operations," lecture presented at The Brookings Institution, May 16.

Hammes, T.X. 2012. "Offshore Control: A Proposed Strategy for an Unlikely Conflict." *Strategic Forum*, No. 258: 2.

Harrison, Todd. 2012. *"Analysis of the FY 2013 Defense Budget and Sequestration."* Washington, DC: Center for Strategic and International Studies.

Indyk, Martin S. 2012. *Bending History: Barack Obama's Foreign Policy*. Wasingtonton, DC: The Brookings Institution.

Jan Van Tol et al. 2010. *AirSea Battle: A Point-Departure Operational Concept* Washington, DC: Center for Strategic and International Studies.

Kazianis, Harry. 2011. "AirSea Battle's identity crisis," *The Geopolitical Conflict Report*. http://gcreport.com/index.php/analysis/194-airsea-battles-identity-crisis.

Kline, Jeffrey, Hughes, Wayne. 2012. "Between Peace and Air-Sea Battle: A War at Sea Strategy." *Naval War College Review* 65, no. 4: 36.

Mann, James. 2012. *The Obamians: The Struggle Inside the White House to Redefine American Power*. New York: Penguin Group.

Obama, President Barack. 2011. "Remarks By President Obama to the Australian Parliament." The White House Office of the Press Secretary, Canberra, Australia, November 17. http://www.whitehouse.gov/the-press-office/2011/11/17/remarks-president-obama-australian-parliament.

O'Rourke, Ronald. 2008. "China Naval Modernization: Implications for US Navy Capabilities—Background and Issues for Congress." *Congressional Research Service Report for Congress*. http://www.fas.org/sgp/crs/row/RL33153.pdf.

Shwartz, Norton. 2012. "Air-Sea Battle Doctrine: A Discussion with the Chief of Staff of the Air Force and Chief of Naval Operations." Lecture presented at The

Brookings Institution, Washington, D.C., May 16. http://www.brookings.edu/~/media/events/2012/5/16%20air%20sea%20battle/20120516_air_sea_doctrine_corrected_transcript.pdf.

U.S. Department of Defense. 2010. *Quadrennial Defense Review Report.*

U.S. Department of Defense. 2011. "Background Briefing on Air-Sea Battle by Defense Officials from the Pentagon." http://www.defense.gov/transcripts/transcript.aspx?transcriptid=4923.

White, Hugh. 2012. *The China Choice: Why America Should Share Power.* Melbourne: Black Inc.

Williams, Noel J. 2011. "Air-Sea Battle: An operational concept looking for a strategy." *Armed Forces Journal.* http://www.armedforcesjournal.com/2011/09/7558138/.

12

The Great Drone Debate

Unmanned aviation systems (UAS), popularly known as drones, are playing an increased role in armed conflicts. They are used both for collecting intelligence and for deploying lethal force. Whereas in 2007 there were seventy-four drone strikes in Afghanistan[1] and five in Pakistan,[2] by 2012 the military was executing an average of thirty-three drone strikes per month in Afghanistan,[3] and the total number of drone strikes in Pakistan has surpassed 330. Drones have been employed in multiple theaters of the counterterrorism campaign, including Yemen, Somalia, Iraq, and Libya.

They are now included in the arsenal of many nations including Israel, China, and Iran. They have even been operated by a nonstate actor (Hezbollah) which has flown at least two drones over Israel.[4] Several nations are currently developing drones that will be able to carry out highly-specialized missions, such as tiny drones able to enter constricted areas through narrow passages. Given the move by the American military away from deploying conventional forces on the ground (in Iraq and Afghanistan) to a "light footprint" strategy of "offshore balancing" (as employed in Libya), drones are likely to play an even more important role in future armed conflicts. Like other new armaments (e.g., long-range cruise missiles and high-altitude carpet bombing) the growing use of drones has triggered a considerable debate over the moral and legal grounds on which they are used. This debate is reviewed here.

I. Excessive Collateral Damage?

Critics argue that a large number of civilians, including women and children, are killed by drones. Some even hold that the number of civilians killed amounts to an overwhelming majority of all those killed. Syed Munawar Hasan, who heads the influential Islamic political party Jamaat-e-Islami in Pakistan, has claimed that the drone strikes "are killing nearly 100 percent innocent people."[5] Former military officers David Kilcullen and Andrew Exum argued in the *New York Times* that in Pakistan drones kill fifty civilians for every militant. Other critics put forward somewhat lower numbers. A study conducted by the Columbia Law School estimates that 35 percent of the victims of drone strikes in 2011 were civilians. In contrast, American counterterrorism officials put the number as low as 2.5 percent. Deputy National Security Advisor for

Homeland Security and Counterterrorism John Brennan claimed that "there hasn't been a single collateral death because of the exceptional proficiency, precision of the capabilities we've been able to develop."[6]

Researchers who conduct comprehensive analyses of the data often provide statistics that fall between these two extremes, though their numbers also differ considerably from one another and fall across a wide range. While the Bureau of Investigative Journalism puts the number as high as 26.5 percent, others estimate that the percentage of civilian casualties falls between 4 percent and 20 percent,[7] and The New America Foundation put the number at a low of 8 percent.

There is no way to settle these differences because often the drone strikes are in areas that are inaccessible to independent observers and the data includes reports by local officials and local media, neither of whom are reliable sources.[8] The most cited statistics on the drone strikes in Pakistan, a data set compiled by the New America Foundation and Peter Bergen, relies completely on local media reports.[9] It is a problem that plagues a majority of the media stories on any particular strike: estimates of civilian casualties are often based exclusively upon other media reports, producing what the Human Rights Clinic at Columbia Law School calls "an echo chamber" effect. In short, there is no fully reliable, or even highly reliable, way to determine the ratio of civilian to militant casualties caused by drone strikes. For reasons that follow we shall see that it stands to reason that these strikes cause less collateral damage than other instruments of warfare, though unfortunately are still likely to cause some.

II. Promiscuous Use?

Critics like the *Atlantic*'s Conor Friedersdorf argue that the drone campaign is an "unprecedented campaign of assassination with no apparent end,"[10] while Glen Greenwald, writing in *Salon.com*, has described it as a set of "ongoing policies of rampant slaughter, secrecy and lawlessness."[11] Army chaplain D. Keith Shurtleff, as quoted by P.W. Singer in the *New Atlantis*, warns that "as war becomes safer and easier, as soldiers are removed from the horrors of war and see the enemy not as humans but as blips on a screen, there is a very real danger of losing the deterrent that such horrors provide."[12] However, the use of drones is actually kept in check by an extensive set of rules, is subject to considerable *a priori* and *a posteriori* review, and is regulated by Congressional oversight.

Drones are used by the US military—especially the Joint Special Operations Command (JSOC)—and by the CIA. Much more is known about the rules that the military is using in its attempts to limit collateral damage in general (that of drones included) than those used by the CIA. Of the three existing drone programs, the one run by the US Air Force in Afghanistan (and to a much lesser extent in Iraq) has the most clearly defined scope and targeting procedures. Drone strikes in Pakistan, which are mostly under the charge of the CIA, and those in Yemen, some of which are operated by the CIA and others by the JSOC, operate with a greater degree of secrecy. As far as is known, these CIA and JSOC strikes follow targeting procedures similar to those used by the military.

The military rules include a long list of "no strike" targets including diplomatic offices, medical facilities, prisons, schools, and structures whose destruction will result in uncontainable environmental damages.[13] They also include a host of other structures which are generally restricted from being targeted, including agricultural facilities, water and power utilities, recreational complexes, parks, restaurants, and retail stores. These regulations also cover a range of potential "dual-use" targets that perform a combination of civilian and military functions. These targets are generally disallowed for military targeting absent higher-level authorization or specific intelligence demonstrating that only the military functions of the building in question are being utilized.

The more sensitive the target, (i.e., the more likely that innocent civilians might be involved), the higher in the ranks that approval must be sought, sometimes extending all the way to the president or the director of the CIA. President Obama is reported to personally review the files of all known terrorists before he approves their inclusion in a hit list.[14]

Michael Scheuer, formerly of the CIA, scoffs at the charge that the review process is not rigorous. He reports that the procedure for nominating individuals for targeted killings is so exhaustive that the CIA was often unable to kill those who ought to have been eliminated. Quoted in a 2011 article for *Newsweek*, Scheuer stated that each nomination, including a short document and "an appendix with supporting information," was passed along to departmental lawyers, who were "very picky. . . . Often this caused a missed opportunity. The whole idea that people got shot because someone has a hunch—I only wish that was true."

John Brennan puts together a weekly "potential target list" based on Pentagon recommendations, which his staff then discusses with other agencies (such as the State Department) before making final recommendations to the president, according to the *Associated Press*. It is the president who then makes the final decision regarding whether to target someone with a kinetic strike.

Further, the Department of Defense employs multiple teams of lawyers that are responsible for determining the legality of specific strikes. These lawyers have undergone "special training in the Geneva conventions," and are instructed to guarantee that each targeted killing upholds international humanitarian law, official rules of engagement, and mission-specific instructions, reports the *Guardian*'s Pratap Chatterjee. The DOD employs some twelve thousand lawyers[15] and during the Iraq War surge, there was one lawyer for every 240 combatants.[16] Some may wish there were even more, but no one should argue that orders to kill terrorists were not subject to close review.

In an op-ed for *Foreign Policy*, Jack Goldsmith argues that the review process for designating an individual for a strike "goes far beyond any process given to any target in any war in American history." In effect, these lawyers and other staff conduct hearings of a sort, in which evidence is presented and lawyers are instructed to guarantee that each targeted killing upholds all applicable laws and rules before the target is approved. I would suggest adding to this process a position for a lawyer explicitly charged with acting as a "guardian" of the terrorists who are essentially tried *in absentia*. Of course, all of these lawyers have and ought to have the proper level of security clearance.

The Senate Foreign Relations committee reports that the military requires "two verifiable human sources" and "substantial additional evidence" that a potential target is an enemy.[17] The first requirement for all drone strikes is to establish "positive identification" of the target in question, which constitutes "reasonable certainty that a functionally and geospatially defined object of attack is a legitimate military target in accordance with the law of war and applicable ROE (rules of engagement)."[18]

As for oversight, Senator Dianne Feinstein, who according to *The Los Angeles Times*, had been previously critical of the drone program's lack of transparency, released a statement on March 7, 2012 affirming that the "Senate Intelligence Committee is kept fully informed of counterterrorism operations and keeps close watch to make sure they are effective, responsible and in keeping with US and international law."[19] Specifically, staffers from the intelligence committees watch footage of the previous month's drone strikes and review the intelligence used to justify the killings. They also learn about the number of civilian casualties. According to Feinstein, the staffers "question every aspect of the program including legality, effectiveness, precision, foreign policy implications and the care taken to minimize noncombatant casualties."[20]

These restraints are maintained despite evidence showing that terrorists are both aware of these self-imposed limitations and use them to their advantage by stationing combatants, supplies, and weapons in mosques, schools, and private homes. In his book *The Wrong War: Grit, Energy, and the Way Out of Afghanistan*, Bing West quotes American servicemen reporting that the "Taliban fight from compounds where there are women and children . . . [so] we can't push the Talibs [sic] out by mortar fire without being blamed for civilian casualties." West also reports that Taliban troops often fired at American soldiers from private homes, mosques, buildings owned by the Red Crescent, and other locales where civilians were likely to be.

Rajiv Chandrasekaran, author of another book on the war in Afghanistan, notes how "In many cases, insurgents would seek refuge in compounds inhabited by women and children—so as to use them as human shields or, if the house was bombed to bits, as pawns in their propaganda campaign to convince the Afghan people that coalition forces were indiscriminate murderers of the innocent."[21] This problem was exacerbated by the fact that the "new rules prevented air strikes on residential buildings unless troops were in imminent danger of being overrun or the house had been observed for more than twenty-four hours to ensure no civilians were inside. If the bad guys ran into a home, they would have a free pass, unless the American's were willing to wait them out." Chandrasekaran further quotes Brigadier General Larry Nicholson, who, citing these rules, worried that "If we have to treat every house like a mosque, it'll result in a whole lot more casualties."

The discussion over drones tends to conflate two issues: should the US set out to kill the particular person in question, and if so, should drones be used rather than Special Forces, bombers, cruise missiles, or some other tool? The drone issue is actually irrelevant to the first question. At the same time it is clear—or at least should be—that if kill we must, drones are the preferable instrument. Compared to Special Forces and even bombers, drones preclude casualties on our side—not a trivial matter.[22] Moreover, because they can linger over the target for hours if need be, often undetected, thereby enabling a much closer review and much more selective targeting process than do other instruments of warfare. This important fact is even recognized by the president of the International Committee of the Red Cross, Jakob Kellenberger. In his 2011 keynote address at the 34th Round Table on Current Issues of International Humanitarian Law, Kellenberger conceded that because drones have "enhanced real-time aerial surveillance possibilities," they "thereby [allow] belligerents to carry out their attacks more precisely against military objectives and thus reduce civilian casualties and damage to civilian objects—in other words, to exercise greater precaution in attack."

Other critics argue that drones strikes engender much resentment among the local population and serve as a major recruitment tool for the terrorists, possibly radicalizing more individuals than they neutralize. This argument has been made especially in reference to Pakistan, where there were anti-American demonstrations following drones strikes, as well as in Yemen.[23] However, such arguments do not take into account the fact that anti-American sentiment in these areas ran high before drone strikes took place and remained so during periods in which strikes were significantly scaled back. Moreover, other developments, such as the release of an anti-Muslim movie trailer by an Egyptian Copt from California or the publication of incendiary cartoons by a Danish newspaper, led to much larger demonstrations. Hence if the use of drones is otherwise justified, and especially given that they are a very effective and low-cost way to neutralize terrorist violence on the ground,[24] stopping drone strikes merely for public relations purposes seems imprudent.

III. Moral Responsibility Rests on Whom?

The main onus for whatever collateral damage is caused by drone strikes is a result of the terrorists' strategy of systematically violating a foundational rule of armed conflict, the rule of distinction. The 1977 Geneva Convention

Article 48 Additional Protocol I states that: "The Parties to the conflict shall at all times distinguish between the civilian population and combatants." The purpose of this rule of armed conflict is to oblige fighting forces that clash with each other not to harm the civilian population—a moral obligation too often ignored during WWII. It is a rule that should apply not only to nation-states but to terrorists as well.

Rather than abide by this principle, however, terrorists exploit it by presenting themselves as civilians, showing their true colors only when they are ready to strike. After attacking US forces, terrorists then switch back to their civilian condition when it suits their purposes, demanding that they be shielded by the law. This practice, exploiting what is known as the "revolving door" of protection, is common with terrorist and insurgent violence. Because the law of armed conflict only permits the targeting of individuals who exercise a "continuous combat function", a person who lays bombs at night but labors as a farmer during the day cannot be attacked in the daytime unless there is indisputable evidence that they are planning to conduct another attack in the near future.[25] In addition, militants have used ambulances to transport suicide vests and bombers, schools and private homes as sniper bases, and mosques as storehouses of ammunition. Above all, they mix in with the civilian population, one moment acting like shepherds and farmers, the next attacking, and soon after returning to the legal safety of their civilian pursuits. These very widespread and deliberate violations of the rule of distinction leave the counterterrorism forces with basically two choices: cause considerable collateral damage and face the wrath of the civilian population, or allow terrorist forces to gain major military advantages. (Although I cannot demonstrate this here, this factor alone explains to a great extent why most counterterrorism campaigns are so long, costly in human and economic terms, and often fail[26]). Moreover, drawing an overbearing military response from counterterrorism forces that harms innocent civilians is a central part of the terrorists' strategy, as such incidents serve as more fodder for their propaganda and recruitment efforts.

In a 2009 brief written by Nils Melzer, The Red Cross states that "at the heart of IHL (International Humanitarian Law) lies the principle of distinction between the armed forces, who conduct the hostilities on behalf of the parties to an armed conflict, and civilians, who are presumed not to directly participate in hostilities and must be protected."[27] However, to protect civilians in practice, it is not enough to expect soldiers to avoid them, but for all who take up arms to separate themselves from peaceful civilians. And if they do not—if they are like someone who carries a white flag claiming to surrender but opens fire when he closes—they ought to be understood as having forfeited some of their rights as fighters or as civilians. If the terrorists observed the rule of distinction, most collateral damage would vanish overnight, although some would still take place due to technical or intelligence failures. This conclusion is borne out by the data regarding civilian casualties in Pakistan. Gregory McNeal found that 70 percent, an overwhelming majority, of incidents of civilian casualties were attributable to failures in the "positive identification" process of differentiating between civilians and militants.[28] Of the remaining civilian casualties, 22 percent were attributable to weapons malfunctions while only 8 percent were the result of "proportionality balancing" decisions wherein the military logic of a strike was considered sufficient to justify potential harm to surrounding civilians.[29] In short, the main onus for collateral damage rests with the terrorists. If they would follow the rules of armed conflict, some innocent civilians would still be killed due to intelligence or technical failures, but the number would be much smaller.

IV. "Extrajudicial Killing" and Outside "Theaters of War"?

Critics employ two lines of legal criticism. One labels the killing of terrorists by drones (or other means) as "extrajudicial killings," implying that only courts can legitimately mete out a death sentence. Michael Boyle, for example, contends in *The Guardian* that "the president has routinized and normalized extrajudicial killing from the Oval Office, taking advantage of America's temporary advantage in drone technology to wage a series of shadow wars."[30] Similarly Conor Friedersdorf has argued in *The Atlantic* that the drone policy is passing death sentences "based on the unchecked authority of the president, who declares himself judge, jury, and executioner."[31] The assumption underlying these criticisms is that terrorists (those who are non-Americans and operating overseas) are nevertheless to be treated as ordinary criminals, that is, captured and tried in American civilian courts. However, these critics do not address the question of how the United States is to treat terrorists that either cannot be captured or can only be captured at a very great risk to our troops and, most likely, through the direct invasion of other countries (for instance, capturing those that make Northern Waziristan their base).

Nor is it clear on what grounds citizens of other nations, attacking our embassies, ships, and forces overseas, should be treated as American citizens, with all the rights thereof. Obviously if they were wearing a uniform or otherwise distinguish themselves from the civilian population (as the rules of armed conflict require) they would be killed and no one would see this as a legal issue. This is what takes place in all instances of war. Why one would hold that we ought to grant numerous extra rights to people just because they fight us in an unfair and illegal way seems difficult to comprehend. In addition, as Philip Bobbitt and Benjamin Wittes have pointed out, trying terrorists in civilian courts would not only force us to reveal sensitive sources and methods used to gather evidence in the first place, but such trials would also tend to lead to plea bargains because the evidence—collected in combat zones—often does not meet the stringent standards of civilian courts.[32] We would also be forced to let terrorists loose once they completed their sentences, which are historically short. By the end of 2011, civilian courts had adjudicated 204 cases of terrorism: 63 percent of convictions were garnered through a plea bargain, 40 percent of the sentences were under five years in length, and 30 percent were between five and ten years. (These statistics and others have been diligently recorded by Karen J. Greenberg et al., in a report published by the Center on Law and Security at the NYU School of Law.[33])

To reiterate, as the preceding discussion has shown, terrorist executions are carefully and extensively reviewed, albeit by different authorities and according to different procedures than those of our civilian courts.

Another line of criticism takes the opposite viewpoint, treating terrorists not as if they were criminals but as if they were soldiers. They hence are to be treated in accordance with the rules of warfare, such as the Geneva Conventions. These rules require that the US strike terrorists only in "declared theaters of war," and treat those it captures as prisoners of war. In a 2010 debate at Fordham Law School, Mary Ellen O'Connell contended that "targeting with the intent to kill an individual is only lawful under international humanitarian law or LOAC (the Law of Armed Conflict) within armed conflict hostilities, and then only members of regular armed forces, members of organized armed groups, or direct participants in those hostilities . . . [thus, because] the United States is only engaged in armed conflict in Afghanistan, targeted killing elsewhere is not commensurate with the law." By this view, drone strikes in Pakistan and elsewhere are legally impermissible.

Regarding the first point—that we must only target terrorists within declared theaters of war—one notes that terrorists readily move from one country to another. Taliban and Al-Qaeda move often and rather freely between Afghanistan and Pakistan. For example, the Pakistani Inter-Services Intelligence (ISI) is working with the Haqqani network that has offshoots in Afghanistan and elsewhere according to the Council on Foreign Relations. Further, the Council reports that Al-Qaeda members and Jihadist fighters are moving in and out of Yemen, Somalia, Mali, and Libya. If we can confirm that a person either is a terrorist or has made plans to kill our troops, civilians, or allies, then the fact that they disregard and cross an unregulated border hardly seems a reasonable criteria for protecting them.

Critics often ask "well if the whole world is now treated as a theater of war, would you kill terrorists even when they were located in a democratic nation?" The question itself is asked rhetorically, the absurdity of such a move assumed to be self-evident. However, one should not be too quick to concede this point, for if Washington had reliable intelligence that some terrorists based in Germany were preparing to strike us, we would ask the German government to deal with them. If the German government refused—perhaps on the grounds that German laws do not allow a response—we surely would neutralize these terrorists one way or another. This is what we are doing in Pakistan, a democratic country who we consider to be our ally, and this is what we did when we captured and surreptitiously removed suspected terrorist Osama

Moustafa Hassan Nasr from Italy. If the current counterterrorism campaign takes the whole world as its theater, the distinction between democratic and authoritarian allies is quickly replaced by the distinction between cooperative and noncompliant counterterrorism partners.

Once captured, treating terrorist suspects as prisoners of war presumes that they can be held until the war is over. However, counterterrorism campaigns as a rule have no clear starting or ending dates; as it has been put elsewhere, in these campaigns there is no ceremonial signing of peace treaties on aircraft carriers. Rather, they tend to peter out slowly, leaving no clear guide for how long we can hold captured terrorists if we to treat them by the rules of war.

As others have pointed out, we need distinct legal procedures and authorities for dealing with terrorists who are neither criminals nor soldiers. So far they have been left in a sort of legal limbo, a legal ambiguity that surrounds not merely drone strikes, but all counterterrorism endeavors.[34] The proper legal status of these individuals will not be cleared up until we move beyond the simplistic dichotomy that terrorists must be viewed either as criminals or as soldiers and instead recognize that they are a distinct breed of enemy, with a distinct legal status: that of fighters who violate the rules of armed conflict and often deliberately target civilian populations in order to wreak terror. To call them soldiers is to unduly honor them; to view them as garden variety criminals is to underestimate both their misbegotten deeds and the danger they pose.

V. "Industrial Warfare?"

Mary Dudziak of the University of Southern California's Gould School of Law opines that "drones are a technological step that further isolates the American people from military action, undermining political checks on . . . endless war." Similarly, Noel Sharkey, in the *Guardian*, worries that drones represent "the final step in the industrial revolution of war—a clean factory of slaughter with no physical blood on our hands and none of our own side killed."

This kind of cocktail-party sociology does not stand up to even the most minimal critical examination. Would the people of the United States, Afghanistan, and Pakistan be better off if terrorists were killed in "hot" blood—say, knifed by Special Forces, blood and brain matter splashing in their faces? Would they be better off if our troops, in order to reach the terrorists, had to go through improvised explosive devices blowing up their legs and arms and gauntlets of machinegun fire and rocket-propelled grenades—traumatic experiences that turn some of them into psychopathic killers?

Perhaps if *all* or *most* fighting were done in a cold-blooded, push-button way, it might well have the effects suggested above. However, as long as what we are talking about are a few hundred drone drivers, what they do or do not feel has no discernable effects on the nation or the leaders who declare war. Indeed, there is no evidence that the introduction of drones (and before that, high-level bombing and cruise missiles that were criticized on the same grounds) made going to war more likely or its extension more acceptable. Anybody who followed the US disengagement in Vietnam after the introduction of high-level bombing, or the US withdrawal from Afghanistan (and Iraq)—despite the considerable increases in drone strikes—knows better. In effect, the opposite argument may well hold: if the United States could not draw on drones in Yemen and the other new theaters of the counterterrorism campaign, the United States might well have been forced to rely more on conventional troops and prolong its involvement in the areas, a choice which would greatly increase US casualties and zones of warfare.

This line of criticism also neglects a potential upside of drones. As philosopher Bradley Strawser notes, this ability to deploy force abroad with minimal US casualties may allow the United States to intervene in emerging humanitarian crises across the world with a greater degree of flexibility and effectiveness.[35] Rather than reliving another "Black Hawk down" scenario, the United States can follow the model of the Libya intervention, where drones were used by NATO forces to eliminate enemy armor and air defenses, paving the way for the highly successful air campaign which followed, as reported by the *Guardian's* Nick Hopkins.

As I see it, however, the main point of moral judgment comes earlier in the chain of action, well before we come to the question of which means are to be used to kill the enemy. The main turning point concerns the question of whether we should go to war at all. This is the crucial decision because once we engage in war, we must assume that there are going to be a large number of casualties on all sides—casualties that may well include innocent civilians. Often, discussions of targeted killings strike me as being written by people who yearn for a nice clean war, one in which only bad people will be killed using "surgical" strikes that inflict no collateral damage. Very few armed confrontations unfold in this way.

Hence, when we deliberate over whether or not to fight, we should assume that once we step on this train, it is very likely to carry us to places we would rather not go. Drones are merely a new stepping stone on this woeful journey. Thus, we should carefully deliberate before we join or initiate any new armed fights, but if fight we must, we should draw on drones extensively. They are more easily scrutinized and reviewed, and are more morally justified, than any other means of warfare available.

Notes

1. Christopher Drew, "Drones are playing a growing role in Afghanistan," *The New York Times* (February 19, 2010), http://www.nytimes.com/2010/02/20/world/asia/20drones.html.

2. "The Bush Years: Pakistan Strikes 2004–2009," *The Bureau of Investigative Journalism* (August 10, 2011), http://www.thebureauinvestigates.com/2011/08/10/the-bush-years-2004-2009/.

3. Noah Shachtman, "Military stats reveal epicenter of US drone war," *Wired. com* (November 9, 2012), http://www.wired.com/dangerroom/2012/11/ drones-afghan-air-war/.
4. "Iran Muscles into the UAV Battlefield," *United Press International* (October 5, 2010), http://www.upi.com/Business_News/Security-Industry/2010/10/05/Iran-muscles-into-the-UAV-battlefield/UPI-47421286303914/?rel=10991287154490.
5. Sebastian Abbot, "New Light on Drone War's Death Toll," *Associated Press* (February 26, 2012), http://news.yahoo.com/ap-impact-light-drone-wars-death-toll-150321926.html.
6. Scott Shane, "C.I.A. Is Disputed on Civilian Toll in Drone Strikes," *The New York Times* (August 11, 2011), http://www.nytimes.com/2011/08/12/world/ asia/12drones.html?pagewanted=all. Brennan's comment was given in June, 2011.
7. Ibid.
8. For discussions of these problems: "Pakistan most unsafe country for journalists - Report," *Yahoo News – India* (October 2, 2012), http://in.news.yahoo. com/pakistan-most-unsafe-country-journalists-reports-113619812.html.
    Also: Conor Friedersdorf, "Flawed Analysis of Drone Strike Data is Misleading Americans," *The Atlantic* (July 18, 2012), http://www.theatlantic. com/politics/archive/2012/07/flawed-analysis-of-drone-strike-data-is-misleading-americans/259836/.
    Also: Sebastian Abbot, "New Light on Drone War's Death Toll," *Associated Press* (February 26, 2012), http://news.yahoo.com/ap-impact-light-drone-wars-death-toll-150321926.html.
    Also: Avery Plaw, Matthew S. Fricker, and Brian Glyn Williams, "Practice Makes Perfect?: The Changing Civilian Toll of CIA Drone Strikes in Pakistan," *Perspectives on Terrorism* 5, no. 6 (December 2011): 51–69.
9. "The Year of the Drone: Methodology," *The New America Foundation*, http://counterterrorism.newamerica.net/drones/methodology, accessed (October 20, 2012).
10. Conor Friedersdorf. "Obama's Execution of the Drone War Should Terrify Even Drone Defenders" *The Atlantic* (July 12, 2012). http://www.theatlantic.com/politics/archive/2012/07/obamas-execution-of-the-drone-war-should-terrify-even-drone-defenders/259704/.
11. Glenn Greenwald. "America's drone sickness" *Salon* (April 19, 2012) http:// www.salon.com/2012/04/19/americas_drone_sickness/.
12. Peter W. Singer. "Military Robots and Laws of War" *The New Atlantis*. Winter 2009. http://www.brookings.edu/research/articles/2009/02/winter-robots-singer.
13. "No-Strike and the Collateral Damage Estimation Methodology," Chairman of the Joint Chiefs of Staff Instruction, (February 13, 2009).
14. Jo Becker and Scott Shane, "Secret 'Kill List' Proves a Test of Obama's Principles and Will," *New York Times* (May 29, 2012), http://www. nytimes.com/2012/05/29/world/obamas-leadership-in-war-on-al-qaeda. html?pagewanted=all.
15. Daniel Klaidman, *Kill or Capture: The War on Terror and the Soul of the Obama Presidency* (New York, NY: Houghton Mifflin Harcourt, 2012), 211.
16. Christopher Caldwell, "Vetted, Altered, Blessed: *Power and Constraint,* by Jack Goldsmith," *The New York Times Book Review* (June 8, 2012), http://

www.nytimes.com/2012/06/10/books/review/power-and-constraint-by-jack-goldsmith.html.

17. Jane Mayer, "The Predator War: What are the Risks of the C.I.A.'s Covert Drone Program?" *The New Yorker* (October 26, 2009), http://www.newyorker.com/reporting/2009/10/26/091026fa_fact_mayer.

18. "No-Strike and the Collateral Damage Estimation Methodology," *Chairman of the Joint Chiefs of Staff Instruction* (February 13, 2009).

19. Ken Dilanian, "Congress Keeps Closer Watch on CIA Drone Strikes," *Los Angeles Times* (June 25, 2012), http://www.latimes.com/news/nationworld/world/middleeast/la-na-drone-oversight-20120625,0,7967691,full.story. Even with robust oversight, it must be acknowledged that mistakes will be made and innocents may be killed. However, regardless of whether the form of attack is a targeted killing or more traditional warfare, "the US government can and sometimes does make mistakes about its targets. There is simply no way to wring all potential error from the system and still carry on a war," See Jack Goldsmith, "Fire When Ready," *Foreign Policy* (March 19, 2012), http://www.foreignpolicy.com/articles/2012/03/19/fire_when_ready?page=0,2.

20. Ken Dilanian, "Congress Keeps Closer Watch on CIA Drone Strikes," *Los Angeles Times* (June 25, 2012), http://www.latimes.com/news/nationworld/world/middleeast/la-na-drone-oversight-20120625,0,7967691,full.story.

21. Rajiv Chandrasekaran, *Little America: The War Within the War for Afghanistan* (New York: Alfred A. Knopf, 2012), 38. Subsequent quotations appear on 39.

22. For a more thorough discussion of this moral argument, see: Bradley Jay Strawser, "Moral Predators: The Duty to Employ Uninhabited Aerial Vehicles," *Journal of Military Ethics* 9, no. 4 (December 2010): 342–368.

23. Owen Bowcott, "Drone Attacks in Pakistan are Counterproductive, Says Report," *The Guardian* (September 24, 2012), http://www.guardian.co.uk/world/2012/sep/25/drone-attacks-pakistan-counterproductive-report.

24. Patrick B. Johnston and Anoop Sarbahi, "The Impact of US Drone Strikes on Terrorism in Pakistan," Working paper, (February 2012), http://patrickjohnston.info/materials/drones.pdf, cited in Trefor Moss, "Obama's Drone War," *The Diplomat* (February 6, 2012), http://thediplomat.com/flashpoints-blog/2012/02/06/obamas-drone-war/.

25. "Targeting Operations with Drone Technology: Humanitarian Law Implications," Human Rights Institute, Columbia Law School (March 25, 2011), Targeting Operations with Drone Technology, 2011, https://s3.amazonaws.com/s3.documentcloud.org/documents/369827/backgroundnoteasilcolumbia.pdf.

26. See, for example, Stathis Kalyvas, "The Paradox of Terrorism in Civil War," *Journal of Ethics* 8 no. 1 (January 2004): 97–138.

27. Nils Melzer "Interpretative Guidance on the Notion of Direct participation in hostilities under International Humanitarian Law" *International Committee of the Red Cross* (May 2009). http://www.icrc.org/eng/assets/files/other/icrc-002-0990.pdf

28. Gregory McNeal, "Are Targeted Killings Unlawful? A Case Study in Empirical Claims Without Empirical Evidence," (November 4, 2011), in *Targeted Killings: Law and Morality in an Asymmetrical World* eds. Claire Finkelstein,

Jens David Ohlin, and Andrew Altman (Oxford: Oxford University Press, 2012). Available at SSRN: http://ssrn.com/abstract=1954795.

29. Ibid.

30. Michael Boyle. "Obama's Drone Wars and the Normalisation of Extrajudicial Murder" *The Guardian* (June 11, 2012). http://www.theguardian.com/commentisfree/2012/jun/11/obama-drone-wars-normalisation-extrajudicial-killing.

31. Conor Friedersdorf. "Obama Plans for 10 More Years of Extrajudicial Killing by Drone" *The Atlantic* (October 24, 2012). http://www.theatlantic.com/politics/archive/2012/10/obama-plans-for-10-more-years-of-extrajudicial-killing-by-drone/264034/.

32. Benjamin Wittes, *Law and the Long War: The Future of Justice in the Age of Terror* (New York: Penguin Books, 2008), especially chapter 6.

    Also: Philip Bobbitt, *Terror and Consent: The Wars for the Twenty-First Century,* (New York: Alfred A. Knopf, 2008), especially chapters 5 and 6.

33. Karen J. Greenberg et al. "Terrorist Trial Report Card: September 11, 2001 – September 11, 2009" *Center on Law and Security, New York University School of Law.* January 2010. http://www.lawandsecurity.org/Portals/0/documents/02_TTRCFinalJan142.pdf.

34. For a discussion of this problem, see Robert M. Chesney, "Beyond the Battlefield, Beyond Al Qaeda: The Destabilizing Legal Architecture of Counterterrorism," *Michigan Law Review* 112, no. 2 (November 2013): 163–224.

35. Rory Carroll, "The Philosopher Making the Moral Case for US Drones," *The Guardian* (August 2, 2012), http://www.guardian.co.uk/world/2012/aug/02/philosopher-moral-case-drones.

13

The Moral and Legal Foundations of Counterterrorism

The paradigms most often employed in conceptualizing and legitimatizing counterterrorism campaigns—the paradigms of law enforcement and war among nations—are ill-suited to meet the contemporary realities of terrorism.[1] The considerable policy mistakes, misjudgments, and above all, morally flawed positions that are caused by the misapplication of these concepts, point to a need for a distinct normative and legal paradigm for dealing with transnational terrorism. This chapter focuses on the normative assumptions of such a paradigm, which have clear legal parallels. Further, this article seeks to develop this distinct paradigm by situating it in ongoing transnational moral dialogues[2] on the just and effective ways to counter terrorism. This distinct paradigm would benefit if it could be consolidated into a new Geneva Convention in the future.

Introduction

The dialogue surrounding the principles that guide the treatment of terrorists is hardly new, although its focus has shifted over the years. In the 1970s, much attention was paid to the ways Britain dealt with terrorists in the wake of "the troubles" in Northern Ireland and to the new anti-terrorism laws the mother of democracy enacted in response. In the 1980s considerable attention was paid to the ways Israel dealt with terrorists. In the aftermath of the 2001 attacks on the United States homeland, attention has shifted from terrorists who limit their activities to their own nations and "lone wolf" terrorists like Timothy McVeigh, to a focus on transnational terrorists and their networks.

The transnational moral dialogue about the issue lost some of its intensity in the decade after 9/11 as terrorist acts in the West were infrequent, often failed, and when successful did not cause massive casualties. In many other parts of the world, however, terrorists continue to pose a major threat. The risk that terrorists will acquire weapons of mass destruction (WMDs) continues to constitute a major security threat. There have been at least six serious terrorist attempts to penetrate storages of nuclear arms in Pakistan alone.[3] Moreover, states continue to wage counterterrorism campaigns across national borders, most notably by the use of drones, Special Forces, and intensified surveillance. This chapter discusses the ways these transnational campaigns ought to be shaped in order to bolster their legitimacy without curtailing their effectiveness. It suggests that a much stronger case can be made for these campaigns by drawing on normative paradigms that break away from the traditional framework of viewing terrorists either as criminals or as soldiers.

First, a few lines about key concepts and their relationships. "Terrorists" are here defined as individuals who seek to drive fear into a population through acts of violence in order to advance their goals in a *sub rosa* manner. Title 18, Section 2331 of the US Code defines terrorism as activities that:

> a) involve violent acts or acts dangerous to human life that are a violation of criminal laws . . . b) appear to be intended—(i) to intimidate or coerce a civilian population; (ii) to influence the policy of a government by intimidation or coercion; or (iii) to affect the conduct of a government by mass destruction, assassination, or kidnapping; and c) occur primarily outside the territorial jurisdiction of the United States.[4]

This definition seems quite clear although there is always room to ask for more specificity. If this is required, one should employ the criteria often used in legal deliberations—what a reasonable person would consider a terrorist act. The establishment of an authority charged with discerning the judgment of reasonable people is given further consideration below. While this article follows the definition just cited, it deals only with those terrorists who strike countries other than their own, that is, only with acts of transnational terrorism.[5]

"Normative paradigm" refers to a set of values that indicates what conduct is morally appropriate and differentiates right from wrong. References to normative paradigms raise the question: whose values? A simple answer is whoever holds them and finds them compelling.[6] Normative paradigms contain both an intellectual element, in the sense that they include moral reasons for holding whatever positions are prescribed, and an affective element that makes those who subscribe to these paradigms emotionally engaged in their support. Unlike codes of law, normative paradigms are informal, rarely embraced by all, and held in varying degrees of intensity by those who subscribe to them.

The relationship between normative paradigms and codes of law is exceedingly complex, and is touched upon here only insofar as such an examination is needed for the following discussion. Some scholars hold that changes in the law can lead to changes in the normative paradigms. For instance, an executive order to desegregate the US military in 1948 is said to have preceded a shift in the normative rules governing the relationship between whites and blacks in the US South.[7] Others hold that normative changes lead to changes in the law. For example, changes in the ways young US citizens view homosexuality is seen as leading to the legalization of same-sex marriage.[8] This chapter assumes that a third position better captures the historical evidence: that in most circumstances normative and legal developments require movement on both "legs." While one kind of development can move ahead of the other, if the two elements move apart a great deal, they endanger the stability of the body of thought and the beliefs at issue. We shall see shortly that the normative paradigms currently applied to terrorists—that we ought to view them either as soldiers (the liberal international order paradigm) or as criminals (the civil society paradigm)—are particularly strained, suggesting the need for a different normative approach. Given that more than a decade has passed since the 2001 attacks on the US homeland, a period in which both Republican and Democratic administrations have shaped the fight against global terrorism, the time is ripe to review which positions withstood the tests of time and political changes and which failed.[9] The time has come to consolidate and institutionalize a new paradigm, if the evidence shows—as the article argues—that one is sorely needed.[10]

There are understandable reasons why once mutually-reinforcing normative paradigms and codes of law are well-ensconced: They resist modification even after the reality changes significantly. Thomas Kuhn pointed out that even scientific paradigms resist change, even though that the essence of the scientific methodology is openness to new evidence.[11] Paradigms are frequently sustained even as more and more facts cast them in doubt (so called "stubborn facts"), until the paradigm can no longer hold and the dam breaks, opening the way for a new paradigm to replace it.

The reason for such persistence is that to form a normative paradigm (and a symbiotic legal code) requires great effort and investment. Decades of moral dialogue, consensus building, legislation, court cases, and public education slowly build such a paradigm. Millions of people come to believe in it, weave it into their worldview and political preferences, and even intertwine it with their personal identities. Hence the strain of dissonance between the paradigm and reality may be quite high before one can expect a paradigm to break down and be replaced with a new one. This chapter suggests that, when possible, a more gradual transition is preferable, and seeks to contribute toward that end.

The discussion focuses on the normative part of the dynamic. That is, although I fully recognize that we must move on both "legs" to proceed, currently the prevailing normative paradigms are particularly lagging behind the new international reality and hence warrant special attention. Also, I focus on the normative rather than the legal because I have no legal training and approach the subject of terrorism as a sociologist, social philosopher, and one who knows of combat first hand.[12] Hence, that the expected review of the legal literature is not provided should not be viewed as a lack of respect for the work of legal scholars on these issues, but as an acknowledgment of my own limitations.

Finally, I should note that the article is written from an American perspective. Although other nations face terrorism in similar terms, there are enough subtle differences, for instance in the contents of the respective constitutions or basic laws, that US normative (and legal) terms cannot be mechanically extended to other nations. Such adaptation requires additional deliberations not here undertaken. However, the challenges confronted here raise issues pertinent to all liberal democracies.

I. Rights and Responsibilities of Nations

1. A Strained Paradigm

The liberal international order is the prevailing paradigm that defines the ways nations ought to treat each other, above all in order to prevent wars and regulate conduct if wars do break out.[13] Prominent among its attending normative principles are the respect for national sovereignty and for the Westphalian principle against armed interference of one nation in the internal affairs of other nations. At issue is not the exact wording of the 1648 Treaty of Westphalia or legal textbook definitions of sovereignty,[14] but the ways these concepts are currently built into the beliefs and worldviews of billions of people. Daily news reminds one that people in very different parts of the world feel personally aggrieved, insulted, and humiliated when they hold that their nation's sovereignty has been violated, even if the troops of another nation merely crossed a minor, vague line in the shifting sands. Millions of people have shown that they are willing to die to protect the sovereignty of their nation, an indication of the depth of their commitment to this precept. The same complex of normative ideas is also tied to the strongly-held precepts of self-determination that played a key role in the dismantling of colonial empires and the rise of independent nation states. The right of state sovereignty is trumpeted by the governments and citizens of both autocracies and democracies, all of whom readily decry foreign intervention into their affairs on nationalist grounds. The liberal international order as a normative paradigm, which is centered on the respect for sovereignty, is ensconced in a slew of international laws and institutions, such as the International Criminal Court (ICC) and most notably in the Charter of the United Nations.[15]

a. *Respect for Borders: "Declared Theaters of War."* Respect for international borders is an important part of a world order based on nation states. They are the markers that separate that which is fully legitimate and that which most assuredly is not. If the soldiers of a given nation are positioned within its boundaries, they are considered a legitimate part of an orderly world composed of nations. If the same soldiers cross a border with hostile intentions, such moves are considered a severe violation of the agreed-upon world order, often leading to massive violent reactions by the invaded nation and the international community.

Seeking to act within the rules of the liberal international order and show respect for sovereignty, the United States provides "concurrent notification" to the Pakistani government when it is conducting drone strikes against suspected terrorists in Pakistan,[16] and its strikes in Yemen have occurred with at least the "tacit consent" of the Yemeni government.[17] Absent such consent, the use of drones (as well as the insertion of Special Forces, as in the killing of Osama bin Laden)[18] is viewed as a violation of national sovereignty and elicits widespread condemnation. On several occasions, these concerns have led to the United States either canceling or greatly limiting its use of drones and Special Forces in pursuing terrorists.

By contrast, terrorists treat borders as a minor inconvenience. They regularly carry multiple passports, falsify documents, and operate in many nations simultaneously. A study published by the Council on Foreign Relations finds that the al Qaeda network has operatives or affiliates in approximately 100 different nations.[19] They attack in one nation but return across the border (say from Afghanistan to Pakistan) for dinner, rest, and medical care, or to train and resupply, with little regard to often poorly marked and poorly enforced borders. That borders are hard to enforce is highlighted by the fact that even the most powerful nation and one with a high level of economic and technological development, the United States, has been unable to stop the flow of controlled substances—or illegal immigrants—into the country. Terrorists exploit this difficulty, taking porous borders as an open invitation to violate the sovereignty of nation states.

It follows that if a nation is prepared to counter terrorism only after terrorists cross a border, or to operate only in those countries that are "declared zones of war" as the liberal international order paradigm is often read to prescribe, that nation is at a great disadvantage.[20]

Even in the face of terrorists' lack of respect for national borders, some scholars still adhere to the existing liberal international order paradigm. For example, Mary Ellen O'Connell, an international law scholar at the University of Notre Dame, argues that "international law has a definition of war [that] refers to places where intense, protracted, organized inter-group fighting occurs. It does not refer to places merely where terrorist suspects are found."[21] She concludes that outside of these narrowly defined theaters of war, the "law of peace" should guide those who seek to counter terrorism. In contrast, legal scholars Jutta Brunnée and Stephen Toope note that the discordance between this paradigm and the legal and military realities of counterterrorism has caused a "confusion of international legal norms that threatens to undermine constraints on the use of force in international society."[22] Vincent-Joël Proulx, a legal scholar and former clerk for the International Court of Justice (ICJ) at The Hague, adds that the present moral paradigm is *already* being subverted, as "well-established legal standards are being distorted or contorted to serve the purposes of the 'war on terror,' or to cater to certain political objectives, while fundamental protections of international law are being eroded in a fashion that the global legal order cannot countenance."[23]

Some scholars argue that it is never permissible, according to international law, to violate another state's sovereignty in order to deal with a nonstate threat. By this interpretation, the UN Charter prohibits "the possibility that states could lawfully resort to forcible measures against terrorists based in another country."[24] Moreover, until the late 1980s, terrorist acts were considered outside of the jurisdiction of the Security Council, meaning that states had little recourse in responding to transnational terrorism within the purview of international law.[25] The Security Council and General Assembly condemned the Israeli attack on the Palestine Liberation Organization headquarters in 1985 and the US strike against Libyan targets in 1986, both responses to terrorist acts (past and expected), as violations of the rules of state sovereignty upheld in the UN Charter.[26] The continued widespread acceptance of the Westphalian paradigm led many who sought the support of the United States and its allies during the 2011 to 2012 civil wars in Libya, Syria and Yemen, even when in dire straits, to oppose the deployment of foreign troops in their lands.

Confronting a global enemy within the constraints of the Westphalian paradigm has posed a significant legal challenge. Philip Bobbitt writes that "there are many good reasons to think that the concept of war is inapplicable to an adversary that has no territory to defend, no capital to seize, no army to surround, no citizenry that can be menaced."[27] He argues that the law, lagging behind the new reality, requires a "fundamental rethinking," and quotes Henry Kissinger as having said, "[While] the US administration has been right to recognize terror as a global problem that is deeply threatening, the US has not been able to implement a response or develop a language to discuss it."[28]

The approach taken by the George W. Bush Administration, and continued by the Obama Administration, interpreted Congress' Authorization for the Use of Military Force (AUMF) in a way that treats the entire globe as a single "theater of war," such that territorial boundaries could not interfere with the conduct of the war on terror.[29] Jack Goldsmith concurs with this interpretation when he points out that "the 2001 [Congressional] authorization contains no geographical limitation."[30] This interpretation was upheld by the Supreme Court in *Hamdan v. Rumsfeld*,[31] which accepts the existing paradigm of international law that restricts the use of military force to defined zones of conflict, but extends that zone across the globe. Such contorted interpretations that strongly challenge widely held normative assumptions are an indication of the great stress that the prevailing paradigm is experiencing. No wonder these interpretations drew significant criticism.[32] Paul Pillar thus observes that "the most important and disturbing aspect" of the current US counterterrorism strategy is "that US military forces are in effect engaging in undeclared hostilities with no effective limits – geographical, temporal, or legal."[33] These legal acrobatics prompted Senator Lindsey Graham to argue that the United

States needs "a whole new legal architecture" for conducting the war on terror, especially with regard to the procedures for dealing with suspected terrorists.[34]

A particularly telling misapplication of the liberal international relations paradigm to counterterrorism comes to light when one considers cyber-attacks. Here, it is very often impossible or at least extremely difficult to establish in which nation the attackers are located, and whether they are the agents of a government or are cyberterrorists—a challenge known as the problem of attribution.[35] As David Post puts it, cyberspace "does not merely weaken the significance of physical location, it destroys it."[36]

b. Misapplied Rules of War. The rules of war—rules fashioned for *nations*— are grounded in basic normative principles (e.g., that all human beings have some basic rights such as freedom from torture, which even the soldiers of the enemy are entitled to) as well as prudential concerns. With respect to the latter, nations seek to ensure that their soldiers will be treated in accordance with the established rules by treating those of the other nation accordingly. Reciprocity is assumed. Terrorists, however, ignore these rules. Some behead, torture, and execute the soldiers they succeed in capturing. They have desecrated their enemies' corpses, for instance in 2006 when the bodies of two US soldiers who had been abducted in Iraq were found mutilated beyond recognition after, according to some witness accounts, being dragged through the streets and beheaded.[37] They have put captured soldiers on display and recorded their execution or desecration on video.[38]

Furthermore, most terrorists are not agents of any state, and hence no government can be held accountable for their behavior. In some cases the government, or some parts of it, support the terrorists indirectly in ways that make it difficult for outsiders to document such links. Also terrorists tend to function in ungoverned or under-governed parts of the world (i.e., where the national government has legal authority but cannot effectively enforce it). These are particularly important areas in that they defy the assumptions built into the rules of war that national governments are in charge of those who fight from within "their" territories.

Moreover, when a nation is punished because it hosts terrorists, often the terrorists are not discouraged but rather benefit. Such countermeasures help the terrorists to recruit more fighters, gain public support, and raise funds, as occurred in the aftermath of US drone attacks on terrorists in Pakistan and Yemen.[39] Transnational terrorism also defies another prominent rule of war: how to deal with captured enemy soldiers. Captured terrorists cannot be handled like conventional prisoners of war because counterterrorism campaigns typically have no clear endpoint or cessation of hostilities enshrined in a treaty between nations but instead gradually peter out, often only after very long periods of time.[40] Terrorists hence must be held until they are no longer a threat, although not indefinitely (more about this below). This disjoint between the laws of war and the practical issues surrounding the capture of terrorist suspects comes to the foreground when one observes the US facilities at Guantanamo Bay. As Ben Wittes argues:

> The administration's critics chronically portray the Guantanamo policy as lawless. This is the wrong vocabulary. The problems that plagued, and still plague, Guantanamo by and large did not stem from defiance of the law. They stemmed, rather, from a mismatch between the assumptions of the laws of war, which the administration tried to adapt for the task at hand, and the realities of that task.[41]

2. Toward a New Paradigm

a. Defining Down Sovereignty.[42] To move toward a new paradigm I suggest one needs to build a case against viewing sovereignty as an absolute value in favor of understanding sovereignty as citizenship. It is a communitarian approach that recognizes that states (like individuals) do not merely command rights, but also have some responsibilities; that they are entitled to self-determination and self-government, but also have some commitment to the common good, such as the protection of the environment, peace, and freedom from terror.

As a starting point for such a case, one had best point out that sovereignty was in fact never absolute. In the mid-twentieth century, Bertrand de Jouvenel argued that the sovereign will, traditionally understood to be of absolute authority, is itself subject to the constraints of morality which are independent of it.[43] Another political philosopher, Jacques Maritain, contended that the concept of sovereignty is intrinsically faulty in that it both separates the will of the state from that of the body politic and creates insurmountable complications for international law.[44]

Stephen Krasner has demonstrated that throughout history the norm of sovereignty has been appealed to by rulers and statesmen when it was advantageous to them in holding onto their positions of power and authority.[45] When it was politically expedient to ignore the Westphalian norm, however Krasner finds that leaders were, by and large, weakly constrained by the norms of sovereignty.

For example, Krasner discusses the many interventions by the Western powers into the internal affairs of the Ottoman Empire during the Empire's decline in the nineteenth century. The 1821 Greek struggle for independence was strictly a domestic affair well within the recognized borders of the Ottoman Empire, yet the revolt eventually drew intervention from Britain, France, and Russia. The 1878 Treaty of Berlin, which marked the end of the conflict, exacted numerous Ottoman concessions for minority and religious rights within the Balkan regions of the Empire. That same treaty imposed the independence of Serbia, Romania, and Montenegro, and settled the status of a semi-autonomous Bulgaria, all previously parts of the Ottoman Empire.

Krasner also highlights the ways Westphalian sovereignty has been sacrificed to both human rights and security concerns. British warships forcibly entered Brazilian ports in 1850 and destroyed those ships suspected of engaging in the slave trade. The pretext was that the Brazilian government was not adequately enforcing its own ban on slavery, which Brazil promised to Britain in an 1826 treaty in exchange for the latter's recognition of Brazilian statehood.

Twentieth century examples of this phenomenon abound. In the first quarter of the century, US marines were deployed to Cuba, Haiti, Honduras, and the Dominican Republic, with each nation being subject to either a US governor or a US-sponsored regime change in the aftermath.

From his survey of the concept's history, Krasner concludes by characterizing the norm of sovereignty as "organized hypocrisy," in that it is universally recognized but at the same time widely violated. Many may well quarrel with Krasner's choice of words but he provides strong evidence that sovereignty was often violated for good and bad causes and thus does not have the inviolate standing those who favor it claim.

The second key to understanding sovereignty as citizenship, is the recognition that no right, whether that of an individual or of a state, is absolute. This famously holds true even for the right many US citizens consider the most absolute of them all, the right of free speech. Beyond the ban on shouting fire in a crowded theater, there are time and place limitations and laws against defamation and incitement. In the same vein, even liberty's most ardent supporters agree that individual freedom ought to be limited by respect for the liberty of others. The same should hold for sovereignty. It cannot be used to harm others, as is the case when a nation's territory serves as a base for terrorists.[46] Much like in the case of humanitarian interventions, where sovereignty is a shield used by dictators to keep out the international community when it seeks to stop a genocide, sovereignty is often used to shield terrorists, or has that effect unintentionally.[47] It should not be automatically heeded in either case.

b. Sovereignty as Conditional. There is growing transnational consensus that sovereignty ought to be conditional. In the wake of World War II, the majority of states drafted and signed the UN's Universal Declaration of Human Rights (1948), thereby codifying the obligation incumbent upon nations to uphold these rights. Although this declaration did not include any enforcement mechanisms, it gave voice to the growing normative consensus that states have an obligation to respect human rights that is simultaneous with, and perhaps even overrides, the right to sovereignty. The Genocide Convention of the same year obliged states to both refrain from and work to punish genocide, an agreement that was then followed by two additional covenants in the mid-1960s, one on civil and political rights and the other on economic and cultural rights.[48]

Yet despite these covenants and conventions, sovereignty remained practically untouchable and sacrosanct. Often when faced with a major humanitarian crisis, even one that clearly rose to the level of genocide,[49] the nations of the world chose to respect sovereignty and not interfere (although there were often additional reasons for such inaction). The international community has responded in an ad hoc and inconsistent way: intervening with the use of force in some of these crises, such as in Bosnia, Kosovo and Libya, but not in many others, such as in Cambodia, Rwanda, Congo, and Sudan.[50]

These humanitarian crises raised further questions about sovereignty. Francis Deng and his associates, in a 1996 book entitled *Sovereignty as Responsibility*,[51] argued that when nations do not conduct their internal affairs in ways that meet internationally recognized standards, other nations have not only the right but the duty to intervene. In effect, such governments forfeit their sovereignty, making it conditional on good conduct. This idea has since been referred to in a sort of shorthand as "the responsibility to protect" (R2P).

This major modification of the Westphalian norm was further developed in a report of the International Commission on Intervention and State Sovereignty (the Evans-Sahnoun Commission, or ICISS), "The Responsibility to Protect," issued in 2001. The commission's report puts sovereignty-as-responsibility at the center of its proposals. It argued:

> "The Charter of the UN is itself an example of an international obligation voluntarily accepted by member states. On the one hand, in granting membership of the UN, the international community welcomes the signatory state as a responsible member of the community of nations. On the other hand, the state itself, in signing the Charter, accepts the responsibilities of membership flowing from that signature. There is no transfer or dilution of state sovereignty. But there is a necessary re-characterization involved: from sovereignty as control to sovereignty as responsibility in both internal functions and external duties."[52]

In 2004, the UN Secretary General's High-Level Panel on Threats, Challenges, and Change (the "High-Level Panel") issued its report, "A More Secure World— Our Shared Responsibility," which lends further support to this reformulation of sovereignty.

While the UN Security Council had previously authorized interventions in states such as Somalia and Haiti, such authorizations have been rare and were made on an ad hoc basis; it had not developed a general case for downgrading national sovereignty. Proponents of the new concept of sovereignty as responsibility sought to legitimate a fundamental shift in the international community's role in the internal affairs of states by establishing an a priori category of conditions under which interventions would be justified. To the extent that this change of the Westphalian norm was accepted, nations that called for armed humanitarian intervention would no longer need to justify them in principle but merely show that a given nation had not lived up to its responsibilities, for instance by allowing a genocide to take place. This much scaled back view of sovereignty was endorsed unanimously by the UN General Assembly.[53] R2P did, however, lose some support when it was employed as a rationale for the 2003 invasion of Iraq and to justify the NATO intervention in Libya during 2011, which shifted from prevention of genocide to regime change.[54]

In 2004, two leading US foreign policy mavens, Lee Feinstein and Anne-Marie Slaughter, sought to further scale back sovereignty by adding a second responsibility that sovereign nations had to discharge, referred to as the "responsibility to prevent." This responsibility amounted to a nation's obligation to refrain from acquiring or developing WMDs. Moreover, it called on the international community to view nations that act irresponsibly in this regard as having lost the privileges of sovereignty and subject to intervention.

In a sense this new responsibility is similar in form to the anti-proliferation norms (or nuclear taboo)[55] behind the Treaty on the Non-Proliferation of Nuclear Weapons (NPT). One hundred and eighty-eight signatory nations agreed that nations that did not have nuclear arms were committed not to acquire them, and those that had them were committed to give them up. However, much like the UN Declaration of Human Rights, the NPT itself has no enforcement mechanism. It leaves it up to the International Atomic Energy Agency (IAEA) to report to the United Nations when nations deviate from the treaty, at which point it will be decided what action, if any, to take. Nor does the NPT explicitly deal with nations that either refused to sign on (such as India, Pakistan, and Israel) or quit (such as North Korea). Thus, Feinstein and Slaughter extend the precept underlying the NPT by defining a universal responsibility to prevent the acquisition of nuclear arms and calling on the nations of the world to enforce it.

c. A Third Responsibility. What is now needed is to take the next step and formulate a third responsibility of sovereign states that takes into account the fading of the old world order of national borders and the evolution of a nascent global regime.[56] We ought to articulate one more condition that states must meet for their sovereignty to be respected, one holding that states forfeit part of their sovereignty if their government (i) uses terrorists as its agents, the way Muammar al-Gaddafi did in Libya and the Pakistani Inter-Services Intelligence has done in Afghanistan; (ii) allows its territory to be used as a safe haven or training grounds, or to raise funds for and by terrorists; (iii) is unable to suppress terrorists on its own, in general or in under-governed or ungovernable regions[57] (as is the case in Pakistan and Yemen).[58] To put it in plain English: if you will not attack us across national borders, we will not hit you back. If a country will prevent terrorists from using its territory to launch attacks in other nations, US drones, Special Forces and other such agents should no longer be used against terrorists within that nation (unless such interventions are requested or consented to by a representative national government).

If a country fails to uphold its Responsibility to Counter Terrorism (R2CT), and if the terrorists from such a nation attack the people of other nations, it should be considered legitimate for counterterrorism measures to be applied in such territories from the outside.[59] Thus, rather than validating the idealized precept of sovereignty and pretending to abide by it while violating it, as for instance the United States does when it couples drone strikes with the provision of "concurrent notice," all sides would benefit from transnational normative dialogues on the reasons sovereignty must be redefined and the ways the new, conditional definitions are going to be worked out. States do have some responsibilities as citizens of an emerging, though nascent, world community. If they fail, they should face corrective measures.

This is the case that ought to be made to change the norms, however gradually, to scale back the emotional outburst that occurs when people hold that their country has been invaded or violated, without acknowledging that they are using their nation to house assassins. This is the brief that must be made and restated by states that employ transnational counterterrorism measures rather than denying that the measures took place, apologizing for them, or claiming that the local government actually consented to them privately—all steps that relegitimate the concept of sovereignty when instead it must be scaled back.

In short, there are numerous compelling and persuasive reasons not to view counterterrorism campaigns as wars and not to treat terrorists as soldiers. The responsibility of nations to prevent terrorists from using their land and assets is one that follows from the recognition that the world of national borders is losing its empirical footing and normative power.

Communitarians stress that individuals do not merely have rights but also responsibilities, to each other and the common good. The balance between rights and responsibilities must be adjusted over time, as either the normative systems tilt in one direction or the other (part of the general tendencies of societies to oversteer and require course correction) or the surrounding reality changes significantly. What is true for individuals also holds for nations. The period of decolonization was a period in which much emphasis was put on the value of independence, self-determination and hence sovereignty for the former colonies. But now, for reasons discussed above, there are strong reasons to treat nations as citizens of the world and expect them to assume more responsibilities for preserving the international order and promoting the common good. Curbing transnational terrorism ranks high on both these lists.

A word of caution. Idealists sometimes—out of a combination of belief in positive thinking, inspiration, rhetoric, and an abiding commitment to progress—are quick to postulate a long list of responsibilities they believe or assume nations should take upon themselves, including fair trade practices, granting of foreign aid, helping to reduce global warming, and cutting pollution. Although the crux of the first part of the sovereignty as citizen paradigm I favor holds that nations have responsibilities in addition to rights, it is important to take into account that as the commitment of nations to the very nascent global community is still rather limited, it cannot impose a great number of missions without potentially undermining itself. Hence we need a sort of moral triage—a focus on those items that are particularly vital. A nation should engage in armed hostilities only if all other means for resolving the conflicts at hand have been exhausted and only if innocent civilians are endangered. That is, only if the conditions of *jus ad bellum* (right to war) of the just war doctrine are met.[60] The use of force in response to the kind of attacks on the US homeland in 2001 meets these criteria.[61] The attack was on innocent civilians rather than on US military forces, and there were no other ways of preventing additional attacks than going after the terrorists before they attacked again.

The three responsibilities of conditional sovereignty considered here—protection, nonproliferation and counterterrorism—all stem from the most fundamental of all human rights, the right to life, which, absent the development of greater world governance, is the only legitimate and prudential ground for justifying intervention in the internal affairs of another nation.[62] In contrast, improving other people's political and economic regimes does not qualify. Regime change and nation-building by outsiders should be limited to nonlethal means rather than the use of force. Because justifying this thesis would require greatly expanding this article, and because I have laid out my case in some detail elsewhere, it is not further discussed here.[63]

One may accept that nations are responsible for the terrorism that comes from their soil but still be concerned about a slippery slope. Would European states be susceptible to intervention when home-grown terrorists have traveled to neighboring states? Would the United States be liable for its citizens who have been recruited on its soil and traveled overseas to train others? Nations should be given a reasonable warning and time to attend to new terrorist threats. If, however, they are unwilling to proceed or clearly unable to do so, they forfeit their right to sovereignty.

As there is considerable, albeit far from universal, agreement that the UN Security Council is the proper authority to determine whether R2P has been violated, it would seem that it would also be the proper authority to rule whether a nation has not met its responsibility to prevent transnational terrorism. However, one can envision situations in which liberal democracies would agree with one another that such a violation has occurred but Russia or China would veto the decision in the UN. In some such cases a coalition of democratic nations might nevertheless feel compelled to proceed (the intervention to prevent atrocities in Kosovo was said to be "legitimate but not legal"). Such decisions are ultimately judged by the informal normative consensus of what is admittedly a vague body—the court of global public opinion.

II. Terrorists as Abusive Citizens: Captured and Not Killed

1. The Misapplication of the Civil Society Paradigm

The other main normative paradigm that is used in strenuous endeavors to conceptualize terrorists and define legitimate ways to deal with them is the civil society paradigm, wherein alleged terrorists are treated like criminals.[64] Members of civil societies are expected to voluntarily obey the law because they hold it to be legitimate and view it as a condition for a safe and peaceful community. The same normative paradigm holds that those who violate the law are to be punished both for the sake of justice and to deter them and others from future transgressions. It is the same normative paradigm that is at least implicitly evoked by those who urge that suspected terrorists are to be treated like other criminals: assumed innocent until proven guilty; tried in civil courts according to similar procedures employed in the trying of other criminals; afforded several layers of appeals if found guilty; and incarcerated and released once they have served their terms.

The following discussion elaborates the reasons this paradigm is misapplied on both normative and prudential grounds when employed to deal with transnational terrorists. I suggest in the following lines that such a paradigm accords terrorists more rights than they are entitled to, and unduly and significantly increases risks to the security of innocent civilians. The discussion focuses first on terrorists who have been captured,[65] then on those that must be confronted in armed conflicts.

It is important to emphasize that this "terrorist class" is not and should not become a code word for Muslims, Arabs, or any other national, ethnic, racial or religious group. One may say that other legal classes, such as minors, can be readily and precisely defined—everyone under eighteen is a member—while the label "suspected terrorist" (referred to henceforth simply as "terrorist") is a conjectural matter. But one could also say the same of those who are labeled legally insane, drug dealers, or undocumented workers, yet they are all treated by the authorities in distinct ways from other categories of suspects. The same should hold for those suspected of having committed terrorism.[66]

a. Prosecution Instead of Prevention. A fatal flaw of the application of the civil society paradigm to terrorists is that it relies on prosecution and incarceration, processes that are typically activated only after a crime has been committed. Dealing with terrorists requires a focus on *preventing* attacks before they occur.[67] This point is particularly evident in light of the concern that terrorists may acquire WMDs. Whatever deterrent benefit their punishment might have,[68] bringing terrorists to trial after they turn part of a major city into a radioactive desert is vastly outweighed by the harm already inflicted.[69] Moreover, there is no reason to hold that those willing to commit suicide during an attack can be deterred by the punishment that follows. Of the nineteen people who attacked the US homeland in 2001, terrorized a nation, and changed the balance between freedom and security for decades, none can be brought to trial. They are viewed by other jihadists not as criminals but as martyrs and heroes, hence even seeking to shame future attackers by affecting the reputation of the previous ones is not practical.

Even terrorists not bent on committing suicide attacks are often "true believers" who are willing to proceed despite whatever punishments the legal system may throw at them.[70] All these kinds of terrorists—those who may use WMDs, suicide bombers, and the "mere" fanatics—cannot be effectively deterred by the criminal justice system.[71] The fact that even the most determined terrorists take into account information when choosing their targets or time of attack does not make them rational actors, as some have argued,[72] at least not actors that can be deterred by risk to their lives or punishment. In short, the civil society law enforcement paradigm assumes that punishment after the fact serves to deter future crimes, and the intent is not to eliminate all crimes but to keep them at a socially acceptable level.[73] Its key premise does not hold when dealing with terrorists because the first priority of counterterrorism is to thwart their designs rather than to try in vain to capture and prosecute terrorists in the aftermath of attacks that often inflict much more damage than most criminal acts.

True, law enforcement can be modified to some extent to adapt to the challenges posed by terrorism.[74] For instance, greater use can be made of statutes already on the books to act against those who engage in conspiracy to commit a crime such as RICO. Note though that when the law is applied in this way, it raises severe concerns by civil libertarians, primarily because it tends to confront suspects *before* they have committed a crime—which is exactly the point when terrorists must be stopped.[75]

Above all, there are critical counterterrorism preventive measures that cannot be accommodated within the standard set of civil laws. These include subjecting a considerable number of people to surveillance and interrogation without any individualized suspicion. The aim in such cases is either to disrupt the *possible* planning of an attack without necessarily charging anybody with anything, or to pry loose some information through what under criminal law would be considered a fishing expedition. For example, in the aftermath of 9/11 the New York Police Department secretly spied on Muslims, monitoring them in their mosques, schools, and places of work, without any suspicion of wrongdoing.[76] The *Associated Press* reporter Matt Apuzzo, who uncovered this operation noted, "While that certainly seems like something you want the police department to do . . . the offshoot of that is that you're collecting personal information on many, many people who have no connection to terrorism, who are completely innocent."[77] However, if one agrees that prevention is crucial, this kind of surveillance is very much needed. What is missing is a systematic justification of when it can be applied, as well as mechanisms to ensure that it will not be excessive and the findings will not be abused.

b. Criminal Procedures: Damaging and Undeserved.[78] The difficulties inherent in attempts to combat terrorism by applying the civil society paradigm become apparent even before a suspect is brought to trial, when terrorists are captured in combat zones or ungoverned regions where it is often difficult to collect evidence in ways such that it will be upheld in criminal courts. One example should suffice to illustrate this point. To obtain DNA samples from people who might have committed a crime, the police draw on samples left behind from when these suspects smoked a cigarette or drank a glass of water. To ensure that DNA evidence will be admissible in a court of law, the rules in New York City that guide the collection of DNA from police station interview rooms include cleaning surfaces with 10-to-1 ratio of water to bleach, replacing all used trash bags beforehand, providing unused ashtrays, offering partially consumable objects (cigarettes, gum) in an unopened "pack" type container, and keeping "unbroken eye contact" with the potential evidence until it is collected.[79] The guidelines are reported to be so onerous that many police officers have given up on using this kind of evidence.

Obviously, following such rules in collecting this or other kinds of evidence, from fingerprints to hair samples, would be much more difficult or impossible in armed conflict zones. It is hard to imagine soldiers fighting terrorists, say in Afghanistan, while carrying fingerprinting equipment and vials for collecting DNA, having to ensure a chain of custody for these materials that would satisfy a civilian court in the United States, and flying witnesses from combat zones to the States to be cross examined during a trial. Eyewitnesses in combat situations can hardly be considered as reliable as those in the streets of a US city, and even the latter are often found lacking.[80]

In addition there is a "mismatch between the manners in which intelligence officers collect information and in which criminal investigators amass evidence [that] can paralyze prosecutors who inherit defendants from intelligence investigations."[81] Unlike law enforcement officials who operate with an eye toward an eventual trial, intelligence officers collect information with the aim of uncovering and preventing attacks. Thus, they may wiretap a phone line without a warrant or continue to cross examine a suspect even if the suspect sought a lawyer because intelligence officers seek *information*, not evidence that will guarantee a conviction in federal court.

Furthermore, counterterrorism campaigns are set back to the extent that they must follow post-Watergate rules that were crafted in response to illegitimate domestic spying by the CIA, FBI and NSA in previous years.[82] The FBI cannot legally monitor religious and political groups even at public meetings—a rule that made sense in the context of the politically motivated domestic spying of the 1960s, but that now seriously restricts the agency in its pursuit of jihadists. In the 1960s the FBI spied on numerous groups that were promoting civil rights, protesting the war in Vietnam, and objecting to nuclear arms—groups that advanced their cause in nonviolent means.

In our own time, mosques have been used in several instances as recruitment grounds for terrorists. At least thirty-five terrorists detained in Guantanamo were radicalized in British mosques, and US intelligence reports describe one such mosque in North London as a "haven for [Islamic] extremists" preparing to fight with al Qaeda in Afghanistan and "an attack planning and propaganda production base."[83] Adam Gadhan, a major English-language spokesman for al Qaeda, was "radicalized in a US mosque" before moving to Pakistan and becoming one of Osama bin Laden's senior operatives.[84]

Although the Patriot Act removed or modified some of these restrictions, Foreign Information Surveillance Act (FISA) rules that prevent inter-agency intelligence sharing coupled with the "minimization rules" created to protect the identities of those US citizens who have had contact with foreigners, have "made it exceedingly difficult for prosecutors to collaborate with intelligence collectors."[85] The "culture of separation" between domestic and international intelligence collection and law enforcement inhibits US agencies in fighting terrorists, while members of al Qaeda respect no such boundaries.[86]

It is difficult to see the normative foundations for rules that direct law enforcement and intelligence officers to follow the same guidelines whether they are searching a US teen suspected of possessing marijuana or a suspected terrorist thought to be constructing a bomb in his apartment.[87] Imagine the FBI receiving an anonymous tip about an apartment where anthrax-laced letters are being prepared. "Could it get a search warrant?" asks Stuart Taylor Jr., "Possibly not: Under current case law, an anonymous tip falls short of the "probable cause" necessary to justify searching an apartment."[88]

Seeking to grant foreign suspected terrorists the same procedural protections accorded to US suspected criminals (some only in recent decades), leads to steps that at best can be described as odd. Taylor continues his scenario by asking what the FBI agent should do if he catches the terrorist placing the anthrax-laced envelope in the mailbox. The answer under current case law is: "read him his *Miranda* rights, and if he asks for a lawyer, ask him no questions."[89] This hypothetical is not as far-fetched as it may seem. In 2009, it was reported that under the Obama administration's Global Justice Initiative, FBI agents in Afghanistan were instructed to read Miranda rights "to enemy combatants caught trying to kill American soldiers."[90] Robert Mueller, the director of the FBI, parried criticism of this approach by effectively confirming it. He stated that there were no new blanket instructions and that "for years, FBI agents have been trained to analyze whether *Miranda* is appropriate to use on a case-by-case basis."[91]

Following the civil society paradigm and hence allowing terror suspects to "lawyer up," imposes a severe opportunity cost: information that can no longer be acquired through questioning. One may suggest that a terrorist could refuse to talk even if he were not granted this privilege. However, adhering to the civil society paradigm requires that if a terrorist asks for legal counsel, the authorities will no longer talk to him, offer deals, give incentives, or let alone apply pressure.

Given that terrorists often act in groups, the notion of being unable to legally address a captured terrorist until an attorney is found and that attorney consents to questioning tilts too far from protecting the common good. On September 11, 2001 the FBI had in custody Zacarias Moussaoui, the alleged "20th hijacker," but because he requested a lawyer, agents "were prevented from even attempting to question [him] on the day of the attacks when, in theory, he could have possessed further information about other co-conspirators."[92] There is already a "public safety" exception to procedural rights that applies to emergency situations. The importance of prevention and the size of the threat argue that this should be the rule, not the exception, for dealing with transnational terrorists.[93]

In addition, the application of criminal procedures such as open arrest records, charging suspects within forty-eight hours under most circumstances, and the guarantee of a speedy trial might undermine the fight against terrorism. Counterterrorism requires time to capture other members of a cell before they realize that one of their members has been apprehended, in order to decipher their records and prevent other attacks that might be underway. Also, security demands that authorities must not reveal their means and methods, and hence terrorists often cannot be allowed to face their accusers.[94]

The nature of the evidence likely to be presented in a terrorist trial is problematic. Much of it is classified and highly sensitive, which puts the government in the position of having to choose between jeopardizing national security in order to gain a conviction or letting terrorists off easy, if not completely, in order to protect vital sources and methods. When Mounir el-Motassadeq, a member of the Hamburg cell which included four 9/11 hijackers, was brought to trial in Germany for abetting mass murder, a judge ordered his immediate release following a successful appeal. His release hinged on the United States' refusal to allow the court to question three detained al Qaeda operatives because of security reasons. The judge stated that el-Motassadeq "must have known that Atta and the others were planning attacks using planes in the US" but without being able to verify the statements made by the prisoners there was not "sufficient proof in either direction."[95]

Furthermore, even evidence which is not classified, such as hearsay or testimony obtained through interrogations (regular ones, not "enhanced"), often does not meet the high standards of civilian courts and cannot be introduced even if it is highly relevant and damaging to the terrorists.

Finally, no matter how strong the case may be against a suspected terrorist, the trial may be compromised or fail due to a technicality,[96] thereby presenting the government with only bad choices: set free someone strongly suspected of plotting mass murder or having committed a terrorist act, or undermine the legitimacy of the US legal system by ignoring the outcome of the trial and continuing to detain the suspect despite their acquittal. Of the 9/11 conspirators, only one, Zacarias Moussaoui, has been tried in federal court. His life-sentence came only after five years of litigation, millions of dollars, and a lucky break for the prosecution. Moussaoui "repeatedly compromised any potential defense by admitting to key elements of the charges against him"[97] in dramatic courtroom speeches and multiple contradictory confessions. A conviction was only obtained after the judge forced him to accept counsel, and he eased the government's job by pleading guilty. In other cases the government may not be so lucky.

In November 2012 a judge in a civil court sentenced three terrorists to five years (or, for one of them, a little under four years) in prison rather than the fifteen years sought by prosecutors because she found that their motivation was financial rather than ideological.[98] In September 2012 a judge threw out evidence that a murderer killed a six-year-old boy because this particular judge held that the evidence that was collected from cell phones violated the defendant's privacy.[99] One may hence assume that judges could also throw out evidence against a terrorist if obtained in a manner whose legality is not fully established. Indeed, the federal appeals court threw out Salim Hamdan's conviction for providing material support for terrorism because he did so before the Military Commissions Act of 2006 was enacted.[100]

The many challenges posed by trial procedures in civilian courts have often led the government to avoid these courts altogether by detaining terrorists without charge. Ghassan Abdullah al Sharbi, accused of conspiring with al Qaeda "to commit terrorism, attack civilians, and murder and destroy property,"[101] openly proclaimed, "I fought the United States, I'm going to make it short and easy for you guys: I'm proud of what I did." Yet he remains detained in Guantanamo without a trial.[102] Two Administrative Review Boards have found Bashir Nasir Al-Marwalah, a professed Arab fighter who "doesn't know" if he is a member of al Qaeda, to be too dangerous to release, yet he has not been designated for a military tribunal, much less a civilian trial.[103] These two examples are not unique: the 2010 Guantanamo Review Task Force found forty-eight detainees "too dangerous to transfer but not feasible for prosecution."[104]

Philip Bobbitt effectively summarizes the intractable position of the government: because the prosecution of terrorists is:

> unlikely to succeed with the current rules of trial practice and evidence, the US administration has taken the position that they can simply be held indefinitely, much like other prisoners of war who await the end of the conflict in which they participated. Yet terrorists can also be interrogated like a spy or partisan or tried like a criminal before a military tribunal (which of course no ordinary criminal could be). This simply amounts to a refusal to follow existing law or create new law that is more responsive to our new situation.[105]

Plea bargaining, the much-utilized alternative to a full trial or indefinite detention, carries its own costs. It is estimated that over 80 percent of the guilty terrorist convictions achieved in civilian courts since 2001 have been the result of plea bargains.[106] Although guaranteeing a guilty verdict, such deals result in lighter sentences. For example, Ali Saleh Kahlah al-Marri, a Qatari citizen, admitted to attending terrorist training camps, meeting with Khalid Sheikh Mohammed, and offering his services to al Qaeda after he entered the United States. Following a plea agreement, which "substantially reduced the possible prison sentence against him," he was sentenced to eight years in prison and is projected to be released in 2015.[107]

A considerable number of terrorists have been successfully tried in civilian courts.[108] In 1994, four of the conspirators of the first World Trade Center bombing were brought to trial in federal court and received life sentences. And in the ten years after 9/11 the civil courts resolved 204 cases where the principal charge concerned acts of terrorism, with a conviction rate close to 87 percent. However, when one looks more closely one finds that US citizens made up the largest contingent of defendants (42 percent) and the most common terrorist affiliation of the others was the Revolutionary Armed Forces of Colombia (FARC). Transnational terrorists made up just 11 percent of the defendants. Furthermore, many of the sentences meted out were relatively light: over 40 percent were under four years in length and an additional 30 percent were between five and ten years. These sentences reflect that the majority of the cases under consideration (66 percent) were "won" by plea bargaining, in which lesser charges and reduced sentences were offered in exchange for a guaranteed conviction.[109] Moreover, the most common convictions by a wide margin are for charges of conspiracy, which raise concern among civil libertarians. Even if such a limited success in civilian court seems acceptable, one ought to keep in mind that many of these cases were handpicked by the government for that forum. In short, it is true that some transnational terrorists can be tried in civil courts, but they are likely to receive relatively light sentences and be released after serving a few years, even if they still pose a major danger to the nation's security.

Ultimately, the procedural barriers that hinder civilian prosecution of terrorists might be overcome, and the excessive burden they place on the military, intelligence, and legal authorities might be tolerated, if this were the only morally defensible course. However, the opposite seems to be the case. Not only are these burdens minimized by treating terrorists as a separate class of dangerous persons, but there is in fact a fundamental normative justification for doing so. As former Attorney General William Barr put it: "Our conventional criminal justice system is designed to apply to people within our political community, but it doesn't make sense to extend those rights to foreign enemies who are trying to slaughter us. These people are just like the Nazi saboteurs."[110] On what ground can terrorists, who are willing to kill and die to undermine the values that undergird the US system of justice, claim to enjoy the very rights and privileges they seek to destroy?[111]

c. Distinct Rights for a Distinct Class. Terrorists abuse and exploit their status as civilians by violating what is arguably the most consequential and essential rule of armed conflicts: the rule of distinction. Historically it has been a standard applied to militaries whereby they are expected to go to great lengths to avoid killing civilians. I suggest that the time has come to significantly broaden the term to refer not only to the obligation of combatants to delineate between hostile combatants and civilians when selecting targets, but also the duty of civilian combatants to clearly and visibly demarcate *themselves* from the rest of the civilian population. Such usage seems to be largely in accordance with the 1977 Geneva Convention Article 48 Additional Protocol I, which states that: "[T]he Parties to the conflict shall at all times distinguish between the civilian population and combatants."[112] It also fits with the purpose of this rule of armed conflict, which is to oblige fighting forces not to harm the civilian population, a rule too often ignored during WWII. Though "fighting forces" connotes state-sponsored militaries, this enhanced rule of distinction applies with equal, if not greater, importance to terrorists.

Terrorists exploit this normative principle by presenting themselves as civilians, and showing their true colors only when they are ready to strike. They then switch back to their civilian status when it suits their purposes, demanding to be shielded by the law. They mix in with the civilian population, one moment acting like shepherds and farmers, the next attacking, and soon after returning to civilian pursuits. These very widespread and deliberate violations of my extended interpretation of the rule of distinction leave the counterterrorism forces with basically two choices: cause considerable collateral damage and face the wrath of the civilian population, or allow terrorism to gain strong advantages.[113] Moreover, part of the terrorists' strategy is drawing from counterterrorism forces a response that harms innocent civilians, as such incidents serve as more fodder for terrorist propaganda. That is, the terrorists' violations of the distinction rule are so consequential that this alone suffices to hold that it is unreasonable to apply the same rules to them that armies apply to one another—or to grant all the rights to them that civilians otherwise command when charged with a crime. In effect they should be charged with a new major ethical and legal violation: abuse of citizen status. The consequences of this charge, if documented, should entail diminished rights. The analogue is someone who benefits from pretending to be a police officer or physician. Such posturing is morally offensive and legally punishable in itself, aside from whatever specific harm the person has wreaked.

Because this point is of critical importance, a hypothetical might help in considering this issue. Assume a US military unit is coming under mortar fire. The US forces identify a person with field glasses on a rooftop overlooking the area. He has a walkie-talkie. As more and more rounds of shells are coming in, it becomes apparent that someone is providing feedback to the attackers, as their aim is improving. If this person was wearing a soldier's uniform, he would not be spared. Should he be spared merely because he donned civilian clothing as his camouflage?

The Red Cross states that "at the heart of IHL [International Humanitarian Law] lies the principle of distinction between the armed forces, who conduct the hostilities on behalf of the parties to an armed conflict, and civilians, who are presumed not to directly participate in hostilities and must be protected."[114] However, in order to protect civilians it is not enough to expect soldiers to separate themselves from civilians, but for *all* who take up arms to separate themselves from peaceful civilians. If they do not, if they abuse their civilian status—like someone who carries a white flag and claims to surrender but opens fire when he draws closer—they ought to be understood as having forfeited some of their rights as fighters or as civilians.

2. Toward a New Paradigm

Despite the inadequacy of the civil society paradigm—in terms of the difficulties both in preventing terrorist activities and successfully bringing to justice many of those who carry out attacks—many insist that suspected terrorists be tried in civilian courts like any ordinary criminal; they oppose treating suspected terrorists as a distinct class of people who have their own set of rights and are subject to distinct procedures and authorities.[115] The very notion that a terrorist—one who pretends to be a civilian and attacks US soldiers in violation of rules of war and of armed conflicts—is entitled to all the legal privileges of a law abiding US citizen—many more than a prisoner of war—seems indefensible on the face of it. There are already many other classes of people we treat differently for a large variety of reasons. Mental patients, incompetent people (those with a very low IQ), noncitizens, soldiers, material witnesses, minors, veterans, and first-time offenders are subject to specialized procedural and administrative processes. The threshold for conviction also varies. For some, the law requires that guilt be established beyond a reasonable doubt while for others merely by the preponderance of specific evidence. Finally, depending on the type of offense, distinct systems are used: FISA, military commissions, ICE, drug courts, family courts, grand juries, and juvenile courts. Given these other categories, it would not be unreasonable to add a legal authority that specializes in dealing with terrorists.[116]

A particularly telling case is that of convicted felons. The extent to which their rights are limited varies from state to state, but most states set a period of time during which they withhold full rights from those who have committed a serious crime. These are US citizens who served the jail sentence meted out by the court but nevertheless cannot vote, cannot practice law, and—depending on their crime and state—cannot leave the jurisdiction of the court. They must report regularly to a probation officer and can be sent back to jail for extended periods of time, with minimal proceedings.[117] There is little reason to treat terrorists as entitled to more rights than convicted felons. On the contrary.

a. National Security Board. Terrorists should indisputably be guaranteed some basic rights. They should be captured rather than killed, if this can be achieved without endangering US troops or innocent civilians. They should not be tortured or turned over to other states that are likely to kill or torture them. As suggested earlier, rather than holding them indefinitely, a needless violation of habeas corpus, they should be subject to a defined period of administrative detention,[118] which could be extended through legally established channels if necessary. While due process requires the opportunity to be heard in front of a neutral decision maker, the US Supreme Court ruled that due process of law does not necessitate judicial process in all circumstances. Rather, the *Mathews* balancing test should be applied to determine whether a trial or hearing is appropriate in each situation.[119]

The trial, hearing, or other legal process should fall under the jurisdiction of a new body, a national security board. Several scholars favor a separate judicial authority for dealing with terrorists and propose a congressionally-created national security court.[120] Because the term "court" is strongly associated with law enforcement within the civil society paradigm, "security board" may be preferable, as it more clearly signals a break from this paradigm. The name, however, matters little; setting up a distinct authority with its own rules and procedures is at the heart of the matter.

One may ask why the United States should not simply use civilian courts with modified procedures and different standards of evidence. Indeed, this approach has been suggested by several critics of the military commission system.[121] Given the extent of changes necessary to convert a civilian court into one that could deal with suspected terrorists, it seems misleading to refer to the modified authority as a civilian court.

Whatever the name, the first step is to determine who would be subject to this new body. Benjamin Wittes includes ununiformed overseas fighters who engaged in or knowingly supported hostilities against the United States, while excluding those captured in the United States or a theater of war where the Geneva Convention applies.[122] This class could be extended to include all foreign transnational terrorists, as the new paradigm does not differentiate between "theaters of war" and other areas, and instead covers whatever areas terrorists spring from.[123] The new paradigm holds that given that transnational terrorists do not respect international borders, neither can those who cope with them. Since a transnational terrorist's state of origin has failed its responsibility to stop acts of transnational terrorism and control their perpetrators, those entrusted with maintaining international order and protecting their citizens are entitled to take the necessary steps to stop this kind of terrorism.

315

Next is the issue of the proper length of detention. Paul Rosenzweig and James Carafano point out that while a comprehensive legal process for terrorist suspects is important, this system cannot be identical to civil courts and must retain a procedure for cases in which preventative detention may be necessary.[124] In Great Britain, the 2006 Terrorism Act permitted a twenty-eight day period of pre-charge detention for those reasonably suspected to be terrorists. The law was allowed to expire in 2010, and the period was subsequently shortened to fourteen days.[125] The specific numbers are not important as long as there is an initial period allowing for the disruption of possible additional attacks, the debriefing of the terrorist, and the deciphering of encrypted documents. In the absence of a clearly defined regime of pre-trial detention and robust status review, the 2012 National Defense Authorization Act, which draws on the war paradigm, enables the President to detain terror suspects in military custody without trial for the duration of the current military conflict. In the war on terror, this may mean indefinitely—an allowance that is currently being challenged in US court, in *Hedges v. Obama*, 12-3176 (2d Cir. 2012). Under the new national review system here championed, all detainees would be granted a meaningful chance to contest their detention and would be afforded an annual review to evaluate whether or not they pose a threat to the United States. If not, they could be released, even if counterterrorism campaigns are still underway.

The national security board would be composed of federal judges with life tenure and expertise in applying rules that protect classified information and national security concerns.[126] Detainees would have the right to fair counsel and to appeal decisions; appeals would then be reviewed by a second set of select federal judges. Unlike, however, a civilian court, detainees would not receive the full array of criminal protections accorded to US citizens. They would not be allowed to face all their accusers, if these included, say, CIA agents working covertly. As Wittes suggests, the standards for admissible evidence would be lower than those of domestic criminal cases; the court would bar the admission of evidence gleaned from torture, but, aside from that, "probative material—even hearsay or physical evidence whose chain of custody or handling would not be adequate in a criminal trial—ought to be fair game."[127]

Given that terrorists cannot gain full access to all the evidence against them without creating very large security risks, I favor allowing terrorists to choose among lawyers who have security clearance.[128] This also greatly curtails the possibility that the lawyers will serve as go-betweens for terrorists and their compatriots, as was the case with lawyer Lynne Stewart.[129]

While many related issues remain to be worked out, the main argument stands: Suspected terrorists are a distinct class of people, and the institutions designed to deal with those that are captured should be tailored to the special challenges they pose, while also protecting those rights to which they are entitled, including freedom from torture and violations of habeas corpus.

III. Norms and Rules for Armed Conflicts with Terrorists

The discussion so far has focused on ways to deal with those terrorists that have been captured. The discussion now turns to those who are confronted in armed conflict and cannot be captured without undue risks to the counterterrorism forces. Although both kinds of terrorists act as abusive civilians, those engaged in armed conflict require—at least on the face of it—a distinct response. The same holds for civilians who support the terrorists engaged in combat.

1. The Main Onus of Responsibility for Collateral Damage

A major challenge faced by counterterrorism forces is that they must seek to minimize killing and harming innocent civilians for both normative and prudential reasons. It is an elementary wrong to kill innocent people, in addition to being a violation of international norms, laws, and treaties. To reiterate, this concern often greatly constrains counterterrorism forces and, in my judgment, is a major reason for their poor performance in most such campaigns including in Iraq and most obviously in Afghanistan.[130]

When counterterrorism forces cause collateral damage, these tragic accidents often lead to apologies and sometimes compensation by the involved militaries. In this way the counterterrorism forces validate and reinforce the perception that they were fighting in violation of the rules of war and are callous about human lives. My argument is not that apologies are a sign of weakness. Indeed, they are often both morally appropriate and helpful. In this case, however, they serve to undergird a way of thinking that is misapplied. The same situations that have elicited apologies should be used to point out that, although collateral damage can never be completely avoided, it would be greatly reduced if terrorists distinguished themselves from the civilian population.

We need to change the terminology that has normative implications. Currently, practically all reports—whether official or in the media—about collateral damage refer to "civilians" and "fighters" (or militants), which reinforces the notion that all civilians are, on the face of it, innocent and thus constitute illegitimate targets. Drawing an additional distinction between two kinds of civilians—between peaceful (or innocent) and abusive civilians—moves the terminology in the direction of more closely reflecting the nature of transnational terrorism.

Furthermore, one should note that current terminology implies that one can readily distinguish peaceful from abusive civilians, while, in fact, the opposite is true. In large parts of the areas involved, many men carry arms and wear the same clothing, headgear, and beards, whether they are herding sheep, farming, or fighting. Moreover, many shift back and forth between their civilian pursuits and combat roles. Hence, flat statements such as X civilians and Y militants were killed are often based on the word of locals or reports by foreign media, which are often wildly off the mark.[131] Post hoc reports show how similar "civilians" and "fighters" were found to be and that, even after the fact, under noncombat conditions and with no time pressures, it is difficult to tell who falls in what category because of the illegitimate ways in which terrorists fight.

2. No Moral Equivalency and Just War Principles

There are those who argue that terrorists' abuse of civilian status is the only way they can fight the United States and its allies, with their powerful war machinery—the only way terrorists can "even the playing field." However, armed conflicts are not tennis matches.

There is no rationale in either moral philosophy or in law for allowing the weaker party to violate fundamental moral precepts, such as the principle of distinction in armed conflict, in order for it to gain an advantage. Most important, terrorists by definition are out to kill, maim, and drive fear into masses of innocent people. They often deliberately target peaceful civilians, including at weddings, funerals, and during prayer. They hardly have the same moral standing as those who are out to prevent such attacks. Terrorists hence should not be favored by the laws of armed conflicts and by the rules of engagement. Provided counterterrorism forces have no goals other than stopping terrorism and they heed the stipulations of just war doctrine, these forces should not be unduly constrained in their operations. This means the use of lethal force in counterterrorism operations must be a measure of last resort undertaken with just cause—self-defense or the protection of innocent lives.[132]

Some of the writings on the subject at hand read as if the authors and officials assume—or at least want to convince the public—that one can conduct a neat, clean war, with "surgical" strikes.[133] They imply that if only the counterterrorism forces would heed the proper rules, restrain themselves, or use some peculiar modes of warfare, these forces could take out the "bad guys" and leave everyone else unharmed. As someone who has actually fought for more than two years, I have no doubt that armed conflicts inevitably cause death and injury to numerous people who should be spared, that armed conflicts are vile and violent, and that however well-intentioned the conflict, the "fog of war" leads to tragic results. Note that even the most disciplined and best-equipped forces have not found a way to avoid the tragic loss of life from "friendly fire." These findings demonstrate that counterterrorism forces cannot completely avoid collateral damage when they set out to curb terrorism.

3. Review and Oversight

Critics argue the United States engages in "extrajudicial" killing.[134] This misapplication of the civil society paradigm implies that the terrorists should not to be targeted until they have been brought before a judge and convicted in a legitimate court of law.[135] Glenn Greenwald characterizes the wide use of drones as a policy "that empowers the President to secretly target people, including American citizens, for instant, due-process-free death . . . beyond the rule of law."[136] Critics also say that the Obama administration's so-called "kill list" lacks proper review procedures, public accountability, and congressional oversight.[137]

This position is reflected in and draws on the International Covenant on Civil and Political Rights, which requires that "sentence of death . . . can only be carried out pursuant to a final judgment rendered by a competent court."[138] Harold Koh, while serving as the State Department's top lawyer during Obama's first term, drew a distinction between "lawful extrajudicial killing" and "unlawful extrajudicial killing," a piece of legal sophistry given that by definition, extrajudicial means "done in contravention of due process of law."[139] Nevertheless, the point itself is actually well taken. By Koh's standards, a strike is deemed "lawful" if a careful study determines the target to be a combatant or planning an attack, and "unlawful" in the absence of such a review. What is missing is an open and full acknowledgement that the review need not take place in a court of law and follow the same procedures as such a court.[140]

At present, considerable review is involved, but it follows different procedures and is carried out outside of courts. When intelligence officials nominate a target, those charged with making the decision are given a file detailing information about the proposed target. To ensure that the intelligence is reliable, US military guidelines require that it must originate from two separate sources.[141]

In addition, officials consider the probability that innocent civilians will be harmed. Although there are circumstances in which civilian casualties cannot be avoided, the administration will "only authorize a strike if we have a high degree of confidence that innocent civilians will not be injured or killed, except in the rarest of circumstances."[142] Involved in this process are "departments and agencies across our national security team," and Congress is notified whenever possible for accountability purposes; never is an isolated group unilaterally responsible for deciding targeted individuals' fates.[143]

To minimize collateral damage, the United States has formulated a collateral damage methodology (CDM), which includes a five-step process to secure a "positive ID" of the targets, a strategy to minimize the loss of life among innocent civilians, and an estimate of damage to property and the environment.[144] It contains a very considerable list of "no strike entities," which include "medical, educational, diplomatic, cultural, religious, and historical sites, or other objects that do not by their nature, location, purpose, or use, effectively contribute to the enemy's war-fighting or war-sustaining capability."[145] The list, which runs to five single-spaced pages, includes medical clinics, sewage facilities, veterinary clinics, prisons, cemeteries, libraries, power stations, agricultural storage, public transit systems, parks, theaters, gas stations, athletic fields, tobacco storage, restaurants, inns, and race tracks, among others.[146]

This restraint is exercised despite the fact that evidence shows that terrorists are aware of these self-imposed limitations. Terrorists use them to their
advantage by both stationing themselves and storing supplies and weapons
in mosques, schools, and private homes. Bing West relays the words of a US
serviceman, who laments the fact that the "Taliban fight from compounds
where there are women and children . . . [so] we can't push the Talibs out by
mortar fire without being blamed for civilian casualties."[147] West notes that
the Taliban often fired at US soldiers from private homes, mosques, buildings
marked by the Red Crescent, and other locales where civilians were likely to
be. In these circumstances, they were free to engage with US ground troops
with minimal risk of attracting US aerial and/or artillery fire, because the US
rules of engagement (ROEs) mandate that "commanders not employ indirect
fires unless they verified that no civilians were endangered—which was impossible to do in many cases."[148]

In several instances, terrorists escaped while soldiers were waiting
for authorization to use force. Two independent sources are required to
confirm a vehicle as a viable target, and that vehicle must be continuously
monitored while awaiting the aerial strike. West relates an account of
Captain Raymond Kaplan, an intelligence officer focused on destroying
the Taliban leadership:

> "One morning, [Kaplan] saw Abdul Rahman[149] climbing into a white
> truck at Pop Rock. He called for an attack by a Predator UAV with
> a Hellfire missile that was on station nearby. The request had to go
> through three layers of bureaucracy. When it was approved twenty-
> five minutes later, Kaplan admitted that he had lost the truck under
> foliage at one point for about ten minutes. Higher [command] decided
> not to fire the missiles."[150]

According to Kaplan, in the average successful operation, only 30 percent of
his efforts were devoted to detective work—the remaining 70 percent focused
on convincing his superiors to permit the use of force.[151] This problem has
endured since the late 1990's, when on more than one occasion CIA officials
sought to gain in a timely manner President Clinton's authorization to proceed
with remote strikes against Osama bin Laden.[152] In short, it is not reasonable
to argue that orders to kill terrorists were not subject to close review.

In addition, there is congressional oversight. Senator Feinstein, who was
critical of the drone program's lack of transparency,[153] stated in March 2012
that the "Senate Intelligence Committee is kept fully informed of counterterrorism operations and keeps close watch to make sure they are effective,
responsible and in keeping with US and international law."[154] Staffers from the
intelligence committees watch footage of the previous month's drone strikes
and review the intelligence used to justify the killings. They also learn about

the number of civilian casualties. According to Feinstein, the staffers "question every aspect of the program including legality, effectiveness, precision, foreign policy implications and the care taken to minimize noncombatant casualties."[155]

In short, one may argue whether the reviews are excessive or could be made more elaborate; one cannot deny, however, that a rather extensive set of reviews is already in place. It is a long way from what has been depicted by critics as a situation worse than the Wild West.[156]

What is missing with regard to the targeted killing program is a shift in the normative paradigm that lays out the moral and legal grounds that justify them without trying to squeeze these justifications into frameworks that were formed for dealing with soldiers or criminals rather than transitional terrorists.[157]

In Conclusion

Critics argue that we increasingly behave like terrorists, especially when we employ drones and Special Forces, and that we are giving up our principles in order to enhance our security. They quote Benjamin Franklin as stating, "Those who would give up essential Liberty, to purchase a little temporary Safety, deserve neither Liberty nor Safety."[158]

Actually, we are different from the terrorists in three major ways: US and allied forces do not set out deliberately to kill innocent civilians, in sharp contrast to the terrorists who make such killing a cornerstone of their strategy. We do not try to terrorize a population to gain their cooperation in fighting terrorists, killing their elected officials and bombing their schools. On the contrary, we are trying to win their hearts and minds by helping them to run free and fair elections and by building schools.

Lastly, we grant suspected terrorists a tight review before their killing is authorized, the kind of review they never grant their victims. Those who are out to counter terrorism are subject to several layers of accountability, oversight, and public scrutiny via the media. One may argue that it should be even tighter, or argue, as I do, that when it comes to the rules of engagement that restrictions are too tight; one cannot, however, seriously claim that our killing of terrorists is wanton and promiscuous.

In the longer run, to the extent that the needed new normative paradigm evolves, based on transnational moral dialogues, we might be ready to form a new Geneva Declaration that will state the Responsibility to Counter Terrorism (R2CT) of nations; warn terrorists to abide by the rules of distinction and articulate their responsibility for the collateral damage that occurs when they ignore this rule; and spell out the rights they are entitled to and those that they forfeit by abusing their civilian status.[159] Such a declaration would serve to put terrorists on notice and guide those who are charged with protecting the rest of us.

Notes

1. Noah Feldman writes:

   "The distinction between crime and war, embodied in international and domestic legal regimes, institutional-administrative divisions, and . . . legislation . . . requires serious rethinking in the light of the terrorist attacks of September 11, 2001. Whether we choose the framework of war, the framework of criminal pursuit and prosecution, or, as is more likely, some complicated combination of the two will have major ramifications in the spheres of law, politics, and policy."

   Noah Feldman, "Choices of Law, Choices of War," *Harvard Journal of Law and Public Policy* 25 (2002): 457, 457.

2. Amitai Etzioni, *The New Golden Rule: Community and Morality in a Democratic Society* (New York: Basic Books, 1996), 102–14, 227–31.

3. Shaun Gregory, "The Terrorist Threat to Pakistan's Nuclear Weapons," *CTC Sentinel* (2009), 2, 7.

   Also: Dean Nelson and Tom Hussain, "Militants Attack Pakistan Nuclear Air Base," *Telegraph* (August 16, 2012), http://www.telegraph.co.uk/news/worldnews/asia/pakistan/9479041/Militants-attack-Pakistan-nuclear-air-base.html.

   Also: Kapil Komireddi, "Take Pakistan's Nukes, Please," *Foreign Policy* (May 24, 2011), http://www.foreignpolicy.com/articles/2011/05/24/take_pakistans_nukes_please.

4. 18 U.S.C. § 2331(1) (2006). For other definitions and their discussion see Bruce Hoffman, who defines terrorism briefly as "the deliberate creation and exploitation of fear through violence or the threat of violence in the pursuit of political change," Bruce Hoffman, *Inside Terrorism* (Columbia University Press 1998), 43. Tamar Meisels defines terrorism as "the intentional random murder of defenseless non-combatants, with the intent of instilling fear of mortal danger amidst a civilian population as a strategy designed to advance political ends," Tamar Meisels, "The Trouble with Terror: The Apologetics of Terrorism—a Refutation," *Terrorism and Political Violence* 18, no. 3 (2006): 465–483, 480. Boaz Ganor defines it more simply as "the deliberate use of violence aimed against civilians in order to achieve political ends," Boaz Ganor, "The Relationship Between International and Localized Terrorism," *Jerusalem Center for Public Affairs* 4, no. 26 (June 28, 2005), http://www.jcpa.org/brief/brief004-26.htm.

5. US citizens who operate as terrorists abroad require a separate discussion that is not taken up here. It should be noted though that from a communitarian viewpoint they add insult to injury by raising arms against their own community, unlike other terrorists, and hence—as the constitution indicates—may be entitled to fewer rather than additional rights. In February 2013, NBC obtained a confidential Justice Department memo that justifies the US government's killing of US citizens who are believed to be "senior operational leaders" of al Qaida or "an associated force." The white paper lays out a three-part test for lawful targeting of US citizens: the suspect must be an "imminent threat," capture must be "infeasible," and the operation must be conducted in line with "law of war principles,"

Michael Isikoff, "Justice Department Memo Reveals Legal Case for Drone Strikes on Americans," *NBC News* (February 4, 2013), http://openchannel. nbcnews.com/_news/2013/02/04/16843014-exclusive-justice-department-memo-reveals-legal-case-for-drone-strikes-on-americans?lite.

6.   The implied issue, whether these values are "good" by some other, independent standard, is exceedingly complex because it raises questions about cultural relativism and ontological principles. My treatment of this subject is laid out in Amitai Etzioni, "On Communitarian and Global Sources of Legitimacy," *The Review of Politics* 73, no. 1 (2011):105–122, 117. For my position in a broader context, see also Don Browning et al., *Universalism vs. Relativism: Making Moral Judgments in a Changing, Pluralistic, and Threatening World* (Lanham, MD: Rowman & Littlefield, 2006).

7.   Charles C. Moskos, Jr., "Racial Integration in the Armed Forces," *American Journal of Sociology* 72, no.2 (September 1966): 132–148, 145–46.

8.   Kathleen E. Hull, "The Cultural Power of Law and the Cultural Enactment of Legality: The Case of Same-Sex Marriage," *Law & Social Inquiry* 28 (2003): 629, 653.

       Also: Jeffrey R. Lax and Justin H. Phillips, "Gay Rights in the States: Public Opinion and Policy Responsiveness," *American Political Science Review* 103 (2009): 367, 382.

9.   For more discussion, see Benjamin Wittes and Ritika Singh, "Two Parties, One Policy: Washington's New Consensus on Terrorism," *Commonweal* (September 14, 2012), http://www.commonwealmagazine.org/two-parties-one-policy.

10.   The Obama administration moved in this direction after he was re-elected, aiming to prepare a framework that would outlast the current administration, sometimes referred to by the bureaucratic term of "disposition matrix," Counterterrorism adviser John O. Brennan led the effort to craft a "playbook"—expected to be submitted for approval by the president in early 2013—that will institutionalize and "impose more consistent and rigorous controls" on targeted-killing operations. Officials say it includes guidelines for adding names to the "kill list," targeting US citizens abroad, and approving drone strikes outside of declared theaters of war. *See* Greg Miller, "Plan for Hunting Terrorists Signals U.S. Intends to Keep Adding Names to Kill Lists," *The Washington Post* (October 23, 2012), http://www.washingtonpost.com/world/ national-security/ plan-for-hunting-terrorists-signals-us-intends-to-keep-adding-names-to-kill-lists/2012/10/23/4789b2ae-18b3-11e2-a55c-39408fbe6a4b_story.html.

       Also: Greg Miller, Ellen Nakashima, and Karen DeYoung, "CIA Drone Strikes Will Get Pass in Counterterrorism 'Playbook,' Officials Say," *The Washington Post* (January 19, 2013), http://www.washingtonpost.com/world/national-security/cia-drone-strikes-will-get-pass-in-counterterrorism-playbook-officials-say/2013/01/19/ca169a20-618d-11e2-9940-6fc488f3fecd_story.html.

11.   Thomas S. Kuhn, *The Structure of Scientific Revolutions* (Chicago: University of Chicago Press, 1996).

12.   Amitai Etzioni, *My Brother's Keeper: A Memoir and a Message* (Lanham, MD: Rowman & Littlefield, 2003), 3, 26.

13.   G. John Ikenberry, *Liberal Leviathan: The Origins, Crisis, and Transformation of the American World Order* (Princeton, NJ: Princeton University Press, 2011), 11–13.

14. The historical question of whether this conception of sovereignty arose out of the Treaty of Westphalia is the subject of significant debate within the literature. For a concurring view, *see* Daniel Philpott, *Revolutions in Sovereignty: How Ideas Shaped Modern International Relations* (Princeton, NJ: Princeton University Press, 2001), 76. For dissenting views, see Daniel Nexon, "Zeitgeist? Neo-idealism and International Political Change," *Review of International Political Economy* 12 (2005): 700–19.

    Also: Stephen D. Krasner, *Sovereignty: Organized Hypocrisy* (Princeton, NJ: Princeton University Press, 1999), 20–25.

15. Dan Philpott, "Sovereignty," *Stanford Encyclopedia of Philosophy* (June 8, 2010), http://plato.stanford.edu/entries/sovereignty/.

    Also: Jack Goldsmith and Daryl Levinson, "Law for States: International Law, Constitutional Law, Public Law," *Harvard Law Review* 122 (2009): 1791, 1844. (The authors discuss "the (perceived) problem of reconciling an all-powerful sovereign (whether a state or a democratic people) with the possibility of legal constraints [which] has played out in international law and constitutional law,").

16. Akbar Nasir Khan, "Legality of Targeted Killings by Drone Attacks in Pakistan," Pakistan Institute for Peace Studies (February 2011), 1, 3, http://san-pips.com/index.php?action=san&id=main&cid=a2.

17. Mary Ellen O'Connell, "Lawful Use of Combat Drones, Testimony at Hearing: Rise of the Drones II: Examining the Legality of Unmanned Targeting," House of Representatives (April 28, 2010), 1–2, http://www.fas.org/irp/congress/2010_hr/042810oconnell.pdf.

    Also: Dana Priest, "Foreign Network at Front of CIA's Terror Fight," *The Washington Post* (November 18, 2005), http://www.washingtonpost.com/wp-dyn/content/article/2005/11/17/AR2005111702070_3.html.

18. Chris Woods, "CIA Drone Strikes Violate Pakistan's Sovereignty, Says Senior Diplomat," *The Guardian* (August 2, 2012), http://www.guardian.co.uk/world/2012/aug/03/cia-drone-strikes-violate-pakistan.

19. Jayshree Bajoria and Greg Bruno, "Al Qaeda (a.k.a. al-Qaida, al-Qa'ida)," Council on Foreign Relations (June 6, 2011), http://www.cfr.org/terrorist-organizations/al-qaeda-k-al-qaida-al-qaida/p9126.

20. Graham Cronogue argues that congressional mandate for war following 9/11 has:

    > "moved beyond its mandate . . . ten years after the attacks, bin Laden is dead and the Taliban is a shadow of its former self. Yet the United States still uses the AUMF to justify the use of force against new terrorist and extremist groups, many of which were not closely involved in 9/11 and may not have even existed in 2001 . . . This "stretching" out of the statute will create significant questions of legality and authorization in times when we cannot afford to hesitate,"

    Graham Cronogue, "A New AUMF: Defining Combatants in the War on Terror," *Duke Journal of Comparative and International Law* 22 (2012): 377, 378.

21. Mary Ellen O'Connell, "When is a War not a War? The Myth of the Global War on Terror," *ILSA Journal of International and Comparative Law* 12 (2005): 2, 5.

22. Jutta Brunnée & Stephen J. Toope, "Canada and the Use of Force: Reclaiming Human Security," *International Journal* 59 (2004): 247, 250.
23. Vincent-Joël Proulx, "If the Hat Fits, Wear It, If the Turban Fits, Run for Your Life: Reflections on the Indefinite Detention and Targeted Killing of Suspected Terrorists," *Hastings Law Journal* 56 (2005): 801, 804.
24. Christian J. Tams, "The Use of Force Against Terrorists," *European Journal of International Law* 20 (2009): 359, 364.
25. Ibid., 366.
26. On the Israeli raid, see also S.C. Res. 573, U.N. Doc. S/RES/573 (October 4, 1985); on the US attacks on Libya, see also G.A. Res. 41/38, U.N. Doc. A/RES/41/38 (November 20, 1986).
27. Philip Bobbitt, *Terror and Consent: The Wars for the Twenty-First Century* (Anchor Books, 2008), 125.
28. Ibid., 19.
    Sir Michael Howard adds another concern—that "to declare war on terrorists or, even more illiterately, on terrorism is at once to accord terrorists a status and dignity that they seek and that they do not deserve. It confers on them a kind of legitimacy," Michael Howard, "What's in a Name?: How to Fight Terrorism," *Foreign Affairs* 81 (January 1, 2002), 8.
29. Daniel Klaidman, *Kill or Capture: The War on Terror and the Soul of the Obama Presidency* (New York, NY: Houghton Mifflin Harcourt, 2012).
30. Jack Goldsmith, "Fire When Ready," *Foreign Policy* (March 19, 2012), http://www.foreignpolicy.com/articles/2012/03/19/fire_when_ready.
31. Kenneth Anderson, "More Predator Drone Debate, in the Wall Street Journal, and What the Obama Administration Should Do as a Public Legal Position," *The Volokh Conspiracy* (January 9 2010), http://www.volokh.com/2010/01/09/more-predator-drone-debate-in-the-wall-street-journal-and-what-the-obama-administration-should-do-as-a-public-legal-position/.
32. Paul R. Pillar, "The Limitless Global War," *The National Interest* (June 19, 2012), http://nationalinterest.org/blog/paul-pillar/the-limitless-global-war-7094.
    For an interesting discussion of the relationship between the war on terror and our understandings of sovereignty and territory, see also Stuart Elden, *Terror and Territory: The Spatial Extent of Sovereignty* (Minneapolis, MN: University of Minnesota Press, 2009).
33. Pillar, Ibid.
34. See note 29 at 152.
35. Reference here is not to cyber spying—which may well not meet the definition of terrorism—but to situations in which cyber agents are employed to inflict physical or economic damage and instill fear, such as by bringing down the electrical grid of a nation. McAfee, "McAfee Virtual Criminology Report: North American Study into Organized Crime and the Internet" (July 6, 2005), http://www.scribd.com/doc/40349191/Mcafee-Na-Virtual-Criminology-Report.\.
    Also: Gregory Larsen and David Wheeler, "Techniques for Cyber Attack Attribution," Institute for Defense Analysis, (October 2003), http://www.dtic.mil/cgi-bin/GetTRDoc?AD=ADA468859&Location=U2&doc=GetTRDoc.pdf.\, 2.
    Also: Jack Goldsmith, "The New Vulnerability," *The New Republic* (June 24, 2010), 23.

36. Stephen J. Kobrin, "Territoriality and the Governance of Cyberspace," *Journal of International Business Studies* 32 (2001): 687, 690.

37. Jonathan Finer and Joshua Partlow, "US Pair Reported Tortured, Beheaded," *Boston Globe* (June 21, 2006), http://www.boston.com/news/world/middlee-ast/articles/2006/06/21/us_pair_reported_tortured_beheaded/?page=full.

38. One may argue that there were occasions in which US troops also defiled corpses, tortured prisoners, and so on. However, in these cases such behavior was widely condemned and those involved were punished, while terrorists and their supporters often cheer such abuses.

39. Leila Hudson, Colin S. Owens, and David J. Callen, "Drone Warfare in Yemen: Fostering Emirates Through Counterterrorism?" *Middle East Policy* 19 (2012): 142, 144.

   Also: Akbar Nasir Khan, "U.S. Policy of Targeted Killings by Drones in Pakistan," *IPRI Journal* 11 (2011): 21, 31.

40. For more on the difficulties of applying the laws of armed conflict to counter-terrorist activities, see Robert M. Chesney, "Beyond the Battlefield, Beyond Al Qaeda: The Destabilizing Legal Architecture of Counterterrorism," Michigan Law Review 112, no. 2 (2013): 163–224.

41. Benjamin Wittes, *Law and the Long War: The Future of Justice in the Age of Terror* (The Penguin Press, 2008), 102.

42. For an excellent discussion on the obsolescence of the concept of sovereignty and ways to define down its legitimacy, see note 27 at 452–83.

43. Bertrand de Jouvenel, *Sovereignty: An Inquiry into the Political Good* (Cambridge University Press, 1957).

44. Jacques Maritain, *Man and the State* (Chicago: University of Chicago Press, 1951).

45. Stephen D. Krasner, *Sovereignty: Organized Hypocrisy* (Princeton, NJ: Princeton University Press, 1999), 85–86, 108, 163–75, 180–82, 202–17.

46. For some discussion of this issue, see Ashley S. Deeks, "Pakistan's Sovereignty and the Killing of Osama Bin Laden," *American Society of International Law* 15 (2011): 11, http://www.asil.org/insights110505.cfm.

47. For example:

   "When al-Qaeda crossed the Durand Line—a scratch on the map ignored by all the local tribes—into Pakistan, the U.S. military, the U.S. Congress, the U.S. President, and the U.S. press stopped as if shocked by an electric current. There was never a serious policy discussion about pursuing and destroying the enemy. By halting on a ridge in the middle of nowhere, we legitimized Pakistan as a sanctuary,"

   Bing West, *The Wrong War: Grit, Energy, and the Way Out of Afghanistan* (New York: Random House, 2012), 123.

48. See note 15.

49. Per the United Nations:

   "Genocide means any of the following acts committed with intent to destroy, in whole or in part, a national, ethnical, racial, or religious group, as such: (a) killing members of the group; (b) causing serious bodily harm or mental harm to members of the group; (c) deliberately inflicting on the group conditions of life calculated to bring about its physical destruction in whole or in part; (d) imposing measures intended to prevent births within the group; (e) forcibly transferring children of the group to another group,"

Amitai Etzioni, *Security First: For a Muscular, Moral Foreign Policy* (New Haven: Yale University Press, 2007), 203.

50. Samantha Power, *A Problem from Hell: America in the Age of Genocide* (New York: Basic Books, 2003).

51. Francis Mading Deng, et al., *Sovereignty as Responsibility: Conflict Management in Africa* (Washington, DC: The Brookings Institution, 1996).

52. UN International Commission on Intervention and State Sovereignty, *Responsibility to Protect* (2001), 13.

53. Security Council Resolution 1674, U.N. Doc. S/RES/1674 (April 28, 2006).

54. *See* Thomas G. Weiss, et al., "The Responsibility to Protect: Challenges & Opportunities in Light of the Libyan Intervention," *e-International Relations* (November 2011), 8, http://www.e-ir.info/wp-content/uploads/R2P.pdf.

Also: Bruce Ackerman, "Obama's Unconstitutional War," *Foreign Policy* (March 24, 2011).

Also: Richard Norton-Taylor, "Libya Campaign 'Has Made UN Missions to Protect Civilians Less Likely,'" *The Guardian* (March 18, 2012), http://www.guardian.co.uk/world/2012/mar/19/libya-un-missions-civilians.

55. Nina Tannenwald, *The Nuclear Taboo: The United States and the Non-Use of Nuclear Weapons Since 1945* (Cambridge University Press, 2007), 247–49.

56. For a discussion of this phenomena and the central place counter-terrorism plays in its dynamics, see Amitai Etzioni, *From Empire to Community* (New York: Palgrave Macmillan, 2004), especially chapters 6 and 9.

57. I will not attempt to define "under-governed" or "ungovernable" here. For those interested in formulating a precise account, a potential starting point is Anne L. Clunnan and Harold A. Trinkunas, *Ungoverned Spaces: Alternatives to State Authority in an Era of Softened Sovereignty* (Stanford, CA: Stanford University Press, 2010), 17–33.

58. Ashley Deeks argues that the test needed to assess whether a state is unwilling or unable to suppress terrorism has yet to be satisfactorily developed and puts forth a "core set of substantive and procedural factors that should inform the 'unwilling or unable' inquiry," Ashley S. Deeks, "Unwilling or Unable: Toward a Normative Framework for Extraterritorial Self-Defense," *Virginia Journal of International Law* 52, no. 3 (2012): 483, 483.

59. A Justice Department white paper states that targeted killings in a foreign nation are "consistent with legal principles of sovereignty and neutrality if it were conducted, for example, with the consent of the host nation's government or after a determination that the host nation is unable or unwilling to suppress the threat posed by the individual targeted," Department of Justice, "Lawfulness of a Lethal Operation Directed Against a US Citizen Who Is a Senior Operational Leader of Al-Qa'ida or an Associated Force," 5, http://msnbcmedia.msn.com/i/msnbc/sections/news/020413_DOJ_White_Paper.pdf.

60. Alexander Moseley, "Just War Theory," *The Internet Encyclopedia of Philosophy* (February 10, 2009), http://www.iep.utm.edu/justwar/.

61.	For more discussion, see Daniel Bethlehem, "Self-Defense Against an Imminent or Actual Armed Attack by Non-state Actors," *American Journal of International Law* 106 (2012): 769.

62.	Amitai Etzioni, *Security First: For a Muscular, Moral Foreign Policy* (New Haven: Yale University Press, 2007), 215–23.

63.	Ibid., parts 1 and 2 (Extensive evidence shows that unless circumstances are uniquely favorable, as they were in post-WWII Germany and Japan, nation building by foreign powers—as attempted by the United States in Iraq, Afghanistan, and scores of other countries—fails. Successful campaigns, such as those in Kosovo, Bosnia, Iraq (in 1991), had limited goals and focused on security. This does not mean the United States should not promote, by nonlethal means, liberal democracies, but that it should not engage in coercive regime changes under most circumstances.); see also, Amitai Etzioni, "The Case for Decoupled Armed Interventions," *Global Policy* 3 (2012): 85, 91.

64.	This line of thought contrasts with the more prevalent post-9/11 treatment of detained terrorists, which has largely occurred within the "rules of war" paradigm: "On November 13, 2001, President Bush issued a Military Order authorizing the Secretary of Defense to constitute 'military commissions' for the purposes of trying noncitizens whom the President determines there is reason to believe either (1) are or were members of Al Qaeda, (2) engaged in, aided or abetted, or conspired to commit 'acts of international terror,' or (3) knowingly harbored Al Qaeda members or international terrorists," See note 1 at 471.

65.	Matthew Alexander, *Kill or Capture: How a Special Operations Task Force Took Down a Notorious al Qaeda Terrorist* (New York: St. Martin's Press, 2011).

66.	Gregory Maggs makes a similar proposal. Gregory E. Maggs, "Assessing the Legality of Counterterrorism Measures Without Characterizing Them as Law Enforcement or Military Action," *Temple Law Review* 80 (2007): 661, 709.

67.	For more on this point, see Amos N. Guiora, "Anticipatory Self-Defence and International Law—A Re-Evaluation," *Journal of Conflict and Security Law* 13, no. 1 (September 8, 2008), 9. ("From experience gained over the years, the state must act pre-emptively in order to either deter terrorists or, at the very least, prevent terrorism,").

68.	See Matthew Kroenig and Barry Pavel, "How to Deter Terrorism," *Washington Quarterly* 35 (2012): 21, 24. ("In contrast [to the Cold War], deterrence against terrorism can only be partial at best. The United States cannot deter all terrorist activity, but as long as Washington can deter certain types of terrorists from engaging in certain types of terrorist activity, deterrence can contribute to national security goals,").

69.	Robert Pape, *Dying to Win: The Strategic Logic of Suicide Terrorism* (New York: Random House, 2005), 75. ("Targets remain willing to countenance high costs for important goals, but administrative, economic, or military adjustments that will prevent suicide attack are harder to make, while suicide attackers themselves are unlikely to be deterred by the threat of retaliation,").

70.	Clearly jihadists do not have a monopoly on this type of fanaticism, and the US criminal court system handles domestic terrorists like Wade Michael Page, who killed six worshippers in a Sikh temple in 2012. But zealots such as these are also best dealt with via preventative measures, and while they make up a tiny percentage of US criminals, they represent a large enough portion of the terrorist population to justify a different level of legal protection.

71. Kenneth Anderson writes that the root cause of the failure of the law enforcement approach "is the process' alleged virtue—the use of models drawn from the fight against organized crime. Organized crime and drug smuggling are, however, essentially problems stemming from material greed. In stark contrast, the motives of Al Qaeda are *apocalyptic and ideological*," Kenneth Anderson, "What to do with Bin Laden and Al Qaeda Terrorists? A Qualified Defense of Military Commissions and United States Policy on Detainees at Guantanamo Bay Naval Base," *Harvard Journal of Law & Public Policy* 25 (2002): 591, 608 (emphasis added).

72. See Paul K. Davis and Brian Michael Jenkins, "Deterrence & Influence in Counterterrorism: A Component in the War on Al Qaeda," no. 1619. Rand Corporation (2002).

73. See Matthew Waxman, "Administrative Detention of Terrorists: Why Detain, and Detain Whom?" *Journal of National Security Law & Policy* 3 (2009) 12–13. ("Criminal justice also has a preventive component . . . criminal law is generally retrospective in focus, in that it addresses past acts,").

74. Scholars have argued that police:

> "are in a good position to learn about and investigate local terrorist threats, and they can work to ensure that vulnerable targets in their jurisdictions are protected. Filling the first of these functions, investigation of terrorists, will require police to extend their normal community policing activities and improve their handling of information,"

Ronald V. Clarke and Graeme R. Newman, "Police and the Prevention of Terrorism," *Policing* 1 (2007): 9, 9. While this is all true, it is only part of the solution in the *global* war of terror.

75. Stephen Murdoch, "Civil Liberties v. National Security," *DC Bar* (March 2012), http://www.dcbar.org/for_lawyers/resources/publications/washington_lawyer/march_2002/civil.cfm.

76. Matt Apuzzo and Adam Goldman, "Inside the Spy Unit that NYPD Says Doesn't Exist," *Associated Press* (August 31, 2011), http://www.ap.org/Content/AP-In-The-News/2011/Inside-the-spy-unit-that-NYPD-says-doesnt-exist.

77. "Stories Put Spotlight on NYPD Surveillance Program," *NPR* (April 18, 2012), http://www.npr.org/2012/04/18/150805767/stories-put-spotlight-on-nypd-surveillance-program.

Civil rights lawyers and Muslim advocates filed a lawsuit against the NYPD for allegedly violating guidelines that limit surveillance activities and bar the police from retaining information not "related to potential terrorist acts or other unlawful activity," "Spying on Law-Abiding Muslims," *The New York Times* (February 9, 2013), http://www.nytimes.com/2013/02/10/opinion/sunday/spying-on-law-abiding-muslim-citizens.html?_r=0.

Also: John Ashcroft, "Success and Strategies in the Effort to Liberate Iraq, Prepared Remarks," (April 17, 2003), http://www.usdoj.gov/archive/ag/speeches/2003/041703effortsliberateIraq.htm.

78. The following line of argumentation was first laid out by Benjamin Wittes of Brookings and Philip Bobbitt of Columbia University.

79. Joseph Goldstein, "Before Lifting DNA, Meticulous Protocol," *The New York Times* (August 28, 2012), http://www.nytimes.com/2012/08/29/nyregion/dna-evidence-in-police-interrogation-rooms-requires-bleach.html?pagewanted=all&_r=1&.

80. Robert Buckout, "Eyewitness Testimony," *Jurimetrics Journal* 15 (1974–1975): 172, 186.

81. See note 41 at 172.

82. See Nicholas Kaufman, "Problems Encountered in Investigating and Prosecuting Conspiracies to Commit Terrorist Offences," (HUMSEC Working Paper Group, Paper no. 7, 2006), available at http://www.humsec.eu/cms/fileadmin/user_upload/humsec/Workin_Paper_Series/Working_Paper_Kaufman.pdf.

83. Steven Swinford, "WikiLeaks: How Britain 'Became a Haven for Migrant Extremists'" *Telegraph* (April 25, 2011), http://www.telegraph.co.uk/news/worldnews/wikileaks/8472784/WikiLeaks-Guantanamo-Bay-terrorists-radicalised-in-London-to-attack-Western-targets.html.

84. Ally Pregulman and Emily Burke, "Homegrown Terrorism," AQAM Futures Project Case Study Series, no. 7 (Washington, DC: Center for Strategic & International Studies 2012), 5.

85. See note 27 at 252.

86. Ibid., 249.

87. Ibid., 248.

88. Stuart Taylor Jr., "The Bill To Combat Terrorism Doesn't Go Far Enough," *National Journal* (October 29, 2001), http://www3.nationaljournal.com/members/buzz/2001/openingargument/102901.htm.

89. Ibid.

90. "GOP Claims Obama Has Ordered FBI to Read Miranda Rights to Terrorist Detainees Captured on the Battlefield," PolitiFact.com (July 7, 2009), http://www.politifact.com/truth-o-meter/statements/2009/jul/14/republican-national-committee-republican/gop-claims-obama-has-ordered-fbi-read-miranda-righ/.

91. Ibid.

92. Coleen Rowley, Center for Research on Globalisation, Memo to FBI Director Robert Mueller (May 21, 2002), available at http://globalresearch.ca/articles/ROW205A.html.

93. The FBI "provides guidance for law enforcement officers confronted with an emergency that may require interrogating a suspect held in custody about an imminent threat to public safety without providing Miranda warnings," Carl A. Benoit, "The 'Public Safety' Exception to Miranda," *FBI Law Enforcement Bulletin* (February 2011), http://www.fbi.gov/stats-services/publications/law-enforcement-bulletin/february2011/legal_digest.

94. Imagine having to bring in a CIA agent or Muslim collaborator that the United States succeeded in placing high in the al Qaeda command in order to have him testify in open court in the United States.

95. El-Motassadeq was later re-tried and convicted but the case demonstrates that "even in the most obvious and dramatic instances of terrorist involvement, substantial conviction cannot always be achieved," Brian Whitaker,

"Member of 9/11 Terror Cell Jailed," *The Guardian* (August 19, 2005), http://www.guardian.co.uk/world/2005/aug/20/september11.usa.

96. See note 41 at 172.

97. Ibid.

98. Benjamin Weiser, "Citing Terror Defendants' Motivation, Judge Shows Sentencing Leniency," *The New York Times* (November 22, 2012), http://www.nytimes.com/2012/11/23/nyregion/judges-ruling-in-qaeda-terror-case-open-ideology-debate.html?pagewanted=all.

99. Somini Sengupta, "Courts Divided over Searches of Cellphones," *The New York Times* (November 25, 2012), http://www.nytimes.com/2012/11/26/technology/legality-of-warrantless-cellphone-searches-goes-to-courts-and-legislatures.html.

100. Charlie Savage, "In Setback for Military Tribunals, Bin Laden Driver's Conviction Is Reversed," *The New York Times* (October 16, 2012), http://www.nytimes.com/2012/10/17/us/politics/dispute-over-clothing-dominates-guantanamo-hearing.html?_r=0.

101. Human Rights First, "Ghassan Abdulla Al Sharbi Case Overview," http://www.humanrightsfirst.org/our-work/law-and-security/military-commissions/cases/ghassan-abdullah-al-sharbi/.

102. Andy Worthington, "Remaining Prisoners in Guantanamo," *Pacific Free Press* (October 9, 2010), http://www.pacificfreepress.com/opinion/7112-remaining-prisoners-in-guantanamo.html.

103. See note 41 at 158.

104. Guantanamo Review Task Force, *Final Report* (January 22, 2010), http://www.justice.gov/ag/guantanamo-review-final-report.pdf.

105. See note 27 at 266.

106. Lucien E. Dervan, "The Surprising Lessons from Plea Bargaining in the Shadow of Terror," *Georgia State University Law Review* 27 (2011): 239, 241.

107. Ali Saleh Kahlah al-Marri, *The New York Times* (May 1, 2009), http://topics.nytimes.com/top/reference/timestopics/people/m/ali_saleh_kahlah_al_marri/index.html.

108. A study that surveyed the federal court's record in trying terrorists in the two decades before 9/11 found that while the government was "relatively successful . . . federal prosecutors have had to deal with courtroom strategies by defense attorneys that jeopardize intelligence and security resources," Brent L. Smith, Kelly R. Damphousse, Freedom Jackson, and Amy Sellers, "The Prosecution and Punishment of International Terrorists in Federal Courts: 1980–1998," *Criminology & Public Policy* 1 (2006): 311, 329. Writing a year after 9/11, they predicted that the government would turn more often to military tribunals which "increase the capacity of the federal government to prosecute international terrorism," Ibid., 330.

109. Karen J. Greenberg, Susan Quatron, et al., "Terrorist Trial Report Card: September 11, 2001–September 11, 2009" Center on Law and Security, NYU School of Law, (2010), 12, http://www.lawandsecurity.org/Portals/0/documents/02_TTRCFinalJan142.pdf.

110. This is a reference to the eight Nazis who entered the United States via submarine with explosives and instructions to destroy vital wartime infrastructure. President Roosevelt set up a military commission for their prosecution. See note 88.

111. Anderson makes a similar point. The constitutional rights and criminal protections granted to US citizens:

> "have developed *within* a particular political community, and fundamentally reflect decisions about rights within a fundamentally domestic, democratic setting in which all of us have a stake in both side of the equation . . . because we are part of the political community which must consider both individual rights and collective security . . . Terrorist who come from outside this society . . . cannot be assimilated into the structure of the ordinary criminal trial,"

See note 71.

112. Protocol Additional to the Geneva Conventions of 12 August 1949, and Relating to the Protection of Victims of International Armed Conflicts art. 48 (June 8, 1977), http://www.icrc.org/ihl.nsf/full/470?opendocument. NOTE: See BB Rule 21.

113. Although I cannot demonstrate this here, this factor alone explains to a great extent why most counterterrorism campaigns are so long and costly in human and economic terms, and often fail.

114. Nils Melzer, "Interpretive Guidance on the Notion of Direct Participation in Hostilities Under International Humanitarian Law," *The International Review of the Red Cross* 90 (2008): 991, 993, available at http://www.icrc. org/eng/assets/files/other/irrc-872-reports-documents.pdf.

115. Gregory E. Maggs chronicles how those involved in the debates over the legality of counterterrorist measures almost always attempt to force terrorists into either the law enforcement paradigm or the military paradigm. See note 66 at 661–710.

    Also: Wayne McCormack, "Military Detention and the Judiciary: Al Qaeda, the KKK, and Supra-State Law," *San Diego International Law Journal* 5 (2004): 7.

    Also: Kenneth Roth, "The Law of War in the War on Terror," *Foreign Affairs* 83 (January 2004), 2

    Also: Evan Perez, "Holder Presses Case for Using Civilian Courts to Try Terrorism Suspects," *The Wall Street Journal* (June 17, 2011), http://blogs. wsj.com/washwire/2011/06/17/holder-presses-case-for-using-civilian-courts-to-try-terrorism-suspects/.

116. It does not matter for the discussion at hand that the normative and legal rationale for treating these various categories of people differently varies; and that the ways they are "qualified" as belonging to these "exceptions" are distinct. What matters is that there is ample precedent for not treating all offenders in the same manner, following the same standards of evidence, in the same forums.

117. Mitchell W. Dale, "Barriers to the Rehabilitation of Ex-Offenders," *Crime & Delinquency* 22 (1976): 322, 327–29.

118. Ashley S. Deeks, "Administrative Detention in Armed Conflict," *Case Western Reserve Journal of International Law* 40 (2009): 403, 436. ("Treaties long have recognized that a state may detain without trial not only opposing armed forces, but also civilians and others who pose threats to its security . . . [t]hese rules [governing detention] impose a high standard for a state to initially detain a person, require the state immediately review that detention,

permit the detainee to appeal the detention decision, require the state to review the detention periodically, and obligate the state to release the detainee when the reasons for his detention have ceased,").

119. The "balancing test" involves three considerations:

> "the private interest that will be affected by the official action; the risk of an erroneous deprivation of such interest through the procedures used, and the probable value, if any, of additional or substitute procedural safeguards; [and] the Government's interest, including the function involved and the fiscal and administrative burdens that the additional or substitute procedural requirement would entail,"

> *Mathews v. Eldridge*, 424 US 319, 335 (1976) (holding that a judicial hearing was not required by the Due Process Clause before the suspension of Social Security Disability benefits on the grounds that holding hearings would incapacitate the government in its ability to process claims); see *Mathews v. Eldridge*, Case Briefs, http://www.casebriefs.com/blog/law/administrative-law/administrative-law-keyed-to-lawson/constitutional-constraints-on-agency-procedure/mathews-v-eldridge/. This position was upheld in *Hamdi v. Rumsfeld*, 542 US 507 (2004); Jared Perkins, "Habeas Corpus in the War Against Terrorism: Hamdi v. Rumsfeld and Citizen Enemy Combatants," *BYU Journal of Public Law* 19 (2005): 437.

120. Jack L. Goldsmith and Neal Katyal, "The Terrorists' Court," *The New York Times* (July 11, 2007), http://www.nytimes.com/2007/07/11/opinion/11katyal.html?_r=0

    Also: Benjamin Wittes & Mark Gitenstein, "A Legal Framework for Detaining Terrorists: Enact a Law to End the Clash over Rights" The Brookings Institution (2008), 12, http://www.brookings.edu/~/media/research/files/papers/2007/11/15%20terrorism%20wittes%20opp08/pb_terrorism_wittes.

121. Serrin Turner & Stephen J. Schulhofer, "The Secrecy Problem in Terrorism Trials," Liberty and National Security Project (2005)

    Also: Interview with Attorney General Eric Holder, *Meet the Press* (May 9, 2010), http://www.nbcnews.com/id/37024384/ns/meet_the_press/print/1/displaymode/1098/. http://www.realclearpolitics.com/articles/2010/05/09/interview_with_attorney_general_eric_holder_105514.html.

122. See note 41 at 163.

123. Matthew Waxman points out that the more difficult question is "what is the standard of certainty a state must exercise in sorting out suspected terrorists from nonterrorists for the purposes of detention?" For his answer, see Matthew C. Waxman, "Detention as Targeting: Standards of Certainty and Detention of Suspected Terrorists," *Columbia Law Review* 198 (2008): 1365, 1367.

124. James Jay Carafano & Paul Rosenzweig, *Winning the Long War: Lessons from the Cold War for Defeating Terrorism and Preserving Freedom* (Washington, DC: Heritage Books, 2005).

125. Gavin Berman & Alexander Horne, "Pre-Charge Detention in Terrorism Cases," Commons Library Standard Note (March 16, 2012), 2, http://www.parliament.uk/briefing-papers/SN05634.

126. Benjamin Wittes & Mark Gitenstein, "A Legal Framework for Detaining Terrorists: Enact a Law to End the Clash over Rights" The Brookings

Institution (2008), 12, available at http://www.brookings.edu/~/media/research/files/papers/2007/11/15%20terrorism%20wittes%20opp08/pb_terrorism_wittes.

127. See note 41 at 19.

128. There is a growing body of such lawyers who have obtained security clearance and specialize in representing defendants charged with terrorism. See Benjamin Weiser, "Terrorism Law Is Niche for a Deepening Pool of Defenders in New York," *The New York Times* (November 25, 2012), http://www.nytimes.com/2012/11/26/nyregion/expertise-in-terror-law-is-a-growing-niche-in-new-york.html?pagewanted=all.

129. Phil Hirschkorn, "Civil Rights Attorney Convicted in Terror Trial," *CNN* (February 14, 2005), http://www.cnn.com/2005/LAW/02/10/terror.trial.lawyer/.

130. Rajiv Chandrasekaran, *Little America: The War Within the War for Afghanistan* (Alfred A. Knopf, 2012).

131. Lucinda Fleeson, "The Civilian Casualty Conundrum," *American Journalism Review* (2002), http://www.ajr.org/article.asp?id=2491.

132. Other principles of *jus ad bellum* (right to war) include right intention (no ulterior motives), declaration by the proper authorities, probability of success, and proportionality. Brian Orend, "War," *Stanford Encyclopedia of Philosophy* (2008), http://plato.stanford.edu/archives/fall2008/entries/war/.

133. John O. Brennan "The Ethics and Efficacy of the President's Counterterrorism Strategy," (transcript) (April 30, 2012), http://www.wilsoncenter.org/event/the-efficacy-and-ethics-us-counterterrorism-strategy.

    Also: "Drone Strikes Kill, Maim and Traumatize Too Many Civilians, US Study Says," *CNN* (September 25, 2012), http://www.cnn.com/2012/09/25/world/asia/pakistan-us-drone-strikes.

    Also: Neta C. Crawford, "'Targeted' Drones Strikes and Magical Thinking," *The Huffington Post* (September 23, 2012), http://www.huffingtonpost.com/neta-crawford/drones-civilian-casualties_b_1907597.html.

134. "ACLU Sues US over Extrajudicial Killings of Americans," *RT* (February 3, 2012), http://rt.com/usa/news/aclu-execution-drone-suit-387/.

    Also: Michael Boyle, "Obama's Drone Wars and the Normalisation of Extrajudicial Murder," *The Guardian* (June 11, 2012), http://www.guardian.co.uk/commentisfree/2012/jun/11/obama-drone-wars-normalisation-extrajudicial-killing.

135. See David Kretzmer, "Targeted Killing of Suspected Terrorists: Extra-Judicial Killing or Legitimate Means of Defence?" *European Journal International Law* 16 (2005): 2.

136. Glen Greenwald, "America's Drone Sickness," *Salon* (April 19, 2012), http://www.salon.com/2012/04/19/americas_drone_sickness/.

137. Tara McKelvey, "Covering Obama's Secret War," Columbia Journal Review (May/June 2011), available at http://www.cjr.org/feature/covering_obamas_secret_war.php?page=all.

    Also: Vicki Divoll, "Targeted killings: Who's Checking the Executive Branch?" *The Los Angeles Times* (March 25, 2012) http://www.latimes.com/news/opinion/commentary/la-oe-divoll-congress-and-targeted-assassinations-20120325,0,5805481.story.

    Also: see note 30.

Also: Glen Greenwald, "Probing Obama's Secrecy Games," *Salon* (June 7, 2012), http://www.salon.com/2012/06/07/probing_obamas_secrecy_games/. Dennis J. Kucinich, John Conyers, Jr. et al., "Letter to the Honorable Barack Obama," (June 12, 2012), http://www.justforeignpolicy.org/sites/default/files/Ltr.%20to%20President%20Obama%20Sig%20Strikes%2006.12.2012.pdf.

Also: Doyle McManus, "Who Reviews the US 'Kill List'?" *The Los Angeles Times* (February 5, 2012), http://articles.latimes.com/2012/feb/05/opinion/la-oe-mcmanus-column-drones-and-the-law-20120205.

Also: Ari Melber, "Breaking with Democrats, Some Activists Target Obama's Kill List," *The Nation* (June 27, 2012), http://www.thenation.com/blog/168617/breaking-democrats-some-activists-target-obamas-kill-list#.

Also: Steven D. Schwinn, "More Justification for Drones," Constitutional Law Professors Blog (April 30, 2012), http://lawprofessors.typepad.com/conlaw/2012/04/more-justification-for-drones.html. Order of authorities R 1.4.

138. International Covenant on Civil and Political Rights (ICCPR), "General Assembly Resolution 2200A (XXI)," U.N. GAOR, 21st Session, Supp. no. 16, U.N. Doc. A/6316, at 52 (Dec. 16, 1966). It should be noted here that the United States never ratified the ICCPR.In 1976, President Gerald Ford issued Executive Order 11,905: "Prohibition on Assassination. No employee of the United States Government shall engage in, or conspire to engage in, political assassination," 3 C.F.R. 90 (1976). Presidents Jimmy Carter and Ronald Reagan extended the ban in 1978 and 1981; Executive Order 12,333 is the version still on the books. 3 C.F.R. 200 (1981).

Also: Gordon L. Bowen, "'Targeted Killings:' US Policy Toward Use of Covert Operations Involving Assassination," Mary Baldwin College (June 7, 2012), http://www.mbc.edu/faculty/gbowen/AssassinationPolicy.htm.

For a discussion of the nuances of the assassination question, see Stephen Knoepfler, "Dead or Alive: The Future of US Assassination Policy Under a Just War Tradition," *New York University Journal of Law & Liberty* 5 (2010): 457.

139. David E. Sanger, *Confront and Conceal: Obama's Secret Wars and Surprising Use of American Power* (New York: Broadway Paperbacks, 2012), 257.

140. In a closely related but (rightly) separate discussion about the use of drones against US citizens who join al Qaeda, some Senators have suggested a "FISA court-like process" to ensure that targets are not killed without due process. In CIA director appointee John Brennan's confirmation hearing, Senator King stated:

> "A soldier on a battlefield doesn't have time to go to court, but if you're planning a strike over a matter of days, weeks or months, there is an opportunity to at least go to something outside of the Executive Branch body, like the FISA court, in a confidential and top-secret way, make the case that this American citizen is an enemy combatant . . . that would be some check on the activities of the Executive,"

Brennan responded that such a court was worth discussing but added that the decisions made in a traditional court of law are:

> "very different from the decisions that are made on the battlefield, as well as actions that are taken against terrorists, because none of those actions are

to determine past guilt for those actions that they took. The decisions that are made are to take action so that we prevent a future action, so we protect American lives,"

"Open Hearing on the Nomination of John O. Brennan to be Director of the Central Intelligence Agency," 113th Cong. (2012).

141. Less is known about the guidelines the CIA follows, but they are reported to be similar. Previously, there were two processes—one for the Defense Department and one for the CIA. The Defense Department maintained a list of "members of the larger al Qaida network," comprised of names nominated based on evidence reviewed by multiple agencies, including the State Department and the National Counterterrorism Center. After thirty days of not being captured or killed, the name was mandated to be reviewed. The CIA's list is reviewed only by "a number of high-ranking staff" and the Covert Action Review Group; it is then given to the CIA's Counterterrorism Center, which executes the strikes. "The Director of National Intelligence, Jim Clapper, is briefed on these actions," "U.S. Uses New System to Decide Terrorist Drone Strikes," *Associated Press* (May 21, 2012), http://www.ctvnews.ca/u-s-uses-new-system-to-decide-terrorist-drone-strikes-1.830005.

142. Ibid.
143. Ibid.
144. Gregory McNeal, "Guest Post: Gregory McNeal," *Lawfare Blog* (November 29, 2011), http://www.lawfareblog.com/2011/11/guest-post-gregory-mcneal/.
145. "Memorandum from the Chairman of the Joint Chiefs of Staff, CJCSI 3160.01: No-Strike and the Collateral Damage Estimation Methodology C1–C2" (Feb. 13, 2009), http://www.aclu.org/files/dronefoia/dod/drone_dod_3160_01.pdf.
146. Ibid., B1–B6.
147. See note 47 at 209.
148. Ibid., 206.
149. Abdul Rahman was a tribal leader operating on the border of Pakistan and Afghanistan in cooperation with the Taliban. He is presumed to have commanded Taliban forces in the battle of Barg-e-Matal, and may or may not currently be alive.
150. See note 47 at 89.
151. Ibid.
152. Nick Wing and Hank Crumpton, "Former CIA Officer: Clinton Wouldn't Authorize Osama Bin Laden Kill in 1999," *The Huffington Post* (May 14, 2012), http://www.huffingtonpost.com/2012/05/14/hank-crumpton-cia-clinton-bin-laden_n_1514895.html.
153. Doyle McManus, "Who Reviews the US 'Kill List'?" *The Los Angeles Times* (February 5, 2012), http://articles.latimes.com/2012/feb/05/opinion/la-oe-mcmanus-column-drones-and-the-law-20120205.
154. Ken Dilanian, "Congress Keeps Closer Watch on CIA Drone Strikes," *The Los Angeles Times* (June 25, 2012), http://www.latimes.com/news/nationworld/world/middleeast/la-na-drone-oversight-20120625,0,7967691,full.story. Even with robust oversight, it must be acknowledged that mistakes will be

made and innocents may be killed. However, regardless of whether the form of attack is a targeted killing or more traditional warfare, "the US government can and sometimes does make mistakes about its targets. There is simply no way to wring all potential error from the system and still carry on a war," See note 30.

155. Ibid.

156. Chris Anders of the ACLU was not swayed by the "more stringent" rules governing the targeted killing process said to be laid out in the Obama administration's new counterterrorism "playbook:"

> "First, secret rules are inconsistent with the rule of law, which is predicated on everyone knowing the rules. Second, the Obama administration's playbook rules will not apply to CIA drone strikes in Pakistan for at least a year if not more, according to the Post. Third, and most importantly, the rules undergirding the program, secret or not, violate the Constitution and international law,"

Matthew Harwood, "Obama's Playbook: Still Killing Outside the Lines," ACLU (January 25, 2013), http://www.aclu.org/blog/national-security/obamas-playbook-still-killing-outside-lines.

157. Micah Zenko makes recommendations for a "well-articulated and internationally supported normative framework, bolstered by a strong US example, [which] can shape armed drone proliferation and employment in the coming decades," Micah Zenko, "Reforming US Drone Strike Policies" Council on Foreign Relations, Special Report no. 65 (2013). He argues for more limited use of drone strikes, greater accountability to Congress, the public and the UN, and the development of a "code of conduct" among drone powers. Ibid.

158. Benjamin Franklin, *The Papers of Benjamin Franklin*, Vol. 6 (Leonard W. Labaree ed., 1963), 242.

159. The Red Cross' "Interpretive Guidance on the Notion of Direct Participation in Hostilities under International Humanitarian Law," adopted in 2009, provides some foundations for such a convention. *See* note 114 at 991.

14

MAR: Mutually Assured Restraint

To avoid the United States and China falling into the Thucydides trap, both nations will be served if they embrace a strategy of Mutually Assured Restraint (MAR). Political scientists argue that history shows, since the days of the ancient Greeks, that when a new power arises and the old superpower does not yield ground quickly enough, wars ensue.[1] However, the record shows that there are no historical Iron Laws. Thus, Harvard's Graham Allison points to four cases out of fifteen since the 16th century that were not followed by war—including the rise of the US as a global power in the 1890s.[2]

The distrust between the US and China has increased in recent years, with the Chinese accusing the U.S of attempting to "sabotage the Communist Party's leadership" and Americans alleging that the PRC's mercantilist policies "harm the chances of American economic recovery."[3] China is building up its military[4] and the US is developing an AirSea Battle plan widely understood as aimed at China.[5] At the same time, both nations face well documented, well known, and important domestic needs. Hence the merits of the following approach that seeks to inject substance into the vague phrases mouthed by both powers: statements that China ought to have a "new model of major-country relations" with the U.S[6] and that the US is looking to build a "cooperative partnership" with China.[7]

Mutually Assured Restraint (MAR) is a foreign policy based on mutual respect, a quest for confidence building, and new institutionalized arrangements that will move both powers away from situations that could escalate into major conflicts. In short, a policy that prevents them from falling into the Thucydides trap. Accordingly, each side would limit its military build-up and coercive diplomacy as long as the other side limits itself as well, and these self-restraint measures would be vetted. Thus, China would be free to take the steps it holds are necessary for its self-defense and the maintenance of its relations with its allies, without extending them to the point that they threaten other nations or the international commons. At the same time, the United States would likewise be free to take the steps it holds as necessary for self-defense, as well as those needed to live up to its obligations to its allies in the region and preserve the international order.

339

Agreements or understandings would spell out ways both powers would be able to rest assured that the other power is limiting itself as indicated. In this sense, MAR would follow President Ronald Reagan's line of "trust but verify," a concept whose value is reflected in START, the vetted treaty between the US and Russia that limits strategic weapons. It should be noted that aside from relying on various technological means for verification, START also stipulates on-site inspections in the United States by Russians and vice-versa, including examinations of the location and number of intercontinental missiles and nuclear warheads.[8]

The author cannot stress enough that the following pages merely provide bare sketches of the kind of policies that could be instituted to develop MAR. Each move requires considerable deliberation, modification, and elaboration as well as give and take among the powers involved.

I. Limiting Anti-Access/Area Denial (A2/AD) Weapons

China holds that it needs Anti-Access/Area Denial weapons (A2/ AD), especially anti-ship missiles, for self-defense.[9] The US views these weapons as a threat to its ability to discharge its obligations to Taiwan, Japan and other states, and to freedom of navigation in the region.[10] Both powers should agree to limit the number and range of these missiles; that these limitations should be verified by agreed methods; and that such short-range, defensive missiles could be provided to other nations in the region, such as Japan, thus curbing a major source of the current pressure on China's neighbors to build up their military forces.

This element of MAR has been criticized on the grounds that one cannot necessarily differentiate defensive from offensive weapons.[11] Thus Michael Haas argues that "MAR burdens itself with the dubious presupposition that offensive and defensive weapons are clearly distinguishable."[12] Although it is true that one can imagine circumstances in which defensive arms will aid an offensive strategy—there are clearly differences between the two. As Harvard's Sean M. Lynn-Jones points out, one can assess whether a particular weapons system is more efficient at furthering an offensive strategy or a defensive one, and categorize it on that basis. For example, though tanks can serve defensive purposes, they are absolutely essential for offensive maneuvers.[13]

Similarly, Charles L. Glaser and Chaim Kaufmann, professors of international relations at George Washington and Lehigh University, respectively, point out that "nearly all historical advances in military mobility—chariots, horse cavalry, tanks, motor trucks, aircraft, mobile bridging equipment—are generally considered to have favored the offense, while major counter-mobility innovations—moats, barbed wire, tank traps, land mines—have favored defense."[14]

The same holds for the range, placement, and number of anti-ship missiles. Indeed, this particular application of MAR is both important in itself and serves well to illustrate the whole approach.

II. Cyberspace

MAR is particularly important for weapons, like cyber-arms, that favor those who strike first—as they are particularly destabilizing. Exploring ways to curb this category of weapons—via shared understandings and verification—should be granted a high priority.

A draft code that seeks to curb conflicts involving cyber-arms has already been proposed. In September 2011, four countries—China, Russia, Tajikistan, and Uzbekistan—submitted an "International Code of Conduct for Information Security" to Secretary General Ban Ki-moon. The draft calls for reaching a "consensus on the international norms and rules standardizing the behavior of countries concerning information and cyberspace at an early date."[15] The document further asks states to pledge "not to use information and communication technologies including networks to carry out hostile activities or acts of aggression and pose threats to international peace and security," as well as insists on "curbing dissemination of information which incites terrorism, secessionism, extremism or *undermines other countries' political, economic and social stability, as well as their spiritual and cultural environment.*"[16]

This last clause is understood by several American and European observers to mean that the cyber code could be used to suppress freedom of expression and human rights—consequently rendering the document unacceptable to them. The preceding clause could be interpreted as applicable to transnational surveillance, or in plain English, electronic spying on other countries. However, the collection of information about another power's military and economy follows a long-standing practice in international relations of intelligence collection and it may be unrealistic to try to ban the use of cyber tools for this purpose.

However, if one reads the text as a call on all powers to agree to restrain their preparations for using cyber tools for kinetic attacks, this may well be an important step toward curbing a highly destabilizing element in international relations. Such an understanding might entail a commitment by the powers to not plant malware in another country's systems. Such an agreed restraint could be vetted. To reiterate, these lines merely serve to illustrate MAR as an approach; developing specific arrangements requires considerable deliberation as well as future negotiation.

III. A Buffer Zone

The US has formed military alliances, signed agreements allowing the placement of American troops and other military assets in allied states, as well as conducted joint military exercises with many of the countries neighboring China. The US views these arrangements as agreements between sovereign nations—a way of burden sharing and part of a drive to contain or "counterbalance" China. China perceives these moves as an attempt at Cold War-era encirclement. The PRC has also been seeking out military alliances of its own with neighboring countries, adding to the tension.

These moves position American and Chinese military forces closer to each other, a proximity that could potentially lead to accidental clashes and conflagrations. This risk was highlighted in the April 2001 incident involving the collision of a US surveillance aircraft and People's Liberation Army Navy fighter jet approximately 65 miles southeast of the PRC's Hainan Island over the South China Sea as well as an additional encounter between a PLAN Jianghu III-class frigate and an American surveillance ship, the USS Bowditch, in the Yellow Sea near South Korea a month earlier.[17]

Moreover, the various treaties and understandings in effect have given several states in the region a finger on the trigger of a gun belonging to their superpower sponsor, as these arrangements stipulate that if the nation in question enters a war with one super-power, the other one will come to its aid. Some treaties quite explicitly entail such a commitment (e.g. The Treaty of Mutual Cooperation and Security between the United States and Japan, which is said to cover the Senkaku Islands.) Others are ambiguous and easily misconstrued by the countries involved (e.g. The Mutual Defense Treaty between the United States and the Philippines and the relationship between China and North Korea.)

It is hence particularly troubling that some of these smaller states have engaged in rather provocative moves, moves that could lead not only to war between them and other states in the region, but could also potentially drag both super-powers into a confrontation with each other. This is most obvious in the case of the two Koreas. Other examples are much less dramatic and conflict-prone, but nonetheless still of concern. For example, in 2012, the Philippine Navy boarded Chinese fishing vessels—allegedly discovering illegally collected corals, giant clams and live sharks—and attempted to arrest the Chinese fishermen. However, Chinese surveillance crafts blocked the arrest by situating their vessels between the Chinese fishing boat and the Philippine navy, leading to a tense stand-off.[18]

If China and the US would embrace MAR, both would treat these nations as neutral buffer zones, similar to the way Austria, and for a while Yugoslavia, were treated during the Cold War. While both powers would be free to continue engaging these nations economically—investing, trading, and providing foreign aid—MAR involves avoiding military commitments, military exercises and the placement of military assets in this zone. Initially, this would only entail no new steps in a militaristic direction. Eventually and gradually, old military ties would be rolled back as well. Above all, both powers would make it clear to their allies that they should not assume the automatic, guaranteed involvement of the US or China if these third nations engage in an armed conflict or war with either of the two powers.

IV. Dealing with North Korea

MAR would make a particularly important contribution if it was applied to American and Chinese positions regarding the future of North Korea—particularly in the aftermath of a government collapse. The RAND Corporation provides the following scenario:

"As chaos develops in North Korea, the ROK, the United States, and China would all likely send special operations forces (SOF) into the North for special reconnaissance, focused in particular on North Korean WMD facilities. Somewhere, the Chinese SOF would make contact with ROK and US SOF, and unintended or accidental conflict could develop[19] . . . if conflict were to begin between the ROK-U.S. forces and the Chinese forces, that conflict could escalate significantly in ways that neither side would want."[20]

The RAND report further recommends that both the United States and the PRC minimize the risk of confrontation by defining a "separation line for Chinese forces versus R.O.K and United States forces," whereby Chinese forces would stay north of the line and both American and South Korean forces would remain south of the demarcation.[21]

MAR can draw on the RAND suggestions and other similar ideas to favor an understanding between the US and China that if North Korea's regime were to collapse, neither American nor Chinese troops would move into the country. Both sides and the world would be much better off if American troops were not based next to the Yalu River, and if Chinese forces were not massed next to the DMZ. Given today's technological means, the neutrality of such a buffer zone—that is, the absence of military forces from both sides—is relatively easy to verify.

In addition, consideration should be given to the possibility of positioning United Nations peacekeeping forces in the area to supervise the removal of nuclear weapons, facilitate the destruction of chemical weapons, as well as provide humanitarian aid so as to avoid a massive flood of refugees from North Korea into China or South Korea.

Such an understanding would make it far more likely that China would be willing to do more to encourage North Korea to stop developing its nuclear arsenal, consider returning to the NPT, and refrain from provocative behavior.

V. The Contested Islands

In recent years, tensions between China and Japan over the Senkakus/Diaoyus—a tiny chain of uninhabited islands in the East China Sea—have escalated. The most recent round of tensions, triggered in part by Japan's nationalization of three of the five islands, has witnessed moves viewed as provocative by both countries. Chinese surveillance and patrol ships have navigated the waters surrounding the islands with greater frequency; PLA military planes have made multiple flights near disputed airspace;[22] and Japan's Ground Self-Defense Forces and US Marines have conducted joints exercises simulating Japan's seizure of "unnamed" islands.[23]

On the diplomatic front, Beijing has demanded that Tokyo acknowledge the existence of a territorial dispute as well as consent to a twelve-nautical-mile no entry zone around the islands as a pre-condition for holding a Sino-Japanese summit. Japan has refused.[24] As such, diplomacy between the two countries remains at an impasse. China has further criticized international, and particularly American, attempts to intervene in the dispute—insisting on bilateral negotiations as the mechanism for reaching a resolution.[25]

At the same time both China and Japan have taken steps that show a measure of self-restraint (visible and hence easy to verify) which, if extended, would serve MAR well. Thus the Japanese Coast Guard has worked to prevent nationalists from landing on the islands[26] and China has assiduously avoided involving its military in the area, instead relying on civilian agencies and the Coast Guard.

Much more needs to be done. Among the suggestions for defusing the situation, three stand out:

- The two states could submit the dispute for review by the International Tribunal for the Law of the Sea or the International Court of Justice. The review is likely to take several years, and during that time, both states would have strong incentives to engage in serious bilateral negotiations before a decision is reached. This idea has been suggested by Jerome Cohen, an internationally renowned China law scholar.
- A framework for the joint administration of resources in and around the islands could be established and the issue of sovereignty shelved. In the past, most notably in the 2008 "principled consensus," arrangements for the joint development of oil and gas resources in the disputed areas were made by Japan and China but never fully implemented. Alternatively, sovereignty over the territory could be awarded to one state but resource-related rights could be assigned to all claimants. Both these recommendations have been put forward by the Carter Center.
- Finally, the two nations may consider the formation of a supra-national organization which would be authorized to exploit and manage resources in the disputed areas. Japan and China's conflicting claims to territorial sovereignty would be effectively overridden by a supra-national governing body similar to the European Coal and Steel Community—an idea advanced by former Japanese ambassador to Iran and Iraq, Magosaki Ukeru.

Although a rational observer may hold that it is irrational to anticipate the possibility that the US and China will be drawn into a war over what some have referred to dismissively as small piles of rocks, wars have started over less important matters once national pride has entered the equation and other factors predispose the parties to conflict. MAR has a significant contribution to make here and can defuse a major source of the tension.

VI. Pathways

China is highly dependent on the import of raw materials and energy. A great deal of these imports reach China via the sea. China sees itself as highly vulnerable because the United States, which has a very strong naval presence, could block these imports quite readily.[27] Some American commentators openly discuss the option of such a blockade, which is considered a moderate way of confronting China relative to the AirSea Battle Plan.[28]

In response to these concerns and as a result of the PRC's broader interest in commercial expansion, China has somewhat increased its naval presence in the South China Sea as well as developed a network of ports in the Indian and Pacific Oceans termed the "string of pearls".[29] China has additionally attempted to reduce the country's reliance on shipping lanes by developing plans for the land transportation of oil and gas resources. These include new Silk Roads.[30] Indeed, a system of roads, railways and pipelines are now extending across continental Asia.[31]

Some Americans view these pathways as a sign of China's expansionist tendencies and interest in asserting global dominance.[32] Some Chinese view American opposition to select pathways (for instance a pipeline from Iran to China) as attempts to contain China's rise. Under MAR, the US would assume—unless clear evidence is presented to the contrary—that extending land-based pathways for the flow of energy resources and raw materials will make China less inclined to build up its military, particularly naval forces needed to secure ocean pathways—a win-win for both powers.

VII. Strategic Reassurance

Applying MAR to Chinese Intercontinental Ballistic Missiles may well be impossible at this stage, as China is so far behind the US in this category of weapons that it would likely refuse to even explore a START-like agreement.[33] However, in the long run, MAR may include what some call "strategic reassurance,"[34] a cap on the ICBMs and similar strategic weapons by both powers.

For instance, according to Hui Zhang (a Senior Research Associate at the Project on Managing the Atom at Harvard University), this scheme might entail Washington accepting "certain measures, including mutual deterrence with Beijing [by] limiting its missile defenses so they do not threaten the potential effectiveness of China's small arsenal."[35]

In contrast to other issues that require attention in the near future, however, these matters do not need to be urgently addressed because—as indicated—the parties are almost certainly unwilling to limit themselves at this stage.

VIII. R2P, Yes; Coercive Regime Change, No

In 2005, 188 countries, including China and the United States, endorsed the "responsibility to protect" doctrine (R2P). Accordingly, the international community pledged "to use appropriate diplomatic, humanitarian and other means to protect populations" from genocide, war crimes, ethnic cleansing and crimes against humanity if the State—characterized as primarily responsible for protecting its own people—failed to meet this obligation.

However in 2011, the UK, France, and the United States turned an armed humanitarian intervention aimed at preventing the large scale killing of civilians in Libya into a coercive regime change. Also in 2011, when a humanitarian crisis developed in Syria, Western powers openly called not just for ending the civil war but for forcing Assad out of power. Russia strongly opposed these kinds of interventions and China supported Russia in this matter. The two countries invoked the long established Westphalian norm which holds that no state should interfere by use of force in the internal affairs of another nation. At the same time, China has increased its contributions to UN peacekeeping forces.

It follows that if the United States and its European allies limit humanitarian interventions to only those interventions aimed at stopping genocide, subsequently leaving the nations involved to sort out their own political futures, and to peacekeeping operations sanctioned by the United Nations, China (and Russia) might very well reactivate their support for R2P, benefitting all nations and peoples.

IX. Beyond MAR

MAR is not the only foundation on which to base a more cooperative Sino-American relationship. There is a long list of areas in which both powers have identical or complimentary interests, and in which they can work together. These include reducing the dangers of nuclear proliferation, climate change, terrorism and financial/economic instability.

X. Basic Strategy

MAR has been criticized as dealing with the symptoms rather than the underlying causes of friction between the United States and China as well as failing to acknowledge that the strategic goals of the two countries are inherently in conflict.[36] Regarding the first point, there are situations in which reducing a rising fever is of value while one searches for more profound cures. In relation to the second point, MAR does hold that the differences between the United States and China do not concern significant national (or so called "core") interests and that there are no signs that China seeks to become a global, let alone hegemonic power. On the contrary, China seems quite content to allow the United States to absorb the costs and risks of ensuring the global flow of oil, free passage on the seven seas, and to stabilize the governments in the Middle East (Iraq and Afghanistan included).

346

As for regional differences, once one scraps away symbolic importance that can be attached to anything—including a pile of rocks—and ceases to view every conciliatory move as a sign of weakness, one finds that these problems can be worked out quite smoothly. Or at least this is a thesis worth testing as both powers have a major shared interest in avoiding an arms race—let alone a war—and face pressing needs which demand that they invest whatever uncommitted resources and available attention they have to nation-building at home.

Notes

1. Sean Clark, "Deadly Decay: Great Power Decline and Cataclysmic War," *International Journal* (Toronto) 65, no. 2 (Spring 2010), 477.
2. Graham T. Allison Jr.,"Obama and Xi Must Think Broadly to Avoid a Classic Trap," *The New York Times* (June 6, 2013), http://www.nytimes.com/2013/06/07/opinion/obama-and-xi-must-think-broadly-to-avoid-a-classic-trap.html?_r=0.
3. Kenneth Lieberthal and Wang Jisi, "Addressing U.S.-China Strategic Distrust," The Brookings Institution (March 2012), http://www.brookings.edu/~/media/research/files/papers/2012/3/30%20us%20china%20lieberthal/0330_china_lieberthal.pdf, viii–ix.
4. Anthony H. Cordesman, Ashley Hess, and Nicholas S. Yarosh, "Chinese Military Modernization and Force Development: A Western Perspective," Center for Strategic and International Studies (August 23, 2013), http://csis.org/files/publication/130725_chinesemilmodern.pdf, 15.
5. Amitai Etzioni, "Who Authorized Preparations for War with China," *Yale Journal of International Affairs* (Summer 2013), http://icps.gwu.edu/files/2013/06/Who-Authorized-Preparations-for-War-With-China.pdf, 41.
6. Speech by Foreign Minister Wang Yi, "Toward a New Model of Major-Country Relations Between China and the United States," Ministry of Foreign Affairs of the People's Republic of China (September 20, 2013), http://www.fmprc.gov.cn/eng/zxxx/t1078768.shtml.
7. "U.S.-China Cooperation in the Asia-Pacific Region," US Department of State (July 12, 2012), http://www.state.gov/r/pa/prs/ps/2012/07/194891.htm.
8. "New START Treaty Inspection Activities," US Department of State, http://www.state.gov/t/avc/newstart/c52405.htm.
9. Sam Goldsmith, "China's Anti-Access and Area-Denial Operational Concept and the Dilemmas for Japan," Australian National University (2012) https://digitalcollections.anu.edu.au/bitstream/1885/9721/1/Goldsmith_ChinasAntiAccess2012MastersThesis.pdf.
10. Major Christopher J. McCarthy, "Anti-Access/Area-Denial: The Evolution of Modern Warfare," *Luce.nt: A Journal of National Security Studies* (Spring 2010), http://www.usnwc.edu/Lucent/OpenPdf.aspx?id=95&title=The%20Global%20System%20in%20Transition, 3.
11. Michael Haas, "A MARred Alternative: Offense, Defense and U.S.-China Relations," *The Diplomat* (October 28, 2013), http://thediplomat.com/the-editor/2013/10/08/a-marred-alternative-offense-defense-and-u-s-china-relations/.
12. Ibid.

13. Sean M. Lynn-Jones, "Offense-Defense Theory and Its Critics," *Security Studies* 4, no. 4 (Summer 1995), http://slantchev.ucsd.edu/courses/pdf/lynn-jones%20-%20offense-defense%20theory%20and%20its%20critics.pdf, 676.

14. Charles L. Glaser and Chaim Kaufmann, "What is the Offense-Defense Balance and Can We Measure it?" *International Security* 22, no. 4 (Spring 1998), 63.

15. "China, Russia and Other Countries Submit the Document of International Code of Conduct for Information Security to the United Nations," Ministry of Foreign Affairs of the People's Republic of China (September 13, 2011), http://www.fmprc.gov.cn/eng/wjdt/wshd/t858978.htm.

16. Ibid.

17. "China-U.S. Aircraft Collision Incident of April 2001: Assessments and Policy Implications," Congressional Research Service (October 2001), http://www.fas.org/sgp/crs/row/RL30946.pdf.

18. "Filipino Warship in Standoff with Chinese Boats," *CBS* (April 10, 2012), http://www.cbsnews.com/8301-202_162-57412182/filipino-warship-in-standoff-with-chinese-boats/.

19. Bruce W. Bennett, *Preparing for the Possibility of a North Korean Collapse* (RAND Corporation, 2013), http://www.rand.org/content/dam/rand/pubs/research_reports/RR300/RR331/RAND_RR331.pdf, 96.

20. Ibid., 97.

21. Ibid., 274.

22. Hannah Beech, "Angry Skies: Japanese Jets Scramble as Tensions With China Escalate," *Time Magazine* (September 18, 2013), http://world.time.com/2013/09/18/angry-skies-japanese-jets-scramble-as-tensions-with-china-escalate/#ixzz2i5XRvtQV.

23. Yuka Hayashi, "U.S., Japan Train for Island Defense," *The Wall Street Journal* (September 24, 2012), http://online.wsj.com/news/articles/SB10000872396390444083304578013692399658834.

24. "China Demands No-Entry Zone Around Senkakus to Hold Summit Talks," *Kyodo News International* (June 21, 2013), http://www.globalpost.com/dispatch/news/kyodo-news-international/130621/china-demands-no-entry-zone-around-senkakus-hold-summi.

25. John Ruwitch, "China Warns U.S., Japan, Australia Not to Gang Up in Sea Disputes," *Reuters* (October 6, 2013), http://www.reuters.com/article/2013/10/07/us-asia-southchinasea-china-idUSBRE99602220131007.

26. "Japan Nationalists Return After Nearing Islands Disputed with China," *NBC* (August 18, 2013), http://worldnews.nbcnews.com/_news/2013/08/18/20073241-japan-nationalists-return-after-nearing-islands-disputed-with-china.

27. Wen Han, "Hu Jintao Urges Breakthrough in 'Malacca Dilemma'", *Wen Wei Po* (January 14, 2004). Also: "China Builds Up Strategic Sea Lanes," The Washington Times (January 17, 2005), http://www.washingtontimes.com/news/2005/jan/17/20050117-115550-1929r/#ixzz2i68i42Hy.

28. T.X. Hammes, "Sorry, AirSea Battle is No Strategy," *The National Interest* (August 7, 2013), http://nationalinterest.org/commentary/sorry-airsea-battle-no-strategy-8846.

29. "China Builds Up Strategic Sea Lanes," *The Washington Times* (January 17, 2005), http://www.washingtontimes.com/news/2005/jan/17/20050117-115550-1929r/#ixzz2i68i42Hy.

30. "New Silk Roads," *The Economist* (April 8, 2010), http://www.economist. com/node/15872888.
31. "Russia-China Oil Pipeline Opens," *BBC News* (January 1, 2011), http:// www.bbc.co.uk/news/world-asia-pacific-12103865.
32. Ariel Cohen, "U.S. Interests and Central Asia Energy Security," The Heritage Foundation (November 15, 2006), http://www.heritage.org/research/ reports/2006/11/us-interests-and-central-asia-energy-security.
33. Hui Zhang, "Chinese Nuclear Modernization: Assuring a Limited but Reliable Counterattack Capability," *Power & Policy* (September 7, 2012), http://www. powerandpolicy.com/2012/09/07/chinese-nuclear-modernization-assuring- a-limited-but-reliable-counterattack-capability/#.UmGOTXewXTp.
34. James Steinberg, "China's Arrival: The Long March to Global Power," Center for a New American Security (Keynote Address) (September 24, 2009), http://www.cnas.org/files/multimedia/documents/Deputy%20Secretary%20 James%20Steinberg%27s%20September%2024,%202009%20Keynote%20 Address%20Transcript.pdf.
35. See note 33.
36. See note 11.

V

Public Philosophy

15

Public/Private Divide

This chapter argues that the frequently-employed distinction between the public and the private realms is becoming increasingly obsolete, because the two realms are intertwined, move in tandem, and seem to be co-determined. It follows that many of the most commonly made statements in public discourse about the government and the market, or the state and individual rights, must be reexamined. Such a re-examination is warranted because if it is true that the two realms are driven by the same historical forces—blurring the boundaries and making them prone to moving in unison—it becomes increasingly difficult to assume that one realm is either the main benefactor or the main cause of harm inflicted on the other realm. This observation challenges those who blame the government for interfering in the marketplace and damaging the economy, or for running a surveillance state that undermines privacy and other individual rights, as well as those who see the government as protecting the people from exploitation by private corporations and banks, or as the main protector of the rights of consumers, workers, minorities, and the poor.

My main aim is at public discourse. As my colleagues correctly point out, social science has long established that the public/private distinction is much less clear and sharp than public discourse about political and social matters takes for granted. However, one should note that there are segments of social science that also rely heavily on this distinction. For instance, major segments of neoclassical economics, the dominant school of economics in the United States., regularly draw a strong line between market forces (those of supply and demand) and government actions (e.g., regulations). The same holds true for major segments of jurisprudence. Thus, the Bill of Rights is typically viewed as protecting citizens from the government, but not from private actors, for instance corporate ones. In addition not all political scientists and sociologists have fully taken into account the significance of high interpenetration of the two realms.

The divide that undergirds these competing public philosophies is the divide between public and private. "Over the course of decades," notes Andrew Stark, a political scientist, "commentators have offered scores of master narratives to interpret American political conflict. None is more popular than the idea that, in one way or another, political controversy in America consists of an unfolding series of struggles between the values of the public and the private realms."[1] Law professors Alan Freeman and Elizabeth Mensch observe that "nothing is more central to our experience in American culture than the split between public and private. It is the premise which lies at the foundation of American legal thought, and it shapes the way in which we relate to each other in our daily lives. We consistently take for granted that there is both a public realm and a private realm."[2]

While social scientists have long observed that the public/private distinction is much less productive than public discourse simply assumes, I attempt to show below that since the advent of cyberspace, the distinction has become even less fruitful.

The preceding claims are so far-reaching that they almost collapse under the weight of their own audacity. If validated, they have considerable implications for the philosophies, ideologies, and policy debates that dominate our public discourse, as well as some segments of social science. On one side are the public philosophies of libertarianism, civil libertarianism, laissez-faire conservatism, and right-wing populism, which distrust the government and extol the private realm. On the other side are the philosophies of social liberalism, social democracy, socialism and progressive populism, which fear unrestrained market forces and cast the government in a much more positive light. These conflicting viewpoints are so familiar—they have played a key role in public discourse for at least two hundred years—that they need no elaboration here. They are often captured in evocative words and phrases such as Big Brother and Wall Street. In earlier ages, these phrases included the Bosses, the Trusts, Tammany Hall, the Establishment, and the Invisible Hand. They are still echoed in sound bites such as "that government which governs best governs least" and "government, even in its best state, is but a necessary evil."

In the following pages I present four case studies that seek to go beyond simply providing more evidence that the assumption that the private and the public realms can be clearly distinguished is an erroneous one and that the blurring of the realms has increased since the advent of cyberspace. They seek to show that is a mistake to assume that the forces that drive societal change are mainly in one realm and that they drive the other. Forces in both sectors combine, and both are affected by forces that located elsewhere, arguably within the civil society. I present first one case study to illustrate the key claims of this article. I then turn to matters of definition, before three other case studies are presented.

I. Case Study – The Rise of a National (Public-Private) Personal Identifier

Social Security numbers (SSNs) were widely used in both the public and private realm long before the cyber age, and they contributed to efficiency and raised privacy concerns from their inception. We shall see shortly, however, that they acquired a much greater import in both realms after digitization.

The creation of SSNs in 1936 resulted from the Social Security Act of 1935, which authorized the Social Security Administration to establish a record-keeping system to track employees' earnings and eligibility for Social Security benefits. Prior to the creation of SSNs, other tracking methods were envisioned, including names and even fingerprints, but numbers were preferred. Soon SSNs were assigned to virtually all Americans and most legal residents.[3]

From the outset, the public was concerned about privacy and confidentiality issues. "The Social Security Board issued releases at various times assuring the public that the information on the application would be kept confidential, with access limited to government employees for whom job duties under the Social Security Act required it."[4] In June 1937, the Social Security Board issued a regulation to this effect.[5] In short, the SSN was initially meant to be a tracking device used only in the public realm—and within that realm, only for very limited and closely-regulated purposes.

The expansion of SSN use in the public realm became apparent in 1943 when an executive order mandated that all federal agencies exclusively use the SSN to set up new identification systems for individuals, though it was not until the 1960s that Federal agencies outside the Social Security Administration context adopted SSNs as general government identifiers.[6] In 1962 the IRS began to use the SSN as a taxpayer identification number. SSNs were employed by other federal programs including Medicaid, food stamps, welfare programs, and child support programs. The Commercial Motor Vehicle Safety Act of 1986 required states to collect SSNs for use in a nationwide database of drivers' license information.[7] The Illegal Immigration Reform and Immigrant Responsibility Act of 1996 provides employers with a voluntary system to verify the validity of employees' SSNs.[8] The 2001 USA Patriot Act requires financial institutions to verify a person's identity, using SSNs for American citizens and legal residents.[9] However, federal laws have restricted the disclosure of SSNs for purposes unrelated to the specific functions of the federal agencies using them.

The private sector found SSNs to be highly useful for verifying identities and matching records for management purposes, keeping records on customer history, and exchanging data with other organizations. This was because other forms of identification, such as names, are often not unique to individuals, and if distinct numbers are assigned to various individual records, data exchanges among corporations become cumbersome and costly. Credit bureaus maintain information on ninety percent of the American adult population using individuals' SSNs, information which is "freely sold and traded, virtually without legal limitations."[10] Banks employ these bureaus to investigate customer history and assess the likelihood that an individual will repay loans. Health care providers and insurers use SSNs to track patient care across multiple providers.

Digitization made the collection, processing, and analysis of information much more efficient and productive. Although the differences between the paper world and the computerized one are very well known, they are briefly listed here because it is difficult to express the magnitude of the change in any other way (coming up with quantitative measurements is problematic because comparing efficiency before and after digitization is akin to comparing the speed of a car to the speed of light). Law enforcement, national security, medical care, research, and commerce were extremely hampered as long they had to rely on paper records. Thus, information about crime used to be kept in local police ledgers, which made it next to impossible to determine whether the same suspect, modus operandi, or associates found in one crime may have been also involved in others. Information about health care, still often kept in paper files in the offices of physicians, makes review and analysis across patients and offices extremely challenging. Combining two, let alone more, bodies of data about the same populations was very costly and slow before digitization.

While all this is generally known, is it important to note that none of the enormous increases in efficiency and productivity provided by digitization could be achieved without the introduction of an effective way to identity people across databases and accounting systems and records, both private and public. SSNs became the major way this identification is carried out in both realms.

This case study illustrates—albeit on matters of limited scope—that the difference between the public and the private realms is much smaller than is often assumed in public discourse and by some segments of social science, and that since the advent of cyberspace, this difference has been further diminished. Both realms came to rely on a nearly universal tracking device to identify people, keep records on them, locate them, and correlate information about one facet of their lives with others. And the tracking device is one and the same in both realms. I use the term "intertwined" to refer to such conversions and the resulting links between the two realms.

Although the SSN was initially introduced by the government for its own use, over the decades that followed the government came to require some parts of the private sector to use SSNs (for instance, to verify the immigration status of prospective employees, to prevent terrorists and drug dealers from using banks, and to prevent financial institutions from laundering money). At the same time, major forces in the private sector promoted the use of the same number for their purposes. From the private sector's viewpoint, if the number did not exist, it would have had to be invented because of the considerable ways in which a universal tracking device enhances profit-making. Thus, although the government was surely the first to introduce the national identifier and to promote its use, private sector forces promoted it strongly for their own reasons. Moreover, each use by one realm fed into the use by the other, and both realms moved in tandem in the same direction: to expand the use of SSNs.

The same tendency toward moving in tandem is revealed in response to new concerns about identity theft and old concerns about privacy. Such concerns led both realms to introduce some (limited) curbs on the use of SSNs. States also deleted SSNs from drivers' licenses. The 1999 Gramm-Leach-Bliley Act imposed restrictions on the ability of financial institutions to disclose non-public personal information, including SSNs, to nonaffiliated third parties. In the private realm, colleges and investment houses moved to allow applicants to use identifiers other than SSNs. Still, for those concerned about violations of privacy and anonymity emanating from the use of SSNs—concerns that, historically, were mainly focused on the government—the intertwining of the realms pointed to a need for reconsideration. A large number of profit-making corporations currently track Americans by the use of SSNs in various ways, including keeping details and intimate dossiers on them. There seems to be no way to reverse course without simultaneously limiting the usage of SSNs in both realms. I will introduce more case studies before discussing which forces are driving both realms to curb the use of SSNs and protect privacy from both Big Brother and his corporate brethren.

II. Definitions and Background

Now that the subject at hand has been illustrated, I turn to matters of definitions and introduce essential qualifications of the main thesis. By "public philosophy" I mean those values, ideologies, and worldviews that undergird the wider social and political discourse. I use this term from here on to include the ideologies and rationales used by public leaders and elected officials to support various public policies and to legitimate court decisions. The term also refers to public understanding of what the Constitution, and more generally the law, means. These are not to be equated with academic bodies of thought that often carry the same name such as libertarianism and social liberalism; these academic texts tend to be much more nuanced, qualified, and varied.

The terms "private" and "public" have many meanings and definitions. For instance, there are those who treat not-for-profit institutions (of which there are hundreds of thousands in the United States alone) as public entities, and others who treat them as private ones. According to historian William J. Novak, "The most compelling analyses of American power have always refused to split the problem along a single either-or, public-private binary (e.g., the people vs. the interests; public good vs. private right; the state vs. the individual; regulation vs. the market). Instead, realistic and pragmatic approaches to American state development emphasize the interpenetration of public and private spheres—the convergence of public and private authority in everyday policymaking."[11] Elisabeth S. Clemens, who writes about a private/public "tangle," sees it as "a misrecognition of public services as private ... publicly subsidized benefits are understood as privacy owned and privately earned."[12]

For the purposes at hand, I follow a common practice in public discourse that uses "public" more or less synonymously with governmental and "private" to refer to all the rest.

To support the thesis that the public and private realms are increasingly intertwined, I will attempt to show that developments in one realm are often and increasingly paralleled or closely followed by changes in the other. I cannot stress enough that the thesis is not that the two realms are becoming indistinguishable, but merely that the walls that were presumed to separate them—and which were never nearly as tall as the dominant public philosophies assume—have already been significantly breached and are in the process of being further scaled down since the advent of the cyber age. In other words, there is considerable "slack" in the sense that developments in one realm can take place to a large extent without parallel developments in the other, but such developments are limited compared to those that are conjoined, and the extent of such slack is declining.

Among the many scholars who have written on related subjects, five stand out. Grant McConnell's position differs from the one laid out here in that he did not view the changes in the private and public sectors as inclined to move in tandem. On the contrary, he held that the weaker and more dispersed public power becomes, the stronger and more centralized private power becomes.[13] E. E. Schattschneider saw a parallel between private and public conflicts. However, he held that these conflicts originate in the private realm and studied the conditions under which they become public.[14] C. Wright Mills did see a convergence of political (public) and economic (private) power, which could lead the two power elites to function as one,[15] a thesis also reflected in the term "military-industrial complex." For Theodore Lowi and Mancur Olson, interest groups bridged the two realms, and could be viewed as a force that moves them in tandem.[16] Though some of these writings, in particular those by C. Wright Mills, gained currency outside academic circles, public discourse is very often still conducted as if the two realms are distinct and one largely drives the other. One merely has to point to the Tea Party and Paul Ryan to note how popular the assumption about the divide is.

Critics may argue that references to public philosophies are actually references to "elite talk," that the public's thinking is actually more nuanced. One way this claim is supported is by pointing out that the majority of Americans have for decades opposed the expansion of the government (or have favored scaling it back) while also demanding the delivery of more government services (or at least insisting that they not be scaled back).[17] Hence, Americans are said to be philosophically conservative (meaning laissez-faire conservative) and operationally liberal. This division was well-captured in the often-quoted demands by opponents of the 2010 health care law that the government stay out of "their" Medicare.[18] (Adam Sheingate showed that this inability to see the proper role of the state extends well beyond Medicare.[19]) However, this complexity does not contradict the thesis at hand. Both positions view one realm as the source of good and the other as threatening, rather than treating them as intertwined and asking: what is the locus and nature of the forces that propel history, if they are not found in one realm or the other?

The following discussion uses the term "propel" rather than "cause," because the latter term raises methodological questions that need not be tackled here. The observation that the two realms are increasingly intertwined and tend move in tandem suffices to support the thesis that the sharp divide between the two realms has lost much of its explanatory power. However, this development could be due to forces in both realms that work on each other and supplement each other, pushing in the same direction (as we have seen so far in the brief study of Social Security numbers), like chemical changes on both sides of the same coin. However, to support the thesis that the main locus of the powers that propel developments in both realms is not located in either realm, as is so often assumed—to show that the realms are codetermined—I need to show that there is another force, located elsewhere, that drives changes in both the public and private realms—that they are, in effect, intermediating variables, not independent ones (to use the language of social science). I turn to this part of my argument in the last segment of this essay. First, I seek to support the thesis that the two realms are intertwined and move largely in tandem.

No attempt is made to analyze in any depth the case studies that follow. They are merely introduced to support the key thesis at hand. All are drawn from American society; applying the same analysis to other societies would require a separate treatment.

III. Case Study – Privacy—Big Brother and his Corporate Brethren

In 2010, the Obama administration began seeking an update to the 1994 Communications Assistance to Law Enforcement Act. One new provision would bring new forms of Internet communications under the scope of the law, allowing the government to require services like Skype and Facebook to maintain the capacity to execute a wiretap order.[20] Another provision would ensure that upgrades to phone and broadband networks will not diminish the government's ability to conduct wiretaps.[21]

Privacy advocates have opposed both proposals, just as they have done with many previous measures that have been suggested to enhance national security. Kevin Bankston of the Electronic Frontier Foundation called the first proposal "a drastic anti-privacy, anti-security, anti-innovation solution in search of a problem."[22] Christopher Calabrese, legislative counsel for the ACLU, argued that "under the guise of a technical fix, the government looks to be taking one more step toward conducting easy dragnet collection of Americans' most private communications."[23]

The reactions of privacy advocates to this news—along with their reactions to many other such reports—clearly show that they view the government as the threat to a major element of the private realm, that of privacy. More generally, individual rights are typically considered first and foremost as checks on the power of the government, protecting individual rights from encroachment by the state, not by private actors such as corporations.

Following the development of the Internet, though, major violations of privacy are the work of private actors, mainly corporations. (We shall discuss shortly whether these violations are more or less serious than those carried about by the government.) There are two kinds of corporations that keep track of what Internet users buy, read, or visit; whom they call, e-mail, befriend, or date; what they watch on television, how they vote, and much else.[24] Some corporations merely track users' activity on their site as part of their regular business, recording purchases and viewed products to better target their advertisements to particular customers. This is true for many thousands of corporations, including nearly every major online retailer from Amazon to Zappos. Other corporations make shadowing Internet users, assembling very detailed dossiers on them, and selling the use of such dossiers their main line of business. In 2005, just one such company—Choicepoint—had records on over 220 million people.[25] As of 2003, another such company, Acxiom, had records on at least 176 million.[26] According to law professor Christopher Slobogin, such corporations offer clients information about "any of us," including "basic demographic information, income, net worth, real property holdings, social security number, current and previous addresses, phone numbers and fax numbers, names of neighbors, driver records, license plate and VIN numbers, bankruptcy and debtor filings, employment, business and criminal records, bank account balances and activity, stock purchases, and credit card activity."[27]

New technologies are expanding this practice. Cell phone companies offer a service by which their customers can be tracked—and cannot refuse the tracking.[28] Computer-savvy users do not even need the assistance of the cell phone company: if they have the target's cell phone number, they can trace them without the service provider's help.[29] This capability has been used by stalkers to find out where their victims are located.

Other new violations of privacy arise out of the rapidly-changing nature of "cookies," the tools which have long been used by websites to track Internet behavior. Vigilant Internet users were once able to clear cookies from their computer. However, this is changing as the Internet's coding language is upgraded to HTML5. The new language can provide dossier-builders with months of individuals' accumulated data, including a "user's location, time zone, photographs, text from blogs, shopping cart contents, e-mails and a history of the Web pages visited."[30] Moreover, these tracking tools, including "Flash cookies" and "supercookies," are difficult to detect and often reinstall themselves if removed.[31]

Using pseudonyms and multiple names and accounts does not protect one from intrusions. Some companies have developed software that match pseudonyms used on message boards and blogs with real names and personal e-mail addresses.[32] The subjects of this tracking include people who use online pseudonyms to discuss sensitive topics, such as mental illness.[33]

Privacy advocates have sharply objected to the government's use of deep packet inspection (DPI)—a powerful tool used to analyze the contents of communications transmitted over the Internet—in large part because it is much more intrusive than merely tracking who is communicating with whom. The difference is akin to reading letters vs. examining the outside of an envelope to see who sent the letter and to whom it is addressed. Now, private companies are offering to perform DPI for anyone who meets their fees.[34]

Moreover, individuals cannot protect themselves from corporations by choosing to deal only with those that promise to respect their privacy. Transparency about their privacy policies does little good, because the privacy statements corporations post are often written in complex legal terms, and there is no realistic way for individuals to ensure that corporations abide by their statements.

In short, corporations do most everything that the federal government has been banned from doing under various laws, in particular the Privacy Act of 1974. One may argue that the private sector merely uses this information for commercial purposes, while the government may use it to jail people, suppress free speech, and otherwise violate individual rights. However, one must note that the violation of privacy by private agents often has the same effects as identical violations committed by government agents. Thus, when gay people who seek to keep their sexual orientation private are "outed" by the media, or banks call in loans of those they find out have cancer, or employees refuse to hire people because they find out about their political or religious views, privacy is violated in a manner just as consequential as if the same violations had been carried out by a government agency. As people learn that if they hold dissenting views or engage in experimental behavior, such actions will not be kept private, they will be "chilled" even if their fear of disclosure is merely due to corporate actors and not to governmental ones.

Most importantly, *the information corporations amass is available to the government.* The thesis that what is private does not stay private is far from hypothetical. For instance, Choicepoint, which amasses extensive dossiers on most Americans, has at least 35 contracts with government agencies, including the Department of Justice (through which it provides its databases to the FBI), as well as the DEA, the IRS, and the Bureau of Citizenship and Immigration Services.[35] Choicepoint is not alone; commercial data banks regularly work with law enforcement officials to provide background information on individuals, including financial reports, felony checks, and more.[36] The federal government paid $12 million dollars to a corporate data miner called SeisInt to develop a database that includes individuals' "criminal histories, photographs, property ownership, SSNs, addresses, bankruptcies, family members, and credit information."[37] Even before the 9/11 attacks, the US Marshals Service alone performed up to forty thousand searches every month using private data banks.[38] The exact number of contracts the government has made with corporate data miners is unknown, because many of the contracts are classified.[39] However, one government study found that as far back as 2004, at least fifty-two federal agencies had launched—or were planning to launch—at least 199 data-mining projects.[40]

In short, whether the data banks loaded with extensive dossiers of most adult Americans are in the FBI headquarters or in some corporate office matters little. At most, they are just a click away.

Laws prevent the government from ordering a private company to conduct surveillance or generate dossiers that the government itself is banned from generating. In other words, the government is prohibited from treating companies as government agents. However, the government can and does use data already in place. Nor do laws exist that prevent private corporations from collecting and analyzing personal data with an eye toward the government's needs and shaping their privacy-violating databanks in ways that make them more attractive to government purchases of their services.

Finally, privacy advocates argue that even if one is not concerned about those currently holding public office, once data banks are amassed of, say, the DNA of millions of people, a less-benign government may exploit them in the future. A future Nixon may employ these data banks to harm those on his enemy list, and a future House Un-American Activities Committee could employ them to cause people to lose their jobs and livelihood. Some even worry about what will happen if a totalitarian government takes over. These concerns, though, tend to ignore that in all these circumstances, databanks held in the private realm are subject to the same abuses as those in the public one.

The key question relevant to the current discussion is whether the divide between public and private realms still serves as the major way to organize our deliberations and policies about privacy. It seems that, no matter how one approaches the topic, one should pay much less mind to the private/public divide and instead seek approaches that treat both realms as intertwined. Thus, one may argue that by default, explicit consent should be required before a person's information is released or stored. People would "own" information about themselves, and their permission would be needed before it could be used by either private or public actors. Or one could take the position that to protect privacy one must limit surveillance and the assembling of dossiers on individuals—disregarding whether the data purveyors are private or public—unless special circumstances prevail and special authorization has been granted (say, if the subject of tracking is suspected of a crime, as demonstrated to a judge).

So far, though, neither of these approaches has found wide currency in the United States, nor have any other cross-realm approaches. Nor have the normative, legal, and political concepts needed to analyze and guide action in such an amalgamated way been worked out. Thus, when one suggests that the 4th Amendment should also apply to private actors, the surprised response highlights how far-reaching the traditional way of thinking is.

IV. Case Study – Cybersecurity: A Cross-Realm Challenge

That national security is the role of the state is a very widely-accepted observation. Still, the private sector has long played a major role in providing national security in the United States. As of 2010, the Pentagon's spending on private contractors amounted to about $400 billion, or nearly 60 percent,[41] of its roughly $700 billion annual budget.[42] The private sector manufactures nearly everything the military uses, including "big ticket" items, such as fleets of airplanes, aircraft carriers, and submarines, as well as smaller items like handguns, grenades, and Kevlar vests. Private contractors also provide a wide array of services including "logistical support, transportation, engineering, construction, skilled and unskilled laborers, maintenance, technical expertise, and other paramilitary operations."[43] Their work ranges from "highly specialized tasks requiring extensive training and experience" to "unskilled general labor in dining halls, laundry facilities, and construction projects."[44] One further notes that although the press has usually referred to the size of the US military force in Afghanistan after the surge as roughly one hundred thousand, as of December 2010, there were roughly 87,000 private contractors working for the Pentagon in Afghanistan,[45] and they have been dying at a rate sometimes higher than US soldiers,[46] making it a rather joint public-private mission. Private contractors are employed in capturing suspected terrorists, interrogating detainees, analyzing terrorist networks, training new spies, and protecting CIA directors as they travel.[47] The reliance on the private sector for security work was significantly expanded during the Bush administration and has been scaled back only to a limited extent during the Obama administration.

As a result, various attributes of the private security industry deeply affect public security endeavors. Thus, when private contractors kill civilians or torture prisoners, the US military's reputation and the cooperation of the local populations are affected. When the private sector finds that producing so called "big ticket" items (e.g., ships) is more profitable than producing small ones (e.g., body armor) because of more oligopolistic opportunities in big items, the US ends up with more warships than experts say it needs, but not enough bulletproof vests.[48] Furthermore, overdue deliveries and vast private cost overruns limit what the US Defense Department can purchase and what is available to the military.

The intertwining of the realms is significantly higher in all matters concerning cybersecurity, a sector whose importance has been growing rapidly over the last decade. This is because practically all the equipment and machinery the military uses is computerized in some way, drawing on both hardware and software produced in the private sector—components which are often produced overseas,[49] including in China.[50] Private computer technology is used by the military, the intelligence community, the US Department of Homeland Security, and other law enforcement and security agencies to process, store, retrieve and analyze information, to communicate commands, and to coordinate policies and actions. In short, computers are an important part of the national security brain and nervous system.

Thus, the extent to which public security assets are themselves secure depends, to a very great extent, on the security of their privately produced components. Although the military produces some technology in-house, the widespread use of privately made technology means that the private and public facets of security are highly intertwined.

At first blush, one might expect the private sector to strongly support new measures that enhance cybersecurity. Many of the crimes committed in cyberspace, including identity theft and financial crimes, impose considerable costs on the private sector. The same holds for industrial espionage, especially from other countries, which deprives American corporations of the fruits of long investments in R&D and grants major advantages to unfair competitors. If cyber warfare were to break out, many of the assets that would likely be damaged are private sector assets. Finally, American businesses are largely operated by citizens who, one assumes, are concerned about their nation's security.

As a matter of fact, though, American businesses have not revealed much support for enhanced cybersecurity. Some security experts argue that this is the case because incentives to secure private computer systems are not aligned in ways that would motivate the private sector to take the needed action.[51] For example, despite the rapid rise of Internet bank theft, for example, the costs of added protections are higher than the losses from the cyber thefts, making added security an unattractive business proposition for financial institutions.[52] In addition, the effects of industrial espionage are often not in evidence for several years and are therefore beyond the horizons of many CEOs concerned with the short-term profits and stock prices of their corporations.

Government-led measures to enhance cybersecurity in the private sector are essential, given the high level of intertwining between public and private cyber equipment and processes. However, these measures have encountered resistance by private-sector actors who argue that forcing companies to comply with cybersecurity regulations will harm their profits, flexibility, and ability to innovate.[53] Furthermore, businesses consider it unfair and inappropriate for the government to impose security requirements on private industries, a task businesses consider a private-sector responsibility.[54] Such requirements are viewed as "unfunded mandates."[55] Stewart Baker, who served as Assistant Secretary for Policy at the Department of Homeland Security, has discussed the fate of one cybersecurity proposal advocated by Richard Clarke, the first White House cybersecurity czar. According to Baker, the proposal "sidled up toward new mandates for industry," would have formed a "security research fund" that would have drawn on contributions from technology companies, and would have increased pressure on Internet companies to provide security technology with their products.[56] However, these requirements were viewed as too onerous for business by many within the George W. Bush administration, and ultimately "anything that could offend industry, anything that hinted at government mandates, was stripped out."[57]

The net result is that cybersecurity is weak for work carried out in and by the private sector—and therefore in the public sector as well. Major security breaches have taken place in recent years at major defense contractors such as General Dynamics, Boeing, Raytheon, and Northrop Grumman.[58] In 2007, unknown attackers probably working for a foreign government stole several terabytes of information from the Departments of State and Defense, among others. The amount stolen was nearly equal to the amount of information in the Library of Congress.[59]

The military's own computers—produced by the private sector, run with software from the private sector, and often maintained and served by the private sector—are not well protected. The networks of the US Department of Homeland Security are also inadequately protected.[60] Cybersecurity expert James Lewis finds that the nation's digital networks are "easily" accessed by foreigners, both competitors and opponents.[61] Lewis flatly states that "the market has failed to secure cyberspace. A ten-year experiment in faith-based cybersecurity has proven this beyond question."[62]

Moreover, it is unclear who is responsible for maintaining the security of many critical assets. Currently, the US Department of Homeland Security is working to secure the .gov and .com domains,[63] but not critical infrastructure.[64] President Obama stated in 2009 when unveiling his administration's cybersecurity policy review, "Let me be very clear: My administration will not dictate security standards for private companies."[65] This is a statement of considerable import given that a very large part of the kind of missions carried out in other states by the military (including by state-owned and managed industries) is carried out in United States by the private sector. It is not much of an exaggeration to hold that because of the high degree of collaboration, joined projects, and links and exchanges between the private security sector and the public one, vulnerabilities in the private sector lead to vulnerabilities in the public one.[66]

One essential security measure is separating critical infrastructure from the Internet. Such a measure has not been taken because it cannot be done without additional federal regulation, and representatives of the affected industries tend to oppose regulation. For example, lobbyists from the power industry believe that "95 percent of their assets should be left unregulated with regard to cybersecurity."[67]

Indeed, federal policy is moving in the opposite direction—toward greater connectivity for America's energy grid. The "smart grid" initiative advanced by the Obama administration is designed to save money and update an aging energy grid by integrating various power suppliers into one system by using a digital network.[68] However, research shows that a smart grid will "introduce new problems, such as increasing the vulnerability to cyber attack as power grid resources become increasingly linked to the internet."[69]

The United States could significantly enhance its protection from cyber attacks by working toward greater security for computer-component supply chains. Former Assistant Attorney General Jack Goldsmith and cybersecurity expert Melissa Hathaway, who led the Obama Administration's cybersecurity review, warn of the "excessive security vulnerabilities" that result from "the use of commercial off-the-shelf software produced in a global supply chain in which malicious code can be embedded by stealth."[70] However, the government is continuing to use generic software and hardware, including those produced overseas.

In short, given the realities of computer network, the Internet, and other elements of cyberspace, there can be no elevated cybersecurity in the public realm unless there is also heightened cybersecurity in the private realm. I am not arguing that the two realms are now one; merely that they are so intertwined that they act, to a significant extent, as if they were one system.

V. Case Study – Preferences—the Byproducts of Culture and Society

This case study differs greatly from the preceding ones. While they deal with recent developments, mainly ones that took place since the advent of cyberspace, this case study deals with factors that have been at work for as far back as history allows us to explore. It deals with long-standing and in this sense "permanent" reasons why the public-private divide should be accorded much less interpretive power than it commands, while the other case studies deal with recent and additional reasons in support of the same overarching thesis. One can think about the study of preference as the foundation, and the other case studies as floors recently added. Moreover, this case study is the most telling of them all, not merely due to the scope of its reach, but also because it points to a locus of power beyond the private/public divide.

Major segments of public philosophy, which assumes a clear and deep public/private divide, start with the individual, whose *privately* formed preferences ought to be respected because they express one's will, and they ought to guide the *public* sphere. Thus, modern democratic theory, in its basic form, assumes that each voter will deliberate, make up his or her own mind, and then privately, in the secrecy of the ballot box, express his or her preference. Out of the aggregation of these private choices, the polity as a public domain gains its direction. Similarly, the "consumer sovereignty" theory starts with millions of individual consumers choosing what to purchase, in line with their personal preferences, and out of the accumulation of these choices, the economy as a whole gains its direction. Constitutional rights exist to prevent the government as the public agent from interfering in these and myriad other private choices expressing private preferences. The very well-known debates that follow from this widely-held assumption focus on the conditions under which exceptions are justified, in which public considerations may trump private, individual preferences—say, for national security or public health.

To highlight the importance that major segments of public philosophy accord this high respect for private preferences, it may serve to assume for a moment, strictly for thought experimental purposes, that the opposite were true. Assume that these driving preferences reflect not the person, but rather are somehow implanted by a public agency through mass propaganda – like something out of *1984*. Then, these implanted preferences would not command anything like the respect they have in the prevailing narratives. Above all, the very private/public divide would become much less important, because the public domain would dominate both sides of the divide. A private/public conflict would be like a fight between a ventriloquist and his dummy.

The position next advanced is not nearly as extreme as the one just used as a thought experiment, but it nevertheless holds that private preferences are significantly influenced by collective societal forces, although individuals do have varying degrees of freedom. That is, preferences are co-determined. It follows that preferences should be accorded a much lower normative standing than they have in the major segments of public philosophies.

The societal influence on private preferences is most clearly revealed by examining young children and the ways they grow up. When one studies the work of parents and educators, one cannot but realize that children's preferences are, initially, largely not their own, but rather reflect the preferences of their families, neighborhoods, and subculture—in short their community. Indeed, a major goal of education (as distinct from teaching) is to foster internalization of societal values in children and thus form and affect their preferences.[71] This is accomplished through such nonrational processes as affective attachments and identification with authority figures.[72]

True, children are born with broad, vague predispositions. For instance, they are predisposed to food over hunger—but these general predispositions are translated into specific preferences, in line with the particular values they internalize. Thus, while children have an inborn need for food, and perhaps even for variation and combinations in food (e.g., proteins and carbohydrates), the specific foods they consider desirable—whether Kosher, soul, organic, or traditional—tend to be those their parents or peers cherish, and are thus acquired tastes. Moreover, the acquisition is often not the result of any individual, conscious reasoning. American teenagers do not prefer Coke and French fries because they have calculated that such consumption will enhance their peer standing; they *feel* that these are the right foods to consume and typically are unaware how they gained such tastes. All this holds for many other areas of behavior. In all of them, initially, biological predispositions are deeply shaped by societal values, and additional preferences are implanted and become an integral part of the self. Thus, a child born in the United States is much less likely to become a Muslim than one born in Saudi Arabia, a Communist if born in North Korea, or a Jew if born in Tel Aviv—not because they each happen to choose their ideational identity and values out of some kind of a normative menu, but because they initially gain their values, expressed in their preferences, from their communities.[73]

Once children become adults, their preferences do not suddenly become immutable (like the "Rocky Mountains," as Stigler and Becker put it),[74] independent, or hermetically sealed. Nonrational processes—peer pressure, for instance—continue to affect them. These effects occur "under the radar." That is, they occur without the individual being aware of the penetrating, preference-changing influences, and without the individual being able to screen them and deliberate whether or not to allow them in. This point is important because, if the inputs were subject to scrutiny and blocking, individuals would be much more able to protect their private identity from public influence.

Persuasion is the term often used to refer to the nonrational processes through which adult preferences are changed.[75] Persuasion works by nonrational means, such as identification with authority figures and group enthusiasm generated through rituals and appeals. Persuasion is also part of processes such as acculturation (especially of immigrants from other countries or of people moving within the same society from one area to another, where the subculture is different), religious conversions, or joining a cult. Leadership, propaganda, and commercials are all forms of persuasion.

One may wonder why the discussion so far has focused on societal values while omitting other public factors, such as the coercive role of the government and macroeconomic forces. The main reason is that although all these public factors constrain and even affect private preferences, societal values are much more consequential in terms of blurring the private/public divide. Coercive and economic factors change private choices, but overall they do not affect a person's will. People may drive more slowly if the penalties on speeding are increased or if the cost of gas rises, but they will still prefer to drive faster. The private/public divide thus remains relevant. However, if people internalize the value of driving at a lower speed, they will come to hold this choice as an expression of their will.[76] When such changes in preferences take place, as they often do, the private/public divide becomes much less important than it otherwise seems, as the private preferences of voters and consumers, workers and investors—which guide the polity and the economy—are themselves in part shaped by a collective realm, albeit not by what is usually understood as the public one, as we shall see next.

VI. Beyond the Divide: The Loci of Power

The preceding case studies illustrate the thesis that the deep divide between the public and the private realms (which plays a cardinal role in public discourse and is drawn upon in several segments of social science) is not nearly as deep as is often assumed, and that the two realms are intertwined and tend to change in tandem. Moreover, we often face the same forces on both sides of the divide; that is, they have a private and a public face but are actually often one and the same actor. Finally, the blurring of the realms has increased since the advent of cyberspace, although—as the study of preferences shows—it was happening long before the 1980s.

These overarching observations lead one to ask what new precepts ought to guide our analyses and public philosophies as we seek the loci of power that propel history, foster changes in both realms, and, to put it in popular terms, can cause much harm and promote great good.

The fact that the two realms are deeply intertwined and move in tandem can be accounted for in three different ways: the forces in one realm can largely shape the other, the two realms can interact to fashion a shared format and course, or there is one power or multiple powers that drive both realms. In any case, we seek to know where the levers are, which forces propel societal change, and in what ways these forces may be redirected, changing the course of history.

I am tempted to respond to these questions by pointing out that the purpose of this essay is to call attention to the growing obsolescence of one of the most important normative precepts, and leave it to others to find out where the loci of power might be found. Therefore, only some rather preliminary thoughts follow.

One way to proceed is to explore the thesis that the main loci of the forces that propel many key changes in both realms lies in a third term. A reader may, for good reason, pause here and demand to know: what realm is there beyond the public and the private? The response comes in two parts. The first is of some import and is very familiar. The second is of considerably more significance, but it is much more contested. The first part of the response deals with the nature of the third realm; the second part with driving forces located within it.

While the public discourse often draws on the opposition between the public and the private realm, academics and public intellectuals have long and often noted the difficulties in two-realm conceptions and the merit of recognizing the distinctive role of community (or civil society) as a third realm.[77] It is a thesis often associated with Alexis de Tocqueville. This communal realm includes relationships among the members of nuclear and extended families; webs of friendships; bonds of affinity in residential, ethnic, racial, religious, professional, and other communities; and many thousands of voluntary associations and not-for-profit corporations, which include, in the U.S., many of the most highly-regarded and influential universities, medical centers, and cultural institutions, among others.

While public discourse has hardly ignored civil society (and if asked, many citizens are likely to acknowledge its import), when the major issues of the day are considered—from improving the economy to protecting the nation from terrorism to improving the climate to reducing drug abuse—the third realm is often overlooked or considered a marginal player. I shall try shortly to suggest that it is not.

One reason the third realm is often overlooked in public discourse is that the discourse is highly polarized, favors clear opposition and dichotomies, and abhors complexity, nuances, and "third" positions. Moreover, much of the public discourse is conducted in terms of liberal versus conservative, associated with the public (government) and private (free market, individual rights) realms. Still, as I already noted, the argument that it is intellectually productive to divide the societal world into three realms is familiar and uncontroversial. It is merely often overlooked in public discourse when the main issues of the day are debated.

My thesis that the major communal force is that of social movements is likely to be much more contested. Key examples include movements of national liberation, socialism, religious movements (such as radical Islam), and movements that seek to protect the environment. These movements differ greatly from one another, in particular in terms of the values they promote. They share, though, several sociological features, despite their major normative and historical differences: they can withdraw legitimacy and political support from a declining regime and lay the foundations for a new one, in the process affecting both the private and the public realms. Thus, if one compares Russia before and after 1917, or China before and after 1949, one observes that socialism radically changed both the private and the public realm. If one looks at societies that established *sharia* law after being won over by Islamist movements—for instance, Iran following the overthrow of the Shah, and Afghanistan following the Taliban takeover—one realizes that the effects encompass most facets of public and private life in those societies, from the ways judgments are rendered in courts to the ways music and alcohol are consumed. The American civil rights movement affected both laws and private interpersonal relations. Thus, a key reason both realms tend to move mainly in tandem, despite significant differences in the pace and scope of change, is that major changes in both realms are to a significant extent initiated and propelled by communal factors, in particular, social movements.

Critics may argue that social movements themselves arise because other factors "prepared the ground" for them. For instance, one reason the civil rights movement arose after WWII is because African-Americans who served in the army returned home equipped with organizational skills and self-confidence.

However, for every immediate cause, one can always find some preceding one. All that I suggest is that the immediate forces that often propel *major* changes in both the public and private realm are social movements. This is especially the case when one focuses, as this article does, on normative changes and changes in the public discourse.

The social movement that affected changes in both the public and the private realms in the three cases here studied—in the use of SSN, privacy, and cybersecurity—might be called the Conservative Reaction or Reaganism. It is a blend of laissez-faire conservatism and libertarianism amplified by Neoconservative ideas. I do not mean the small groups of public intellectuals and leaders who are associated with these ideas, but a wide array of anti-government sentiments widely held by people who do not formally affiliate with any organization or school of thought. These ideas have of course played a key role in American society, polity, and economy from their inception. However, these themes lost some of their sway during the New Deal, the Great Frontier, and the Great Society eras as well as the heydays of the civil rights, women's rights, sexual liberation, and counterculture movements. Even during the Nixon era (1969–1974) pro-government normative themes and societal following still were relatively widespread, as evidenced by the rise of the environmental movement that changed both the private (e.g., voluntary recycling) and public (e.g., formation of the EPA) realms.

A Conservative Reaction arose during and in the wake of the Reagan administration in the United States (1981–1989) and the Thatcher administration in United Kingdom (1979–1990). It was somewhat mitigated during the Clinton era (1993–2001), although it was he who declared the end of big government, ended "welfare as we know it," and put a five-year freeze on social spending to balance the budget. President George W. Bush (2001–2009) greatly amplified these conservative themes and forces, leading to the unfettering of capitalism in the public realm and additional increases in inequality in the private one. During the first Obama administration, these conservative forces were so strong that they limited what he could do to move in the opposite direction.

It would take a another essay at least as long as this one to trace the specific ways the Conservative Reaction affected the cases at hand, but basically the effect was to strengthen the private actors, which led to the spread of the use of SSNs by businesses, gross violations of privacy by private actors, and strong resistance to cybersecurity by the private sector. All of these changes were legitimated by the Conservative Reaction. Its champions were often unaware that in the process they also affected the public realm, allowing government agents to use private information amassed by private actors, undermining the cybersecurity of the public sector and granting the government (until recently) a much freer hand in the use of SSNs. Historians will understandably find this kind of sociological shorthand annoying. It is but a very sketchy outline, which has to be fleshed out and documented, but it does indicate the connection between the Conservative Reaction and the cases at hand during the cyber age.

Cyberspace was not created by the Conservative Reaction nor did it generate Reaganite ideology, although—despite the fact that it was created by the government—it was considered a government-free zone from its inception.[78] It still is much less taxed and regulated than the offline world. The fact that cyberspace rose in the same era as that of Reaganism was largely coincidental. However, it did play a very major role in providing the technological and economic underpinning that enabled Reaganite policies to be advanced. The wide use of SSNs, violation of privacy, and of course the undermining of cybersecurity were all enabled by cyberspace.

While all these changes occurred, preferences continued to be largely shaped by the third realm and much changed by social movements. For instance, the environmental movement led people to prefer "green" products. Public discourse continued to treat individual preferences as being entitled to great respect, ignoring the fact that they often expressed collective forces rather than individual choices. This respect provided a consistent underpinning to the ideas at the center of the Conservative Reaction.

One may disagree that social movements are the main force that emanates from the third realm and plays a key role in shaping the two others while still agreeing with the main thesis of this essay: that both realms are increasingly intertwined and tend to move in tandem. It would still follow from this agreement that such observations urge re-examinations of several key assumptions of public philosophy.

Notes

1.   Andrew Stark, *Drawing the Line: Public and Private in America* (Washington, D.C.: Brookings Institution Press, 2010), 191.
2.   Alan Freeman and Elizabeth Mensch, "The Public-Private Distinction in American Law and Life," *Buffalo Law Review* 36 (Spring 1987): 237–58.
3.   Carolyn Puckett, "The Story of the Social Security Number," *Social Security Bulletin* 69, no. 2 (2009), http://www.ssa.gov/policy/docs/ssb/v69n2/v69n2p55.html.
4.   Ibid.
5.   Ibid.
6.   Kathleen S. Swendiman, "The Social Security Number: Legal Developments Affecting Its Collection, Disclosure, and Confidentiality," Congressional Research Service (February 21, 2008), http://www.fas.org/sgp/crs/misc/RL30318.pdf.
7.   "Government and Commercial Use of the Social Security Number is Widespread" Government Accountability Office, Report to the Chairman, Subcommittee on Social Security, Committee on Ways and Means, House of Representatives (February 1999).
8.   "Social Security Number Chronology," Social Security Administration (November 9, 2005), http://www.ssa.gov/history/ssn/ssnchron.html.

9. US Department of the Treasury, Office of Public Affairs. *Fact Sheet: Final Regulations Implementing Customer Identity Verification Requirements under Section 326 of the USA PATRIOT Act*, April 30, 2003. http://www.treasury.gov/press-center/press-releases/Documents/js7432.doc.

10. Flavio L. Komuves, "We've Got Your Number: An Overview of Legislation and Decisions to Control the Use of Social Security Numbers as Personal Identifiers," *John Marshall Journal of Computer & Information Law* 16 no. 3 (1998).

11. William J. Novak, "The Myth of the 'Weak' American State," *American Historical Review* 113 (2008), 769–770.

   See also Karl Polanyi, *The Great Transformation: The Political and Economic Origins of Our Time* (Boston, MA: Beacon Press, 2001).

12. Elisabeth S. Clemens, "Lineages of the Rube Goldberg State: Building and Blurring Public Programs, 1900–1940," in Ian Shapiro, Stephen Skowronek, and Daniel Golen (eds.), *Rethinking Public Institutions: The Art of the State* (New York: New York University Press, 2006), 208–209.

13. Grant McConnell, *Private Power and American Democracy* (New York: Knopf, 1966).

14. E. E. Schattschneider, *The Semi-Sovereign People: A Realist's View of America* (Chicago: Holt, Rinehart, and Winston, 1960).

15. C. Wright Mills, *The Power Elite*, New Edition (Oxford: Oxford University Press, 2000).

16. Theodore Lowi, *The End of Liberalism*, 2nd ed. (New York: Norton, 1979); Mancur Olson, *The Rise and Decline of Nations* (New Haven, CT: Yale University Press, 1982).

17. See Lloyd A. Free and Hadley Cantril, *The Political Beliefs of Americans: A Study of Public Opinion* (New York: Simon and Schuster, 1967).

   Also: Sara Murray, "Obstacle to Deficit Cutting: A Nation on Entitlements," *The Wall Street Journal* (September 14, 2010), http://online.wsj.com/article/SB10001424052748703791804575439732358241708.html. The author describes a *Wall Street Journal*/NBC poll taken in August 2010 which found that 61% of American voters were "enthusiastic" or "comfortable" with congressional candidates who want to cut federal spending in general—but 56% expressed the same level of support for candidates who voted to extend unemployment benefits.

18. See for example Philip Rucker, "S.C. Senator Is a Voice of Reform Opposition," *The Washington Post* (July 28, 2009): "In other pockets of the state, the reaction to Democratic proposals has been strong, too. At a recent town-hall meeting in suburban Simpsonville, a man stood up and told Rep. Robert Inglis (R-S.C.) to 'keep your government hands off my Medicare.'"

19. Adam Sheingate, "Why Can't Americans See the State?" *The Forum* 7, no. 4 (2009): 1–13.

20. Charlie Savage, "U.S. Tries to Make It Easier to Wiretap the Internet," *The New York Times* (September 27, 2010), http://www.nytimes.com/2010/09/27/us/27wiretap.html?pagewanted=all.

21. Charlie Savage, "Officials Push to Bolster Law on Wiretapping," *The New York Times* (October 18, 2010), http://www.nytimes.com/2010/10/19/us/19wiretap.html.

22. Ellen Nakashima, "U.S. Seeks Ways to Wiretap the Internet," *The Washington Post* (September 28, 2010), http://www.washingtonpost.com/wp-dyn/content/article/2010/09/27/AR2010092706637.html.

23. Lolita C. Baldor, "U.S. Works to Make Internet Wiretaps Easier," *The Huffington Post* (September 9, 2010), http://www.huffingtonpost.com/2010/09/27/internet-wiretaps-would-b_n_740064.html.

24. See for example Julia Angwin and Steve Stecklow, "'Scrapers' Dig Deep for Data on Web," *The Wall Street Journal* (October 12, 2010), http://online.wsj.com/article/SB10001424052748703358504575544381288117888.html.

   Other kinds of prescription drug tracking may not come specifically from tracking Internet use, but from purchasing records from pharmaceutical companies. See also Jessica Vascellaro, "TV's Next Wave: Tuning Into You," *The Wall Street Journal* (March 7, 2011), http://online.wsj.com/article/SB10001424052748704288304576171251689944350.html.

25. Paul Magnusson, "They're Watching You," *Bloomberg Businessweek* (January 23, 2005). http://www.businessweek.com/stories/2005-01-23/theyre-watching-you.

26. Ryan Singel, "Acxiom Opts Out of Opt-Out," *Wired* (November 17, 2003).

27. Christopher Slobogin, "Data Mining and the Fourth Amendment," *University of Chicago Law Review* 75, no. 1 (2008), 320.

28. Justin Scheck. "Stalkers Exploit Cellphone GPS," *The Wall Street Journal* (August 3, 2010), http://online.wsj.com/news/articles/SB10001424052748703467304575383522318244234.

29. Ibid.

30. Tanzina Vega, "New Web Code Draws Concern Over Privacy Risks," *The New York Times* (October 11, 2010), http://www.nytimes.com/2010/10/11/business/media/11privacy.html?pagewanted=all.

31. Julia Angwin, "The Web's New Gold Mine: Your Secrets," *The Wall Street Journal* (July 30, 2010), http://online.wsj.com/news/articles/SB10001424052748703940090457539507351298940.

32. See note 24.

33. Ibid.

34. Steve Stecklow and Paul Sonne, "Shunned Profiling Technology on the Verge of Comeback," *The Wall Street Journal* (November 24, 2010), http://online.wsj.com/news/articles/SB10001424052748704243904575630751094784516.

35. "The Surveillance-Industrial Complex: How the American Government Is Conscripting Businesses and Individuals in the Construction of a Surveillance Society," American Civil Liberties Union (2004), http://www.aclu.org/FilesPDFs/surveillance_report.pdf, 26.

36. Christopher Hoofnagle, "Big Brother's Little Helpers: How ChoicePoint and Other Commercial Data Brokers Collect, Process, and Package Your Data for Law Enforcement," *North Carolina Journal of International Law and Commercial Regulation* 29 no. 4 (2004).

37. Daniel Solove, *The Digital Person: Technology And Privacy In The Information Age* (New York: New York University Press, 2004) 170.

38. See note 27 at 320.

39. Arshad Mohammed and Sara Kehaulani Goo, "Government Increasingly Turning to Data Mining," *The Washington Post* (July 15, 2006), http://www.washingtonpost.com/wp-dyn/content/article/2006/06/14/AR2006061402063.html.

40. Ibid.

41. US Department of Defense, *Overview of the DOD Fiscal 2010 Budget Proposal* (May 7, 2009), http://www.defense.gov/news/2010%20Budget%20Proposal.pdf. The "base budget" refers to the budget request before "contingency operations" – i.e., the wars in Afghanistan and Iraq – are factored in.

42. Elaine Wilson, "Gates Unveils Strategy to Cut Costs, Boost Efficiency," US Department of Defense. Press Release (September 14, 2010), http://www.defense.gov/news/newsarticle.aspx?id=60854.

    See also: Pat Towell, "Defense: FY2011 Authorization and Appropriations," Congressional Research Service (November 23, 2010).

43. Deborah C. Kidwell, "Public War, Private Fight? The United States and Private Military Companies," Global War on Terrorism Occasional Paper 12, Combat Studies Institute Press, Fort Leavenworth, KS (2005), http://www.dtic.mil/cgi-bin/GetTRDoc?AD=ADA446127, 1.

44. Ibid., 2.

45. Moshe Schwartz, "Department of Defense Contractors in Iraq and Afghanistan: Background and Analysis," Congressional Research Service (July 2, 2010), 10.

46. T. Christian Miller, "This Year, Contractor Deaths Exceed Military Ones in Iraq and Afghanistan," *ProPublica* (September 23, 2010), http://www.propublica.org/article/this-year-contractor-deaths-exceed-military-ones-in-iraq-and-afgh-100923/.

47. Dana Priest and William M. Arkin, "National Security Inc.," *The Washington Post* (July 20, 2010), http://projects.washingtonpost.com/top-secret-america/articles/national-security-inc/.

48. Government Accountability Office, "Defense Logistics: Actions Needed to Improve the Availability of Critical Items during Current and Future Operations," (April 2005), http://www.gao.gov/new.items/d05275.pdf, 4.

49. Jack Goldsmith and Melissa Hathaway, "The Cybersecurity Changes We Need," *The Washington Post* (May 29, 2010), http://www.washingtonpost.com/wp-dyn/content/article/2010/05/28/AR2010052803698.html.

50. U.S.-China Economic And Security Review Commission. *2008 Report to Congress of the U.S.-China Economic And Security Review Commission* (November 2008), http://www.uscc.gov/annual_report/2008/annual_report_full_08.pdf. 167.

51. Bruce Schneier, "Eliminating Externalities in Financial Security," *Schneier on Security* (September 23, 2009), http://www.schneier.com/blog/archives/2009/09/eliminating_the.html.

52. See Jeremy Kirk, "IBM Looks to Secure Internet Banking with USB Stick," *PCWorld* (March 3, 2009), http://www.pcworld.com/businesscenter/article/160575/ibm_looks_to_secure_internet_banking_with_usb_stick.html. If developing, distributing, and supporting the USB sticks or card readers developed by IBM cost banks even $3 per customer, losses would need to approach $1B in order to economically justify providing every banking customer in the United States with the additional security. See also McAfee Labs, "2010 Threat Predictions," http://www.mcafee.com/us/local_content/white_papers/7985rpt_labs_threat_predict_1209_v2.pdf.

53. Business Software Alliance. "Cybersecurity Bill Clears Senate Committee," Press Release (June 24 2010), http://www.bsa.org/country/News%20and%20Events/News%20Archives/en/2010/en-06242010-cybersecbill.aspx

Also: Grant Gross, "Industry Groups Question Regulations in Cybersecurity Bill," *PCWorld* (April 2, 2010), http://www.pcworld.com/businesscenter/article/193286/industry_groups_question_regulations_in_cybersecurity_bill.html.

54. Richard Clarke and Robert K. Knake, *Cyber War: The Next Threat To National Security and What To Do About It* (New York: HarperCollins, 2010), 144.

55. For an excellent discussion of this subject, see Jack Goldsmith, "Against Cyberanarchy," *University of Chicago Law Review* 65, no. 4 (1998): 1199–1250.

56. Stewart Baker *Skating on Stilts: Why We Aren't Stopping Tomorrow's Terrorism* (Stanford: Hoover Institution Press 2010), 233.

57. Ibid.

58. Andy Greenberg, "For Pentagon Contractors, Cyberspying Escalates," *Forbes* (February 17, 2010), http://www.forbes.com/2010/02/17/pentagon-northrop-raytheon-technology-security-cyberspying.html.

59. CBS, "Cyber War: Sabotaging the System," *60 Minutes* (November 8, 2009), http://www.cbsnews.com/stories/2009/11/06/60minutes/main5555565.shtml.

60. Ellen Nakashima and Brian Krebs, "Contractor Blamed in DHS Data Breaches," *The Washington Post* (September 24, 2007), http://www.washingtonpost.com/wp-dyn/content/article/2007/09/23/AR2007092301471.html.

61. James Lewis, "Innovation and Cybersecurity Regulation," Center for Strategic and International Studies (March 2009), http://csis.org/files/media/csis/pubs/090327_lewis_innovation_cybersecurity.pdf.

62. Ibid.

63. William J. Lynn III, "Defending a New Domain: The Pentagon's Cyberstrategy," *Foreign Affairs* 89 no. 5 (2010), 104.

64. See note 54 at 121.

65. White House, "Remarks by the President on Securing Our Nation's Cyber Infrastructure," (May 29, 2009), http://www.whitehouse.gov/the_press_office/Remarks-by-the-President-on-Securing-Our-Nations-Cyber-Infrastructure/.

66. One may argue that the president merely said he will not "dictate" which security standards must be followed, but will find some other ways of making or persuading the private sector adhere to them. However, he has neither declared nor followed such a course, nor have previous administrations.

67. See note 54, 167.

68. National Institute of Standards and Technology, "Smart Grid FAQs," (December 23, 2010), http://www.nist.gov/smartgrid/faq.cfm.

69. Kim Zetter, "Feds' Smart Grid Race Leaves Cybersecurity in the Dust," *Wired* (October 28, 2009), http://www.wired.com/threatlevel/2009/10/smartgrid/#ixzz12AxBDsEi.

70. See note 49.

71. Lawrence Kohlberg, "Moral Development," *International Encyclopedia of the Social Sciences*, ed. David Sills (New York: MacMillan, 1968), 483.

72. See, e.g., B. Stilwell, M. Galvin, M. Kopta, R. Padgett, and J. Holt, "Moralization of Attachment: A Fourth Dimension of Conscience Functioning," *Journal of the American Academy of Child and Adolescent Psychiatry* 36, no. 8 (1997): 1140–1147.

73. See Kingsley Davis, *Human Society* (New York: MacMillan, 1949). On the difference between treating people as a product of their social status versus the creation of their project, see Arthur Schlesinger, Jr., *The Disuniting of America: Reflections on a Multicultural Society* (Knoxville, TN: Whittle Books, 1991).

74. See George Stigler and Gary Becker, "De Gustibus Non Est Disputandum," *American Economic Review* 67 no. 2 (1977), 76.

75. While it often flows from authority figures or elites to followers, this need not always be the case. Members of a community can work out a shared position in which peers persuade those who may initially have differed on normative issues, drawing on nonrational means. For additional discussion, see the examination of moral dialogues in Amitai Etzioni, *The Moral Dimension: Towards a New Economics* (New York: The Free Press, 1988), 85–118.

76. See Amitai Etzioni, *A Comparative Analysis of Complex Organizations* (New York: The Free Press, 1961).

77. See for example Amitai Etzioni, "The Third Way is a Triumph," *New Statesman* (June 25, 2001): ". . . Society is like a stool that rests on three legs, two of which (the state and the market) are too long and one too short. The third leg is the things people do for one another as members of families and neighborhoods, as friends and co-workers."

78. John Perry Barlow, "A Declaration of the Independence of Cyberspace," *Electronic Frontier Foundation,* 1996, https://projects.eff.org/~barlow/Declaration-Final.html.

Acknowledgments

All papers appearing in this book have been modified from their original form, some extensively so. Melissa Paul for helping to put this book to bed. The author gratefully acknowledges the following publishers and publications for permission to use previously-published material:

"The New Normal" includes a section from a paper originally published in *Sociological Forum* 26, no. 4 (December 2011): p. 779–789.

"Limit the Freedom of the Press?" originally published as "A Liberal Communitarian Approach to Security Limitations on the Freedom of the Press" in *William & Mary Bill of Rights Journal* 22, no. 4 (2014): 1141–1181.

"How Much Surveillance is Legitimate?" originally published as "NSA: National Security vs. Individual Rights" in *Intelligence and National Security*, TK.

"Should American Terrorists Be Tried Differently From Others?" originally published as "American Terrorists as Perpetrators of Communitarian Assaults" in *The American University International Law Review* 47, no. 1 (2013): 123–144.

"A Cyber Age Privacy Doctrine" originally published as "A Cyber Age Privacy Doctrine: A Liberal Communitarian Approach," in *I/S: A Journal of Law and Policy for the Information Society* 10, no. 2 (Summer 2014).

"The Privacy Merchants" originally published as "The Privacy Merchants: What Is To Be Done?" in *University of Pennsylvania Journal of Constitutional Law* 14, no. 4 (March 2012): 929–951.

"Is There a Gridlock?" originally published as "Gridlock?" in *The Forum* 10, no. 3, (2012): 1–44.

"The Scope of Corruption" originally published as "Political Corruption in America: A Design Draft," in *PS: Political Science & Politics* 47, no. 1 (January 2013): 141–144.

"Regulatory Capture" originally published as "Legislation in the Public Interest: Regulatory Capture and Campaign Reform," in *Agenda for Social Justice: Solutions 2012*. Glenn W. Muschert, Kathleen Ferraro, Brian V. Klocke, Robert Perrucci, and Jon Shefner, editors. Knoxville, TN: University of Tennessee, 2012. 11–19.

"Is Transparency the Best Disinfectant?" originally published in *Journal of Political Philosophy* 18, no. 4 (December 2010): 389–404.

"Cutting 'Entitlements'?" originally published as "Rationing by Any Other Name" in *Policy Review*, 173 (June & July 2012): 19–28.

"Who Authorized Preparations for a War With China?" originally published in *Yale Journal of International Affairs* (June 2013).

"MAR: Mutually Assured Restraint" originally published in *Brown Journal of World Affairs* FORTHCOMING.

"The Great Drone Debate," originally published in *Military Review* (March–April 2013): 2–13.

"The Moral and Legal Foundations of Counterterrorism Policies" originally published as "A Liberal Communitarian Paradigm for Counterterrorism," in *Stanford Journal of International Law* 49, no. 2 (2013): 330–370.

"Public Private Divide" originally published as "The Bankruptcy of Liberalism and Conservatism," *Political Science Quarterly* 128, no. 1 (May 2013): 39–65.

I am also indebted to Alex Platt, Ashley McKinless, Courtney Kennedy, Danielle Kerem, Erin Syring, Jeffrey Gianattasio, Jesse Spafford, Marissa Cramer, Nathan Pippenger, and S. Riane Harper for their research assistance on various sections of the book. My thanks also goes out to Steven Bellovin, and Shaun Spencer for their comments on "A Cyber Age Privacy Doctrine"; Larry DeWitt for his comments on the Social Security Numbers section of "Public/Private Divide"; Orin Kerr and Gina Stevens for their comments on "The Privacy Merchants"; *Journal of Political Philosophy* referees for their comments on "Is Transparency the Best Disinfectant?"; T.X. Hammes and Elbridge Colby for their comments on "Who Authorized Preparations for a War with China?"; and Peter Raven-Hansen, Kenneth Anderson, Wells Bennett, Burrus Carnahan, Miriam Galston, Michael Matheson, Sean Murphy, Gary Solis, Paul Pillar and David Shinn for their comments on "The Moral and Legal Foundations of Counterterrorism Policies."

Other Books by Amitai Etzioni:

Hot Spots: American Foreign Policy in a Post-Human-Rights World (New Brunswick, N.J.: Transaction Publishers, 2012)

Security First: For A Muscular, Moral Foreign Policy (New Haven: Yale University Press, 2007)

From Empire to Community: A New Approach to International Relations (New York: Palgrave Macmillan, 2004)

How Patriotic is the Patriot Act? (New York: Routledge, 2004)

The Common Good (Cambridge, Mass.: Polity Press, 2004)

My Brother's Keeper: A Memoir and a Message (Lanham, MD: Rowman and Littlefield, 2003)

Political Unification Revisited: On Building Supernational Communities (Lexington Books, 2001)

The Limits of Privacy (New York: Basic Books, 1999)

The New Golden Rule: Community and Morality in a Democratic Society (New York: Basic Books, 1997)

A Comparative Analysis of complex Organizations rev. ed. (New York: The Free Press, 1975)

The Moral Dimension: Toward a New Economics (New York: The Free Press, 1968)

The Active Society: A Theory of Societal and Political Processes (New York: The Free Press, 1968)

Winning Without War (Garden City, NY: Doubleday, 1964)

Index